The Hillier
Colour Dictionary of
Trees and Shrubs

The Hillier Colour Dictionary of Trees and Shrubs

David & Charles
Newton Abbot

British Library Cataloguing in Publication Data

The Hillier colour dictionary of trees and shrubs.
  1. Shrubs – Dictionaries
  I. Hillier Nurseries (Winchester) Ltd
  635.9'7603   SB435

  ISBN 0-7153-8192-X

Acknowledgements
The basic text for this book was prepared and verified by Hillier Nurseries (Winchester) Ltd., and especially by the following members of the Hillier team; Sid Cox, Allen Coombes, Stan Dolding, John Hillier, Robert Hillier, Brian Humphrey, Bill Stillwell and Sarah Stride.

The majority of the photographs are by Michael Warren, but additional pictures were provided by Pat Brindley, Valerie Finnis, Brian Humphrey, Roy Lancaster and Dennis Woodland.

Co-ordinating editor: Don Snelling, Blair Bowden Associates Limited, Southampton

Design and layout: Ad Infinitum Limited, Southampton

© Hillier Nurseries (Winchester) Ltd 1981
First published 1981
Second impression 1982
Third impression 1984
Fourth impression 1988
Fifth impression 1990
Sixth impression 1991

Printed in Hong Kong
by Regent Publishing Services
for David & Charles plc
Brunel House Newton Abbot Devon

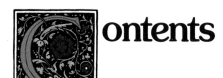ontents

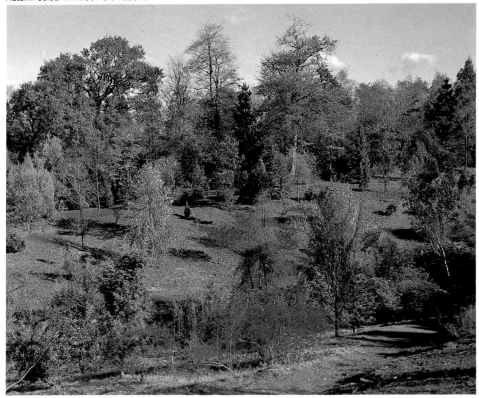

he Hillier Arboretum

Jermyns Lane, Ampfield, Romsey, Hampshire.
Telephone Braishfield (0794) 68787 (Curator: Keith Rushforth, BSc (For), MIFor.)

To secure the future of the unique collection which he had founded as both a national and an international asset, Harold Hillier C.B.E. presented the Arboretum as a gift to Hampshire County Council in October 1977. A charitable trust has been established, in which the County Council have responsibility for the Arboretum as corporate trustee, advised by a committee of experts.

New plantings and expansions are continuing to enhance the international status of the collection, to increase the Arboretum's role in the important areas of education and conservation and to bring year-round pleasure to its many visitors.

Situated between the Hampshire villages of Ampfield and Braishfield, 3 miles east of Romsey and 9 miles west of Winchester the Arboretum is open to the public from 9am-4.30pm, Monday-Friday throughout the year and from 1pm-6pm on Saturdays, Sundays and Bank Holidays from Easter until the last Sunday of October. A small charge is made for admission to help towards maintenance costs.

Preface

In an era when gardening books, many of dubious authenticity and doubtful value, tumble like secondhand confetti from the publishers' presses, *Hillier's Manual of Trees and Shrubs*, first published in 1971 and now in its fourth edition, stands out as a classic that will hold its own among the great reference works on gardening for many decades, and perhaps centuries, to come. Both amateur and professional gardeners regard it as an essential aid to their hobby or profession and many, as I do myself, take a copy on every visit to a garden or nursery to use as a *vade mecum* which accurately presents concise but detailed information on the widest range of trees and shrubs known and grown in the northern hemisphere. It is, in short, indispensable.

Today, with inflation outstripping even that most rampant of climbers *Polygonum baldschuanicum* in growth, and economic pressures battering the horticultural trade on all sides, it is clearly, if regrettably, impracticable for any one nursery to stock permanently the enormous range of trees and shrubs for which the name of Hillier is known throughout the gardening world. Among the 8,000 or more items described in the Manual are some which, although fascinating to the botanist and collector, have little general garden appeal. Many hundreds of others, however, excellent garden plants in their own right, are scarcely known and seldom available from other sources.

It is, therefore, a very great pleasure to provide this preface for a new and complementary publication, *The Hillier Colour Dictionary of Trees*

and Shrubs, which describes over 3,500 trees, shrubs, climbers and conifers carefully selected for their garden value and illustrates in colour over 600 of the plants included. These have been chosen with particular care to ensure that they represent the best available species and cultivars for garden decoration. The information provided is neatly distilled from the descriptions in the Manual and together with the very wide range of colour illustrations, unmatched in any other comparable work, provides both the beginner and the enthusiast with an invaluable reference and guide.

As an ardent believer in the need to conserve our garden plants it is particularly pleasing to find included many uncommon plants which should, in my view, be more widely grown for their beauty and aesthetic appeal but, through lack of publicity, are in danger of being lost.

This new *Colour Dictionary* should, through its illustrations, descriptions and other helpful information, stimulate all those interested in woody plants and seems destined to become as indispensable as the Manual. Certainly I shall now need a second 'poacher's pocket' in my coat to accommodate them both when visiting gardens and nurseries.

CHRISTOPHER D. BRICKELL, BSc (Hort) VMH
Director of The Royal Horticultural Society's Garden, Wisley

Introduction

In 1864, after having gained a knowledge and love of plants in some of the leading horticultural establishments of his day, Edwin Hillier bought a small nursery business and florist's shop in the centre of Winchester. Gradually, the business expanded, more land was acquired and the range of plants increased. Regular deliveries of flowers and plants were made by horse and cart to the great houses and estates in and around the ancient city, and as the Hillier reputation for quality began to spread, greater use of the nearby railway was made, to despatch plants further afield.

Edwin's two sons, Edwin Lawrence Hillier and Arthur Richard Hillier and Edwin's son in turn, Harold, continued the tradition, and, through their particular dedication to woody plants raised the firm to international pre-eminence, with a range of plants running into thousands and a complex of nurseries covering around 800 acres in Hampshire.

The family's commitment to the introduction, identification and conservation of trees and shrubs is evidenced by the fact that around 200 cultivars, sub-species or varieties have been raised, selected or named by Hillier's.

Harold Hillier CBE, FLS, VMH is still active as President of the Hillier organisation and, since his notional "retirement", has travelled many thousands of miles, obtaining new specimens and sharing his knowledge with plantsmen in the UK and overseas.

The 110 acre Hillier Arboretum (see page 6) founded in the early 1950s and presented to the Hampshire County Council in 1977, is a botanist's paradise containing and conserving one of the most diverse collections of trees and shrubs in the temperate regions of the world. Harold Hillier is also continuing to pursue his long-standing interest in the almost 'Mediterranean' Ventnor Botanic Garden on the Isle of Wight, and has been an enthusiastic contributor to the Royal Horticultural Society's new arboretum at Wisley Garden in Surrey.

Each year the Hillier show team travels enormous distances to stage fascinating living displays at leading horticultural shows in Britain and, from time to time, overseas, and the nurseries have been awarded more than 30 gold medals at Chelsea Shows alone.

Today, the family tradition is being upheld by Harold's two sons, John and Robert Hillier.

Much has changed in the day to day running of the nurseries, with a high degree of mechanisation, the use of modern materials, chemicals and fertilisers, the increasing proportion of container-grown plants and even the sophisticated computerisation of production schedules and stock control.

One thing, however, remains constant – a total dedication to producing plants which will bring pleasure and an element of environmental stability in an ever-changing world.

ymbols & Abbreviations

Plants not marked are suitable for most situations.

(E)	Evergreen	ST	Small tree (Eventual height 4.5–9m)
♥	Spreading tree		
♠	Conical tree	MT	Medium tree (Eventual height 10–18m)
♥	Broadly columnar tree		
♦	Columnar (fastigiate) tree	LT	Large tree (Eventual height over 18m)
♠	Weeping tree	PS	Prostrate (Creeping) shrub
Hort.	Name used in horticultural (garden) context.	DS	Dwarf shrub (.3–.6m)
Hdg (1.0m)	Suitable for hedging or edging (Figure in brackets indicates recommended planting distance)	SS	Small shrub (1–1.5m)
		MS	Medium shrub (1.5m–3m)
†	Not recommended for exposed positions without some protection	LS	Large shrub (over 3m)
		Cl	Self clinging
✗	Will not tolerate alkaline or chalky conditions	☐	Thrives in full sun
		◑	Thrives in partial shade
×	Hybrid origin	●	Thrives in dense shade
+	Chimera (graft hybrid)	GC	Suitable for use as ground cover

Royal Horticultural Society Awards (Followed by year of award)

AGM	Award of Garden Merit	FCC	First Class Certificate
AM	Award of Merit	FCCT	First Class Certificate after trial at the RHS Gardens, Wisley
AMT	Award of Merit after trial at the RHS Gardens, Wisley		

ow to use the Plant List

For ease of reference, the plant list is divided into three sections: Trees and Shrubs, Climbers and Conifers The plants in each section are then listed in strict alphabetical order, by GENERA, in bold capital letters, like this:

ACER

Immediately after the generic name the FAMILY to which that genus belongs is shown in **bold type**, with a capital initial, followed by one or more abbreviations or symbols (as listed on page 9,) and, perhaps, a common name, enclosed in double inverted commas, like this:

ACER – Aceraceae SS-LT "Maples"
genus   family   range from
                               small shrubs
                               to large trees
                               commonly called
                               'Maples'

Next you will find a paragraph in *italic* type, describing the general characteristics of the genus and its broad requirements in terms of soil and situation, where these are important. There may also be a guide to pruning (see page 33) where pruning requirements are common to the whole or most of the genus.

Below each generic description, there then follows a descriptive list of individual species, sub-species or varieties, and cultivars.

Species

These appear in bold type, with a small initial letter.
e.g. in the **ACER** section,

– campestre

indicates the species **campestre** of the genus.

Sub-species and varieties

Wild varieties and sub-species are shown in bold type with small initial letter, following the species to which they belong, so, under the genus **BERBERIS**, species **hookeri**, you will find the (natural) variety **viridis** listed like this:

– – viridis

Cultivars

Garden varieties and selected forms from the wild maintained in cultivation normally follow the species to which they belong. They are shown in bold type with a capital initial, and in single inverted commas. Thus, under the genus **ACER**, species **campestre** the cultivar **'Postelense'** appears like this:

– – 'Postelense'

Clones

A clone is a group of plants derived originally from a single plant and maintained in cultivation true to type by vegetative propagation. Most of the cultivars described in this book are clonal in origin.

Hybrids

Hybrids between two or more species, forms, etc. are normally given a collective Latin name, shown as for a species, but preceded by a multiplication sign, e.g., under the genus **ABELIA**, you will find

– × grandiflora

Sometimes, a group of hybrids is given a collective English name – (e.g. **RHODODENDRON – Lady Chamberlain**,) which is then followed

by the various named clones, e.g.
–– **'Chelsea'**
–– **'Exbury'** etc.

Where no collective name is available for a hybrid which consists only of a single clone, its clonal name is given and treated in the same way as a cultivar,
e.g. **CISTUS**
   – **'Silver Pink'**

Bi-generic hybrids
Natural (sexual) hybrids between species of two different genera are shown in bold capitals, preceded by a multiplication sign, followed by the names of the parents, italicised and in parenthesis, like this:
   × **MAHOBERBERIS** (*MAHONIA* × *BERBERIS*)

Names of bi-generic hybrids which have originated artificially as a result of grafting species of two different genera are preceded by a 'plus' sign, and names of the parents are similarly linked, thus:
   + **LABURNOCYTISUS** (*LABURNUM* + *CYTISUS*)

Sections and series
The larger genera are normally sub-divided into sections or series, and where it is thought these may be useful for reference, they have been added in parenthesis after the individual species
e.g. **FRAXINUS**
   – **mariesii** (Ornus Sect)
or **RHODODENDRON**
   – **forrestii** (S. Neriiflorum)

Groups
Where named clones of a variable hybrid have been listed separately, reference to the hybrid is made in parenthesis after the clone concerned.
e.g. **COTONEASTER**
   – **'Cornubia'** (Watereri Group)

Synonyms
Plant names can and do change for a variety of reasons. Names by which plants were formerly known, or which are not accepted in this book, are shown in parenthesised italics after the accepted name
e.g. **COTONEASTER**
   dammeri (*humifusus*)

Alternative names are frequently also cross-referenced.
Where the abbreviation HORT follows a synonym, it indicates that the plant in question is known by this name only in Horticulture (Gardens)
e.g. **COTONEASTER**
   – **distichus** (*rotundifolius* HORT)

Common names
Frequently used common names are given in double inverted commas after the botanical names to which they relate
e.g. **ARBUTUS**
   – **unedo** "Killarney Strawberry Tree"

The more familiar common names are also included alphabetically among the genera, and cross referenced to the appropriate botanical name
e.g. **"LILAC"** see *SYRINGA*

Awards
Many plants of particular merit are given awards by the Royal Horticultural Society. The most important of these are given at the end of the relevant plant descriptions, and are described in the key to abbreviations and symbols. (page 9)

Heights

The ultimate height of a tree will
depend upon many factors, (including
soil, aspect and local climate), and
may take many years to attain.
The abbreviations used in this book
relate to a scale devised to give British
gardeners the probable height range
of each plant growing under average
conditions:

Trees

LT – Large tree growing to over 18m
　　　(over 60ft)
MT – Medium tree, growing to 10-18m
　　　(35 – 60ft)
ST – Small tree, growing to 4.5-9m (15 –
　　　30ft)

Shrubs

LS – Large shrub, growing to over 3m
　　　(over 10ft)
MS – Medium shrub, growing to 1.5-3m
　　　(5 – 10ft)
SS – Small shrub, growing to 1-1.5m (3
　　　– 5ft)
DS – Dwarf shrub, growing to .3-.6m (1
　　　– 2ft)
PS – Prostrate shrub, – creeping habit

Flowering periods

Flowering periods will inevitably vary
according to locality and from year to
year, depending upon the vagaries of
the season.
Those given in this book should
therefore be taken as approximate.

Pruning

Advice on pruning, and the key to the
pruning symbols used in the text, will
be found on pages 33-34

Leaf Forms

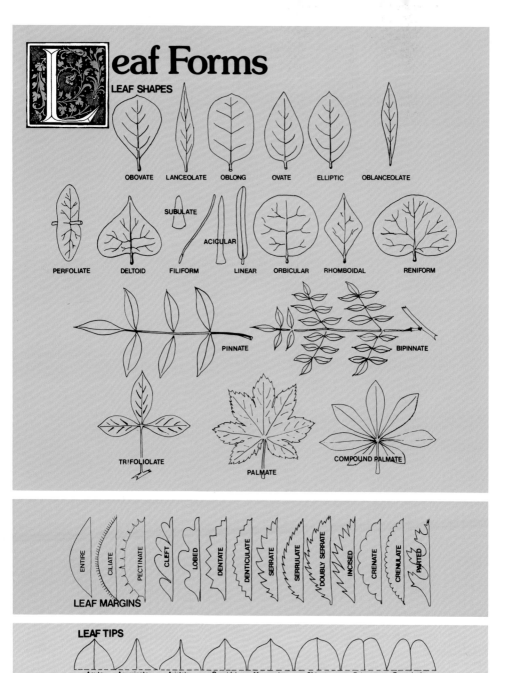

LEAF SHAPES

OBOVATE   LANCEOLATE   OBLONG   OVATE   ELLIPTIC   OBLANCEOLATE

SUBULATE

ACICULAR

PERFOLIATE   DELTOID   FILIFORM   LINEAR   ORBICULAR   RHOMBOIDAL   RENIFORM

PINNATE   BIPINNATE

TRIFOLIOLATE   PALMATE   COMPOUND PALMATE

LEAF MARGINS

ENTIRE   CILIATE   PECTINATE   CLEFT   LOBED   DENTATE   DENTICULATE   SERRATE   SERRULATE   DOUBLY SERRATE   INCISED   CRENATE   CRENULATE   PARTED

LEAF TIPS

Acute   Acuminate   Aristate   Cuspidate   Mucronate   Obtuse   Retuse   Emarginate

LEAF BASES

Cuneate   Attenuate   Obtuse   Cordate   Auriculate   Sagittate   Hastate   Truncate   Oblique

nflorescences

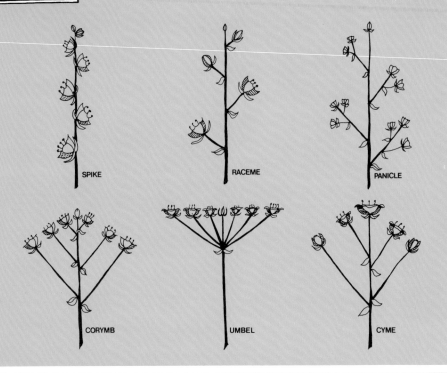

SPIKE

RACEME

PANICLE

CORYMB

UMBEL

CYME

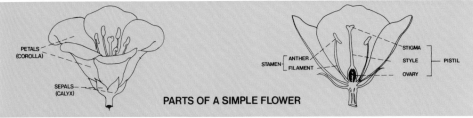

PETALS
(COROLLA)

SEPALS
(CALYX)

STAMEN — ANTHER
— FILAMENT

STIGMA
STYLE — PISTIL
OVARY

PARTS OF A SIMPLE FLOWER

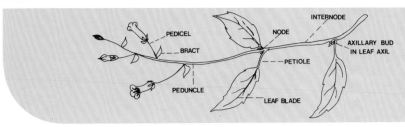

INTERNODE

PEDICEL

NODE

BRACT

AXILLARY BUD
IN LEAF AXIL

PETIOLE

PEDUNCLE

LEAF BLADE

Understanding Plant Names & Classification

Plant names can sometimes appear difficult to understand and even harder to pronounce! The reason is that, because plants are international, we have to stick to agreed 'Codes' to meet the needs of many countries.

Two codes are internationally accepted – the 'International Code of Botanical Nomenclature' covering wild plants, and the 'International Code of Nomenclature for Cultivated Plants', for cultivars.

As man's knowledge of plant variations and plant relationships expands, so the re-classification of many plants inevitably results. This, together with the remorseless application of the 'Rule of Priority' (i.e. standardisation on the earliest legitimate name known for a plant) means a number of imposed changes in the names of plants which may have been familiar to us.

For various reasons, not all changes are accepted in this book, but much attention has been paid to appending and cross-referencing synonyms for 'accepted' names.

This is described more fully in the section 'How to Use the Plant Lists' (commencing on page 10) as are the other main factors in plant nomenclature and classification.

Botanical names are latinised so that they can be accepted the world over, to avoid further translation and the confusion which can so easily arise in national or even regional differences in 'common names'.

Fortunately, one does not have to be a devoted Latin scholar to gain a reasonable grasp of the more commonly used elements of botanical names and their meanings – and as these become more familiar, so we learn more about the plants they describe.

Don't be put off by a long name. It's the beauty and interest of the plant that matters.

Generic names

These are always nouns. Their origins and meanings are occasionally obscure, but the majority are derived from older names in Greek, Latin, Arabic and other languages.

Some generic names are based on characters in Greek mythology, e.g.

DAPHNE named after the river god's daughter

ANDROMEDA named after the daughter of Cepheus and Cassiope

PHYLLODOCE name of a sea nymph

Whilst others commemorate people, such as botanists, patrons etc., e.g.

BUDDLEIA named after Rev. Adam Buddle

DEUTZIA named after J. Deutz

ESCALLONIA named after Signor Escallon

FUCHSIA named after Leonard Fuchs

LONICERA named after Adam Lonicer

Specific epithets

The names used to describe species are varied and fall into four main categories, namely:–

A. Names which indicate the origin of the plant, e.g. continent, country, region, etc.

B. Names that describe the habitat of a plant (where it grows in the wild). e.g., in woods, or mountains, by rivers, etc.

C. Names that describe a plant or a particular feature, such as size, habit, leaf shape, colour of flower, etc.

D. Names which commemorate

people, e.g. botanists, plant collectors, patrons, famous horticulturists, etc.

Here is a selection of the most commonly used names (specific epithets) and their meanings.

Names describing Habit

arborea(um)(us)	tree-like
fastigiata(um)(us)	erect, the branches
fruticosa(um)(us)	shrubby
horizontale(is)	horizontally spreading
humile(is)	low growing
major(us)	greater
minor(us)	lesser
nana(um)(us)	dwarf
pendula(um)(us)	pendulous, weeping
procera(um)(us)	very tall, high
procumbens	procumbent, creeping
prostrata(um)(us)	prostrate, hugging the ground
repens	creeping and rooting
suffruticosa(um)(us)	woody at base

Names describing Habitat

alpina(um)(us)	alpine, of the Alps or growing in alpine regions
arvense(is)	of fields or cultivated land
aquatica(um)(us)	of water, or growing by water
campestre(is)	of plains or flat areas
littorale(is)	of sea shores
maritima(um)(us)	by the sea
montana(um)(us)	of mountains
palustre(is)	of swamps or marshes
rivulare(is)	of streams and brooks
rupestre(is)	of rocks or cliffs
sylvatica(um)(us)	of woods

Names which are Geographical

atlantica(um)(us)	of the Atlas Mountains (North Africa)
australe(is)	southern
boreale(is)	northern
californica(um)(us)	of California
capense(is)	of the Cape (South Africa)
europaea(um)(us)	of Europe
himalaica(um)(us)	of the Himalaya
hispanica(um)(us)	of Spain
japonica(um)(us)	of Japan
lusitanica(um)(us)	of Portugal
nipponica(um)(us)	of Japan
occidentale(is)	western
orientale(is)	eastern
sinense(is)	of China

Names describing Leaves

angustifolia(um)(us)	narrow-leaved
arguta(um)(us)	sharp
coriacea(um)(us)	coriaceous, leathery
crassifolia(um)(us)	thick-leaved
crenata(um)(us)	with shallow, rounded teeth
decidua(um)(us)	deciduous, dropping its leaves
glabra(um)(us)	glabrous, without hairs
glutinosa(um)	sticky
heterophylla(um)(us)	variable-leaved
hirsuta(um)(us)	hairy
incana(um)(us)	grey-downy
integerrima(um)(us)	without teeth
laciniata(um)(us)	cut into narrow pointed lobes
laevigata(um)(us)	smooth and polished

lanceolata(um)(us)	lance shaped
latifolia(um)(us)	broad-leaved
macrophylla(um)(us)	large-leaved
maculata(um)(us)	spotted, blotched
marginata(um)(us)	margined
microphylla(um)(us)	small leaved
molle(is)	soft
nitida(um)(us)	shining
ovata(um)(us)	egg-shaped
parvifolia(um)(us)	small-leaved
picta(um)(us)	painted, coloured
pinnata(um)(us)	pinnate
platyphylla(os)(um)(us)	broad-leaved
reticulata(um)(us)	net-veined
rotundifolia(um)(us)	round-leaved
sempervirens	always green, evergreen
serrata(um)(us)	saw-toothed
splendens	glittering, shining
tomentosa(um)(us)	covered with a short dense pubescence
variegata(um)(us)	variegated, two coloured
velutina(um)(us)	velvety

Names describing Flowers

(flora(um)(us) = flower)

campanulata(um)(us)	bell-shaped
floribunda(um)(us)	free-flowering
grandiflora(um)(us)	large-flowered
macropetala(um)(us)	many-petalled
nudiflora(um)(us)	naked, without leaves
nutans	nodding
paniculata(um)(us)	flowering in panicles
parviflora(um)(us)	small-flowered
pauciflora(um)(us)	few-flowered
polyantha(um)(us)	many-flowered
racemosa(um)(us)	flowers in racemes
spicata(um)(us)	flowers in spikes
stellata(um)(us)	starry
triflora(um)(us)	flowers in threes
umbellata(um)(us)	flowers in umbels
uniflora(um)(us)	one-flowered

Names describing Colours

alba(um)(us)	white
argentea(um)(us)	silvery
aurantiaca(um)(us)	orange
aurea(um)(us)	golden
bicolor	two coloured
carnea(um)(us)	flesh-coloured
caerulea(um)(us)	blue
cinerea(um)(us)	ash grey
coccinea(um)(us)	scarlet
concolor	of the same colour
discolor	two-coloured
ferruginea(um)(us)	rusty brown
flava(um)(us)	pale yellow
glauca(um)(us)	sea-green
lactea(um)(us)	milk white
lilacina(um)(us)	lilac
lutea(um)(us)	yellow
nigra(um)(us)	black
punicea(um)(us)	crimson
purpurea(um)(us)	purple
rosea(um)(us)	rose-coloured
rubra(um)(us)	red
sanguinea(um)(us)	blood red
tricolor	three-coloured
variegata(um)(us)	variegated – two-coloured
versicolor	variously coloured, or changing colour

violacea(um)(us)	violet	williamsiana(um)(us)	after Mr. J.C. Williams
viride(is)	green	willmottiana(um)(us)	after Miss Ellen Willmott
		wilsoniae	after Mrs. E.H. Wilson

Names describing Aromas and Scents

aromatica(um)(us)	aromatic
citriodora(um)(us)	lemon-scented
foetida(um)(us)	strong-smelling, unpleasant
fragrans	fragrant
fragrantissima(um)(us)	most fragrant
graveolens	smelling unpleasantly
odorata(um)(us)	sweet-scented
odoratissima(um)(us)	sweetest-scented
moschata(um)(us)	musk-scented
suaveolens	sweet-scented

Names alluding to Other Plants

bignoniodes	Bignonia-like
jasminea	Jasmine-like
liliiflora(um)(us)	Lily-flowered
pseudoplatanus	False Plane
salicifolia(um)(us)	Willow-leaved
tulipifera(um)(us)	Tulip-bearing

Names which are Commemorative

delavayi	after the Abbé Delavay
harryana(um)(us)	after Sir Harry Veitch
henryana(um)(us)	after Dr. Augustine Henry
hookeri	after Sir Joseph Hooker
thunbergii	after Carl Peter Thunberg

Miscellaneous Names

affine(is)	related (to another species)
alata(um)(us)	winged
amabile(is)	lovely
ambigua(um)(us)	doubtful (identity?)
amoena(um)(us)	charming, pleasant
bella(um)(us)	pretty
commune(is)	common, occurring in plenty
confusa(um)(us)	confused (identity?)
dulce(is)	sweet
edule(is)	edible
florida(um)(us)	free-flowering
formosa(um)(us)	handsome, beautiful
hybrida(um)(us)	hybrid
insigne(is)	outstanding
intermedia(um)(us)	intermediate
media(um)(us)	middle, midway between
officinale(is)	of the shop (herbal)
praecox	early
pulchella(um)(us)	beautiful
speciosa(um)(us)	showy
sativa(um)(us)	sown, planted or cultivated
utile(is)	useful
vernale(is)	spring
vulgare(is)	common

hoosing Trees & Shrubs

Reasons for choosing trees and shrubs can appear to be almost as many and varied as the range of plants available.

Personal taste plays an important rôle, as do factors such as whether the plants are required for a public or private place, a small or large garden, or for their effect in a particular season.

At the end of this section, you will find tables designed to give you clues to selecting trees and shrubs for particular purposes or with certain characteristics.

The suggestions are by no means exhaustive. They are simply intended as a guide – or perhaps, just a reminder – of trees and shrubs suitable for some of the many different soils, situations and conditions found in the

British Isles – and even within one site.

In the majority of cases, the tables list complete genera, leaving the pleasure of final selection to the reader, by browsing through the detailed descriptions of plants within a particular genus. In some cases, however, certain species or forms 'break the rules' of their genus by proving to have marked characteristics or tolerance of conditions which differ from those of most of their close relatives – and thus offer prospects of success in conditions in which other plants of the same genus might fail. Thus, you will find some plants listed more specifically in the tables.

When thinking about planting new trees and shrubs, it makes good sense to take a walk around the area in which you live, visiting public parks, or private gardens which may be open to the public at different seasons, and even looking over fences, making notes of those subjects which appear to do well. If yours is a chalk-soil district, for instance, you probably won't find any rhododendrons or azaleas, whereas shrubs such as the potentillas, with their long flowering season, will probably thrive.

The three main factors controlling the growth of a plant (and, consequently, its selection for the garden) are soil, situation and hardiness.

Most of us think of soil as being either clay, sandy or chalky, and wet or dry, but there are obviously many degrees of these conditions. Many shrubs which are weak and miserable in a **shallow** soil over chalk will grow well in a **deep** soil over chalk.

The Importance of Soil pH

The pH scale is a means of measuring the acid or alkaline reaction of the soil. A pH reading of seven is neutral. Soils rich in lime are said to be alkaline, and show progressive readings above seven on the scale, whilst readings below this figure indicate progressive acidity.

Simple proprietary soil testing kits are readily available, and are a worthwhile investment. A kit may well cost appreciably less than a single tree or shrub, and a few minutes spent in using it may save expensive disappointment by warning you to steer clear of a particular plant or indicating how conditions for it might be improved.

Most ornamental plants thrive best in soils with a pH between 5.7 and 6.7, but, happily, one can find cultivated trees and shrubs which will tolerate the most extreme conditions at either end of the scale. For example, some species in the family Ericaceae will flourish in soils with a pH as low as 4 whereas some members of the

Oleaceae, Rosaceae and other families will thrive in limey soils with readings as high as 8.5.

In some cases (Holly, Beech, Yew, etc.) plants have a very wide range of tolerance to both acidity and alkalinity – from, say, pH3.6 to above 8.

The relationship between soil pH and plant growth is extremely complex, and secondary factors certainly play an important part in a plant's reaction. Hard and fast rules are therefore difficult, and one may well find, for example, that a Rhododendron will do well in one type of soil with a pH of 6.5 (slightly acid) but may fail in a different type of soil with the same reading.

The most profound influence of pH on plant growth is its effect on the availability of soil chemical elements to the plant. In the pH range between 5.7 and 6.7 the greatest number of nutrients are in a soluble state, the state in which they can most easily be absorbed.

As the pH rises, such important major elements as nitrogen, phosphorus and potassium gradually become less available and minor elements such as iron become increasingly unobtainable. As the pH decreases and the soil becomes more acid, availability of the three major elements again decreases, and the important minor element, calcium, is deficient. At the same time, other minor elements such as iron, manganese and aluminium become only too readily available, giving rise to toxic symptoms.

The choice of worthwhile trees and shrubs is so vast that, as a rule, there is not much point in struggling to grow subjects in soils which are really unsuitable. However, excessively acid soils may be improved by adding chalk or limestone, whilst the pH of alkaline soils may be lowered by applying iron sulphate, ammonium sulphate or Flowers of Sulphur.

Gardeners wishing to grow acid loving plants on alkaline soils can often achieve satisfactory results by applying the missing elements in chelated form – as Iron Sequestrene.

What is Hardiness?

The hardiness of plants is something about which the gardener is always wondering – and frequently baffled!

Why is it that trees which thrive in the harshness of Northern Europe, Russia or Siberia may fail in the comparatively warmer and apparently kinder conditions of southern England? One answer is that our treacherous springs, with mild spells followed by sharp frosts trick these unsuspecting trees into early growth, only to cut them back, again and again, until the tree is exhausted and dies. Plants from the milder countries, such as New Zealand or Chile are not so easily fooled. They wait for the more settled weather of late spring before making their move.

As most experienced gardeners know to their cost, few plants may confidently be described as being sure to withstand any condition in any part of Britain. Conversely it is surprising (and encouraging) just how many 'suspect' subjects may be grown with very little protection.

It is known and accepted that in general, the milder, moister areas of western Britain are more hospitable to tender plants than the often colder or drier areas of central and eastern regions. What is not always appreciated is that many tender subjects may be, (and are) grown in central, eastern and northern gardens where careful positioning or sheer good luck has provided adequate protection.

Fortunately, a combination of legislation, advancing technology and increasing environmental awareness have decreased the volume of atmospheric pollution in industrial and urban areas – and lessened the extent to which it affects the well-being of plants. It is happily rarer nowadays to find leaves coated with grime, soil defiled by sulphur dioxide or 'evergreens' which have become wholly or partly deciduous because of chemical 'burn'.

As a result it is encouraging to see town gardens which contain as many beautiful and interesting plants as those in rural areas. Indeed the microclimate in some favoured town situations enables successful cultivation of a number of exotic plants which are less likely to succeed in the harsher climate of nearby country districts.

Trees

Key to symbols & abbreviations

□   Suitable for conditions or having marked characteristics listed in column headings

■   Suitable for extreme conditions or having indicated characteristic to an intense degroo

S   Semi-evergreen

Figures in "Flowering time" column indicate months (i.e. 1 = January, and so on).

	CLAY	DRY	CHALK	MOIST/BOGGY	COLD EXPOSED INLAND	COASTAL	EVERGREEN (S–Semi)	DECIDUOUS	LARGE	MEDIUM	SMALL	WEEPING HABIT	UPRIGHT NARROW HABIT	RED OR PURPLE FOLIAGE	GOLD OR YELLOW FOLIAGE	GREY OR SILVER FOLIAGE	VARIEGATED FOLIAGE	AUTUMN COLOUR	BOLD ARCHITECTURAL FOLIAGE	AROMATIC FOLIAGE	ORNAMENTAL FRUIT	ORNAMENTAL BARK	FLOWERING TIME	FRAGRANT FLOWERS	HEDGING/SCREENING	SOUTH/WEST WALLS	SHADE TOLERANT
ACER campestre & cultivars ("Field Maple")	□	■		□				□		□								□			□	□					
ACER capillipes & other "Snake Barks"	□	□						□		□								□				□	□				
ACER griseum ("Paper Bark Maple")	□	□						□		□								■				□					
ACER negundo & cultivars ("Box Elder")	□	■		□				□	□						□		□										
ACER platanoides & cultivars ("Norway Maple")	□	■	□	□		□		□					□	□			□	□				4					
ACER pseudoplatanus & cultivars ("Sycamore")	□	□	■	□	□	□		□	□					□	□		□										
ACER rubrum & cultivars ("Red Maple")	□							□	□		□						□										
ACER saccharinum & cultivars ("Silver Maple")	□	□	□					□			□						□										
AESCULUS ("Horse Chestnut")	□		■					□	□					□				5/6			□						
AILANTHUS altissima ("Tree of Heaven")	□	□						□	□								□										
ALNUS ("Alder")	■			■	□			□	□				□									3					
AMELANCHIER ("Snowy Mespilus")	□		□					□		□				□				4/5									
ARBUTUS ("Strawberry Tree")		□		□	□			□			□				□	□	10/11										
BETULA ("Birch")	□	□	□	□	□			□	□	□		□	□				□			□							
CARAGANA ("Pea Tree")	□	□						□		□	□							5/6							□		
CARPINUS ("Hornbeam")	□		■	□	□			□	□				□				□				□					□	
CARYA ("Hickory")		□						□	□								□				□						
CASTANEA ("Sweet Chestnut") ✗		□			□			□	□								□					7					
CATALPA ("Bean Tree")		□				□		□	□				□	□			□					7					
CEDRELA		□				□		□	□							□	□					6	□				
CELTIS ("Hackberry")		□				□		□	□																		
CERCIDIPHYLLUM	□	□				□		□								□	□										
CERCIS ("Judas Tree")		□	■			□		□		□							□					5					
CLADRASTIS		□						□		□						□						6/7	□				
CORNUS ("Dogwood")	□	□						□		□						□						5					
CORYLUS colurna ("Turkish Hazel")	□	□		□				□	□								□				□						
COTONEASTER		□			□	S	□			□	□						□					6					
CRATAEGUS ("Thorn")	■		■	■	□	□		□		□	□	□	□				□	■				5		□	□	
DAVIDIA ("Pocket Handkerchief Tree")		□						□	□		□											5					

Key to symbols & abbreviations

□ Suitable for conditions or having marked characteristics listed in column headings

■ Suitable for extreme conditions or having indicated characteristic to an intense degree

S Semi-evergreen

Figures in "Flowering time" column indicate months (i.e. 1 = January, and so on).

	CLAY	DRY	CHALK	MOIST/BOGGY	COLD EXPOSED INLAND	COASTAL	EVERGREEN (S=Semi)	DECIDUOUS	LARGE	MEDIUM	SMALL	WEEPING HABIT	UPRIGHT NARROW HABIT	RED OR PURPLE FOLIAGE	GOLD OR YELLOW FOLIAGE	GREY OR SILVER FOLIAGE	VARIEGATED FOLIAGE	AUTUMN COLOUR	BOLD ARCHITECTURAL FOLIAGE	AROMATIC FOLIAGE	ORNAMENTAL FRUIT	ORNAMENTAL BARK	FLOWERING TIME	FRAGRANT FLOWERS	HEDGING/SCREENING	SOUTH/WEST WALLS	SHADE TOLERANT
DIOSPYROS ("Persimmon")			□					□			□							□	□		□		7				
EMBOTHRIUM ("Chilean Fire Bush") ↙				□			□				□												5/6				
EUCALYPTUS ("Gum")	□		□			□	□									□						□					
EUCRYPHIA ↙				□			□	□		□	□							□					7/8/9	□			
EUODIA			■					□		□									□								
FAGUS ("Beech")			■		□			□	□			□	□	□	□			□							□		
FRAXINUS ("Ash")	■	□	■		□	□		□	□	□	□	□					□	□				□	5/6				
GLEDITSIA		□	□		□			□	□	□	□	□			□						□						
GYMNOCLADUS			□					□		□								□	□		□						
HALESIA ("Snowdrop Tree") ↙				□				□			□												5				
IDESIA								□		□									□		□		6				
ILEX ('Holly")	■	□				□	□	□		□	□	□	□		□		□				□				□		□
JUGLANS ("Walnut")			□					□	□	□									□								
KOELREUTERIA ("Pride of India")		□	□					□		□			□								□		7/8				
LABURNUM	□		■		□			□			□	□			□								6	□			
LIGUSTRUM ("Privet")			□				□			□	□						□						8	□			
LIQUIDAMBAR ↙				□				□	□								□	■									
LIRIODENDRON ("Tulip Tree")			□					□	□	□			□				□	□	□				6/7				
MAACKIA			□					□			□								□				7/8				
MAGNOLIA (Some ↙)	□		□	□			□	□	□	□	□								□				8/9	□		□	
MALUS ("Flowering Crabs")	□		■					□		□	□	□		□				□			□		4/5	□			
MORUS ("Mulberry")			■					□		□	□	□									□						
NOTHOFAGUS ("Southern Beech") ↙				□			□	□	□	□																	
NYSSA ↙				□				□		□	□							■									
OSTRYA ("Hop Hornbeam")			□					□	□	□								□			□						
PARROTIA			□					□			□							■				□					
PAULOWNIA			□					□	□	□									□				5	□			
PHELLODENDRON ("Amur Cork Tree")			□					□		□								□	□	□							
PHILLYREA			□			□	□				□												5	□			
PLATANUS ("Plane")	□		□					□	□								□		□								
POPULUS ("Poplar")	■	□	□	□	□	□		□	□			□	□		□	□	□	□	□	□							
PRUNUS ("Almond", "Cherry", "Peach", "Purple Leaf Plum")	□		■				□	□		□	□	□	□	□				□				□	2 to 12	□	□		
PTEROCARYA	□		□	□				□	□										□				6				
PYRUS ("Pear")	□		□	□				□		□	□	□				□		■					4				
QUERCUS ("Oak")	□		□	□	□	□	□	□	□	□		□	□	□	□		□	□	□						□		
RHUS ("Sumach")			□					□			□							□	□								
ROBINIA ("False Acacia")		□	□					□	□		□		□		□								6	□			

Key to symbols & abbreviations

☐ Suitable for conditions or having marked characteristics listed in column headings

■ Suitable for extreme conditions or having indicated characteristic to an intense degree

S Semi-evergreen

Figures in "Flowering time" column indicate months (i.e. 1 = January, and so on).

	CLAY	DRY	CHALK	MOIST/BOGGY	COLD EXPOSED INLAND	COASTAL	EVERGREEN (S=Semi)	DECIDUOUS	LARGE	MEDIUM	SMALL	WEEPING HABIT	UPRIGHT NARROW HABIT	RED OR PURPLE FOLIAGE	GOLD OR YELLOW FOLIAGE	GREY OR SILVER FOLIAGE	VARIEGATED FOLIAGE	AUTUMN COLOUR	BOLD ARCHITECTURAL FOLIAGE	AROMATIC FOLIAGE	ORNAMENTAL FRUIT	ORNAMENTAL BARK	FLOWERING TIME	FRAGRANT FLOWERS	HEDGING/SCREENING	SOUTH-/WEST WALLS	SHADE TOLERANT
SALIX ("Willow")	■		☐	■	☐			☐		☐	☐	☐	☐	☐	☐	☐							3				
SASSAFRAS ✓			☐					☐			☐							☐									
SOPHORA			☐						☐	☐				☐	☐												
SORBUS ("Mountain Ash/Whitebeam")	☐		☐	☐	☐	☐		☐	☐	☐	☐		☐			☐		☐			☐		5/6	☐			
STEWARTIA ✓			☐					☐		☐			☐					☐				☐	7/8				
STYRAX ("Snowbell")			☐					☐		☐			☐										6	☐			
TETRACENTRON																							6				
TILIA ("Lime")	☐		☐	☐				☐	☐	☐	☐											☐	7/9	☐			
ZELKOVA			☐					☐	☐	☐								☐									

Conifers as trees

Key to symbols & abbreviations

☐ Suitable for conditions or having marked characteristics listed in column headings

■ Suitable for extreme conditions or having indicated characteristic to an intense degree

S Semi-evergreen

Figures in "Flowering time" column indicate months (i.e. 1 = January, and so on).

	CLAY	DRY	CHALK	MOIST/BOGGY	COLD EXPOSED INLAND	COASTAL	EVERGREEN	DECIDUOUS	LARGE	MEDIUM	SMALL	WEEPING	UPRIGHT NARROW	GOLD OR YELLOW FOLIAGE	GREY OR SILVER FOLIAGE	VARIEGATED FOLIAGE	AUTUMN COLOUR	AROMATIC FOLIAGE	ORNAMENTAL CONES	ORNAMENTAL BARK	HEDGING/SCREENING	SHADE TOLERANT
ABIES ("Silver Firs")	☐		☐	☐		☐	☐		☐	☐	☐		☐						☐			☐
ARAUCARIA ("Monkey Puzzle")	☐		☐	☐		☐	☐			☐												
CALOCEDRUS ("Incense Cedar")	☐		■			☐	☐		☐	☐			☐					☐				
CEDRUS ("Cedar")	☐		☐				☐		☐	☐		☐		☐	☐				☐			
CHAMAECYPARIS lawsoniana & cultivars ("Lawson Cypress")	☐	☐	■	☐			☐		☐	☐	☐	☐	☐	☐	☐	☐					☐	
CHAMAECYPARIS nootkatensis ("Nootka Cypress")	☐	☐	☐	☐	☐		☐		☐	☐		☐						☐		☐	☐	
CHAMAECYPARIS obtusa & cultivars ("Hinoki Cypress")	☐	☐	☐	☐	☐		☐			☐	☐			☐		☐						
CHAMAECYPARIS pisifera & cultivars ("Sawara Cypress")	☐	☐	☐	☐	☐		☐			☐	☐			☐								
CHAMAECYPARIS thyoides & cultivars ("White Cypress")	☐	☐					☐			☐				☐								
CRYPTOMERIA ("Japanese Cedar")	☐		☐	☐			☐		☐	☐	☐						☐			☐		
CUNNINGHAMIA ("Chinese Fir")	☐	☐				☐			☐													
× CUPRESSOCYPARIS ("Leyland Cypress")	☐	☐	☐	☐	☐	☐	☐		☐					☐							☐	
CUPRESSUS ("Cypress")	☐	■	■			☐	☐		☐	☐	☐		☐	☐	☐						☐	
GINKGO ("Maidenhair Tree")	☐	☐	☐					☐	☐				☐				☐					

Key to symbols & abbreviations

□ Suitable for conditions or having marked characteristics listed in column headings

■ Suitable for extreme conditions or having indicated characteristic to an intense degree

S Semi-evergreen

Figures in "Flowering time" column indicate months (i.e. 1 = January, and so on).

	CLAY	DRY	CHALK	MOIST/BOGGY	COLD EXPOSED INLAND	COASTAL	EVERGREEN	DECIDUOUS	LARGE	MEDIUM	SMALL	WEEPING	UPRIGHT NARROW	GOLD OR YELLOW FOLIAGE	GREY OR SILVER FOLIAGE	VARIEGATED FOLIAGE	AUTUMN COLOUR	AROMATIC FOLIAGE	ORNAMENTAL BARK	ORNAMENTAL CONES	HEDGING/SCREENING	SHADE TOLERANT
JUNIPERUS ("Juniper")	□	■	■	□	□	□	□		□	□	□		□	□	□	□					□	
LARIX ("Larch")	□	□	□		□			□	□	□		□	□				□		□			
METASEQUOIA ("Dawn Redwood")	□	□	□	■				□	□								□					
PICEA ("Spruce")	□		□	□	□		□		□	□	□	□	□							□		
PINUS ("Pine")	□	■	■		□	□	□		□	□	□				□	□					□	
PSEUDOTSUGA ("Douglas Fir")	□		□		□		□		□	□	□	□				□	□					
SEQUOIA ("Californian Redwood")	□		□		□		□		□										□			
SEQUOIADENDRON ("Wellingtonia")	□		□		□		□		□			□										
TAXODIUM ("Swamp Cypress")	■		■					□	□	□							□		□			
TAXUS ("Yew")	□	□	■		□		□			□	□		□	□		□					□	
THUJA ("Arborvitae")	□	□	■		□		□			□	□		□	□		□		□		□	□	
THUJOPSIS	□	□	■		□		□			□	□											
TORREYA	□	□	■				□			□	□											
TSUGA ("Hemlock")	□		□	□			□		□			□										□

Shrubs

Key to symbols & abbreviations

□ Suitable for conditions or having marked characteristics listed in column headings

■ Suitable for extreme conditions or having indicated characteristic to an intense degree

S Semi-evergreen

Figures in "Flowering time" column indicate months (i.e. 1 = January, and so on).

	CLAY	DRY	CHALK	MOIST/BOGGY	COLD EXPOSED INLAND	COASTAL	EVERGREEN (S = Semi)	DECIDUOUS	LARGE	MEDIUM	SMALL	DWARF	GROUND COVER	RED OR PURPLE FOLIAGE	GOLD OR YELLOW FOLIAGE	GREY OR SILVER FOLIAGE	VARIEGATED FOLIAGE	AUTUMN COLOUR	BOLD ARCHITECTURAL FOLIAGE	AROMATIC FOLIAGE	ORNAMENTAL FRUIT	ORNAMENTAL BARK	FLOWERING TIME	FRAGRANT FLOWERS	HEDGING/SCREENING	NORTH/EAST WALLS	SOUTH/WEST WALLS	SHADE TOLERANT
ABELIA	□		□				S			□	□												6/9				□	□
ABELIOPHYLLUM	□		□					□		□													2				□	□
ABUTILON		□	□					□	□	□					□	□							5/9				□	□
ACACIA ("Wattle") ✗ †		□				□			□						□	□							1/2	□			□	
ACER japonicum, palmatum & cultivars ("Japanese Maples")	□		□					□		□	□			□	□			□										
AESCULUS ("Horse Chestnut")	□		■					□	□										□	□			5/7					
AMELANCHIER ("Snowy Mespilus")	□		□					□	□	□								□					4/5					
ANDROMEDA ✗				□			□					□									□		5/6					
ANTHYLLIS		□	□					□			□												6/7					

Key to symbols & abbreviations

□ Suitable for conditions or having marked characteristics listed in column headings

■ Suitable for extreme conditions or having indicated characteristic to an intense degree

S Semi-evergreen

Figures in "Flowering time" column indicate months (i.e. 1 = January, and so on).

Plant	Flowering time
ARALIA	7/9
ARBUTUS ("Strawberry Tree")	10/11
ARCTOSTAPHYLOS ✗	4/5
ARONIA ("Chokeberry")	4
ARTEMESIA	
ARUNDINARIA ("Bamboo")	
ATRIPLEX	
AZARA	3
AUCUBA	
BALLOTA	7
BERBERIS ("Barberry")	4
BUDDLEIA	5/6 & 8/9
BUPLEURUM	7
BUXUS ("Box")	
CALLICARPA	8
CALLISTEMON ("Bottle Brush")	7
CALLUNA ("Ling") ✗	7/10
CALYCANTHUS ("Allspice")	7
CAMELLIA ✗	2/5
CARAGANA ("Pea Tree")	5
CARPENTERIA	7
CARYOPTERIS	8
CASSINIA	7
CASSIOPE ✗	4
CEANOTHUS ("California Lilac")	5 & 8
CERATOSTIGMA ("Plumbago")	8/10
CERCIS ("Judas Tree")	5
CHAENOMELES ("Japonica")	3/4
CHAMAEROPS ("Fan Palm")	
CHIMONANTHUS ("Winter Sweet")	1
CHIONANTHUS ("Fringe Tree")	6/7
CHOISYA ("Mexican Orange")	5/6
CISTUS ("Sun Rose")	6/7
CLERODENDRUM	8/9
CLETHRA ✗	7/8
CLIANTHUS ("Lobster's Claw") †	6
COLLETIA	7/8
COLUTEA ("Bladder Senna")	6/8
COMPTONIA ("Sweet Fern") ✗	3
CONVOLVULUS	5
CORNUS ("Dogwood")	2/5/6

Column headings (left to right): CLAY · DRY · CHALK · MOIST/BOGGY · COLD EXPOSED INLAND · COASTAL · EVERGREEN (S = Semi) · DECIDUOUS · LARGE · MEDIUM · SMALL · DWARF · GROUND COVER · RED OR PURPLE FOLIAGE · GOLD OR YELLOW FOLIAGE · GREY OR SILVER FOLIAGE · VARIEGATED FOLIAGE · AUTUMN COLOUR · BOLD ARCHITECTURAL FOLIAGE · AROMATIC FOLIAGE · ORNAMENTAL FRUIT · ORNAMENTAL BARK · FLOWERING TIME · FRAGRANT FLOWERS · HEDGING/SCREENING · NORTH/EAST WALLS · SOUTH/WEST WALLS · SHADE TOLERANT

	CLAY	DRY	CHALK	MOIST/BOGGY	COLD EXPOSED INLAND	COASTAL	EVERGREEN (S = Semi)	DECIDUOUS	LARGE	MEDIUM	SMALL	DWARF	GROUND COVER	RED OR PURPLE FOLIAGE	GOLD OR YELLOW FOLIAGE	GREY OR SILVER FOLIAGE	VARIEGATED FOLIAGE	AUTUMN COLOUR	BOLD ARCHITECTURAL FOLIAGE	AROMATIC FOLIAGE	ORNAMENTAL FRUIT	ORNAMENTAL BARK	FLOWERING TIME	FRAGRANT FLOWERS	HEDGING/SCREENING	NORTH/EAST WALLS	SOUTH/WEST WALLS	SHADE TOLERANT
COROKIA		□	□		□	□				□											□		5/6					
CORONILLA		□	□				□			□	□				□	□							5/7	□			□	
CORYLOPSIS	□	□						□	□	□			□										3/4	□				
CORYLUS ("Hazel")	□	□	□	□				□	□					□	□				□		□		2		□			□
COTINUS ("Smoke Tree")		□	□					□	□	□				□				□					6/7					
COTONEASTER	□	□	□	□	□	□	□	□	□	□	□	□	□					□			□		6		□	□		□
CRINODENDRON ✓				□			□			□													5			□	□	
CYATHODES ✓				□			□				□												5					
CYTISUS ("Broom")	□	□	□					□	□	□	□	□											5/7					
DABOECIA ("Irish Heath") ✓			□				□				□	□											6/8					
DANAE ("Alexandrian Laurel")	□	□			□		□				□																	□
DAPHNE		□	□				□	□			□	□							□				2/6	□				□
DECAISNEA		□	□					□	□												□							□
DESFONTAINEA ✓			□				□			□													7/9			□		
DEUTZIA	□	□	■		□			□		□	□												6/7					
DIERVILLA	□	□	□		□			□		□									□				6/7					
DIPELTA		□	□					□	□	□													5	□				
DIPTERONIA	□	□						□	□	□								□										
DISANTHUS ✓ ◑	□	□		□				□	□									□					10					
DISTYLIUM	□				□		□		□	□													4					
DRIMYS				□			□		□	□													4/5	□	□			
ELAEAGNUS	□	□	□		□	□	□	□	□	□					□	□					□	□	5/6 & 10	□	□			
ENKIANTHUS ✓	□			□				□	□	□								□					5					
ERICA, tall forms ("Heath") ✓		□			□	□	□			□	□												3/5	□				
ERICA carnea, mediterranea, terminalis and × darleyensis		□	□				□				□	□	□	□	□		□						4/5 & 9	□				
ERICA, others ✓		□		□	□	□	□				□	□		□	□		□						6/10					
ERIOBOTRYA ("Loquat")	□						□		□										□							□	□	
ESCALLONIA	□	□	□			□	□			□	□												6/7		□			
EUONYMUS	□	□	■	□	□	□	□	□	□	□	□						□	□			□	□	5/6		□	□		□
EXOCHORDA	□		□					□	□	□	□												5					
FABIANA			□		□		□			□									□				5/6					
× FATSHEDERA	□	□	□				□			□									□									□
FATSIA	□	□	□				□			□									□				10					□
FORSYTHIA	□	□	■	□				□	□	□		□											3/4		□	□		
FOTHERGILLA ✓	□			□				□		□	□							□					4	□				
FREMONTODENDRON (FREMONTIA) †		□	□				□		□														6/8				□	
FUCHSIA		□		□				□		□	□	□											7/9				□	
GARRYA	□	□			□		□			□													1/2			□		
× GAULNETTYA ✓		□	□		□		□				□		□								□		5/6					□
GAULTHERIA ✓				□			□				□	□	□								□		5/6	□				□

Key to symbols & abbreviations

☐ Suitable for conditions or having marked characteristics listed in column headings

■ Suitable for extreme conditions or having indicated characteristic to an intense degree

S Semi-evergreen

Figures in "Flowering time" column indicate months
(i.e. 1 = January, and so on).

	CLAY	DRY	CHALK	MOIST/BOGGY	COLD EXPOSED INLAND	COASTAL	EVERGREEN (S = Semi)	DECIDUOUS	LARGE	MEDIUM	SMALL	DWARF	GROUND COVER	RED OR PURPLE FOLIAGE	GOLD OR YELLOW FOLIAGE	GREY OR SILVER FOLIAGE	VARIEGATED FOLIAGE	AUTUMN COLOUR	AROMATIC FOLIAGE	ORNAMENTAL FOLIAGE	BOLD ARCHITECTURAL FOLIAGE	ORNAMENTAL FRUIT	ORNAMENTAL BARK	FLOWERING TIME	FRAGRANT FLOWERS	HEDGING/SCREENING	NORTH/EAST WALLS	SOUTH-/WEST WALLS	SHADE TOLERANT
GENISTA ("Broom")		☐	☐				☐	☐		☐	☐													5/9					
GREVILLEA ⚲ †		☐			☐		☐			☐														6/7				☐	
GRISELINIA †		☐	☐		☐	☐	☐		☐								☐									☐			
× HALIMIOCISTUS ("Sun Rose")		☐	■			☐	☐			☐						☐								5/9					
HALIMIUM ("Sun Rose")		☐	☐			☐	☐				☐	☐				☐								5/6					
HALIMODENDRON ("Salt Tree")		☐	☐		☐	☐		☐								☐								6/7					
HAMAMELIS ("Witch Hazel")	☐			☐				☐	☐									☐						12/3	☐				
HEBE ("Veronica")		☐	■			☐	☐			☐	☐	☐					☐	☐						6/10					
HEDYSARUM		☐	☐					☐																7/9					
HELIANTHEMUM ("Rock Rose")		☐	■			☐	☐					☐	☐											5/9					
HELICHRYSUM		☐	☐			☐	☐					☐				☐				☐				7					
HIBISCUS		☐	■					☐		☐	☐													7/10					
HIPPOPHAE ("Sea Buckthorn")	☐	☐	☐	■	☐	☐		☐	☐							☐					☐								
HOHERIA		☐	☐					☐	☐							☐								6/7	☐		☐		
HOLODISCUS		☐	■					☐		☐														7					
HYDRANGEA	☐		☐	☐				☐		☐	☐		☐				☐	☐						6/9					☐
HYPERICUM	☐		■				S	☐		☐	☐	☐	☐							☐				6/10					☐
ILEX ("Holly")	☐	☐	☐	☐	☐	☐	☐		☐						☐		☐				☐					☐			
ILLICIUM		☐					☐			☐									☐					5/6					
INDIGOFERA	☐	☐	■					☐		☐							☐							6/9				☐	
ITEA ilicifolia	☐		☐				☐			☐														8	☐		☐		
JASMINUM ("Jasmine")	☐		☐					☐		☐													☐	11/12 & 6/7	☐		☐	☐	
KALMIA ⚲			☐				☐			☐														4/6					
KERRIA	☐		■					☐		☐					☐									4/5					☐
KOLKWITZIA ("Beauty Bush")	☐	☐	■					☐		☐														5/6					
LAURUS ("Sweet Bay")	☐	☐	■		☐	☐	☐		☐										☐						☐			
LAVANDULA ("Lavender")		☐	■				☐			☐		☐				☐			☐					7		☐			
LEDUM ⚲				☐			☐			☐														4/6					
LEIOPHYLLUM ⚲			☐				☐				☐													5/6					
LEPTOSPERMUM		☐				☐	☐			☐														5/6					
LESPEDEZA	☐	☐	☐					☐		☐														8/9					
LEUCOTHOE ⚲			☐				☐				☐			☐	☐									5/8					☐
LEYCESTERIA	☐		☐		☐			☐		☐											☐	☐		6/9					
LIGUSTRUM ("Privet")	☐	☐	■			☐	☐	☐		☐							☐					☐		6/9		☐			☐
LINDERA ⚲				☐				☐		☐																			
LIPPIA ("Lemon Plant") †		☐	☐					☐		☐									☐					8			☐		
LOMATIA ⚲				☐			☐			☐	☐													7	☐				
LONICERA ("Honeysuckle")	☐	☐	■			☐	☐	☐		☐			☐									☐		1/3 & 5/6	☐	☐			
MAGNOLIA	☐		☐	☐			☐	☐	☐		☐											☐		7/9 & 3/4	☐			☐	
× MAHOBERBERIS	☐	☐	■		☐	☐	☐			☐										☐				4					☐
MAHONIA		☐	■				☐			☐	☐	☐								☐		☐		12/4	☐				☐

26

Key to symbols & abbreviations

□ Suitable for conditions or having marked characteristics listed in column headings

■ Suitable for extreme conditions or having indicated characteristic to an intense degree

S Semi-evergreen

Figures in "Flowering time" column indicate months (i.e. 1 = January, and so on).

	CLAY	DRY	CHALK	MOIST/BOGGY	COLD EXPOSED INLAND	COASTAL	EVERGREEN (S=Semi)	DECIDUOUS	LARGE	MEDIUM	SMALL	DWARF	GROUND COVER	RED OR PURPLE FOLIAGE	GOLD OR YELLOW FOLIAGE	GREY OR SILVER FOLIAGE	VARIEGATED FOLIAGE	AUTUMN COLOUR	AROMATIC FOLIAGE	BOLD ARCHITECTURAL FOLIAGE	ORNAMENTAL FRUIT	ORNAMENTAL BARK	FLOWERING TIME	FRAGRANT FLOWERS	HEDGING/SCREENING	NORTH/EAST WALLS	SOUTH/WEST WALLS	SHADE TOLERANT
MENZIESIA ⚹				□				□			□												5					
MYRICA	□	□		□	□			□		□	□										□	□	4/5					
MYRICARIA		□						□			□												6/7					
MYRTUS ("Myrtle") †		□	□			□	□				□								□	□			7/8				□	
NANDINA ("Sacred Bamboo")		□	□				□			□	□			□				□					6/7					
NEILLIA	□		■					□		□	□												5/6					
OLEARIA ("Daisy Bush")	□	□	■			□	□			□	□					□							5/8		□□			
ONONIS		□	■								□												6/7					
OSMANTHUS	□	□	□				□			□							□						4/5 & 9	□				
× OSMAREA	□	□	□				□			□													4/5					
OZOTHAMNUS		□	□				□			□													7	□				
PACHYSANDRA	□		□	□			□					□	□										2/3					□
PAEONIA ("Tree Paeony")			■					□			□									□			5/6					
PARAHEBE	□	□	□				□					□	□										7/8					
PARROTIA	□	□						□	□									□				□	3					
PERNETTYA ⚹	□	□		□	□		□				□										□		5/6					□
PEROWSKIA		□	□					□			□					□			□				8/9					
PETTERIA		□	□					□		□													5/6	□				
PHILADELPHUS ("Mock Orange")	□	□	■	□				□	□	□	□				□								6/7	□				□
PHILESIA ⚹				□			□				□	□											6/7					
PHILLYREA	□	□	□				□			□	□												5	□				□
PHLOMIS		□	□				□				□					□			□				6					
PHORMIUM		□	□			□	□			□				□			□			□			7/9					
PHOTINIA	□	□	□				□			□				□				□			□		5/6					
PHYGELIUS ("Cape Figwort")		□	□								□												7/9				□	
PHYLLODOCE ⚹			□	□			□					□	□										5/6					
PHYLLOSTACHYS ("Bamboo")				□			□			□										□								□
PHYSOCARPUS	□	□	□	□				□							□								6					
PIERIS ⚹				□			□			□				□									3/5	□				
PIPTANTHUS ("Evergreen Laburnum")		□	□				S			□													5				□	
PITTOSPORUM	□	□	□			□	□			□							□	□	□				5/6	□	□□			
POLYGALA ⚹				□			□				□	□											4/6					
PONCIRUS ("Bitter Orange")	□	□	□					□		□											□□		5	□				
POTENTILLA	□	■	■	□	□			□		□	□	□				□			□				6/11		□			□
PRUNUS	□	□	■	□	□			□	□	□	□			□				□			□□		3/6	□	□			□
PTELEA ("Hop Tree")	□							□	□	□					□								6	□				
PTEROSTYRAX	□		□					□	□	□													6/7	□				
PUNICA ("Pomegranate") †		□	□					□	□	□							□						9/10				□	
PYRACANTHA ("Firethorn")	□	□	■			□	□			□	□										□		6		□□□	□	□	□
RAPHIOLEPIS		□	□				□				□												6	□			□	

27

	CLAY	DRY	CHALK	MOIST/BOGGY	COLD EXPOSED INLAND	COASTAL	EVERGREEN (S = Semi)	DECIDUOUS	LARGE	MEDIUM	SMALL	DWARF	GROUND COVER	RED OR PURPLE FOLIAGE	GOLD OR YELLOW FOLIAGE	GREY OR SILVER FOLIAGE	VARIEGATED FOLIAGE	AUTUMN COLOUR	BOLD ARCHITECTURAL FOLIAGE	AROMATIC FOLIAGE	ORNAMENTAL FRUIT	ORNAMENTAL BARK	FLOWERING TIME	FRAGRANT FLOWERS	HEDGING/SCREENING	NORTH/EAST WALLS	SOUTH/WEST WALLS	SHADE TOLERANT
RHAMNUS ("Buckthorn")	□	□	■	□	□	□	□	□	□	□	□											□						
RHODODENDRON ✗	□		□				□		□	□	□	□							□				1/8	□	□			□
RHODODENDRON AZALEA, deciduous ✗	□				□			□		□								□					5/6	□				
RHODODENDRON AZALEA, evergreen ✗	□					□					□	□	□										4/5					□
RHODODENDRON – (See also charts "Choosing Rhododendrons")																												
RHODOTYPOS	□	□	■					□														□	5/7					
RHUS ("Sumach")	□	□	■			□		□		□								□	□									
RIBES ("Currants" and "Gooseberries")	□	□	■		□		□	□		□	□								□				2/5					
ROBINIA ("False Acacia")	□	□	□					□	□	□													6					□
ROMNEYA ("Tree Poppy")		□	□			□				□						□							7/10	□				
ROSA ("Rose species")	□	□	□			□		□		□	□									□	□		5/7					
ROSE ("Shrub Roses")	□		□			□		□		□	□										□		6/9	□	□		□	
ROSMARINUS ("Rosemary")		□	■			□	□			□	□									□			5		□			
RUBUS ("Brambles")	□	■	□	□	□	□	□	□		□	□											□	5/8					□
RUSCUS ("Butcher's Broom")	□	□	□	□			□				□										□							□
RUTA ("Rue")		□	□			□					□					□				□			6/8					
SALIX ("Willow")	■		□	■	□			□	□	□	□	□										□	2/3					
SALVIA		□	□			S	□		□	□	□					□	□						8/9				□	
SAMBUCUS ("Elder")	□	□	■	□		□		□	□	□					□		□				□		6	□				□
SANTOLINA ("Cotton Lavender")		□	□		□	□					□					□				□			7					
SARCOCOCCA ("Christmas Box")	□		■				□				□	□											2	□				□
SASA ("Bamboo")	□		□	□			□			□	□								□									□
SENECIO	□	□	■		□	□	□				□					□			□				6/7					
SKIMMIA	□	□	□			□	□				□	□									□	□	4/5	□				□
SORBARIA	□	□	■	□	□		□		□	□	□								□				6/8					
SORBUS reducta	□	□	□									□						□			□	□	5					
SPARTIUM ("Spanish Broom")	□	□	■		□	□				□						□							6/8	□				
SPIRAEA	□	□	■	□	□			□		□	□							□			□		4/8					
STACHYURUS	□	□	□					□		□													8					
STAPHYLEA ("Bladder Nut")	□		□					□		□											□		5/6					
STEPHANANDRA	□							□		□	□	□	□					□				□	6					
STRANVAESIA	□		□		□		□		□									□			□		6		□			□
STYRAX ("Snowbell") ✗	□							□		□													6					
SYCOPSIS	□	□					□				□												2/3					□
SYMPHORICARPOS	□	□	■	□	□	□		□		□			□								□				□			□
SYRINGA ("Lilac")	□		■					□	□	□	□												5/6	□				
TAMARIX ("Tamarisk")	□	□	□		□	□		□		□													3 & 7/9					
TELOPEA ("Waratah") ✗	□		□	□			□			□													6					
TETRACENTRON	□		□					□		□									□				6/7					

Key to symbols & abbreviations

□ Suitable for conditions or having marked characteristics listed in column headings

■ Suitable for extreme conditions or having indicated characteristic to an intense degree

S Semi-evergreen

Figures in "Flowering time" column indicate months (i.e. 1 = January, and so on).

Column headings (left to right): CLAY · DRY · CHALK · MOIST/BOGGY · COLD EXPOSED INLAND · COASTAL · DECIDUOUS · EVERGREEN (S = Semi) · LARGE · MEDIUM · SMALL · DWARF · GROUND COVER · RED OR PURPLE FOLIAGE · GOLD OR YELLOW FOLIAGE · GREY OR SILVER FOLIAGE · VARIEGATED FOLIAGE · AUTUMN COLOUR · AROMATIC FOLIAGE · ORNAMENTAL FRUIT · ORNAMENTAL BARK · BOLD ARCHITECTURAL FOLIAGE · FLOWERING TIME · FRAGRANT FLOWERS · HEDGING/SCREENING · NORTH/EAST WALLS · SOUTH/WEST WALLS · SHADE TOLERANT

Plant	Flowering time
TEUCRIUM	6/8
TROCHODENDRON ✗	5/6
ULEX ("Gorse")	3/5 & 8/10
VACCINIUM ✗	
VIBURNUM	11/3 & 4/6
VINCA ("Periwinkle")	4/6
VITEX ("Chaste Tree")	9/10
WEIGELA	5/6
YUCCA	7/8
ZENOBIA ✗	6/7

Conifers as shrubs

Key to symbols & abbreviations

□ Suitable for conditions or having marked characteristics listed in column headings

■ Suitable for extreme conditions or having indicated characteristic to an intense degree

S Semi-evergreen

Figures in "Flowering time" column indicate months (i.e. 1 = January, and so on).

Column headings (left to right): CLAY · DRY · CHALK · MOIST/BOGGY · COLD EXPOSED INLAND · COASTAL · EVERGREEN (S = Semi) · LARGE · MEDIUM · SMALL · DWARF · GROUND COVER · UPRIGHT, NARROW · GOLD OR YELLOW FOLIAGE · GREY OR SILVER FOLIAGE · VARIEGATED FOLIAGE · AUTUMN COLOUR · AROMATIC FOLIAGE · ORNAMENTAL CONES · SHADE TOLERANT

- ABIES ("Silver Fir")
- CEDRUS ("Cedar")
- CEPHALOTAXUS
- CHAMAECYPARIS lawsoniana & cultivars ("Lawson Cypress")
- CHAMAECYPARIS obtusa & cultivars ("Hinoki Cypress")
- CHAMAECYPARIS pisifera & cultivars ("Sawara Cypress")
- CHAMAECYPARIS thyoides & cultivars ("White Cypress")
- CRYPTOMERIA ("Japanese Cedar")
- JUNIPERUS ("Juniper")
- PICEA ("Spruce")
- PINUS ("Pine")
- PODOCARPUS

29

Key to symbols & abbreviations
□ Suitable for conditions or having marked characteristics listed in column headings
■ Suitable for extreme conditions or having indicated characteristic to an intense degree
C Semi-evergreen
Figures in "Flowering time" column indicate months
(i.e. 1 = January, and so on).

Column headings (conifers): CLAY · DRY · CHALK · MOIST/BOGGY · COLD EXPOSED INLAND · COASTAL · EVERGREEN (S=Semi) · LARGE · MEDIUM · SMALL · DWARF · UPRIGHT, NARROW · GROUND COVER · GOLD OR YELLOW FOLIAGE · GREY OR SILVER FOLIAGE · VARIEGATED FOLIAGE · AUTUMN COLOUR · AROMATIC FOLIAGE · ORNAMENTAL CONES · SHADE TOLERANT

- PSEUDOTSUGA ("Douglas Fir")
- TAXUS ("Yew")
- THUJA ("Arborvitae")
- TSUGA ("Hemlock")

Climbers

Key to symbols & abbreviations
□ Suitable for conditions or having marked characteristics listed in column headings
■ Suitable for extreme conditions or having indicated characteristic to an intense degree
S Semi-evergreen
Figures in "Flowering time" column indicate months
(i.e. 1 = January, and so on).

Column headings (climbers): CLAY · DRY · CHALK · COASTAL · EVERGREEN (S=Semi) · DECIDUOUS · VIGOROUS · MEDIUM · GROUND COVER · SELF CLINGING · TWINING · RED OR PURPLE FOLIAGE · GOLD OR YELLOW FOLIAGE · VARIEGATED FOLIAGE · AUTUMN COLOUR · BOLD ARCHITECTURAL FOLIAGE · ORNAMENTAL FRUIT · FLOWERING TIME · FRAGRANT FLOWERS · NORTH/EAST WALLS · SOUTH/WEST WALLS · SHADE TOLERANT

Plant	Flowering time
ABELIA	4
ACTINIDIA	7/8
AMPELOPSIS	
ARISTOLOCHIA	6
BERBERIDOPSIS	7/8
CAMPSIS ("Trumpet Vine")	8/9
CELASTRUS	
CLEMATIS	4/10
HEDERA ("Ivy")	
HUMULUS ("Hop")	
HYDRANGEA, climbing	6
JASMINUM ("Jasmine")	8/9
LONICERA ("Honeysuckle")	5/10
PARTHENOCISSUS	
PASSIFLORA ("Passion Flower") †	6/9
PILEOSTEGIA	8/9
POLYGONUM ("Russian Vine")	7/9
RUBUS ("Bramble")	
SCHIZANDRA	5 & 8/9
SCHIZOPHRAGMA	7
SENECIO	9/11
SOLANUM	7/10
TRACHELOSPERMUM	7/8
VITIS ("Vines")	
WISTERIA	5/6

Choosing Rhododendrons

The genus RHODODENDRON is so vast that the range of choice can sometimes appear to be overwhelming.

The table below, based upon a representative selection of species and hybrids, has been designed to facilitate selection by three main factors – height, colour and flowering period.

Names commencing with a small initial letter are those of species; those starting with a capital letter (with or without quotation marks) are hybrids.

Figures following the names indicate the flowering period (depending on location and season). A figure 1 represents January, and so on.

Information on relative hardiness and other characteristics is incorporated within individual plant descriptions.

TALL

REDS
– arboreum	1–3
– 'Bagshot Ruby'	5–6
– barbatum	3–4
– 'Britannia'	5–6
– cinnabarinum roylei	5–6
– 'Cynthia'	5–6
– 'Fire Bird'	5–6
– 'Hugh Koster'	5–6
– 'Kluis Sensation'	5–6
– mallotum	3–4
– 'Michael Waterer'	6–7
– Nobleanum	1–3
– 'Rocket'	3–4
– 'Romany Chal'	6–7
– 'Tally Ho'	6–7
– thomsonii	4–5

YELLOWS
– 'Beatrice Keir'	5–6
– 'Brookside'	5–6
– 'Cool Haven'	5–6
– 'Crest'	5–6
– Damaris 'Logan'	4–5
– falconeri	4–5
– 'Goldsworth Yellow'	5–6
– 'Harvest Moon'	5–6
– 'Hawk'	5–6
– Jalisco 'Janet'	6–7
– 'Jervis Bay'	5–6
– macabeanum	3–4
– 'Marcia'	4–5
– 'New Comet'	4–5
– 'Roza Stevenson'	5–6
– xanthocodon	5–6

MEDIUM

REDS
– 'Arthur Osborn'	6–7
– beanianum	3–5
– chaetomallum	3–4
– 'Choremia'	4–5
– 'Doncaster'	5–6
– 'Elizabeth'	4–5
– haematodes	5–6
– 'May Day'	5–6
– 'W.F.H'	5–6

YELLOWS
– 'Bo-peep'	3–4
– 'Caerhays Philip'	4–5
– campylocarpum	4–5
– lutescens	2–4
– 'Moonstone'	4–5
– 'Remo'	3–4
– 'Unique'	4–5
– wardii	5–6
– 'Yellow Hammer'	3–4

DWARF

REDS
– calostrotum 'Gigha'	5–6
– campylogynum	5–6
– 'Carmen'	5–6
– 'Elisabeth Hobbie'	4–5
– ferrugineum	6–7
– forrestii repens	4–5
– 'Humming Bird'	4–5
– 'Jenny'	5–6
– 'Little Ben'	3–4
– saluenense	4–5
– 'Scarlet Wonder'	5–6

YELLOWS
– 'Chikor'	5–6
– chrysanthum	5–6
– chryseum	4–5
– 'Cowslip'	5–6
– 'Curlew'	4–5
– flavidum	3–4
– glaucophyllum luteiflorum	4–5
– hanceanum 'Nanum'	4–5
– keiskei	3–5
– sargentianum	4–5

Continued

TALL

PINKS
- Albatross 'Townhill Pink'   5-6
- 'Alice'   5-6
- 'Betty Wormald'   5-6
  'Cornish Cross'   4-5
- discolor   6-7
- fargesii   3-4
- fortunei   5-6
- 'Lady Clementine Mitford'   6-7
- Lady Roseberry 'Pink
  Delight'   5-6
- Loderi 'Venus'   4-5
- 'Mrs G.W. Leak'   5-6
- Naomi 'Exbury'   4-5
- orbiculare   3-4
- 'Pink Pearl'   5-6
- 'Sir Frederick Moore'   5-6
- Vanessa 'Pastel'   5-6

WHITES
- Albatross 'Townhill White'   5-6
- auriculatum   7-8
- 'Beauty of Littleworth'   5-6
- 'Carex White'   3-4
- decorum   5-6
- fictolacteum   4-5
- 'Gomer Waterer'   6-7
- 'July Fragrance'   6-7
- Loderi 'King George'   4-5
- 'Loder's White'   5-6
- 'Mrs Lionel de Rothschild'   5-6
- 'Mrs P.D. Williams'   5-6
- 'Polar Bear'   7-8
- 'Sappho'   5-6
- 'Snow Queen'   5-6
- 'White Glory'   4-5

BLUES
- augustinii   4-5
- 'Arthur Bedford'   5-6
- 'Blue Peter'   5-6
- 'Countess of Athlone'   5-6
- 'Electra' (see augustinii)   4-5
- 'Fastuosum Flore Pleno'   5-6
- 'Lavender Girl'   5-6
- 'Purple Splendour'   5-6
- 'Susan'   5-6

MEDIUM

PINKS
- 'Brocade'   4-5
- bureavii   4-5
- 'Christmas Cheer'   3-4
- davidsonianum   4-5
- fittianum   4-5
- makinoi   5-6
- 'Oudijk's Sensation'   5-6
- 'Praecox'   2-3
- 'Racil'   4-5
- spiciferum   4-5
- 'Winsome'   5-6

WHITES
- 'Arthur Stevens'   5-6
- Cilpinense   3-4
- flavidum 'Album'   3-4
- quinquefolium (azalea
  series)   4-5
- roxianum   4-5
- yakushimanum   5-6

BLUES
- 'Augfast'   3-4
- 'Bluebird'   4-5
- 'Blue Diamond'   4-5
- Russautinii   5-6
- 'Saint Tudy'   4-5
- 'Songster'   4-5

DWARF

PINKS
- 'Bow-Bells'   4-5
- campylogynum 'Crushed
  Strawberry'   5-6
- 'Elizabeth Lockhart'   4-5
- Fittra   4-5
- imperator   5-6
- kotschyi   5-7
- pemakoense   3-4
- 'Pink Drift'   5-6
- racemosum 'Forrest's
  Dwarf'   3-4
- 'Treasure'   4-5
- williamsianum   4-5

WHITES
- 'Bric-a-Brac'   3-4
- leucaspis   2-3
- microleucum   4-5
- 'Ptarmigan'   3-4
- Sarled   5-6

BLUES
- 'Blue Tit'   4-5
- fastigiatum   4-5
- hippophaeoides 'Inshriach'   3-4
- impeditum   4-5
- intricatum   4-5
- 'Intrifast'   5-6
- nitens   6-7
- orthocladum   4-5
- russatum   4-5
- 'Sapphire'   4-5
- scintillans, F.C.C. Form   4-5

runing Garden Shrubs and Climbers

Although the methods and times of pruning are (and will probably remain) a controversial subject, there are some useful guidelines which can be confidently recommended.

The aim of pruning should primarily be to remove any dead, diseased, weak or straggly growth. This ensures a healthy open framework within which air can circulate freely.

The majority of trees and shrubs need little further pruning provided due regard was paid to their ultimate height and spread when they were sited. It is better to thin out and transplant trees and shrubs if they were placed too close together initially than to clip them all round every year as a means of restriction.

However, others, particularly shrubs which tolerate frequent clipping, such as Yew, (*Taxus*), Bay (*Laurus*), Box (*Buxus*), etc., may be formed, if desired, into hedges, arches, or examples of the topiarist's art. Annual or bi-annual removal of old flowering wood encourages many shrubs to produce a greater number of flowers.

'Dead-heading' reduces competition for nutrients between developing seeds and the rest of the plant, so that further flowering and a better flush of vegetative growth is often encouraged. New basal growth can be stimulated in plants such as laurel, yew, holly, some rhododendrons, cotoneaster and viburnums, which have become bare at the base, by cutting back hard into the old wood in April. Similarly brightly coloured new shoots of shrubs such as *Cornus alba* are induced by cutting the old shoots near to the ground in winter or early spring.

Large cuts should always be coated with a bituminous dressing or a proprietary wound sealant.

Shrub types and pruning key

Throughout this book abbreviated guides to pruning have been incorporated in the generic descriptions, or appended to the descriptions of individual types wherever this is thought to be helpful or the need for pruning is significant.
A capital letter indicates the general extent to which pruning may be required, as defined below:

A – In general, little pruning required
B – Cut back to within two or three buds/15-30cm (6 to 12ins) of ground level
C – On young or semi-mature plants, cut back each flowering shoot *as soon as the blossoms have faded*, leaving one or two young shoots at the base of each
D – Cut out as much old wood as possible *during the winter* consistent with leaving last year's growth for the following year's flowering
E – Shorten back side shoots of current season's growth to within five or six buds during August or September
· **A small letter in parenthesis** gives supplementary pruning information and/or details of method, as follows:
(a) To increase size, a framework of old wood may be built up, in which case prune to within two or three buds of the old wood
(b) If damaged by frost or straggly in habit, cut back to sound wood
(c) As (b), but damage may be so severe as to require cutting back to ground level

(d) Where grown as a foliage shrub, may be cut to within a bud or two of ground level to maintain compact growth

(e) Makes a small tree. Attend to formation in the early stages by preventing crossing or touching branches and lopsided growth

(f) Restrict growth as desired

(g) Occasionally, thin out older wood and unproductive shoots to encourage new basal growths

(h) If vigorous, leave unpruned for one season

(i) Remove seed pods immediately after flowering

(j) Remove seed pods and weaker shoots immediately after flowering

(k) Remove suckers (understock), preferably during the dormant season

(l) Trim lightly after flowering to retain compact growth

A figure (1-12) indicates the month of the year when the work should be carried out

Thus, for example, Buddleias of the species davidii carry the pruning guide B(a)4 in the main text, most forsythias are classified A(g)1,2,3, and Wisterias E(f) 8 and 11

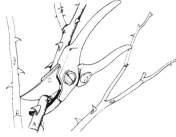

Pruning cuts should be made just above a bud, with the cut sloping backwards, as shown above

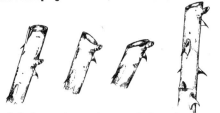

Only the pruning cut shown on the far right is correct

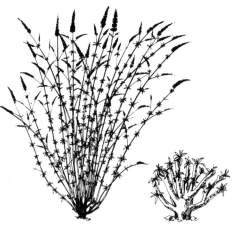

A *Buddleia davidii* before and after pruning (Type B(a)4)

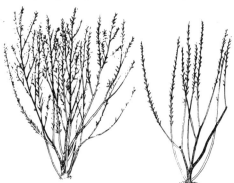

A Forsythia, (Type A(g)1,2,3,) before and after pruning

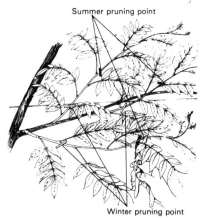

Summer pruning point

Winter pruning point

Pruning a Wisteria (Type E(f) 8 and 11)

Trees and Shrubs

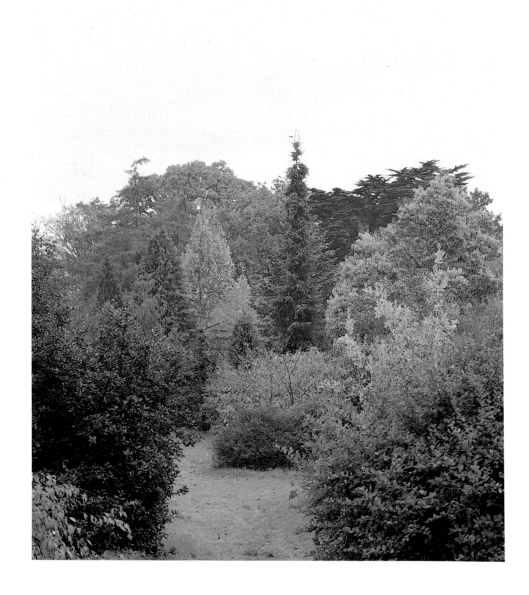

ABELIA -Caprifoliaceae SS-LS ○
Graceful shrubs with tubular flowers,
abundant summer – autumn. A (b) 5
– chinensis MS ○
Fragrant flowers, white flushed rose, freely
produced July – August. AM 1976. A (b) 5

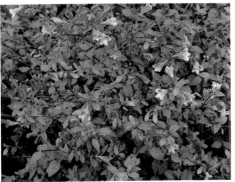

ABELIA 'Edward Goucher'

– 'Edward Goucher' SS Semi-(E) ○
Lilac pink flowers freely produced July-
September. A (b) 5
– englerana SS-MS ○
Flowers rose coloured borne in pairs June
onwards. A(b) 5
– floribunda MS Semi-(E) ○
Abundant cherry red flowers up to 5cm long in
June. Best against a warm wall. A (b) 5

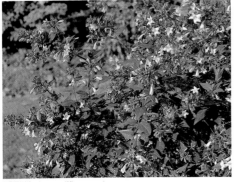

ABELIA × grandiflora

– × grandiflora SS-MS Semi-(E) ○
Pink and white flowers, continuously
July-September. AGM 1962. A (b) 5
– – 'Francis Mason' SS ○
Golden-yellow foliage. Scented flowers, white
flushed rose. A (b) 5
– schumannii SS ○
Prolonged display of abundant lilac pink
flowers, late summer. Liable to damage in
very cold winters. AM 1926. A (b) 5
– triflora LS ○
Clusters of fragrant flowers white, flushed rose
produced in threes, June. Erect habit.
AM 1959. A (b) 5
ABELIOPHYLLUM -Oleaceae SS ◑
Monotypic genus

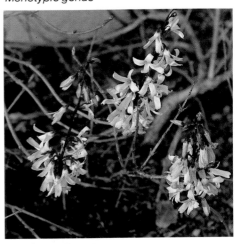

ABELIOPHYLLUM distichum

– distichum SS ◑
Scented star-shaped flowers, white, flushed
pink, produced February on bare stems. Slow
growth. AM 1937 FCC 1944
ABUTILON – Malvaceae SS-LS ○
Elegant shrubs for south wall. Bell or saucer-
shaped flowers over long period.
– 'Ashford Red' MS ○ †
Apple green leaves. Large bell-shaped
flowers of deep crushed strawberry.

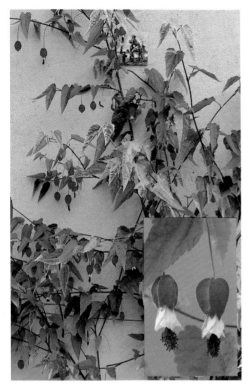

ABUTILON megapotamicum

– megapotamicum SS-MS ☼
Attractive, pendulous, bell-shaped flowers
with red calyces, yellow petals and purple
anthers, summer-autumn. South wall.
AM 1949. A (b) 5
– – 'Variegatum' MS ☼
As above. Leaves green mottled yellow.
– ochsensii MS ☼ †
Flowers lavender blue with darker centres,
cup-shaped. Warm wall. AM 1962
– × suntense MS-LS ☼
Abundant, saucer-shaped flowers 3-5cm,
and vine-shaped grey 'felted' leaves. AGM
1973. We recommend the following clones:
– – 'Jermyns' MS-LS ☼
Clear dark mauve flowers.
– – 'White Charm' MS ☼
White flowers.
– vitifolium LS ☼
Saucer-shaped flowers, 3-5cm, and vine-
shaped felted grey leaves. The following
clones are in cultivation:

– – 'Tennant's White' LS ☼
Pure white flowers, freely borne. A (b) 5
– – 'Veronica Tennant' LS ☼
Abundant large mauve flowers. A (b) 5
ACACIA – Leguminosae LS-ST (E) ☼ †
"Wattle"
Yellow blossom winter-spring. Only hardy in
the mildest areas – elsewhere requiring full
sun and shelter. Most are intolerant of alkaline
soils.
– baileyana LS (E) ☼ † "Cootamundra
Wattle"
Leaves glaucous. Abundant bright yellow
flowers in racemes winter and spring.
AM 1927 FCC 1936

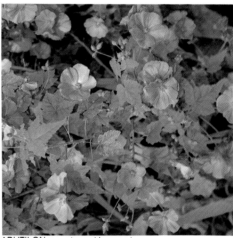

ABUTILON × suntense 'Jermyns'

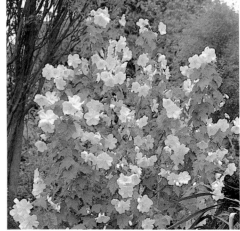

ABUTILON vitifolium 'Tennant's White'

37

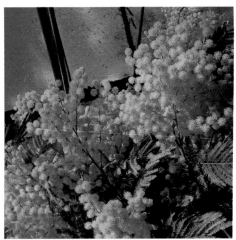

ACACIA dealbata

– **dealbata** LS (E) ☼ † "Mimosa"
"Silver Wattle".
Dainty silvery green fern-like leaves. Clusters
of scented, fluffy golden balls, winter-spring.
AM 1935 FCC 1971. A (c) 5
– **mucronata** LS (E) ☼ †
The hardiest of the genus, making a small tree
in mild areas. Leaves lance-shaped.
"ACACIA, FALSE" see *ROBINIA*
pseudoacacia
ACER – Aceraceae SS-LT "Maples"
Extensive, variable genus, mostly easy to
grow and hardy. Leaves noted for rich autumn
colours. Flowers inconspicuous, except
where indicated otherwise. Stems often
attractively striated.
– **campestre** MT ♥ Hdg (0.5m) "Field or
Hedge Maple"
Foliage turns clear yellow occasionally
flushed red, in autumn.
– – **'Postelense'** MT ♥
Young leaves golden, striking in spring.
– – **'Pulverulentum'** MT ♥
Leaves attractively mottled and blotched
white.
– – **'Schwerinii'** MT ♥
Leaves rich reddish purple.
– **capillipes** ST ♥
'Snakebark' with silvery-green striations.
Young growths coral red. Leaves tinted red in
autumn. AGM 1969 AM 1975
– **cappadocicum** MT-LT ♥
Elegant habit. Leaves turn butter-yellow in
autumn.

– – **'Aureum'** MT ♥ ☀
Young foliage red, turning golden yellow.
AGM 1969
– – **'Rubrum'** LT ♥
Striking blood-red young foliage, turning
through green to red and gold by autumn.

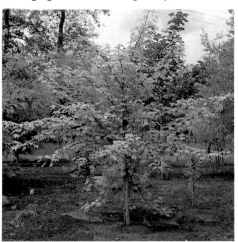

ACER cappadocicum 'Aureum'

– **carpinifolium** ST ♥ "Hornbeam Maple"
Leaves similar to native hornbeam, turning
gold and brown in autumn.
– **circinatum** LS ☼ "Vine Maple"
Leaves almost circular, turning orange and
red in autumn. Flowers plum red and white
produced in April.
– **davidii** ST ♥
'Snakebark' with attractive green and white
striations. Green fruits, suffused red, hang
along branches in autumn. Following clone is
recommended.
– – **'George Forrest'** ('*Horizontalis*') ST ♥
Excellent form. Vigorous spreading branches.
Large dark green leaves with red stalks,
variously autumn tinted. AM 1975 (for fruit)
– **distylum** MT ♥
Undivided leaves, cream and pink tinged
when young. Butter yellow autumn hues.
– **forrestii** ST ♥ ✗
'Snake bark' with attractive striations. Young
growths coral red.
– **ginnala** LS-ST ♥
Vigorous. Bright green, 3-lobed leaves,
turning fiery red in autumn.
– **griseum** ST ♥ "Paperbark Maple"
Attractive bark, peels revealing cinnamon

coloured underbark. Trifoliolate leaves have glorious fiery autumn tints. AM 1922 AGM 1936

– heldreichii MT ♥

Distinct for its deeply divided 3-lobed leaves not unlike those of 'virginia creeper'. Conspicuous red seed wings.

– hersii (*grosseri hersii*) ST ♥

Leaves with or without lobes. Marbled bark. Yellow racemes of flowers followed by conspicuous seed. Red autumn colour.

– japonicum LS-ST ♥

Usually a large shrub with soft green leaves and autumn colour. Natural shelter from cold winds is desirable. The following clones are recommended:

– – 'Aconitifolium' (*'Laciniatum'*) (*'Filicifolium'*) LS

Leaves deeply lobed and cut, turning ruby crimson in autumn. AGM 1957

– – 'Aureum' MS ◑

Slow growing form with attractive soft yellow leaves. FCC 1884 AGM 1969

– – 'Vitifolium' LS

Large, fan shaped leaves which turn brilliant red in autumn. FCC 1974 (for autumn foliage)

– lobelii LT ♥

Distinctive columnar habit. Rich green palmately lobed leaves turning yellow in autumn.

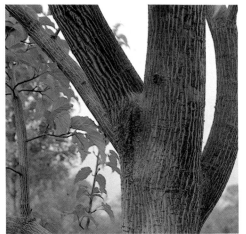

ACER davidii 'George Forrest'

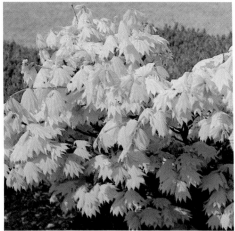

ACER japonicum 'Aureum'

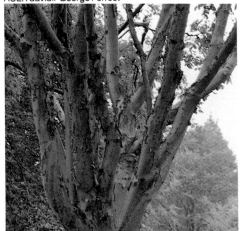

ACER griseum

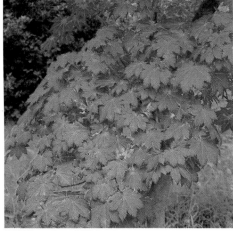

ACER japonicum 'Vitifolium'

– **macrophyllum** LT ♥ "Oregon Maple"
Large, shiny, dark green leaves, turning orange in autumn. Conspicuous seeds.
– **maximowiczii** ST ♥
Leaves 3-5 lobed tinted red in summer, more 30 in autumn. Striated stems.
– **micranthum** LS-ST ♥
Small 5-lobed leaves tinted through growing season, usually red in autumn.
– **mono** MT ♥
Leaves 5-7 lobed, generally turning bright yellow in autumn.
– **monspessulanum** ST ♥ "Montpelier Maple"
Neat habit, often shrubby. 3-lobed leaves. Resembles *Acer campestre*.
– **negundo** MT-LT ♥ "Box Elder"
Bright green, pinnate leaves, normally 3-5 separate leaflets. Fast growing.
– – **'Auratum'** MT ♥
Bright golden leaves. Slow growing. AM 1901
– – **'Elegans'** (*'Elegantissimum'*) MT ♥
Leaves irregularly margined bright yellow, fading to cream. FCC 1898

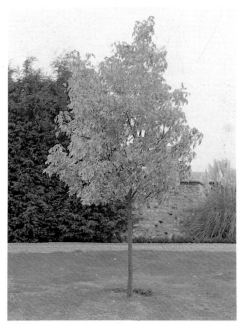

ACER negundo 'Variegatum'

– – **'Variegatum'** (*'Argenteovariegatum'*) MT ♥
Leaves irregularly margined white. AGM 1973

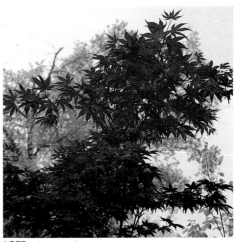

ACER palmatum 'Atropurpureum'

– – **violaceum** MT ♥
Young shoots purple with white bloom. Long reddish pink flower tassels in spring. AM 1975 when shown by us in flower.
– **nikoense** ST-MT ♥ "Nikko Maple"
Trifoliolate leaves. Fiery autumn tints. FCC 1971
– **opalus** LT ♥ "Italian Maple"
Conspicuous yellow flowers before sycamore-like leaves in March. AM 1967
– **palmatum** LS-ST ♥ "Japanese Maple"
Elegant habit. 5 or 7 lobed, bright green leaves, turning orange/red in autumn. AGM 1969. Many cultivars with beautiful autumn colour. Natural shelter from cold winds is desirable.
– – **'Atropurpureum'** MS
Brilliant purple summer foliage turning rich crimson purple in autumn. AGM 1928
– – **'Chitoseyama'** MS
Deep cut green/bronze leaves. Rich autumn colour. Becomes mound-like with age.
– – **'Corallinum'** DS
Young stems coral pink. Small 5-lobed leaves, bright shrimp pink when young, turning to pale mottled green. Slow growth.
– – **coreanum** MS-LS ◑
Leaves crimson in autumn, longer lasting than most.
– – **'Crippsii'** SS-MS
Bronze-red finely cut leaves. Elegant and slow growing. AM 1903
– – **(Dissectum Group)** SS-MS
Group of clones with deeply cut and finely

divided fern like leaves. Mushroom shaped, ultimately dense rounded habit.

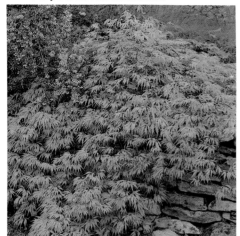

ACER palmatum 'Dissectum'

‐‐**'Dissectum'** SS
Soft green leaves, turning red in autumn, occasionally yellow. AGM 1956
‐‐**'Dissectum Atropurpureum'** SS
Bronze-purple leaves. Red in autumn. AGM 1969
‐‐**'Dissectum Nigrum'** SS
Purple-red leaves, brighter in autumn.
‐‐**'Dissectum Ornatum'** SS
Bronze tinted leaves, turning red in autumn.
‐‐**(Heptalobum Group)** (*Septemlobum Group*)
The following have leaves larger than the type, generally with 7 lobes, finely doubly serrate.
‐‐**'Heptalobum Elegans'** LS
Fresh green, attractive, deeply toothed leaves, up to 13cm long.

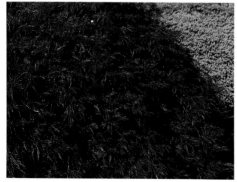

ACER palmatum 'Dissectum Atropurpureum'

‐‐**'Heptalobum Elegans Purpureum'** MS
Leaves beautiful dark burnished crimson.

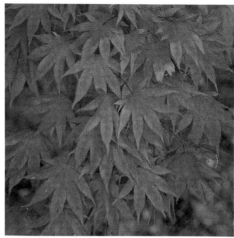

ACER palmatum 'Heptalobum Elegans'

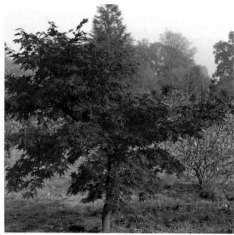

ACER palmatum 'Heptalobum Osakazuki'

‐‐**'Heptalobum Osakazuki'** LS
Green leaves change through various shades to brilliant flame scarlet in autumn. Spectacular. AGM 1969
‐‐**'Heptalobum Rubrum'** MS
Large leaves, deep red when young, paling as they age.
‐‐**'Linearilobum'** (*'Scolopendrifolium'*) MS
Green leaves divided into long narrow lobes. AM 1896
‐‐**'Linearilobum Atropurpureum'** MS
As above but leaves of delightful burnished red.

-- **'Nigrum'** MS
Leaves of deep plum-purple.
-- **'Reticulatum'** (*'Flavescens'*) MS
Soft yellow-green leaves with distinct green
margins and dark veins.
-- **'Ribesifolium'** (*'Shishigashira'*) LS
Distinct upright form, but with a broad crown.
Slow growing. Dark green leaves turning
old-gold in autumn.

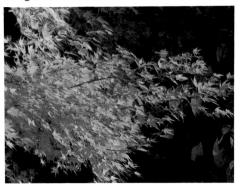

ACER palmatum 'Senkaki'

-- **'Senkaki'** (*'Sangokaku'*) LS "Coral Bark
Maple"
Conspicuous coral-red branches, particularly
effective in winter. Leaves colouring soft
yellow in autumn. AM 1950 AGM 1969
-- **'Shishio Improved'** LS
Deeply lobed leaves, crimson when young.
- **pensylvanicum** (*striatum*) ST ♥
Young stems pale green with white striations.
Large 3-lobed leaves turn to buttercup-yellow
in autumn. Not good on shallow chalk soils.
-- **'Erythrocladum'** ST ♥
Delightful form. Juvenile shoots shrimp-pink
with pale striations, conspicuous in winter.
AM 1976 FCC 1977
- **pentaphyllum** ST ♥
Green leaves, glaucous beneath with 5 linear-
lanceolate segments on elongated scarlet
leaf stalks. Handsome and rare.
- **platanoides** LT ♥ "Norway Maple"
Magnificent, fast growing. Green leaves, turn
buttercup yellow, occasionally red, in autumn.
Conspicuous yellow flowers in clusters on
naked stems from April make this one of the
most outstanding large trees in the British
landscape. AM1967 AGM 1969
-- **'Columnare'** LT ♥
Erect form with closely packed branches.

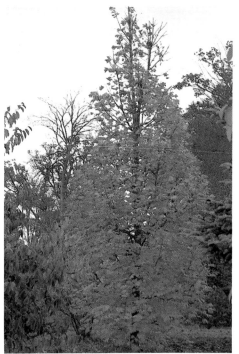

ACER platanoides 'Columnare'

-- **'Crimson King'** LT ♥
Striking form with deep crimson-purple
leaves. AGM 1969
-- **'Drummondii'** MT-LT ♥
Leaves with broad, creamy-white margins.
Elegant. AM 1956 AGM 1969

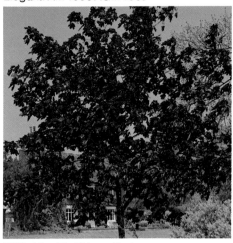

ACER platanoides 'Crimson King'

– –'Globosum' ST
Short branches forming a dense globular crown which glows golden autumn.
– –'Lorbergii' MT ♥
Pale green palmate leaves, lobes have long pointed tips.
– –'Reitenbachii' MT ♥
Young leaves are red, turning to green and finally red tinted in autumn.
– –'Schwedleri' MT-LT ♥
Young growths and leaves rich crimson-purple, improved by hard pruning in alternate autumns.
– pseudoplatanus LT ♥ "Sycamore"
Magnificent green leaved tree, tolerant of virtually all conditions and soils other than waterlogged sites.
– –'Atropurpureum' (*'Purpureum Spaethii'*) LT ♥
Form with purple undersides to leaves.

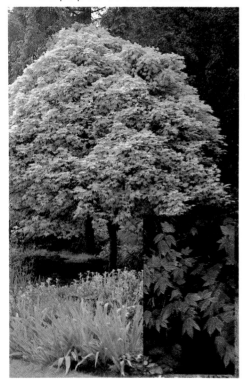

ACER pseudoplatanus 'Brilliantissimum' (Young foliage)

– –'Brilliantissimum' ST ♥
Spectacular. Delightful, shrimp-pink young foliage. Slow grower. AM 1925 AGM 1973

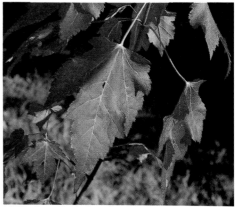

ACER rubrum 'Schlesingeri'

– –'Erectum' (*'Fastigiatum'*) LT ❦
Strongly ascending branches.
– –'Leopoldii' MT ♥
Variegated foliage, initially yellowish-pink then green with yellow and pink splashes and speckles. FCC 1865
– –'Nizetti' LT ♥
Leaves with yellow, pink and white markings, purple beneath.
– –'Prinz Handjery' ST ♥
Leaves bright shrimp-pink in spring changing to green. Undersides tinged purple. FCC 1890
– –'Worleei' MT ♥ "Golden Sycamore"
Beautiful soft golden leaves, turning green in high summer.
– rubrum LT ♥ ⚮ "Red Maple" "Canadian Maple"
Dark green, palmate leaves with bluish green undersides, turning red or scarlet in autumn. Rarely colours well on chalk. AM 1969
– –'Scanlon' MT ♥
Rich autumn hues. Excellent for smaller gardens and restricted spaces.
– –'Schlesingeri' MT ♥
Early autumn colour of deep scarlet. AM 1976
– rufinerve MT ♥
Snake bark. Older stems and trunk green with white striations. 3-lobed leaves turn scarlet and yellow in autumn.
– saccharinum (*dasycarpum*) (*eriocarpum*) LT ♥ "Silver Maple"
A remarkably fast growing tree with large, deeply five-lobed leaves, silvery beneath. Good autumn colour.

– – **laciniatum** MT-LT
Graceful tree with gently drooping branches and finely and deeply cut leaves.
– – **'Pyramidale'** (*'Fastigiatum'*) LT
Upright growing form.
– **saccharinum** LT "Sugar Maple"
5-lobed leaves turn crimson, orange or gold in a good autumn.
– – **'Temple's Upright'** (*'Monumentale'*) MT
Slow growing erect tree. Striking orange autumn colour.
– **'Silver Vein'** ST
Perhaps the most spectacular snake bark maple. The large leaves turn yellow in autumn.
– **triflorum** ST
Dark brown furrowed bark. Trifoliolate leaves, glaucous beneath; consistently brilliant autumn colour. Rare and slow growing.
– **wilsonii** LS-ST
Generally 3-lobed leaves, shrimp-pink when young, changing to coral and finally soft green.
– × **zoeschense** (*neglectum*) MT
5-lobed leaves of dark green, tinged purple.

ADENOCARPUS – Leguminosae SS -MS (E) ☼
Very leafy with golden yellow 'broom-like' flowers.
– **decorticans** MS (E) ☼
Vigorous. Flowers in dense upright racemes, May-June. Best against sunny wall. AM 1947

AESCULUS – Hippocastanaceae "Horse Chestnut" MT-LT
Ornamental late spring/early summer flowering. Leaves compound, palmate, flowers in erect racemes. Easy cultivation. Any soil.
– **californica** ST
Low spreading growth. Fragrant flowers white or pink flushed, in dense erect panicles.
– × **carnea** (*rubicunda*) MT-LT "Red Horse Chestnut"
Magnificent deep pink 'candles' up to 20cm long in May.
– – **'Briotti'** MT-LT
More compact form. Flowers a richer shade of rose-pink. AM 1965
– **flava** (*octandra*) MT-LT "Sweet Buckeye"
Flowers creamy-yellow with red markings. Leaves normally have good autumn colour.
– **hippocastanum** LT "Common Horse Chestnut"
Impressive, especially in May with erect

panicles of white flowers. "Conkers" produced in autumn.
– – **'Baumannii'** (*'Flore Pleno'*) LT
Double white form, does not set seed, therefore of no attraction to stone throwing boys.
– **indica** LT "Indian Horse Chestnut"
Superb tree with slender panicles of pink flushed flowers up to 40cm long, June-July. AM 1922 FCC 1933 AGM 1969

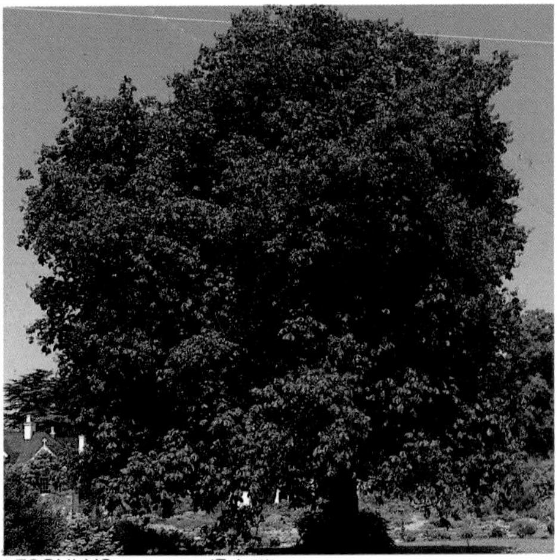

AESCULUS × carnea 'Briotti'

– – **'Sydney Pearce'** LT
Dark olive green leaves. Free flowering, with large panicles with petals white marked yellow and tinged pink. AM 1967 AGM 1969
– × **mutabilis** LS-ST
Flowers red and yellow May-June. We recommend the form:

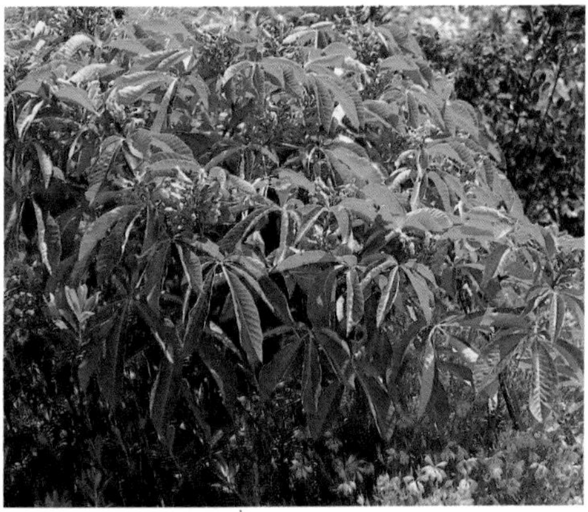

AESCULUS × mutabilis 'Induta'

–– 'Induta' (*'Rosea Nana'*) LS-ST ♀
Delightful apricot flowers with yellow markings in early summer.
– neglecta MT ♀
Leaves attractively coloured in autumn. Panicles of pale yellow flowers, May-June. The following forms are recommended:
–– 'Erythroblastos' MT ♀ ◑
Young leaves delightful shrimp pink, changing pale yellow/green and finally orange and yellow in autumn. Slow grower. AM 1962
–– georgiana (*A. georgiana*) LS
Broad, dense panicles of flame coloured flowers.
– parviflora (*Pavia macrostachya*) MS
Panicles of white flowers with red anthers, freely produced July-August. Good autumn leaf colour. AM 1955 AGM 1969
– pavia (*Pavia rubra*) LS-ST ♀ "Red Buckeye"
Crimson flowers in panicles June. We recommend selected form:

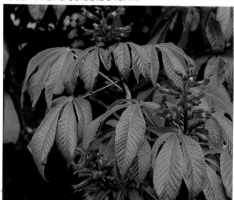

AESCULUS pavia 'Atrosanguinea'

–– 'Atrosanguinea' LS-ST ♀
Beautiful form with deep crimson flowers, June.
– splendens LS
Delightful long panicles of scarlet flowers, May.
– turbinata LT ♀ "Japanese Horse Chestnut"
Fast growing large tree with leaves the largest of the genus. Good autumn colour. Long panicles of creamy flowers with red markings, June.
AILANTHUS – Simaroubaceae LT ❢
Elegant, fast growing. Tolerant of most soils and conditions – including industrial pollution.

– altissima (*glandulosa*) LT ❢ "Tree of Heaven"
Large, ash-like leaves to 1m long. Reddish "key"-like fruits in conspicuous bunches on female trees. AM 1953
ALBIZIA – Leguminosae LS-ST ♀ ○
Mimosa-like, attractive foliage and fluffy heads of flowers.
– julibrissin LS-ST ○
Deeply divided fern-like foliage. Pink flowers in summer: We commend the following form:
–– 'Rosea' LS-ST ○
Dense heads of deep rose-pink flowers. Withstands severe frosts.
"ALMOND" see *PRUNUS dulcis*
ALNUS – Betulaceae MS-LT "Alder"
Tolerant of most soils, except shallow chalk. Ideal for damp sites. Often bear attractive catkins.
– cordata (*cordifolia*) MT ♦ "Italian Alder"
Fresh green glistening foliage. Attractive cone-shaped fruiting heads. Grows rapidly – even on chalk.
– firma ST ♀
Long, tapering, sharply toothed, oval leaves, remaining green until late autumn.
– glutinosa MT ♀ "Common Alder"
Smooth grey bark. Sticky young growths. Leaves green and shiny, retained until late autumn. Yellow catkins in March.

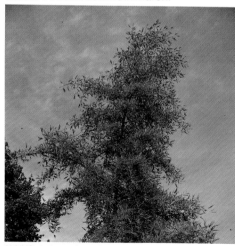

ALNUS glutinosa 'Imperialis'

–– 'Imperialis' MT ♦
Attractive form with finely cut feathery leaves. AM 1973

–**incana** ST ♥ "Grey Alder"
Oval to round leaves with grey undersides.
Extremely hardy; ideal for cold wet situations.
Fast growth.
– –**'Aurea'** LS
Young shoots and foliage yellow. Catkins red
tinted. Bright orange wood in winter. Slow
growth. AGM 1973
– –**'Pendula'** ST ♠
Weeping branches and grey green foliage
forming a dense mound. Bright catkins in
January.
× **spaethii** MT ♥
Large, green leaves. Showy catkins.
AMELANCHIER – Rosaceae MS-ST "Snowy
Mespilus" "June Berry"
Beautiful genus with abundant racemes of
white flowers in spring. Often rich autumn
colour. Best in lime-free soils. A (E) 2
– **asiatica** LS
Flowers produced May and intermittently over
long period. Ripe fruits resemble
blackcurrants. Fairly lime tolerant. A (E) 2
– **canadensis** MS
Suckering shrub with erect racemes of
flowers. Good in moist situations. AM 1938
A (E) 2
– **laevis** ST ♥
Fragrant, white flowers in early May. Delicate
pink young foliage. Leaves richly coloured in
autumn.
A (E) 2

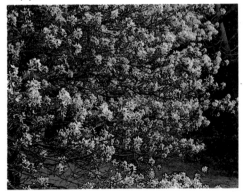

AMELANCHIER lamarckii

– **lamarckii** ST ♥
Silky, coppery-red young leaves, turning
scarlet in autumn. Clusters of starry flowers in
lax racemes.
A (E) 2

– –**'Rubescens'** (× *grandiflora 'Rubescens'*)
ST ♥
Flowers pink tinged, darker in bud. A (E) 2
AMYGDALUS see *PRUNUS dulcis*
ANDROMEDA – Ericaceae DS-SS (E) ✗ ●
Slender stemmed shrubs for damp acid soils
or rock garden.
– **polifolia** DS (E) ✗ ● "Bog Rosemary"
Narrow glaucous green leaves, white
beneath. Terminal clusters of soft pink
flowers, May-June. We recommend the forms:

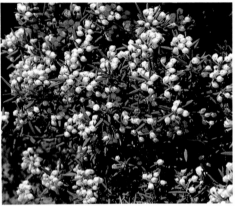

ANDROMEDA polifolia 'Compacta'

– –**'Compacta'** DS (E) ✗ ●
Bright pink flowers, May onwards. Compact
habit. AM 1964
– –**'Major'** SS (E) ✗ ●
Broader leaves. Taller.
"ANGELS TRUMPET" see *DATURA*
suaveolens
ANTHYLLIS – Leguminosae DS-SS ☼
Sun-loving shrubs or herbs. The following
species is in cultivation.
– **hermanniae** DS ☼
Abundant, small pea flowers, yellow with
orange markings on standards, produced
June-July.
ARALIA – Araliaceae LS-ST ☼
Handsome, large, compound leaves. Hardy
but prefer some shelter to protect leaves.
– **elata** LS ☼ "Japanese Angelica Tree"
Huge, "Angelica"-like leaves, forming ruffs at
ends of branches. Crowned by large
branched heads of white flowers in early
autumn. AM 1959
– –**'Aureovariegata'** LS
Leaflets margined and splashed yellow,
turning silver-white later in summer.

– –**'Variegata'** LS
Leaflets margined creamy white, turning
silver-white later in summer. AM 1902
– **sieboldii** see *FATSIA japonica*
– **spinosa** LS ○ "Hercules Club" "Devil's
Walking Stick"
Vicious spiny stems. Flowers greenish white in
panicles July. AM 1974
ARBUTUS – Ericaceae ST-MT ♥ (E)
"Strawberry trees"
*Ornamental evergreens with dark green
leathery leaves. Clusters of white, pitcher-
shaped flowers followed by strawberry-like
fruits.*
– **andrachne** ST ♥ (E) † "Grecian Strawberry
Tree"
Flowers in spring. Cinnamon-brown stems.
Tender when young, hardy when mature.
– × **andrachnoides** ST ♥ (E)
Attractive peeling cinnamon red bark. Flowers
late autumn and winter. Lime tolerant and
hardy. AM 1953 AGM 1969
– **menziesii** MT ♥ (E) ∠ "Madrona"
Flowers in conspicuous panicles late spring,
followed by orange yellow fruits. AM 1926
AGM 1973

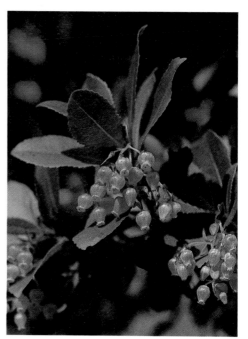

ARBUTUS unedo 'Rubra'

– –**'Rubra'** ST ♥ (E)
More compact form with pink flushed flowers
and abundant fruit. AM 1925
ARCTOSTAPHYLOS – Ericaceae PS-ST (E)
∠ ○
*Variable genus allied to Rhododendrons and
needing similar conditions.*
– **manzanita** MS (E) ∠
Sea green leaves. Dark reddish brown stems.
Spikes of pink/white pitcher-shaped flowers.
FCC 1923
– **uva-ursi** PS (E) ∠ GC "Red Bearberry"
Creeping alpine with small white, pink tinged
flowers. Red fruits.
ARONIA – Rosaceae SS-MS
*White flowers in spring, followed by red or
black berries. Bright autumn foliage. Not for
shallow chalk.*
– **arbutifolia** MS "Red Chokeberry"
Bright red fruits and brilliant autumn foliage.
– **melanocarpa** SS "Black Chokeberry"
Hawthorn-like spring flowers followed by
shiny black fruits. AM 1972
We recommend the form:
– –**'Brilliant'** SS
Exceptionally fine autumn colour.

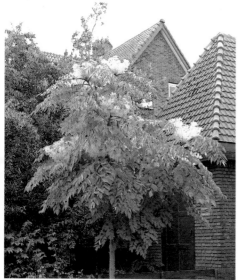

ARALIA elata

– **unedo** ST ♥ (E) "Killarney Strawberry Tree"
Gnarled trunk with brown shredding bark.
Flowers and fruit borne simultaneously late
autumn. Lime tolerant. FCC 1933 AGM 1969

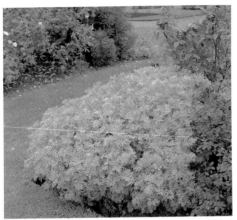

ARTEMISIA arborescens

ARTEMISIA – Compositae MS-SS ○
Attractive grey or green foliage. Aromatic.
– arborescens SS ○ †
Rounded habit. Filigree of silvery leaves.
AM 1966
ARUNDINARIA – Gramineae DS-LS (E)
*Clump-forming or spreading bamboos. The
spreading species are useful for ground
cover or screens, depending on their size.*
– anceps LS (E)
Vigorous, wide-spreading species good for
screens and hedges. Erect, glossy green
canes useful in the garden when mature.
– auricoma See *A. viridistriata*
– fortunei See *A. variegata*
– 'Gauntlettii' SS (E)
Bright green, later purple, clump-forming
canes. Rare.
– hindsii MS (E)
Vigorous, thicket-forming habit with erect
olive-green canes and thickly clustered
sea-green leaves.
– japonica LS (E)
Most commonly cultivated bamboo, with
dense thickets of tall, olive-green canes,
arching at the tips with lush masses of dark,
glossy, green leaves.
– murielae LS (E)
Canes bright green, becoming yellow-green,
arching and making dense, non-rampant
clumps. AGM 1973
– nitida LS (E)
Purple-flushed, arching canes making a
dense clump. Delicate, narrow leaves.
FCC 1898 AGM 1930

– pumila DS (E) GC
Dense carpets of slender, purplish canes.
– pygmaea DS (E) GC
Wide-spreading, carpet-forming species with
slender stems.
– ragamowskii see *SASA tesselata*
– simonii LS (E)
Vigorous clump-forming species with erect,
olive-green canes, bloomed when young.
Luxuriant foliage. Makes a good screen.
– spathiflora LS (E)
Dense, clump-forming species with erect
stems, drooping at the tips. Canes bright
green, bloomed when young, becoming
tinged purplish pink.
– vagans DS (E) GC
Vigorous, carpeting plant with bright green
foliage. Canes bright green, becoming deep
olive-green.
– variegata SS (E)
Dense, tufted species with erect, zig-zag,
pale green canes. Leaves dark green striped
with white.

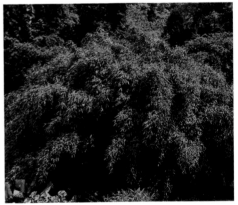

ARUNDINARIA murielae

– viridistriata SS-MS (E)
Erect, slender, purplish-green canes forming
small patches. Leaves dark green, striped
rich yellow. AM 1972
"ASH" see *FRAXINUS*
"ASPEN" see *POPULUS tremula*
ASTERANTHERA ovata see under
CLIMBERS
ATRIPLEX – Chenopodiaceae MS Semi-(E)
○
*Striking silvery-grey foliage. Thrives on saline
soil. Excellent seaside plant.*

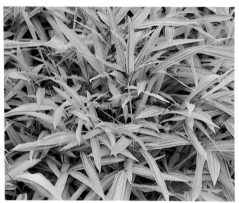
ARUNDINARIA viridistriata

– **canescens** MS Semi-(E) ○
Lax bush with greyish-white narrow leaves.
– **halimus** MS Semi-(E) ○ "Tree Purslane"
Silvery-grey leaves.
AUCUBA – Cornaceae SS-MS (E)
Handsome rounded shrubs, with glossy green or variegated leaves. Male and female (berrying) forms. Suitable for almost all soils and situations.
– **japonica** MS (E)
Wild type with green leaves. FCC 1864 AGM 1969. We recommend selected forms:
– – **'Crassifolia'** SS (E)
Thick, broad, deep green leaves – upper half toothed. Male. AGM 1969
– – **'Crotonifolia'** (*'Crotonoides'*) MS (E)
Large leaves boldly speckled gold. Male. AGM 1969

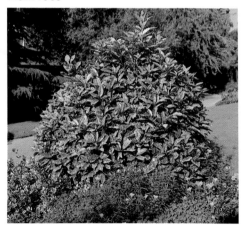
AUCUBA japonica 'Crotonifolia'

– – **'Gold Dust'** MS (E)
Leaves boldly speckled gold. Female.
– – **'Hillieri'** MS (E)
Large, glossy, dark green leaves. Pointed fruits. Female.
– – **'Lance Leaf'** MS (E)
Glossy, green, lance-shaped leaves. Male.
– – **'Longifolia'** MS (E)
Long, bright green leaves. Female. FCC 1864
– – **'Nana Rotundifolia'** SS (E)
Small, rich green leaves, toothed in upper half. Sea green stems. Free berrying, female form. AGM 1969
– – **'Picturata'** MS (E)
Richly variegated, with elongated splashes of gold. Male.

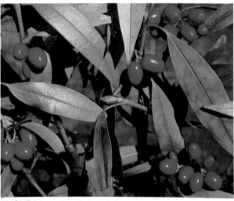
AUCUBA japonica 'Salicifolia'

– – **'Salicifolia'** MS (E)
Narrow leaved, free berrying, female form.
– – **'Variegata'** MS (E) (*'Maculata'*)
Yellow blotched leaves. Female. FCC 1865
AZALEA and × **AZALEODENDRON** see under *RHODODENDRON*
AZARA – Flacourtiaceae LS-ST (E) †
Attractive leaves and fragrant flowers, early spring. Best against a wall.
– **microphylla** ST (E) †
Dainty, divided leaves. Vanilla scented, yellow flowers in clusters, early spring. FCC 1872.
– – **'Variegata'** ST (E) †
Leaves attractively variegated cream. Slow growing.
– **petiolaris** LS (E) †
Comparatively large leathery leaves. Fragrant, small yellow flowers, February-March. AM 1933

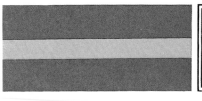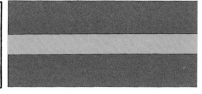

BALLOTA – Labiatae DS ☼
Sub-shrubs for sunny, well-drained sites.
– pseudodictamnus DS ☼
Leaves orbicular-cordate, whole shrub
greyish-white, woolly. Flowers lilac-pink, July.
"BAMBOOS" see *ARUNDINARIA,*
CHUSQUEA, PHYLLOSTACHYS, SASA and
SHIBATAEA
"BARBERRY" see *BERBERIS*
"BAY" see *LAURUS nobilis*
"BEAUTY BUSH" see *KOLKWITZIA amabilis*
"BEECH" see *FAGUS*
"BEECH SOUTHERN" see *NOTHOFAGUS*
BENZOIN see *LINDERA benzoin*
BERBERIS – Berberidaceae DS-LS
Variable genus with evergreen and
deciduous members. Spring flowers from
pale yellow to orange. Showy fruits. Many
have brilliant autumn foliage. Easy cultivation,
any soil not waterlogged.

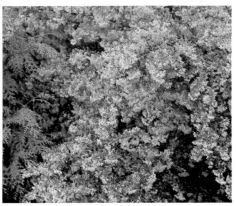
BERBERIS darwinii

– aggregata MS
Dense habit. Clusters of flowers, followed by
red autumn berries. Rich autumn leaf colour.
AM 1913
– × antoniana SS (E)
Rounded habit. Almost spineless leaves.
Single, long-stalked deep yellow flowers.
Blue-black berries.

– 'Barbarossa' MS
Vigorous. Branches weighed down by
masses of red berries.
– bealei see *MAHONIA bealei* and *MAHONIA*
japonica
– 'Blenheim' MS (E)
Dense habit. Leaves sharply toothed. Flowers
golden.
– 'Bountiful' SS
Spreading habit. Clusters of coral red berries
on arching branches in autumn.
– 'Buccaneer' MS
Erect. Brilliant autumn leaf colour. Clusters of
large deep red berries, lasting until
December.
– buxifolia MS Semi (E)
Early flowers, followed by grape-like purple
blue berries. AM 1961
– – 'Nana' DS (E)
Dense, mound like habit. Slow growing.
– calliantha SS (E)
Small, holly-like leaves, grey beneath.
Crimson young stems. Flowers single or in
pairs, pale yellow. Blue-black fruits. AM 1942
– candidula SS (E)
Dense dome-shaped habit. Small dark green,
glossy leaves, silvery beneath. Single, bright
yellow flowers.
– 'Chenaultii' SS
Dense habit. Warty stems. Dull green leaves
with wavy, spiny margins.
– chrysophaera MS (E)
Narrow, glossy, green leaves, white beneath.
Large canary-yellow flowers.
– coxii MS (E)
Leathery leaves up to 5cm long, glaucous
beneath. Blue-black berries. Handsome.
– darwinii MS (E) Hdg (0.5m)
Glossy dark green, three pointed leaves.
Spectacular deep-yellow flowers in racemes
April-May. Purplish-blue berries. AGM 1930
FCC 1967

– dictyophylla (*dictyophylla 'Albicaulis'*) MS
Red young stems, clothed in white bloom.
Leaves white beneath – good autumn colour.
Large, single, red berries with white bloom.

– francisci-ferdinandii LS
Vigorous. Large drooping clusters of sealing-wax-red berries.

– × frikartii 'Amstelveen' SS (E)
Dense, mound-like habit. Yellow flowers.

– gagnepainii SS (E) Hdg (0.5m)
Dense habit. Makes excellent impenetrable hedge. Narrow undulate leaves. Black berries with blue bloom.

– hakeoides LS (E)
Distinctive, loose habit. Rounded, spiny leaves in pairs. Clusters of golden-yellow flowers along shoots, April-May. AM 1901

– hookeri SS (E)
Leaves glaucous beneath. Dense, compact habit. Berries green, turning black.

– – viridis SS (E)
Leaves green beneath. Small black berries.

– hypokerina SS (E) ⚹
Thicket of purple stems. Holly-like leaves, silver beneath up to 10cm long. Dark blue berries with white bloom. AM 1932

– × interposita SS (E)
Dense mound of arching stems. Vigorous. Spiny, glossy dark green leaves.

– × irwinii and cultivars see under *BERBERIS × stenophylla*

– julianae MS (E)
Dense habit. Spiny stems and stiff, narrow leaves, copper tinted when young. Yellow, slightly scented, flowers in axillary clusters.

– kawakamii SS (E)
Short, broad, spiny leaves, copper tinged when young. Rich yellow flowers in clusters, March-April.

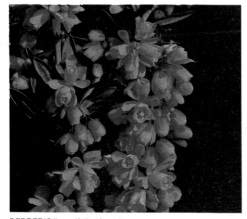

BERBERIS linearifolia 'Jewel'

– linearifolia MS (E)
Erect habit. Glossy, dark green, spineless leaves. Orange-red flowers, early spring and sometimes autumn. FCC 1931

– – 'Jewel' MS (E)
Conspicuous flowers, scarlet in bud, opening bright orange. AM 1978

– – 'Orange King' MS (E)
Form with larger rich orange flowers.

– × lologensis MS (E)
Leaves variable, entire and spiny on same plant. Apricot yellow flowers. A lovely shrub. AM 1931

– montana LS
Large, yellow and pale orange flowers. Black berries. AM 1935 AGM 1969

– morrisonensis SS "Mt Morrison Barberry"
Compact habit. Free flowering. Bright red berries and brilliant autumn leaf colour.

– orthobotrys MS
Vigorous, upright habit. Large, oval berries, bright red. Bright autumn leaves. AM 1919. We recommend the form:

– – canescens MS
A form with narrower leaves, bloomy beneath.

– × ottawensis MS
Oval or rounded green leaves and drooping clusters of red berries. We recommend the form:

– – 'Purpurea' (*'Superba'*) MS
Vigorous form with rich purple foliage. Flowers yellow, followed by red berries.

– panlanensis SS (E) Hdg (0.5m)
Compact, neat habit. Spiny, sea-green, linear leaves.

– 'Parkjuweel' SS Semi-(E) ☼
Dense, prickly habit. Leaves almost spineless, colouring well in autumn (occasionally lasting until spring).

– 'Pirate King' SS
Dense habit. Vigorous. Orange-red berries.

– prattii MS
Flowers in erect panicles. Beautiful in autumn when laden with coral red, ovoid berries. AM 1953

– pruinosa MS (E)
Vigorous. Spiny sea-green leaves, white beneath. Soft-yellow flowers. Abundant blue-black bloomy berries. AM 1924

– replicata SS (E)
Slow growing. Narrow leaves, glaucous beneath. Blackish-purple, ellipsoid berries. AM 1923

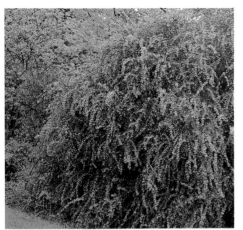

BERBERIS × stenophylla

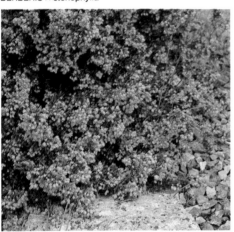

BERBERIS × stenophylla 'Corallina Compacta'

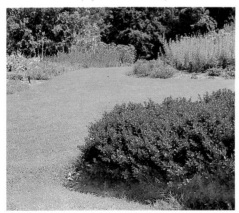

BERBERIS thunbergii 'Atropurpurea Nana'

– × **rubrostilla** SS
Large, showy, coral-red, oblong berries.
FCC 1916 AGM 1969
– **sargentiana** MS (E)
Leathery net-veined leaves up to 13cm. Blue-black berries. Upright habit. AM 1915
FCC 1916
– × **stenophylla** MS (E) Hdg (0.5m)
Long, arching branches. Golden-yellow
flowers, April-May. FCC 1864 AGM 1923
– – **'Coccinea'** SS (E)
Crimson buds opening orange. AM 1925
AGM 1969
– – **'Corallina'** SS (E)
Lax habit. Coral red buds, opening yellow
AGM 1969
– – **'Corallina Compacta'** DS (E)
Coral-red buds, opening yellow. AGM 1969
– – **'Irwinii'** SS (E)
Deep yellow flowers. AGM 1969
– – **'Pink Pearl'** SS (E)
Leaves dark green or mottled and striped pink
and cream. Variable flower colour – creamy
yellow, orange, pink or bicoloured on same
plant.
– – **'Prostrata'** (*darwinii* 'Prostrata') DS (E)
Orange buds opening golden-yellow.
– **temolaica** MS
Vigorous, striking shrub. Glaucous young
growths, shoots dark purple-brown and
glaucous with age. Egg-shaped, red, bloomy
berries.
– **thunbergii** SS Hdg (0.5m)
Compact growth. Bright red berries and
brilliant autumn foliage. FCC 1890 AGM 1927
– – **atropurpurea** SS Hdg (0.5m)
Reddish-purple foliage, becoming richer in
colour towards winter. AM 1926 AGM 1932
– – **'Atropurpurea Nana'** DS Hdg (0.4m)
Dwarf form with purple foliage, ideal for rock
gardens or dwarf hedge. AGM 1969
– – **'Aurea'** SS
Yellow leaves, turning pale green by late
summer.
– – **'Kobold'** DS
Glossy, green foliage, grey green beneath.
– – **'Red Chief'** SS
Rich wine-red foliage on upright branches.
– – **'Red Pillar'** SS
Fastigiate form with reddish-purple leaves.
– – **'Rose Glow'** SS
Young leaves purple, mottled silver-pink and
bright rose, later becoming purple.

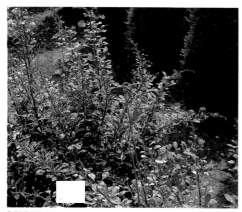
BERBERIS thungbergii 'Rose Glow'

– tsangpoensis DS
Wide spreading, mound-forming habit. Red berries and good autumn colour.

– valdiviana LS (E)
Elegant, distinctive plant. Large leathery, almost spineless leaves. Saffron-yellow flowers in drooping racemes. AM 1939

– veitchii MS (E)
Long, lanceolate, spiny leaves; red young shoots. Bronze-yellow flowers on long stalks. Black berries.

– verruculosa MS (E)
Slow growing, compact habit. Warty stems with small, glossy, dark green leaves, white beneath. Golden-yellow flowers. AM 1911 AGM 1929

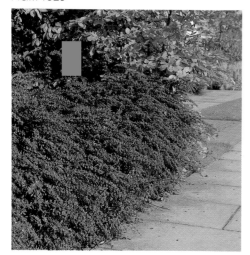
BERBERIS verruculosa

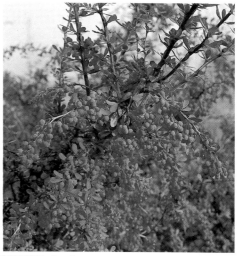
BERBERIS wilsoniae

– wilsoniae SS
Dense, mound-like habit. Small, sea-green leaves, turning attractive colours in autumn. Coral-red berries. FCC 1907 AGM 1969

– yunnanensis MS
Rounded habit. Vivid autumn leaf colour. Bright red berries.

BETULA – Betulaceae SS-LT "Birch"
Many noteworthy for stem colour, and beautiful yellow autumn leaves. Good on most soils, but do not attain full height on shallow chalk.

– alba
See *BETULA pendula* and *BETULA pubescens*

– albo-sinensis septentrionalis MT ♦
Shining orange-brown bark with a pink and grey "bloom".

– caerulea – grandis ST ▀
Conspicuous white bark. Large, ovate leaves and showy catkins.

– costata MT ♥
Superb creamy-white exfoliating bark. Golden-yellow autumn colour.

– ermanii LT ♥
Peeling, creamy-white bark, tinted pink, branches orange brown.

– × fetisowii MT ▀
Graceful habit. Chalk-white, peeling bark.

– jacquemontii MT ♥
Beautiful white, peeling bark. Ovate, serrated leaves. Excellent species. AGM 1969

53

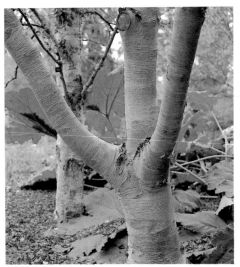

BETULA ermanii

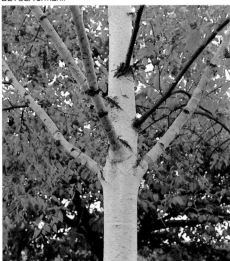

BETULA 'Jermyns'

– **'Jermyns'** MT ♥
Creamy-white stems. Peeling, orange-brown or coppery bark on trunk and main branches. Good autumn colour.
– **luminifera** LT ♥
Large, deep green, lustrous leaves, persisting until sharp frosts in late autumn.
– **lutea** MT ♥
Attractive peeling bark of amber or golden brown. Rich yellow autumn leaves.
– **mandschurica** see BETULA platyphylla

– – **szechuanica** see BETULA platyphylla szechuanica
– **maximowicziana** MT ♥
Fast growing. Orange-brown trunk, finally greyish. Large, heart-shaped leaves, clear butter yellow in autumn.
– **nana** SS "Dwarf Birch"
Tiny, neat, rounded leaves.
– **nigra** ST ♥ "River Birch"
Shaggy bark. Diamond shaped, soft green leaves. Excellent for damp, but not waterlogged, ground.
– **papyrifera** LT ♥ "Paper Birch" "Canoe Birch"
White, papery bark. Yellow autumn leaf colour.
– – **kenaica** MT ♥
White bark, tinged orange.
– **pendula** (verrucosa) MT ♠ "Common Silver Birch"
White bark and rough warty shoots. Drooping branchlets with diamond shaped leaves. AGM 1969
– – **'Dalecarlica'** LT ♥ "Swedish Birch"
Slender tree with gracefully drooping branchlets. Deeply cut, long pointed leaves. AGM 1969
– – **'Fastigiata'** MT ♥
Form with erect stiff habit. AGM 1969
– – **'Purpurea'** MT ♥ "Purple Leaf Birch"
Ornamental, slow growing form with purple leaves. FCC 1874
– – **'Tristis'** LT ♥
Graceful, drooping branches, forming a narrow symmetrical head. AGM 1969
– – **'Youngii'** ST ♠ "Young's Weeping Birch"
Broad, mushroom-headed habit. Branches ultimately reaching the ground. AGM 1969
– **platyphylla** (mandschurica) LT ♥
White bark. Larger leaves than BETULA pendula. We recommend the following:
– – **szechuanica** (mandschurica szechuanica) MT ♥
Chalky-white bark. Vigorous.
– **pubescens** (alba in part) MT ♥ "Common White Birch"
Thrives in all soils, especially damp locations. Reddish bark and smooth downy shoots.
– **utilis** MT ♥ "Himalayan Birch"
Orange to brown or deep coppery-brown, peeling bark.
– **verrucosa** see BETULA pendula
"BILBERRY" see VACCINIUM myrtillus

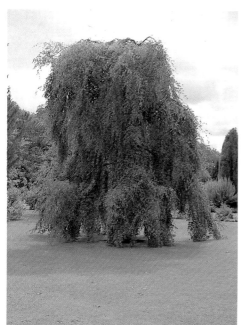

BETULA pendula 'Youngii'

"BIRCH" see *BETULA*
"BITTER NUT" see *CARYA cordiformis*
"BLACKTHORN" see *PRUNUS spinosa*
"BLADDER NUT" see *STAPHYLEA*
"BLADDER SENNA" see *COLUTEA*
"BLUEBERRY" see *VACCINIUM*
"BOTTLEBRUSH" see *CALLISTEMON*
"BOX" see *BUXUS*
"BOX ELDER" see *ACER negundo*
BRACHYGLOTTIS – Compositae LS (E) †
○
Genus of two species. Large leaves and large panicles of mignonette-scented flowers. Mildest areas or conservatory only.
– repanda LS (E) † ○
Soft green leaves, white beneath.
–– 'Purpurea' LS (E) † ○
Purple leaves, white beneath.
"BRAMBLE" see *RUBUS*
"BRIDAL WREATH" see *SPIRAEA × arguta*
"BROOM" see *CYTISUS* and *GENISTA*
"BROOM, BUTCHER'S" see *RUSCUS aculeatus*
"BROOM, HEDGEHOG" see *ERINACEA anthyllis*
"BROOM, SPANISH" see *SPARTIUM junceum*

BROUSSONETIA-Moraceae LS-ST
Small genus. Dioecious flowers – male pendulous catkins, female decorative globular heads.
–papyrifera LS/ST ♀ "Paper Mulberry"
Variously lobed, hairy leaves. Female has globular heads of orange-red fruits.
"BUCKEYE" see *AESCULUS*
"BUCKTHORN" see *RHAMNUS*
"BUCKTHORN, SEA" see *HIPPOPHAE rhamnoides*
BUDDLEIA – Loganiaceae MS-LS ○
"Butterfly Bush"
Opposite leaves except BUDDLEIA *alternifolia. Generally flowering July to September. Thriving in virtually all soils.*

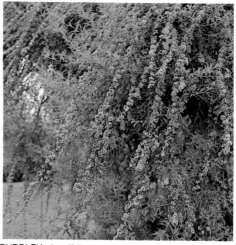

BUDDLEIA alternifolia

–alternifolia LS ○
Narrow, dark green, alternate leaves on arching branches. Fragrant, lilac flowers, June. AM 1922. AGM 1924
–– 'Argentea' MS ○
Leaves covered in silky hairs, giving a silvery sheen.
– colvilei LS ○
Dark green leaves. Large tubular flowers in terminal drooping panicles, June. Vigorous. FCC 1896. We recommend the form:-
–– 'Kewensis' LS ○
Rich red flowers. AM 1947
– crispa MS-LS ○
Leaves and stems covered in white felt. Scented flowers lilac with orange throat, in terminal panicles, September. AM 1961

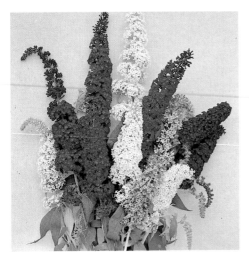

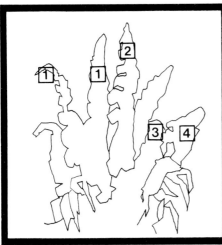

BUDDLEIA davidii cultivars:

1. 'Royal Red'
2. 'White Cloud'
3. nanhoensis
4. 'Black Knight'

– **davidii** MS ○
Fragrant flowers in long racemes are very attractive to butterflies. Best when pruned hard in March. AM 1898 AGM 1941. We recommend:-
– – **'Black Knight'** MS ○
Dark violet flowers. AGM 1969. B (a) 4
– – **'Border Beauty'** MS ○
Compact habit. Deep crimson purple flowers. B (a) 4

– – **'Empire Blue'** MS ○
Flowers rich violet blue with orange eye. AGM 1969 B (a) 4
– – **'Harlequin'** MS ○
Leaves variegated creamy white. Reddish-purple flowers. B (a) 4

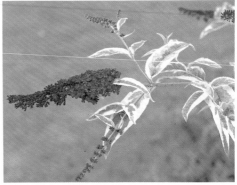

BUDDLEIA davidii 'Harlequin'

– – **'Ile de France'** MS ○
Rich violet flowers in long racemes. B (a) 4
– – **nanhoensis** MS ○
Slender branches and narrow leaves. Long panicles of mauve flowers. B (a) 4

– – **'Peace'** MS ○
Large panicles of white flowers. B (a) 4

– – **'Pink Pearl'** MS ○
Flowers lilac-pink with soft yellow eye. B (a) 4

– – **'Royal Red'** MS ○
Red-purple flowers in huge panicles. AM 1950. AGM 1969 B (a) 4

– – **'White Cloud'** MS ○
Pure white flowers in dense panicles. B (a) 4

– **fallowiana** MS ◑
White woolly stems and leaves. Pale lavender, fragrant flowers in large panicles. Requires shelter. B (a) 4

– – **'Alba'** MS ◑
Creamy-white flowers with orange eye. B (a) 4

– **globosa** MS ○ "Orange Ball Tree"
Sweetly scented, orange ball-like inflorescences, May. A (g) 5

– **'Lochinch'** MS ○
Grey, pubescent young shoots, leaves later green, white beneath. Flowers scented, violet-blue, orange eye. AM 1969.

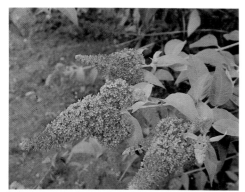

BUDDLEIA fallowiana

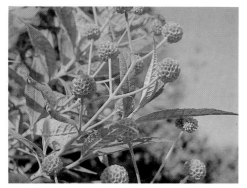

BUDDLEIA globosa

– × **weyerana** MS ☼
Ball shaped heads of flowers in long panicles
on the young wood in summer.
We recommend the form:-
– – **'Golden Glow'** LS ☼
Interrupted spikes of mauve flowers, suffused
yellow.
BUPLEURUM – Umbelliferae
Generally sub shrubs and herbs. The
following is the only woody species in open
cultivation in Britain.
– **fruticosum** MS (E) ☼
Sea green foliage. Yellow flowers, July to
September. Excellent for exposed coastal
sites. AM 1979.
"BUTCHER'S BROOM" see *RUSCUS*
aculeatus
BUXUS-Buxaceae DS-LS (E)
Thriving in most soils. Many forms useful for
hedging.
– **microphylla** DS (E)
Dense rounded habit. Narrow, oblong leaves.

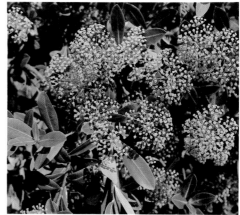

BUPLEURUM fruticosum

– **sempervirens** LS (E) Hdg (0.6m) "Common
Box"
Dense mass of small dark green leaves.
– – **'Elegantissima'** SS (E)
Dense dome-shaped habit. Leaves have
irregular creamy-white margin. Slow grower.
– – **'Gold Tip'** LS (E)
Yellow tips usually on leaves of the terminal
shoots.

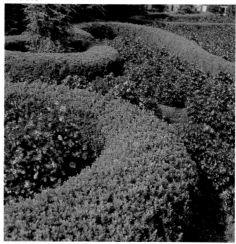

BUXUS sempervirens

– – **'Handsworthensis'** LS (E) Hdg (0.6m)
Thick, tough, dark green leaves. Excellent tall
hedge or screen.
– – **'Suffruticosa'** DS (E) "Edging Box"
Rounded, shiny, green leaves. Used as low
formal edging to paths and flower beds.

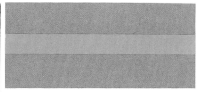

"CABBAGE TREE" see *CORDYLINE*
CAESALPINIA-Legumimosae LS † ○
Spectacular inflorescences. Bright yellow flowers with clusters of scarlet stamens, in erect racemes.
– **gilliesii** *(Poinciana gilliesii)* LS † ○ "Bird of Paradise"
Dainty, doubly pinnate, leaves. Flowers as many as 30 together in racemes, July-August. Requires a hot sunny wall. AM 1927
– **japonica** LS † ○
Prominent spines. Acacia-like soft green leaves. Flowers, 20 to 30 to a raceme, June. FCC 1888.
CALCEOLARIA – Scrophulariaceae SS (E) † ○
Requires well drained position. "Pouch-like" flowers in terminal panicles.
– **integrifolia** SS (E) † ○
Large yellow flowers late summer.
– **violacea** see *JOVELLANA violacea*
"CALICO BUSH" see *KALMIA latifolia*
CALLICARPA-Verbenaceae SS-MS
Leaves have soft rose-madder autumn colour. Small pink flowers. Conspicuous lilac/purple fruits, freely produced when several shrubs planted in group.
– **bodinieri** MS ◑
Foliage rose-purple in autumn. We recommend the forms:
– – **giraldii** MS ◑
Lilac flowers, late summer. Masses of small fruits, dark lilac or pale violet. FCC 1924
– – **'Profusion'** MS ◑
NEW. Pale pink flowers. Very free fruiting form – purple-blue berries.
– **dichotoma** SS ◑
Compact growth. Coarsely serrated leaves. Flowers July, followed by deep lilac fruits. AM 1962.
– **japonica** SS ◑
Compact growth. Oval leaves. We recommend the form:
– – **'Leucocarpa'** SS ◑
White fruits.

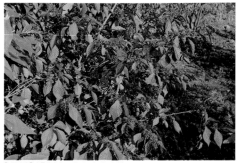
CALLICARPA bodinieri giraldii

CALLISTEMON-Myrtaceae MS (E) † ○
"Bottle Brush"
Flowers in cylindrical spikes with long showy stamens. Not for shallow chalk.
– **citrinus** MS (E) † ○
Vigorous, spreading habit. Narrow leaves, lemon scented when crushed. We recommend the form:

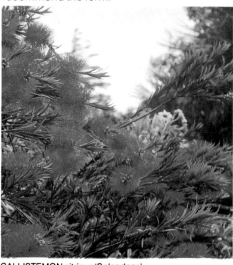
CALLISTEMON citrinus 'Splendens'

– – **'Splendens'** MS (E) † ○
Graceful shrub. Brilliant scarlet flowers throughout summer. AM 1926

CALLISTEMON – Continued

– linearis MS (E) † ○
Small narrow leaves. Long cylindrical spikes of scarlet flowers.
– salignus MS (E) † ○
Narrow willow-like leaves. Pale yellow flowers. One of the hardiest. AM 1948.
CALLUNA-Ericaceae DS (E) ⨼
Genus of a single species with many forms.
– vulgaris *(Erica vulgaris)* DS (E) ⨼ "Heather" "Ling"
AGM 1969. Many forms cultivated, varying in habit, foliage and flower colour. Flowering times are as follows:

      Early – July-August
      Mid – August-September
      Late – October-November

C (e) 9 or 10
We recommend the following:
– – 'Alportii' DS (E) ⨼
Tall, erect. Crimson flowers, Mid. 0.6m.
AGM 1947

CALLUNA vulgaris – Continued

– – 'Alba Plena' *('Alba Flore Pleno')* DS (E) ⨼
Free flowering, double white, Mid. 0.5m.
AM 1938 AMT 1969 AGM 1969
– – 'Beoley Gold' DS (E) ⨼
Strong growing form. Golden foliage. White flowers. Mid. 45cm.
– – 'Blazeaway' DS (E) ⨼
Green foliage, turning rich red in winter. Lilac mauve flowers. Mid. 0.5m.
– – 'County Wicklow' *('Camla')*
Spreading. Double shell-pink flowers. Mid.
AMT 1969 FCCT 1961 AGM 1969
– – 'C.W.Nix' DS (E) ⨼
Dark green leaves. Dark crimson flowers in long racemes. Mid 0.6m. AMT 1961
– – 'Darkness' DS (E) ⨼
Dense habit. Bright green foliage. Deep rose-purple flowers. Mid. 0.3m.

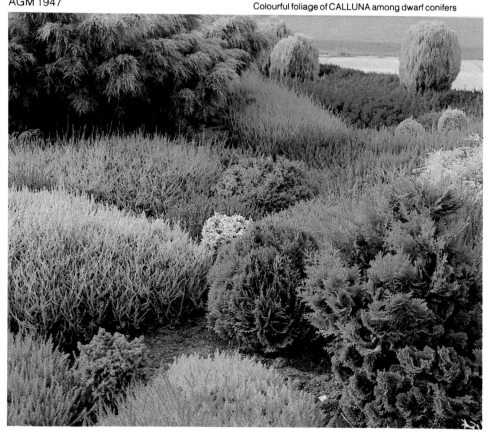
Colourful foliage of CALLUNA among dwarf conifers

59

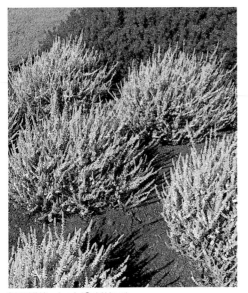

CALLUNA vulgaris 'Gold Haze'

--'**Gold Haze**' DS (E) ⊬
Bright gold foliage. White flowers. Mid. 0.5m.
AMT 1961 FCCT 1963 AGM 1969
--'**Goldsworth Crimson**' DS (E) ⊬
Flowers dark crimson. Mid to late. 0.8m
--'**H. E. Beale**' DS (E) ⊬
Long racemes of bright rose, double flowers.
Mid–Late 0.6m. AGM 1942 FCC 1943
--'**Ineke**' DS (E) ⊬
Golden foliage. Rosy-violet flowers. Mid.
30cm.
--'**J. H. Hamilton**' DS (E) ⊬
Large pink, double flowers. Early 0.25m
AM 1935 AMT 1960 FCCT 1961 AGM 1962
--'**Joy Vanstone**' DS (E) ⊬
Golden foliage, turning rich orange in winter.
Orchid pink flowers. Mid. 0.5m. AMT 1971
--'**Mair's Variety**' DS (E) ⊬
White flowers. Mid. 0.8m. AMT 1961
FCCT 1963
--'**Mullion**' DS (E) ⊬
Semi prostrate. Deep pink flowers. Mid. 0.2m.
AMT 1963
--'**Orange Queen**' DS (E) ⊬
Gold young foliage, turning orange. Pink
flowers. Mid. 0.6m.
--'**Peter Sparkes**' DS (E) ⊬
Long racemes of double pink flowers. Mid-
Late. 0.5m. AM 1958 FCCT 1962
AGM 1969

--'**Robert Chapman**' DS (E) ⊬
Golden foliage, turning orange, then red. Soft
purple flowers. Mid. 0.3m-0.6m. AMT 1962
AGM 1965
--'**Serlei**' DS (E) ⊬
Erect. Dark green foliage. White flowers.
Mid–Late. 0.6m. AMT 1961 FCCT 1962 AGM
1969
--'**Silver Queen**' DS (E) ⊬
Silver-grey foliage. Pale mauve flowers. Mid.
0.6m.
--'**Sister Anne**' DS (E) ⊬
Mounds of grey foliage. Pink flowers. Mid.
0.1m.
--'**Sunset**' DS (E) ⊬
Variegated foliage – gold, orange and yellow.
Pink flowers. 0.3m. AMT 1967 FCCT 1968
--'**Tib**' DS (E) ⊬
Double rosy red flowers. Early 0.3-0.6m.
AMT 1960 FCCT 1962
CALYCANTHUS-Calycanthaceae MS
"Allspice"
Aromatic shrubs with red-brown flowers.
Summer – early autumn. Easy cultivation.
–**fertilis** MS
Glossy leaves. Flowers throughout summer.
We recommend the form:
--'**Purpureus**' MS
Undersides of leaves tinged purple.
–**floridus** MS "Carolina Allspice"
Reddish-purple, fragrant flowers. Undersides
of leaves downy. Rare.

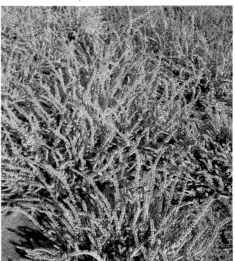

CALLUNA vulgaris 'H. E. Beale'

CAMELLIA – Theaceae SS-LS (E) ✗ ○ or ◑
Beautiful hardy spring flowering shrubs. Acid or neutral peat soil. Light shade or sheltered sunny position – avoid early morning spring sunshine, which can damage frost covered flowers. Ideal for tubs or cool greenhouse.
Flower Form:
Single – single row of up to 8 petals, conspicuous stamens
Semi-double – two or more rows of petals, conspicuous stamens
Anemone – one or more rows of large petals, central convex mass of petaloids and stamens
Paeony – convex mass of petals, petaloids and sometimes stamens.
Double – Imbricated petals, stamens in concave centre
Formal Double – Many rows of fully imbricated petals, no stamens
Flower diameter:
Small 5 to 7.5cm
Medium 7.5 to 10cm
Large 10 to 12.5cm
Very large 12.5cm+

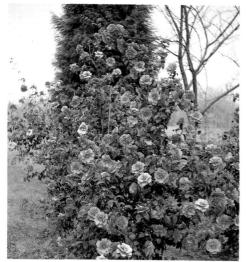

CAMELLIA 'Inspiration'

– **'Arch of Triumph'** LS (E) ✗ ◑
Deep pink to wine-red. Very large, loose paeony form. Vigorous, bushy, upright habit.
– **'Barbara Clark'** MS (E) ✗ ◑
Rose-pink, medium, semi-double, notched petals. Vigorous, compact, upright habit.

– **'Cornish Snow'** MS (E) ✗ ◑
Masses of white flowers along branchlets.
AM 1948 AGM 1963
– **cuspidata** LS (E) ✗ ◑
Small leaves, copper tinged when young. Small creamy white flowers. AM 1912
– **'Felice Harris'** LS (E) ◑
Medium semi-double, very pale pink with deeper veins. Vigorous, upright, compact habit. AMT 1979
– × **heterophylla** LS (E) ✗ ◑
Hardy hybrids between *C. japonica* and *C. reticulata*. We recommend the following:
– – **'Barbara Hillier'** LS (E) ✗ ◑
Large glossy leaves. Large, single satin-pink flowers.
– – **'Dr Clifford Parks'** LS (E) ✗ ◑
Red with orange cast. Very large, semi-double to loose paeony form or anemone form. Vigorous.
– – **'Royalty'** LS (E) ✗ ◑
Bright pink, deeper in the centre. Very large, semi-double with wavy petals.
– **'Inspiration'** MS (E) ✗ ◑
Large, semi-double, deep pink flowers.
AM 1954 FCCT 1980

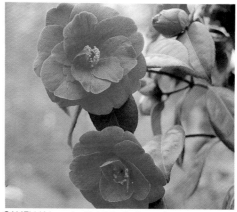

CAMELLIA japonica 'Adolphe Audusson'

– **japonica** LS (E) ✗ ◑ "Common Camellia"
Parent of many cultivars. Majority are MS, flowering within range Feb to mid-May. Size and colour depend on age, season and conditions. We recommend the following:
– – **'Adolphe Audusson'** MS (E) ✗ ◑
Blood red, conspicuous stamens; large, semi-double. Vigorous, compact. AM 1934
FCC 1956 AGM 1969

– –**'Alba Plena'** (*'Alba Grandiflora'*) MS (E)
⚲ ◑
White; large, formal double. Erect, bushy.
AM 1948

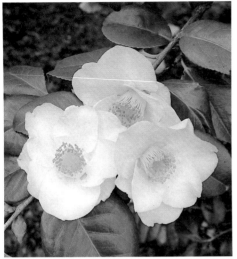

CAMELLIA japonica 'Alba Simplex'

– –**'Alba Simplex'** MS (E) ⚲ ◑
White, conspicuous stamens; large, single.
AGM 1969
– –**'Alexander Hunter'** MS (E) ⚲ ◑
Crimson, medium, single with occasional
petaloids. Upright habit.
– –**'Apollo'** MS (E) ⚲ ◑
Rose-red, occasionally with white botches;
medium, semi-double. Vigorous open growth.
AM 1956 AGM 1969
– –**'Apple Blossom'** (*'Joy Sander'*) MS (E)
⚲ ◑
Pale blush pink, deeper at edges; medium,
semi-double. AM 1933
– –**'Are-jishi'** MS (E) ⚲ ◑
Rose-red; medium, paeony form. Distinctive
leaves, thick, coarsely toothed.
– –**'Australis'** MS (E) ⚲ ◑
Rose-red, medium, paeony form. Vigorous,
compact, upright habit.
– –**'Ballet Dancer'** MS (E) ⚲ ◑
Cream, shading to coral pink at the edges.
Medium, full paeony form. Compact, upright
habit.
– –**'Benten'** MS (E) ⚲ ◑
Leaves conspicuously variegated creamy
white. Flowers rose-red, single. Compact
habit.

– –**'Betty Sheffield Supreme'** MS (E) ⚲ ◑
White, petals edged pink-red; large, semi-
double to paeony form.
– –**'Bob Hope'** MS (E) ⚲ ◑
Black-red, large, semi-double with irregular
petals. Slow, compact growth.
– –**'Bob's Tinsie'** MS (E) ⚲ ◑
Brilliant red, small, anemone form. Compact,
upright habit.
– –**'Carter's Sunburst'** MS (E) ⚲ ◑
Pale pink striped or marked deeper pink.
Large to very large, semi-double to paeony
form or formal double. Compact habit.
– –**'Cecile Brunazzi'** MS (E) ⚲ ◑
Pale pink, medium, semi-double to loose
paeony form. Large outer petals and twisted,
upright centre petals.
– –**'Chandleri Elegans'** see *'Elegans'*
– –**'Clarise Carleton'** MS (E) ⚲ ◑
Red, large to very large, semi-double.
Vigorous, upright habit.

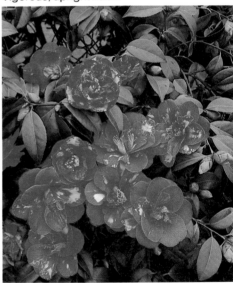

CAMELLIA japonica 'Donckelarii'

– –**'C.M. Hovey'** MS (E) ⚲ ◑
Carmine; medium, formal double. Vigorous,
compact. FCC 1879
– –**'C.M. Wilson'** MS (E) ⚲ ◑
Light pink; very large, anemone form.
AM 1956
– –**'Contessa Lavinia Maggi'** MS (E) ⚲ ◑
White-pale pink with dark rose stripes; large,
formal double. FCC 1862 AGM 1969

--'**Coquetti**' MS (E) ✗ ◑
Rose; medium, double. Erect, slow growth.
AM 1956 AGM 1969
--'**Devonia**' MS (E) ✗ ◑
White, medium, single. Vigorous, erect.
AM 1900
--'**Donckelarii**' MS (E) ✗ ◑
Red, sometimes with white marbling; large,
semi-double. Slow, bushy. AM 1960
AGM 1969
--'**Drama Girl**' MS (E) ✗ ◑
Deep salmon pink; very large, semi-double.
Vigorous. Slightly pendulous. AM 1966
FCC 1969

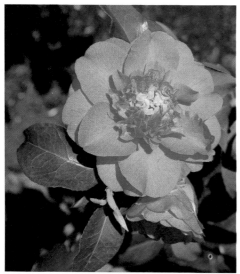

CAMELLIA japonica 'Elegans'

--'**Elegans**' (*'Chandleri Elegans'*) MS (E)
✗ ◑
Deep peach; very large, anemone. Spreading
form. AM 1953 FCC 1958 AGM 1969
--'**Elegans Champagne**' MS (E) ✗ ◑
Sport of *'Elegans'*, white with creamy petaloid
stamens.
--'**Elegans Supreme**' MS (E) ✗ ◑
A beautiful sport with deeply serrated,
rose-pink petals.
--'**Frau Minna Seidel**' see *'Pink Perfection'*
--'**Extravaganza**' MS (E) ✗ ◑
White, vividly marked and striped light red.
Large to very large, anemone form. Compact,
Compact, upright habit.
--'**Furo-an**' MS (E) ✗ ◑
Soft pink; medium, single. AM 1956

--'**General Lamorciere**' see *'Marguerite
Gouillon'*
--'**Gloire de Nantes**' MS (E) ✗ ◑
Rose pink; large, semi-double. Erect,
compact. AM 1956 AGM 1969
--'**Grand Slam**' MS (E) ✗ ◑
Brilliant, dark red. Large to very large
semi-double to anemone form. Vigorous,
open, upright habit.
--'**Guest of Honor**' MS (E) ✗ ◑
Salmon pink; very large, semi-double to loose
paeony form. Vigorous compact and erect.
Best under glass. AM 1967
--'**Guilio Nuccio**' MS (E) ✗ ◑
Coral pink; very large, semi-double. Vigorous.
Erect. AM 1962
--'**Haku-rakuten**' MS (E) ✗ ○
White; large, semi-double to loose paeony
form. Vigorous. Erect.
--'**Hawaii**' MS (E) ✗ ◑
Pale pink, medium to large, paeony form with
fringed petals.
--'**Joy Sander**' See *'Apple Blossom'*
--'**Jupiter**' MS (E) ✗ ○
Scarlet blotched white sometimes; medium,
single to semi-double, conspicuous stamens.
Vigorous, erect.
--'**Kouron-jura**' MS (E) ✗ ◑
Dark red; medium, formal double. Semi-erect.
AM 1960
--'**Lady Buller**' see *'Nagasaki'*
--'**Lady Clare**' MS (E) ✗ ◑
Deep, clear peach pink; large, semi-double.
Vigorous spreading. AM 1927 AGM 1969
--'**Lady de Saumerez**' MS (E) ✗ ◑
Red blotched white; medium, semi-double.
Vigorous, compact.
--'**Lady Vansittart**' MS (E) ✗ ◑
White striped rose pink; medium,
semi-double. Bushy.
--'**Latifolia**' MS (E) ✗ ◑
Soft rose-red; medium, semi-double.
Vigorous, bushy.
--'**Madame Victor de Bisschop**' MS (E)
✗ ◑
White, medium, semi-double. Vigorous.
--'**Magnoliiflora**' MS (E) ✗ ◑
Blush pink; medium, semi-double. Compact.
AM 1953
--'**Marguerite Gouillon**' (*'General
Lamorciere'*) LS (E) ✗ ◑
Pale pink, flecked deeper pink; medium,
paeony form. Vigorous, bushy.

--**'Mars'** MS (E) ✓ ◑
Turkey red; large, semi-double. Conspicuous stamens. Open, loose growth.
--**'Mathotiana'** (*'Mathotiana Rubra'*) MS (E) ✓ ◑
Crimson; large double to formal double. Upright.

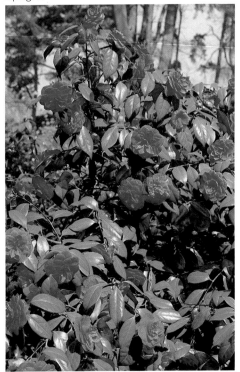
CAMELLIA japonica 'Rubescens Major'

--**'Mathotiana Alba'** MS (E) ✓ ◑
White, rarely spotted pink; large, formal double. Shelter required.
--**'Mathotiana Rosea'** MS (E) ✓ ◑
Clear pink; large, formal double. Vigorous, erect. AM 1954
--**'Mercury'** MS (E) ✓ ◑
Deep crimson, darker veins; large, semi-double. Compact. AM 1948
--**'Mrs. D. W. Davis'** MS (E) ✓ ◑
Blush pink; very large, semi-double. Vigorous. AM 1960 FCC 1968
--**'Nagasaki'** (*'Lady Buller'*) MS (E) ✓ ◑
Rose pink, white marbling; large, semi-double. Leaves sometimes blotched yellow. AM 1953 AGM 1969

--**'Nobilissima'** MS (E) ✓ ◑
White shaded yellow; medium, paeony form. Erect. Early flowering.
--**'Pink Champagne'** LS (E) ✓ ◑
Soft pink; large, semi-double-paeony form. Vigorous. AM 1960
--**'Pink Perfection'** (*'Frau Minna Seidel'*) LS (E) ✓ ◑
Shell pink; small, formal double. Erect, vigorous.
--**'Premier'** MS (E) ✓ ◑
Clear rose-red. Large, full paeony form. Vigorous, upright habit.
--**'Preston Rose'** (*'Duchess de Rohan'*) LS (E) ✓ ◑
Salmon pink; medium, paeony form. Vigorous. AGM 1969
--**'R. L. Wheeler'** LS (E) ✓ ◑
Rose pink; very large, semi-double-anemone form. Vigorous. AM 1959 FCC 1975
--**'Rubescens Major'** MS (E) ✓ ◑
Crimson, dark veins, large double. Bushy. AM 1959 AGM 1969
--**'Sieboldii'** see *'Tricolor'*
--**'Souvenir de Bahaud Litou'** MS (E) ✓ ◑
Light pink; large, formal double. Vigorous, erect.
--**'Sylvia'** MS (E) ✓ ◑
Carmine red, white flecks; medium, single.
--**'Tinker Bell'** MS (E) ✓ ◑
White, striped pink and rose red. Small, anemone form. Vigorous, upright habit.
--**'Tomorrow'** MS (E) ✓ ◑
Rose; very large, semi-double-paeony form. Vigorous, slightly pendulous. Best in cool greenhouse. AM 1960
--**'Tomorrow's Dawn'** MS (E) ✓ ◑
Deep soft pink fading to white at margins; very large, semi-double-paeony form. Vigorous, open. Best in cool greenhouse.
--**'Tricolor'** (*'Sieboldii'*) MS (E) ✓ ◑
White streaked carmine; medium, semi-double.
-**'Leonard Messel'** LS (E) ✓ ◑
Rich clear pink; large, semi-double. Dark green leaves. AM 1958 FCC 1970
-**reticulata** LS (E) ✓ ◑
Rose pink, large single flowers trumpet shaped before opening. Produced freely late winter-early spring. AM 1944. We recommend the following selected clones which require a conservatory, except in mild areas:

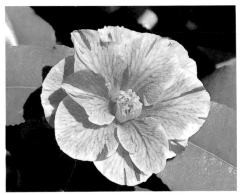

CAMELLIA japonica 'Tricolor'

– –**'Captain Rawes'** (*'Semi-plena'*) LS (E)
↑ ↙ ◑
Carmine pink; very large, semi-double. FCC
1963
– –**'Robert Fortune'** (*'Pagoda'*) (*'Flore Pleno'*) LS (E) ↑ ↙ ◑
Dark crimson; large, double. Compact.
FCC 1865
– **saluenensis** LS (E) ↑ ↙ ◑
Soft pink flowers, medium, single, in great
profusion.
– **sasanqua** MS (E) ↙ ◑
Small, fragrant usually white flowers
produced winter-early spring. Require wall
protection. FCC 1892. We recommend the
following forms:
– –**'Crimson King'** MS (E) ↙ ◑
Red; small, single.
– –**'Narumi-gata'** MS (E) ↙ ◑
Creamy white, pink towards margins; large,
fragrant. AM 1953
– **sinensis** (*thea*) (*Thea sinensis*) SS (E)
↑ ↙ ◑ "Tea Plant"
Small white flowers in spring. Slow, compact.
Hardy in a sheltered position.
– **'Spring Festival'** LS (E) ↙ ◑
Medium pink, fading to light pink in centre.
Miniature, semi-double. Narrow, upright
habit.
– **'William Hertrich'** LS (E) ↙ ◑
Deep cherry red, very large, semi-double,
with slightly reflexed outer petals. Vigorous,
bushy habit.
– × **williamsii** MS (E) ↙ ◑
Best camellia for general planting. Free
flowering over long period from November to
May. We recommend the following cultivars:

– –**'Anticipation'** MS (E) ↙ ◑
Deep rose, large, paeony form. Upright habit
AMT 1974 FCCT 1975
– –**'Bow Bells'** MS (E) ↙ ◑
Bright rose; semi-double.
– –**'Brigadoon'** MS (E) ↙ ◑
Rose pink, medium, semi-double. Compact,
upright habit. AMT 1974
– –**'Caerhays'** MS (E) ↙ ◑
Lilac rose; medium, anemone form.
Pendulous habit. AM 1969
– –**'Charles Michael'** MS (E) ↙ ◑
Pale pink; large, semi-double.
– –**'China Clay'** MS (E) ↙ ◑
White, medium, semi-double. Open habit.
– –**'Daintiness'** MS (E) ↙ ◑
Salmon pink, large, semi-double. Open habit.
– –**'Debbie'** MS (E) ↙ ◑
Clear pink, large, semi-double. AM 1971

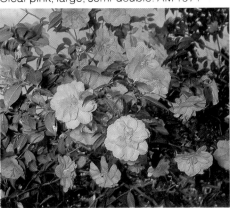

CAMELLIA × williamsii 'Donation'

– –**'Donation'** LS (E) ↙ ◑
Orchid pink; large, semi-double. Erect
vigorous. AM 1941 AM 1952 AGM 1958
FCCT 1974
– –**'E. G. Waterhouse'** MS (E) ↙ ◑
Light pink; medium, formal double. Upright.
– –**'Elizabeth Rothschild'** MS (E) ↙ ◑
Soft rose; medium, semi-double.
– –**'Elsie Jury'** MS (E) ↙ ◑
Clear pink, large, full paeony form. FCCT 1975
– –**'Francis Hanger'** MS (E) ↙ ◑
White; single. Leaves undulate. Erect.
AM 1953
– –**'Glenn's Orbit'** MS (E) ↙ ◑
Deep orchid pink, large, semi-double to loose
paeony form. Vigorous, upright habit.
AMT 1976

--**'J. C. Williams'** MS (E) ⚊ ◑
Phlox pink; medium, single. FCC 1942
AGM 1949

--**'Lady Gowrie'** MS (E) ⚊ ◑
Pink; large, semi-double. Vigorous, compact.

--**'Mary Christian'** MS (E) ⚊ ◑
Clear pink; small, single. AM 1942

--**'Mildred Veitch'** MS (E) ⚊ ◑
Orchid pink, large, semi-double to anemone
form. AM 1977 FCCT 1979

--**'November Pink'** MS (E) ⚊ ◑
Phlox pink; medium, single. Early flowering.
AM 1950

--**'Rose Parade'** MS (E) ⚊ ◑
Deep rose pink, medium, formal double.
Vigorous, compact, upright habit.

--**'Rosemary Williams'** MS (E) ⚊ ◑
Rose pink, medium, single. Compact, upright
habit.

--**'St. Ewe'** MS (E) ⚊ ◑
Rose pink; medium, single. AM 1947 FCCT
1974

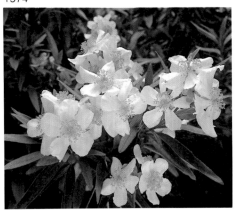

CARPENTERIA californica

CANTUA – Polemoniaceae ST (E) ↑ ☼
*Small S. American genus. The following
species is cultivated:*
–**buxifolia** (*dependens*) SS (E) ↑ ☼
Tubular cherry red flowers in drooping
corymbs. April. Semi (E) in mild areas.
Requires sheltered wall. AM 1905

CARAGANA – Leguminosae SS-ST
*Yellow pea flowers, early summer. Compound
leaves, often spiny.*
–**arborescens** ST ♥ "Pea Tree"
Shrubby habit. Flowers in May. Succeeds in
exposed situations and most soils.

--**'Lorbergii'** LS
Graceful form with very narrow leaflets.

--**'Pendula'** ST ♠
Weeping form.

CARMICHAELIA – Leguminosae SS ☼
Broom-like shrubs requiring well drained soil.
–**enysii** DS-SS ☼
Mound-like mat of branchlets. Small lilac-pink
flowers.

–**petriei** SS ☼
Stout branchlets. Fragrant violet purple
flowers in racemes.

CARPENTERIA – Philadelphaceae MS
(E) ☼
*Monotypic genus, native of California, best as
a wall shrub in sunny position.*
–**californica** MS (E) ☼
Large white flowers with golden anthers, July.
FCC 1888 AGM 1935. A (b) 5

CARPINUS – Carpinaceae ST-MT ♥
"Hornbeams"
*Hardy trees for any fertile soil. Produce
clusters of hop-like fruits.*
–**betulus** MT ♥ Hdg (0.5m) "Common
Hornbeam"
Characteristic grey fluted bark. Strongly
ribbed and toothed leaves turn yellow in
autumn. As a hedge, leaves retained into
winter, like beech.

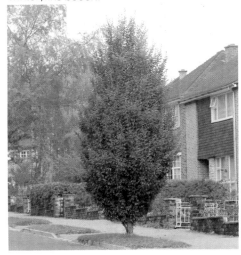

CARPINUS betulus 'Fastigiata'

--**'Fastigiata'** (*'Pyramidalis'*) MT ♦
Narrow as a young tree, broadening with age.
AGM 1969

–**caroliniana** ST ♥ "American Hornbeam"
"Blue Beech"
Grey fluted bark. Glossy apple-green leaves,
tinted in autumn.
–**japonica** ST ♥
Prominently corrugated leaves. Conspicuous
fruiting catkins.
–**laxiflora macrostachya** MT ♥
Drooping branches and slender pointed
leaves, bright red when young. Conspicuous
fruit clusters.
–**turczaninowii** ST ♥
Slender stems and small leaves. Young
leaves bright red.
CARYA – Juglandaceae MT-LT ♥ "Hickory"
*Large compound leaves turn clear yellow in
autumn. Grey trunks attractive in winter. Fast
growing, but best planted small.*
–**cordiformis** (*amara*) LT ♥ "Bitter Nut"
Thin brown scaly bark. Characteristic yellow
winter buds. Best "Hickory" for general
planting.
–**illinoensis** (*olivaeformis*) LT ♥
Numerous leaflets – 11 to 17 per leaf.

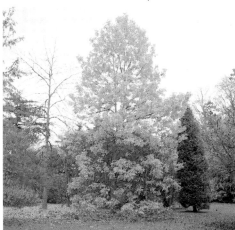

CARYA ovata

–**ovata** MT ♥ "Shagbark Hickory"
Leaves of 5 pointed leaflets, the 3 upper ones
large. Rich yellow autumn colour.
CARYOPTERIS – Verbenaceae SS ○
*Aromatic leaves. Blue flowers late summer.
Well drained soil. Ideal for chalk.*
– × **clandonensis** SS ○
Variable hybrid of which two good forms are
grown:

––**'Arthur Simmonds'** SS ○
Attractive bright blue flowers August-
September AM 1933 FCC 1041 AGM 1942
A (b) (g) 5
––**'Heavenly Blue'** SS ○
Deeper blue flowers. Compact habit.
A (b) (g) 5
CASSIA – Leguminosae MS † ○
*Enormous genus of mainly tropical species.
The following species requires a warm
sheltered wall.*
–**obtusa** MS † ○
Large deep yellow flowers in terminal clusters,
late summer-autumn. Vigorous.
CASSINIA – Compositae SS-MS (E) ○
Heath like shrubs, requiring well drained soil.
–**fulvida** (*Diplopappus chrysophyllus*) SS
(E) ○
Small massed leaves have golden
appearance. Flowers white, July. Young
growth sticky.

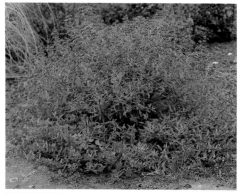

CARYOPTERIS × clandonensis 'Heavenly Blue'

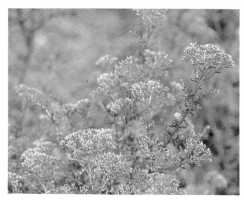

CASSINIA fulvida

– **vauvilliersii** SS (E) ☼
Slightly taller than *C. fulvida* with larger leaves, dark green. The following is the best form:
– – **albida** SS (E) ☼
White hoary leaves and stems.
CASSIOPE (*ANDROMEDA* in part)
Ericaceae PS-DS (E) ⚋ ◑
Shrublets needing moist peaty soil. White bell flowers in spring.

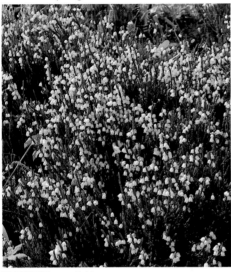

CASSIOPE lycopodioides

– **lycopodioides** PS (E) ⚋ ◑
Mat of thread like branches. Flowers on slender stalks. AM 1937 FCC 1962
– **'Muirhead'** DS (E) ⚋ ◑
Characteristic curved forked shoots. Small nodding flowers. AM 1953 FCC 1962
CASTANEA – Fagaceae LT ♥ "Chestnuts"
Long lance shaped serrated leaves. Small white flowers in slender racemes. Moderately lime-tolerant but chlorotic on shallow chalk.
– **sativa** LT ♥ "Sweet Chestnut" "Spanish Chestnut"
Pale yellow catkins, July. Hot summers necessary for worthwhile crop of edible nuts. Old trees develop characteristic grooved, spiralling bark. Fast growing.
– – **'Albomarginata'** LT ♥
Leaves have creamy white margins. AM 1964
– – **'Marron de Lyon'** LT ♥
Nuts borne at early age – best fruiting clone.
CASTANOPSIS chrysophylla see
CHRYSOLEPIS chrysophylla

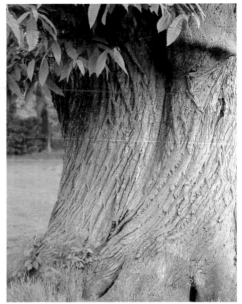

CASTANEA sativa

CATALPA – Bignoniaceae MT ♥
Large leaves. Foxglove-like flowers in conspicuous panicles (on older trees) late summer. All well drained soils.
– **bignonioides** MT ♥ "Indian Bean Tree"
Large heart-shaped leaves. White, yellow and purple marked flowers July and August.
AM 1933 AGM 1960

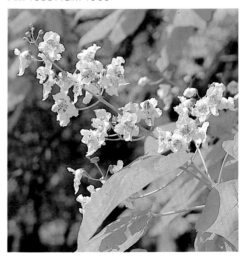

CATALPA bignonioides

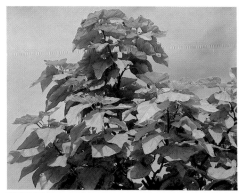

CATALPA bignonioides 'Aurea'

– – **'Aurea'** LS-MT ♥ "Golden Indian Bean Tree"
Large velvety soft yellow leaves.
– × **erubescens** MT ♥
Broad ovate leaves. Small numerous flowers late July, similar to *C. bignonioides*. We recommend the form:
– – **'Purpurea'** MT ♥
Young leaves and shoots dark, almost black-purple, becoming dark green with age. AM 1970
– **fargesii** MT ♥
Lilac pink flowers with reddish brown spots and yellow staining, 7 to 15 together in corymbs. AM 1973. We recommend the form:
– – **duclouxii** MT ♥
Leaves less hairy with conspicuous acuminate lobes. AM 1934
– **speciosa** MT ♥
Large heart shaped leaves. White flowers with purple spots, July. AM 1956
CEANOTHUS – Rhamnaceae PS-LS ○
"Californian Lilacs"
Variable genus incorporating evergreen and deciduous members. Mainly blue flowers. Require shelter and good drainage. Not for shallow chalk.
– **arboreus** MS (E) † ○
Large leaved species. Deep blue flowers, spring, in large panicles. We recommend the form:
– – **'Trewithen Blue'** MS (E) † ○
Slightly scented deep blue flowers in large panicles. A (b) 5
– **'A.T. Johnson'** MS (E) † ○
Rich blue flowers in spring and autumn. AM 1934. A (b) 5

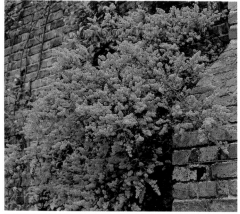

CEANOTHUS 'Cascade'

– **'Autumnal Blue'** MS (E) ○
Abundant deep blue flowers late summer and autumn. Hardy. AM 1930. A (b) 5
– **'Blue Mound'** DS (E) ○
Dense mound-like habit. Mid-blue flowers, May-June.
– **'Burkwoodii'** MS (E) † ○
Rich dark blue flowers summer and autumn. AM 1930. A (b) 5
– **'Cascade'** MS (E) † ○
Bright blue flowers in long stalked clusters, spring. AM 1946. A (b) 5
– **'Delight'** MS (E) ○
Rich blue spring flowers in long panicles. Hardy. AM 1933 AGM 1957. A (b) 5
– **dentatus** MS (E) † ○
Bright blue flowers, May. Tiny glandular leaves. A (b) 5

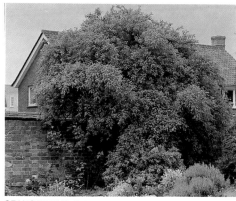

CEANOTHUS 'Delight'

– **'Gloire de Versailles'** MS ○
Powder blue flowers in large panicles, summer and autumn. FCC 1872 AGM 1925. B (a) 4

– **'Henri Desfosse'** MS ○
Violet blue flowers in panicles, summer. AM 1926. B (a) 4

– **impressus** MS (E) ↑ ○
Deep blue flowers, spring. Small leaves with deeply impressed veins. AM 1944 FCC 1957 AGM 1969. A (b) 5

– – **'Puget Blue'** MS (E) ↑ ○
Selected form with deep blue flowers. AM 1971. A (b) 5

– × **lobbianus** MS (E) ↑ ○
Bright blue flowers May and June. AGM 1969 A (b) 5

– **papillosus** LS (E) ↑ ○
Rich blue flowers late spring. Long narrow sticky leaves. We recommend the form:

– – **roweanus** LS (E) ↑ ○
Darker blue flowers. A (b) 5

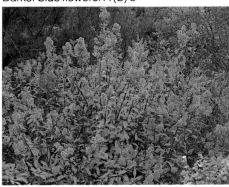

CEANOTHUS 'Perle Rose'

– **'Perle Rose'** MS ○
Rose carmine flowers, summer. B (a) 4

– **prostratus** PS (E) ○ "Squaw Carpet"
Creeping form. Bright blue flowers, spring. AM 1935

– **rigidus** MS (E) ↑ ○
Purple blue flowers, spring. Distinctive wedge-shaped leaves. A (b) 5

– **'Southmead'** MS (E) ○
Rich blue flowers, May-June. Small oblong leaves, dark glossy green above. AM 1964. A (b) 5

– **thyrsiflorus** LS (E) ○
Bright blue flowers, early summer. Hardy. AM 1935. A (b) 5

– – **repens** PS (E) GC ○ "Creeping Blue Blossom"
Light blue flowers. Vigorous, mound forming.

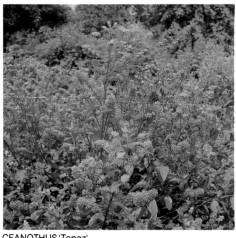

CEANOTHUS 'Topaz'

– **'Topaz'** MS ○
Light indigo blue flowers, summer. AM 1961 AGM 1969. B (a) 4

– × **veitchianus** MS (E) ○
Deep blue flowers, May-June. Hardy. AGM 1925. A (b) 5

CEDRELA – Meliaceae MT ♥
Mainly tropical genus. We recommend:

– **sinensis** (*Ailanthus flavescens*) MT ♥
Large pinnate leaves. Panicles of fragrant white flowers. Yellow autumn tints. Fast growing.

CELTIS – Ulmaceae ST-MT ♥ "Nettle trees" "Hackberries"
Allied to the Elms. Fast growing.

– **occidentalis** MT ♥ "North American Hackberry"
Warty corky bark and profusions of black fruits on mature trees.

CERATOSTIGMA – Plumbaginaceae DS-SS ○ "Hardy Plumbago"
Blue flowers, early autumn. Dry well drained soils.

– **griffithii** SS ○
Deep blue flowers. Often conspicuous red autumnal tints.

– **minus** (*polhillii*) DS ↑ ○
Slate-blue flowers. Slender form.

– **willmottianum** SS ○
Rich blue flowers July to autumn. Red tinted foliage in autumn. AM 1917 AGM 1928

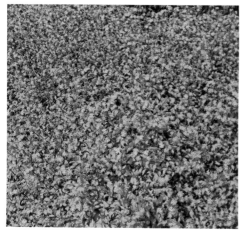

CERATOSTIGMA willmottianum

CERCIDIPHYLLUM – Cercidiphyllaceae MT
Elegant, autumn colouring trees. Flowers insignificant. Moist well drained soils.

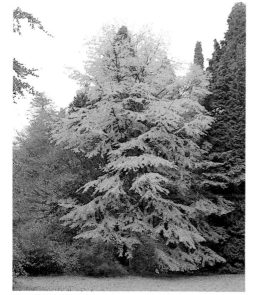

CERCIDIPHYLLUM japonicum

– japonicum MT ♥
Slightly pendulous branches. Bright green leaves turn smoky-pink or yellow in autumn and evict pungent aroma of burnt sugar.
– magnificum MT ♥
Smoother bark and larger leaves than *C. japonicum*. Yellow autumn leaves. Rare.

CERCIS – Leguminosae LS-ST ○
Distinctive foliage. Pea-flowers in spring. Usually low branched large shrubs, though attaining tree-size after many years. Good drainage.
– canadensis ST ♥
Pale pink flowers May-June. We recommend:
– – 'Forest Pansy' ST ♥
Magnificent new introduction. Deep reddish-purple foliage, retaining colour throughout the season.
– racemosa MT ♥
Flowers in hanging racemes, May, on mature trees. AM 1927

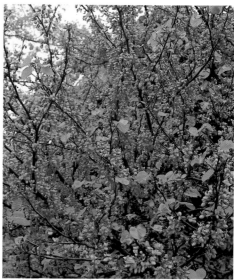

CERCIS siliquastrum

– siliquastrum ST ♥ "Judas Tree"
Branches laden with clusters of rosy lilac flowers, May. Conspicuous red seed pods July onwards. Legendary tree from which Judas hanged himself. AGM 1927
– – 'Alba' ST ♥
White flowers. AM 1962
– – 'Bodnant' ST ♥
Deep purple flowers. FCC 1944
CESTRUM – Solanaceae MS (E) † ○
Shrubs for warm wall or conservatory.
– aurantiacum MS (E) † ○
Orange yellow tubular flowers in panicles. AM 1961
– 'Newellii' MS (E) † ○
Large orange red flowers. FCC 1876 AM 1951

71

CHAENOMELES – Rosaceae DS-LS ○ or ◑
"Japonica"
Saucer-shaped flowers in spring, followed by yellow quinces. Easy growing in open or against a wall. Prune wall grown shrubs only.
C4/E9
– **cathayensis** LS ○ or ◑
Spiny branches and long narrow toothed leaves. White, salmon-pink tinted, flowers. Fruits very large.
– **japonica** (*Cydonia japonica*) (*Cydonia maulei*) SS ○ or ◑
Bright orange flame flowers. FCC 1890 AGM 1943
– – **alpina** DS ○ or ◑
Form with creeping stems and ascending branchlets.
– **speciosa** (*lagenaria*) (*Cydonia speciosa*) MS ○ or ◑ "Japonica"
With spreading, branched habit. AGM 1927 Many forms of varying flower colour are in cultivation, of which we recommend the following:
– – **'Cardinalis'** MS ○ or ◑
Crimson scarlet. AM 1893 AGM 1969
– – **'Moerloosei'** MS ○ or ◑
Pink and white. AM 1957 AGM 1969

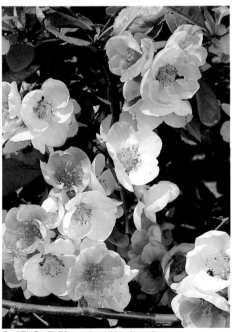
CHAENOMELES speciosa 'Moerloosei'

– – **'Nivalis'** MS ○ or ◑
Large pure white. AGM 1969
– – **'Rosea Plena'** MS ○ or ◑
Double rose-pink.
– – **'Rubra Grandiflora'** SS ○ or ◑
Very large, crimson. Low spreading habit.
AGM 1969
– – **'Simonii'** DS ○ or ◑
Semi-double, flat, blood red. AM 1907
AGM 1924
– × **superba** SS-MS ○ or ◑
Vigorous habit. We recommend the following forms:
– – **'Crimson & Gold'** MS ○ or ◑
Crimson petals and golden anthers.
AGM 1969 AM 1979
– – **'Hever Castle'** MS ○ or ◑
Shrimp pink.
– – **'Knap Hill Scarlet'** MS ○ or ◑
Bright flame, profuse spring – early summer.
AM 1961 AGM 1969
– – **'Nicoline'** SS ○ or ◑
Scarlet. Spreading.
– – **'Pink Lady'** SS ○ or ◑
Rose pink. spreading.
– – **'Rowallane'** MS ○ or ◑
Large blood-red, spreading habit. AGM 1957
CHAMAEROPS – Palmaceae SS (E) ↑ ○
Only two species of which we recommend:
– **humilis** SS (E) ↑ ○
Miniature palm rarely higher than 1.5m. Hardy in mild areas.
"CHASTE TREE" see *VITEX agnus-castus*
"CHERRY" see *PRUNUS*
"CHERRY, CORNELIAN" see *CORNUS mas*
"CHESTNUT, GOLDEN" see *CHRYSOLEPIS chrysophylla*
"CHESTNUT, HORSE" see *AESCULUS hippocastanum*
"CHESTNUT, SPANISH" see *CASTANEA sativa*
"CHILEAN FIRE BUSH" see *EMBOTHRIUM*
CHIMONANTHUS – Calycanthaceae MS ○
"Winter Sweet"
Best against sunny wall. Any well drained soil – good on chalk.
– **praecox** (*fragrans*) (*Calycanthus praecox*) MS ○
Pale waxy yellow flowers, purple at centre on bare branches, winter. Sweetly scented. E2
– – **'Grandiflorus'** MS ○
Deeper yellow flowers with red centre.
AM 1928

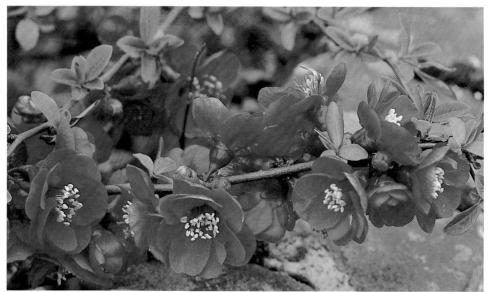

CHAENOMELES × superba 'Crimson and Gold'

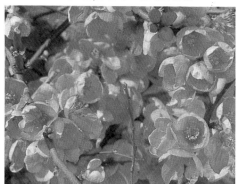

CHAENOMELES × superba 'Pink Lady'

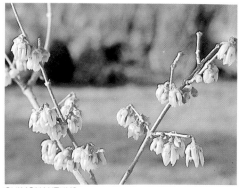

CHIMONANTHUS praecox

– –**'Luteus'** MS ○

Large clear waxy yellow flowers, opening later. AM 1948 FCC 1970

CHIONANTHUS – Oleaceae LS ○ "Fringe Tree"

White flowers with strap shaped petals, produced abundantly June-July, on older plants. Easy cultivation.

– **retusus (FORREST FORM)** LS ○ "Chinese Fringe Tree"

Handsome shrub. Flowers followed by damson-like fruits. FCC 1885

– **virginicus** LS ○ North American "Fringe Tree"

Slightly fragrant white flowers. AM 1931

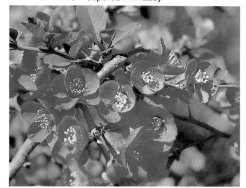

CHAENOMELES × superba 'Rowallane'

73

CHOISYA – Rutaceae MS (E) ☼ or ●
Small genus of attractive shrubs.

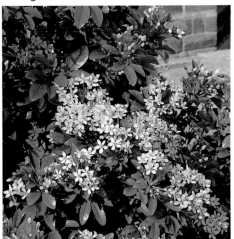

CHOISYA ternata

– **ternata** MS (E) ☼ or ● "Mexican Orange Blossom"
Rounded habit. Glossy dark green leaves, aromatic when bruised. White sweetly scented flowers late spring – early summer. FCC 1880 AGM 1969. A (b) 5

"CHOKEBERRY" see *ARONIA*

CHORDOSPARTIUM – Leguminosae MS ☼
Monotypic genus:
– **stevensonii** MS ☼
Broom-like leafless shrub. Racemes of lavender-pink flowers, summer. Weeping habit. Rare. AM 1943

"CHRIST'S THORN" see *PALIURUS spina-christi*

CHRYSOLEPIS – Fagaceae LS-ST (E)
Shrubs or small trees with fruits resembling those of "Sweet Chestnut".
– **chrysophylla** (*Castanopsis chrysophylla*) LS-ST (E) ♥
"Golden Chestnut". Leathery pointed leaves. Fruits in dense green prickly clusters. Well drained acid or neutral soil. AM 1935

CHUSQUEA – Gramineae
Distinguished from other bamboos by the solid stems.
– **culeou** LS (E)
Rare bamboo forming broad, dense clumps. Deep olive green. Canes bear dense clusters of slender, short, leafy branches along their entire length. AM 1974

CISTUS – Cistaceae DS-MS (E) ☼ "Sun Roses"
Except otherwise stated, white flowers June-July. Ideal for rock gardens, dry banks. Resent frost, but wind and salt tolerant. Good on chalk.
– × **aguilari** SS (E) † ☼
Very large flowers. Vigorous. We recommend the form:
– – **'Maculatus'** SS (E) † ☼
Flowers have ring of crimson blotches in centre. AM 1936
– **'Anne Palmer'** SS (E) † ☼
Upright habit. Pink flowers. AM 1964
– **canescens 'Albus'** SS (E) ☼
Flowers 5cm across. Grey leaves.
– × **corbariensis** SS (E) ☼
Crimson tinged buds, opening white. Hardy.
– × **cyprius** MS (E) ☼
Large flowers with crimson basal blotches. Hardy. AMT 1925 AGM 1926
– **'Elma'** MS (E) † ☼
Very large flowers. Deep green glossy lance-shaped leaves. Sturdy bushy habit. AM 1949
– **ladanifer** MS (E) † ☼ "Gum Cistus"
Large flowers with chocolate basal stain, frilled petals. Lance-shaped leaves.
– **laurifolius** MS (E) ☼
Flowers with yellow centres. Dark green leathery leaves. Erect habit. Hardy. AGM 1969
– × **loretii** DS (E) ☼
Large flowers with crimson basal blotches.
– × **lusitanicus** SS (E) ☼
Large flowers with crimson basal blotches.

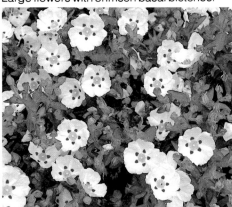

CISTUS × lusitanicus 'Decumbens'

– – **'Decumbens'** DS (E) ☼ GC
Wide spreading form.

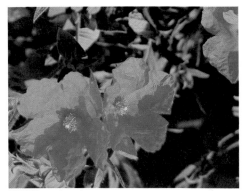

CISTUS × pulverulentus

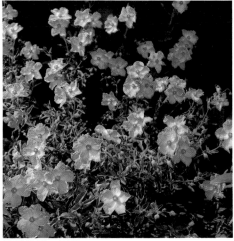

CISTUS 'Silver Pink'

– **palhinhae** SS (E) † ☼
Large pure white flowers. Glossy, sticky leaves. Distinctive. AM 1944
– **'Pat'** SS (E) ☼
Large flowers with maroon blotches. Hardy. AM 1955
– **'Peggy Sammons'** MS (E) ☼
Pale pink flowers. Grey green leaves. Erect habit.
– **populifolius** SS (E) ☼
Flowers white with central yellow blotches. Leaves small hairy and poplar-like. Erect habit. AM 1930. We recommend the form:
– – **lasiocalyx** SS (E) ☼
Large, wavy flowers with inflated calyx.
– × **pulverulentus** DS (E) † ☼
Bright cerise flowers. Sage-green wavy leaves.
– × **purpureus** SS (E) † ☼
Large rosy-crimson flowers with chocolate basal blotches. AMT 1925 AGM 1927
– **'Silver Pink'** SS (E) ☼
Silver-pink flowers in long clusters. Very hardy. AM 1919 AGM 1930
– × **skanbergii** SS (E) † ☼
Clear pink flowers.
× **CITRONCIRUS webberi** (*CITRUS sinense* × *PONCIRUS trifoliata*) LS Semi-(E) † ☼ "Citrange"
Spiny shrub. Large trifoliolate leaves with narrow winged petioles. Flowers, when produced, large white, fragrant. Orange or yellow fruit.

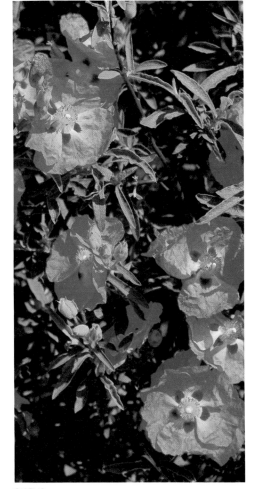

CISTUS × purpureus

CITRUS – Rutaceae S-T Semi-(E) ↑ ○
Grown for their fruits. In this country require
sunny wall or conservatory. White flowers,
when produced.
– **ichangense** MS Semi-(E) ↑ ○ "Ichang
Lemon"
Leaves with conspicuous winged leaf stalks.
Lemon-shaped fruits.
– **japonica** see *FORTUNELLA japonica*

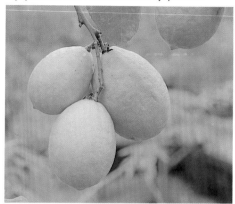

CITRUS 'Meyer's Lemon'

– **'Meyer's Lemon'** LS Semi-(E) ↑ ○
Large dark-green elliptic leaves. Fragrant
flowers. Large fruits.
- **trifoliata** see *PONCIRUS trifoliata*
CLADRASTIS – Leguminosae MS ♥
Ornamental trees with pinnate leaves.
Fragrant flowers in panicles – not on young
trees.
– **amurensis** see *MAACKIA amurensis*
– **lutea** (*tinctoria*) MT ♥ "Yellow Wood"
Long hanging panicles of white flowers, June.
Leaves turn yellow in autumn. AM 1924
– **sinensis** MT ♥ "Chinese Yellow Wood"
Soft green compound leaves. White, pink-
tinged flowers July. AM 1923 AM 1938
CLEMATIS see climbers
CLERODENDRUM – Verbenaceae MS-LS
Valuable late summer and autumn flowering
shrubs.
– **bungei** (*foetidum*) MS ◑
Semi-woody, suckering. Large heart-shaped
leaves. Dense corymbs of fragrant rosy-red
flowers August-September. AM 1926
– **trichotomum** LS ○
Fragrant star-like flowers August-September.
China-blue berries in crimson calyces follow.
FCC 1893

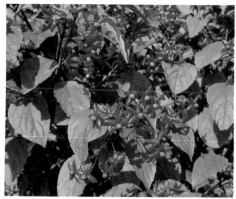

CLERODENDRUM trichotomum fargesii

– – **fargesii** LS ○
Smooth stems and leaves. Usually fruits more
freely than the type. AM 1911
CLETHRA – Clethraceae MS ⚲
Fragrant, white flowers July-August.
– **alnifolia** MS ⚲ "Sweet Bush"
Scented flowers in terminal racemes, August.
AGM 1969 We recommend the selected
forms:

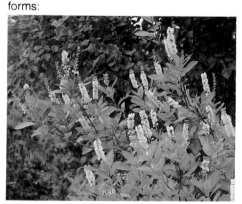

CLETHRA alnifolia 'Paniculata'

– – **'Paniculata'** MS ⚲
Flowers in terminal panicles AM 1956
AGM 1969
– – **'Rosea'** MS ⚲
Buds and flowers, pink-tinged. Glossy
leaves.
– **barbinervis** (*canescens*) MS ⚲
Long racemes of flowers. Autumn leaf colour
red and yellow.
– **fargesii** (*wilsonii*) MS ⚲
Long pure-white panicles of flowers, July.
Rich yellow autumn leaf colour. AM 1924

CLEYERA – Theaceae LS (E) ✓
A small genus of which we recommend:
– **fortunei** (*Eurya fortunei*) LS (E) ✓
Leathery blunt tipped leaves – dark glossy-
green with grey marbling. Margins cream,
sometimes flushed deep pink.
CLIANTHUS – Leguminosae MS † ☉
*Require well drained soil. For sheltered sunny
position or conservatory.*

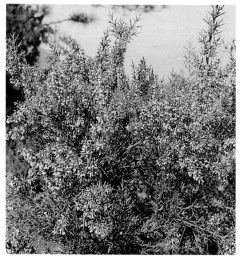

COLLETIA armata 'Rosea'

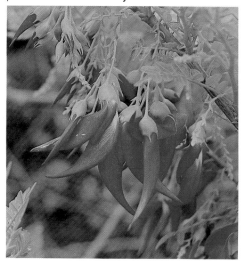

CLIANTHUS puniceus

– **puniceus** MS Semi-(E) † ☉ "Lobster's
Claw"
Pinnate leaves. Distinctive claw-like flowers
bright-red, in pendulous racemes, early
summer. AM 1938
COLLETIA – Rhamnaceae SS-MS
*Spiny shrubs. Fragrant flowers, late summer
and autumn.*
– **armata** MS
Stout rounded spines. Small white pitcher-
shaped flowers smother branches. AM 1973
– – **'Rosea'** MS
Flower buds pink. AM 1972
– **cruciata** (*bictoniensis*) SS
Branchlets comprised of flat triangular spines.
Pitcher-shaped white flowers. Slow growing.
AM 1959
COLUTEA – Leguminosae MS-LS "Bladder
Sennas"
*Pinnate leaves. Pea-flowers throughout
summer. Inflated seed pods.*
– **arborescens** LS
Yellow flowers. Vigorous

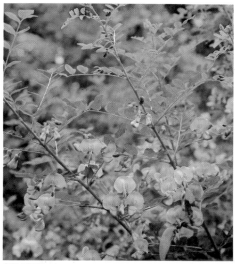

COLUTEA arborescens

– × **media** MS
Greyish leaves. Bronze-yellow flowers.
Vigorous.
– **orientalis** MS
Glaucous leaves. Coppery flowers. Rounded
habit.
COMPTONIA – Myricaceae SS ✓ ☉
Monotypic genus:
– **peregrina** SS ✓ ☉ "Sweet Fern"
Frond-like narrow leaves. Small brown
catkins, spring. Aromatic, suckering shrub.

CONVOLVULUS – Convolvulaceae
Large genus composed mainly of perennials. The following shrubby species is cultivated.

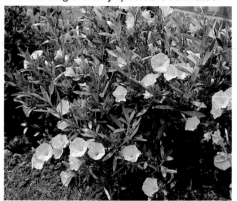

CONVOLVULUS cneorum

– cneorum SS (E) † ☼ GC
Silky silver leaves. Large pink and white funnel-shaped flowers, May. Needs well drained sunny site.

COPROSMA – Rubiaceae PS-MS (E) ☼
Variable genus. Separate male and female plants required to produce fruits.
– petriei PS (E) ☼
Rock garden plant, forming dense mats. Conspicuous blue berries on female.

CORDYLINE (*DRACAENA* in part) – Agavaceae ST (E) † ❢
Distinctive trees or shrubs. Only the following species is commonly grown.
– australis ST (E) † ❢ "Cabbage Tree"
Single trunk with stout ascending branches, dense mass of sword-like leaves. Small fragrant creamy flowers in panicles early summer. AM 1953
– 'Atropurpurea' ST (E) † ❢
Purple leaves.

CORIARIA – Coriariaceae DS-MS
Frond-like leaf arrangements. Flower petals ultimately thick and fleshy enclosing the seeds.
– japonica DS GC
Arching stems. Conspicuous red fruits. Good autumn leaf colour. AM 1908
– terminalis DS GC
Sub-shrub with rich autumn leaf colour. Black fruits. AM 1931. We recommend the form:
– – xanthocarpa DS GC
Translucent yellow fruits. FCC 1970

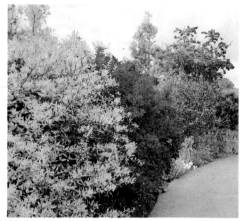

CORNUS alba 'Elegantissima'

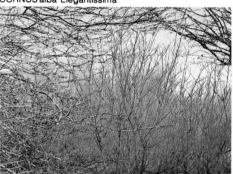

CORNUS alba 'Sibirica'

– thymifolia DS GC
Suckering shrub, making dense fern-like clumps. Small black currant-like fruits.

CORNUS – Cornaceae SS-MT "Dogwoods"
Extensive genus, containing many variable garden plants.
– alba MS "Red barked Dogwood"
Forms thicket of stems – young ones red in winter. Good autumn leaf colour. Tolerant of wet soils. B (a) 4
– – 'Aurea' MS
Soft yellow leaves. B (a) 4
– – 'Elegantissima' (*'Sibirica Variegata'*) MS
Leaves with white margins and mottling. AGM 1969 B (a) 4
– – 'Kesselringii' MS
Purplish-black stems. B (a) 4
– – 'Sibirica' (*'Atrosanguinea'*) MS
"Westonbirt Dogwood"
Bright crimson winter shoots. AM 1961
AGM 1969 B (a) 4

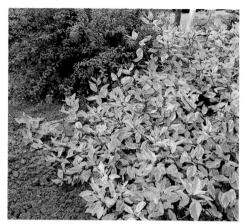

CORNUS alba 'Spaethii'

–– **'Spaethii'** MS
Golden margined leaves. FCC 1889
AGM 1969 B (a) 4
–– **'Variegata'** MS
Grey-green leaves with cream margins.
B (a) 4
– **alternifolia** LS-ST
Horizontal spreading branches. Alternate
small leaves, sometimes colouring in autumn.
–– **'Argentea'** (*'Variegata'*) MS
Small leaves with creamy margins. Dense
habit.
– **amomum** MS
Purple winter shoots. Blue fruits. AM 1968

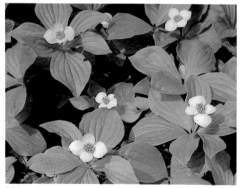

CORNUS canadensis

– **canadensis** PS ◑ GC "Creeping
Dogwood"
Herbaceous species. Makes thick carpet,
white flowers in summer. Bright red fruits.
AM 1937

– **capitata** LS-ST (E) † ♥
Flowers encircled by sulphur yellow bracts,
June-July. Strawberry like fruits. AM 1922
– **controversa** ST ♥
Layered branches with broad heads of cream
flowers May. Small black fruits. Purple-red
autumn foliage.

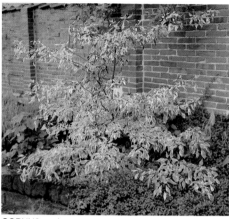

CORNUS controversa 'Variegata'

–– **'Variegata'** ST ♥
Silver variegated leaves.
– **'Eddie's White Wonder'** LS
Large white flower heads in spring. AM 1972
FCC 1977
– **florida** MS-LS North American "Flowering
Dogwood". Flowers have 4 conspicuous
white bracts, May. Colourful autumn foliage.
Not for shallow chalk. AM 1951
–– **'Apple Blossom'** MS
Pale pink flower bracts.

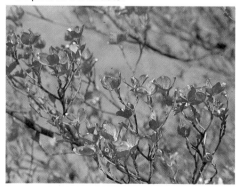

CORNUS florida 'Cherokee Chief'

–– **'Cherokee Chief'** MS
Deep rose-red flower bracts.

– –**'Rainbow'** MS
Dense habit. Leaves margined bright yellow; rich-red autumn colour.

– –**rubra** MS
Rose pink bracts. Red young leaves. FCC 1927 AGM 1937

– –**'Tricolor'** MS
Green leaves variegated cream flushed rose. In autumn turn bronzy-purple edged deep rose.

– –**'White Cloud'** MS
Free flowering, pure white bracts. Bronzed foliage.

–**kousa** LS
Flowers with conspicuous white bracts, June. Strawberry-like fruits. Bronze and crimson autumn foliage. FCC 1892 AM 1958 AGM 1969

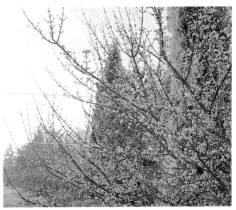

CORNUS mas

–**mas** LS "Cornelian Cherry"
Small yellow flowers, before leaves, February. Edible cherry-like red fruits. Red-purple autumn foliage. AGM 1924 AM 1929

– –**'Aurea'** LS
Leaves suffused yellow

– –**'Elegantissima'** (*'Tricolor'*) MS
Leaves variegated yellow, tinged pink. FCC 1872

– –**'Variegata'** LS
Conspicuous white leaf margins. AGM 1973

–**nuttallii** MT ❦
Flowers with large white bracts, occasionally flushed pink, May. Yellow (occasionally red) autumn foliage. Not for shallow chalk. FCC 1970 AM 1971

– –**'Portlemouth'**
A form with very large flower heads.

–**officinalis** LS-ST
Exfoliating bark. Yellow flowers before leaves, February. Red fruits. Rich autumn foliage. AM 1970

–**sanguinea** MS "Common Dogwood"
Greenish red stems. Black fruits. Purple autumn foliage.

–**stolonifera** MS
Suckering shrub forming dense thickets of stems. We recommend the form:

– –**'Flaviramea'** MS
Young shoots yellow to olive-green. Good on wet soils. B (a) 4

COROKIA – Cornaceae SS-MS (E) ○
Small star-like yellow flowers. Orange fruits.

–**cotoneaster** SS (E) ○ "Wire-netting bush"
Stiff intertwined branchlets. Small dark-green leaves, white felted beneath. AM 1934

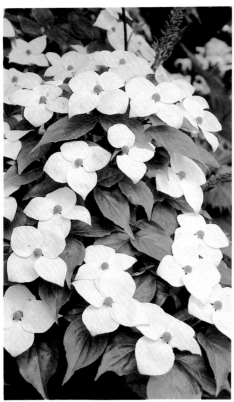

CORNUS kousa chinensis

– –**chinensis** LS
Taller, more open form. Larger leaves. FCC 1924 AM 1959 AGM 1969

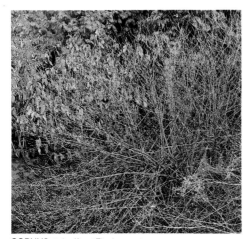

CORNUS stolonifera 'Flaviramea'

– × **virgata MS** (E) ○
Erect habit. Floriferous and free fruiting.
AM 1934

CORONILLA – Leguminosae MS ○
*Bright yellow pea-flowers produced freely
through the season.*
– **emerus** MS ○
Flower clusters in leaf axils. Slender seed
pods, articulated, like a scorpions tail.

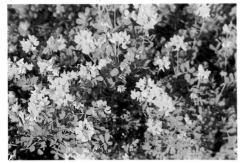

CORONILLA glauca

– **glauca** MS (E) ↑ ○
Glaucous leaves. Flowers mainly April, but
intermittently throughout year. Requires a
warm wall. AM 1957
– – **'Variegata'** MS (E) ↑ ○
Conspicuous creamy variegation to leaves.
CORREA – Rutaceae SS (E) ↑ ○
For mildest areas or cool greenhouse.
Abundant flowers late winter.
– × **harrisii** SS (E) ↑ ○
Rose scarlet flowers.

CORYLOPSIS – Hamamelidaceae SS-LS
*Drooping racemes of fragrant primrose yellow
flowers before leaves, spring.*
– **glabrescens** MS
Wide spreading. Slender tassels of flowers.
AM 1960 FCC 1968 AGM 1969

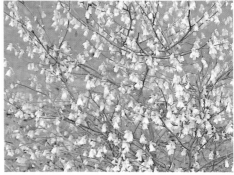

CORYLOPSIS pauciflora

– **pauciflora** SS ⤢
Bristle toothed leaves, pink when young.
Cowslip-scented flowers in short racemes,
March. FCC 1893 AGM 1923
– **sinensis** LS
Lemon yellow flower tassels. AM 1967
– **spicata** MS
Narrow racemes of bright yellow flowers with
dark purple anthers. AM 1897
– **veitchiana** LS
Large racemes of flowers with conspicuous
brick-red anthers. AM 1912 FCC 1974
– **willmottiae** MS
Leaves often purple or reddish-purple when
young. Dense racemes of flowers. AM 1912
FCC 1965

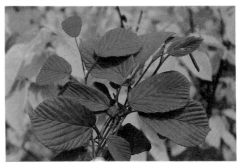

CORYLOPSIS willmottiae 'Spring Purple'

– – **'Spring Purple'** MS
Pium purple young growths.

CORYLUS – Corylaceae MS-LT "Hazels"
Many cultivated for their nuts. Any soils. Will tolerate bleak sites.
– **avellana** LS "Hazel"
Long yellow "lamb tails", February. Leaves yellow in autumn. Good for screening.
– – **'Aurea'** MS ◑
Soft yellow leaves.
– – **'Contorta'** MS "Corkscrew Hazel" "Harry Lauder's Walking Stick"
Unusual twisted branches. Showy catkins, February. AM 1917
– **colurna** LT ♥ "Turkish Hazel"
Striking bark with corky corrugations.
– **maxima** LS "Filbert"
Large rounded heart-shaped leaves. Large nuts. We recommend the form:
– – **'Purpurea'** (*'Atropurpurea'*) LS "Purple-leaf Filbert"
Rich purple leaves.
COTINUS *RHUS* in part) – **Anacardiaceae** MS-LS
The "Smoke Trees". Distinctive in-florescences. Rich autumn leaf colour.
– **coggygria** (*Rhus cotinus*) LS "Venetian Sumach" "Smoke Tree"
Smooth, rounded, green leaves. Fawn plume-like inflorescences June-July turn grey by late summer. AGM 1969

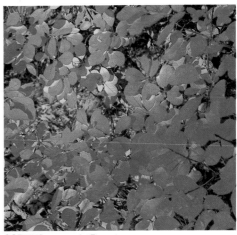

COTINUS coggygria 'Flame'

– – **'Flame'** LS
The best form for brilliant orange, autumn colour. Flowers pink.
– – **'Foliis Purpureis'** LS
Rich plum-purple leaves turn light red, autumn. AM 1921 AGM 1930

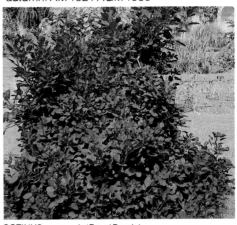

COTINUS coggygria 'Royal Purple'

– – **purpureus** (*'Atropurpureus'*) "Burning Bush"
Green leaves. Inflorescences resemble puffs of pink smoke. AM 1948 AGM 1969
– – **'Royal Purple'** LS
Deep wine purple leaves, reddening towards autumn. AGM 1969
– **obovatus** (*americanus*) (*Rhus cotinoides*) LS
Leaves colour brilliantly in autumn. AM 1904

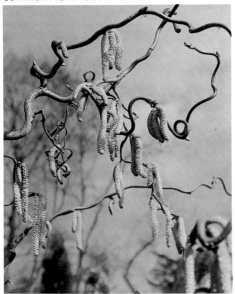

CORYLUS avellana 'Contorta'

COTONEASTER – Rosaceae PS-ST
Variable genus evergreen and deciduous.
Bright autumn colour of leaf or fruit. Almost all
soils and conditions.
– adpressus DS GC
Small leaves scarlet in autumn. Bright red
fruits. Spreading habit.
– – praecox (*C. praecox*) SS GC
Arching branches. Large orange-red berries.
Vigorous.
– apiculatus SS
Arching branches. Small rounded leaves.
Solitary red fruits.
– bullatus LS
Large, conspicuously corrugated leaves
colour well in autumn. Large bright-red fruits.
We recommend the forms:

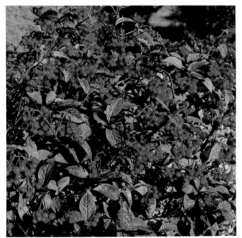

COTONEASTER bullatus floribundus

– – floribundus MS
Slightly larger leaves. Fruits in clusters.
– – macrophyllus MS
Large dark-green corrugated leaves.
AM 1912
– buxifolius DS (E)
Dense habit. Small dull-green leaves. Small
obovoid red fruits.
– congestus DS (E) GC
Mounds of small bluish-green leaves. Red
fruits.
– conspicuus MS (E)
Arching branches. Small leaves. White
flowers smother branches early summer.
Abundant bright-red fruits. Spreading habit.
AM 1933

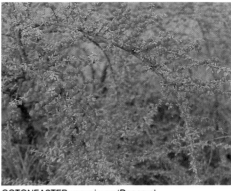

COTONEASTER conspicuus 'Decorus'

– – 'Decorus' DS (E)
Free fruiting. AGM 1947 FCC 1953
– – 'Highlight' MS (E)
Dense mound of arching shoots. Large
orange-red fruits.
– 'Coral Beauty' DS (E) GC
Glossy green leaves. Orange-red fruits. Wide
spreading.

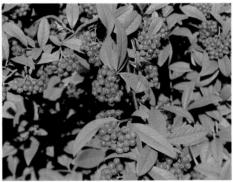

COTONEASTER 'Cornubia'

– 'Cornubia' (Watereri Group) LS-ST Semi-(E)
Semi-(E)
Long leaves. Profuse large red fruits weigh
down branches. AM 1933 FCC 1936
AGM 1969
– dammeri (*humifusus*) PS (E)
Leaves to 4cm long. Long trailing shoots.
Sealing wax-red fruits.
– – radicans PS (E) GC
Smaller leaves. Flowers usually in pairs.
– distichus (*rotundifolius* HORT) MS
Stiff rigid branches. Small, polished leaves.
Large bright scarlet fruits persist until spring.
AGM 1927. We recommend:

COTONEASTER distichus – Continued

--tongolensis MS
Mound of arching branches. Rich autumn leaf colour. Scarlet obovoid fruits.
--divaricatus MS
Rich autumn leaf colour. Dark red fruits.
FCC 1912 AGM 1969
-'Exburiensis' (Watereri Group) LS (E)
Apricot-yellow fruits, pink-tinged in winter.
AGM 1969
-franchetii MS Semi-(E)
Very graceful habit. Sage-green foliage.
Ovoid orange scarlet fruits.
--sternianus (*wardii* HORT) MS Semi-(E)
Hdg (0.5m)
Sage-green leaves, silver-white beneath.
Abundant fruits. AGM 1953
-frigidus LS-ST
Large broad elliptic leaves, large heavy clusters of crimson fruits, autumn and winter.
Spreading habit. AGM 1925 AM 1966
-glaucophyllus LS (E)
Oval leaves. July flowering. Berries orange-red. AM 1924. We recommend the forms:
--serotinus (*C. serotinus*) LS (E)
Leathery roundish leaves. Later berries.
FCC 1919
--vestitus LS (E)
Abundant flowers, July. Berries colouring red December. Vigorous.
-harrovianus MS (E)
Arching branches. Conspicuous in flower.
Red fruits colouring late December. AM 1905
-horizontalis PS GC
Spreading "herring-bone" branches. Rich autumn coloured leaves and fruit. Excellent wall shrub. FCC 1897 AGM 1925
--'Saxatilis' PS GC
Distinctive fan-like branches and small leaves.

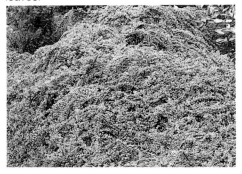

COTONEASTER horizontalis 'Variegatus'

COTONEASTER horizontalis – Continued

--'Variegatus' PS GC
Small cream variegated leaves, suffused red in autumn.

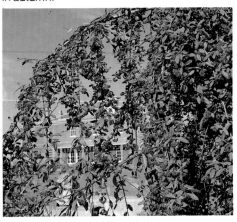

COTONEASTER 'Hybridus Pendulus'

-'Hybridus Pendulus' ST ⬆ or PS (E) GC
Glossy leaves. Abundant brilliant red fruits autumn and winter. When grown on a stem makes small weeping tree.
-'John Waterer' (Watereri Group) LS Semi-(E)
Spreading branches. Abundant bunches of red fruits, autumn. AM 1951 AGM 1969
-lacteus MS (E) Hdg (0.5m)
Large oval leathery leaves grey beneath. Late ripening clusters of red fruits last beyond Christmas. AM 1935 AGM 1969

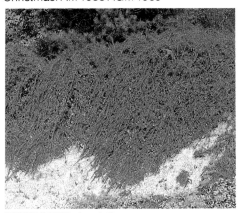

COTONEASTER microphyllus

-microphyllus DS (E) GC
Glossy small leaves. Extra large round scarlet fruits.

COTONEASTER microphyllus – Continued

–– **cochleatus** PS (E) GC
Slow growing. Paler broader leaves than the type. AM 1930
–– **thymifolius** SS (E) GC
Dainty shrub, very small, narrow shining, deep green leaves.
– **pannosus** MS (E)
Slender arching branches. Sage-green leaves. Small deep red fruits.
– **'Pink Champagne'** (Watereri Group) LS (E)
Slender arching branches. Narrow leaves. Abundant, small yellow fruits, become pink-tinged.
– **praecox** see *C. adpressus praecox*
– **prostratus** (*rotundifolius*) (*microphyllus uva-ursi*) SS (E)
Small glossy leaves. Large rose-red fruits. Semi-prostrate, long arching branches. AGM 1927
–– **'Eastleigh'** LS (E)
Dark-green leaves. Large blood-red fruits. Vigorous, much branched tall shrub.
– **racemiflorus** LS
Slender arching branches. Rounded leaves, grey-white beneath. Brick-red fruits.

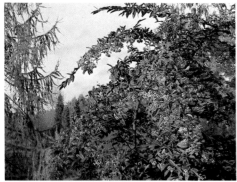
COTONEASTER 'Rothschildianus'

– **'Rothschildianus'** (Watereri Group) LS (E)
Light green leaves. Creamy-yellow fruit clusters. Spreading habit when young.
– **rotundifolius** see *C. distichus* and *C. prostratus*
– **'St. Monica'** (Watereri Group) LS Semi-(E)
Leaves colour well in autumn. Abundant small bright red fruits.
– **salicifolius** LS (E)
Profuse bright red berries, autumn. Many clones:
–– **'Autumn Fire'** ('Herbstfeuer') SS Semi-(E)
Lax habit. Masses of orange-red fruits.

COTONEASTER salicifolius – Continued

–– **floccosus** MS (E)
Distinctive glossy narrow leaves, woolly white beneath on slender drooping stems. Abundant small red berries. AM 1920
–– **'Gnom'** DS (E) GC
Mound forming with prostrate branches.
–– **'Parkteppich'** DS (E) GC
Scrambling partially prostrate form. Small red berries.
–– **'Repens'** (*'Avondrood'*) PS (E) GC
Very narrow leaves. Small red fruits.
–– **rugosus** (*C. rugosus*) MS (E)
Broader dark glossy leaves, tomentose beneath. Red fruits.
– **'Salmon Spray'** (Watereri Group) MS (E)
Salmon-red fruit clusters.

– **serotinus** see *C. glaucophyllus serotinus*
– **simonsii** MS Semi-(E) Hdg (0.5m)
Large scarlet fruits. Erect growing.
– **'Skogholm'** DS (E) GC
Small leaves. Large, coral-red obovoid berries. Wide spreading.
– **splendens** MS
Arching shoots with small greyish-green rounded leaves. Bright orange obovoid berries. We recommend the clone:
–– **'Sabrina'** (*C. 'Sabrina'*) MS
Free fruiting. AM 1950
– **'Valkenburg'** DS GC
Long spreading stems. Leaves colour well in autumn.

– **wardii** MS
Stiff, erect branched shrub. Dark glossy leaves, white beneath. Bright flame top-shaped berries. AM 1939

– × **watereri** LS-ST Semi-(E)
Variable hybrids. Long leaves. Profuse red or orange-red berries. Strong vigorous growth. AM 1951

"COTTONWOOD, BLACK" see *POPULUS trichocarpa*

"CRAB APPLE" see *MALUS*

"CRANBERRY" see *VACCINIUM oxycoccos*

"CRAPE MYRTLE" see *LAGERSTROEMIA indica*

CRATAEGUS – Rosaceae LS-ST-MT
''Thorns''
Attractive autumn leaf colour. Generally white flowers, red fruits. Tolerant of most soils and conditions, even windswept coastal areas.

× **carrierei** see *C.* × *lavallei*
– **cordata** see *C. phaenopyrum*
– **crus-galli** ST ♥ "Cockspur Thorn"
Spreading, glabrous tree with thorns up to
8cm. Fruits last into New Year.
– × **grignonensis** ST ♥
Leaves green until winter. Late, large red
fruits.
– **laciniata** (*orientalis*) ST ♥
Deeply cut downy leaves, grey beneath.
Large fruits, coral – or yellowish red. AM 1933
FCC 1970 AGM 1973
– × **lavallei** (× *carrierei*) ST ♥
Long, shiny dark green leaves. Orange-red
persistent fruits. AM 1924 AGM 1925
– **mollis** MT ♥ "Red Haw"
Downy leaves. Large red fruits in clusters.
– **monogyna** MT ♥ Hdg (0.5) "Common
Hawthorn" "May" "Quick"
Strongly fragrant flowers. Mass of red "haws"
in autumn.
– – **'Biflora'** (*'Praecox'*) ST ♥ "Glastonbury
Thorn"
Earlier leafing. Occasionally flowers during
winter.
– – **'Pendula Rosea'** ST ♠
Pink flowers. Graceful pendulous branches.
– – **'Stricta'** (*'Fastigiata'*) ST ❦
Erect branches.
– – **'Variegata'** ST ♥
Leaves splashed and mottled creamy-white.
– **oxyacantha** (*oxyacanthoides*) ST ♥
May flowering species. The following clones
are probably hybrids between *C. oxyacantha*
and *C. monogyna.*
– – **'Masekii'** ST ♥
Double pale pink flowers.

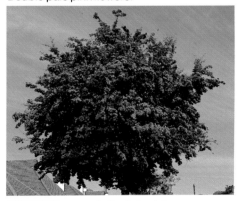

CRATAEGUS oxyacantha 'Paul's Scarlet'

– – **'Paul's Scarlet'** (*'Coccinea Plena'*) ST ♥
Double scarlet flowers. FCC 1867 AGM 1969
– – **'Plena'** ST ♥
White, double flowers. AGM 1969
– – **'Punicea'** ST ♥
Single, scarlet flowers.
– – **'Rosea'** ST ♥
Single, pink flowers.
– – **'Rosea Flore Pleno'** ST ♥
Double, pink flowers.
– **phaenopyrum** (*cordata*) ST ♥ "Washington
Thorn"
Glossy, maple like leaves. Small dark crimson
fruits, freely borne.
– **pinnatifida** ST ♥
Large conspicuously lobed leaves. Crimson
fruits. We recommend the form:
– – **major** ST ♥
Rich red autumn leaves. Glossy crimson
fruits. FCC 1886

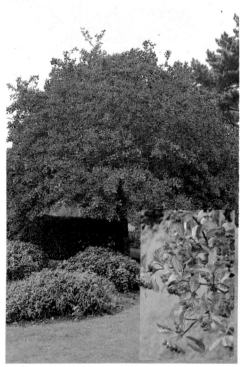

CRATAEGUS prunifolia

– **prunifolia** ST ♥
Glossy oval leaves, colour well in autumn,
persistent showy fruits. AGM 1969

–tanacetifolia ST 🍷 "Tansy-leaved Thorn" Grey, downy leaves. Usually thornless. Large yellow fruits like small apples.

CRINODENDRON (*TRICUSPIDARIA*)– **Elaeocarpaceae** LS (E) † ✗ ◑

Attractive shrubs for mild areas.

–hookeranum (*Tricuspidaria lanceolata*) LS (E) † ✗ ◑

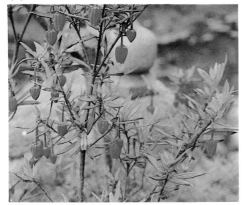

CRINODENDRON hookeranum

Dense habit. Long, narrow, deep-green leaves. Crimson "lantern" flowers on long stalks, hang along branches May-June. FCC 1916

"CUCUMBER TREE" see *MAGNOLIA acuminata*

"CURRANT, FLOWERING" see *RIBES*

CYATHODES – Epacridaceae PS-SS (E) ✗ ◑

Heath-like shrubs with small white "pitcher" flowers. Attractive foliage.

–colensoi PS (E) ✗ ◑ Glaucous foliage. White or red fruits. AM 1962

CYDONIA japonica see *CHAENOMELES speciosa*

CYDONIA maulei see *CHAENOMELES japonica*

CYTISUS – Leguminosae PS-LS ○ "Brooms"

Typical pea-shaped flowers – yellow unless stated otherwise.

Pruning: Trim young plants after flowering to maintain compact growth.

Shorten long growths on mature bushes immediately after flowering.

–ardoinii PS ○ Miniature alpine. Flowers bright yellow, April-May. AM 1955

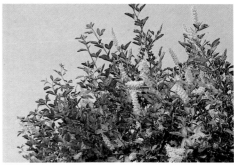

CYTISUS battandieri

–battandieri LS ○ Silky grey leaves. Pineapple scented flowers in cone-shaped clusters, July. Excellent for a high wall. AM 1931 FCC 1934 AGM 1938

––'Yellow Tail' LS ○ Long spikes of flowers.

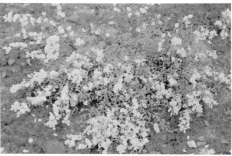

CYTISUS × beanii

– × beanii DS ○ Golden yellow flowers, May. FCC 1955 AGM 1969

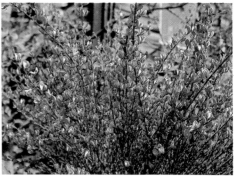

CYTISUS 'Burkwoodii'

–'Burkwoodii' MS ○ Cerise flowers, wings deep crimson edged yellow, May-June. AMT 1973

– **demissus** PS ☼
Large, yellow flowers with brown keels, May.
AM 1932

– **'Dorothy Walpole'** MS ☼
Dark cerise flowers, crimson wings,
May-June. AM 1923

– **'Johnson's Crimson'** MS ☼
Clear crimson flowers. AMT 1972 FCCT 1973

– × **kewensis** DS ☼
Mass of cream flowers, May. Semi-prostrate
habit. AGM 1951

– **'Killiney Red'** MS ☼
Rich red flowers, darker velvety wings,
May-June.

– **'Lady Moore'** MS ☼
Large, creamy-yellow flowers, tinted rose on
standard and flame on wings. May-June.
AM 1928

– **'Lord Lambourne'** MS ☼
Pale cream standard, dark red wings,
May-June. AM 1927

CYTISUS × kewensis

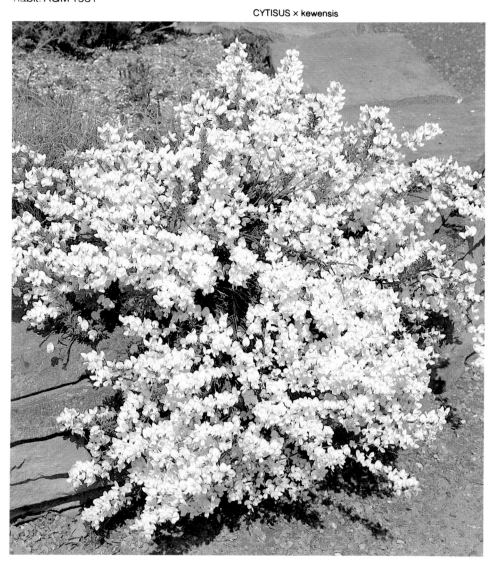

–'**Minstead**' MS ○
Small white flowers, tinged lilac, darker on
wings May-June. AM 1949
– **multiflorus** MS ⚹ ○ "White Spanish
Broom"
Small white flowers, May-June. Erect habit.
AGM 1926
– **nigricans** (*carlieri*) SS
Long terminal racemes of flowers
continuously late summer. AGM 1948
–'**Porlock**' LS Semi-(E) † ○
Racemes of fragrant butter yellow flowers,
April-May. AM 1931
– × **praecox** SS ○ "Warminster Broom"
A tumbling mass of rich cream flowers, May.
AGM 1933
––'**Albus**' SS ○
White flowers.
––'**Allgold**' SS ○
Arching sprays of bright yellow flowers.
AGM 1969 FCCT 1976
– **procumbens** DS ○
Prostrate, branching, flowers in leaf axils,
May-June. AM 1948
– **purpureus** DS ○ "Purple Broom"
Lilac-purple flowers, May. AM 1980
––**albus** DS ○
White flowers.
––'**Atropurpureus**' DS ○
Deep purple flowers.
– **scoparius** MS ○ "Common Broom"
Rich butter-yellow flowers, May. AGM 1969.
Not suitable for shallow chalk.
––'**Andreanus**' MS ○
Flowers marked with brown-crimson.
FCC 1890 FCCT 1973
––'**Cornish Cream**' MS ○
Cream flowers. AM 1923 AGM 1969
FCCT 1973
––'**Dragonfly**' MS ○
Deep yellow standard, crimson wings,
May-June. Strong growing.
––'**Firefly**' MS ○
Yellow standard, bronze stained wings.
AM 1907 AGM 1969
––'**Fulgens**' MS ○
Orange yellow flowers with crimson wings,
June. Dense, compact habit.
––'**Golden Sunlight**' MS ○
Rich yellow flowers. Strong growing.
AGM 1969 AMT 1973

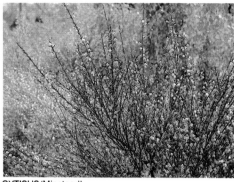

CYTISUS 'Minstead'

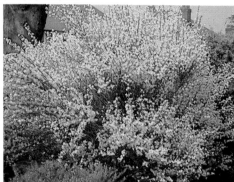

CYTISUS × praecox 'Allgold'

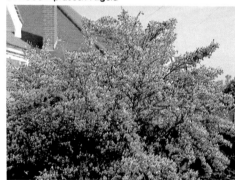

CYTISUS scoparius 'Dragonfly'

––**prostratus** DS ○
Large yellow flowers spreading. AM 1913
– **supranubius** see *SPARTOCYTISUS
nubigenus*
–'**Windlesham Ruby**' MS ○
Dark mahogany-crimson flowers.
–'**Zeelandia**' SS ○
Standard lilac and cream, wings pinkish and
creamy, May-June. FCCT 1974

DABOECIA – Ericaceae DS (E) ⚹ ☼
Dwarf, heath-like shrubs related to Erica.
– **azorica** DS (E) † ⚹ ☼
Rich crimson flowers. Requires shelter.
AM 1932
– **cantabrica** DS (E) ⚹ ☼ "Connemara Heath"
Long racemes, rose-purple flowers June to
November. AGM 1930
We recommend the following forms:
– – **'Alba'** DS (E) ⚹ ☼
White flowers. AGM 1969
– – **'Atropurpurea'** DS (E) ⚹ ☼
Dark rose-purple flowers. AGM 1969
– – **'Bicolor'** DS (E) ⚹ ☼
Flowers white, rose-purple, or striped – often
all on same raceme. AGM 1969
– – **'Porter's Variety'** DS (E) ⚹ ☼
Small rose-purple flowers.

– – **'Praegerae'** DS (E) ⚹ ☼
Rich pink flowers. AMT 1970
"DAISY BUSH" see *OLEARIA*
DANAE – Liliaceae SS (E) ●
*Monotypic genus. Hermaphrodite flowers in
terminal racemes.*
– **racemosa** (*Ruscus racemosus*) SS (E) ●
"Alexandrian Laurel"
Arching sprays of narrow, glossy leaves.
Orange berries. AM 1933
DAPHNE – Thymelaeaceae PS-MS ☼ or ◑
*Generally fragrant, evergreen and deciduous
shrubs. Ideal for rock garden. Good drainage
and loamy soil necessary.*
– **arbuscula** DS (E) ☼
Narrow leaves. Fragrant pink flowers. Yellow-
brown fruits. AM 1915 FCC 1973

Grouped DABOECIA

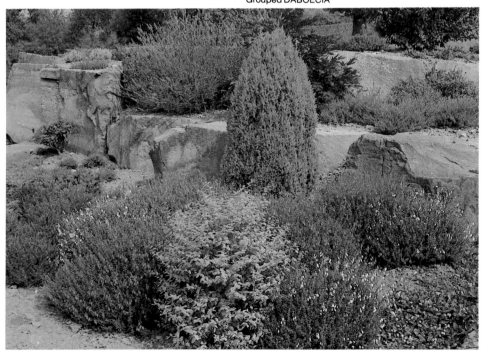

– **aurantiaca** SS ☼ "Golden-flowered daphne"
Fragrant, rich yellow flowers, May. Slow growth. FCC 1927

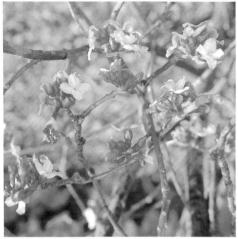

DAPHNE bholua 'Gurkha'

– **bholua 'Gurkha'** MS ☼
Richly scented, purplish-rose flowers. December to February. Black fruits.
– **blagayana** DS ◑
Terminal clusters of fragrant, creamy-white flowers, March-April. Whitish fruits. Best in deep leaf mould. FCC 1880

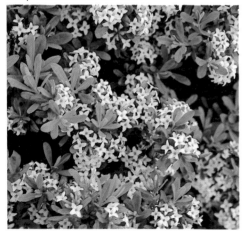

DAPHNE × burkwoodii

– × **burkwoodii** SS Semi-(E) ☼
Fragrant pale pink flowers in clusters along branches, May-June AM 1935. NB The clone 'Somerset' is almost identical.

– **cneorum** PS (E) ◑
Clusters of richly scented, rose-pink flowers, April-May. Brownish-yellow fruits. AGM 1927
– – **'Alba'** PS (E) ◑
White, free flowering form. AM 1920
– – **'Eximia'** PS (E) ◑
Larger leaves and flowers. Crimson buds opening rose-pink. AM 1938 FCC 1967
– – **'Pygmaea'** PS (E) ◑
Rose pink, free flowering. Branches flat on ground.
– – **'Variegata'** PS (E) ◑
Leaves margined cream. Vigorous.
– **collina** DS (E) ☼
Blunt, deep green leaves. Terminal clusters of fragrant rose-purple flowers, May. AM 1938

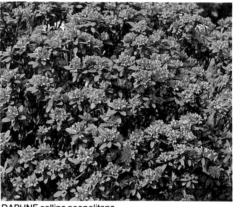

DAPHNE collina neapolitana

– – **neapolitana** DS (E) ☼
Rose pink flowers April-June. AGM 1969
– **dauphinii** See *D. × hybrida*
– **genkwa** SS ◑
Light green leaves. Lilac-blue flowers before leaves, April-May. FCC 1885
– **giraldii** DS ☼
Clusters of fragrant, yellow flowers May-June. Bright red fruits.
– **gnidium** SS (E) ☼
Fragrant creamy-white flowers, June-August. Red fruits.
– × **hybrida** (*dauphinii*) SS (E) ☼
Very fragrant, reddish purple flowers, late autumn through winter.
– **jasminea** DS (E) † ☼
Very fragrant white flowers, rose-pink in bud. AM 1968
– **julia** DS (E) ☼
Very fragrant rose-pink flowers. Rare.

– laureola SS (E) ❀ "Spurge laurel"
Leathery, green leaves. Yellowish-green, fragrant flowers in clusters, February-March. Black fruits.
– – philippi DS (E) ○
Dwarf form with smaller flowers.

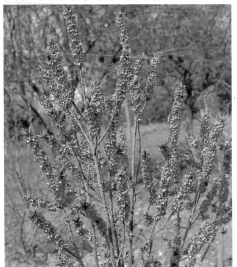

DAPHNE mezereum

– mezereum SS ○
Scented purple-red flowers, February-March before leaves. Red, poisonous berries. Good on chalk. AGM 1929
– – 'Alba' SS ○
White flowers. Clear amber fruits.
– – 'Grandiflora' (*'Autumnalis'*) SS ○
Larger flowers, September onwards.
– – 'Rosea' SS ○
Clear rose-pink flowers.
– odora (*indica 'Rubra'*) SS (E) ○
Very fragrant purple-pink flowers, winter-early spring.
– – 'Alba' SS (E) ○
White flowers.
– – 'Aureomarginata' SS (E) ○
Leaves with creamy-white margins. AGM 1973
– oleoides (*buxifolia*) DS (E) ○
Thick leaves with bristle-like tips. Fragrant clusters of pale pink or cream flowers. Red fruits.
– petraea (*rupestris*) DS (E) ○
Small gnarled shrublet 5 to 7.5cm high. Fragrant, rose-pink flowers, June. AM 1906

– – 'Grandiflora' DS (E) ○
Larger flowers. AM 1918 FCC 1924
– pontica SS (E) ❀
Bright green, glossy leaves. Spidery yellow-green flowers, April-May. Blue-black fruits.
– retusa DS (E) ○
Fragrant deep rose-purple flowers, May-June. AM 1927 AGM 1946
– rupestris see *D. petraea*
– sericea DS (E) ○
Blunt olive-green leaves. Terminal clusters of fragrant, pink flowers. Orange red fruits. AM 1931
– 'Somerset' see under *D.* × *burkwoodii*
– tangutica DS (E) ○
Terminal clusters of fragrant flowers, white, tinged purple on inside, rose-purple outside, March-April. AM 1929 AGM 1949

DAPHNIPHYLLUM – Daphniphyllaceae
LS (E)
Large rhododendron-like leaves. Inconspicuous flowers.
– macropodum (*glaucescens*) LS (E)
Pale green leaves, glaucous beneath. Clusters of pungent, pink and green flowers, late spring. FCC 1888

"DATE PLUM" see *DIOSPYROS lotus*

DATURA – Solanaceae LS † ○
Tree-like shrubs with large pendulous trumpet flowers.
– sanguinea LS † ○
Large hairy leaves. Orange-red trumpets May-June.
– suaveolens (*Brugmansia suaveolens*) LS † ○ "Angel's Trumpet"
Flannel-like leaves. Fragrant, white trumpets June-August.
– versicolor 'Grand Marnier' LS † ○
Large peach-coloured trumpets.

DAVIDIA – Davidiaceae MT ❦
Hardy trees for all fertile soils. Small inconspicuous flowers in May, each accompanied by two large conspicuous white bracts.
– involucrata MT ❦ "Pocket Handkerchief Tree" "Dove Tree" "Ghost Tree"
Heart-shaped leaves, felted beneath. Conspicuous handkerchief-like bracts. AGM 1969 AM 1972
– – vilmoriniana MT ❦
Leaves glabrous beneath. FCC 1911 AGM 1969

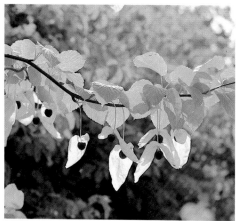

DAVIDIA involucrata

DECAISNEA – Lardizabalaceae MS
Requires moist well-drained soil.

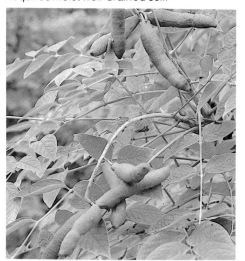

DECAISNEA fargesii

– fargesii MS
Pinnate leaves 0.6-1.0m long. Yellowish green flowers in racemes. Metallic blue "broadbean" pods.

DENDROMECON – Papaveraceae LS (E)
† ○
Entire green leaves. Poppy-like yellow flowers.
– rigida LS (E) † ○
Rigid, narrow glaucous leaves. Buttercup-yellow flowers intermittently over long period. AM 1913

DESFONTAINEA – Potaliaceae MS (E)
† ∠ ◑
Small holly-like leaves. Tubular flowers. Not for shallow chalk.
– spinosa (*hookeri*) MS (E) † ∠ ◑
Scarlet flowers with yellow mouth, late summer. AM 1931
– – 'Harold Comber' MS (E) † ∠ ◑
Vermilion-orient-red, 5cm long flowers. AM 1955

DESMODIUM penduliforum see
LESPEDEZA thunbergii

DEUTZIA – Philadelphaceae MS
Attractive June flowering shrubs for all fertile soils. D (h) 2 or (b) 5
– chunii MS
Flowers with pink petals, white inside, reflexed, displaying golden anthers. Produced in panicles along branches, July.
– – 'Pink Charm' MS
Conspicuous pink flowers.

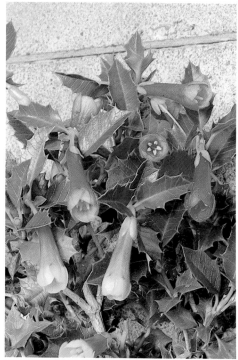

DESFONTAINEA spinosa

– compacta SS
Sweetly scented white flowers, pink in bud, in wide corymbs, July.

––**'Lavender Time'** MS
Lilac flowers, turning pale-lavender.
– × **elegantissima** MS
Fragrant, rose-tinted flowers, in paniculate
corymbs. AM 1914 AGM 1954
––**'Rosealind'** MS
Deep carmine-pink flowers. AM 1972
– **longifolia** MS
Long narrow leaves. Clusters of flowers, June-
July. AM 1912. We recommend the form:
––**'Veitchii'** MS
Rich lilac-pink tinted flowers. AM 1912
FCC 1978

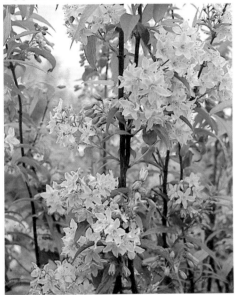

DEUTZIA 'Magicien'

– **'Magicien'** MS
Large flowers with pink-tinted, white-edged
petals. Prominent purple streak on reverse.
AGM 1969
– × **magnifica** MS
Large panicles of double, white flowers.
AM 1916. AGM 1926
– **monbeigii** MS
Small leaves, white beneath. Mass of star-like,
small white flowers; late. AM 1936
– **'Mont Rose'** MS
Profuse rose-pink flowers, tinted darker.
AGM 1957 AM 1971
– **pulchra** MS
White flowers in racemes, resembling
drooping spikes of lily-of-the-valley.

– × **rosea** SS
Bell-shaped, pink flowers on arching
branches. We recommend the form:

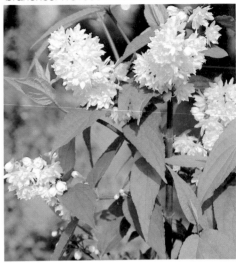

DEUTZIA × magnifica

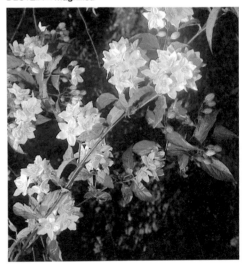

DEUTZIA × rosea 'Carminea'

––**'Carminea'** SS
Rose-carmine flushed flowers. AGM 1969
– **scabra** LS
Large panicles of white flowers June-July.
AGM 1928. We recommend the forms:
––**'Plena'** LS
Double flowers, rose-purple tinted on outside.
FCC 1863

– – **'Watereri'** LS
Single flowers tinted carmine.
– **setchuenensis** MS
Corymbs of small starry white flowers July-
August. AM 1945. We recommend the form:
– – **corymbiflora** MS
Form with broader leaves. One of the most
beautiful flowering shrubs. AM 1945
"DEVIL'S WALKING STICK" see *ARALIA
spinosa*
DIERVILLA – Caprifoliaceae SS
*Yellow, two-lipped, tubular flowers. Easy
cultivation.*
– **lonicera** (*canadensis*) SS
Pale yellow, honeysuckle-like, flowers June-
July. Good autumn leaf colour.
DIOSMA pulchella see *BAROSMA pulchella*
DIOSPYROS – Ebenaceae ST-MT ♥
*Large genus of mainly tropical trees and
shrubs. Male and female flowers on separate
plants.*
– **kaki** (*chinensis*) ST ♥ "Chinese
Persimmon"
Large leaves turn yellow-orange to red-purple
in autumn. Orange, tomato-like fruits most late
summers.
– **lotus** ST ♥ "Date Plum"
Dark, glossy green, tapered leaves. Tomato-
like purple or yellow fruits.
– **virginiana** MT ♥ N. American "Persimmon"
Good autumn leaf colour. Rugged tessellated
bark.
DIPELTA – Caprifoliaceae LS
*Tall shrubs with funnel shaped flowers,
resembling* Weigela.
– **floribunda** LS
Fragrant pink flowers with yellow throat
produced abundantly May. AM 1927
– **ventricosa** LS
Lilac-rose flowers with swollen base,
produced spring.
– **yunnanensis** LS
Cream flowers with orange markings.
DIPLACUS see *MIMULUS*
DIPLOPAPPUS chrysophyllus see
CASSINIA fulvida
DIPTERONIA – Aceraceae LS
Pinnate leaves. Clusters of winged seeds.
– **sinensis** LS
Inconspicuous flowers. Large clusters of pale
green fruits turning red. AM 1922
DISANTHUS – Hamamelidaceae MS ⟋
Monotypic genus. Moist well-drained soil.

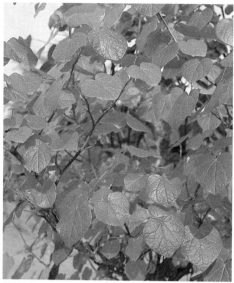

DISANTHUS cercidifolius

– **cercidifolius** MS ⟋ ◑
Leaves colour claret and crimson in autumn.
Tiny purplish flowers October. AM 1936
FCC 1970
DISTYLIUM – Hamamelidaceae LS-ST (E) ◑
Shiny leathery leaves. Flowers in racemes.
– **racemosum** LS (E) ◑
Wide spreading, slow. Flowers with no petals,
conspicuous red stamens, April.
"DOGWOOD" see *CORNUS*
DORYCNIUM – Leguminosae DS ○
*Sub-shrubs and herbs. Well-drained situation
in most soils.*
– **hirsutum** DS ○
Silvery, hairy plant. Pink-tinged, white, pea
flowers on erect stems, late summer-autumn.
Red-tinged fruit pods.
"DOVE TREE" see *DAVIDIA involucrata*
DRACAENA australis see *CORDYLINE
australis*
DRIMYS – Winteraceae LS (E) † ◑
*Handsome shrubs for sheltered situations –
ideal against a wall.*
– **colorata** see *PSEUDOWINTERA colorata*
– **lanceolata** (*aromatica*) LS (E) † ◑
Neat habit. Young growths coppery. Small
creamy white flowers April-May. AM 1926
– **winteri** LS (E) † ◑ "Winter's Bark"
Large leathery leaves. Fragrant ivory flowers
in loose umbels, May. AM 1971

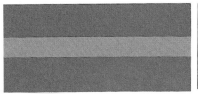

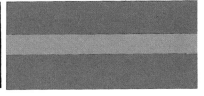

EDGEWORTHIA – Thymelaeaceae SS
Small genus related to Daphne.
– **chrysantha** (*papyrifera*) SS
Fragrant, yellow flowers in terminal clusters, covered by silky hairs on outside. AM 1961
ELAEAGNUS – Elaeagnaceae MS-LS ☼
Fast growing deciduous and evergreen. Very resilient – ideal shelter belts for exposed and maritime areas. Abundant small fragrant flowers. Not for shallow chalk.
– **angustifolia** LS ☼ "Oleaster"
Spiny shrub with silver-grey willow-like leaves. Fragrant flowers, June. Silvery amber fruits. AM 1978

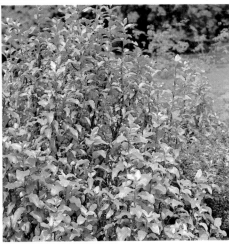

ELAEAGNUS commutata

– **commutata** MS ☼ "Silver Berry"
Silver leaves and small egg-shaped fruits. Flowers, May. AM 1956
– × **ebbingei** LS (E) ☼
Large leaves, silvery beneath. Silvery scaly flowers, autumn. Orange, silver speckled, fruits, spring. AGM 1969
– – **'Gilt Edge'** LS (E) ☼
Leaves margined golden yellow. AM 1971
– – **'Limelight'** LS (E) ☼
Leaves with a broad central blotch of deep yellow.

– **macrophylla** LS (E) ☼
Silvery, round leaves, becoming green. Flowers autumn. AM 1932. AGM 1969
– **pungens** LS (E) ☼
Shiny green leaves, dull white speckled with brown scales beneath. Flowers, autumn.

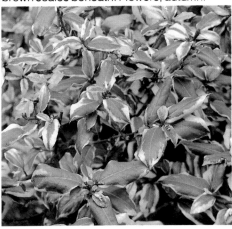

ELAEAGNUS pungens 'Dicksonii'

– – **'Dicksonii'** (*'Aurea'*) MS (E) ☼
Irregular wide golden margins to leaves. Slow.
– – **'Maculata'** MS (E) ☼ Hdg (0.5)
Golden central splash to leaves. FCC 1891. AGM 1969
– – **'Variegata'** LS (E) ☼
Thin creamy margin to leaves.
– **umbellata** LS ☼
Leaves silvery beneath. Yellow-brown shoots. Flowers, May-June. Small orange fruits. AM 1933
"ELDER" see *SAMBUCUS*
"ELDER, BOX" see *ACER negundo*
"ELM" see *ULMUS*
ELSHOLTZIA – Labiatae SS ☼
Aromatic sub-shrubs. Late flowering. Any fertile soil.
– **stauntonii** SS ☼
Leaves smell of mint when crushed. Abundant lilac-purple flowers in panicles, August-October.

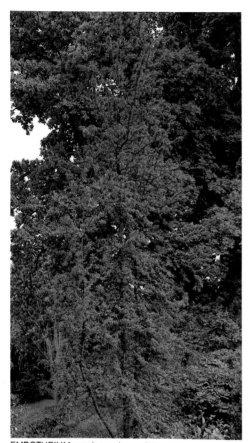

EMBOTHRIUM coccineum lanceolatum

– –'**Alba**' SS ○
A form with white flowers.
EMBOTHRIUM – Proteaceae LS (E) ✗ ◑
Spectacular flowering shrubs. Deep moist well-drained soil.
– **coccineum** LS Semi-(E) ✗ ◑ "Chilean Fire Bush"
Profusion of brilliant orange scarlet flowers, May-early June. AM 1928
– – **lanceolatum** LS Semi-(E) ✗ ◑
Form with linear – lanceolate leaves. Hardy.
ENKIANTHUS – Ericaceae MS-LS ✗ ◑
Distinctive shrubs with outstanding autumn leaf colour. Drooping flowers, cup or urn-shaped, produced May.
– **campanulatus** MS ✗ ◑
Cup-shaped flowers, sulphur-bronze produced abundantly. Autumn foliage yellow through shades to red. AM 1890 AGM 1932

– **cernuus rubens** MS ✗ ◑
Deep red, fringed flowers. Brilliant autumn colour. AM 1930
– **chinensis** (*himalaicus*) (*sinohimalaicus*) LS ✗ ◑
Flowers yellow and red with darker veins, in umbles. Leaves generally with red petioles, good autumn colour. AM 1935

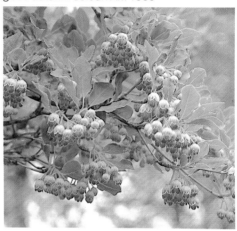

ENKIANTHUS campanulatus

– **perulatus** (*japonicus*) MS ✗ ◑
Urn-shaped, white flowers freely borne, with the leaves, spring. Scarlet autumn colour. AM 1979
EPIGAEA – Ericaceae PS (E) ✗ ◑
Creeping shrubs requiring peaty soil.
– **asiatica** PS (E) ✗ ◑
Rose-pink, urn-shaped flowers, in racemes April. AM 1931
– **repens** PS (E) ✗ ◑
Fragrant, white or rose tinted, flowers in terminal heads, April. AM 1931

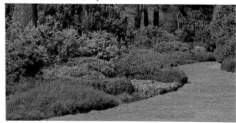

A colourful heath garden at Wisley

ERICA – Ericaceae DS-LS (E) "Heath"
Conspicuous colourful corollas. A prolonged show of flowers can be obtained by planting different species and varieties. Generally lime-hating. C(I)

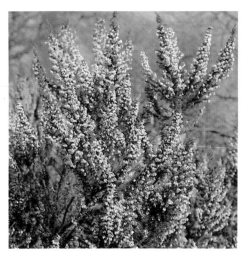

ERICA arborea 'Alpina'

– **arborea** LS (E) ✗ "Tree Heath"
Fragrant, white, globular flowers, early spring.
– – **'Alpina'** LS (E) ✗
Brighter green foliage. Hardier. AGM 1933
AM 1962
– **australis** MS (E) ✗ "Spanish Heath"
Rose-purple flowers, April-May. AM 1935
FCC 1962 AGM 1969
– – **'Mr. Robert'** MS (E) ✗
White flowers. AM 1929 AGM 1941
– – **'Riverslea'** MS (E) ✗
Fuchsia-purple flowers. AM 1946
– **canaliculata** LS (E) † ✗ "Tree Heath"
White or pink-tinged flowers, protruding
brown anthers, January-March.
– **carnea** DS (E) GC
Rosy-red flowers through winter. AGM 1924
Numerous cultivars, all lime tolerant.
Flowering season: **Early** November-
December
Mid January-March
Late April
Height 15-23cm
We recommend the following:
– – **'Adrienne Duncan'**
Dark bronze green foliage. Carmine-red
flowers. Mid
– – **'Ann Sparkes'** DS (E)
Golden foliage. Rich-purple flowers.
– – **'Aurea'** DS (E)
Golden spring and summer foliage. Deep
pink flowers, paling to white. Mid-Late.
AMT 1971

– – **'Eileen Porter'** DS (E)
Carmine-red flowers, October to April. Dark
corollas with pale calyces. AM 1956
– – **'Foxhollow'** DS (E)
Yellow foliage, tinged red in winter. Pale pink
flowers.
– – **'King George'** see *'Winter Beauty'*
– – **'Loughrigg'** DS (E)
Dark green foliage. Rose-purple flowers, Mid.
AMT 1966

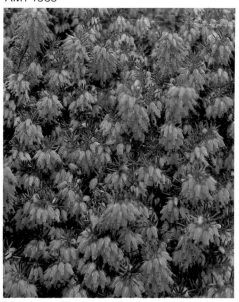

ERICA carnea 'Myretoun Ruby'

– – **'Myretoun Ruby'** DS (E)
Dark green foliage. Large, deep rose-pink
flowers.
– – **'Praecox Rubra'** DS (E)
Deep rose-red. Early-Mid. AMT 1966
FCCT 1968
– – **'Ruby Glow'** DS (E)
Bronzed foliage. Rich dark-red flowers, late.
AMT 1967 AGM 1969
– – **'Springwood Pink'** DS (E)
Clear rose-pink flowers. Mid. AMT 1964 AGM
1969
– – **'Springwood White'** DS (E)
Superb white, urn-shaped flowers. Mid.
AGM 1930 AGM 1940 FCCT 1964
– – **'Vivellii'** (*'Urville'*) DS (E)
Bronze-red winter foliage. Vivid carmine
flowers. Mid. AMT 1944 FCCT 1965 AGM
1969

– –'**Winter Beauty**' ('*King George*') DS (E)
Rose-pink flowers. December onwards.
AM 1922 AGM 1927
– **ciliaris** DS (E) ✗ "Dorset Heath"
Large rose-red flowers July-October. We
recommend the forms:
– –'**Mrs. C. H. Gill**' DS (E) ✗
Dark green foliage. Clear-red flowers. Up to
0.3m.
– –'**Stoborough**' DS (E) ✗
Long racemes of white flowers. 0.5–0.6m.
– **cinerea** DS (E) ✗ "Bell Heather"
Purple flowers, June-September. Wiry stems.
Generally 23/30cm. We recommend the
following forms:
– –'**Alba Minor**' DS (E) ✗
White flowers. 15cm. AMT 1967 FCCT 1968
– –'**Atrorubens**' DS (E) ✗
Bright red flowers in long sprays, distinctive.
AM 1915
– –'**Atrosanguinea Smith's Variety**'
DS (E) ✗
Dark foliage. Intense scarlet flowers. 15cm.
– –'**C. D. Eason**' DS (E) ✗
Deep pink. FCCT 1966 AGM 1969
– –'**Cevennes**' DS (E) ✗
Lavender-rose, prolonged display. AMT 1968
– –'**Domino**' DS (E) ✗
White flowers with ebony calyces. AMT 1970
– –'**Eden Valley**' DS (E) ✗
Lilac-pink, paler at base. 15cm. AM 1933
AGM 1969

– –'**Golden Drop**' DS (E) ✗
Golden-copper summer foliage, turning rust-
red in winter. Pink flowers seldom produced.
15cm.
– –'**Golden Hue**' DS (E) ✗
Golden foliage turning red in winter. 0.5m.
– –'**P.S.Patrick**' DS (E) ✗
Bright purple flowers. AMT 1967 AGM 1969
– –'**Rosea**' DS (E) ✗
Bright pink. AGM 1928 AMT 1966
– –'**Velvet Night**' DS (E) ✗
Blackish-purple flowers.
– **corisica** see *E. terminalis*
– × **darleyensis** DS (E)
Flowering throughout winter. Lime tolerant,
but not for shallow chalk. 0.5-0.6m high. We
recommend the clones:
– –'**Arthur Johnson**' DS (E)
Magenta flowers in long sprays. AM 1952
AGM 1969
– –'**Darley Dale**' DS (E)
Pale pink flowers. AM 1905 AGM 1924
– –'**George Rendall**' DS (E)
Rich pink flowers. AGM 1969
– –'**Jack H. Brummage**' DS (E)
Foliage yellow, turning gold, tinged red in
winter. Flowers deep pink.
– –'**Silberschmelze**' ('*Molten Silver*') DS (E)
Sweetly scented white flowers. AMT 1968
AGM 1969
– **hibernica** see *E. mediterranea*
– **lusitanica** (*codonodes*) LS (E) ✗ "Portugal
Heath" "Tree Heath"
With pale green, plumose stems. Fragrant
white flowers, pink in bud, December
onwards. AM 1972
– **mackaiana** (*mackaii*) DS (E) ✗
Rose crimson flowers in umbels July-
September. 15cm. We recommend the form:
– –'**Lawsoniana**' DS (E) ✗
Dwarf habit. Rose pink flowers.
– **mediterranea** (*hibernica*) SS (E)
Fragrant rose-red flowers, March-May. Lime
tolerant but not for shallow chalk.

– –'**Brightness**' SS (E)
Bronze-red buds opening rose-pink.
0.6-1.0m. AM 1972

– –'**Superba**' MS (E)
Pink flowers. 2m. AM 1972 AGM 1973

– –'**W. T. Rackliff**' SS (E)
Dark green foliage. Pure white flowers with
brown anthers. 1-1.2m. AM 1972

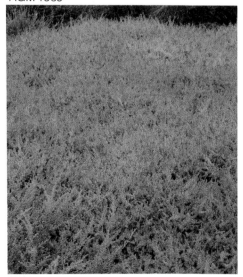

ERICA cinerea 'Golden Drop'

– **pageana** SS (E) † ⚊
Clusters of waxy-yellow, bell-shaped flowers,
spring. AM 1937
– **terminalis** (*stricta*) (*corsica*) MS (E)
"Corsican heath"
Rose coloured flowers late summer, fading
brown and remaining throughout winter.
Good on chalk.
– **tetralix** DS (E) ⚊ "Cross-leaved Heath"
Rose coloured flowers June-October.
0.2-0.5m. We recommend the forms:

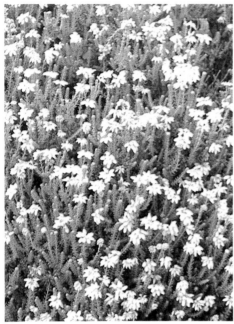

ERICA tetralix 'Alba Mollis'

– – **'Alba Mollis'** (*'Mollis'*) DS (E) ⚊
Grey foliage. White flowers. AM 1927
AGM 1973
– – **'Con Underwood'** DS (E) ⚊
Grey-green foliage. Crimson flowers.
AGM 1973
– – **'Lawsoniana'** see *E. mackaiana*
'Lawsoniana'
– – **'L. E. Underwood'** DS (E) ⚊
Silver-grey foliage. Pale-pink flowers,
terracotta in bud.
– – **'Pink Glow'** DS (E) ⚊
Grey foliage. Bright pink flowers.
– **umbellata** DS (E) †
Cerise-pink flowers, chocolate anthers,
throughout summer. Lime tolerant. AM 1926

– **vagans** DS (E) ⚊ "Cornish Heath"
Flowers in long sprays, July-October. We
recommend:
– – **'Cream'** DS (E) ⚊
White flowers. 0.6m. AMT 1968
– – **'Fiddlestone'** DS (E) ⚊
Rose-cerise flowers. 0.5-0.6m.
– – **'Kevernensis Alba'** DS (E) ⚊
Small racemes of white flowers. 0.3m.
AMT 1971
– – **'Lyonesse'** DS (E) ⚊
White flowers, protruding brown anthers.
0.5-1.0m. AM 1928 AGM 1969
– – **'Mrs. D. F. Maxwell'** DS (E) ⚊
Deep cerise. 0.5m. AM 1925 AGM 1969
FCCT 1970
– – **'Pyrenees Pink'** DS (E) ⚊
Pink flowers. 0.5m.
– – **'St. Keverne'** (*'Kevernensis'*) DS (E) ⚊
Clear rose-pink flowers 0.5m. AM 1914
AGM 1927 FCCT 1971
– – **'Valerie Proudley'** DS (E) ⚊
Golden-yellow foliage. White flowers.
– × **veitchii** MS (E) ⚊
A "Tree Heath", the following clone is in
cultivation:
– – **'Exeter'** MS (E) ⚊
Bright green foliage. Plumes of fragrant, white
flowers, spring. AM 1905
– **vulgaris** see *CALLUNA vulgaris*
– × **watsonii** DS (E) ⚊
Hybrid of which we recommend the clone:
– – **'Dawn'** DS (E) ⚊
Young spring foliage yellow. Large rose-pink
flowers, July-October. 23cm.
– × **williamsii** DS (E) ⚊
Hybrid, of which we recommend the clone:
– – **'P. D. Williams'** DS (E) ⚊
Growth tips yellow in spring, bronze in winter.
Rose-pink flowers in umbels, July-September.
0.3-0.6m.
ERINACEA – Leguminosae DS ○
Monotypic genus
– **anthyllis** (*pungens*) DS ○ "Hedgehog
Broom"
Spiny, slow growing shrub. Slate-blue flowers,
April-May. AM 1922 FCC 1976
ERIOBOTRYA – Rosaceae LS-ST (E)
Small genus of which we recommend:
– **japonica** LS (E) "Loquat"
Leathery, corrugated leaves up to 0.3m long.
Pungent, hawthorn-like flowers, after a hot
summer, intermittently Nov-April.

Occasionally globe or pear-shaped yellow fruits, produced. Best against a wall.

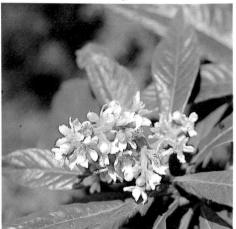

ERIOBOTRYA japonica

ERYTHRINA – Leguminosae S-T † ○
Large genus. Trifoliolate leaves and prickly stems.
– **crista-galli** MS † ○ "Coral Tree"
Waxy, deep scarlet, "Sweet Pea" flowers, summer. Requires sunny wall and winter protection. AM 1954

ESCALLONIA – Escalloniaceae SS-LS (E)
Useful shrubs tolerating lime and drought. Most withstand salt laden winds. Good hedges and windbreaks. Small leaves and abundant small flowers, summer-autumn. Generally A (b) 5 or C7
– **'Apple Blossom'** MS (E)
Pink and white flowers. Slow. AM 1946 AGM 1951
– **'C.F. Ball'** MS (E)
Large leaves, aromatic when crushed. Crimson flowers. Excellent coastal shrub. AM 1926
– **'Crimson Spire'** MS (E)
Dark glossy green leaves. Bright crimson flowers. Vigorous.
– **'Donard Beauty'** MS (E)
Large leaves, aromatic when bruised. Rose-red flowers. AM 1930
– **'Donard Brilliance'** MS (E)
Arching branches. Large leaves and large, rose-red flowers. AM 1928
– **'Donard Gem'** MS (E)
Small leaves. Large, fragrant, pink flowers. AM 1927

– **'Donard Radiance'** MS (E)
Large, glossy leaves. Large chalice-shaped flowers, rose-red. Strong growth. AM 1954
– **'Donard Seedling'** MS (E)
Large leaves. White flowers, pink in bud. Vigorous. AM 1916 AGM 1969

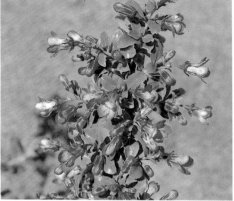

ESCALLONIA 'Donard Star'

– **'Donard Star'** MS (E)
Large leaves. Large, rose-pink flowers. AM 1967
– **'Edinensis'** MS (E)
Small leaves. Shell-pink flowers, carmine in bud. Neat habit. AM 1918 AGM 1969
– **'Ingramii'** LS (E) Hdg (0.5m)
Large leaves, aromatic when crushed. Rose-pink flowers. Good coastal shrub.
– **'Iveyi'** LS (E) †
Large, glossy leaves. Large panicles of white flowers, autumn. Vigorous. AM 1926

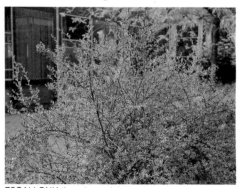

ESCALLONIA 'Langleyensis'

– **'Langleyensis'** MS (E)
Arching branches. Small leaves. Rose-pink flowers. AM 1897 AGM 1926

– **coccifera** LT (E) ♀ "Tasmanian Snow Gum"
Patchwork grey and white bark. Silvery-grey
adult leaves. AM 1953
– **coriacea** see *E. pauciflora*
– **dalrympleana** MT (E) ♀
Cream, brown and grey patchwork bark.
Grey-green adult leaves are bronzed when
young. Fast growth. AM 1953
– **gunnii** LT (E) ♀
Sage-green, sickle-shaped, adult leaves.
Silver-blue, rounded juvenile foliage, for floral
art. AM 1950
– **johnstonii** (*subcrenulata*) LT (E) ♀
Reddish bark. Glossy, apple-green leaves.

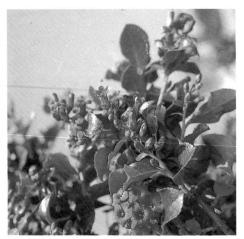

ESCALLONIA macrantha

– **macrantha** LS (E) Hdg (0.5m)
Glossy, aromatic leaves. Rose-crimson
flowers. Excellent for coast.
– **'Peach Blossom'** MS (E)
Clear peach-pink flowers. Slow growth.
AGM 1969
– **'Pride of Donard'** MS (E)
Dark, glossy leaves. Large, bright rose, bell-
shaped flowers, June onwards.
– **punctata** (*sanguinea*) LS (E) Hdg (0.5m)
Large leaves, aromatic when crushed. Deep
crimson flowers. Good coastal windbreak.
– **'Red Elf'** MS (E)
Dark, glossy green leaves and deep crimson
flowers.
– **rubra** (*microphylla*) MS (E)
Leaves aromatic when bruised. Red flowers in
panicles, July. We recommend the form:
– – **'Woodside'** (*'Pygmaea'*) SS (E)
Small crimson flowers. Neat spreading habit.
– **'Slieve Donard'** MS (E)
Small leaves. Large panicles of apple-
blossom-pink flowers.
– **'William Watson'** MS (E)
Small leaves. Bright red flowers.
EUCALYPTUS – Myrtaceae ST-LT (E)
♀ or ♀ "Gum Tree"
Fast growing trees noted for their attractive
stems and leaves and unusual white flowers.
Leaves of mature trees often completely
different from those of saplings. Will tolerate a
variety of soils – not shallow chalk, except
E. parvifolia. *Best spring planted as young pot*
grown plants.

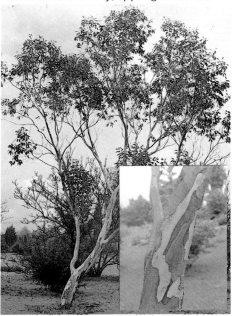

EUCALYPTUS niphophila with detail of bark

– **niphophila** ST (E) ♀ "Snow Gum"
Attractive grey, green and cream "Python's
Skin" bark. Scimitar-shaped, grey-green
adult leaves. Slow growth.
– **nitens** LT (E) ♀ "Silver Top"
Long, ribbon-like, glaucous leaves.
– **parvifolia** MT (E) ♀
Narrow, blue-green adult leaves. Smooth grey
bark. Tolerant of chalk.
– **pauciflora** (*coriacea*) ST (E) ♀ "Cabbage
Gum"
White trunk. Adult leaves sickle shaped, up to
20cm.

– subcrenulata see *E. johnstonii*
– urnigera MT (E) ❦
Greyish, peeling bark. Dark green leaves.
EUCOMMIA – Eucommiaceae MT ❦
A monotypic genus, suitable for all fertile soils.
– ulmoides MT ❦
Large, leathery, glossy, elm-like leaves. Only
known latex-producing hardy tree.
EUCRYPHIA – Eucryphiaceae LS-MT ◑
*Highly ornamental. White flowers with
conspicuous stamens July-September, when
mature. Prefers moist loam with shade at
roots, preferably non-calcareous.*
– billardieri see *E. lucida*
– cordifolia LS (E) † ◑
Heart-shaped leaves. Cup-shaped flowers.
Relatively lime tolerant. AM 1936
– glutinosa (*pinnatifolia*) LS ◑
Glossy, dark green, pinnate leaves turning
orange and red in autumn. Abundant flowers,
July-August. FCC 1880. AGM 1935
– × intermedia ST (E) ❦
Leaves varying, single to trifoliolate. Mass of
small flowers, August-September. Fast
growing. We recommend the form:
– –'Rostrevor' ST (E) ❦
Fragrant flowers crowd the slender branches.
AM 1936
– lucida (*billardieri*) ST (E) ❦
Oblong leaves, glaucous beneath. Fragrant,
pendulous flowers, June-July. AM 1936
– milliganii (*lucida milliganii*) ST ❦ (E) † ◑
Small, glossy, dark green leaves. Miniature
cup-shaped flowers freely borne, June-July.
Narrow habit. AM 1978
– × nymansensis MT (E) ❦
Dark green leaves, simple and compound on
the same plant. We recommend the form:
– –'Nymansay' MT (E) ❦
Flowers, 6cm across, crowd branches
August-September. Rapid growth. AM 1924
FCC 1926
EUGENIA ugni see *MYRTUS ugni*
EUODIA (*EVODIA*) **– Rutaceae** MT ❦
*Simple or compound leaves. White flowers. All
soils.*
– daniellii MT ❦
Large pinnate leaves. Corymbs of small,
pungent flowers, late summer. Black fruits.
– hupehensis MT ❦
Compound leaves. Panicles of flowers. Bright
red fruits on female trees. Excellent for shallow
chalk soil. AM 1949

EUONYMUS – Celastraceae PS-LS
*Evergreen or deciduous shrubs. Flowers,
green or purplish, early summer. Often showy
fruits, persisting into winter. Suitable for most
soils, particularly chalk.*

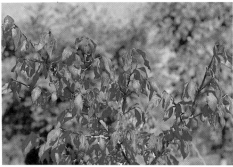
EUONYMUS alatus

– alatus MS
Broad, corky wings on the branchlets.
Excellent autumn leaf colour. Slow growth.
AGM 1932
– –'Compactus' SS
Dense, compact form – makes a good low
hedge.
– europaeus LS "Spindle"
Green stemmed shrub. Abundant, rosy-red ·
fruit capsules. Brilliant autumn foliage. AGM
1969
– –'Albus' (*'Fructo-albo'*) MS
White fruits. AGM 1969

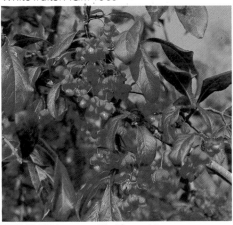
EUONYMUS europaeus 'Red Cascade'

– –'Red Cascade' MS
Branches weighed down in autumn by mass
of fruits. AM 1949 AGM 1969

–fortunei PS (E) GC
Trailing or climbing evergreen. Small, pale-green flowers. Pink fruits. We recommend:
– –'Coloratus' PS (E) GC
Trailing or climbing. Shiny, green leaves assume purplish tints throughout winter.
– –'Emerald and Gold' SS (E) GC
Dwarf bushy habit. Bright golden variegated leaves, tinged bronzy-pink in winter. AM 1978

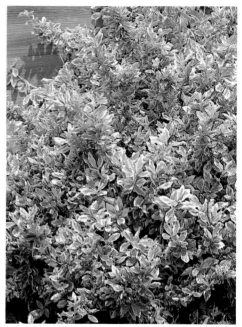

EUONYMUS fortunei 'Silver Queen'

– –'Silver Queen' MS (E)
Green foliage, variegated creamy-white, tinted rose in winter. Compact habit.
– –'Variegatus' PS (E) GC
Trailing or climbing. Greyish leaves, margined white, tinged pink.
–grandiflorus LS Semi-(E)
Conspicuous straw-yellow flowers. Yellow fruit capsules with red seeds. Autumn leaf colour often wine-purple. AM 1927
–hamiltonianus sieboldianus 'Coral Charm' LS
Spreading habit, pale-yellow autumn colour. Abundant, pale-pink fruits opening to show red seeds.
–japonicus LS (E)
Glossy green, leathery leaves. Extremely versatile – tolerant of salt spray and smog.
– –'Aureopictus' (*'Aureus'*) LS (E)
Leaves with broad green margins and golden centre.
– –'Macrophyllus Albus' LS (E)
Conspicuous white margins to leaves, which are larger and broader than the type.
– –'Microphyllus Pulchellus' (*'Microphyllus Aureus'*) SS (E)
Small leaves, variegated with gold.

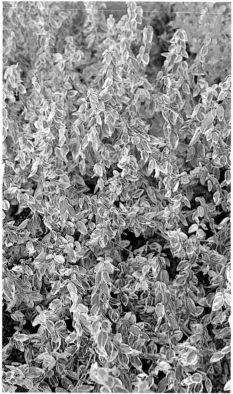

EUONYMUS fortunei 'Emerald and Gold'

– –'Emerald Charm' PS (E) GC
Deep green leaves with conspicuous white venation. Will climb if supported.
– –'Emerald Galety' SS (E) GC
Upright and spreading. Leaves margined white.
– –'Kewensis' PS (E) GC
Minute leaves on prostrate stems. Hummock forming. Will climb if supported.
– –'Silver Pillar' MS (E)
Erect habit. Narrow leaves with broad white margins.

– – **'Microphyllus Variegatus'** SS (E)
Small leaves with white margins.
– – **'Ovatus Aureus'** (*'Aureovariegatus'*)
LS (E)
Leaves margined and suffused creamy
yellow. Slow compact growth.
– **latifolius** LS
Large scarlet fruits. Brilliant autumn foliage.
AM 1916
– **nanus** (*rosmarinifolius*) PS Semi-(E) GC
Narrow leaves. Tiny purplish-brown flowers.
Mat forming. AM 1920
– **oxyphyllus** MS
Carmine-red fruit capsules. Red and purple
autumn leaf colour. Slow growth.
– **phellomanus** MS
Corky winged shoots. Conspicuous pink
fruits. FCC 1924
– **sachalinensis** (*planipes*) LS
Rich autumn leaf colour. Large scarlet fruits.
AM 1954 AGM 1969
– **wilsonii** LS (E)
Lanceolate leaves. Hedgehog-like fruits
covered in awl-like spines.
– **yedoensis** LS
Large leaves turning brilliant red and yellow in
autumn. Conspicuous rose-pink fruits.
AM 1924 AGM 1969

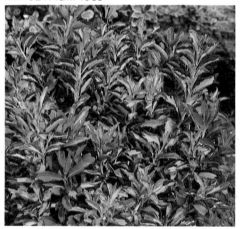

EUONYMUS japonicus 'Aureopictus'

EURYA – Theaceae DS-SS (E) ◑
Generally toothed leaves. Dioecious flowers.
– **japonica** SS (E) ◑
Leathery leaves. Tiny yellow flowers, spring.
Purplish-black berries. FCC 1861. We
recommend the form:

– – **'Variegata'** DS (E) ◑
Pale green leaves with dark green margins.
FCC 1894
– **ochnacea** see *CLEYERA japonica*
EURYOPS – Compositae DS-SS (E) ○
*Conspicuous, yellow, daisy flowers. Require
well drained soil.*
– **acraeus** (*evansii* HORT) DS (E) ○
Small, narrow, silvery-grey leaves. Canary-
yellow flowers, freely borne May-June.
AM 1952
– **pectinatus** SS (E) ○
Downy, grey shoots and leaves. Rich yellow
flowers May-June.
EVODIA see *EUODIA*
EXOCHORDA – Rosaceae LS
*Long arching branches. Conspicuous
racemes of large paper-white flowers, May.
Not suitable for shallow chalk soils.* D2 or 7
– **giraldii** LS
Large flowers freely borne. We recommend
the form:
– – **wilsonii** LS
Even larger flowers up to 5cm across.
AM 1931
– **korolkowii** (*albertii*) LS
Vigorous. Best species for chalk. AM 1894.
AGM 1933
– × **macrantha** LS
Abundant large flowers, late spring. AM 1917.
We recommend the form:

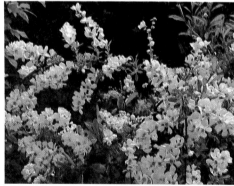

EXOCHORDA × macrantha 'The Bride'

– – **'The Bride'** SS
Weeping habit making a low dense mound.
Free flowering. AM 1973
– **racemosa** (*grandiflora*) LS ⚹ "Pearl Bush"
Spreading habit. Not for shallow chalk.
AM 1978

FABIANA – Solanaceae SS-MS (E) ○
*Heath-like shrub. Requires moist, well-
drained soil. Will not tolerate shallow chalk
soil.*

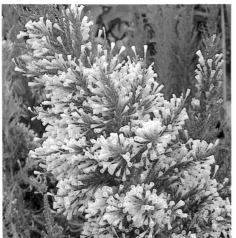

FABIANA imbricata

– imbricata MS (E) † ○
Abundant, tubular white flowers along
branches, June. AM 1934
––'Prostrata' SS (E) † ○
Mound-like habit. Small, pale-mauve tinted
flowers, May-June.
––violacea MS (E) † ○
Lavender-mauve flowers. FCC 1932
FAGUS – Fagaceae ST-LT "Beech"
*Small genus containing several beautiful
large, hardy trees. Important for timber,
windbreaks and hedges.*
– crenata (*sieboldii*) LT ♥
Similar to *F. sylvatica* but more obovate
leaves.
– englerana MT ♥
Glaucous, sea-green foliage. Rare.
– orientalis LT ♥ "Oriental Beech"
Obovate leaves turn butter-yellow in autumn.
– sylvatica LT ♥ "Common Beech" Hdg
(0.5m)
Large, noble tree. Leaves turning golden-

copper in autumn. Requires well drained soil.
Tolerates most soils, including chalk.
When trimmed as hedge retains brown leaves
through winter.
––'Asplenifolia' see under *heterophylla*
––'Atropurpurea' see under *'Riversii'*
––'Aurea Pendula' ST ♠ ◑
Pendulous branches. Golden yellow leaves.
––'Cockleshell' MT ♦
Small, rounded leaves.

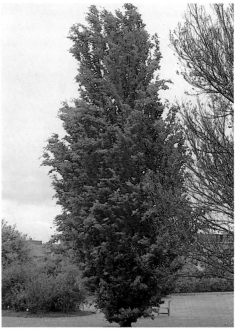

FAGUS sylvatica 'Dawyck'

––'Dawyck' (*'Fastigiata'*) LT ♦ "Dawyck
Beech"
Slender tree, broadening in maturity.
AGM 1969
––'Dawyck Gold' MT ♦ "Golden Dawyck"
Form with golden leaves
––'Dawyck Purple' MT ♦ "Purple Dawyck"
NEW. Form with purple leaves. FCC 1973.
Subject to Plant Breeder's Rights.

--**'Fastigiata'** see *'Dawyck'*
--**heterophylla** LT ♥ "Fern-leaved Beech"
"Cut-leaved Beech"
Graceful tree with narrow leaves, variously cut
and lobed. Several forms including
'Asplenifolia' AGM 1969
--**'Latifolia'** (*'Macrophylla'*) LT ♥
Larger leaves up to 15cm long, 10cm wide.
--**'Pendula'** LT ↑ "Weeping Beech"
High, arching and weeping branches.
--**'Prince George of Crete'** LT ♥
Very large leaves.
--**purpurea** LT ♥ "Purple Beech"
Covers a number of forms with purplish
leaves, see also *'Riversii'*

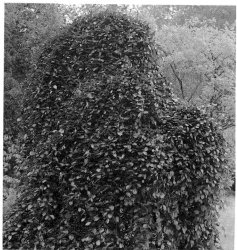

FAGUS sylvatica 'Purpurea Pendula'

--**'Purpurea Pendula'** ST ↑ "Weeping
Purple Beech"
Mushroom-headed. Dark purple leaves.
--**'Riversii'** LT ♥ "Purple Beech"
Large dark-purple leaves. *'Atropurpurea'* is
similar
--**'Rohanii'** MT ♦
"Fern-leaved Beech" with purple leaves.
--**'Roseomarginata'** LT ♥
Purple leaves with irregular pale-pink
margins.
--**'Tortuosa'** ST ♥
Twisted, contorted branches, weeping at the
tips.
--**'Zlatia'** MT ♥
Soft yellow leaves, turning green by late
summer. Slow growing.

× **FATSHEDERA** (*FATSIA* × *HEDERA*) –
Araliaceae MS (E) GC
Tolerant of pollution and salt winds. For all
soils.

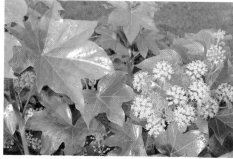

× FATSHEDERA lizel

–**lizei** MS (E) GC
Large, leathery, palmate leaves. Loose habit.
Round heads of small white flowers, autumn.
--**'Variegata'** MS (E)
Greyish-green leaves, irregularly margined
with white.
FATSIA – Araliaceae LS (E) ◑
*A monotypic genus, succeeding in all well
drained soils.*

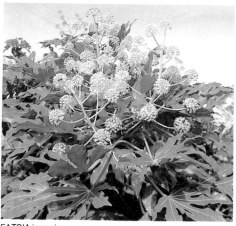

FATSIA japonica

–**japonica** (*Aralia sieboldii*) MS-LS (E) ◑
Large polished, dark green, palmate leaves.
Panicles of milk-white, globular flower-heads,
October. Excellent for seaside gardens.
--**'Variegata'** MS (E) ◑
Lobes of leaves white at tips
FEIJOA – Myrtaceae LS (E) † ○
Summer flowering, monotypic genus.

– **sellowiana** LS (E) † ○
Grey-green leaves. Flowers have fleshy red
and white petals, and long crimson stamens.
Large egg-shaped berries after a hot
summer. Edible petals and fruit are aromatic.
AM 1927

– – **'Variegata'** LS (E) † ○
Cream and white variegated leaves. AM 1969

FICUS – Moraceae S-T
*Large variable genus; evergreen and
deciduous. Very few hardy in this country.*

– **carica** LS-ST ♥ "Common Fig"
Handsome, lobed leaves and edible fruits in
autumn. Best against a sunny wall. Several
good fruiting forms are cultivated.

– **pumila** (*stipulata*) SS (E) † ◑
Shrub with climbing stems. Bears flowers and
fruit under favourable conditions. We
recommend the form:

– – **'Minima'** (*stipulata 'Minima'*) PS (E) † ◑
Slender creeper with minute leaves, forms a
carpet. Ideal for rockery or low walls.

"FIG, COMMON" see *FICUS carica*

"FIRETHORN" see *PYRACANTHA*

FORSYTHIA – Oleaceae DS-LS
*Generally golden-yellow flowers cover
branches, early spring. Very hardy and easy
to grow.*

– **'Beatrix Farrand'** MS
Erect, dense habit. Very large, canary-yellow
flowers. AM 1961 A (g) 1,2,3

– × **intermedia** MS
Vigorous. Flowers late March-April. AM 1894
A (g) 1,2,3. We recommend the forms:

– – **'Densiflora'** MS
Compact growth. Abundant flowers, smother
branches.

– – **'Spectabilis'** MS
Profusion of flowers, hiding branches.
AM 1915 AGM 1923 FCC 1935

– **'Lynwood'** MS
Abundant large flowers with broad petals.
AM 1956 FCC 1966 A (g) 1,2,3

– **ovata** SS
Ovate leaves. Amber-yellow flowers early
March. AM 1941 AGM 1947 A (g) 1,2,3

– **suspensa** LS
Rambling habit. Flowers on slender stalks
March-April. C2 or 3, wall shrubs.

– – **'Nymans'** LS
Bronze-purple branches. Large, primrose-
yellow flowers. C2 or 3, wall shrubs.

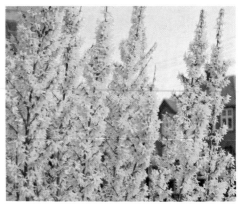
FORSYTHIA 'Lynwood'

– **viridissima** MS
Square stemmed shrub. Flowers April
onwards. We recommend the form:

– – **'Bronxensis'** DS
Mass of twiggy branchlets. AM 1958
A (g) 1,2,3

FORTUNAEA chinensis see *PLATYCARYA
strobilacea*

FOTHERGILLA – Hamamelidaceae DS-MS
↙
*Conspicuous bottle-like flower spikes, spring.
Rich autumn leaf colour.*

– **gardenii** (*alnifolia*) (*carolina*) DS ↙
Erect, scented inflorescences – clusters of
white stamens, April-May.

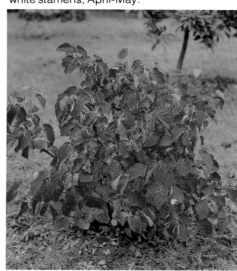
FOTHERGILLA major

– **major** (*monticola*) MS ✕
Conspicuous white flower clusters before leaves. Rich autumn leaf colour. AM 1927 AGM 1946 FCC 1969

FRANKLINIA – Theaceae LS ✕ ○
Delightful autumn flowering shrub for a continental climate.

– **alatamaha** (*Gordonia alatamaha*) LS ✕ ○
Large, shining green leaves, crimson in autumn. Large white, cup-shaped flowers, open only during hot, late summer.

FRAXINUS – Oleaceae ST-LT "Ash"
Fast growing trees with pinnate leaves. Tolerate wind, salt and atmospheric pollution. All soils.

– **americana** (*alba*) LT ♥ "White Ash"
Brown winter buds. Fast growing.

– **angustifolia** LT ♥
Glabrous slender pointed leaflets. Brown winter buds. Fast growing.

– **chinensis** MT ♥ "Chinese Ash"
Leaves sometimes turn wine-purple in autumn. Grey winter buds. Scented flowers. We recommend the form:

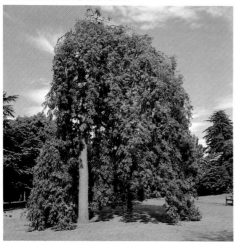

FRAXINUS excelsior 'Pendula'

– – **rhyncophylla** MT ♥
Large terminal leaflets.

– **excelsior** LT ♥ "Common Ash"
Valuable timber tree. Black winter buds. Named clones include:

– – **'Diversifolia'** (*'Monophylla'*) LT ♥ "One-leaved Ash"
Usually simple, jagged-toothed leaves. Vigorous.

– – **'Jaspidea'** MT ♥ "Golden Ash"
Yellowish branches and golden young shoots. Leaves clear-yellow in autumn. Vigorous.

– – **'Pendula'** MT ♠ "Weeping Ash"
Mound-like form with weeping branches.

– – **'Westhof's Glorie'** LT ❶
Strong growing form. Glossy dark green leaves open late.

– **latifolia** (*oregona*) MT ♥ "Oregon Ash"
Large leaves. Brown winter buds. Fast growth.

– **mariesii** (Ornus Sect.) ST ♥
Beautiful "Flowering Ash". Creamy-white flowers in panicles, June. Slow growing. AM 1962

– **ornus** (Ornus Sect.) MT ♥ "Manna Ash" "Flowering Ash"
Abundant white flowers in panicles, May. AGM 1973

– **oxycarpa** LT ♥
Small leaves. Winter buds dark brown. We recommend the form:

– – **'Raywood'** LT ♥ "Claret Ash"
Leaves turn plum-purple in autumn.

– **paxiana** (Ornus Sect.) MT ♥
Glabrous twigs. Winter buds coated in brownish down. Large panicles of white flowers, May-June.

– **pennsylvanica** (*pubescens*) MT ♥ "Red Ash"
Downy shoots, large leaves. Winter buds brown. Fast growth. We recommend the following:

– – **lanceolata** MT ♥ "Green Ash"
Bright green, glabrous shoots and narrow leaflets.

– – **'Variegata'** MT ♥
Silver-grey leaves, margined and mottled creamy white.

– **spaethiana** ST ♥
Large leaves. Large swollen petiole bases often reddish-brown. Large flower panicles.

– **velutina** MT ❶ "Arizona Ash"
Leaves and shoots coated in grey, velvety down. Winter buds brown.

FREMONTODENDRON (*FREMONTIA*) – **Sterculiaceae** LS (E) † ○
Conspicuous flowers with colourful calyx. Require good drainage. Good on chalk.

– **'California Glory'** LS (E) † ○
Yellow flowers up to 5cm. South facing wall.

– **californicum** LS (E) † ☼
Freely borne large yellow flowers. Three-lobed leaves. South facing wall. FCC 1866
– **mexicanum** LS (E) † ☼
Five-lobed leaves. Yellow flowers. AM 1927
"FRINGE TREE" see *CHIONANTHUS*

FUCHSIA – Onagraceae DS-MS
Flowers freely borne, summer-autumn. Red sepals unless stated otherwise. All well-drained soils. B or (a) or (b) 4
– **'Alice Hoffman'** SS
Purple tinged leaves. Small flowers, calyx scarlet, petals white.
– **'Blue Gown'** DS
A dwarf, floriferous plant of compact habit. Corolla double, deep purple, calyx scarlet.
– **'Brilliant'** SS †
Large flowers. Scarlet calyx, rose-purple, broad petals. AMT 1962
– **'Chillerton Beauty'** SS
Medium flowers. Calyx white, tinged rose, soft-violet petals. AGM 1973
– **'Corallina'** SS
Scarlet and violet flowers. Spreading.
– **'Dunrobin Bedder'** SS
Scarlet and violet flowers. AM 1890
– **'Graf Witte'** SS
Scarlet sepals, violet-purple petals. AMT 1978

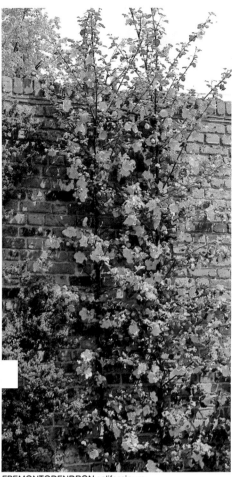

FREMONTODENDRON californicum

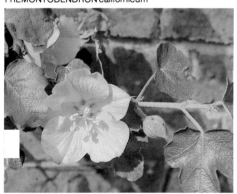

FREMONTODENDRON californicum

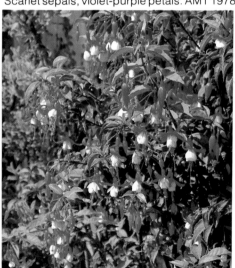

FUCHSIA 'Madame Cornelissen'

– **'Madame Cornelissen'** MS †
Large flowers; red calyx, white petals.
AM 1941 AMT 1965 AGM 1969

– magellanica MS
Long slender flowers; calyx scarlet, petals violet.

– – 'Alba' MS
Shorter flowers, white tinged mauve. AM 1932

– – gracilis MS
Small flowers, scarlet and violet. AGM 1930

– – 'Pumila' DS
Tiny flowers; scarlet and violet.

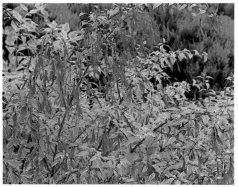

FUCHSIA magellanica 'Variegata'

– – 'Variegata' (*F. gracilis 'Variegata'*) SS
Green leaves, margined creamy yellow, tinged pink. Small scarlet and purple flowers. AGM 1969

– – 'Versicolor' SS
Grey-green leaves, rose tinted when young, variegated creamy-white when mature. AMT 1965 AGM 1969

– 'Margaret' MS
Semi-double flowers; crimson and violet purple. AMT 1965

– 'Margaret Brown' DS
Large flowers; crimson and magenta.

– 'Mrs. Popple' SS
Large flowers; scarlet and violet. Protruding crimson stamens and style. AM1934 AGM 1958 AMT 1962

– 'Prosperity' SS
Vigorous upright habit to 1m. Flowers very large, double; corolla white veined pink, calyx deep rose pink. One of the most spectacular hardy fuchsias.

– 'Riccartonii' (*magellanica 'Riccartonii'*) LS
Scarlet calyx, broad violet petals. AGM 1927 AMT 1966

– 'Tom Thumb' DS
Abundant flowers; rose-scarlet and violet. AMT 1938 FCCT 1962 AGM 1969

"FURZE" see *ULEX*
"FURZE, NEEDLE" see *GENISTA anglica*

FUCHSIA 'Mrs Popple'

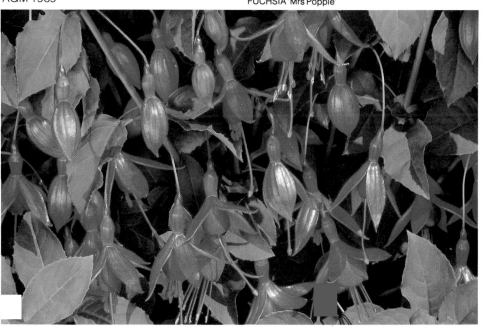

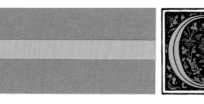

GARRYA – Garryaceae LS (E)

Leathery leaves. Dioecious; ornamental catkins. Withstand atmospheric pollution and coastal spray. All well-drained soils.

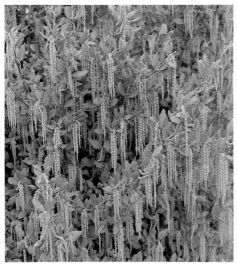

GARRYA elliptica (male form)

– elliptica LS (E)
Male plant has magnificent grey-green catkins. January-February. Female has clusters of purple brown fruits. AM 1931 AGM 1960 (male form). We recommend the form:

– – 'James Roof' LS (E)
Vigorous, male form with extra long catkins. AM 1974

– 'Pat Ballard' LS (E)
Free flowering male hybrid with long catkins.

– × thuretii LS (E)
Dark green, glossy leaves. Vigorous. Withstands wind well.

× GAULNETTYA – Ericaceae DS-SS (E) ⤸ GC
Hybrid origin (GAULTHERIA × PERNETTYA) (× GAULTHETTYA)

– wisleyensis SS (E) ⤸ GC
We recommend the following clones:

– – 'Pink Pixie' DS (E) ⤸ GC
White pitcher-shaped flowers, tinged pink, May. Purplish-red fruits.

– – 'Wisley Pearl' SS (E) ⤸ GC
Dull, dark-green leaves. Large ox-blood-red fruits, autumn and winter. AM 1939

GAULTHERIA – Ericaceae PS-MS (E) ⤸
Mainly tufted shrubs. White urn-shaped flowers, late spring, early summer.

– cuneata DS (E) ⤸
Compact habit. Narrow oblanceolate leaves. White fruits. Smell of 'Germalene' when crushed. AM 1924

– forrestii PS (E) ⤸
Waxy white, scented flowers in white stalked racemes. Blue fruits. AM 1927 AM 1937

– hookeri (*veitchiana*) DS (E) ⤸
Leathery, glandular toothed leaves. Bristly stems. White flowers, May. Blue fruits. AM 1943 FCC 1945

– miqueliana DS (E) ⤸
Shiny, green leaves. Flowers in short racemes, June. White or pink edible fruits. AM 1948

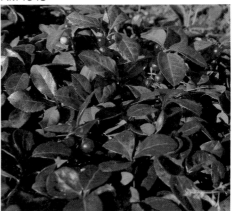

GAULTHERIA procumbens

– procumbens PS (E) ⤸ GC
"Checker-berry"
Creeping carpet of dark green leaves. Bright-red fruits.

GAULTHERIA – Continued

– **semi-infera** DS (E) ⚻
Glossy, green leaves. Bristly shoots. White or occasionally blush flowers. Generally dark-blue fruits. AM 1950
– **shallon** MS (E) ⚻
Broad, leathery leaves. Pinkish white flowers. Clusters of dark-purple fruits. Vigorous.
– **veitchiana** see *G. hookeri*
– **wardii** SS (E) ⚻
Bristly shoots. Leathery leaves with impressed veins. White flowers, May-June. Milky-blue fruits. AM 1933
× **GAULTHETTYA** see × *GAULNETTYA*
GAYA lyallii see *HOHERIA glabrata* and *H. lyallii*
– **ribifolia** see *HOHERIA lyallii*
"GEAN" see *PRUNUS avium*
GENISTA – Leguminosae PS-LS ○
Allied to Cytisus. *Generally have yellow flowers. Lime-tolerant, succeed in acid or neutral soils.*
– **aetnensis** LS ○ "Mount Etna Broom"
Slender, nearly leafless shoots. Flowers freely borne, July. AGM 1923 FCC 1938
– **cinerea** HORT see *G. tenera 'Golden Shower'*

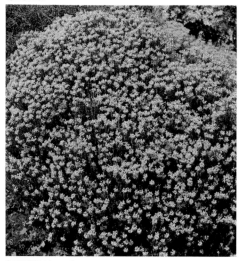

GENISTA hispanica

– **hispanica** SS ○ GC "Spanish Gorse"
Mass of flowers, May-June. Ideal for dry banks. AGM 1969
– **januensis** (*triquetra*) PS ○ "Genoa Broom"
Winged branches. Flowers, May. Rare. AM 1932

GENISTA – Continued

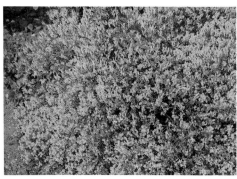

GENISTA lydia

– **lydia** (*spathulata*) DS GC ○
Slender drooping branchlets. Abundant golden flowers May-June. AM 1937 AGM 1946 FCC 1957
– **pilosa** DS GC ○
Cascades of golden flowers, May.
– **sagittalis** PS GC ○
Broadly winged branches. Flowers, June.
– **tenera** LS ○
Mass of flowers, June-July. AGM 1923

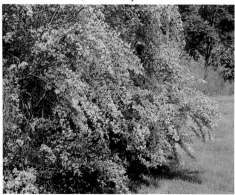

GENISTA tenera 'Golden Shower'

– – **'Golden Shower'** (*G. cinerea* HORT) LS ○
Hanging branches, wreathed in flowers in June.
– **tinctoria** SS ○ "Dyer's Greenweed"
Flowers in long terminal racemes, June-September. We recommend the forms:
– – **'Plena'** DS ○
Double flowers, freely borne. Excellent rock garden shrub. AGM 1969
– – **'Royal Gold'** SS ○
Mass of flowers throughout summer. AGM 1969

113

–**virgata** see *G. tenera*
"GHOST TREE" see *DAVIDIA involucrata*
GLEDITSIA (*GLEDITSCHIA*) –
Leguminosae MS-LT ○
*Delightful foliage trees. Trunk and branches
generally barbed with vicious spines. Seeds
in flattened pods. All well-drained soils.
Tolerates atmospheric pollution.*
–**triacanthos** LT ♥ ○ "Honey Locust"
Feathery, green leaves, yellow in autumn.
Long, shining, brown seed pods.
––**'Bujoti'** (*'Pendula'*) LS ○
Slender pendulous branchlets.
––**'Elegantissima'** LS-ST ♥ ○
Large fern-like leaves. Slow.
––**inermis** ST ♥ ○
Thornless.

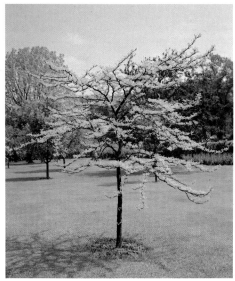

GLEDITSIA triacanthos 'Sunburst'

––**'Sunburst'** (*'Inermis Aurea'*) MT ♥
Spineless stems. Bright-yellow young foliage.
AGM 1973
"GOLDEN RAIN" see *LABURNUM*
GORDONIA – **Theaceae** LS (E) † ↙ ◑
*Camellia-like shrubs with conspicuous
flowers.*
–**axillaris** (*anomala*) LS (E) † ↙ ◑
Large, leathery, green leaves. Creamy-white
flowers, November to May. AM 1929
"GORSE, COMMON" see *ULEX europaeus*
"GORSE, SPANISH" see *GENISTA
hispanica*

GREVILLEA – **Proteaceae** DS-MS (E)
† ↙ ○
*Flowers like those of honeysuckle, but
smaller, produced over long period. Good
drainage essential.*
–**alpina** DS (E) † ↙ ○
Grey-green needle-like leaves. Red and
cream flowers. AM 1936
–**rosmarinifolia** MS (E) † ↙ ○
Deep green, needle-like leaves. Crimson
flowers in long terminal racemes. AM 1932
–**sulphurea** MS (E) † ↙ ○
Bright green, needle-like leaves. Canary-
yellow flowers in terminal racemes. AM 1974
GRINDELIA – **Compositae** SS (E) ○
Small genus. We recommend the following:
–**chiloensis** (*speciosa*) SS (E) ○
Narrow hoary leaves. Cornflower-like, yellow
flowers on tall thick stems, June-October.
AM 1931
GRISELINIA – **Cornaceae** MS-LS (E) †
*Densely leafy shrubs, ideal for hedging.
Insignificant flowers.*
–**littoralis** LS (E) † Hdg (0.50m)
Leathery apple-green leaves. All soils. Ideal
coastal hedge plant.

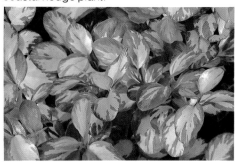

GRISELINIA littoralis 'Dixon's Cream'

––**'Dixon's Cream'** MS (E) † ◑
Leaves splashed and mottled creamy white.
––**'Variegata'** MS (E) † ◑
White margined leaves. AM 1978
"GUELDER ROSE" see *VIBURNUM opulus*
"GUM TREE" see *EUCALYPTUS*
GYMNOCLADUS – **Leguminosae** MT ♥
Pod bearing trees with bipinnate leaves.
–**dioica** (*canadensis*) MT ♥ "Kentucky
Coffee Tree"
Large compound leaves, pink tinged when
unfolding, clear-yellow in autumn. Whitish-
grey young twigs.

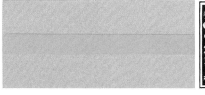

"HACKBERRY" see *CELTIS*

HAKEA – Proteaceae MS-LS (E) ○
Ideal shrubs for sunny, arid sites. Not good on chalk.
– **microcarpa** LS (E) ○
Rounded habit. Needle-like leaves. Clusters of creamy-white, fragrant flowers in leaf axils, May. Brown seed capsules.
– **sericea** (*acicularis*) LS (E) ○
Awl-shaped leaves, 2.5-7.5cm long. White flowers in leaf axils May-July.

HALESIA – Styracaceae LS-ST ♥ ✗
Delightful small trees producing snowdrop-like flowers along branches, before leaves, May. Small, green, winged fruits.
– **carolina** (*tetraptera*) ST ♥ ✗ "Snowdrop Tree"
White, nodding, flowers in clusters of 3 or 5. Pear-shaped, winged fruits. AGM 1946 AM 1954
– **diptera** ST ♥ ✗
More shrubby and less free-flowering than *H. carolina*. AM 1948. We recommend the form:
– –**'Magniflora'** LS ✗
Larger flowers, 2 to 3cm long. AM 1976
– **monticola** ST ♥ ✗
Larger tree with larger flowers and fruit than *H. carolina*. AM 1930
– –**'Rosea'** ST ♥ ✗
Flowers of delicate blush-pink.
– –**vestita** ST ♥ ✗
Superb form with even larger flowers, white, sometimes rose-tinted. AM 1958

× **HALIMIOCISTUS** (*HALIMIUM* × *CISTUS*)
– **Cistaceae** DS (E) ○
Attractive hybrids requiring good drainage.
– **'Ingwersenii'** (*Helianthemum clusii*) DS (E) ○
Pure white flowers, over a long period.
– **sahucii** DS (E) ○
Linear leaves. Pure white flowers, May-September. AGM 1969
– **wintonensis** DS (E) † ○
Grey foliage. Pearly-white flowers, stained yellow at petal bases, with maroon pencilled zone. AM 1926

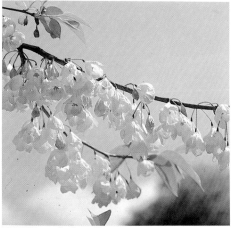
HALESIA monticola vestita

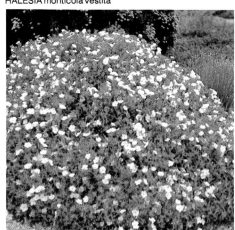
× HALIMIOCISTUS 'Ingwersenii'

HALIMIUM – Cistaceae DS-SS (E) ○
Low spreading shrubs for a sunny, well-drained site.
– **lasianthum** (*Cistus formosus*) SS (E) ○
Greyish leaves. Golden-yellow flowers with dark basal-blotches, May. AM 1951
– **libanotis** (*Helianthemum rosmarinifolium*) DS (E) ○
Linear leaves. Golden flowers, June.

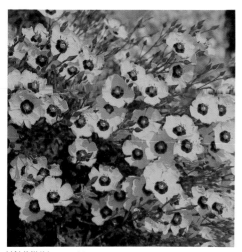

HALIMIUM ocymoides

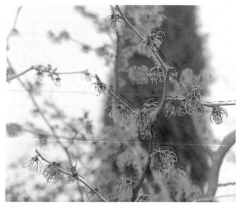

HAMAMELIS × intermedia 'Jelena'

– **ocymoides** (*Helianthemum algarvense*)
DS (E) ○
Grey leaves. Bright yellow flowers with black-brown basal markings. AGM 1932

HALIMODENDRON – Leguminosae MS ○
A monotypic genus suitable for all well-drained soils.

– **halodendron** (*argenteum*) MS ○ "Salt Tree"
Spiny shrub. Silvery leaves. Abundant purple-pink, pea flowers June-July.

HAMAMELIS – Hamamelidaceae MS-LS
Delightful, fragrant, winter flowering shrubs. Spidery yellow or reddish flowers, December-March, before leaves. Good autumn leaf colour.
Flower size:

> *Large over 3cm across*
> *Medium 2 to 3cm across*
> *Small up to 2cm across*

– × **intermedia** LS
Medium to large flowers. Following clones are recommended:

– – **'Allgold'** LS
Deep yellow flowers with reddish calyces, in clusters. Autumn leaves, yellow.

– – **'Carmine Red'** (*japonica 'Carmine Red'*) LS
Large, pale bronze flowers, coppery at tips. Yellow autumn leaves.

– – **'Diane'** LS
Coppery-red flowers. Rich autumn leaf colour. AM 1969

– – **'Jelena'** (*'Copper Beauty'*) LS
Dense clusters of large flowers, yellow, suffused coppery red – appearing orange. Flame autumn leaf colours. AM 1955

– – **'Moonlight'** LS
Pale sulphur-yellow flowers, tinged red at base, strongly scented. Yellow autumn leaves.

– **japonica** LS "Japanese Witch Hazel"
Glabrous, shiny leaves. Small to medium, wavy-petalled flowers, December-March. Rich autumn leaf colour. We recommend the form:

– – **'Arborea'** LS
Characteristic horizontal branching. Dense clusters of small, yellow flowers; red calyces. Yellow autumn leaves. FCC 1881

– – **'Carmine Red'** see *H × intermedia 'Carmine Red'*

– **mollis** LS "Chinese Witch Hazel"
Large, golden, broad-petalled flowers, December-March. Strong, sweet scent. Yellow autumn leaves. FCC 1918. AGM 1922

– – **'Coombe Wood'** LS
Spreading habit. Slightly larger flowers.

– – **'Goldcrest'** LS
Large, golden flowers, suffused claret at base. Red on backs of petals, appearing orange in bud. AM 1961

– – **'Pallida'** LS
Dense clusters of large, sulphur-yellow flowers. AM 1932. FCC 1958 AGM 1960

– **vernalis** MS "Ozark Witch Hazel"
Abundant small flowers, January-February, pale yellow to red. Heavily scented. Good autumn leaf colour. We recommend the form:

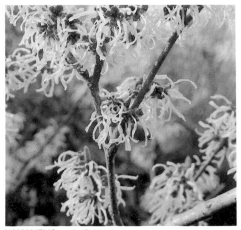

HAMAMELIS mollis 'Pallida'

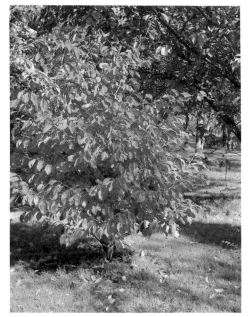

HAMAMELIS vernalis 'Sandra'

– – 'Sandra' MS
Purplish young leaves, turning green, purple
beneath, flame autumn colour. Cadmium-
yellow flowers.
"HAWTHORN" see *CRATAEGUS monogyna*
and *C. oxyacantha*
"HAZEL" see *CORYLUS*
"HEATHER" see *CALLUNA, DABOECIA &
ERICA*

HEBE (*VERONICA* in part)
– Scrophulariaceae DS-MS (E) ○
*Useful genus of variable species, invaluable
for industrial and coastal areas. Useful for
hedging, and ground cover. All well drained
soils. Generally white flowers, spring to
autumn flowering.* A (b) 5

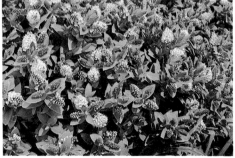

HEBE albicans

– albicans DS (E) ○
Dense, rounded habit. Glaucous leaves.
– 'Alicia Amherst' (*'Veitchii'*) (*'Royal Purple'*)
SS (E) † ○
Long racemes of deep-purple flowers, late
summer.
– × andersonii MS (E) † ○
Long racemes of soft-mauve flowers, fading
to white, August-September. Vigorous.
– – 'Variegata' MS (E) † ○
Leaves margined and splashed cream.
– anomala SS (E) ○
Small bright green leaves. Flowers June-July.
Slow. AM 1891
– 'Aoira' see *H. recurva*

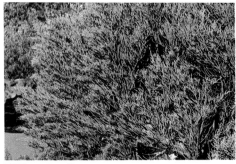

HEBE armstrongii

– armstrongii DS (E) ○
Ochre-yellow, "whipcord" foliage. Flowers
July-August. AM 1925.

117

– **'Autumn Glory'** SS (E) ○
Glossy, green leaves, tinged purple. Intense-violet flowers, continuously June-October. AGM 1969

– **'Bowles' Hybrid'** DS (E) ○
Racemes of mauve flowers, spring and summer. Fairly hardy.

– **brachysiphon** (*traversii* HORT) SS (E) ○
Rounded habit. Abundant flowers, June-July.

–– **'White Gem'** DS (E) ○
Mass of flowers, June.

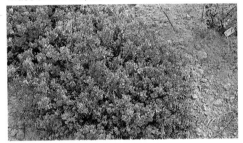
HEBE 'Carl Teschner'

– **'Carl Teschner'** DS (E) ○ GC
Mound-like habit. Small leaves and violet, white-throated flowers June-July. AM 1964 AGM 1969

– **'Carnea'** SS (E) † ○
Long racemes of rose-pink flowers, fading to white, freely borne, May-September. AM 1925

– **colensoi 'Glauca'** DS (E) ○
Dense habit. Glaucous-blue foliage. Flowers July-August.

– **cupressoides** SS (E) ○
Distinctive, dense, rounded habit. Long slender branches resemble a *Cupressus*. Pale-blue flowers, June-July. FCC 1894

–– **'Boughton Dome'** DS (E) ○
Dwarf form.

– **darwiniana** see *H. glaucophylla*

– × **franciscana** (*lobelioides*) SS (E) ○
Excellent hybrid. We recommend the clones:

–– **'Blue Gem'** SS (E) ○
Compact, dome shape. Racemes of bright-blue flowers. Extremely hardy. FCC 1869

–– **'Variegata'** SS (E) ○
Broad, creamy leaf margins.

– **glaucophylla** (*darwiniana*) SS (E) ○
Narrow, greyish-green leaves. Flowers July-August.

–– **'Variegata'** (*darwiniana 'Variegata'*) SS (E) ○
Slender, wiry shoots. Creamy leaf margins.

– **'Gloriosa'** (*'Pink Pearl'*) SS (E) † ○
Compact habit. Long racemes of bright pink flowers.

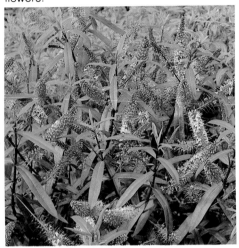
HEBE 'Great Orme'

– **'Great Orme'** SS (E) ○
Compact. Long, tapering, racemes of bright pink flowers. Fairly hardy. AGM 1961

– **'Hagley Park'** DS (E) ○
Long, terminal panicles of rose-purple flowers.

– **'Hielan Lassie'** SS (E) ○
Compact. Narrow leaves. Violet-blue flowers, July-September.

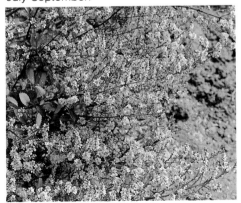
HEBE hulkeana

– **hulkeana** SS (E) ○
Loose habit. Glossy, green leaves. Panicles of soft lavender-blue flowers, May-June. FCC 1882.

– **'La Seduisante'** (*'Diamant'*) SS (E) ○
Large racemes of bright-crimson flowers.
AM 1897.
– **'Lindsayi'** SS (E) ○
Short racemes of pink flowers. Very hardy.
– **macrantha** DS (E) † ○
Leathery, toothed leaves. Flowers up to 2cm
across. AM 1952.
– **'Marjorie'** SS (E) ○
Long racemes of pale violet and white flowers,
July-September. Very hardy.

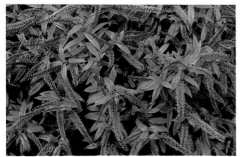

HEBE 'Midsummer Beauty'

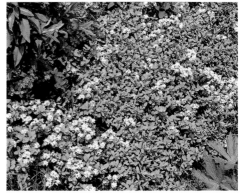

HEBE pinguifolia 'Pagei'

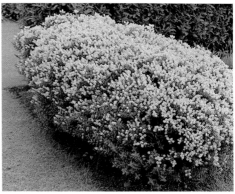

HEBE rakaiensis

– **'Midsummer Beauty'** SS (E) ○
Light green leaves, reddish beneath. Long
racemes of lavender flowers throughout
summer. Moderately hardy. AM 1960
– **'Mrs. E. Tennant'** SS (E) ○
Long racemes of pale-violet flowers, July-
September, fairly hardy.
– **'Mrs Winder'** MS (E) ○
Purple foliage. Bright-blue flowers.
Moderately hardy. AM 1978
– **pimeleoides 'Glaucocaerulea'** PS (E) ○
Small, glaucous-blue leaves. Pale lavender
flowers June-July.
– **pinguifolia 'Pagei'** (*Veronica pageana*)
PS (E) ○ GC
Small, glaucous-grey, leaves. Abundant,
small white flowers, May. AM 1958 AGM 1969
– **'Purple Queen'** SS (E) † ○
Large racemes of purple flowers. AM 1893.
– **rakaiensis** (*subalpina* HORT) DS (E) ○
Dense, rounded habit. Small, pale-green
leaves. Flowers, June-July.
– **recurva** (*'Aoira'*) SS (E) ○
Open, rounded habit. Narrow leaves,
glaucous above. Slender racemes of flowers.
– **salicifolia** MS (E) ○
Bright, green leaves. Long racemes of white
or lilac-tinted flowers, June-August.

– – **'Spender's Seedling'** SS (E) ○
Fragrant, white flowers, abundant. AM 1954
– – **'Variegata'** SS (E) ○
Leaves with creamy-white margins.
– **'Simon Delaux'** SS (E) † ○
Rounded habit. Large racemes of crimson
flowers.
– **subalpina** see *H. rakaiensis*
– **traversii** see *H. brachysiphon*
– **'Tricolor'** SS (E) † ○
Grey-green leaves with darker veins. Margins
yellowish white, flushed purple when young.
Long racemes of magenta flowers, turning
white in time.
HEDYSARUM – Leguminosae SS ○
Large genus, easy cultivation. We
recommend:
– **multijugum** SS ○
Sea-green, pinnate leaves. Racemes of rosy-
purple pea flowers, summer. Lax habit.
AM 1898

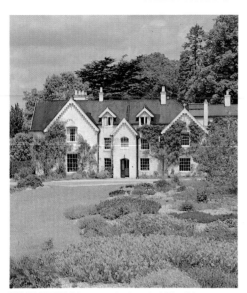

HELIANTHEMUM on scree beds at the Hillier Arboretum

HELIANTHEMUM – Cistaceae DS (E) ○
"Rock Rose" "Sun Rose"
*Green and grey-leaved plants. Abundant,
brilliant flowers, throughout summer. Ideal for
dry, sunny positions.*
– **algarvense** see *HALIMIUM ocymoides*
– **alpestre** DS (E) ○
Grey-green foliage. Yellow flowers, June-July.
AMT 1925
– **clusii** see *HALIMIOCISTUS 'Ingwersenii'*
– **lunulatum** DS (E) ○
Cushion-like alpine. Yellow flowers with
orange basal spots, June-July. AGM 1973
– **nummularium** (*chamaecistus*) (*vulgare*)
DS (E) ○ GC "Common Sun Rose"
Many hybrids and cultivars excellent for poor
dry soils. We recommend the following:
– – **'Afflick'** DS (E) ○ GC
Green foliage. Orange-yellow flowers with
deeper centre.
– – **'Amy Baring'** DS (E) ○ GC
Compact habit. Green foliage. Buttercup-
yellow flowers.
– – **'Coppernob'** DS (E) ○ GC
Foliage grey-green. Deep glowing copper
flowers with bronze-crimson centre.
– – **'Firedragon'** DS (E) ○ GC
Neat growth. Flame-orange flowers.
– – **'Golden Queen'** DS (E) ○ GC
Green foliage. Golden flowers.

– – **'Jubilee'** DS (E) ○ GC
Green foliage. Drooping, double, primrose-
yellow flowers. AGM 1969
– – **'Mrs. C. W. Earle'** DS (E) ○ GC
Dark-green foliage. Double, scarlet flowers
with yellow bases. AGM 1969
– – **'Praecox'** DS (E) ○ GC
Grey foliage. Bright yellow flowers.
– – **'Red Dragon'** DS (E) ○ GC
Green foliage. Scarlet flowers, yellow centres.
– – **'Rhodanthe Carneum'** DS (E) ○ GC
Silver-grey foliage. Pale rhodamine-pink
flowers, orange centres.
– – **'Snowball'** DS (E) ○ GC
Green foliage. Double, creamy flowers, pale
yellow centre.
– – **'Sudbury Gem'** DS (E) ○ GC
Neat habit. Deep rose-pink flowers with flame
centre.
– – **'Supreme'** DS (E) ○ GC
Grey-green foliage. Crimson flowers.
– – **'Wisley Pink'** DS (E) ○ GC
Soft pink flowers on grey foliage.
– – **'Wisley Primrose'** DS (E) ○ GC
Grey-green foliage. Primrose-yellow flowers,
deeper centre. AGM 1960 AMT 1970
HELICHRYSUM – Compositae DS-SS (E) ○
Attractive foliage, often aromatic. Bright
yellow flowers. Well drained, poor soil.
– **italicum** (*rupestre* HORT) DS (E) ○
Long, narrow, grey leaves. Clusters of flowers,
summer.
– **ledifolium** see *OZOTHAMNUS ledifolius*
– **plicatum** (*anatolicum*) DS (E) † ○
Narrow, silvery-white, downy leaves. Clusters
of flowers, July.
– **rosmarinifolium** see *OZOTHAMNUS
rosmarinifolius*
– **selago** DS (E) † ○
Tiny, scale-like leaves, adpressed to upright
stems. Leaves are white on inside giving
chequered look to the stems. We recommend:.
– – **'Major'** DS (E) † ○
Thicker stems and larger leaves.
– **serotinum** (*angustifolium*) DS (E) ○
"Curry Plant"
Narrow, sage-green leaves, with curry-like
smell. Heads of yellow flowers in mid-summer.
– **splendidum** (*triliniatum*) SS (E) ○
Silvery-grey leaves, with three longitudinal
ridges. Everlasting flowers keep colour into
the following year.

HESPEROYUCCA whipplei see *YUCCA whipplei*

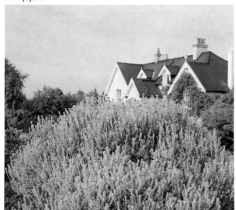

HELICHRYSUM splendidum

HIBISCUS – Malvaceae MS ○
Late summer, early autumn flowering shrubs.
– sinosyriacus MS ○
Vigorous. Sage-green leaves. Large trumpet-shape flowers, September-October, until the frosts. Rounded open habit. We recommend the clones:
– – 'Lilac Queen' MS ○
White, lilac-tinted petals, garnet red at base.

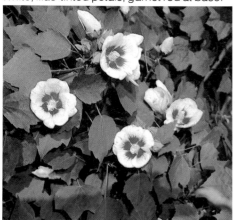

HIBISCUS sinosyriacus 'Ruby Glow'

– – 'Ruby Glow' MS ○
White petals, cerise base.
– syriacus MS ○
Trumpet-shaped flowers, successively July-October. Compact upright habit. AGM 1934. We recommend the following clones:

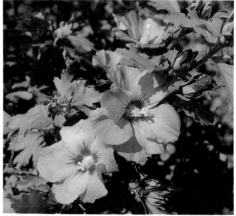

HIBISCUS syriacus 'Blue Bird'

– – 'Blue Bird' ('Oiseau Bleu') MS ○
Single, violet-blue flowers, darker eye.
AM 1965 AGM 1969
– – 'Diana' MS ○
Large, single, pure-white flowers.
– – 'Hamabo' MS ○
Large, single, blush flowers, crimson eye.
AM 1935 AGM 1969
– – 'Lady Stanley' (*'Elegantissimus'*) MS ○
Nearly double, white flowers, shaded blush, with maroon base.
– – 'Monstrosus' MS ○
Single white flowers, maroon eye.
– – 'Red Heart' MS ○
White flowers with a conspicuous red centre.

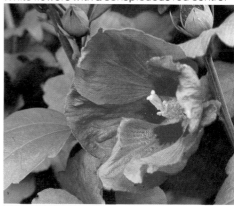

HIBISCUS syriacus 'Woodbridge'

– – 'Woodbridge' MS ○
Large, single, rose-pink flowers, carmine eye.
AM 1937 AGM 1969

121

"HICKORY" see *CARYA*
HIPPOPHAE – Elaeagnaceae LS-ST ○
Silvery or sage-green, willowy leaves. Female plants have orange berries. Good maritime wind break.

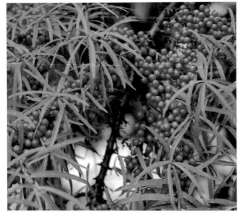

HIPPOPHAE rhamnoides

– **rhamnoides** MS ○ "Sea Buckthorn"
Silvery leaves. Berries last through to following February. Plant in groups to ensure pollination of females. AM 1944
HOHERIA – Malvaceae LS ○ or ◑
Variable genus, some evergreen, which require protection. White flowers, mid-late summer.

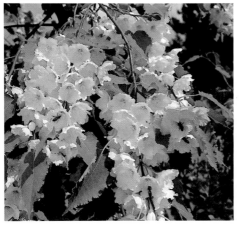

HOHERIA glabrata

– **glabrata** (*Gaya lyallii* KIRK) (*Plagianthus lyallii* HOOK) LS ○
Mass of fragrant, almost translucent, flowers, June-July. AM 1911 FCC 1946

– **'Glory of Amlwch'** LS Semi-(E) ○
Leaves retained in mild winters. Large flowers smothering stems, summer. AM 1960
– **lyallii** (*Gaya lyallii* BAKER) (*Gaya lyallii ribifolia*) (*Plagianthus lyallii* GRAY) LS ○
Usually silvery-grey heart-shaped leaves. Numerous flowers, July. AGM 1926 AM 1955 FCC 1964
– **populnea** LS (E) † ◑
Flowers in dense clusters, late summer-autumn. AM 1912
– – **'Alba Variegata'** LS (E) † ◑
Dark-green leaves, irregularly margined creamy-white.
– **sexstylosa** (*populnea lanceolata*) LS (E) † ◑
Grey-green, lanceolate leaves. Flowers borne freely. Hardier than *H. populnea*. FCC 1924 AM 1964
"HOLLY" see *ILEX*
HOLODISCUS – Rosaceae LS
Spiraea-like shrubs. Finely divided leaves. Feathery flower panicles, July. Hardy.
– **discolor** (*Spiraea discolor*) LS ○
Greyish-white leaves, tomentose beneath. Creamy-white flowers. AGM 1949 AM 1978
"HONEY LOCUST" see *GLEDITSIA triacanthos*
"HONEYSUCKLE" see *LONICERA*
"HOP HORNBEAM" see *OSTRYA carpinifolia*
"HORNBEAM" see *CARPINUS*
"HORSE CHESTNUT" see *AESCULUS hippocastanum*
HYDRANGEA – Hydrangeaceae DS-LS ◑ or ○
Attractive summer-autumn flowering shrubs with generally dome-shaped or flattened heads. Easy cultivation, but resent dryness at roots.
Pruning for all (except H. paniculata*) A (g) 10 or 4*
– **arborescens** SS ◑
Flowers with conspicuous, creamy, marginal ray florets, July-September. We recommend the following:
– – **'Annabelle'** ◑
Large, hemispherical heads of white, nearly all sterile, flowers. AM 1978
– – **'Grandiflora'** SS ◑
Large globular heads of creamy sterile florets. AM 1907 AGM 1969
– **aspera** MS ◑
Large leaves. Pale blue flowers with lilac-pink

or white ray florets, June-July.
– **'Ayesha'** (*'Silver Slipper'*) SS ◑
Distinctive shrub. Glossy, green leaves.
Greyish-lilac-pink, flattened flower heads,
with thick cup-shaped florets. AM 1974
– **cinerea** SS ◑
Leaves tomentose beneath. Flowers with few
white ray florets, June-July. We recommend
the form:
– – **'Sterilis'** SS ◑
Globular heads of sterile cream florets.
– **heteromalla** LS ◑
Dark green leaves, whitish beneath. White
flowers with conspicuous ray florets. We
recommend the forms:
– – **'Bretschneideri'** (*H. bretschneideri*) LS ◑
Peeling, brown bark. Broad, flattened
lacecaps, July.
– – **'Snowcap'** LS ◑
Large heart-shaped leaves. Flowers in large,
flattened corymbs, 20-25cm across.
Tolerates sun, wind or drought.
– **involucrata** SS ◑
Blue or rosy-lilac flowers, margined with white
or tinted ray florets.
– – **'Hortensis'** SS ◑
Double, creamy-white florets, tinted pink in
the open. AM 1956
– **macrophylla** DS-LS ◑
Large group incorporating the **HORTENSIAS**
and the **LACECAPS**:
HORTENSIAS "Mop-headed hydrangeas"
*Large globular heads of sterile florets, pink,
red, white, blue or combination. A hydrangea
colourant is necessary in alkaline soils to
retain blue shades.*
*Excellent maritime plants, also thrive in inland
sheltered gardens.* We recommend:

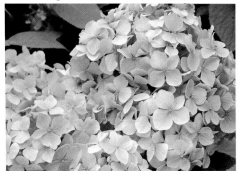

HYDRANGEA macrophylla 'Altona' (HORTENSIA)

– – **'Altona'** SS ◑
Rose coloured, large florets. Blues well if
treated. AM 1957

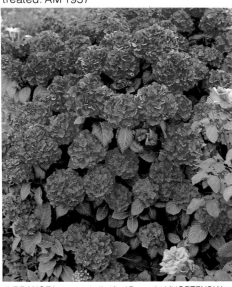

HYDRANGEA macrophylla 'Ami Pasquier' (HORTENSIA)

– – **'Ami Pasquier'** DS ◑
Deep red. AM 1953
– – **'Ayesha'** see *H. 'Ayesha'*
– – **'Deutschland'** MS ◑
Deep pink. Good autumn leaf colour. AM 1927
– – **'Europa'** SS ◑
Deep pink, large florets.
– – **'Generale Vicomtesse de Vibraye'** SS ◑
Vivid rose. Blues well if treated. AM 1947
– – **'Goliath'** MS ◑
Rich pink or purple-blue. Small head of large
florets.
– – **'Hamburg'** SS ◑
Deep rose-purple. Large florets.
– – **'Heinrich Seidel'** SS ◑
Rich red-purple. Large fringed florets.
– – **'King George'** SS ◑
Rose pink. Large florets with serrated sepals.
AM 1927.
– – **'Madame Emile Mouilliere'** SS ◑
White, with pink or blue centre. Large florets
with serrated sepals. AM 1910.
– – **'Marechal Foch'** SS ◑
Rosy-pink, purple to deep blue in acid soil.
AM 1923.
– – **'Niedersachsen'** MS ◑
Pale pink. Blues well if treated. AM 1968

LACECAPS
Large corymbs of fertile flowers, ringed by sterile, coloured ray florets. Similar requirements to **HORTENSIAS**. We recommend:

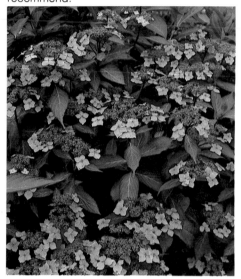

HYDRANGEA macrophylla 'Blue Wave' (LACECAP)

– – **'Blue-Wave'** MS ◑
Blue, fertile flowers with large ray florets, varying pink to blue. Beautiful gentian-blue in suitable soils. AM 1956 FCC 1965

– – **'Lanarth White'** MS ◑
Bright blue or pink fertile flowers, ringed with white ray florets. AM 1949

– – **'Mariesii'** SS ◑
Rosy-pink flowers, very large ray florets. Rich blue in suitable soils. FCC 1881 AGM 1938

– – **'Sea Foam'** (*maritima 'Seafoam'*) SS ◑
Blue fertile flowers, white ray florets.

– – **'Tricolor'** MS ◑
Pale pink to white flowers. Variegated leaves of green, grey and pale yellow. FCC 1882

– – **'Veitchii'** MS ◑
Blue fertile flowers, ray florets white to pale pink. AM 1974

– – **'White Wave'** (*'Mariesii Alba'*) SS ◑
Pink or blue fertile flowers, pearl-white ray florets. AM 1948

– **paniculata** MS-LS ○
Dense, terminal panicles of both fertile and large, creamy sterile florets, late summer-autumn. AGM 1936. AM 1964 B (a) 4. We recommend the forms:

– – **'Grandiflora'** LS ○
Massive panicles of sterile florets, white, turning to pink. FCC 1869 AGM 1969

– – **'Praecox'** LS ○
Smaller panicles of dentated, ray florets, early July. AM 1956 AGM 1960 FCC 1973

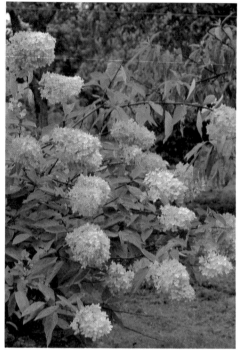

HYDRANGEA paniculata 'Grandiflora'

– – **'Tardiva'** LS ○
More numerous ray florets, September-October. Short stiff, erect branches.

– – **'Unique'** LS ○
Larger panicles than *H. paniculata 'Grandiflora'*.

– **petiolaris** see under CLIMBERS

– **'Preziosa'** see *H. serrata 'Preziosa'*

– **quercifolia** MS ◑
White flowers. Superb autumn leaf colour. AM 1928

– **sargentiana** MS ◑
Large, bluish flowers with white ray florets, July-August. Large, velvety leaves and hairy shoots. AM 1912.

– **serrata** (*macrophylla serrata*) DS ◑
Flattened corymbs of white or blue flowers; pink, white or blue ray florets, sometimes crimson in autumn. We recommend the forms:

−−**'Bluebird'** (*H. acuminata 'Bluebird'*) SS ◑
Slightly dome-shaped corymbs of blue, fertile
flowers, ringed by large red-purple ray florets
– sea-blue on acid soil. AM 1960 AGM 1969
−−**chinensis** DS ◑
Flattened corymbs, lilac-blue ray florets –
powder-blue on acid soils. Downy leaves.
−−**'Grayswood'** SS ◑
Blue fertile flowers, white ray florets, turning
rose, then crimson. AM 1948.
−−**'Intermedia'** SS ◑
Pink fertile flowers, white ray florets, turning to
crimson.
−−**koreana** DS ◑
Lilac ray florets, sky-blue on acid soils.

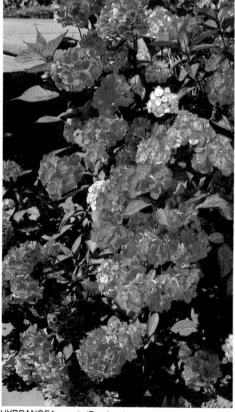

HYDRANGEA serrata 'Preziosa'

−−**'Preziosa'** SS ◑
Globular heads of rose-pink, florets, reddish-
purple in autumn. Purplish-red stems. Leaves
tinged purple when young. AM 1963
FCC 1964 AGM 1973

−−**'Rosalba'** SS ◑
White ray florets, turning crimson. Large
leaves. AM 1939
– **serratifolia** see under CLIMBERS

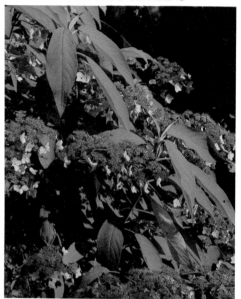

HYDRANGEA villosa

– **villosa** MS ◑
Large lilac-blue flowers with serrated
margined sepals. Leaves and stems hairy.
AM 1950
– **xanthoneura** LS ○
Large flat flower heads, creamy-white ray
florets, June. We recommend the form:
−−**wilsonii** LS ○
White florets. Large, lustrous leaves.
HYMENANTHERA – Violaceae PS-MS (E) or
Semi-(E) ○
*Rigid habit. Small genus of which we
recommend:*
– **crassifolia** PS Semi-(E) ○
Spreading habit. Obovate leaves. White
berries on underside of branches. FCC 1892
HYPERICUM – Guttiferae PS-MS
*Abundant yellow flowers, summer and
autumn. Almost all well drained soils.*
– **androsaemum** DS "Tutsan"
Small flowers, conspicuous anthers. Berry-
like capsules, red turning black, autumn.
– **beanii** (*patulum henryi* BEAN) SS
Arching branches with slightly drooping
flowers. AM 1904. We recommend the form:

– – **'Gold Cup'** SS
Deep yellow cup-shaped flowers 6cm across.
– **calycinum** DS (E) GC "Rose of Sharon"
Large leaves. Large golden flowers. Excellent
in dry and in shady places. AM 1978
– **coris** PS (E)
Flowers in terminal panicles. Excellent for rock
garden, dry wall or scree.
– **'Eastleigh Gold'** SS Semi-(E)
Drooping reddish-brown branchlets.
Abundant flowers, late June-October.
– **elatum 'Elstead'** see *H. × inodorum 'Elstead'*
– **empetrifolium oliganthum** PS (E)
Small linear leaves. Flowers in small erect
panicles. Ideal rock garden or scree plant.
AM 1937
– **forrestii** (*patulum forrestii*) (*patulum henryi*
HORT) SS
Leaves have rich autumn colour. Abundant
saucer-shaped flowers, summer and autumn.
AM 1922. AGM 1924

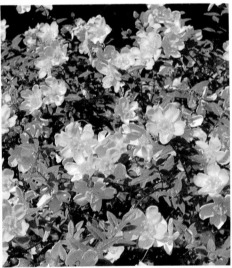

HYPERICUM 'Hidcote'

– **'Hidcote'** (*patulum 'Hidcote'*) MS Semi-(E)
Compact habit. Abundant, large saucer-
shaped flowers, July-October. AM 1954. AGM
1954
– × **inodorum** (*elatum*) (*multiflorum* HORT)
SS
Small pale-yellow flowers in terminal cymes.
Red fruits. We recommend the form:
– – **'Elstead'** (*elatum 'Elstead'*) SS
Brilliant salmon-red fruits. AM 1933

– **kouytchense** (*penduliflorum*) (*patulum
grandiflorum*) (*patulum 'Sungold'*) SS
Semi-(E)
Golden-yellow flowers with conspicuous
stamens, June-October. Bright red long-
styled capsules.
– × **moseranum** DS GC
Arching, reddish stems. Flowers with
conspicuous reddish anthers, July-October.
FCC 1891

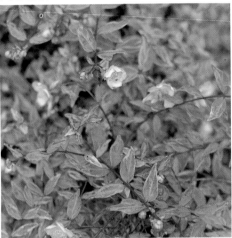

HYPERICUM × moseranum 'Tricolor'

– – **'Tricolor'** DS ◑
Leaves variegated pink, white and green.
AM 1896
– **patulum forrestii** see *H. forrestii*
– **patulum grandiflorum** see *H. kouytchense*
– **patulum henryi** see *H. forrestii* and
H. pseudohenryi
– **patulum 'Hidcote'** see *H. 'Hidcote'*
– **patulum 'Sungold'** see *H. kouytchense*
– **pseudohenryi** (*patulum henryi* HORT) SS
Mound-like habit. Arching stems. Abundant
flowers with conspicuous stamens, July-
August.
– **reptans** PS
Mat-forming shrublet. Terminal, solitary
flowers June-September. Excellent for scree
or rock garden. AGM 1927
– **'Rowallane'** MS Semi-(E) †
Rich golden flowers, to 7.5cm wide. Graceful
habit. AM 1943
– **xylosteifolium** SS
Suckering shrub. Small flowers, intermittently
July-September.

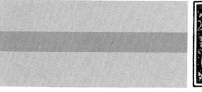

IDESIA – Flacourtiaceae MT ♀

Monotypic. Dioecious. Prefers neutral to acid soil.

– polycarpa MT ♀

Large ovate leaves. Terminal panicles of small yellowish-green flowers, summer on older trees. Bunches of red berries, autumn, on female trees. AM 1934

ILEX – Aquifoliaceae DS-MT

Variety of forms, many evergreen. Generally dioecious. Great variety of leaf and berry. Many withstand industrial pollution and maritime exposure. Some make excellent hedges

A (f) 5 (all evergreens).

– × altaclarensis LS-ST (E) Hdg (0.5m)

Vigorous growth. Large leaves. Tolerant of maritime and industrial atmosphere. Good hedges and screens. We recommend several forms:

– –'Camelliifolia' (*aquifolium 'Camelliifolia'*) LS (E)

Pyramidal habit. Long, generally spineless, shiny, dark green leaves, reddish-purple when young. Purple stems. Large fruit. AGM 1931

– –'Camelliifolia Variegata' LS (E)

Dark green leaves with paler marbling, and gold margins. Part or whole leaves sometimes gold.

– –'Golden King' (*aquifolium 'Golden King'*) LS (E)

Broad, green, almost spineless leaves, with golden margin. Female. AM and FCC 1898 AGM 1969

– –'Hodginsii' ST (E) ♀

Dark green, rounded or oval leaves, variously many or sparsely spined. Purple stems. Male. AGM 1969

– –'Lawsoniana' LS (E)

Generally spineless leaves with central yellow splash. Female. FCC 1894

– –'Mundyi' LS (E)

Spiny, oval leaves with heavy veining. Male.

– –'Purple Shaft' ST (E) ♀

Strong, dark-purple young shoots. Abundant fruit.

– –'Silver Sentinel' LS (E)

Erect habit. Deep green leaves, mottled grey and pale-green, with creamy margin. Few spines. Female.

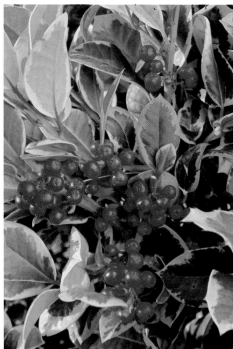

ILEX × altaclarensis 'Golden King'

– –'Wilsonii' LS (E)

Dome-shaped habit. Prominently veined, spiny leaves. Female. FCC 1899 AGM 1969

– aquifolium MT (E) ♀ Hdg (0.5m) "Common Holly"

Spiny, glossy dark-green leaves. Male and female forms. Excellent hedges. Tolerant of most conditions. Variety of clones.

– –'Amber' LS (E)

Large bronze-yellow fruits.

‒‒**'Argentea Marginata'** LS (E) "Broad-leaved Silver Holly"
Leaves margined white. We recommend the female form. AGM 1969

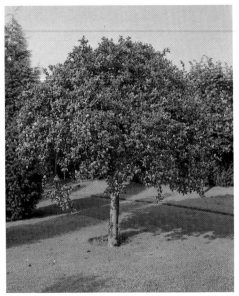

ILEX aquifolium 'Argentea Marginata'

‒‒**'Argentea Pendula'** ST (E) ♠ "Perry's Silver Weeping Holly"
Strongly weeping branches. Leaves margined white. Free fruiting.
‒‒**'Argentea Regina'** see *'Silver Queen'*
‒‒**'Bacciflava'** (*'Fructuluteo'*) LS (E) "Yellow Fruited Holly"
Abundant, bright yellow fruits.

‒‒**'Camelliifolia'** see *I. × altaclarensis 'Camelliifolia'*
‒‒**'Ferox'** MS (E) "Hedgehog Holly"
Small leaves, short sharp spines on upper surface. Male.

‒‒**'Ferox Argentea'** MS (E) "Silver Hedgehog Holly"
Creamy-white margins and spines. Purple twigs. Male.

‒‒**'Ferox Aurea'** MS (E) "Gold Hedgehog Holly"
Leaves with golden central splash. Male.
‒‒**'Flavescens'** (*'Clouded Gold'*) LS (E) "Moonlight Holly"
Leaves suffused yellow-old gold. Female.

‒‒**'Fructuluteo'** see *'Bacciflava'*

‒‒**'Golden King'** see *I × altaclarensis 'Golden King'*
‒‒**'Golden Milkboy'** (*'Aurea Mediopicta Latifolia'*) MS (E)
Flattened, spiny, green leaves, with central golden splash. Male.
‒‒**'Golden Queen'** (*'Aurea Regina'*) MS (E)
Green or reddish young shoots. Dark green spiny leaves, shaded grey and pale green, margined yellow. Male. AGM 1969

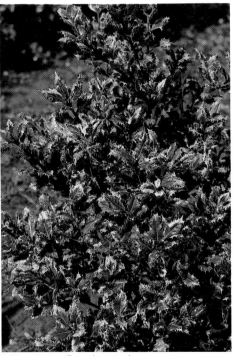

ILEX aquifolium 'Ferox Argentea'

‒‒**'Golden van Tol'** LS (E)
Leaves margined gold. Female.
‒‒**'Green Pillar'** MT (E) ♦
Dark green spiny leaves. Female.
‒‒**'Handsworth New Silver'** LS (E)
Purple stems. Leaves mottled grey, broad creamy-white margin. Female. AGM 1969
‒‒**'J.C. van Tol'** (*'Polycarpa'*) LS (E)
Glossy, dark green, almost spineless leaves. Abundant red berries. AGM 1969
‒‒**'Madame Briot'** LS (E)
Purple stems. Spiny green leaves, mottled and margined dark yellow. Female. AGM 1969

––**'Ovata Aurea'** MS (E)
Purple stems. Thick, short spined leaves,
margined gold. Male.
––**'Pendula'** ST (E) ♠
Dark green spiny leaves. Abundant fruits.
––**'Polycarpa'** see *'J. C. van Tol'*
––**'Pyramidalis'** MT (E) ♥
Conical when young, broadening in maturity.
Bright green leaves. Abundant fruit.
AGM 1969

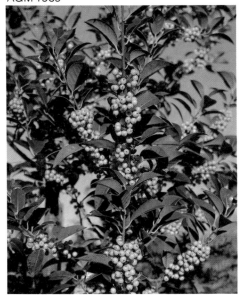

ILEX aquifolium 'Pyramidalis Fructuluteo'

––**'Pyramidalis Fructuluteo'** MT (E) ♥
Abundant bright yellow fruits. Perhaps the
best yellow-fruited holly.
––**'Silver Milkboy'** (*Argentea Mediopicta'*)
LS (E)
Dark green spiny leaves, with central cream
blotch. Male.
––**'Silver Queen'** (*'Argentea Regina'*) LS (E)
Dark green leaves, grey marbling, creamy
white margins. Purple young shoots. Male.
–**cornuta** MS (E)
Unusual rectangular leaves, generally 5-
spined. Large red berries. Slow.
––**'Burfordii'** SS (E)
Glossy leaves with single terminal spine. Free
fruiting.
–**crenata** SS (E)
Tiny leaves. Small, shiny black berries. Slow.
We recommend the forms:

––**'Convexa'** SS (E)
Free fruiting. Excellent low hedge.
––**'Golden Gem'** DS (E)
Yellow leaves.
–**fargesii** LS (E)
Narrow oblong leaves. Small red berries. AM
1926
–**'Jermyns Dwarf'** DS (E)
Mound-like habit. Arching stems. Dark green,
spiny leaves. Female.
–**kingiana** (*insignis*) (*nobilis*) ST (E) ♥ †
Leathery, few spined, leaves – very spiny on
young plants. Large red fruits. AM 1964
– × **koehneana** LS (E)
Purple-tinged young shoots. Glossy dark
green leaves. Large red berries on female
plants. We recommend the form:
––**'Chestnut Leaf'** (*castaneifolia* HORT)
Thick, yellowish-green leaves, with strong
spines.

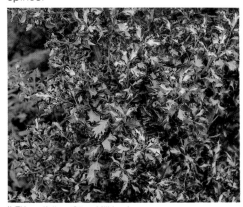

ILEX aquifolium 'Silver Milkboy'

–**latifolia** ST (E) ♥
Huge, glossy dark green leaves, oblong with
serrated margins. Abundant scarlet berries.
AM 1952 (foliage and fruit) AM 1977 (flowers)
–**'Lydia Morris'** MS (E)
Compact pyramidal habit. Glossy, strongly
spiny leaves. Large red berries.
–**pernyi** ST (E) ♦
Small, almost triangular, spined leaves. Small
bright red fruits. FCC 1908
–**verticillata** (*Prinos verticillatus*) LS ⨍
Deciduous. Purple-tinged leaves, yellow in
autumn. Bright red fruits. AM 1962. We
recommend the form:
––**'Christmas Cheer'** LS ⨍
Female form with abundant persistent fruits.

ILLICIUM – Illiciaceae MS (E) ◑
Aromatic shrubs with unusual many petalled flowers.
– **anisatum** (*religiosum*) MS (E) ◑
Thick, fleshy, glossy leaves. Pale yellow flowers, spring. AM 1930
  floridanum MS (E) ◑
Broadly oval, leathery leaves. Maroon-purple flowers, May-June.

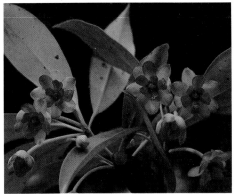

ILLICIUM henryi
– **henryi** MS (E) ◑
Shiny, leathery leaves. Bright rose flowers.
"INDIAN BEAN TREE" see *CATALPA bignonioides*

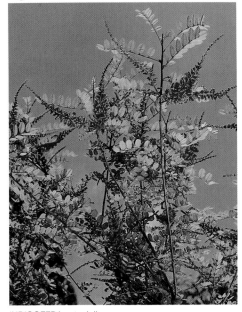

INDIGOFERA potaninii

INDIGOFERA – Leguminosae SS-MS ○
Pinnate leaves. Racemes of flowers in leaf axils of growing shoots, all summer and autumn. All soils. Excellent on dry sites. A (b) 4
– **hebepetala** MS ○
Spreading habit. Rose coloured flowers with crimson standard.
– **heterantha** (*gerardiana*) SS ○
Bright purple-pink flowers. AM 1977
– **potaninii** MS ○
Clear pink flowers continuously June to September.
– **pseudotinctoria** SS ○
Dense racemes of pink flowers. Vigorous. AM 1965
"IRONWOOD" see *OSTRYA virginiana*
ITEA – Iteaceae SS-MS ◑
Unusual evergreen and deciduous shrubs. Summer flowering.

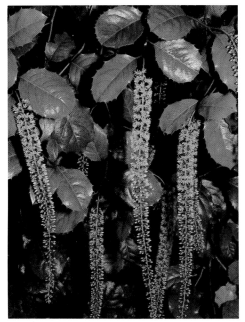

ITEA ilicifolia

– **ilicifolia** MS (E) ◑
Lax, holly-like shrub. Drooping racemes of fragrant, greenish-white flowers, late summer. AM 1911
– **virginica** SS ✗ ◑
Deciduous. Leaves often colour well, autumn. Upright racemes of fragrant, creamy-white flowers, July. AM 1972

JASMINUM – Oleaceae DS-MS "Jasmine"
"Jessamine"
More or less deciduous. Green stems. Bright yellow flowers. All soils. For climbing species see under CLIMBERS.
– **humile** (*farreri*) (*pubigerum*) MS Semi-(E)
Semi-climbing growth. Trifoliolate leaves.
Terminal clusters of flowers, June-July. We recommend the form:
– – **'Revolutum'** (*J. revolutum*) MS (E)
Deep green leaves, with 5 to 7 leaflets.
Slightly scented flowers, in cymose clusters, summer.

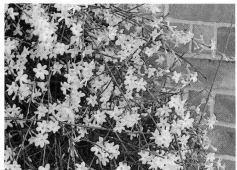
JASMINUM nudiflorum

– **nudiflorum** MS "Winter Jasmine"
Bright yellow flowers on naked green branches, November-February. Excellent against walls. AGM 1923 C2 or 3
– **parkeri** DS
Mound-like habit. Small pinnate leaves. Small flowers, summer. Ideal for rock garden.
AM 1933
– **subhumile** see CLIMBERS
"JERUSALEM SAGE" see *PHLOMIS fruticosa*
JOVELLANA – Scrophulariaceae DS-SS
† ◑
Attractive shrubs flowering June-July.
– **violacea** (*Calceolaria violacea*) SS (E) † ◑
Small neat leaves. Pale violet flowers with darker markings. AM 1930
"JUDAS TREE" see *CERCIS siliquastrum*

JUGLANS – Juglandaceae ST-LT ♣
"Walnuts"
Often large, pinnate leaves. Generally fast growing, all soils, but site where late frosts unable to damage emerging foliage.
– **ailantifolia** (*sieboldiana*) MT ♣
Large handsome leaves, up to 1m long.
– **cinerea** MT ♣ "Butternut"
Large hairy leaves. Sticky shoots. Large fruits.
– **microcarpa** (*rupestris*) ST ♣ "Texan Walnut"
Graceful shrubby tree. Numerous thin narrow leaflets.
– **nigra** LT ♣ "Black Walnut"
Deeply furrowed bark. Large leaves. Large round fruits.

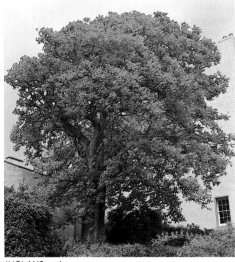
JUGLANS regia

– **regia** LT ♣ "Common Walnut"
Slow growing, valuable timber tree. Clones which will fruit at an early age are also available.
– – **'Laciniata'** LT ♣ "Cut-leaved Walnut"
Deeply cut leaflets. Pendulous branchlets.
AM 1960
"JUNE BERRY" see *AMELANCHIER*

KALMIA – Ericaceae DS-MS ✗ ◑
Conspicuous saucer-shaped flowers, spring-early summer. Moist soil for maximum flowering.
– angustifolia SS (E) ✗ ◑
Spreading habit. Leaves in twos or threes. Rose-red flowers, June. We recommend the form:
– – 'Rubra' SS (E) ✗ ◑
Deep green foliage. Rich rosy flowers, over long period.

– latifolia MS (E) ✗ ◑ "Calico Bush"
Rhododendron-like shrub with shiny leaves. Clusters of bright pink flowers, June. AGM 1948
– – 'Clementine Churchill' MS (E) ✗ ◑
Form with red flowers. AM 1952 AGM 1969
– polifolia (*glauca*) DS (E) ✗ ◑
Wiry shrub with narrow leaves. Terminal clusters of bright rose-purple flowers, April.

KALMIA latifolia

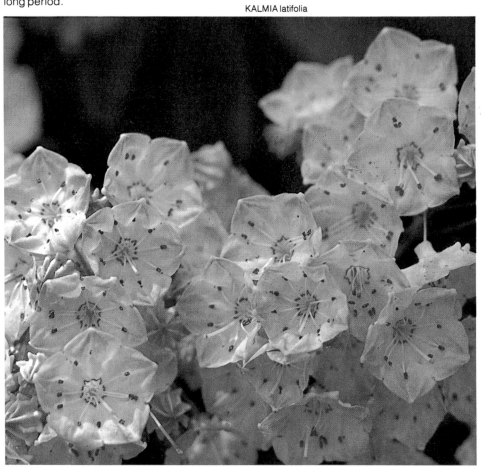

KALMIOPSIS – Ericaceae DS (E) ✗ ◑
Monotypic genus with kalmia-like blooms.
– **leacheana** DS (E) ✗ ◑
Rare, choice shrub. Terminal, leafy racemes
of pink flowers, March-May. AM 1937
KALOPANAX – Araliaceae ST ♥
*Monotypic genus, with 5-7 lobed leaves, over
30cm across in young plants.*
– **pictus** (*septemlobus*) (*Acanthopanax
ricinifolius*) ST ♥
Branches and suckers bear stout prickles.
Clusters of white flowers in flattish heads,
autumn.
"KENTUCKY COFFEE TREE" see
GYMNOCLADUS dioica
KERRIA – Rosaceae SS-MS ○
*Monotypic genus. Suckering shrub with
alternate leaves and yellow flowers, April-
May. May be thinned and pruned after
flowering.*
– **japonica** MS ○
Green stems. Arching branches. Rich yellow,
buttercup-like flowers. AGM 1928

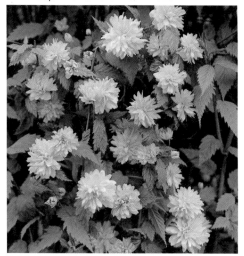

KERRIA japonica 'Pleniflora'

– – **'Pleniflora'** (*'Flore Pleno'*)MS ○
Double flowered form. Taller and more
vigorous than type. AGM 1925 AM 1978
– – **'Variegata'** (*'Picta'*) SS ○
Spreading habit. Creamy-white variegated
leaves.
KOELREUTERIA – Sapindaceae ST-MT ♥
*Long pinnate leaves. Large panicles of small
yellow flowers, July-August. All soils.*

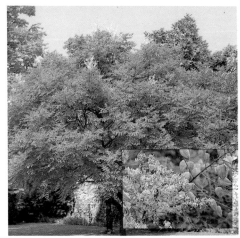

KOELREUTERIA paniculata (with flower and fruit detail)

– **paniculata** MT ♥ "Pride of India" "China-
tree" "Golden rain-tree"
Flowers followed by bladder-like fruits.
Leaves turn yellow, autumn. AM 1932
– – **'Fastigiata'** ST ❶
Narrow columnar habit. Slow.
KOLKWITZIA – Caprifoliaceae MS ○
*Monotypic genus. Graceful, twiggy bush, with
peeling brown stems. Delightful fox-glove-like
flowers.* D (h) 2 or 7

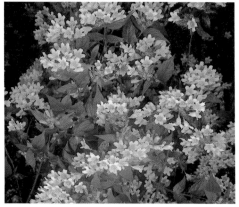

KOLKWITZIA amabilis

– **amabilis** MS ○ "Beauty Bush"
Drooping branches laden with soft pink,
yellow-throated flowers, May-June. AM 1923.
– – **'Pink Cloud'** MS ○
Superb pink-flowered seedling. '*Rosea*' is a
similar clone. FCC 1963 AGM 1965

+ **LABURNOCYTISUS** (*LABURNUM +
CYTISUS*) – **Leguminosae** ST ♥
*Graft hybrid (chimera) with laburnum as the
core, enclosed by broom.*
– **adamii** ST ♥
Branches bear either yellow laburnum flowers
or clusters of purple broom. Also intermediate
coppery-pink flowers produced.
LABURNUM – Leguminosae ST ♥ "Golden
Rain"
*Yellow pea flowers in drooping racemes, late
spring-early summer. Poisonous seeds. All
soils; particularly good on dry shallow chalk.*
– **alpinum** ST ♥ "Scotch Laburnum"
Shiny, green leaves, paler and sparsely hairy
beneath. Long drooping flower racemes,
early June. Shiny flattened pods.
– **anagyroides** (*vulgare*) ST ♥ "Common
Laburnum"
Dull green leaves, hairy beneath. Flowers late
May-early June. Hairy pods.
– – **'Aureum'** ST ♥ "Golden-leaved
Laburnum"
Soft yellow leaves. FCC 1875
– – **'Pendulum'** ST ♠
Long slender drooping branches.
– × **watereri** (*'Parkesii'*) ST ♥
Glossy leaves. Long slender racemes, June.
We recommend the form:
– – **'Vossii'** ST ♥
Free flowering, long racemes. Produces little
seed. AGM 1928
"LABURNUM, EVERGREEN" see
PIPTANTHUS laburnifolius
LAGERSTROEMIA – Lythraceae LS-ST
† ○
*Large genus, some evergreen, requiring
warm, sunny well-drained site. Only one
species in general cultivation:*
– **indica** LS † ○ "Crape Myrtle"
Main stem mottled pink, grey and cinnamon.
Lilac-pink flowers in terminal panicles,
autumn, opening after a long hot summer.
AM 1924
– – **'Rosea'** LS † ○
Deep pink flowers.

"LAUREL, ALEXANDRIAN" see *DANAE
racemosa*
"LAUREL, CALIFORNIAN" see
UMBELLULARIA californica
"LAUREL, COMMON" or **"CHERRY"** see
PRUNUS laurocerasus
"LAUREL, PORTUGAL" see *PRUNUS
lusitanica*
LAURUS – Lauraceae LS (E)
*Small, yellow, dioecious flowers, April. Shiny
black fruits on female trees. All well-drained
soils.*
– **nobilis** LS (E) ○ Hdg (0.5m) "Sweet Bay"
"Bay Laurel"
Dense, pyramidal habit. Glossy dark green,
wavy margined leaves – aromatic when
crushed, used for flavouring. Excellent
coastal hedge.

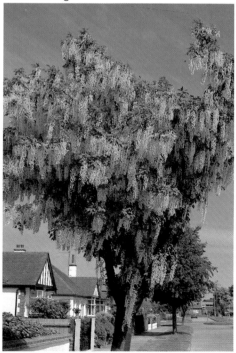

LABURNUM × watereri 'Vossii'

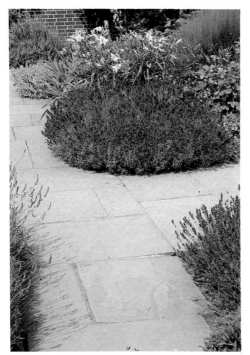

LAVANDULA as an edging to paved areas

– – **angustifolia** (*'Salicifolia'*) LS (E) ◁
"Willow-leaf Bay"
Long narrow pale green leaves.
– – **'Aurea'** LS (E) ◑
Golden-yellow leaves.
"LAURUSTINUS" see *VIBURNUM tinus*
LAVANDULA – Labiatae DS-SS (E) ○
"Lavender"
Aromatic shrubs. Excellent maritime plants, good dwarf hedging. All well-drained soils.
(j) 8 or (c) 3 *Spring pruning preferable*
– **angustifolia** (*spica* in part) SS (E) ○ "Old English Lavender"
Flowers on long stems in dense spikes.
AMT 1962. Several clones are recommended.
– – **'Alba'** SS (E) ○
Robust. Long, narrow grey-green leaves.
White flowers, late July.
– – **'Grappenhall'** SS (E) ○
Robust. Broad grey-green leaves. Lavender-blue flowers, late July.
– – **'Hidcote'** SS (E) ○
Compact. Narrow, grey-green leaves. Violet flowers, early July. AM 1950 FCCT 1963
AGM 1965

– – **'Munstead'** DS (E) ○
Compact. Narrow, green leaves. Lavender-blue flowers, early July. AMT 1963
– – **'Nana Alba'** DS (E) ○
Compact. Broad, grey-green leaves. White flowers, early July.
– – **'Rosea'** SS (E) ○
Compact. Narrow, green leaves. Soft pink flowers, early-mid July.
– – **'Vera'** SS (E) ○ "Dutch Lavender"
Robust. Broad, grey leaves. Lavender-blue flowers, early July. AMT 1962
– **lanata** DS (E) † ○
White-woolly leaves and stems. Fragrant, bright violet flowers, July-September.
– **spica** see *L. angustifolia*
– **stoechas** DS (E) ○ "French Lavender"
Narrow leaves. Dark purple flowers in terminal heads, summer. AM 1960
LAVATERA – Malvaceae MS ○
Palmate leaves. Hollyhock-like flowers. All soils. Excellent for coastal sites.
– **olbia 'Rosea'** MS ○
Downy grey stems and leaves. Large pink-red flowers, summer. AM 1912
"LAVENDER" see *LAVANDULA*
LEDUM – Ericaceae DS (E) ↙ ◑
Neat leaves, woolly-white or rust beneath. White flowers in terminal clusters.
– **buxifolium** see *LEIOPHYLLUM buxifolium*
– **groenlandicum** (*latifolium*) DS (E) ↙ ◑
"Labrador Tea"
Conspicuous flowers, April-June.
– **palustre** DS (E) ↙ ◑ "Wild Rosemary"
Variable species. Flowers, April-May. We recommend the form:
– – **dilatatum** (*hypoleucum*) (*nipponicum*) DS (E) ↙ ◑
Dark green, oval leaves, rusty beneath.
AM 1938
LEIOPHYLLUM – Ericaceae DS (E) ↙
Monotypic genus. Small, glabrous, box-like leaves.
– **buxifolium** (*Ledum buxifolium*) DS (E) ↙ ◑
Compact, rounded habit. Clusters of white flowers, May-June. AM 1955
– – **prostratum** DS (E) ↙ ◑ GC
Loosely spreading or prostrate form. AM 1945
"LEMON PLANT" see *LIPPIA citriodora*
LEPTOSPERMUM – Myrtaceae PS-MS (E) ○
Small leaves. Generally white flowers, May-June. Well drained neutral or acid soil.

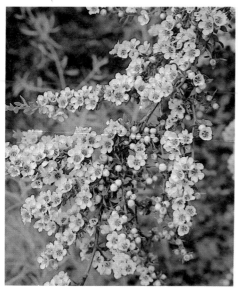

LEPTOSPERMUM cunninghamii

–cunninghamii MS (E) ○
Silvery-grey leaves, reddish stems. Flowers, July. Hardy. AM 1959
–humifusum (*scoparium prostratum* HORT) PS (E) ○
Carpet of reddish stems and small leathery leaves. Small flowers on older plants. Very hardy.
–lanigerum (*pubescens*) SS (E) ○
Long silvery leaves, bronzing towards autumn. Hardier than most.
–scoparium MS (E) † ○ "Manuka" "Tea-tree"
Flowers single, white. AM 1972
This species has given rise to many forms, the best of which are the following.
––'Chapmanii' MS (E) † ○
Brownish-green leaves. Bright rose flowers.
––'Keatleyi' MS (E) † ○
Young shoots and leaves, silky crimson. Large, soft pink flowers. AM 1961
––'Nanum' DS (E) † ○
Rose-pink flowers. Free flowering. AM 1952
––'Nichollsii Grandiflorum' MS (E) † ○
Dark purplish-bronze foliage. Large carmine red flowers.
––prostratum see *L. humifusum*
––'Red Damask' MS (E) † ○
Deep red, double, persistent flowers. AM 1955

LESPEDEZA – Leguminosae SS-MS ○
"Bush Clover"
Trifoliolate leaves. Abundant racemes of pea-flowers, late summer.
–bicolor MS ○
Bright rose-purple flowers. Semi-erect habit.

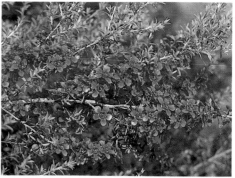

LEPTOSPERMUM scoparium 'Nichollsii Grandiflorum'

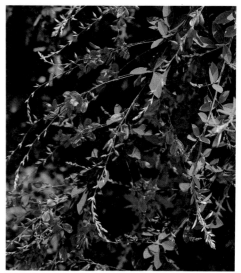

LESPEDEZA thunbergii

–thunbergii (*sieboldii*) (*Desmodium penduliflorum*) SS ◑
Arching stems. Huge panicles of rose-purple flowers, September. FCC 1871
LEUCOTHOE – Ericaceae DS-SS ✗
Attractive summer flowering shrubs. Some members evergreen.
–davisiae (*Andromeda davisiae*) DS (E) ✗
Shiny dark green leaves. Erect panicles of white flowers, June. FCC 1883

– **fontanesiana** (*catesbaei* HORT) SS (E)
✗ GC
Arching stems. Leathery leaves, tinged red or
bronze – purple in winter. Pendant, white
pitcher flowers, May. AM 1972
– –**'Nana'** SS (E) ✗ GC
More compact habit. Lower growing.
– –**'Rainbow'** (*'Multicolor'*) SS (E) ✗ GC
Leaves variegated yellow, pink and cream.
– **grayana** SS Semi-(E) ✗
Stout green stems, deep red in winter.
Leaves, bronze-purple in autumn. Pale green
flowers, July-August.
– **keiskei** SS (E) ✗ GC
Arching, red tinged shoots. Cylindrical white
flowers in nodding racemes, July. AM 1933
LEYCESTERIA – Caprifoliaceae MS ○
Hollow stemmed shrubs. All fertile soils.

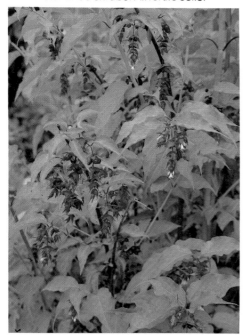

LEYCESTERIA formosa

– **formosa** MS ○ "Flowering Nutmeg"
"Pheasant Berry"
White flowers in drooping panicles of claret-
red bracts, June-September. Shiny, reddish-
purple berries. B3
LIGUSTRUM – Oleaceae MS-ST ♥ "Privets"
Evergreen or semi-evergreen, for all soils.
Generally white flowers. Fast growing.

– **chenaultii** LS Semi-(E)
Narrow, lance-shaped leaves. Flowers in
large panicles, late summer.

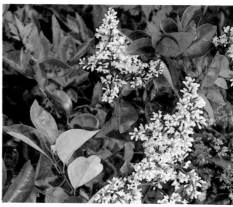

LIGUSTRUM japonicum

– **japonicum** LS (E)   "Japanese Privet"
Shiny, olive-green, camellia-like foliage.
Large panicles of flowers, late summer.
Excellent for screening.
– –**'Macrophyllum'** LS (E)
Black-green broad shiny leaves.
– –**'Rotundifolium'** (*'Coriaceum'*) MS (E)
Round, leathery, black-green leaves.
Compact habit. Slow.
– **lucidum** ST (E) ♥
Shiny, long pointed, large leaves. Large
panicles of flowers, autumn. AM 1965
AGM 1973

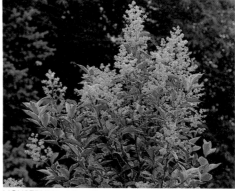

LIGUSTRUM lucidum 'Excelsum Superbum'

– –**'Excelsum Superbum'** ST (E) ♥
Leaves variegated creamy-white and deep
yellow. AGM 1973

––**'Tricolor'** ST (E) ♥
Narrow leaves margined white, tinged pink,
when young. AGM 1973
– **ovalifolium** LS (E) Hdg (0.5m) "Oval-leaf
Privet"
Commonly grown species. Useful for
hedging. Loses leaves in cold areas.
––**'Aureum'** MS ○ "Golden Privet"
Rich yellow leaves, generally green centred.
AGM 1973 AM 1977
– **quihoui** MS
Large flower panicles, August-September.
Elegant habit.
– **sinense** LS
Oval leaves. Dense sprays of flowers, July.
Black-purple fruits. We recommend the form:
––**'Variegatum'** LS
Soft grey-green leaves, margined white.
– **vulgare** MS Hdg (0.5m) "Common Privet"
Conspicuous shiny black fruits in long
clusters, autumn.
"LILAC" see *SYRINGA*
"LIME" see *TILIA*
LINDERA – Lauraceae MS ∠ ◑
Aromatic shrubs. Small unisexual flowers.
Attractive leaves.

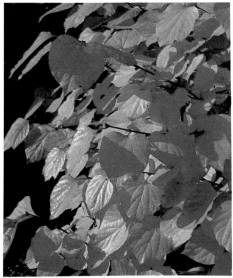

LINDERA benzoin

– **benzoin** (*Benzoin aestivale*) MS ∠ ◑
"Spice Bush"
Leaves turn clear yellow, autumn. Yellowish
green flowers. Red berries on female plants.

– **obtusiloba** MS ∠ ◑
Large ovate or obovate leaves, butter-yellow
with rich pink tints in autumn. Mustard-yellow
flowers, early spring. AM 1952
"LING" see *CALLUNA*
LINUM – Linaceae DS ○
Glaucous leaves. Yellow flowers, summer.
Ideal for rock garden. Good drainage.
– **arboreum** DS (E) ○
Spreading shrub with narrow leaves. Loose
terminal clusters of golden flowers.
LIPPIA (*ALOYSIA*) – **Verbenaceae** MS ⊺ ○
Large genus, of which only one shrubby
species is commonly cultivated.
– **citriodora** MS ⊺ ○ "Lemon Plant"
Lemon-scented, lanceolate leaves. Tiny, pale
purple flowers, August.
LIQUIDAMBAR – Hamamelidaceae ST-LT ♥
♥ ∠
Generally 5-lobed, maple-like leaves,
colouring richly in autumn. Insignificant
flowers. Prefer moist, well drained soil. Not for
shallow chalk.
– **formosana** ST ♥ ∠
Leaves tinted red in spring and again in
autumn. We recommend the form:
––**monticola** ST ♥ ∠
Large 3-lobed leaves, colouring well in
autumn. AM 1958
– **styraciflua** LT ♥ ∠ "Sweet Gum"
Handsome tree. Glossy, maple-like leaves
turn shades of crimson and purple in autumn.
––**'Aurea'** MT ♥ ∠
Leaves blotched and striped yellow.
––**'Golden Treasure'** MT ♥ ∠
Leaves conspicuously margined golden
yellow.
––**'Lane Roberts'** LT ♥ ∠
Reliable rich black crimson-red autumn leaf
colour.
––**'Variegata'** MT ♥ ∠
Leaf margins creamy-white, flushed rose in
late summer.
LIRIODENDRON – Magnoliaceae MT-LT ♥
"Tulip Tree"
Fast growing trees for all fertile soils –
including chalk. Distinctive lobed leaves turn
clear yellow, in autumn.
– **chinense** MT ♥
Similar to *L. tulipifera*. Narrower waisted
leaves, more glaucous beneath. Smaller
green flowers with yellow inside. AM 1980

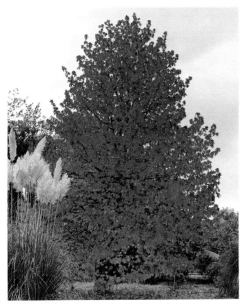

LIQUIDAMBAR styraciflua 'Lane Roberts'

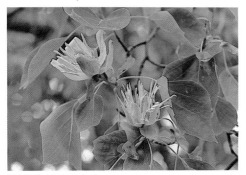

LIRIODENDRON tulipfera

– tulipifera LT ♥ "Tulip Tree"
Tulip-shaped flowers, yellowish-green with
orange internal markings, June-July – not on
young trees. AM 1970 AGM 1973
– – 'Aureomarginatum' MT ♥
Leaves margined yellow or greenish-yellow.
AM 1974
– – 'Fastigiatum' (*'Pyramidale'*) MT ❢
Columnar form, ideal for limited spaces.
LITHOCARPUS – Fagaceae ST (E) ♥ ⚋
Evergreen trees related to Quercus.
– edulis (*Quercus edulis*) ST (E) ♥ ⚋
Glabrous young shoots. Leathery glabrous
leaves, yellowish-green above, scaly when
young.

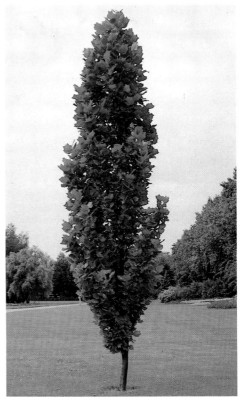

LIRIODENDRON tulipfera 'Fastigiatum'

– henryi (*Quercus henryi*) ST (E) ♥ ⚋
Very long, lanceolate, slender pointed leaves.
Slow. A remarkable hardy tree.
LITHOSPERMUM – Boraginaceae PS-DS ○
*Low growing, blue flowered plants. Ideal for
rock garden.*
– diffusum (*prostratum*) PS (E) ⚋ ○
Forms a large mat, smothered in flowers, late
spring-early summer. Not for shallow chalk.
We recommend the forms:
– – 'Heavenly Blue' PS (E) ⚋ ○
Delightful blue flowers. AM 1909 AGM 1925
– oleifolium PS (E) ○
Semi-prostrate. Azure bell-shaped flowers,
June-September. AM 1938
– petraeum see *MOLTKIA petraea*
– rosmarinifolium DS † ○
Rosemary-like, with narrow leaves and bright
blue flowers, winter-early spring.
"LOBSTER'S CLAW" see *CLIANTHUS
puniceus*

LOMATIA – Proteaceae SS-LS (E) ⚊ ◑
Attractive flower and foliage shrubs, excellent for floral art. Not for shallow chalk.
– ferruginea LS (E) † ⚊ ◑
Large, deep green, fern-like leaves. Rust coloured velvety stems. Buff and scarlet flowers. AM 1927

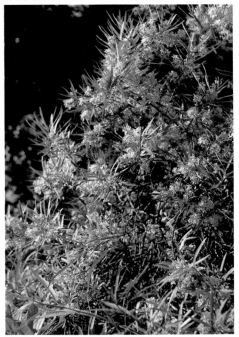

LOMATIA myricoides

– myricoides (*longifolia*) MS (E) ⚊ ◑
Long, narrow, toothed leaves. Fragrant white flowers, July. AM 1955
– silaifolia SS (E) ⚊ ◑
Finely divided leaves. Large panicles of creamy-white flowers, July.
– tinctoria SS (E) ⚊ ◑
Suckering shrub. Pinnate or doubly pinnate leaves. Creamy-white flowers, deep yellow in bud. AM 1948
"LOMBARDY POPLAR" see *POPULUS nigra 'Italica'*
"LONDON PLANE" see *PLATANUS × hispanica*
LONICERA – Caprifoliaceae DS-MS
Shrubby honeysuckles. Flowers in pairs, followed by completely or partially fused berries. All soils. For climbing species see CLIMBERS.

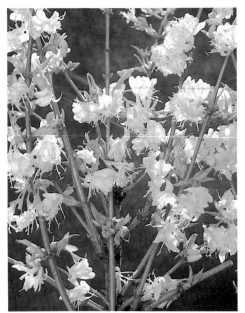

LONICERA fragrantissima

– chaetocarpa MS
Bristly stems and leaves. Primrose yellow flowers with two conspicuous bracts, May-June. Red berries. Erect habit. A (g) 3 or 7

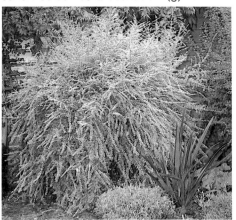

LONICERA nitida 'Baggesen's Gold'

– fragrantissima MS Semi-(E)
Fragrant cream flowers, late winter-spring. Red berries, May. A (g) 3 or 7
– nitida MS (E) Hdg (0.25m)
Dense habit. Small leaves. Useful for hedging. We recommend the clones:

--**'Baggesen's Gold'** MS (E)
Yellow leaves, turning yellow-green in
autumn.
--**'Elegant'** SS (E)
Arching shoots. Glossy bright green leaves.
--**'Ernest Wilson'** MS (E) Hdg (0.25m)
Arching branches. Tiny ovate leaves. This is
the form commonly used for hedging.
AM 1911

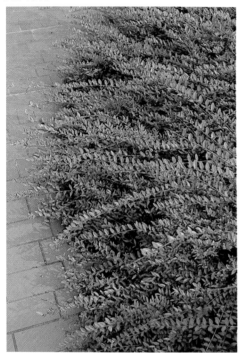

LONICERA pileata

-**pileata** DS Semi-(E) GC
Small, bright green leaves. Clusters of
translucent violet berries. AM 1910
-× **purpusii** MS Semi-(E)
Vigorous. Cream coloured, fragrant flowers,
winter. AM 1971 A (g) 3 or 7
--**'Winter Beauty'** MS Semi-(E)
Free flowering over a long period. A (g) 3 or 7
-**pyrenaica** SS ○
Small sea-green leaves. Cream and pink
funnel-shaped nodding flowers. May-June.
Orange red berries. AM 1928 A (g) 3 or 7
-**setifera** MS
Bristly stems. Clusters of fragrant, tubular pink
and white flowers on bare stems, winter-early
spring. A (g) 3 or 7 AM 1980

-**standishii** MS Semi-(E)
Bristly stems. Fragrant, winter flowers. Red
berries, June. A (g) 3 or 7
-**syringantha** SS
Small leaves. Fragrant, tubular, soft lilac
flowers, May-June. A (g) 3 or 7
-**tatarica** MS
Vigorous. Abundant pink flowers, May-June.
Red berries. A (g) 3 or 7
We recommend the form:
--**'Hack's Red'** MS
Rose-pink flowers. A (g) 3 or 7
"LOQUAT" see *ERIOBOTRYA japonica*
LUCULIA – Rubiaceae MS ↑ ○
*Delightful shrubs for conservatory or mildest
gardens.*
-**gratissima** MS Semi-(E) ↑ ○
Fragrant almond-pink flowers, winter.
AM 1938
LUPINUS – Leguminosae MS ○
Shrubby lupins
-**arboreus** MS (E) ○ "Yellow Tree Lupin"
Scented flowers in dense racemes,
throughout summer. Fast growth. We
recommend the forms:
--**'Golden Spire'** MS (E) ○
Deep yellow flowers.
--**'Snow Queen'** MS (E) ○
White flowers. AM 1899
LYCIUM-Solanceae MS ○
*Rambling shrubs. Small, generally violet
flowers. Conspicuous berries. Excellent
coastal plants.*
-**barbarum** (*halimifolium*) (*chinense*)
(*europaeum* HORT) MS ○
"Duke of Argyll's Tea Tree"
Purple flowers, June-September. Egg-
shaped orange or scarlet small berries. The
form '*Carnosum*' has pink flowers.
LYONIA – Ericaceae MS ⋋ ◑
Closely related to Pieris.
-**ligustrina** (*Andromeda paniculata*) MS
⋋ ◑
White pitcher-shaped flowers in panicles,
July-August. Moist peaty or sandy loam.
LYONOTHAMNUS – Rosaceae ST (E)
❢ ↑ ⋋
Monotypic genus.
-**floribundus asplenifolius** ST (E) ❢ ↑ ⋋
Chestnut brown and grey shreddy bark.
Glossy, green, fern-like leaves, grey, hairy
beneath. Slender spiraea-like panicles of
creamy-white flowers, early summer.

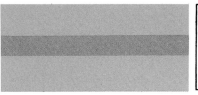

MAACKIA – Leguminosae ST ♥
Slow growing trees related to Cladrastis.
– amurensis (*Cladrastis amurensis*) ST ♥
Pinnate leaves, white flowers tinged pale
slate-blue, in upright racemes, July-August.
MACLURA – Moraceae MT ♥
Monotypic genus. Dioecious.
– pomifera (*aurantiaca*) MT ♥ "Osage
Orange"
Thorny branches. Fleshy yellow roots. Large
pale yellow, orange-like fruits on mature
female trees.
"MADRONA" see *ARBUTUS menziesii*
MAGNOLIA – Magnoliaceae MS-LT
*Variety of forms, some evergreens. Include
magnificent flowering varieties. Require good
drainage, plenty of moisture. Very tolerant of
heavy clay and atmospheric pollution. Shelter
early flowering kinds from cold winds and
spring frosts. Flowers of deciduous species
produced before leaves, unless stated
otherwise.*

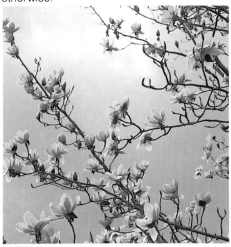

MAGNOLIA campbellii

– acuminata LT ♥ "Cucumber Tree"
Vigorous. Greenish, metallic blue and yellow
flowers with leaves, May-June. Cucumber-like
fruit clusters.

– auriculata see *M. fraseri*
– campbellii LT ♥ ⤱ "Pink Tulip Tree"
Large goblet–shaped flowers opening like
water lilies, February-March. Deep rose-pink
petals outside, paler within. Flowers not
produced until approximately twenty years
old. Colour variation from white to deep rose-
purple. FCC 1903
– – alba LT ♥ ⤱
Seed raised plants usually available, variable
white blooms. FCC 1951
– – 'Charles Raffill' LT ♥ ⤱
Vigorous. Large flowers, deep rose in bud
opening rose-purple outside, white flushed
marginally, pinkish-purple within. AM 1963
FCC 1966
– – 'Darjeeling' LT ♥ ⤱
Dark rose-coloured flowers.
– – 'Ethel Hillier' MT ♥ ⤱
Vigorous. Very large white flowers, tinged pink
at the base on outside.
– – 'Lanarth' (*williamsiana 'Lanarth'*) MT ♥ ⤱
Very large "water-lily" flowers, cyclamen-
purple with darker stamens. FCC 1947
– – mollicomata (*M. mollicomata*) MT ♥ ⤱
Very large pink to rose-purple "water-lily"
flowers, produced at ten to fifteen years of
age. FCC 1939
– – 'Princess Margaret' LT ♥ ⤱
Large flowers reddish-purple outside,
creamy-white marked with purple inside.
FCC 1973
– – 'Wakehurst' LT ♥ ⤱
Superb form resembling '*Charles Raffill*' but
flowers darker.
– 'Charles Coates' ST ♥ ⤱
Distinctive fragrant creamy-white flowers with
conspicuous reddish stamens, May-June
(with the leaves) AM 1973 AGM 1973
– conspicua see *M. denudata*
– cordata (*acuminata cordata*) ST ♥
Soft canary-yellow flowers produced in
summer with leaves, and again autumn.
– cylindrica LS ⤱ ○
Elegant white cup-shaped flowers, April.
Cylindrical fruits. AM 1963

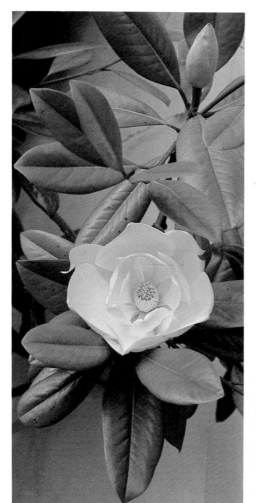

MAGNOLIA grandiflora 'Exmouth'

– **dawsoniana** MT ♀ ✗
Long leathery leaves, glaucous beneath.
Large pale-rose flowers, suffused purple
outside, spring – on mature trees. AM 1939
– **delavayi** LS (E) † ◑
Huge sea-green leaves, glaucous beneath.
Slightly fragrant, creamy-white flowers up to
20cm across, late summer-early autumn. Best
against a wall. FCC 1913
– **denudata** (*conspicua*) LS ✗ ○ "Yulan"
"Lily Tree"
Pure white, cup-shaped fragrant flowers with
thick fleshy petals, early spring. AGM 1936
FCC 1968

– **glauca** see *M. virginiana*
– **globosa** (*tsarongensis*) LS ○
Brown-felted buds, young shoots and
undersides of leaves. Fragrant, creamy-white,
somewhat globular flowers on stout felted
stems, June. AM 1931
– **grandiflora** LS (E) ○
Leathery, glossy leaves, often rust coloured
beneath. Huge, fragrant creamy-white flowers
up to 25cm across, summer-autumn.
Excellent wall shrub. We recommend the
forms:
– – **'Exmouth'** (*'Exoniensis'*) LS (E) ○
Very large flowers at an early age. AGM 1969
– – **'Goliath'** LS (E) ○
Shorter, broader leaves, green beneath. Very
large globular flowers, at an early age.
AM 1931 FCC 1951 AGM 1969
– – **'Purple Eye'** LS ✗ ○
Wide spreading habit. Large, fragrant, white
flowers, stained purple at base of inner petals.
– **fraseri** (*auriculata*) MT ♀ ✗
Rare, leaves up to 40cm long. Large,
parchment-coloured, slightly fragrant flowers,
produced May-June, with leaves. Rose-
coloured fruit clusters.

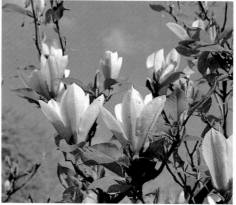

MAGNOLIA 'Heaven Sent'

– **'Heaven Sent'** MT ♀ ✗
Large white, goblet-shaped flowers, streaked
rose-purple on outside, spring.
– **hypoleuca** (*obovata*) MT ♀ ✗
Very large obovate leaves. Fragrant, creamy-
white flowers with central ring of red stamens,
June. Attractive large fruit clusters.
– **'Kewensis'** ST ♦
Slender habit. White flowers 6cm long, April.
AM 1952

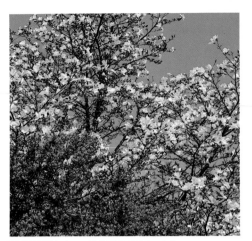

MAGNOLIA kobus with BERBERIS darwinii

– kobus ST ♥
Slightly fragrant, white flowers freely borne, April, after about 15 years. Tolerates chalk. AGM 1936 AM 1942
– × lennei see *M. × soulangiana 'Lennei'*
– liliiflora (*discolor*) (*purpurea*) MS ✗ ○
Wide spreading habit. Slender tulip-like flowers, creamy-white inside, flushed purple outside, late April-June and recurrently summer. AGM 1973
– – 'Nigra' MS ✗ ○
More compact. Dark vinous-purple flowers, creamy-white stained purple within. AM 1907 AGM 1969

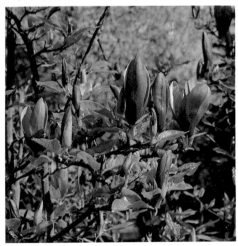

MAGNOLIA liliiflora 'Nigra'

– × loebneri 'Leonard Messel' LS ○
Lilac-pink flowers, deeper in bud, strap-like petals. AM 1955 FCC 1969
– – 'Merrill' LS ○
Large white, fragrant flowers, freely borne.
– macrophylla ST ♥ ✗
Enormous leaves sometimes exceeding 0.6m length. Very large, ivory coloured, fragrant flowers with central purple blotch, early summer. FCC 1900
– 'Manchu Fan' MT ♥ ✗
White, purple flushed, goblet-shaped flowers, spring.
– 'Maryland' LS (E)
Leaves like *M. grandiflora* but smaller, fragrant, creamy white small flowers, late summer-autumn.
– 'Michael Rosse' LT ♥ ✗
Large soft-purple flowers. AM 1968
– mollicomata see *M. campbellii mollicomata*
– nicholsoniana see *M. sinensis* and
M. wilsonii
– obovata see *M. hypoleuca*
– officinalis ST ♥ ✗
Yellowish-grey young shoots. Large, obovate leaves. Large, fragrant flowers, early summer. We recommend the form:
– – biloba ST ♥ ✗
Leaves deeply notched at apex. Parchment coloured, cup-shaped flowers with maroon centre.
– parviflora see *M. sieboldii*
– 'Peppermint Stick' LT ♥ ✗
Upright habit. White narrowly goblet-shaped flowers, flushed pale purple at base.
– purpurea see *M. liliiflora*
– salicifolia ST ♦ ✗
Narrow willow-like leaves. Fragrant, white, narrow-petalled flowers, April. Leaves, bark and wood lemon scented when bruised. AM 1927 AGM 1941 FCC 1962
– – 'Jermyns' LS ✗ ○
Broader leaves, glaucous beneath. Larger flowers.
– sargentiana MT ♥ ✗
Leathery leaves. Huge, rose-pink, water-lily-like flowers, paler pink inside produced April-May on mature specimens. FCC 1935
– – robusta MT ♥ ✗
Longer narrower leaves. Rose-crimson flowers, paler inside. Larger fruits. FCC 1947
– 'Sayonara' LT ♥ ✗
Superb large white globular flowers.

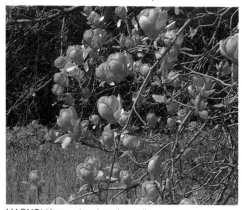

– – **'Nigra'** see *M. liliiflora 'Nigra'*

– – **'Picture'** LS ✗ ○

Large leaves. Vinous-purple flowers, white inside. Vigorous, erect habit. AM 1969

– – **'Rustica Rubra'** (*'Rubra'*) LS ✗ ○

Vigorous. Rich rosy-red cup-shaped flowers. AM 1960 AGM 1969

– **sprengeri** (*sprengeri diva*) (*denudata purpurascens*) MT ♥ ✗

Goblet-shaped, fragrant, rose-carmine flowers, April. AM 1942

– – **elongata** LS ✗ ○

Pure white flowers, narrower petals. AM 1955

MAGNOLIA × soulangiana 'Lennei'

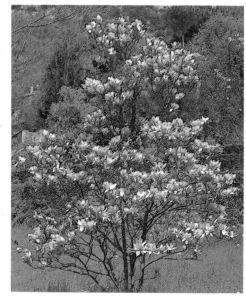

MAGNOLIA × soulangiana 'Rustica Rubra'

MAGNOLIA sieboldii

– **sieboldii** (*parviflora*) LS ✗ ○

Wide-spreading. Fragrant, cup-shaped, pendent flowers, white with crimson stamens, produced with leaves intermittently May-August. Spectacular crimson fruit clusters. FCC 1894 AGM 1935

– **sinensis** (*globosa sinensis*) (*nicholsoniana* HORT) LS ○

Lemon-scented, white nodding flowers, with central red staminal cone, produced with leaves, June. AM 1927 FCC 1931 AGM 1969

– × **soulangiana** LS ✗ ○

Wide spreading. Large tulip-shaped white flowers stained rose-purple at the base, April-early May before the leaves. Flowers when young. Not for shallow chalk. AGM 1932

– – **'Alba Superba'** (*'Alba'*) LS ✗ ○

Fragrant white flowers. AGM 1969

– – **'Amabilis'** (*'Alba'*) LS ✗ ○

Ivory-white flowers, faint-purple flush at base of inner petals.

– – **'Brozzonii'** LS ✗ ○

Superb large white, elongated flowers, purple at the base. FCC 1929 AGM 1969

– – **'Lennei'** (*M. × lennei*) LS ✗ ○

Vigorous, spreading. Huge goblet-shaped rose-purple flowers, creamy-white stained soft purple inside, April-May and sometimes autumn. FCC 1863 AGM 1969

– – **'Lennei Alba'** LS ✗ ○

Globular ivory-white flowers.

– **stellata** (*halliana*) (*kobus stellata*) MS ○
Slow. Compact, rounded habit. Fragrant,
white flowers with strap-like petals, March-
April. FCC 1878 AGM 1923
– – **'Rosea'** MS ○
Pink flushed flowers, deeper in bud.

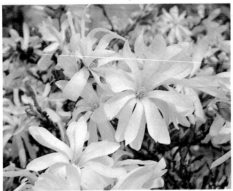
MAGNOLIA stellata 'Water Lily'

– – **'Water Lily'** MS ○
Larger flowers with more petals.
– **'Susan'** LS ⚹ ○
Erect habit. Flowers deep purple in bud,
opening white, stained purple, April-June.
– × **thompsoniana** LS ○
Wide spreading. Large, fragrant, parchment-
coloured flowers, intermittently through
summer – even on young plants. AM 1958
– **tripetala** MT ♥ ⚹ "Umbrella Tree"
Pungently scented, cream flowers, May-June.
Red, cone-shaped fruit clusters.
– × **veitchii** MT ♥ ⚹
Very vigorous. Goblet-shaped flowers. The
following is the original clone.
– – **'Peter Veitch'** MT ♥ ⚹
White flowers, flushed purple-pink, April.
FCC 1921
– **virginiana** (*glauca*) LS Semi-(E) ○ "Sweet
Bay" "Swamp Bay"
Fragrant, creamy-white, rather small globular
flowers, June-September.
– **'Wada's Memory'** ST ♥
Abundant, fragrant, white flowers.
– **wilsonii** (*nicholsoniana*) LS ◑
Wide spreading. Pendulous saucer-shaped
flowers, white, with crimson stamens, May-
June. AM 1932 FCC 1971
× **MAHOBERBERIS** (*MAHONIA* ×
BERBERIS) – **Berberidaceae** SS (E)
Hybrid for any soil and exposure.

– **aquisargentii** SS (E)
Dense habit. Variable dark green glossy
leaves, on slender stalks with regularly
spined, long leaves, or short stalks with
viciously spined, ovate-lanceolate leaves.
Terminal clusters of soft yellow flowers. Black
berries.
MAHONIA – Berberidaceae DS-ST (E)
*Attractive pinnate leaves. Racemes of yellow
flowers, winter or spring. Generally, blue-
black berries. Most well drained soils,
including chalk.*
– **acanthifolia** ST ♦ †
Erect habit. Enormous leaves in dense collars
at ends of stems. Clusters of slightly scented
mimosa-yellow flowers, autumn-winter.
AM 1953 FCC 1958

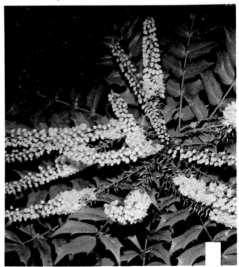
MAHONIA aquifolium

MAHONIA 'Charity'

– **aquifolium** SS (E) "Oregon Grape"
Glossy green leaves, sometimes red in winter.
Terminal clusters of rich yellow flowers, early
spring. Decorative berries. AGM 1930
– – **'Atropurpurea'** SS (E)
Rich red-purple leaves, winter-early spring.
– – **'Moseri'** SS (E)
Bronze-red young leaves turn through apple-
green to dark green.
– – **'Orangee Flame'** MS (E)
Young leaves rust orange in spring.
– **bealei** MS (E)
Short, erect racemes of flowers, winter.
AM 1916
– **'Buckland'** MS (E)
Long leaves, composed of paired leaflets.
Long, lax, flower racemes.
– **'Charity'** MS (E)
Upright. Long spreading and ascending
terminal racemes of fragrant flowers, autumn-
early winter. AM 1959 FCC 1962 AGM 1969
– **fortunei** MS (E) ◑
Slender erect habit. Distinctive matt-green,
lanceolate leaflets. Upright, slender, terminal
racemes, September-November.
– **fremontii** SS (E) ○
Blue-green leaves with small spiny leaflets.
Small flower clusters, May-June. Inflated
yellowish or red berries.
– **japonica** MS (E)
Magnificent deep-green leaves. Fragrant,
lemon-yellow flowers in long pendulous or lax
terminal racemes, late autumn-early spring.
AM 1916 AGM 1962
– **'Lionel Fortesque'** MS (E)
Bright yellow, fragrant flowers in erect
racemes in late autumn and winter.
– **lomariifolia** LS (E) † ◑
Erect habit. Long leaves with narrow, rigid,
paired leaflets. Erect, dense, terminal
racemes of deep yellow flowers, winter.
AM 1938 FCC 1939
– **'Moseri'** see *M. aquifolium 'Moseri'*
– **nervosa** DS ○
Suckering. Lustrous leaves, often reddening
in winter. Flower, May-June. Not good on
chalk.
– **pinnata** (*fascicularis*) MS (E)
Sea-green prickly leaflets. Racemes in
clusters along stems, late winter. AGM 1947
AM 1948
– **pumila** DS (E) ○
Neat habit. Sea-green, spiny edged leaflets.

Flowers, spring. Large clusters of bloomy
black fruits.
– **repens** DS (E)
Suckering. Matt-green leaflets. Terminal
flower racemes. We recommend the form:
– – **rotundifolia** SS (E)
Sea-green, spineless, rounded leaves. Large
plumes of rich yellow flowers, May. Black
bloomy berries.

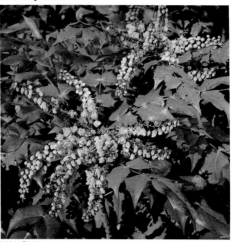
MAHONIA japonica

– **trifolioliata** MS (E) ○
Leaves of three spiny, heavily veined leaflets.
Flower clusters, spring. Redcurrant-like
berries. Best against a sunny wall. We
recommend the form:
– – **glauca** MS (E) ○
Leaflets conspicuously glaucous above.
– **'Undulata'** MS (E)
Lustrous, dark green leaves, leaflets having
undulate margins. Deep yellow flowers,
spring. AGM 1960 AM 1971
– **'Winter Sun'** MS (E)
Erect, dense racemes of fragrant, yellow
flowers.
"MAIDENHAIR TREE" see *GINKGO biloba*
under CONIFERS
MALUS – Rosaceae ST-MT ♥ "Flowering
Crabs"
*Attractive April-May flowering trees. Many
have attractive fruits in autumn, some
persisting late into winter. For all fertile soils.*
– × **atrosanguinea** ST ♥
Glossy-green leaves. Rose-pink flowers,
crimson in bud. Yellow fruits with red flush.

– **baccata** MT ♥ "Siberian Crab"
Fragrant white flowers. Small yellow or red berry-like fruits. We recommend the form:
– – **mandshurica** MT ♥
Fruits slightly larger. AM 1962 FCC 1969
– **coronaria** ST ♥
Strong growing. Large shell-pink, fragrant flowers, late May. Often richly coloured leaves, autumn. We recommend the form:
– – **'Charlottae'** (*'Flore Pleno'*) ST ♥
Large lobed leaves, colouring in autumn. Large semi-double flowers, violet scented.
– **'Crittenden'** ST ♥
Attractive pale pink flowers. Heavy crops of edible, bright scarlet, persistent fruits. AM 1961 FCC 1971
– **'Echtermeyer'** (*purpurea 'Pendula'*) ST ♠
Wide-spreading, weeping branches. Bronze green-purple leaves. Rose-crimson flowers, darker in bud. Reddish-purple fruits.
– **'Elise Rathke'** (*pumila 'Pendula'*) ST ♠
Pendulous branches. Large white flowers, pink in bud. Large yellow, edible fruits.

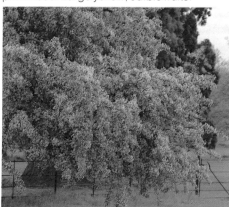

MALUS floribunda

– **floribunda** ST ♥ "Japanese Crab"
Long arching branches. Crimson flower buds opening white or blush. Small yellow and red fruits. AGM 1923
– **'Golden Hornet'** ST ♥
White flowers. Abundant bright yellow persistent fruits. AM 1949 FCC 1961 AGM 1969
– **halliana** ST ♥
Narrow, shiny, dark green leaves. Shell-pink flowers, carmine in bud. Small purple fruits. AM 1935. We recommend the form:

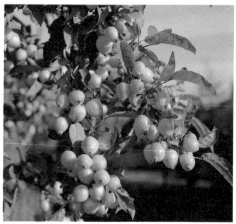

MALUS 'Golden Hornet'

– – **'Parkmanii'** ST ♥
Semi-double flowers hanging on deep crimson stalks.
– **'Hillieri'** ST ♥
Semi-double, bright pink flowers, crimson in bud, wreathing arching stems.

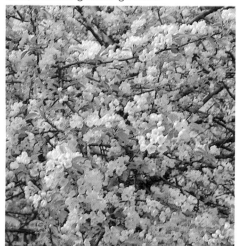

MALUS hupehensis

– **hupehensis** (*theifera*) ST ♥
Stiff, ascending branches. Abundant, fragrant, white flowers, soft pink in bud, May-June. Yellow fruits, red tinged. AM 1928 AGM 1930
– **'John Downie'** ST ♥
White flowers. Large, conical, edible fruits bright orange and red. AM 1895 AGM 1969

– **'Kaido'** see *M. × micromalus*
– **'Katherine'** ST ♥
Dense globular head. Semi-double, pink flowers, fading white. Bright red fruits, flushed yellow. AM 1967
– **'Lemoinei'** ST ♥
Purplish-green shoots and leaves. Deep wine-red flowers. AM 1928, AGM 1937
– × **micromalus** (*'Kaido'*) ST ♥
Clear deep-pink flowers. Small red or yellow fruits.
– **'Prince George's'** ST ♥
Light pink, fully double flowers, late.

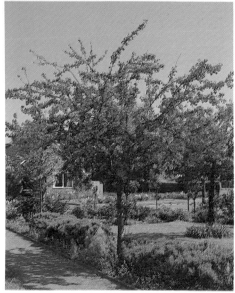

MALUS 'Profusion'

– **'Profusion'** ST ♥
Coppery-crimson young leaves. Abundant wine-red flowers, slightly fragrant. Small, dark red fruits. AGM 1969
– **pumila 'Pendula'** see *M. 'Elise Rathke'*
– × **purpurea 'Pendula'** see *M. 'Echtermeyer'*
– **'Red Jade'** ST ♠
Weeping branches. Pink and white flowers. Persistent red fruits.
– **'Red Sentinel'** ST ♥
White flowers. Large clusters of persistent deep red fruits. AM 1959
– × **robusta** MT ♥
White or pinkish flowers. Cherry-like red or yellow persistent fruits. AM 1957 AGM 1958
We recommend:

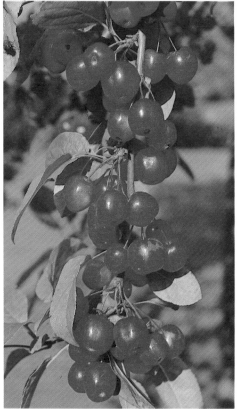

MALUS × robusta 'Red Siberian'

–– **'Red Siberian'** MT ♥
Red fruits.
–– **'Yellow Siberian'** MT ♥
Yellow fruits.
– **'Royalty'** ST ♥
Reddish-purple leaves. Crimson flowers. Dark red fruits.
– **sargentii** MS
Abundant white flowers with golden anthers, spring: Small red cherry-like fruits. AM 1915 AGM 1927
– **theifera** see *M. hupehensis*
– **transitoria** ST ♥
Slender habit. Creamy-white flowers. Small, rounded yellow fruits. Good autumn leaf colour.
– **trilobata** MT ♥
Distinctive erect habit. Maple-like, 3-lobed leaves, tinted in autumn. White flowers. Yellowish fruits, seldom produced.

149

–**tschonoskii** MT ❢

Erect conical habit. Excellent autumn leaf colour. White flowers, tinged pink. Yellow-green, round fruits, tinged reddish-purple. AM 1962

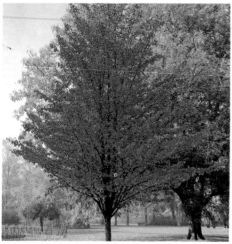

MALUS tschonoskii

–'**Van Eseltine**' ST ❢

Stiffly erect branches. Semi-double, shell pink flowers white within, rose-scarlet in bud. Yellow fruits.

–**yunnanensis** MT ♥

Ovate, occasionally lobed leaves, colouring well in autumn. White flowers. Deep red fruits. We recommend the form:

––**veitchii** MT ♥

Erect branches. Cordate, lobed leaves. Bright-red fruits. AM 1912

"MANUKA" see *LEPTOSPERMUM scoparium*

"MAPLE" see *ACER*

MARGYRICARPUS – Rosaceae PS (E) ○
Deep green, pinnate leaved shrubs. All well drained soils.

–**pinnatus** (*setosus*) PS (E) ○ "Pearl Berry"
Finely cut leaves. White berries. Ideal for rock garden.

MARSDENIA – Asclepiadaeae MS ○
For all well drained soils.

–**erecta** (*Cionura erecta*) MS ○
Lax habit. Silvery-green leaves. Milky sap. Fragrant, white flowers in cymes, May-July.

"MAY" see *CRATAEGUS monogyna*

MAYTENUS – Celastraceae LS (E) ○
For all well drained soils.

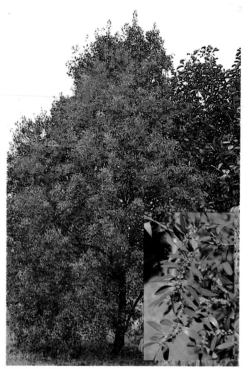

MAYTENUS boaria

–**boaria** (*chilensis*) LS (E) ○
Graceful, slender branches. Glossy, narrow, finely toothed leaves. Insignificant flowers.

"MEDLAR" see *MESPILUS germanica*

MELIANTHUS – Melianthaceae DS (E) † ○
Sub-shrubs, suitable only for very mild areas. Attractive foliage, unusual flowers.

–**major** DS (E) † ○
Spreading, hollow stems. Deeply serrated, glaucous, pinnate leaves. Tawny-crimson tubular flowers in erect terminal racemes, summer. FCC 1975

MELIOSMA – Sabiaceae ST ♥
Attractive leaves. White, spiraea-like, paniculate inflorescences. Prefers deep neutral soil, although lime tolerant.

–**veitchiorum** ST ♥
Stout branches, large pinnate leaves and prominent winter buds. Panicles of fragrant, creamy flowers, May. Violet fruits.

MENZIESIA – Ericaceae SS ✗ ◑
Waxy flowers in terminal clusters. Best sited where protected from late frosts.

– ciliicalyx SS ✗ ◑
Hairy leaves. Nodding pitcher-shaped
flowers in clusters, May – colour varies cream
to soft purple. AM 1938
– – purpurea SS ✗ ◑
Spiny-tipped leaves. Larger flowers of rose-
purple, May-June. Slow.

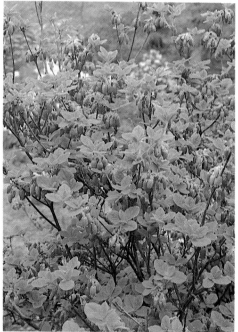

MENZIESIA ciliicalyx

MESPILUS – Rosaceae ST ♥
A monotypic genus related to Crataegus.
– germanica ST ♥ "Medlar"
Large, hairy leaves, warm russet in autumn.
Large, white flowers, May-June. Brown,
edible fruits. Low spreading habit. We
recommend the clone *'Nottingham'*.
"MESPILUS, SNOWY" see *AMELANCHIER*
METROSIDEROS – Myrtaceae LS – ST (E)
† ○
*Spectacular "bottle-brush" flowers, mainly
composed of stamens. Not for shallow chalk.*
– excelsa (*tomentosa*) LS (E) † ○
"Christmas Tree" of New Zealand. Brilliant
crimson flowers, freely borne, summer.
– lucida LS (E) † ○
Dense, bushy habit. Glossy, myrtle-like
leaves, coppery when young. Bright crimson
flowers, late summer, on mature shrubs.

– robusta ST (E) ♥ † "Rata"
Thick, rounded, dark-green leaves. Coppery-
scarlet flowers, late summer. AM 1050
"MEXICAN ORANGE BLOSSOM" see
CHOISYA ternata
"MEYER'S LEMON" see *CITRUS 'Meyer's
Lemon'*
MICHELIA – Magnoliaceae LS-ST (E) † ✗
*Glossy, dark-green leathery leaves. Flowers
borne in leaf axils.*
– doltsopa ST Semi-(E) ♥ † ✗
Heavily scented flowers, white and
multipetalled, formed in autumn, opening
spring. AM 1961
MICROGLOSSA (*AMPHIRAPHIS*)
– Compositae SS ○
Resembling and related to Aster. *Any well
drained soil.*
– albescens (*Aster albescens*) SS ○
Pale lilac-blue, daisy-like flowers, July.
MIMULUS (*DIPLACUS*)
– Scrophulariaceae SS (E) † ○
*Suitable for sheltered sunny positions. Lime
tolerant.*
– aurantiacus (*glutinosus*) SS (E) † ○
"Shrubby Musk"
Sticky stems. Orange or salmon-yellow
flowers, throughout summer-autumn.
AM 1938
– puniceus (*aurantiacus puniceus*) SS (E)
† ○
Small brick red or orange-red flowers.
MITCHELLA – Rubiaceae PS (E) ✗ ●
*Creeping sub-shrubs for ground-cover or
rock garden in shade.*
– repens PS (E) ✗ ● "Partridge Berry"
Mat-forming. Tiny, glossy, dark-green leaves.
Small, fragrant, pink or white flowers, June-
July. Scarlet fruits. AM 1951
MITRARIA – Gesneriaceae DS (E) † ◑
Monotypic genus.
– coccinea DS (E) † ◑
Spreading habit. Small, glossy leaves. Bright
flame-coloured tubular flowers, late spring-
summer. Not for shallow chalk. AM 1927
"MOCK ORANGE" see *PHILADELPHUS*
MOLTKIA – Boraginaceae DS ○
Sub-shrub related to Lithospermum. *Requires
well drained soil.*
– petraea (*Lithospermum petraeum*) DS ○
Neat habit. Tubular, violet-blue flowers, pink in
bud, June-July. FCC 1871

"MONKEY PUZZLE" see *ARAUCARIA araucana* under CONIFERS
MORUS – Moraceae ST ♥ "The Mulberries"
Any well drained soil. Ideal for town or maritime gardens.

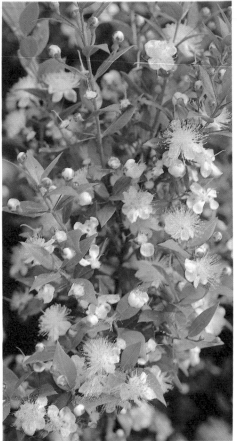

MYRTUS communis

– alba ST ♥ "White Mulberry"
Heart-shaped leaves. Sweet, edible fruits, whitish turning reddish-pink. Silk worms are fed on the leaves.
– –'Pendula' ST ♠
Dense weeping branches hang perpendicularly, like a curtain. AM 1897 AGM 1973
– nigra ST ♥ "Black Mulberry"
Architectural tree, becoming gnarled with age. Heart-shaped rough leaves, downy beneath. Edible, purplish-red fruits.

"MOUNTAIN ASH" see *SORBUS aucuparia*
"MULBERRY" see *MORUS*
"MULBERRY, PAPER" see *BROUSSONETIA papyrifera*
MYRICA – Myricaceae SS-LS ⚹ ◑
Aromatic shrubs. Unisexual flowers.
– cerifera (*caroliniensis*) LS (E) ⚹ ◑ "Wax Myrtle"
Narrow leaves. Glaucous wax covering fruits, used for candles. Excellent for damp site.
– gale SS ⚹ ◑ "Sweet Gale" "Bog Myrtle"
Dense habit. Golden-brown male and female catkins, April-May on separate plants. Tolerates acid, boggy swamp.
MYRICARIA – Tamaricaceae MS ○
Related to and resembling Tamarix.
– germanica (*Tamarix germanica*) MS ○
Feathery, blue-green foliage on wand-like stems. Fluffy, light pink flowers, throughout summer. Best in neutral or acid soil.
"MYROBALAN" see *PRUNUS cerasifera*
"MYRTLE" see *MYRTUS*

MYRTUS – Myrtaceae PS-ST (E) "Myrtles"
Aromatic, generally white flowered, shrubs. Any well drained soil. Excellent for coastal planting.
– apiculata (*luma*) ST (E) ♥ †
Attractive, peeling, cinnamon outer bark, reveals young cream surface beneath. Flowers, late summer-early autumn. Edible, sweet red and black fruits.
– communis LS (E) ○ "Common Myrtle"
Aromatic, densely leafy. Profuse flowers, July-August. Purplish-black berries. AM 1972
– –'Flore Pleno' LS (E) ○
Double flowers.
– –tarentina ('*Jenny Reitenbach'*) MS (E) ○
Compact. Narrow leaves. Abundant flowers, white berries.
– –tarentina 'Variegata' MS (E) ○
Leaves variegated creamy-white.
– –'Variegata' MS (E) ○
Leaves variegated creamy-white.
– nummularia PS (E) ○
Wiry, reddish stems. Tiny, rounded leaves. Flowers, May-June. Pink berries. Completely hardy. AM 1967
– ugni (*Eugenia ugni*) MS (E) † ○ "Chilean Guava"
Stiff, erect habit. Leathery leaves. Waxy pink bells. Edible, aromatic, mahogany-red berries. AM 1925

NANDINA – Berberidaceae SS-MS (E) ☼
Monotypic genus. Any well drained soil, sheltered position.

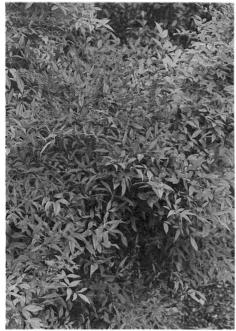

NANDINA domestica

– **domestica** MS (E) ☼ "Sacred Bamboo"
Large, compound, green leaves, tinged red, spring and autumn. Small white flowers in large terminal panicles, summer. AM 1897
– – **'Nana Purpurea'** SS (E) ☼
Compact habit. Young foliage red-purple throughout season.
NEILLIA – Rosaceae MS
Easy cultivation. For all but very dry soils.
– **thibetica** (*longiracemosa*) MS
Erect, downy stems. Slender-pointed, often 3-lobed leaves. Pink, tubular flowers in terminal racemes, May-June. AM 1931
"NETTLE TREE" see *CELTIS*
"NEW ZEALAND FLAX" see *PHORMIUM tenax*

"NORWAY MAPLE" see *ACER platanoides*
NOTHOFAGUS – Fagaceae ST-LT ↙
"Southern Beech"
Ornamental, generally fast growing trees, some evergreen. Small leaves. Like deep, moist, well drained soil – not shallow chalk. Poor wind resisters.
– **antarctica** MT ❢ "Antarctic Beech"
Dark-green, glossy, rounded and heart-shaped, serrated leaves, turning yellow in autumn.
– **betuloides** MT (E) ❢
Densely leafy. Dark-green, glossy, serrated leaves, ovate or rounded.
– **dombeyi** MT (E) ❀
Vigorous. Shiny, dark-green, doubly-toothed leaves. May shed leaves in cold winters.
– **fusca** ST (E) ❀ "Red Beech"
Oval or rounded, toothed leaves, often coppery in autumn. Flaking old bark.

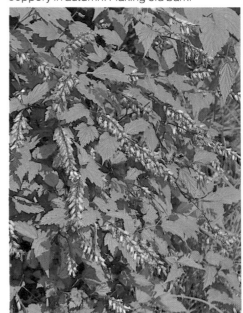

NEILLIA thibetica

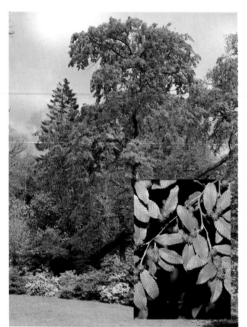

NOTHOFAGUS obliqua

– obliqua LT ♥ "Roblé Beech"
Elegant and fast growing, branches often droop gracefully at tips. Leaves larger than most, uneven at base.
– procera LT ♥
Fast growing. Comparatively large leaves, prominent venation. Generally rich autumn colour.
– solandri MT (E) ♥ "Black Beech"
Slender habit. Ascending fan-like branches. Tiny leaves arranged neatly on wiry branchlets.
NOTHOPANAX see *PSEUDOPANAX*
NOTOSPARTIUM – Leguminosae MS ○
Broom-like shrubs for any well drained soil.
– carmicheliae MS ○ "Pink Broom"
Graceful, arching habit. Lilac-pink pea-flowers smother leafless stems, July.
FCC 1889
NUTTALLIA see *OSMARONIA*
NYSSA – Nyssaceae LS-MT ✗
Noted for fine autumn leaf colour. Insignificant flowers and fruit. Require moist soil. Best planted young, as resent disturbance.
– sinensis LS ✗ ○
Young growths red throughout season. Leaves turn glorious shades of red, autumn.

– sylvatica (*multiflora*) MT ♥ ✗ "Tupelo"
Slow growing, glossy, dark-green leaves turn rich shades of red, yellow and orange, autumn. AM 1951 FCC 1968 AGM 1969
– – 'Sheffield Park' MT ♥ ✗
Selected form with splendid autumn leaf colour, turning two to three weeks earlier.

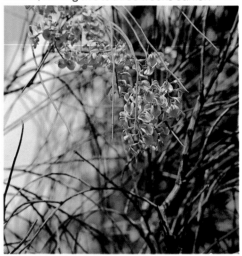

NOTOSPARTIUM carmicheliae

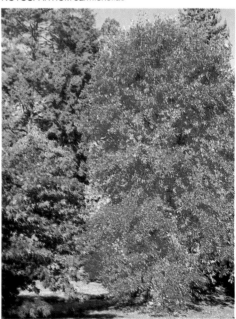

NYSSA sylvatica

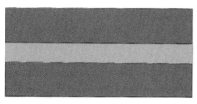

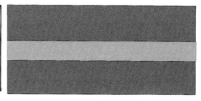

"OAK" see *QUERCUS*
OLEA – Oleaceae LS-ST (E) †
Opposite, leathery leaves. Any well drained soil.
– europaea LS-ST (E) † "Olive"
Grey-green, leathery leaves. Fragrant, small white flowers, late summer. Olive oil is extracted from fruits. Only suitable for mildest areas.
OLEARIA – Compositae SS-LS (E) ○ "Daisy Bushes" "Tree Daisies"
Daisy-like flower-heads, generally white or cream. Easy growing shrubs for all well drained soils. Excellent on chalk. Wind resistant and tolerant of salt and atmospheric pollution. A (b) 4
– avicenniifolia MS (E) ○ Hdg (0.5m)
Pointed leaves, whitish beneath. Fragrant flowers, August-September. Excellent for hedging.
– chathamica SS (E) † ○
Pale violet, purple centred flower heads, borne singly on long stalks, June. AM 1938
– frostii SS (E) † ○
Downy shrub with sage-green leaves. Large, double, mauve flower-heads, borne singly.
– gunniana see *O. phlogopappa*
– gunniana 'Splendens' see *O. stellulata 'Splendens'*

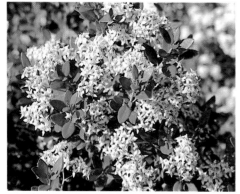

OLEARIA × haastii

– × haastii MS (E) ○ Hdg (0.5m)
Rounded habit. Small leaves, white-felted beneath. Abundant, fragrant flower-heads, July-August. Good for hedging. FCC 1873 AGM 1928
– ilicifolia MS (E) ○
Dense habit. Leathery, grey-green leaves, white-felted beneath. Fragrant flowerheads, June. "Musky" smell to shrub. AM 1972
– insignis see *PACHYSTEGIA insignis*
– macrodonta (*dentata* HOOK.f) MS (E) Hdg (0.5m) "New Zealand Holly"
Strong growing. Sage-green, holly-like leaves, silvery beneath. Fragrant flower-heads, June. "Musky" odour. Excellent for hedging. FCC 1895
– – 'Major' MS (E)
Larger leaves and flower-heads.

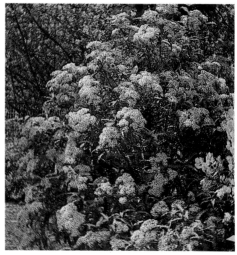

OLEARIA macrodonta 'Major'

– mollis SS (E) ○
Rounded habit. Silvery-grey, wavy-edged leaves. Flower-heads, May.
– nummulariifolia MS (E)
Small, thick, yellowish-green leaves, crowd the stems. Small, fragrant, single flower-heads in leaf-axils, July.

– phlogopappa (*gunniana*) (*stellulata* BENTH) MS (E) † ○ "Tasmanian Daisy Bush"
Narrow, toothed, aromatic leaves. Flower-heads in crowded panicles along stems, May. FCC 1885
– × scilloniensis MS (E) † ○
Rounded, compact habit. Grey leaves. Abundant flower-heads, May. AM 1951
– semidentata MS (E) † ○
Grey-green leaves, silvery beneath. Large, hanging, aster-like flower-heads, lilac with purple centres, June. AM 1916
– stellulata SS (E) † ○
Lax habit. Flower-heads in panicles, May. AM 1893.
We recommend the form:
– – 'Splendens' (*gunniana 'Splendens'*) SS (E) † ○
Flower-heads resembling Michaelmas daisies. Blue, lavender or rose colours are available.
– traversii LS (E) †
Fast growing. Dense white-felted shoots and leaf undersides. Leaf upper surface glossy, green. Insignificant flower-heads. Excellent coastal windbreak.
– virgata (*Eurybia virgata*) MS-LS
Dense habit. Long wiry stems. Small flowers, June.
We recommend the form:
– – lineata (*O. lineata*) LS
Loose, graceful habit. Slender, angular, hanging branches. Narrow, linear leaves.
– 'Waikariensis' SS (E) ○
Olive-green, lanceolate leaves, white beneath. Flower-heads in axillary clusters.
– 'Zennorensis' MS (E) † ○
Dark olive, narrow, sharply-toothed leaves, white beneath. Pale brown tomentum on leaf stalks and young stems. Excellent coastal foliage plant.
"OLEASTER" see *ELAEAGNUS angustifolia*
"OLIVE" see *OLEA europaea*
ONONIS – Leguminosae SS ○
Trifoliolate leaves. Pea-shaped flowers. Any well drained soil including shallow chalk.
– fruticosa SS ○
Compact mound-like habit. Narrow leaflets. Clusters of bright rose-pink flowers throughout summer. AM 1926
"OSAGE ORANGE" see *MACLURA pomifera*
"OSIER, COMMON" see *SALIX viminalis*

OSMANTHUS – Oleaceae MS-LS (E)
Holly-like shrubs. Small, white or cream, generally fragrant flowers. Suit almost all soils.
– armatus LS (E)
Dense habit. Thick, rigid leaves, edged with stout, often hooked, spiny teeth. Scented flowers, autumn.

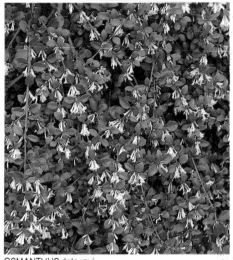
OSMANTHUS delavayi

– delavayi (*Siphonosmanthus delavayi*) MS (E)
Slow-growing. Small leaves. Abundant, fragrant, white, jasmine-like flowers, April. AM 1914 AGM 1923 FCC 1931
– × fortunei LS (E)
Fairly vigorous. Dense habit. Glossy, dark green, conspicuously veined leaves, edged with spiny teeth. Fragrant flowers, autumn.
– heterophyllus (*aquifolium*) (*ilicifolius*) LS (E)
Slow-growing, dense habit. Glossy, dark green, entire or spiny leaves. Sweetly scented flowers, autumn. FCC 1859
– – 'Aureomarginatus' (*Aureovariegatus*) LS (E)
Leaves margined yellow.
– – 'Gulftide' LS (E)
Strongly spiny, twisted or lobed leaves. Dense habit.
– – 'Latifolius Variegatus' LS (E)
Silver variegated, broad leaves.
– – 'Purpureus' LS (E)
Young growths purple, changing to green, tinged purple.

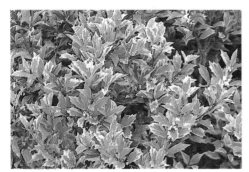

OSMANTHUS heterophyllus 'Variegatus'

– –**'Variegatus'** (*'Argenteomarginatus'*) LS (E)

Leaves margined creamy-white.

–**ilicifolius** see *O. heterophyllus*

–**yunnanensis** (*forrestii*) LS (E)

Dark olive-green leaves, varying from undulate and toothed to flat and entire. Fragrant, ivory flower, late winter. AM 1967

× **OSMAREA** (*OSMANTHUS* × *PHILLYREA*) **-Oleaceae** MS (E)

Conspicuous, small tubular white flowers. Good on all fertile soils – including shallow chalk.

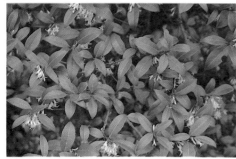

× OSMAREA burkwoodii

–**burkwoodii** MS (E)

Compact habit. Lustrous green, toothed leaves. Very fragrant flowers, April-May. AGM 1950 AM 1978

OSMARONIA (*NUTTALLIA*) **-Rosaceae** MS *Monotypic genus. Male and female flowers, usually on different plants. All fertile soils but may become chlorotic on shallow chalk.*

–**cerasiformis** MS "Oso Berry"

Suckering shrub. Sea-green leaves. Hanging racemes of fragrant, white flowers, February-March. Brown, plum-like fruits, turning purple when ripe.

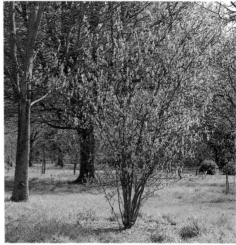

OSMARONIA cerasiformis

OSTRYA – Carpinaceae ST-MT

"Hornbeam"-like trees with hop-like fruits and good autumn colour.

–**carpinifolia** (*vulgaris*) MT ❦ "Hop Hornbeam"

Toothed leaves, clear yellow in autumn. Long, drooping catkins in spring.

–**virginiana** ST ❦

Similar to above but with glandular shoots. Warm yellow autumn colour. Rare.

OXYCOCCUS macrocarpus see *VACCINIUM macrocarpum*

–**palustris** see *VACCINIUM oxycoccos*

OXYDENDRUM – Ericaceae LS-ST ⚮

A monotypic genus.

–**arboreum** (*Andromeda arborea*) LS-ST ⚮ "Sorrel Tree"

Slender, drooping racemes of white flowers at shoot tips, late summer-autumn; crimson and yellow autumn colour. AGM 1947 AM 1951 (for autumn colour) AM 1957 (for flowers) FCC 1972

OZOTHAMNUS – Compositae SS-MS (E) ○ *Summer flowering shrubs related to Helichrysum.*

–**ledifolius** (*Helichrysum ledifolium*) MS (E) ○ Narrow, aromatic leaves, yellow beneath. Flowers reddish in bud opening white; honey scented seed heads.

–**rosmarinifolius** (*Helichrysum rosmarinifolium*) MS (E) † ○ Dark green, narrow leaves; white, scented flowers, red in bud. AM 1968

PACHYSANDRA – Buxaceae DS ● GC
Dwarf, carpeting shrubs for a moist position.
– terminalis DS (E) GC ●
Toothed leaves clustered at stem tips,
greenish-white flower spikes, February-
March. AGM 1969
– – 'Variegata' DS (E) ● GC
Leaves variegated white.

PACHYSTEGIA – Compositae DS (E) †
Monotypic genus.
– insignis (*Olearia insignis*) DS (E) †
Obovate leaves to 15cm, dark-green, white
felted beneath. Aster-like, large, white, yellow
centred flowers, late summer. Good in
maritime exposure. AM 1915

PAEONIA – Ranunculaceae MS ○
*The "Tree Paeonies" make handsome
flowering shrubs for any well-drained soil.*
– delavayi MS ○
Crimson flowers with golden anthers, May.
Good foliage. AM 1934
– × lemoinei MS ○
Large, yellow flowers, May. We recommend
the following cultivars:
– – 'Alice Harding' MS ○
Fully double, canary-yellow. AMT 1960
– – 'Chromotella' MS ○
Double, sulphur-yellow.
– – 'Souvenir de Maxime Cornu'
Fragrant, very large, bright yellow, edged with
carmine.
– lutea MS ○
Cup-shaped, golden-yellow flowers in May-
June. FCC 1903
– – ludlowii MS ○
Larger, saucer-shaped flowers. AM 1954
AGM 1963
– suffruticosa MS ○ "Moutan Paeony"
Large flowers up to 15cm across, May.
Various named varieties are offered, generally
semi-double, or double, in shades of pink,
red, crimson, also white.
Young growth needs protection from spring
frosts.
"PAGODA TREE" see *SOPHORA japonica*

PALIURUS – Rhamnaceae MS-LS ○
*The following is the most commonly cultivated
species:*
– spina-christi (*aculeatus*) LS ○ "Christ's
Thorn"
Spiny shrub with glossy leaves, yellow in
autumn. Small yellowish flowers, late summer.

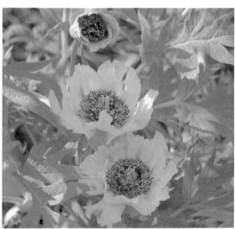

PAEONIA lutea

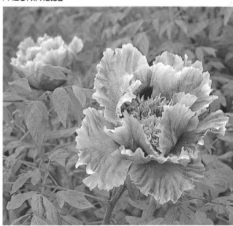

PAEONIA suffruticosa

"PALM, HARDY" see *CHAMAEROPS* and
TRACHYCARPUS

PARAHEBE PS-DS ○
Sub-shrubs, intermediate between Hebe *and*
Veronica.
– catarractae DS ○ GC
Small leaved, spreading plant, making low
mounds. Flowers blue, in erect racemes, late
summer.
– – 'Diffusa' DS ○ GC
Leaves smaller, flowers white, veined rose-
pink.

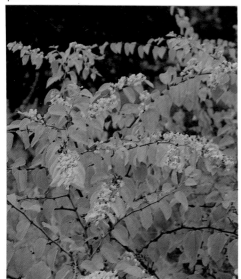

PALIURUS spina-christi

PARROTIA – Hamamelidaceae ST ♥
A monotypic genus.
– persica ST ♥
Large "Beech-like" leaves, crimson and gold
in autumn, flaking bark like the "London
Plane". FCC 1884 AGM 1969
"PARTRIDGE BERRY" see *MITCHELLA*
repens
PASANIA edulis see *LITHOCARPUS edulis*
"PASSION FLOWER" see *PASSIFLORA*
under Climbers
PAULOWNIA – Scrophulariaceae ST-LT ♥
Large leaved trees with erect panicles of
foxglove-like flowers, in spring.
– fargesii LT ♥
Flowers fragrant, heliotrope, speckled dark
purple with yellow stain in throat.
– tomentosa (*imperialis*) MT ♥
Fragrant, blue-purple flowers like huge
foxgloves. AM 1934

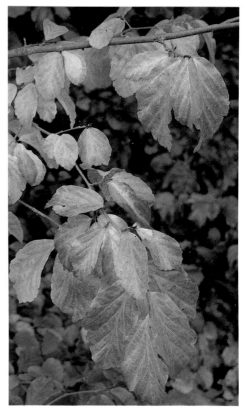

PARROTIA persica

"PEACH" see *PRUNUS persica*
"PEAR" see *PYRUS*
"PEARL BERRY" see *MARGYRICARPUS*
pinnatus
PENSTEMON – Scrophulariaceae
The following are suitable for the rock garden.
– heterophyllus 'Blue Gem' DS ○
Azure-blue, tubular flowers in long racemes,
summer.
– newberryi DS (E) ○
Abundant, scarlet flowers, June.
– scouleri DS ○
Large flowers in erect racemes, June. AM
1951. We recommend the following form:
– – 'Albus' DS ○
Flowers white.
"PERIWINKLE" see *VINCA*
PERNETTYA – Ericaceae DS (E) ⋌ GC
Low growing, densely leafy, shrubs for peaty
soils. White flowers and conspicuous berries.

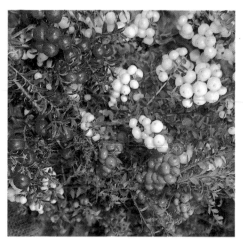

PERNETTYA mucronata 'Pink Pearl', 'Cherry Ripe' and 'White Pearl'

– mucronata DS (E) ⚹ GC
Masses of heath-like white flowers, May-June. Showy marble-like berries in profusion on females. A male is needed for pollination. We recommend:
– –'Bell's Seedling' DS (E) ⚹ GC
Hermaphrodite. Berries large, dark red. AM 1928 AGM 1969
– –'Cherry Ripe' DS (E) ⚹ GC
Berries bright cherry-red.
– –'Lilacina' DS (E) ⚹ GC
Abundant reddish-lilac berries. FCC 1878
– –Male DS (E) ⚹ GC
Proven male plants.
– –'Mulberry Wine' DS (E) ⚹ GC
Berries large, magenta, ripening to deep-purple.
– –'Pink Pearl' DS (E) ⚹ GC
Lilac-pink berries.
– –'Rosie' DS (E) ⚹ GC
Large berries, pink, flushed deep-rose.
– –'Sea Shell' DS (E) ⚹ GC
Berries shell-pink, ripening to rose.
– –'Thymifolia' SS (E) ⚹ GC
A male form of neat habit. Abundant white flowers.
– –'White Pearl' DS (E) ⚹ GC
Gleaming white berries.
– prostrata PS (E) ⚹ GC
We recommend the following form:
– –pentlandii PS (E) ⚹ GC
Vigorous creeper. Glossy, green leaves. Black berries. AM 1957

PEROVSKIA – Labiatae SS ○
Valuable late summer and autumn flowering sub-shrubs.
– atriplicifolia SS ○
Grey foliage. Long, narrow panicles of lavender-blue flowers. AM 1928 AGM 1935

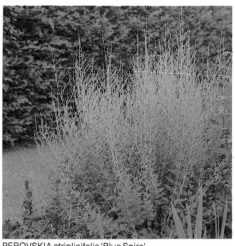

PEROVSKIA atriplicifolia 'Blue Spire'

– –'Blue Spire' SS ○
Deeply cut, grey-green leaves. Large panicles of lavender-blue flowers. AM 1962 AGM 1969
– 'Hybrida' SS ○
Finely-cut, grey-green leaves. Very long panicles of deep lavender-blue flowers.
"PERSIMMON, CHINESE" see *DIOSPYROS kaki*
PETTERIA – Leguminosae MS ○
A monotypic genus.
– ramentacea MS ○
Like a shrubby "Laburnum". Trifoliolate leaves. Erect racemes of yellow, pea flowers.
PHELLODENDRON – Rutaceae ST-MT ♥
Very hardy trees with pinnate leaves, yellow in autumn. Small yellowish-green flowers. Black fruits.
– amurense MT ♥ "Amur Cork Tree"
Bright green leaves with 5-11 leaflets. Older branches corky.
PHILADELPHUS – Philadelphaceae SS-LS ○ "Mock Orange"
Fragrant, white flowers, June-July. D (h) 2
– 'Beauclerk' MS ○
Flowers single, 6cm across with broad petals, cerise centres. AM 1947 FCC 1951 AGM 1955

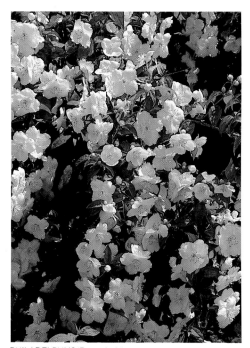

PHILADELPHUS 'Beauclerk'

– **'Belle Etoile'** MS ○
Very fragrant, single flowers, 5cm across,
maroon centres. AM 1930 AGM 1936
– **'Boule d'Argent'** SS ○
Large, double, pure white flowers in dense
clusters. FCC 1895
– **'Bouquet Blanc'** SS ○
Double, orange-scented flowers in dense
clusters. AM 1912
– **'Burfordensis'** MS ○
Large, cup-shaped, single flowers with
conspicuous yellow stamens. AM 1921 FCC
1969
– **coronarius** MS ○
A commonly cultivated species. Creamy-
white, richly scented flowers.
– – **'Aureus'** MS ◑
Young leaves bright yellow. Foliage tends to
burn in hot sun.
– – **'Variegatus'** MS ○
Leaves with a creamy-white margin.
– **'Coupe d'Argent'** SS ○
Large, single, fragrant flowers, almost square
in outline. AM 1922
– **delavayi** LS ○
We recommend the following form:

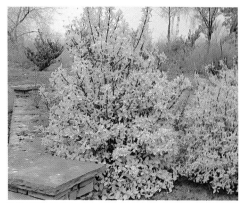

PHILADELPHUS coronarius 'Aureus'

– – **calvescens** LS ○
Heavily scented flowers to 4cm across, in
dense racemes, calyx purple. Vigorous, large
leaved shrub.
– **'Enchantment'** SS ○
Abundant, sweetly scented, double flowers.
AM 1966
– **'Erectus'** SS ○
Small, richly scented flowers, freely borne.
AGM 1946
– **'Etoile Rose'** MS ○
Large, fragrant, single flowers. Elongated
petals, blotched carmine-rose at base.

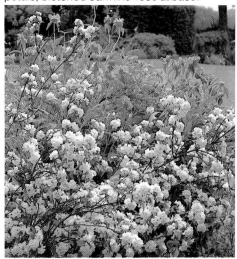

PHILADELPHUS 'Manteau d'Hermine'

– **'Manteau d'Hermine'** DS ○
Creamy-white, double, fragrant flowers.
Compact habit.

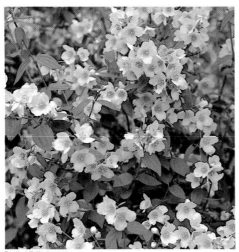

PHILADELPHUS microphyllus

– microphyllus SS ○
A dainty plant. Small leaves. Small, richly fragrant, single flowers. FCC 1890
– 'Minnesota Snowflake' MS ○
Arching branches and double, fragrant flowers.
– 'Sybille' SS ○
Flowers single, orange-scented, purple-stained petals. Graceful, arching habit. AM 1954 AGM 1955

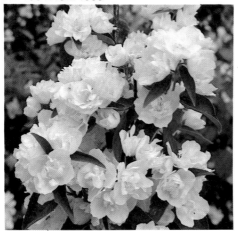

PHILADELPHUS 'Virginal'

– 'Virginal' LS ○
A deservedly popular, vigorous shrub, with richly fragrant, double flowers. FCC 1911 AGM 1926

PHILESIA – Philesiaceae DS (E) † ↙ ◑
A monotypic genus related to Lapageria.
– magellanica DS (E) † ↙ ◑
Suckering shrub. Narrow, rigid leaves. Crimson, tubular flowers 5cm long, summer-autumn. AM 1937
PHILLYREA – Oleaceae MS-ST (E)
Handsome and useful, hardy evergreens.
– angustifolia MS (E)
We recommend the following form:
– – 'Rosmarinifolia' MS (E)
Neat compact bush. Dark-green, narrow leaves. Small, fragrant, creamy-yellow flowers, May-June. Tolerates salt spray.
– decora (*Osmanthus decorus*) MS (E)
Dome-shaped. Large, glossy, leathery leaves. Small fragrant, white flowers – spring. Purplish-black fruits. FCC 1888
– latifolia LS-ST (E) ♥
Elegant clive-like plant. Drooping branches, glossy, dark-green leaves. Small ivory-white flowers, late spring.
PHLOMIS – Labiatae DS-SS (E) ○
Shrubs or sub-shrubs with woolly leaves and conspicuous flowers. A (b) 5
– chrysophylla SS (E) ○
Yellow-tinged, sage-like leaves. Golden-yellow flowers, June.
– 'Edward Bowles' SS (E) ○
Large, heart-shaped leaves. Sulphur-yellow flowers, late summer-autumn.

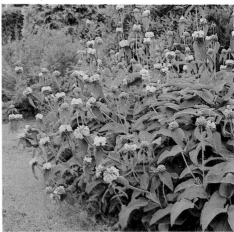

PHLOMIS fruticosa

– fruticosa SS ○
Bright yellow flowers, late summer-autumn. AM 1925 AGM 1929

– italica DS (E) † ○

White-hairy stems and leaves. Pale-lilac flowers, summer.

PHORMIUM – Agavaceae SS-MS (E) ○

Handsome plants with tufts of sword-like leaves. Fairly hardy in all but coldest areas.

– 'Bronze Baby' SS (E) ○

Leaves bronze, drooping at the tips.

– cookianum (*colensoi*) MS (E) ○

Differs from *P. tenax* in its smaller stature and lax leaves. We recommend the following form:

– – 'Tricolor' MS (E) ○

Leaves conspicuously edged creamy-yellow, with a thin red strip on the margin.

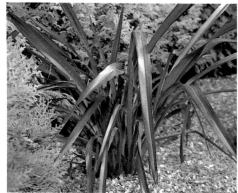

PHORMIUM 'Dazzler'

– 'Dazzler' MS (E) ○

A striking plant. Leaves deep red, rose-red in centre.

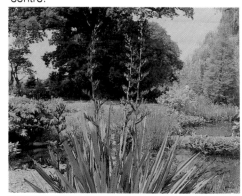

PHORMIUM tenax

– tenax MS (E) ○

Rigid, sword-like leaves. Flowers bronze-red in panicles up to 4.5m.

– – 'Purpureum' MS (E) ○

Leaves bronze-purple.

PHOTINIA – Rosaceae MS-ST

Evergreen and deciduous shrubs and small trees.

– beauverdiana ST ♥

Pinkish young leaves. White flowers followed by dark-red fruits. Good autumn colour.

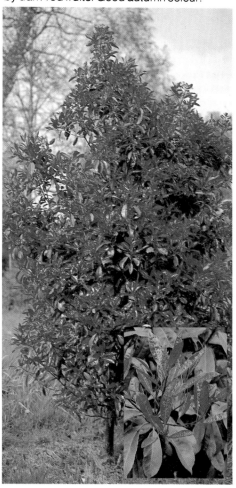

PHOTINIA × fraseri 'Robusta'

– × fraseri LS (E)

Dark, glossy-green leaves. Attractively coloured when young. We recommend the following forms:

– – 'Red Robin' LS (E)

Young leaves brilliant red.

– – **'Robusta'** LS (E)
Brilliant coppery-red young leaves. AM 1974
– **glabra** MS (E)
We recommend the following form:
– – **'Rubens'** MS (E)
Young leaves bright, sealing-wax red. Dense habit. AM 1972

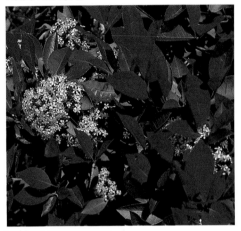

PHOTINIA glabra 'Rubens'

– **serrulata** LS-ST (E) ❦
Glossy, green, coarsely toothed leaves, coppery-red when young.
– **villosa** (*variabilis*) ST ❦
Small, white flowers, May. Bright red fruits. Leaves scarlet and gold in autumn. AM 1932 AGM 1969
PHYGELIUS – Scrophulariaceae SS ○
South African sub-shrubs with conspicuous flowers.
– **capensis** SS ○ "Cape Figwort"
We recommend the following form:
– – **'Coccineus'** SS ○
Nodding, tubular, crimson-scarlet flowers, in late summer-autumn. AM 1926
× **PHYLLIOPSIS – Ericaceae** DS (E) ⚘ ●
Hybrid between PHYLLODOCE *and* KALMIOPSIS *which occurred in our nursery. Only one form is known.*
– **hillieri 'Pinocchio'** DS (E) ⚘ ●
Small, glossy, green leaves. Conspicuous racemes of small, rich pink flowers. AM 1976
PHYLLODOCE – Ericaceae DS (E) ⚘ ●
Dainty, heath-like shrubs for moist soils.
– **aleutica** DS (E) ⚘ ●
Spreading habit. Small, creamy-white or pale-yellow flowers, May-June. AM 1939

– **caerulea** DS (E) ⚘ ●
Cushion forming. Bluish-purple flowers in May-June. AM 1938
– **nipponica** DS (E) ⚘ ●
Compact, erect habit. White, or pink-tinged flowers, May. AM 1938 FCC 1946
PHYLLOSTACHYS – Gramineae MS-LS (E)
Tall, graceful bamboos, usually less invasive than Arundinaria *with zig-zag stems flattened or grooved on alternate sides.*
– **aurea** MS (E)
Bright green canes, later creamy-yellow, forming large clumps. Nodes crowded at the base.
– **bambusoides** (*quilioi*) LS (E)
Canes shining deep-green, becoming deep yellow-green, then brown. Forms large clumps.
– – **'Sulphurea'** (*'Allgold'*) LS (E)
Canes rich yellow, sometimes striped with green.
– **flexuosa** MS (E)
Slender, somewhat wavy canes, zig-zag at the base, bright green at first, darkening with age. Makes a good screen.
– **nigra** °LS (E) "Black Bamboo"
We recommend the following form:
– – **'Boryana'** LS (E)
Luxuriant masses of arching, leafy canes, green at first, becoming yellow, splashed with purple.
– **quilioi** see *P. bambusoides*
– **ruscifolia** see *SHIBATAEA kumasasa*

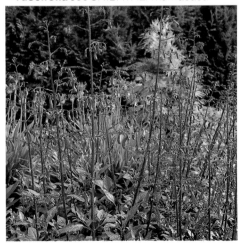

PHYGELIUS capensis 'Coccineus'

× PHYLLOTHAMNUS – Ericaceae DS (E) ⚹ ◗

A hybrid between PHYLLODOCE *and* RHODOTHAMNUS

– erectus DS (E) ⚹ ◗
Narrow leaves. Terminal clusters of delicate rose flowers, April-May. AM 1958 FCC 1969

PHYSOCARPUS – Rosaceae MS
A small genus of shrubs related to Neillia. *We recommend the following:*

– opulifolius MS "Nine Bark"
Three-lobed leaves. Dense clusters of pink-tinged, white flowers, June.

– – 'Luteus' MS
Young leaves clear yellow.

PICRASMA – Simaroubaceae ST ❦
Mainly tropical trees related to Ailanthus. *The following is completely hardy.*

– quassioides (*ailanthoides*) ST ❦
Pinnate leaves, orange and scarlet in autumn. Small, green flowers. Red, pea-like fruits.

PIERIS – Ericaceae MS-LS (E) ⚹ ◗
Conspicuous, usually white, Lily-of-the-valley-like flowers, spring. Often attractive young foliage.

– floribunda MS (E) ⚹ ◗
We recommend the following form:

– – 'Elongata' (*'Grandiflora'*) MS (E) ⚹ ◗
Dense, rounded habit. Long panicles of white flowers, April. AM 1938

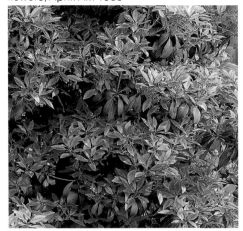

PIERIS 'Forest Flame'

– 'Forest Flame' MS (E) ⚹ ◗
Large drooping flower panicles. Young leaves brilliant red, turning pink, creamy white, then green. AM 1973 AGM 1973

– formosa LS (E) ◗
Magnificent shrub. Glossy dark-green, leathery leaves. White flowers in May. AM 1894 AGM 1973
The forms we recommend belong to the following variety·

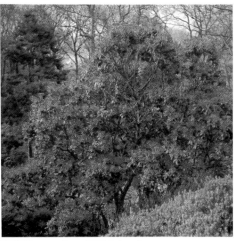

PIERIS formosa forrestii 'Wakehurst'

– – forrestii LS (E) ◗
Long, conical panicles of slightly fragrant flowers in April. Young leaves, brilliant red. AM 1924 FCC 1930 AGM 1944. The following forms are recommended:

– – – 'Charles Michael' LS (E) ⚹ ◗
Large white flowers in large panicles.

– – – 'Jermyns' MS (E) ⚹ ◗
Red flower buds throughout winter, opening white. AM 1959

– – – 'Wakehurst' LS (E) ⚹ ◗
Vivid-red young foliage. Glistening white flowers. Vigorous growth. AM 1957

– japonica MS (E) ⚹ ◗
Glossy-green leaves, coppery when young. Drooping panicles of white flowers, March-April. FCC 1882 AGM 1924

– – 'Blush' MS (E) ⚹ ◗
Flowers rose in bud, opening pale blush-pink.

– – 'Christmas Cheer' MS (E) ⚹ ◗
Flowers flushed deep-rose at the tip, often produced in winter.

– – 'Purity' MS (E) ⚹ ◗
Comparatively large, snow-white flowers.

– – 'Scarlett O'Hara' MS (E) ⚹ ◗
Abundant white flowers in dense panicles. Scarlet young foliage.

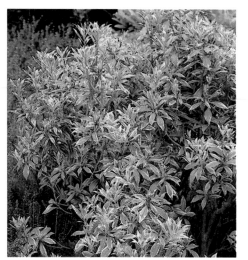

PIERIS japonica 'Variegata'

– – **'Variegata'** MS (E) ⚹ ◗
Leaves margined creamy-white, flushed pink
when young. AGM 1969
– **taiwanensis** MS (E) ⚹ ◗
White flowers, March-April. Bronze or bronze-
red young foliage. AM 1922 FCC 1923
AGM 1963
PIMELEA – Thymelaeaceae PS-SS (E)
Australasian shrubs related to Daphne *and*
requiring similar treatment. Not suitable for
shallow chalky soils.
– **prostrata** PS (E) ○ GC
Carpeting shrubs with small, grey-green
leaves. Clusters of fragrant, white flowers,
summer. Fleshy, white fruits.
PIPTANTHUS – Leguminosae LS (E) ○
Only one species is commonly cultivated.
– **laburnifolius** (*nepalensis*) LS (E) ○
"Evergreen Laburnum"
Evergreen or semi-evergreen, with trifoliolate
leaves and large bright yellow, pea-flowers in
May. AM 1960 A (b) 5
PISTACIA – Anacardiaceae LS ○
Genus related to Rhus.
We recommend the following:
– **chinensis** LS ○ "Chinese Pistachio"
Glossy, green, pinnate leaves, brilliantly
coloured in autumn.
PITTOSPORUM – Pittosporaceae MS-LS (E)
Attractive foliage plants excellent for mild
coastal areas. Several produce small,
fragrant flowers.

– **crassifolium** LS (E)
Leathery leaves, white-felted beneath. Deep
purple flowers. Makes an excellent hedge in
coastal areas.
– – **'Variegatum'** LS (E)
Grey-green leaves, margined creamy-white.
AM 1977
– **dallii** LS (E)
Rounded habit, leathery matt-green leaves.
Reddish-purple shoots and leaf stems. Hardy.
– **eugenioides** LS (E) † "Tarata"
Glossy, green, undulate leaves. Pale yellow
honey-scented flowers, spring.
We recommend the following:
– – **'Variegatum'** LS (E) †
Leaves margined creamy-white.

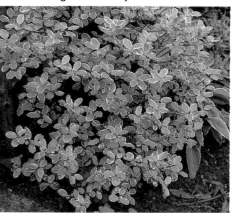

PITTOSPORUM 'Garnettii'

– **'Garnettii'** LS (E) †
Broadly columnar habit. Grey-green leaves,
margined white, marked pink in winter.
– **nigricans** see *P. tenuifolium*
– **ralphii** LS (E)
Similar to *P. crassifolium* with longer leaves.
Dark crimson flowers with yellow anthers.
– **'Saundersii'** (*tenuifolium 'Saundersii'*) LS
(E) †
Resembles *P. 'Garnettii'* but leaves more grey
and of more compact habit.
– **tenuifolium** (*nigricans*) LS-ST (E) ♦ †
Glossy, pale-green, undulate leaves on black
shoots. Small, chocolate-purple, honey-
scented flower, spring. Makes excellent
hedge in mild areas. AM 1931
– – **'Eila Keightley'** (*'Sunburst'*) LS (E) †
Pale-green leaves, conspicuously blotched
with yellow.

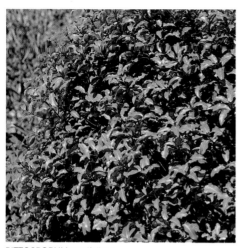

PITTOSPORUM tenuifolium

‑‑**'Garnettii'** see *P. 'Garnettii'*
‑‑**'Irene Paterson'** LS (E) †
Young leaves creamy-white, becoming deep green, marbled white, pink tinged in winter.
‑‑**'Purpureum'** LS (E) †
Young leaves pale-green, becoming deep purple.
‑‑**'Silver Queen'** LS (E) †
Leaves suffused silvery-grey. AM 1914
‑‑**'Saundersii'** see *P. 'Saundersii'*
‑‑**'Sunburst'** see *'Eila Keightley'*
‑‑**'Variegatum'** LS (E)
Leaves broadly margined creamy-white.
‑‑**'Warnham Gold'** LS (E) †
Young leaves greenish-yellow, becoming golden yellow.
‑**tobira** (*chinense*) LS (E) †
Whorls of glossy, bright-green leaves. Conspicuous, cream, orange-blossom-scented, flowers in summer.
‑‑**'Variegatum'** LS (E) †
Leaves with a creamy-white margin.
PLAGIANTHUS – Malvaceae
Australasian shrubs and trees.
We recommend the following:
‑**betulinus** ST ♀
Slender tree with variable leaves. Up to 7.5cm long. Large, dense panicles of tiny, white flowers, May.
‑**lyallii** see *HOHERIA glabrata* and *H. lyallii*
"PLANE" see *PLATANUS*
PLATANUS – Platanaceae LT ♥
Large trees with attractive, flaking bark.

‑ × **hispanica** (× *acerifolia*) LT ♥ "London Plane"
Large, palmately lobed leaves and patchwork, flaking bark. Very tolerant of atmospheric pollution.
‑‑**'Suttneri'** MT ♥
Leaves boldly variegated creamy-white.
‑**orientalis** LT ♥ "Oriental Plane"
Deeply five-lobed leaves. Attractive flaking bark. AM 1966 AGM 1973
‑‑**digitata** LT ♥
Leaves deeply divided into three to five finger-like lobes.
PLATYCARYA – Juglandaceae ST ♥
A monotypic genus related to Pterocarya.
‑**strobilacea** ST ♥
Rare tree with pinnate leaves. Flowers in catkins, late summer.
"PLUMBAGO, HARDY" see
CERATOSTIGMA willmottianum
"POCKET HANDKERCHIEF TREE" see
DAVIDIA involucrata

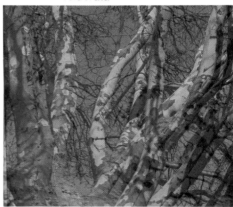

PLATANUS × hispanica

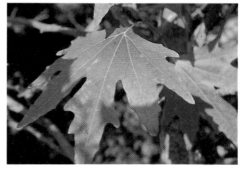

PLATANUS orientalis

POLYGALA – Polygalaceae PS-DS (E) ✗
The following are suitable for a cool, moist position on the rock or peat garden.
– chamaebuxus DS (E) ✗
Low, mat-forming shrub. Creamy-white, tipped bright yellow, flowers, April-June.
– – grandiflora DS (E) ✗
Flowers purple and yellow. AM 1896
– vayredae PS (E) ✗
Flowers reddish-purple, tipped bright yellow. March-April.
"POMEGRANATE" see *PUNICA granatum*
PONCIRUS – Rutaceae MS ○
A monotypic genus related to Citrus.

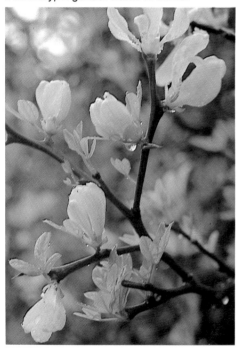

PONCIRUS trifoliata

– trifoliata (*Citrus trifoliata*) MS ○ "Japanese Bitter Orange"
Stout green stems and spines. Large, white, sweetly-scented, flowers in spring. Fruits like miniature oranges, green, becoming yellow.
"POPLAR" see *POPULUS*
POPULUS – Salicaceae MT-LT
Fast-growing trees for nearly all soils, even very wet, but usually not at their best on shallow chalk. Several have scented leaves. Others have attractive catkins.

– alba LT ♥ "White Poplar"
Leaves irregularly lobed, white-woolly beneath. Autumn colour yellow. Good in exposed sites and coastal areas. Lime tolerant.
– – 'Pyramidalis' LT ♦
Resembles the "Lombardy Poplar" in habit, but slightly broader.
– – 'Richardii' MT ♥
Leaves bright golden-yellow above. AM 1912
– balsamifera (*tacamahaca*) LT ♦ "Balsam Poplar" Erect branches. Large sticky buds. Young leaves balsam-scented.
– balsamifera × **trichocarpa** see *'Tacatricho 32'*
– × berolinensis LT ♦ "Berlin Poplar"
Broadly columnar habit. Downy shoots and sticky buds. Much planted as street tree on the continent.
– × candicans MT ♥ "Ontario Poplar" "Balm of Gilead Poplar"
Broad-headed tree. Downy twigs and leaves grey-white beneath, strongly balsam-scented when young.
– – 'Aurora' MT ♥
Young leaves marbled creamy-white, tinged pink. AM 1954

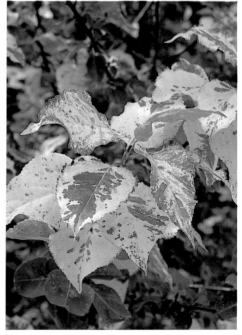

POPULUS × candicans 'Aurora'

- canescens LT ♀
Commonly planted tree. Lobed leaves, grey-white beneath. Attractive catkins, late winter. Yellow, or occasionally red, autumn colour. We recommend the following form:
– –**'Macrophylla'** LT ♀ "Picart's Poplar"
A very vigorous, large-leaved form.
– **'Eugenei'** MT ♂
Narrow habit. Young leaves coppery. Canker resistant.
– × **generosa** LT ♀
Vigorous tree, with very large leaves when young. Attractive catkins, April.
– **koreana** MT ♀
Conspicuous, large, bright apple-green leaves, produced very early in spring.
– **lasiocarpa** MT ♀
Magnificent tree with stout shoots and huge leaves up to 30cm long. FCC 1908
– **nigra** LT ♀ "Black Poplar"
We recommend the following forms:
– –**betulifolia** LT ♀ "Manchester Poplar"
Bushy-headed tree. Very tolerant of atmospheric pollution.
– –**'Italica'** LT ♂ "Lombardy Poplar"
Very effective as a tall screen.
– **'Robusta'** LT ♀
Vigorous tree with a straight trunk and open crown. Young leaves coppery-red.
– **'Serotina'** LT ♀
Very vigorous, openly-branched tree. Leaves coppery-red when young. Catkins with conspicuous red anthers
– **'Serotina Aurea'** MT ♀ "Golden Poplar"
Leaves clear golden-yellow in spring and early summer, becoming greenish-yellow. Golden-yellow in autumn.
– **tacamahaca** see *P. balsamifera*
– **'Tacatricho 32'** (*balsamifera* × *trichocarpa*) (*TT 32*) LT ♂
Very fast growing tree of narrow habit.
– **tremula** MT ♀ "Aspen"
Prominently toothed leaves which tremble in the breeze. Clear yellow in autumn. Long, grey catkins, late winter.
– –**'Pendula'** ST ♠ "Weeping Aspen"
Weeping form, particularly effective in winter when laden with purplish-grey catkins.
– **trichocarpa** LT ♂ "Black Cottonwood"
Largest and fastest growing balsam poplar, peeling bark and large, sticky buds. Young leaves strongly scented. Rich yellow in autumn.

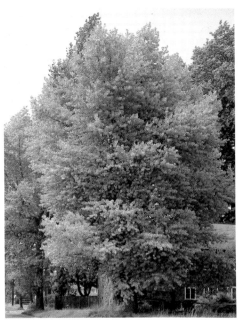
POPULUS 'Serotina Aurea'

– **violascens** LT ♀
Vigorous very large leaved tree related to *P. lasiocarpa*.
– **wilsonii** MT ♀
Resembles *P. lasiocarpa* but with smaller bright sea-green leaves.
"PORTUGAL LAUREL" see *PRUNUS lusitanica*
POTENTILLA – Rosaceae DS-MS
Invaluable plants for a shrub border, flowering over a long period.
– **arbuscula** DS
Large, rich-yellow flowers mid summer-late autumn. Sage-green leaves. AM 1925 AMT 1965 AGM 1969
– –**'Beesii'** DS
Golden-yellow flowers and silvery foliage. AGM 1956 AMT 1966
– **dahurica** DS-SS
Variable white flowered species. We recommend the following forms:
– –**'Abbotswood'** DS
Spreading habit. Dark foliage. Flowers profusely over long period. AMT 1965
– –**'Farrer's White'** SS
Erect habit.

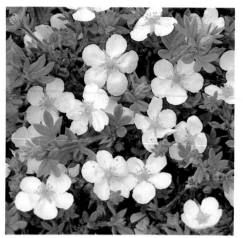

POTENTILLA dahurica 'Manchu'

– –**'Manchu'** (*fruticosa mandschurica* HORT)
DS GC
Dwarf, spreading habit. Greyish foliage.
Continuous flowering. AM 1924 AGM 1969
– –**veitchii** SS
Graceful arching habit. AGM 1969
– **'Daydawn'** SS
Flowers peach-pink, suffused cream.
– **'Elizabeth'** SS GC
Dome-shaped bush. Large, rich canary-
yellow flowers late spring-autumn. AMT 1965
AGM 1969
– **fruticosa** SS
Parent of many hybrids often listed under this
species.

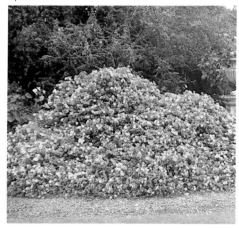

POTENTILLA 'Elizabeth'

– **'Goldfinger'** SS
Compact habit. Large, rich-yellow flowers.
– **'Katherine Dykes'** MS
Dome-shaped, with arching branches. Large,
yellow flowers, continuously produced.
AM 1944 AGM 1969
– **'Longacre'** DS GC
Dense, mat-forming habit. Large, bright
yellow flowers. AMT 1965
– **parvifolia** (*fruticosa farreri*) SS
Small leaves and relatively small rich yellow
flowers. AGM 1969. We recommend the
following:

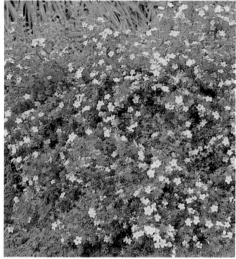

POTENTILLA parvifolia 'Klondike'

– –**'Klondike'** DS
Dwarf habit, larger bright, golden-yellow
flowers throughout summer. AMT 1965
– **'Primrose Beauty'** SS
Primrose-yellow flowers deeper in centre.
Grey-green foliage. Arching branches.
AMT 1965 AGM 1969
– **'Red Ace'** DS
Glowing red flowers over a long period.
FCC 1975 (Subject to Plant Breeders Rights)
– **'Sunset'** SS
Deep orange to brick red flowers.
– **'Tangerine'** DS
Wide-spreading, mound-forming. Flowers
pale, coppery-yellow.
– **'Vilmoriniana'** MS
Erect branched. Silvery leaves and cream
flowers. AGM 1926 AMT 1965

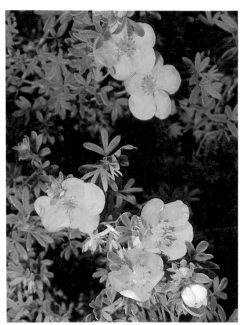

POTENTILLA 'Tangerine'

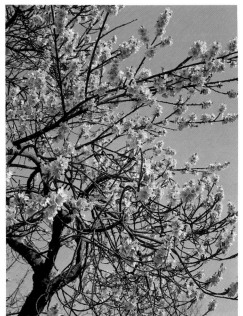

PRUNUS × amygdalo-persica 'Pollardii'

PROSTANTHERA – Labiatae SS-MS
(E) † ○
Floriferous, aromatic, Australasian shrubs for mild areas. We recommend the following:
– rotundifolia SS (E) † ○
Dense shrub with tiny leaves and masses of heliotrope flowers in spring. AM 1924
PRUNUS – Rosaceae PS-MT
A large genus containing many beautiful flowering trees.
*Peaches and almonds (*Prunus persica,
P. × amygdalo-persica *and* P. dulcis) *must be sprayed in mid-February and in early March with lime-sulphur, as a control for "Peach Leaf Curl".*
– 'Accolade' ST ♥
Semi-double, rich pink flowers, 4cm across, in profusion, early spring. AM 1952 AGM 1961
– × amygdalo-persica ST ♥
A hybrid between the peach and almond of which we recommend the following:
– – 'Pollardii' ST ♥
Rich pink, almond-like flowers. FCC 1935 AGM 1937
– amygdalus see *P. dulcis*
– armeniaca ST ♥ "Apricot"
We recommend the following form:

– – ansu 'Flore Pleno' (*P. mume 'Grandiflora'*)
ST ♥
Semi-double flowers, carmine in bud, opening pink. March-April. AM 1934
– avium MT ♥ "Gean" "Wild Cherry"
Dense clusters of white, cup-shaped flowers, April-May. Small, glossy, red-purple fruits.
– – 'Plena' (*'Multiplex'*) MT ♥ "Double Gean"
Masses of drooping, double-white flowers. AGM 1924 FCC 1964
– × blireana ST ♥
Metallic, coppery-purple leaves. Double rose-pink flowers, April. AM 1914 FCC 1923 AGM 1928
– cerasifera (*myrobalana*) ST ♥ Hdg (0.5m)
"Myrobalan" "Cherry Plum"
Myriads of small white flowers, February-March. Mature trees bear red or yellow, edible "cherry-plums".
– – 'Nigra' ST ♥ Hdg (0.5m)
Leaves and stems blackish-purple. Flowers prolific, single pink fading blush. FCC 1939
– – 'Pissardii' (*'Atropurpurea'*) ST ♥
Hdg (0.5m) "Purple-leaved Plum"
Dark-red young foliage, turning deep-purple. Abundant flowers pink in bud, opening white. FCC 1884 AGM 1928

--**'Rosea'** LS-ST ♀
Young leaves bronze-purple, turning bronze-green, then green. Flowers salmon-pink.
- **cerasus** ST ♀ "Sour Cherry"
We recommend the following:
--**'James H. Veitch'** see *'Fugenzo'* under Japanese Cherries
--**'Rhexii'** (*P. ranunculiflora*) ST ♀
Very showy, double, white flowers.

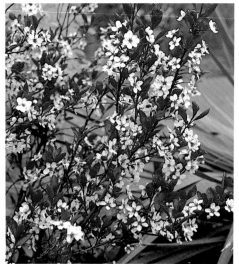

PRUNUS × cistena

- × **cistena** MS Hdg (0.5m) "Purple-leaf Sand Cherry"
Rich red leaves, white flowers in spring. Black-purple fruits.
- **conradinae** ST ♀
We recommend the following:
--**'Semiplena'** ST ♀
Long lasting, semi-double flowers, late February-March. AM 1935
- **davidiana** ST ♦
One of the earliest trees to bloom, January to March. We recommend the following:
--**'Alba'** ST ♦
Flowers white. FCC 1892 AGM 1927
--**'Rubra'** ST ♦
Flowers pink.

- **dulcis** (*amygdalus*) T ♀ "Common Almond"
One of the most popular spring-flowering trees. We recommend the following:
--**'Macrocarpa'** ST ♀
Large, very pale-pink or white flowers. Large fruits. AM 1931

--**nana** see *P. tenella*
--**'Roseoplena'** ST ♀ "Double Almond"
Double pale pink flowers.
- **glandulosa** SS ○ "Chinese Bush Cherry"
Neat, bushy habit with slender, erect shoots.
We recommend the following:
--**'Albiplena'** SS ○
Pendant shoots wreathed with double, white flowers, early May. AM 1950
--**'Sinensis'** (*japonica 'Flore Roseoplena'*) SS ○
Double, bright-pink flowers. AM 1968
- **'Hally Jolivette'** LS-ST ♀
Slender, willowy stems, covered in early spring with small, semi-double, blush-white flowers.
- × **hillieri** MT ♀
Abundant, soft-pink flowers in spring. Gorgeous autumn colour. AM 1959
--**'Spire'** ST ♦
Narrow habit, soft-pink flowers and good autumn colour. Excellent for restricted spaces.
- **incisa** LS-ST ♀ "Fuji Cherry"
Abundant, small white flowers, pink-tinged in bud, March. AM 1927 AGM 1930
--**'Praecox'** LS-ST ♀
Flowers during late winter. AM 1957 FCC 1973
- × **juddii** ST ♀
Pale pink flowers in late April or early May. Deep crimson autumn colour.
- **kurilensis** (*nipponica kurilensis*) ST ♦
We recommend the following:

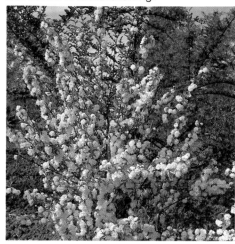

PRUNUS glandulosa 'Albiplena'

-–**'Ruby'** ST ☀
Narrow tree with masses of pale-pink flowers, early April.

-**Kursar** ST ♀
Small, rich deep-pink flowers, March-early April. Young leaves reddish-bronze. AM 1952

-**laurocerasus** LS (E) "Cherry Laurel"
Vigorous shrub with glossy leaves and white flowers in erect racemes, April. Black, cherry-like fruits. For chalky soils and very cold areas *P. lusitanica* is more suitable. We recommend the following forms:
A (f) 5

-–**'Greenmantle'** LS (E)
A wide spreading form of open habit.

-–**'Latifolia'** LS (E)
Tall, vigorous, large-leaved form.

-–**'Magnoliifolia'** LS (E)
Very large, glossy leaves.

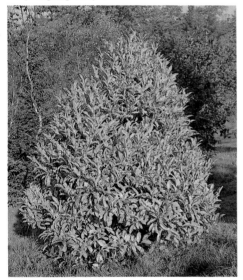

PRUNUS laurocerasus 'Marbled White'

-–**'Marbled White'** (*'Variegata'*) LS (E)
Slow-growing, dense, broadly conical habit. Leaves conspicuously marbled with grey-green and white.

-–**'Otto Luyken'** SS (E) GC
Outstanding form of dense, dome-shaped habit with narrow, glossy dark-green leaves. AM 1968 AGM 1973

-–**'Rotundifolia'** MS (E) Hdg (0.5m)
Bushy form with short leaves. Recommended for hedging.

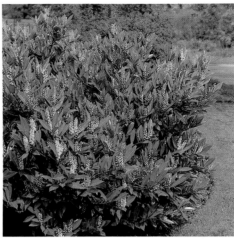

PRUNUS laurocerasus 'Otto Luyken'

-–**'Schipkaensis'** MS (E) GC
Spreading habit, narrow leaves, free flowering. AM 1959

-–**'Zabeliana'** SS (E) GC
Horizontally branched, with very narrow leaves. Very free flowering. AGM 1973

-**lusitanica** LS-ST (E) ♀ "Portugal Laurel"
Hdg (0.5m)
Glossy, dark-green ovate leaves, with red leaf stalks. White flowers in erect racemes. Dark purple fruits. Good on chalk. A (f) 5

-–**azorica** LS (E)
Magnificent densely bushy shrub with larger, bright green leaves, red when young.
FCC 1866

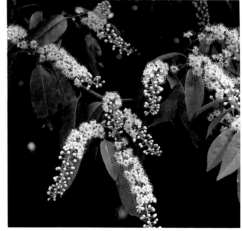

PRUNUS lusitanica

– – **'Myrtifolia'** (*'Angustifolia'*) (*'Pyramidalis'*)
LS (E)
Dense, conical habit. Smaller leaves. A good
substitute for *Laurus nobilis* ("Bay Tree") in
cold areas.
– – **'Variegata'** LS (E)
Leaves conspicuously margined white,
sometimes flushed pink in winter.
– **maackii** ST ♥ "Manchurian Cherry"
Shining, golden-brown, flaking bark. Small
white flowers, April.
– **mume** ST ♥ "Japanese Apricot"
Pink, almond-scented flowers, late winter-
early spring. We recommend the following
forms:
– – **'Alboplena'** ST ♥
Semi-double, white flowers.
– – **'Alphandii'** ST ♥
Semi-double, pink flowers.
– – **'Beni-shi-don'** ST ♥
Strongly fragrant, double, rich madder-pink
flowers. AM 1981
– – **'Rosea Plena'** see *P. armeniaca ansu*
'Flore Pleno'
– **mutabilis** see *P. serrulata spontanea*
– **myrobalana** see *P. cerasifera*
– **nana** see *P. tenella*
– **'Okame'** ST ♥
Masses of carmine-rose flowers in March.
Attractive autumn tints. AM 1947 AGM 1952
– **padus** MT ♥ "Bird Cherry"
Racemes of small, white, almond-scented
flowers, May.
– – **'Albertii'** MT ♥
Vigorous, free-flowering form.
– – **'Colorata'** MT ♥
Flowers pale pink, young leaves coppery-
purple. AM 1974
– – **'Watereri'** (*'Grandiflora'*) MT ♥
Flowers in conspicuous racemes up to 20cm
long. AGM 1930 AM 1969
– **'Pandora'** ST ♥
Masses of pale, shell-pink flowers, March-
early April. AM 1939 AGM 1959
– **persica** LS-ST ♥ "Peach"
We recommend the following ornamental
form:
– – **'Klara Meyer'** (*'Flore Roseoplena'*) LS ○
Double, peach-pink flowers. AGM 1939
– **'Pink Shell'** ST ♥
Elegant tree with drooping branches,
abundant, delicate shell-pink flowers.
AM 1969

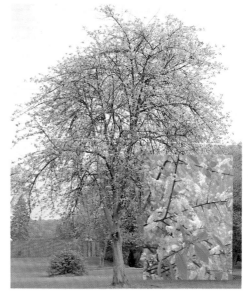

PRUNUS padus 'Watereri"

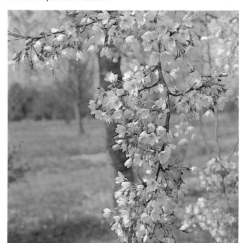

PRUNUS 'Pink Shell'

– × **pollardii** see *P. × amygdalo-persica*
'Pollardii'
– **prostrata** DS ○ "Rock Cherry"
Wide, spreading habit. Pale-pink flowers,
April.
– **pumila** "Sand Cherry"
We recommend the following form:
– – **depressa** PS ○ GC
Wide spreading shrub. Small white flowers,
May. Good autumn colour.

– **rufa** ST ♥ "Himalayan Cherry"
Small clusters of pale-pink flowers. Often has attractive, peeling reddish-brown or amber bark.

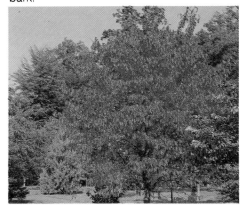

PRUNUS sargentii

– **sargentii** (*serrulata sachalinensis*) MT ♥
One of the loveliest of all cherries. Flowers single, pink, late March-early April. Young leaves bronze-red. Gorgeous autumn colours. AM 1921 FCC 1925 AGM 1928
– – **'Rancho'** MT ❋
A form of narrow growth with upswept branches.
– × **schmittii** MT ❋
Vigorous tree with polished brown bark. Pale-pink flowers, spring.

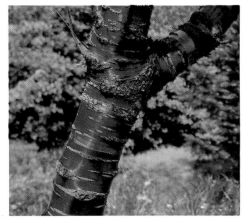

PRUNUS serrula

– **serrula** ST ♥
Glossy, red-brown, mahogany-like bark. Small, white flowers, late April. AM 1944

– **serrulata** ST-MT ♥
We recommend the following forms:
– – **'Autumn Glory'** ST-MT ❋
Abundant, pale-blush flowers. Consistent rich-red autumn colour. AM 1966
– – **erecta** see *'Amanogawa'* under Japanese Cherries
– – **longipes** see *'Shimidsu Sakura'* under Japanese Cherries
– – **rosea** see *'Kiku-shidare Sakura'* under Japanese Cherries
– – **sachalinensis** see *P. sargentii*
– – **spontanea** (*P. mutabilis*) (*P. jamasakura*) MT ♥ "Hill Cherry"
Young foliage bronze. Flowers white or pink, late April. AM 1936
– **'Snow Goose'** ST ❋
Masses of pure white flowers in spring.
– **spinosa** LS Hdg (0.5m) "Blackthorn" "Sloe"
Dense, spiny shrub studded with small white flowers March-early April. Black fruits.
– – **'Purpurea'** MS
Rich purple leaves. White flowers. Dense habit. AGM 1973

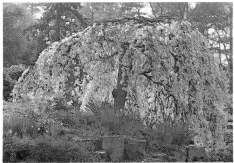

PRUNUS subhirtella 'Pendula Rosea'

– **subhirtella** ST ♥ "Spring Cherry"
We recommend the following forms:
– – **'Autumnalis'** ST ♥ "Autumn Cherry"
Semi-double, white flowers produced over period November to March.
AM 1912 AGM 1924 FCC 1966
– – **'Autumnalis Rosea'** ST ♥
Semi-double, blush-pink flowers. AM 1960
– – **'Fukubana'** ST ♥
The most colourful form with masses of semi-double, rose-madder flowers.
– – **'Pendula Rosea'** ST ↟ "Weeping Spring Cherry"
Mushroom habit. Flowers rich pink in bud, fading to blush, late March-early April.

PRUNUS subhirtella – Continued

– – **'Pendula Rubra'** ST ↟
Deep rose flowers, carmine in bud.
– **tenella** (*nana*) SS "Dwarf Russian Almond"
We recommend the following form:

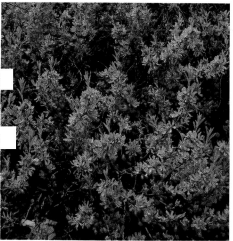

PRUNUS tenella 'Fire Hill'

– – **'Fire Hill'** SS ☼
Erect stems, wreathed with brilliant rose-red
flowers, April. AM 1959 AGM 1969

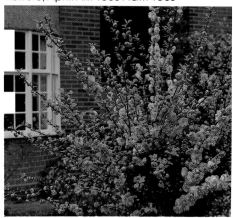

PRUNUS triloba

– **triloba** (*triloba multiplex*) MS
Large, double, rosette-like clear peach-pink
flowers in profusion, late March-early April.
AGM 1935. C (a) 5
– × **yedoensis** MT ♥ "Yoshino Cherry"
Arching branches. Profusion of
almond-scented blush-white flowers, late
March-early April. AM 1927 AGM 1930

PRUNUS × yedoensis – Continued

– – **'Ivensii'** ST ↟
Snow-white cascades of delicately fragrant
flowers, late March-early April.
– – **'Shidare Yoshino'** (*perpendens*)
(*'Pendula'*) ST ↟
Branches weeping to the ground. Pale-pink
flowers, in March-April.

JAPANESE CHERRIES
of Garden Origin
*Mainly small trees of easy cultivation in all
well-drained soils. Often with bronze young
leaves. Flowers single, semi-double or
double, varying from rich pink to white or
cream. Flowering times are indicated as
follows:*

> *Early – Late March-early April*
> *Mid – Mid-late April*
> *Late – Late April-early May*

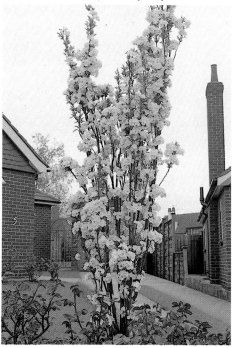

PRUNUS 'Amanogawa'

– **'Amanogawa'** (*serrulata erecta*) ST ❙
Narrow habit. Upright clusters of fragrant,
semi-double, shell-pink flowers. Mid to late.
AM 1931 AGM 1931
– **'Asano'** ST ⚑
Dense clusters of very double, deep pink,
flowers. Early.

– **'Fudanzakura'** ST ♥
Flowers single, white, pink in bud, produced between November and April. AM 1930

– **'Fugenzo'** (*cerasus 'James H. Veitch'*) ST ♥
Flowers large, double, rose-pink, in drooping clusters, very late. FCC 1899

– **'Fukubana'** see *P. subhirtella 'Fukubana'*

– **'Gioiko'** MT ♥
Flowers semi-double, creamy-white, streaked green, and often tinged pink. Mid. AM 1930

– **'Hisakura'** ST ♥
Single deep pink flowers. Mid. *'Kanzan'* is the double, purplish-pink, cherry often erroneously called *'Hisakura'*.

– **'Hokusai'** ST ♥
Vigorous tree. Masses of large, semi-double, pale-pink flowers, in large clusters. Mid.

– **'Ichiyo'** ST ♥
Ascending branches. Double, shell-pink flowers, frilled at the edge, in long-stalked clusters. Mid. AM 1959

– **'Jo-nioi'** ST ♥
Single white, deliciously scented flowers, Mid.

– **'Kanzan'** MT ♥
One of the most popular ornamental cherries. Large, showy, double, purplish-pink flowers. Mid. Vigorous.

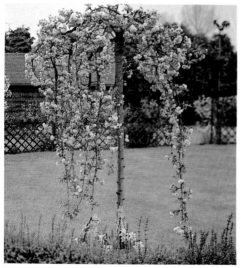

PRUNUS 'Kiku-shidare Sakura'

– **'Kiku-shidare Sakura'** ST ↟
Drooping branches, wreathed with very double, clear, deep pink flowers, early. AM 1915

– **'Ojochin'** ST ♥
Large, single flowers, pink in bud, opening blush, profusely borne in large, long-stalked clusters. Mid. AM 1924 AGM 1926

– **'Pink Perfection'** ST ♥
Flowers double, bright rosy-pink in bud, opening paler, in long, drooping clusters. Mid-late. AM 1945

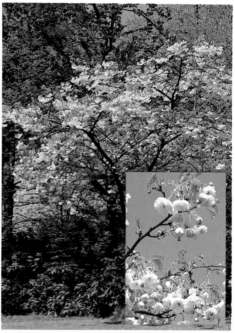

PRUNUS 'Shimidsu Sakura'

– **'Shimidsu Sakura'** (*serrulata longpipes*) ST
♥
Most-attractive. Flowers large, fimbriated double, pink tinged in bud, opening pure white, hanging in long-stalked clusters. Mid-late. AM 1930 AGM 1933

– **'Shirofugen'** MT ♥
Flowers large, double, purplish-pink in bud, opening white, fading to purplish-pink, contrasting well with the copper-coloured young leaves, very late.

– **'Shirotae'** ST ♥
Slightly drooping branches. Very large, single or semi-double, fragrant, snow-white flowers. Mid.

– **'Tai Haku'** MT ♥ "Great White Cherry"
Flowers very large, single, dazzling white. Mid. AM 1931 FCC 1944 AGM 1964

– **'Ukon'** MT ♀
Flowers semi-double, pale yellowish, tinged green, occasionally pink flushed. Mid. Spreading. AM 1923 AGM 1969
– **"Yoshino"** see *P.* × *yedoensis*
PSEUDOPANAX – Araliaceae MS-ST (E) †
○
Unusual and distinctive shrubs or small trees mainly from New Zealand. The leaves vary, depending on the age of the plant.
– **crassifolius** ST (E) ♦ † ○
Leaves on young plants long and rigid, sharply toothed.
– **davidii** (*Nothopanax davidii*) MS (E) † ○
Leaves simple or divided into two or three leaflets. Small greenish flowers in clusters; black fruits.
– **ferox** ST (E) ♦ † ○
Resembles *P. crassifolius* but with shorter leaves with strongly hooked teeth.
PSEUDOSASA japonica see *ARUNDINARIA japonica*
PSEUDOWINTERA – Winteraceae MS (E) †
◑
A monotypic genus related to Drimys.
– **colorata** (*Drimys colorata*) MS (E) † ◑
Remarkable for its unusually coloured oval, leathery leaves – pale yellow-green, flushed pink, edged and blotched deep crimson-purple.

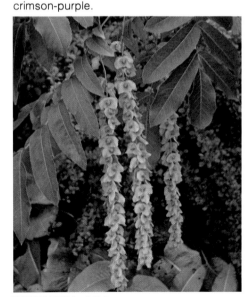

PTEROCARYA fraxinifolia

PTELEA – Rutaceae LS-ST
We recommend the following:
– **trifoliata** LS "Hop Tree"
Trifoliolate leaves. Small, very fragrant, yellowish flowers, June. Dense clusters of persistent, green-winged fruits.

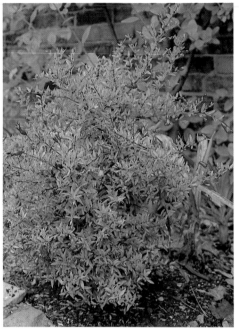

PUNICA granatum 'Nana'

– – **'Aurea'** LS
Leaves soft yellow.
PTEROCARYA – Juglandaceae LT ♀
Vigorous trees with handsome, pinnate leaves. Flowers in catkins. Any fertile soil.
– **fraxinifolia** (*caucasica*) LT ♀
Wide-spreading tree. Large leaves, with numerous leaflets. Greenish flowers in pendulous catkins, the female up to 50cm long.
– × **rehderana** LT ♀
Vigorous, suckering tree. Long, fruiting catkins a feature for several months.
PTEROSTYRAX – Styracaceae LS-ST
We recommend the following species:
– **hispida** LS
Drooping panicles of fragrant white flowers, June-July. Five-ribbed fruits. AM 1964
PUNICA – Punicaceae LS † ○
Only one species is in general cultivation.

– **granatum** LS † ○ "Pomegranate"
Glossy-green leaves, coppery when young, yellow in autumn. Funnel-shaped scarlet or orange-red flowers with crumpled petals, late summer-early autumn. Fruits after a long, hot summer. Best on warm wall.

– – **'Nana'** (*'Gracillima'*) DS † ○
Dwarf form with narrow leaves. Orange-scarlet flowers in profusion, September-October. AM 1936

PYRACANTHA – Rosaceae MS-LS (E)
Hdg (0.6m) "Firethorn"
Invaluable, thorny evergreens. Masses of small white flowers in summer, spectacular clusters of yellow, orange or red fruits, autumn-winter. A (f) 5

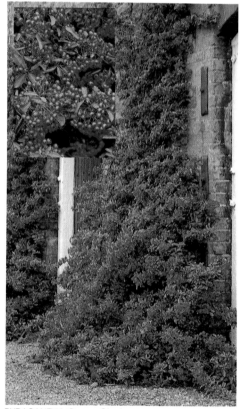

PYRACANTHA 'Orange Glow'

– **angustifolia** MS (E)
Narrow leaves, grey-felted beneath. Clusters of orange-yellow fruits, retained through the winter. FCC 1904

– **atalantioides** (*gibbsii*) LS (E)
Large, glossy, dark-green leaves and long-lasting scarlet fruits. FCC 1918 AGM 1922

– – **'Aurea'** (*'Flava'*) LS (E)
Fruits rich yellow. AM 1936 AGM 1969

– **'Buttercup'** MS (E)
Spreading habit, abundant, small, rich-yellow fruits.

– **coccinea** LS (E)
We recommend the form:

– – **'Lalandei'** LS (E)
Vigorous, erect habit. Abundant, large, orange-red fruits. AGM 1925

– **gibbsii** see *P. atalantioides*

– **'Golden Charmer'** LS (E)
Vigorous, upright habit, orange-yellow fruits.

– **'Mohave'** LS (E)
Wide spreading habit, masses of large, orange-red fruits.

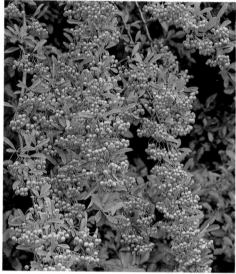

PYRACANTHA rogersiana 'Flava'

– **'Orange Charmer'** LS (E)
Upright habit. Large, deep orange fruits, freely borne.

– **'Orange Glow'** LS (E)
Dense habit. Bright orange-red fruits, persisting into winter. Free fruiting.

– **rogersiana** (*crenulata rogersiana*) LS (E)
Narrow leaves, reddish-orange fruits. Free fruiting. AGM 1937 AM 1953

– – **'Flava'** LS (E)
Fruits bright yellow. FCC 1919 AGM 1969

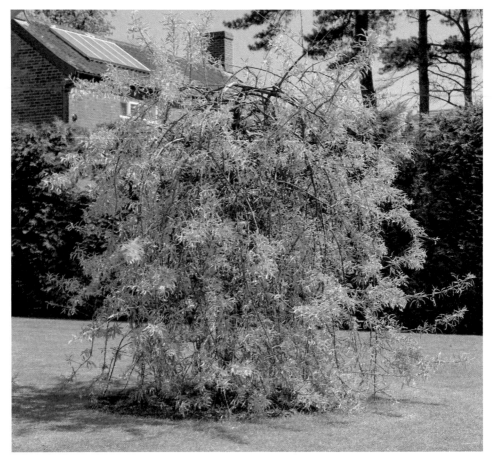

PYRUS salicifolia 'Pendula'

– **'Soleil d'Or'** MS (E)
Spreading habit. Orange-yellow fruits. Very useful as ground cover or for mass bedding.
– **'Watereri'** LS (E)
Compact habit. Abundant, bright-red fruits. AM 1955 AGM 1969

PYRUS – Rosaceae ST-MT
Ornamental trees often with silvery leaves. White flowers, April. Tolerant of atmospheric pollution. All soils.
– **betulifolia** ST ♥
Slender fast-growing tree. Leaves grey-green at first, becoming glossy-green. Small, brown fruits.
– **calleryana** ST ♥
We recommend the following form:
– – **'Chanticleer'** ST ♦
Neat, narrowly conical crown, glossy leaves turn rich purple and claret in autumn.

– **communis** "Common Pear" ST ♥
Apart from fruiting forms we recommend the following:
– – **'Beech Hill'** ST ♦
Upright habit, glossy green leaves – brilliant orange-yellow in autumn.
– **nivalis** ST ♥
Abundant, pure white flowers, April, with the white woolly young leaves. Small, yellowish-green fruits.
– **salicifolia** "Willow-leaved Pear" ST ♥
We recommend the following form:
– – **'Pendula'** ST ♠
Graceful, small tree. Silvery, willow-like leaves. Flowers creamy-white. Brown, top-shaped fruits. AGM 1969

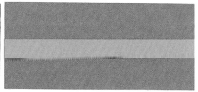

QUERCUS – Fagaceae SS-LT
A large genus of deciduous and evergreen trees. Best on deep, rich soils and mostly lime tolerant, except on shallow chalk soils.
– **acutissima** MT ♥
Glossy, green, chestnut-like leaves with bristle-tipped teeth, persisting well into winter.
– **aegilops** see *Q. macrolepis*
– **alba** MT ♥ ⨍ "White Oak"
Deeply lobed leaves, reddish when young. Purple-crimson in autumn.
– **aliena** ST ♥
Large, coarsely toothed leaves, glossy, green above.
– **ambrozyana** see *Q. × hispanica 'Ambrozyana'*
– **aquatica** see *Q. nigra*
– **bambusifolia** see *Q. myrsinifolia*
– **bicolor** MT ♥ ⨍
Flaking bark, especially on young trees. Shallowly lobed, glossy, green leaves, usually grey- or white-felted beneath.
– **canariensis** (*mirbeckii*) LT ♥ "Algerian Oak"
Fast growing tree for all soils. Large, shallowly lobed, glossy, green leaves persisting until new year. Young trees have narrow habit.
– **castaneifolia** MT ♥ "Chestnut-leaved Oak"
Long, narrow, glossy, green leaves with sharp-pointed teeth.
– – **'Green Spire'** MT ♥
A vigorous form of compact, broadly columnar habit.
– **cerris** LT ♥ "Turkey Oak"
Fast growing tree with shallowly lobed leaves. Excellent on chalk soils and in coastal situations.
– – **'Variegata'** MT ♥
Leaves with a very conspicuous creamy-white margin. Narrow habit when young.
– **coccifera** SS-MS (E) ○
Dense, slow-growing shrub with glossy, green, usually prickly leaves.
– **coccinea** LT ♥ ⨍ "Scarlet Oak"
Deeply lobed leaves, glossy green above,

with bristle-tipped teeth. Glowing scarlet in autumn.
– – **'Splendens'** LT ♥ ⨍
Rich scarlet autumn colour. FCC 1893 AGM 1927
– **conferta** see *Q. frainetto*
– **dentata** ST ♥ ⨍ "Daimyo Oak"
Small, angular tree with very large, obovate, broadly lobed leaves. AM 1901
– **edulis** see *LITHOCARPUS edulis*
– **ellipsoidalis** MT ♥ ⨍
Deeply-lobed, slender-stalked leaves turn deep crimson in autumn.
– **frainetto** (*conferta*) LT ♥ "Hungarian Oak"
Fast growing tree with fissured bark. Leaves deeply and regularly lobed. Excellent on all soils, including chalk.
– **henryi** see *LITHOCARPUS henryi*
– × **hispanica** LT Semi-(E) ♥
Vigorous hybrids between the "Cork Oak" and the "Turkey Oak". Leaves retained until spring.
We recommend the following forms:
– – **'Ambrozyana'** LT Semi-(E) ♥
Leathery, dark green, toothed leaves, white beneath.
– – **'Lucombeana'** (*Q. lucombeana*) LT Semi-(E) ♥ "Lucombe Oak"
Sharply toothed, glossy, green leaves, grey beneath.
– **hypoleucoides** ST (E) ♥ ○
Narrow, leathery, pointed, leaves, grey-downy beneath.
– **ilex** LT (E) ♥ "Evergreen Oak" "Holm Oak"
Leathery, glossy, dark green, entire or toothed leaves. Branches pendulous at tips on old trees. Excellent on chalk or in coastal areas.
– × **kewensis** MT (E) ♥
Vigorous, compact habit with small, dark green, angularly lobed leaves.
– **lanuginosa** see *Q. pubescens*
– **libani** ST ♥ "Lebanon Oak"
Narrow, long, persistent, glossy, green leaves, margined with triangular, bristle-tipped teeth.

– **lucombeana** see *Q.* × *hispanica* *'Lucombeana'*

– × **ludoviciana** LT Semi-(E) ♥ ⚹
Vigorous tree with deeply and irregularly lobed, glossy, green leaves. Rich autumn colours.

lusitanica ST ♥ "Portuguese Oak"
Strongly toothed leaves, grey-felted beneath.

– **macedonica** see *Q. trojana*

– **macranthera** MT ♥
Fast growing tree with stout shoots and large, strongly lobed leaves, softly downy beneath.

– **macrocarpa** MT ⚹ "Burr Oak" "Mossy-cup Oak"
Leaves very large, conspicuously lobed, glossy green, felted beneath.

– **macrolepis** (*aegilops*) "Valonia Oak"
Greyish, olive-green leaves, with bristle tipped lobes, grey-downy beneath.

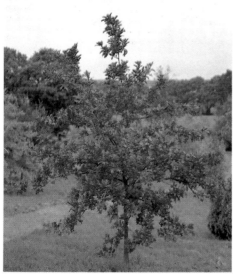

QUERCUS palustris

– **marilandica** ST ♥ ⚹ "Black Jack Oak"
Slow growing tree with very distinct, broadly obovate or almost triangular leaves, three-lobed at the broad apex, glossy green above, tawny-yellow beneath.

– **mirbeckii** see *Q. canariensis*

– **mongolica** ST ♥ ⚹ "Mongolian Oak"
Striking, irregular tree. Large, strongly lobed leaves in dense clusters at ends of branches.

– **myrsinifolia** (*bambusifolia*) (*vibrayeana*) ST (E) ♥

Densely branched, compact habit. Narrow glossy green, pointed and remotely toothed leaves, purplish-red when young.

– **nigra** (*aquatica*) MT ♥ ⚹ "Water Oak"
Obovate, variously lobed or entire leaves, glossy green on both sides.

– **palustris** LT ♥ "Pin Oak"
Leaves deeply and sharply lobed, glossy green, often turning rich scarlet in autumn. Branches droop gracefully at the tips.

– **pedunculata** see *Q. robur*

– **petraea** (*sessiliflora*) LT ♥ "Sessile Oak" "Durmast Oak"
One of our native oaks, differing from *Q. robur* in its long-stalked leaves and sessile acorns. Good on damp soils.

– – **'Columnaris'** MT ⚹
A densely branched form of columnar habit.

– – **'Purpurea'** (*'Rubicunda'*) LT ♥
Young leaves deep, reddish-purple.

– **phellos** LT ♥ ⚹ "Willow Oak"
Leaves glossy green, narrow, usually entire, willow-like, yellow and orange in autumn.

– **phillyreoides** LS-ST ♥ (E) ○
Leathery, glossy green, minutely toothed leaves, bronze tinted when young. Rare.

– **pontica** ST ♥ ⚹ "Armenian Oak"
Rugged tree with stout shoots and large, coarsely toothed leaves. Rich yellow autumn colour.

– × **pseudoturneri** see *Q.* × *turneri*

– **pubescens** (*lanuginosa*) ST ♥
Leaves wavy-edged, deeply lobed, covered with a thick, grey down.

– **pyrenaica** (*toza*) LT ♥ "Pyrenean Oak"
Spreading, slightly drooping branches. Leaves deeply lobed, glossy green above, grey-felted beneath.

– **robur** (*pedunculata*) LT ♥ "Common Oak" "English Oak"
Our best known native species. Leaves shallowly lobed, nearly sessile; stalked acorns.

– – **'Atropurpurea'** ST ♥
Slow growing with young leaves and shoots rich, vinous-purple.

– – **'Fastigiata'** LT ⚹ "Cypress Oak"
A large imposing tree of columnar habit.

– – **'Fastigiata Purpurea'** MT ⚹
Young leaves reddish-purple throughout the growing season.

– – **'Filicifolia'** see *Q.* × *rosacea* *'Filicifolia'*

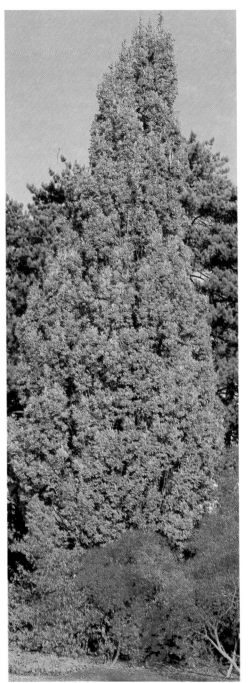

QUERCUS robur 'Fastigiata'

––**'Pectinata'** see *Q.* × *rosacea 'Filicifolia'*
––**'Pendula'** ST ♠ "Weeping Oak"
A form with pendulous branches.
––**'Variegata'** MT ✚
Leaves with irregular, creamy-white margin.
– × **rosacea** LT ♥
A hybrid between our two native oaks.
We recommend the following form:
––**'Filicifolia'** (*robur 'Filicifolia'*) (*robur
'Pectinata'*) LT ♥
Leaves pinnately divided into narrow, forward
pointing lobes.
– **rubra** (*borealis maxima*) LT ♥ ✗ "Red Oak"
Fast growing tree thriving even in industrial
areas. Leaves sharply lobed, matt green; red,
then red-brown in autumn. AM 1971
AGM 1973
––**'Aurea'** ST ♥ ✗ ◑
Young leaves bright yellow. AM 1971
– × **schochiana** MT ♥ ✗
Leaves glossy green, willow-like or with a few
teeth. Bright yellow in autumn.
– **serrata** see *Q. acutissima*
– **shumardii** ST ♥
Attractive, deeply-cut leaves, red or golden-
brown in autumn.
– **suber** MT (E) ♥ "Cork Oak"
Thick, rugged, corky bark. Leaves broadly-
toothed, leathery, glossy green above, grey-
green felted beneath.
– **toza** see *Q. pyrenaica*
– **trojana** (*macedonica*) MT Semi-(E) ♥
"Macedonian Oak"
Densely branched tree. Leaves glossy, taper-
pointed, margined with incurved, triangular
teeth.
– × **turneri** (× *pseudoturneri*) MT Semi-(E) ♥
"Turner's Oak"
Compact, rounded head. Leaves dark green,
toothed.
– **variabilis** LT ♥
Elegant tree with thick, corky bark. Leaves
narrow, chestnut-like with bristle-tipped teeth,
grey pubescent beneath.
– **velutina** LT ♥ ✗ "Black Oak" "Yellow-bark
Oak"
Large, glossy dark-green leaves.
We recommend the following form:
––**'Rubrifolia'** (*'Albertsii'*) LT ♥ ✗
Enormous leaves up to 40cm long, reddish-
brown and yellowish in autumn.
– **vibrayeana** see *Q. myrsinifolia*
"QUICK" see *CRATAEGUS monogyna*

RAPHIOLEPIS – Rosaceae SS (E) ○

Slow growing shrubs with leathery leaves.
Well drained soil. Good on sunny walls.

– × delacourii SS (E) † ○

Obovate, glossy, green leaves. Flowers in erect, terminal panicles in spring or summer. We recommend the following:

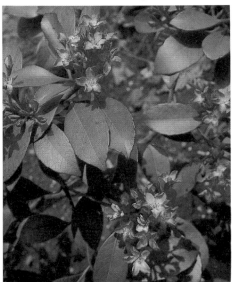

RAPHIOLEPIS × delacourii 'Coates Crimson'

– – 'Coates Crimson' SS (E) † ○

Flowers rose-crimson.

– umbellata (*japonica*) SS (E) ○

Dense, rounded habit with thick, oval, inconspicuously toothed leaves. Clusters of slightly fragrant, white flowers, June. Bronze-black fruits.

REHDERODENDRON – Styracaceae ST ✕

A small genus of Chinese trees.

– macrocarpum ST ✕

Leaves finely serrate, 7.5 to 10cm long. Flowers, in pendulous clusters, white, tinged pink with conspicuous yellow anthers, May. Oblong, pendulous, bright-red fruits. Attractive autumn colour. Rare. AM 1947

RHAMNUS – Rhamnaceae PS-LS

Deciduous or evergreen trees and shrubs
with small but numerous flowers. For all soils in
sun or semi-shade.

– alaterna LS (E)

Vigorous, bushy habit; glossy, dark green leaves. Yellowish green flowers. Fruits red, then black. Good in coastal and industrial areas.

– – 'Argenteovariegata' MS (E)

Leaves green, marbled grey with irregular creamy-white margin.

– cathartica LS "Common Buckthorn"

Slender, spiny branches with glossy, green, finely-toothed leaves. Abundant shining, black fruits. Good on shallow chalk soils.

– frangula LS "Alder Buckthorn"

Entire, glossy, green leaves, yellow in autumn. Fruits red, turning black. Suitable for moist areas.

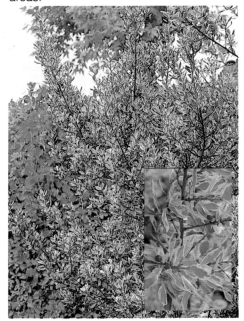

RHAMNUS alaterna 'Argenteovariegata'

– imeritina LS

Very distinct in its stout shoots. Large leaves, downy beneath usually bronze-purple in autumn. Large black buds. Good in damp soils.

– procumbens PS

Low mounds of intricate stems with small, glossy, green leaves; black fruits.

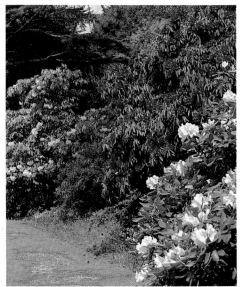

Grouped RHODODENDRONS

RHODODENDRON (including *AZALEA*) –
Ericaceae PS-ST ✗ ◑

Vast group of diverse ornamental plants, both deciduous and evergreen. Primarily noted for magnificent inflorescences. Range of flowering from January-August, although majority are April-June. Many have handsome foliage, some of the deciduous kinds being known for rich autumn leaf colour. They require moist, well drained, lime free soil and relish annual mulching. Large leaved forms require shelter from wind damage. Relative hardiness denoted by use of R.H.S. symbols as follows:

H4 – hardy anywhere in British Isles
H3 – hardy in South and West, and along seaboard and sheltered inland gardens
H2 – requires protection in most sheltered gardens
H1 – should usually only be grown as a greenhouse plant.

RHODODENDRON SPECIES (including
AZALEA series) PS-ST ✗ ◑

Dwarf species make ideal rock garden subjects. Large-leaved species require wind shelter, ideally thin oak woodland with some evergreen protection. The series or section to which each species belongs is indicated in brackets after the name.
Awards given to unnamed forms of species are indicated AM (F) or FCC (F)

– aberconwayi (s. Irroratum) MS (E) ✗ ◑

Rigid, leathery leaves. Loose trusses of saucer-shaped flowers. White, tinged pink and spotted maroon; May-June. AM 1945 H3

– aechmophyllum see *R. yunnanense*

– aemulorum see *R. mallotum*

– aeruginosum see *R. campanulatum aeruginosum*

– albrechtii (*Azalea albrechtii*) (s. Azalea) MS ✗ ◑

Open habit. Leaves clustered at branch tips, turn yellow, autumn. Deep rose flowers, before or with leaves; April-May. AM 1943 AGM 1969 H4

– amagianum (*Azalea amagiana*) (s. Azalea) MS-LS ✗ ◑

Leaves in threes, at branch tips. Funnel-shaped orange-red flowers, 3 or 4 to truss; June-July. AM 1948 H4

– arborescens (*Azalea arborescens*) (s. Azalea) LS ✗ ◑

Glossy leaves, pale green or glaucous beneath, usually colouring autumn. Fragrant, white, funnel-shaped flowers, sometimes flushed pink, long red protruding style; June-July. H4

– arboreum (s. Arboreum) LS-ST (E) ✗ ◑

Leaves, whitish or rust coloured beneath, up to 20cm long, impressed venation. Bell-shaped flowers in dense globular heads; January-April. H2-4.
We recommend the forms:

– – 'Blood Red' LS-ST (E) ✗ ◑

Blood red flowers. H3

– – 'Roseum' LS-ST (E) ✗ ◑

Rich pink flowers, darker spots. AM 1973 FCC 1974 H4

– – 'Sir Charles Lemon' LS-ST (E) ✗ ◑

White flowers. H3

– argyrophyllum (s. Arboreum) LS (E) ✗ ◑

Long leaves silvery or white felted beneath. Lax trusses of bell-shaped flowers. Slow. AM (F) 1934 H4

We recommend:

– – 'Chinese Silver' LS (E) ⊀ ◑
Leaves silver beneath. Pink flowers, darker on the lobes; May. AM 1957 H4

– arizelum (s. Falconeri) LS-ST (E) ⊀ ◑
Large leaves, cinnamon indumentum beneath. Compact heads of creamy yellow bells, sometimes rose-tinted, dark crimson blotch; April. For damp woodland. H3-4

– atlanticum (*Azalea atlantica*) (s. Azalea) SS ⊀ ◑
Stoloniferous. Fragrant, funnel-shaped flowers, white or tinged pink, occasional yellow blotch; May. H4

– aucklandii see *R. griffithianum*

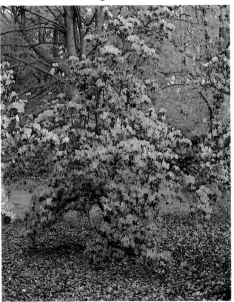

RHODODENDRON augustinii

– augustinii (s. Triflorum) LS (E) ⊀ ◑
Small leaves. Delightful blue flowers; April-May. Excellent woodland shrub. AGM 1924 AM 1926 H3-4

– – chasmanthum (*R. chasmanthum*) LS (E) ⊀ ◑
Larger trusses of pale to deep lavender-mauve flowers, flowering later. AM 1930 FCC 1932 H3

– – 'Electra' LS (E) ⊀ ◑
Clusters of violet blue flowers marked with greenish-yellow blotches, appearing almost luminous en masse. AM 1940 H3

– auriculatum (s. Auriculatum) LS (E) ⊀ ◑
Richly-scented large, white, funnel-shaped flowers in huge trusses; July-August. AM 1922 H4

– barbatum (s. Barbatum) LS-ST (E) ⊀ ◑
Attractive peeling bark. Conspicuous bristles on petioles and branchlets. Dense, globular heads of crimson-scarlet, bell-shaped flowers; March. AM 1954 H3-4

– basilicum (s. Falconeri) LS-ST (E) ⊀ ◑
Large leaves, cinnamon coloured beneath, have winged petioles. Pale yellow flowers sometimes tinged crimson, with deep crimson basal blotch; April. AM (F) 1956 H3-4

– beanianum (s. Neriiflorum) MS (E) ⊀ ◑
Leaves with brown woolly tomentum beneath. Loose trusses of waxy bell-shaped red or pink flowers; March-May. AM (F) 1953 H3-4

– bureavii (s. Taliense) MS (E) ⊀ ◑
Dark shiny leaves, red woolly beneath. Young growths pale fawn to rust. Compact trusses of bell-shaped rose flowers marked crimson; April-May. AM 1939 (for flowers) AM 1972 H4

– caeruleum see *R. rigidum*

– calendulaceum (*Azalea calandulacea*) (s. Azalea) MS-LS ⊀ ◑
Leaves turn orange and red autumn. Funnel shaped flowers of vivid red, orange or scarlet; May-June. H4

– callimorphum (*cyclium*) (s. Thomsonii) MS (E) ⊀ ◑
Small round leaves, glaucous beneath. Loose trusses of bell-shaped, soft pink flowers, occasional crimson basal blotch; April-June. H4

– calophytum (s. Fortunei) LS-ST E ⊀ ◑
Rosettes of long narrow leaves at tips of shoots. Large trusses of bell-shaped, white or pink flowers, maroon basal blotch; March-April. AM (F) 1920 FCC (F) 1933 H4

– calostrotum (*riparium*) (s. Saluenense) DS (E) ⊀ ◑
Grey-green foliage. Large saucer-shaped magenta-crimson flowers; May-June. AM (F) 1935 H4
We recommend the form:

– – 'Gigha' (*'Red Form'*) SS (E) ⊀ ◑
Deep claret-red flowers. AGM 1969 FCC 1971

– caloxanthum (s. Thomsonii) SS (E) ⊀ ◑
Small, rounded leaves. Bell-shaped, citron-yellow flowers, tinged flame in bud, in clusters; April-May. AM(F)1934 H3-4

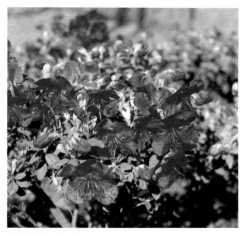

RHODODENDRON calostrotum 'Gigha'

–**campanulatum** (s. Campanulatum) LS (E) ⚮ ◖
Unfurling leaves coated in suede-like fawn or rust indumentum. Bell-shaped flowers varying pale rose to lavender; April-May. H4
We recommend the forms:
––**aeruginosum** (R. aeruginosum) MS (E) ⚮ ◖
Metallic, green-blue young growths. Slow growth.
––**'Knap Hill'** MS (E) ⚮ ◖
Lavender-blue flowers. AM 1925
–**campylocarpum** (s.Thomsonii) MS (E) ⚮ ◖
Glossy green leaves, glaucous beneath. Bell-shaped, clear yellow flowers; April-May. Does not flower when young. FCC 1892 H3-4
–**campylogynum** (s.Campylogynum) DS (E) ⚮ ◖
Small, lustrous leaves. Nodding, waxy, bell-shaped flowers on long stalks; May-June. H3-4.
We recommend the forms:
––**cremastum** (R. cremastum) DS (E) ⚮ ◖
Erect habit. Waxy, rose-purple flowers.
––**'Crushed Strawberry'** DS (E) ⚮ ◖
Strawberry pink flowers.
––**myrtilloides** (R. myrtilloides) DS (E) ⚮ ◖
Smaller, waxy, plum-purple flowers. AM 1925 FCC 1943 H3-4
–**camtschaticum** (s.Camtschaticum) DS ⚮ ◖
Spreading shrub with saucer-shaped, rose-purple flowers, May. Attractive autumn leaf tints. AM 1908 H4

–**canadense** (Rhodora canadensis) (s.Azalea) SS ⚮ ◖
Erect, twiggy habit. Sea-green, narrow leaves. Saucer or bell-shaped, rose-purple flowers; April, before leaves. AM 1928 H4
–**cantabile** see R. russatum
–**chaetomallum** (s.Neriiflorum) MS (E) ⚮ ◖
Undersides of leaves have brown woolly indumentum. Loose trusses of blood-red, waxy, bell-shaped flowers; March-April. AM (F) 1959 H4
–**charianthum** see R. davidsonianum
–**charitopes** (s.Glaucophyllum) SS (E) ⚮ ◖
Leaves glaucous and scaly beneath. Bell-shaped, apple-blossom-pink flowers, speckled crimson; April-May. H4
–**chartophyllum** see R. yunnanense
–**chasmanthum** see R. augustinii chasmanthum
–**chrysanthum** (s. Ponticum) DS (E) ⚮ ◖
Bell-shaped, pale yellow flowers; May-June. H4
–**chryseum** (muliense) (s.Lapponicum) DS (E) ⚮ ◖
Small aromatic leaves. Small trusses of bright yellow funnel shaped flowers; April-May. H4
–**ciliatum** (s.Maddenii) SS (E) ⚮ ◖
Peeling bark and conspicuously hairy leaves. Fragrant, lilac-rose, bell-shaped, nodding flowers; March-April. AM (F) 1953 H3-4
–**cinnabarinum** (s.Cinnabarinum) MS-LS (E) ⚮ ◖
Scaly leaves. Bright cinnabar red, tubular flowers; May-June. H4
––**blandfordiiflorum** MS-LS (E) ⚮ ◖
Red flowers, yellow inside. AM 1945
––**'Mount Everest'** MS-LS (E) ⚮ ◖
Abundant, pale apricot flowers, less tubular than type.
––**roylei** (R. roylei) MS-LS (E) ⚮ ◖
Glaucous leaves. Rose-red to purple-red flowers, shorter than type.
–**concatenans** (s.Cinnabarinum)MS (E) ⚮ ◖
Leaves glaucous-blue when young, scaly beneath. Waxy, apricot-yellow, bell-shaped flowers, faintly tinged purple outside; April-May. FCC 1935 H3
–**concinnum** (yanthinum) (s.Triflorum) LS (E) ⚮ ◖
Scaly leaves. Clusters of funnel-shaped, purple flowers; April-May. H4. We recommend the form:

--**pseudoyanthinum** (*R. pseudoyanthinum*)
LS (E) ✗ ◑
, Deep ruby or purple red flowers. AM 1951
– **cremastum** see *R. campylogynum
cremastum*
– **croceum** see *R. wardii*
– **cyclium** see *R. callimorphum*
– **dauricum** (s. Dauricum) MS Semi-(E) ✗ ◑
1 to 3-flowered trusses of funnel-shaped rose-
purple flowers; January-March. H4. We
recommend the form:
--**'Midwinter'** MS Semi-(E) ✗ ◑
Phlox-purple flowers. AM 1963 FCC 1969
– **davidsonianum** (*charianthum*) (s. Triflorum)
MS-LS (E) ✗ ◑
Lanceolate leaves. Clusters of funnel-shaped
flowers, varying soft pink-purplish-rose. We
recommend a good pale-pink form. FCC 1955
H3-4
– **decorum** (s. Fortunei) LS-ST (E) ✗ ◑
Glabrous leaves. Lax trusses of large fragrant,
funnel-shaped flowers, white or shell pink,
sometimes spotted; May-June. H3-4
– **diaprepes** (s. Fortunei) LS-ST (E) † ✗ ◑
Leaves up to 30cm long. Loose trusses of
fleshy, slightly fragrant flowers, white faintly
flushed rose; June-July. AM 1926 H3
– **dichroanthum** (s. Neriiflorum) SS-MS (E) ✗
◑
Dome-shaped habit. Loose trusses of
generally deep orange bell-shaped flowers;
May-June. AM (F) 1923
– **dilatatum** see *R.reticulatum*
– **discolor** (s. Fortunei) LS (E) ✗ ◑
Huge trusses of fragrant, funnel-shaped, pink
flowers; June-July. AM 1921 AM (F) 1922
FCC (F) 1922 AGM 1969 H4
– **euchaites** see *R. neriiflorum euchaites*
– **eximium** (s. Falconeri) LS-ST (E) ✗ ◑
Large leaves, up to 30cm, and young growths
coated with orange brown indumentum. Pink
or rose, bell-shaped, fleshy flowers, April-
May. AM 1973 H3-4
– **exquisetum** see *R. oreotrephes*
– **falconeri** (s. Falconeri) LS-ST (E) ✗ ◑
Large leaves with deeply impressed veins.
Huge trusses of bell-shaped, waxy creamy-
yellow, blotched purple, flowers; April-May.
AM 1922 H3-4
– **fargesii** (s. Fortunei) LS (E) ✗ ◑
Bell-shaped, generally rose-lilac flowers,
sometimes spotted; March-April. AM (F) 1926
H4

– **fastigiatum** (s. Lapponicum) DS-SS (E) ✗
◑
Dense, dome-shaped habit. Small scaly
leaves. Funnel-shaped lavender-purple
flowers April-May. AM (F) 1914 H4
– **ferrugineum** (s. Ferrugineum) SS (E) ✗ ◑
"Alpen Rose"
Leaves reddish-scaly beneath. Small trusses
of tubular, rose-crimson flowers, June. H4
– **fictolacteum** (s. Falconeri) LS-ST (E) ✗ ◑
Young shoots and leaf undersides brown
tomentose. Large trusses of bell-shaped,
creamy-white flowers, with crimson blotch;
April-May. AM (F) 1923 AGM 1969 H4
– **fittianum** (s. Dauricum) SS-MS (E) ✗ ◑
Funnel-shaped mauve-pink flowers; mid-
April. H4
– **flavidum** (*primulinum*) (s. Lapponicum) SS
(E) ✗ ◑
Erect habit. Small, glossy, aromatic leaves.
Primrose-yellow funnel-shaped flowers;
March. AM 1910 H4
--**'Album'** SS (E) ✗ ◑
Laxer habit. White flowers, larger.
– **forrestii** (s. Neriiflorum) PS (E) ✗ ◑
Mat-forming. Dark green leaves, purple
beneath. Bright scarlet, bell-shaped flowers,
singly or in pairs. April-May. Slow growth. H4.
We recommend the following:

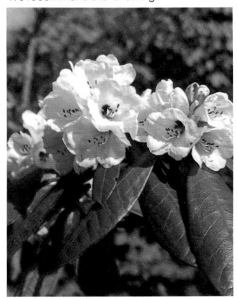

RHODODENDRON fulvum

RHODODENDRON forrestii – Continued

--repens (*R. repens*) PS (E) ✗ ◑
Leaves pale or glaucous green below.
Creeping form. FCC (F) 1935
- fortunei (s.Fortunei) LS-ST (E) ✗ ◑
Bell-shaped, lilac-pink, fragrant flowers in
loose trusses; May. AGM 1969 H4
- fulgens (s.Campanulatum) MS-LS (E) ✗ ◑
Dark shiny leaves, reddish-brown hairy
beneath. Bright scarlet, bell-shaped flowers,
in tight rounded trusses; February-April.
Young shoots have crimson bracts. AM 1933
H4
-- Leonardslee form MS-LS (E) ✗ ◑
A good selected clone.
- fulvum (*fulvoides*) (s.Fulvum) LS-ST (E) ✗
◑
Large, polished, dark green leaves, cinnamon
indumentum beneath. Bell-shaped flowers,
blush to deep rose sometimes with crimson
blotch; March-April. AM (F) 1933 H4
- glaucophyllum (*glaucum*)
(s.Glaucophyllum) SS (E) ✗ ◑
Aromatic. Leaves white beneath. Large leafy
calyx. Bell-shaped flowers varying old rose to
lilac; April-May. H3-4
-- luteiflorum SS (E) ✗ ◑
Lemon yellow flowers. AM (F) 1960
- griersonianum (s.Griersonianum) MS
(E) ✗ ◑
Matt green leaves, buff woolly beneath.
Unusual, narrowly bell-shaped, geranium-red
flowers, June. Long tapered flower buds,
FCC 1924 H3-4
- griffithianum (*aucklandii*) (s.Fortunei)
LS-ST (E) † ✗ ◑
Reddish brown peeling bark. Leaves up to
30cm. Loose trusses of widely bell-shaped
flowers, white, faintly speckled green, sweetly
scented; May. FCC 1866 H1-3
- haematodes (s.Neriiflorum) SS-MS (E) ✗ ◑
Compact, slow growth. Dark green leaves,
rufous felted beneath. Scarlet crimson, bell-
shaped flowers; May-June. FCC 1926 H4
- hanceanum (s.Hanceanum) SS (E) ✗ ◑
Dainty habit. Bronze coloured young growths.
Leaves scaly beneath. Creamy white or pale
yellow, slightly scented, funnel-shaped
flowers, April. H4. We recommend the clone:
--'Nanum' DS (E) ✗ ◑
Hummock forming shrublet. Slow growth.
- hippophaeoides (s.Lapponicum) SS
(E) ✗ ◑
Erect, leafy shrub. Small grey-green leaves.

RHODODENDRON hippophaeoides – Cont.

Usually lavender, lilac or rose, funnel-shaped
flowers, March-April. Tolerant even of
semi-bog conditions, H4. We recommend the
following:
--'Inshriach' SS (E) ✗ ◑
Flowers lavender-mauve, darker at margins,
in comparatively large clusters.
- hodgsonii (s.Falconeri) LS-ST (E) ✗ ◑
Large, dark green leaves, up to 30cm long,
grey or fawn tomentose beneath. Dense
trusses of dark magenta bell-shaped flowers;
April. H4
- impeditum (s. Lapponicum) DS (E) ✗ ◑
Low mounds of scaly branches. Tiny leaves.
Light purplish-blue, funnel-shaped flowers;
April-May. AM (F) 1944 AGM 1969 H4
- imperator (s. Uniflorum) PS-DS (E) ✗ ◑
Small, narrow leaves. Generally, solitary pink
or rose-purple, funnel-shaped flowers; May.
AM (F) 1934 H3-4
- indicum (*macranthum*) (*Azalea indica*)
(*A. macrantha*) (s.Azalea) SS Semi-(E) ✗ ◑
Dense habit. Small narrow leaves, often
crimson or purple in autumn. Widely funnel-
shaped, scarlet to red flowers, singly or in
pairs; June. H2-3
--'Balsaminiflorum' (*R. rosiflorum*) (*Azalea
rosiflora*) DS Semi-(E) ✗ ◑
Double, salmon-pink flowers. FCC 1882
- insigne (s.Arboreum) LS (E) ✗ ◑
Slow growing. Leathery, glossy green leaves,
silvery-white beneath, metallic when young.
Soft pink, bell-shaped flowers, with darker
markings, in large trusses; May-June.
AM 1923 H4
- intricatum (s.Lapponicum) DS (E) ✗ ◑
Densely twiggy. Small, aromatic, olive-green
leaves. Lavender-blue funnel-shaped flowers
in small trusses. April-early May. FCC 1907 H4
- irroratum (s.Irroratum) LS-ST (E) ✗ ◑
Narrowly bell-shaped flowers, coloured
variously white or yellow and marked or
spotted dark crimson; March-May.
AM (F) 1957 H3. We recommend:
--'Polka Dot' LS-ST (E) ✗ ◑
White flowers heavily marked with purple
dots. AM 1957
- kaempferi (*obtusum kaempferi*) (s. Azalea)
MS ✗ ◑ Deciduous or Semi-(E)
Leaves and young shoots hairy. Clusters of 2
to 4, funnel-shaped flowers, varying biscuit,
salmon, orange, red, rose scarlet; May-June.
AM 1953 AGM 1969 H4

– –**'Mikado'** MS ✗ ◑
Apricot-salmon flowers; late June-July.
– **keiskei** (s.Triflorum) DS Semi-(E) ✗ ◑
Abundant, widely funnel-shaped, lemon
flowers in trusses of 3 to 5; March-May.
AM 1929 H3-4
– **keysii** (s.Cinnabarinum) MS LS (E) ✗ ◑
Densely scaly leaves. Clusters of unusual
tubular, cuphea-like orange-red flowers,
tipped yellow; June. H3-4
– **kotschyi** (s.Ferrugineum) DS (E) ✗ ◑
Dense habit. Crenulate leaves, densely scaly
beneath. Clusters of rose-pink, tubular flowers
with spreading lobes; May-July. H3-4
– **lanigerum** (*silvaticum*) (s.Arboreum) LS-ST
(E) ✗ ◑
Grey tomentose young shoots. Large leaves,
tomentose beneath. Round, compact trusses
of bell-shaped flowers, rose-purple to dark
magenta; March-April. AM 1949 AM 1951 H4.
We recommend:
– –**'Chapel Wood'** LS-ST (E) ✗ ◑
Flowers neyron rose. AM 1961 FCC 1967
– **ledifolium** see *R. mucronatum*
– **ledoides** see *R. trichostomum*
– **lepidostylum** (s.Trichocladum) SS Semi-(E)
✗ ◑
Dense, compact habit. Small bristly leaves,
blue-green until winter. Pale yellow,
funnel-shaped flowers, singly or in pairs;
May-June. AM 1969 H4
– **leucaspis** (s.Boothii) DS (E) ✗ ◑
Hairy leaves, scaly stems. Milky white, saucer
shaped flowers, with chocolate anthers, in
clusters of 2 or 3; February-March.
AM (F) 1929 FCC 1944 H3-4
– **litiense** (s.Thomsonii) MS (E) ✗ ◑
Densely glandular young shoots. Widely bell
or saucer-shaped soft yellow flowers; May.
AM 1931 FCC 1953 H3
– **lowndesii** (s.Lepidotum) DS ✗ ◑
Compact. Bright green, hairy leaves. Widely
bell-shaped pale yellow flowers with reddish
spots. Singly or in pairs; June-July. H3-4
– **ludlowii** (s.Uniflorum) DS (E) ✗ ◑
Saucer-shaped, yellow flowers with central
rufous spots, singly or in pairs; April-May.
Large leafy calyx. H3-4
– **lutescens** (s.Triflorum) MS-LS (E) ✗ ◑
Bronze-red young leaves. Primrose-yellow,
funnel-shaped flowers, February to April. We
recommend the clone *'Exbury'* with lemon
yellow flowers. FCC 1938 H3-4

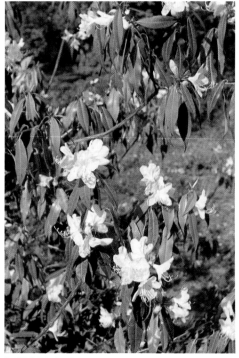

RHODODENDRON lutescens

– **luteum** (*Azalea pontica*) (s.Azalea)
MS-LS ✗ ◑
Common, fragrant yellow azalea. Leaves turn
orange, crimson and purple, autumn. Funnel-
shaped, yellow flowers in rounded trusses,
May. AGM 1930 H4
– **macabeanum** (s.Grande) LS-ST (E) ✗ ◑
Glossy, dark green conspicuously veined
leaves, grey-white tomentose beneath, up to
30cm long. Bell-shaped pale yellow, purple
spotted flowers in large trusses; March-April.
AM 1937 FCC 1938 H3-4
– **macranthum** see *R. indicum*
– **makinoi** (*metternichii angustifolium*)
(s.Ponticum) MS (E) ✗ ◑
White or fawn woolly young growths, late
summer. Soft pink, bell-shaped flowers,
sometimes with crimson dots; June. H3-4
– **mallotum** (*aemulorum*) (s.Neriiflorum)
LS-ST (E) ✗ ◑
Leaves, rufous woolly beneath. Dark crimson,
bell-shaped flowers, March-April. AM 1933
H4
– **maxwellii** see *R. pulchrum 'Maxwellii'*

– **meddianum** (s.Thomsonii) MS (E) ✗ ◑
Glaucous young shoots. Deep crimson or
bright scarlet fleshy, bell-shaped flowers;
April. H2-4. We recommend the following:
– – **atrokermesinum** MS (E) ✗ ◑
Glandular branchlets. Generally larger,
darker flowers. AM 1954
– **metternichii** (s.Ponticum) MS (E) ✗ ◑
Glossy leaves, tawny or rusty tomentose
beneath. Rose coloured bell-shaped flowers;
April-May. H4. We recommend:
– – **angustifolium** see *R. makinoi*
– – **'Wada'** MS (E) ✗ ◑
Compact habit. Leaves cinnamon tomentose
beneath.
– **microleucum** (s.Lapponicum) DS (E) ✗ ◑
Brown, scaly twigs. Densely leafy. Small
clusters of funnel-shaped, white flowers; April.
FCC 1939 H4

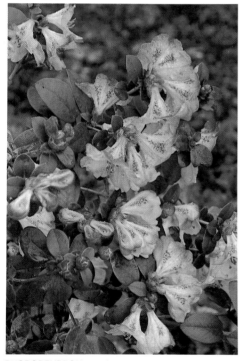

RHODODENDRON moupinense

– **moupinense** (s. Moupinense) SS (E) ✗ ◑
Bristly branchlets. Leaves densely scaly
beneath. Sweetly scented, funnel-shaped
flowers, white, pink or deep rose, sometimes
spotted red; February-March. AM (F) 1914 H4

– – **Pink** SS (E) ✗ ◑
Flowers deep pink, spotted and streaked red.
AM 1937 H4
– **mucronatum** (*ledifolium*) (*Azalea ledifolia*)
(s.Azalea) SS (E) or Semi-(E) ✗ ◑
Dome shaped habit. Dull green, hairy leaves.
Pure white, fragrant, funnel-shaped flowers;
May. AMT 1958 AGM 1969 H4
– **mucronulatum** (s.Dauricum) MS ✗ ◑
Slender habit. Bright rose-purple,
funnel-shaped flowers; January-March.
AM (F) 1924 AGM 1969 H4
– **muliense** see *R. chryseum*
– **myrtilloides** see *R. campylogynum
myrtilloides*
– **nakaharae** (s. Azalea) DS (E) ✗ ◑
Creeping habit. Densely appressed, hairy
shoots. Small clusters of dark brick-red
funnel-shaped flowers; June-July or later. H4
– **neriiflorum** (s.Neriiflorum) MS (E) ✗ ◑
Narrow leaves, gleaming white below.
Trusses of fleshy bell-shaped flowers varying
deep rose to scarlet and crimson, with large
calyx coloured as corolla; April-May. H3-4.
We recommend:
– – **euchaites** (*R. euchaites*) LS (E) ✗ ◑
Taller growth. Larger, crimson-scarlet flowers;
April. AM 1929
– **nitens** (s.Saluenense) DS (E) ✗ ◑
Erect habit. Aromatic leaves. Saucer or widely
funnel-shaped deep purple flowers;
June-July. H4
– **niveum** (s.Arboreum) LS (E) ✗ ◑
Young leaves covered with dense white hairs.
Compact, rounded heads of smoky blue to
rich purple, bell-shaped flowers; April-May.
AM (F) 1951 H4. We recommend the form:
– – **'Clyne Castle'** LS (E) ✗ ◑
Larger leaves. Rich purple flowers. H4
– **nudiflorum** (*Azalea nudiflora*) (s. Azalea)
MS ✗ ◑
Bright green leaves. Clusters of fragrant,
funnel-shaped flowers, pale pink with reddish
tube; May. H4
– **obtusum** (*Azalea obtusa*) (s. Azalea) SS (E)
or Semi-(E) ✗ ◑ "Kirishima Azalea"
Wide spreading. Densely hairy branches.
Small glossy, oval leaves. Funnel-shaped
crimson or scarlet flowers; May. AM 1898 H4
We recommend the forms:
– – **'Amoenum'** (*Azalea amoena*) MS (E) or
Semi-(E) ✗ ◑
Taller. Brilliant magenta or rose-purple

flowers, hose-in-hose. AM 1907 AMT 1965 AGM 1965

– –'**Amoenum Coccineum**' MS (E) or Semi-(E) ⚹ ◑

Carmine rose, hose-in-hose flowers. AGM 1969

  occidentale (*Azalea occidentalis*) (s. Azalea) MS ⚹ ◑

Glossy leaves colouring richly in autumn. Fragrant, widely funnel-shaped flowers, creamy-white to pale-pink with yellow or orange-yellow basal stain; June with the leaves. AM (F) 1944 H4

– **orbiculare** (s. Fortunei) MS-LS (E) ⚹ ◑

Rounded, heart-shaped leaves, glaucous beneath. Bell-shaped, rose-pink flowers, sometimes tinged blue; March-April. AM 1922 H4

– **oreotrephes** (*artosquameum*) (*exquisetum*) (*timeteum*) (s. Triflorum) LS (E) or Semi-(E) ⚹ ◑

Leaves scaly and glaucous beneath. Generally funnel-shaped flowers varying mauve, pink, purple, rose, sometimes with crimson spots; April-May. AM (F) 1932 AM (F) 1937 H4

– **orthocladum** (s. Lapponicum) SS (E) ⚹ ◑

Dense, scaly branches. Small scaly, greyish leaves. Small, funnel-shaped flowers, mauve-purplish-blue, abundant, April. H4

– **pemakoense** (s. Uniflorum) DS (E) ⚹ ◑

Suckering habit. Small leaves. Funnel-shaped lilac-pink or purple flowers, March-April. AM (F) 1933 AGM 1969 H3-4

– **pentaphyllum** (s. Azalea) MS-LS ⚹ ◑

Leaves in whorls at branch tips, colouring crimson and orange, autumn. Saucer or shallow bell-shaped peach-pink flowers, singly or in pairs before leaves, March-April. AM (F) 1942 H4

– **pleistanthum** see *R. yunnanense*

– **ponticum** (s. Ponticum) LS (E) ⚹ ◑

The Common Rhododendron which has become naturalised in British Isles. Mauve to lilac pink flowers; May-June. Excellent for hedging and as shelter belt. H4

– –'**Variegatum**' LS (E) ⚹ ◑

Leaves margined creamy-white.

– **primulinum** see *R. flavidum*

– **proteoides** (s. Taliense) DS (E) ⚹ ◑

Slow growth. Leaves with thick, woolly, rust tomentum beneath. Compact trusses of bell-shaped, creamy-white or white flowers

with crimson spots; April. H4

– **prunifolium** (*Azalea prunifolia*) (s. Azalea) MS-LS ⚹ ◑

Brilliant orange-red, funnel-shaped flowers, 4 or 5 per truss, after the leaves; July-August. H3-4

– **pseudoyanthinum** see *R. concinnum pseudoyanthinum*

– **pulchrum** (*phoenicium smithii*) (s. Azalea) SS-MS (E) ⚹ ◑

Densely hairy twigs. Clusters of funnel-shaped, rose-purple flowers with dark spots; May. H3 We recommend the form:

– –'**Maxwellii**' (*R. maxwellii*) SS (E) ⚹ ◑

Larger flowers, bright rose-red with darker blotch. AMT 1960

– **quinquefolium** (s. Azalea) MS-LS ⚹ ◑

Leaves in whorls at shoot tips, green, bordered reddish-brown when young, colouring autumn. Clusters of pendulous, saucer-shaped, white flowers with green spots; April-May. AM 1931 AM (F) 1958 H4

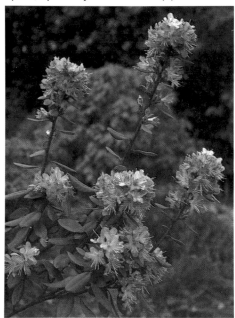

RHODODENDRON racemosum

– **racemosum** (s. Scabrifolium) MS (E) ⚹ ◑

Leathery leaves, glaucous beneath. Pale to bright pink, funnel-shaped flowers forming racemes along branchlets; March-April. FCC 1892 AGM 1930 H4

--**'Forrest's Dwarf'** DS (E) ✗ ◑
Red branchlets. Bright pink flowers.
-**radicans** (s. Saluenense) PS (E) ✗ ◑
Creeping habit. Tiny, bright green leaves.
Generally solitary flattish, rose-purple flowers;
May-June. AM (F) 1926 H4
-**recurvoides** (s. Taliense) SS (E) ✗ ◑
Dense compact habit. Leaves tawny
tomentose beneath, margins recurved.
Compact trusses of bell-shaped, white or rose
flowers with darker spots; April-May.
AM (F) 1941 H4
-**repens** see *R. forrestii repens*
-**reticulatum** (*Azalea reticulata*) (*dilatatum*
MIQ) (*rhombicum* MIQ) (*wadanum*)
(s. Azalea) MS-LS ✗ ◑
Leaves conspicuously reticulate beneath,
purplish when young, colouring vinous-purple
autumn. Bright purple, funnel-shaped flowers,
singly or in pairs before leaves; April-May. AM
1894 H4
-**rex** (s. Falconeri) LS-ST (E) ✗ ◑
Large, shiny, dark green leaves, grey or buff
tomentose beneath. Large trusses of bell-
shaped, rose or white flowers with crimson
basal stain and spots; April-May. FCC (F)
1935 AM (F) 1946 AGM 1969 H4
-**rhombicum** see *R. reticulatum*
-**rigidum** (*caeruleum*) (s. Triflorum) MS (E)
✗ ◑
Twiggy habit. Funnel-shaped flowers, varying
pink to white; March-May. AM (F) 1939 H4
--**'Album'** MS (E) ✗ ◑
White flowers.
-**riparium** see *R. calostrotum*
-**roseum** (*Azalea rosea*) (s. Azalea) MS-LS
✗ ◑
Clusters of clove-scented, funnel-shaped
flowers, pale to deep pink, with the leaves;
May. AM (F) 1955 H4
-**rosiflorum** see *R. indicum 'Balsaminiflorum'*
-**roxieanum** (s. Taliense) SS-MS (E) ✗ ◑
Slow growth. Narrow leaves with fawn or rust
indumentum beneath. Tight trusses of bell-
shaped creamy-white, rose flushed flowers;
April-May – not whilst young. H4
--**oreonastes** SS (E) ✗ ◑
Very narrow, linear leaves. AM 1973
-**roylei** see *R. cinnabarinum roylei*
-**rubiginosum** (s. Heliolepis) LS (E) ✗ ◑
Aromatic leaves with rust-coloured scales
beneath. Pink or lilac, funnel-shaped flowers,
spotted brown; April-May. H4

-**russatum** (S. Lapponicum) SS (E) ✗ ◑
Compact habit, leaves 2.5cm long, densely
scaly beneath. Flowers funnel-shaped, deep
blue-purple to violet, white throat, April-May.
H4
-**saluenense** (s. Saluenense) SS (E) ✗ ◑
Densely matted. Aromatic, small leaves.
Rose-purple to purplish-crimson, funnel-
shaped flowers; April-May. AM (F) 1945 H4
-**sanguineum** (s. Neriiflorum) DS-SS (E) ✗ ◑
Narrow leaves, greyish-white beneath. Bright
crimson, bell-shaped flowers, 3 to 6 per truss,
on older plants; May. H4
-**sargentianum** (s. Anthopogon) DS (E)
✗ ◑
Dense, compact, twiggy habit. Small leaves,
aromatic when crushed. Small tubular lemon
or white flowers; April-May. AM (F) 1923 H4
-**schlippenbachii** (*Azalea schlippenbachii*)
(s. Azalea) LS ✗ ◑
Rounded habit. Large leaves in whorls at
branch tips, suffused purple when young,
colouring richly autumn. Saucer-shaped
flowers pale to rose-pink or white; April-May.
AM (F) 1896 FCC (F) 1944 AGM 1969 H4

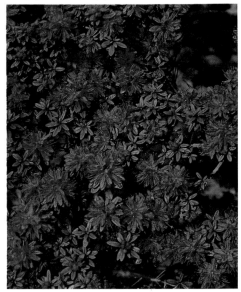

RHODODENDRON scintillans

-**scintillans** (s. Lapponicum) SS (E) ✗ ◑
Tiny, scaly leaves. Lavender blue or purple-
rose, funnel-shaped flowers; April-May.
AM (F) 1924 AGM 1969 H4 We recommend:

– – F.C.C. Form

Flowers deep violet. FCC 1934

– **serotinum** (s. Fortunei) LS (E) ✗ ◑
Sweetly-scented and bell-shaped flowers,
white flushed pink, pink spotted inside and
with yellow basal stain; August-September –
one of the latest to flower. AM (F) 1925 H4

– **setosum** (s. Lapponicum) DS (E) ✗ ◑
Densely bristly branches. Aromatic, bristly,
scaly leaves. Reddish purple, funnel-shaped
flowers; May. H4

– **sheriffii** (s. Campanulatum) MS-LS (E) ✗ ◑
Leaves with dark brown thick indumentum
beneath. Rich carmine, bell-shaped flowers
with bloomy, crimson calyx; March-April.
AM 1966 H4

– **silvaticum** see *R. lanigerum*

– **sinogrande** (s. Grande) LS-ST (E) † ✗ ◑
Huge, glossy-green leaves, with silvery or
fawn indumentum beneath, up to 0.8m long.
Huge trusses of creamy flowers with crimson
blotch; April. AM (F) 1922 FCC (F) 1926 H3-4

– **souliei** (s. Thomsonii) MS (E) ✗ ◑
Leaves almost round. White to soft pink,
saucer-shaped flowers; May-June. FCC (F)
1909 H4

– **sphaeranthum** see *R. trichostomum*

– **spiciferum** (s. Scabrifolium) SS-MS (E)
✗ ◑
Wiry, bristly stems and bristly leaves.
Abundant funnel-shaped rose or pink flowers;
April-May. H3

– **strigillosum** (s. Barbatum) LS (E) ✗ ◑
Bristly young shoots and leaves. Trusses of
brilliant crimson bell-shaped flowers;
February-March. Requires woodland shelter.
AM (F) 1923 H3-4

– **suberosum** see *R. yunnanense*

– **sutchuenense** (s. Fortunei) LS (E) ✗ ◑
Drooping leaves up to 30cm. Beautiful bell-
shaped flowers, pale pink to rosy lilac, spotted
purple; February-March. H4

– **thomsonii** (s. Thomsonii) LS (E) ✗ ◑
Plum- or cinnamon-coloured bark. Loose
trusses of blood red bell-shaped flowers with
large cup-shaped calyx; April-May. Attractive
fruiting clusters. AGM 1925 AM 1973 H3

– **timeteum** see *R. oreotrephes*

– **tosaense** (s. Azalea) SS Semi-(E) ✗ ◑
Narrow leaves colouring crimson-purple,
autumn clusters of lilac-pink, funnel-shaped
flowers, April-May. AM 1974 H4
We recommend:

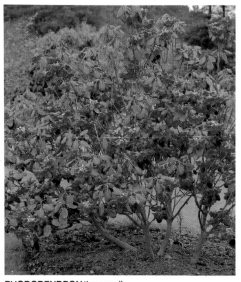

RHODODENDRON thomsonii

– – **'Barbara'** SS Semi-(E) ✗ ◑
Clear pink flowers.

– **trichostomum** (*ledoides*) (*sphaeranthum*)
(s. Anthopogon) SS (E) ✗ ◑
Twiggy aromatic shrub. Terminal heads of
white or rose, tubular, daphne-like flowers;
May-June. AM 1925 H3-4

– **tsangpoense** (s. Glaucophyllum) DS-SS (E)
✗ ◑
Aromatic. Leaves with pale green and pink
scales beneath. Abundant, semi-bell-shaped
flowers varying crushed strawberry to deep
crimson or violet; May-June. AM (F) 1972 H4

– **vaseyi** (*Azalea vaseyi*) (s. Azalea) LS ✗ ◑
Leaves often colouring fiery red, autumn.
Widely funnel-shaped flowers, varying pale
pink, rose or white with flame spots; April-May.
AGM 1927 H4

– **viscosum** (*Azalea viscosa*) (s. Azalea) MS
✗ ◑ "Swamp Honeysuckle"
Bushy habit. Fragrant spicy, narrow, funnel-
shaped flowers. White sometimes pink
stained, sticky on outside; June-July. AM (F)
1921 AGM 1937 H4

– **wardii** (*croceum*) (s. Thomsonii) MS-LS (E)
✗ ◑
Compact habit. Loose trusses of saucer-
shaped clear yellow flowers, sometimes with
crimson basal stain; May. AM (F) 1926 AM (F)
1931 AGM 1969 H4

– **weyrichii** (s. Azalea) MS-LS ✗ ◑
Leaves in clusters at branch tips. Widely
funnel-shaped generally brick-red flowers,
blotched purple, before leaves; April-May. H4
– **williamsianum** (s. Thomsonii) SS (E) ✗ ◑
Spreading habit. Bronze young growths.
Small heart-shaped leaves. Bell-shaped
shell-pink flowers; April. AM 1938 H3
– **wongii** (s. Triflorum) SS (E) ✗ ◑
Densely scaly twigs. Pale yellow funnel-
shaped flowers in terminal clusters; May-
June. H4
– **xanthocodon** (s. Cinnabarinum) MS-LS (E)
✗ ◑
Aromatic. Golden scaly young shoots.
Densely scaly leaves. Waxy, yellow bell- to
funnel-shaped flowers in clusters; May-June.
AM (F) 1935 H4

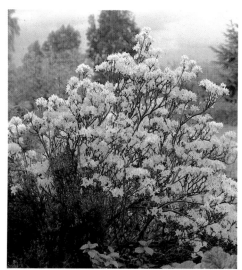

RHODODENDRON yunnanense

– **yunnanense** (*aechmophyllum*)
(*chartophyllum*) (*pleistanthum*) (*suberosum*)
(s. Triflorum) LS (E) ✗ ◑
Funnel-shaped generally pink flowers with
darker spots; May. AM 1903 AGM 1934 H4
RHODODENDRON HYBRIDS PS-ST (E)
✗ ◑
*Original Hardy Hybrids (HH) exhibit ample
foliage, full firm trusses, ability to withstand
exposure and complete hardiness. More
recent introductions show greater variation in
foliage, flower and habit and although
generally hardy, will not tolerate such extreme
conditions.*
*Average height is 1.8 to 3m. Flowering
seasons are:*
            Early – April
            Mid – May-Mid June
            Late – Late June onwards
A (b) (i) (k) 2 *Old plants of hardy hybrids if
straggly may be cut back hard during winter.*
– **'Aladdin'** LS (E) ✗ ◑
Loose trusses of large, open, brilliant salmon-
cerise flowers. Late. AM 1935 H3
– **Albatross** LS-ST (E) ✗ ◑
Terminal leaf clusters. Lax trusses of fragrant,
trumpet-shaped flowers. Mid. AM 1934
AMT 1935 AGM 1969 H3 We recommend:

– – **'Townhill Pink'** LS-ST (E) ✗ ◑
Immense trusses, deep pink, opening shell
pink. Mid. AM 1945

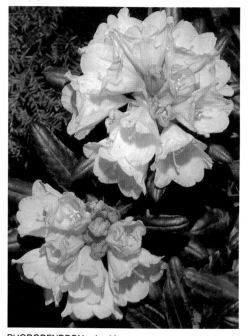

RHODODENDRON yakushimanum

– **yakushimanum** (*metternichii
yakushimanum*) (s. Ponticum) SS (E) ✗ ◑
Compact habit. Young silvery growths. Dark
glossy leaves, densely brown tomentose
beneath. Compact trusses of bell-shaped
flowers, rose in bud opening apple blossom
pink finally white; May. FCC 1947 AGM 1969
H4

– – **'Townhill White'** LS-ST (E) ✗ ◑
White flowers, pale yellowish-green within.
Mid.

– **'Alice'** (HH) LS (E) ✗ ◑
Vigorous upright habit. Tall, conical trusses of
funnel-shaped flowers, rose pink with lighter
centre. Mid. AM 1910 H4

– **'Alison Johnston'** MS (E) ✗ ◑
Dainty habit. Trusses of slender-tubed,
amber, flushed pink flowers. Mid. AM 1945 H4

– **'Anita'** MS (E) ✗ ◑
Deep salmon pink buds, opening apricot,
finally cream, tinged pale pink. Mid. H3

– **'Antonio'** LS (E) ✗ ◑
Richly-scented, funnel-shaped, pink flowers,
blotched crimson within, deep pink in bud.
Mid. AM 1939 H3

– **'Arthur Osborn'** SS (E) ✗ ◑
Drooping, funnel-shaped, ruby flowers with
orange-scarlet tube. Late – sometimes
continuing until early autumn. AM 1933 H3

– **'Arthur Stevens'** MS (E) ✗ ◑
Rounded habit. Bright yellow buds and
petioles. Bell-shaped flowers in loose trusses.
Pale pink, fading white, with deep rose basal
stain. Mid. H3

– **'Augfast'** SS (E) ✗ ◑
Dense, rounded habit. Scaly young shoots
Terminal clusters of small funnel-shaped
flowers, varying dark lavender to heliotrope
blue. Early. H4

– **'Avalanche'** LS (E) ✗ ◑
Conspicuous red pedicels and bracts. Huge
fragrant, widely funnel-shaped, white flowers
with inner red basal stain, pink flushed in bud.
Early. AM 1934 FCC 1938 H3

– **'Azor'** LS (E) ✗ ◑
Large, trumpet-shaped, soft salmon pink
flowers in trusses. Late. AM 1933 H3-4

– **'Bagshot Ruby'** MS (E) ✗ ◑
Vigorous. Widely funnel-shaped, ruby flowers
in rounded trusses. Mid. AM 1916 H4

– **'Beatrice Keir'** LS (E) ✗ ◑
Large trusses of funnel-shaped, lemon yellow
flowers. Early. H3

– **'Beauty of Littleworth'** (HH) LS (E) ✗ ◑
Huge conical trusses of white, crimson-
spotted flowers. Mid. FCC 1904 FCCT 1953
H4

– **'Beefeater'** MS (E) ✗ ◑
Flat-topped trusses of geranium-lake flowers.
Mid. AM 1958 FCC 1959

– **'Betty Wormald'** (HH) MS (E) ✗ ◑
Huge trusses of funnel-shaped, wavy-edged
flowers, crimson in bud, opening deep rose,
lighter in centre and marked blackish crimson
within. Mid. AMT 1935 FCCT 1964 AGM 1969
H4

– **'Bluebird'** DS (E) ✗ ◑
Small leaves. Small, compact trusses of violet-
blue flowers. Early. AM 1943 AGM 1969 H4

– **'Blue Diamond'** SS (E) ✗ ◑
Slow, to 1m high. Lavender-blue flowers in
terminal clusters. Early. AM 1935 FCC 1939
AGM 1969 H4

– **'Blue Peter'** (HH) MS (E) ✗ ◑
Vigorous upright habit. Conical trusses of
funnel-shaped, frilly-edged, cobalt-violet
flowers, paling to white at throat with ray of
maroon spots. Mid. AMT 1933 FCCT 1958
AGM 1969 H4

– **'Blue Tit'** DS-SS (E) ✗ ◑
Dense, rounded habit. Small, widely funnel-
shaped flowers, lavender-blue, in clusters at
tips of branches. Mid. First class small shrub
for rock or heather garden. H4

– **'Bo-peep'** MS (E) ✗ ◑
Slender, loose habit. Primrose-yellow flowers
with inner darker ray, in clusters of 1 or 2;
March. AM 1937 H3

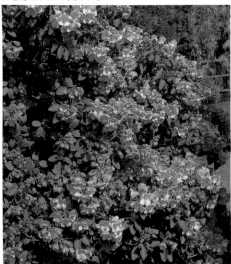

RHODODENDRON 'Brocade'

–**'Bow Bells'** MS (E) ✗ ◑
Bushy habit. Coppery young growths. Widely bell-shaped, shell-pink flowers, deep cerise in bud. Early-Mid. AM 1935 H4

–**'Bray'** MS (E) ✗ ◑
Deep pink buds opening mimosa-yellow flushed pale pink outside. Mid. AM 1960 H3

–**'Bric-a-brac'** SS (E) ✗ ◑
Neat habit. White, open flowers with chocolate anthers, March. AM 1945 H3

–**'Britannia'** (HH) MS (E) ✗ ◑
Compact habit. Slow. Glowing crimson scarlet flowers in compact trusses. Mid. AM 1921 FCCT 1937 AGM 1965 H4

–**'Brocade'** MS (E) ✗ ◑
Dome-shaped habit. Loose trusses of frilly, bell-shaped, peach-pink flowers, carmine in bud. Early-Mid. H4

–**'Brookside'** MS (E) ✗ ◑
Ochre yellow, tubular flowers shaded flame and pale yellow, blood red in bud. Mid. AM 1962 H3-4

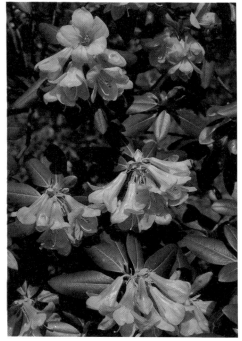

RHODODENDRON 'Caerhays John'

–**'Caerhays John'** MS (E) ✗ ◑
Erect, bushy habit. Deep apricot funnel-shaped flowers. Mid. H4

–**'Caerhays Philip'** MS (E) ✗ ◑
Funnel-shaped yellow flowers in loose trusses. Early. AM 1966 H4

–**'Carex White'** LS (E) ✗ ◑
Tall, pyramidal habit. Fragrant, bell-shaped white flowers, spotted maroon inside, flushed pink in bud; March-April. H4

–**Carita** LS (E) ✗ ◑
Large, bell-shaped pale lemon flowers with inner cerise basal blotch. Early. AM 1945 H3-4
We recommend:

–**'Charm'** LS (E) ✗ ◑
Cream flushed and overlaid peach pink, deep pink in bud.

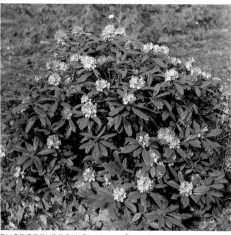

RHODODENDRON 'Christmas Cheer'

–**'Carmen'** DS (E) ✗ ◑
Dark crimson, waxy, bell-shaped flowers. Mid. H4

–**'Chikor'** DS (E) ✗ ◑
Small leaves. Clusters of yellow flowers. Mid. AM 1962 FCCT 1968 H4

–**'China'** MS (E) ✗ ◑
Large loose trusses, cream flowers with rose-carmine basal blotch. Mid. AM 1940 AMT 1948 H4

–**'Chink'** SS (E) ✗ ◑
Chartreuse green, drooping bell-shaped flowers in lax trusses; March. AM 1961 H4

–**'Choremia'** MS (E) ✗ ◑
Waxy bright crimson-scarlet, bell-shaped flowers. Early. AM 1933 FCC 1948 H3

–**'Christmas Cheer'** (HH) MS (E) ✗ ◑
Dense, compact habit. Flowers pink in bud, fading white; March. H4

– **Cilpinense** SS (E) ✗ ◑
Neat rounded habit to 1m high. Shallowly bell-shaped, white flowers, flushed pink, deeper in bud; March. AM 1927 FCC 1968 AGM 1969 H4

– **'Cinnkeys'** LS (E) ✗ ◑
Dense clusters of tubular, orange-red flowers, shading to yellow in lobes. Mid. AM 1935 H4

– **'Cool Haven'** MS (E) ✗ ◑
Widely funnel-shaped, pale yellow flowers, flushed pink outside, with ray of crimson spots. Slightly fragrant. Mid. H3

– **'Cornish Cross'** LS (E) ✗ ◑
Open habit. Lax trusses. Waxy, narrowly bell-shaped, mottled rose pink flowers, darker outside. Early-Mid. H3

– **'Countess of Athlone'** (HH) MS (E) ✗ ◑
Compact habit. Conical trusses. Widely funnel-shaped, frilled flowers, purple in bud, opening mauve, marked greenish-yellow at base. Mid. H4

– **'Countess of Haddington'** MS (E) † ✗ ◑
Straggling habit. Fragrant, trumpet-shaped, white, flushed pale rose, flowers, in umbels of 2 to 4. Early. FCC 1862 H1

– **'Cowslip'** SS (E) ✗ ◑
Neat rounded habit. Loose trusses. Cream or pale-primrose bell-shaped flowers, flushed pale pink when young. Mid. AM 1937 H4

– **'Creeping Jenny'** see *R. 'Jenny'*

– **'Crest'** MS (E) ✗ ◑
Large trusses. Bell-shaped, primrose yellow flowers, darker in throat. Mid. FCC 1953 H3

– **'Cunningham's White'** (HH) LS (E) ✗ ◑
Lax trusses. Funnel-shaped flowers mauve, opening white with pale purple ray and brown markings inside. Mid. H4

– **'Curlew'** DS (E) ✗ ◑
Spreading habit. Widely bell-shaped flowers about 5cm across, pale yellow, marked with greenish-brown. Mid. FCC 1969 H4

– **'Cynthia'** (HH) LS (E) ✗ ◑
Vigorous. Conical trusses. Widely funnel-shaped rose-crimson flowers, with ray of blackish-crimson markings within. Mid. AGM 1969 H4

– **Damaris** MS (E) ✗ ◑
Dome-shaped. Lax trusses, pale canary-yellow, widely bell-shaped flowers, ivory towards margins. Early-Mid. H3
We recommend:

–– **'Logan'** MS (E) ✗ ◑
Dresden-yellow flowers, Early-Mid. AM 1948

– **'Doncaster'** (HH) SS (E) ✗ ◑
Dome-shaped habit. Very dark green, leathery leaves. Dense trusses. Funnel-shaped, crimson-scarlet flowers, ray of black markings within. Mid. H4

– **'Earl of Athlone'** MS (E) ✗ ◑
Compact trusses. Deep blood red, bell-shaped flowers. Early-Mid. FCCT 1933 AGM 1969 H3

– **'Electra'** see *R. augustinii 'Electra'* under species

– **'Elisabeth Hobbie'** DS (E) ✗ ◑
Translucent, scarlet, bell-shaped flowers in loose umbels. Early. H4

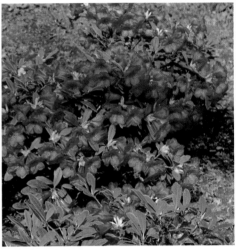

RHODODENDRON 'Elizabeth'

– **'Elizabeth'** DS (E) ✗ ◑
Clusters of rich dark red, trumpet-shaped flowers; April. AM 1939 FCC 1943 AGM 1969 H4

– **'Elizabeth Lockhart'** SS (E) ✗ ◑
Mound-like habit. Leaves bronze-purple most of season. Deep-red, bell-shaped flowers. Early. H4

– **'Emerald Isle'** MS (E) ✗ ◑
Bell-shaped, chartreuse green flowers; May. AM 1956 H4

– **Fabia** SS (E) ✗ ◑
Dome-shaped bush. Loose flat trusses, scarlet, funnel-shaped flowers, orange inside and speckled pale brown. Mid. AM 1934 H4

–– **'Waterer'** SS (E) ✗ ◑
Compact habit. Salmon pink, tinged orange. Late. H4

– 'Fastuosum Flore Pleno' (HH) LS (E) ✗ ◑
Dome-shaped bush. Lax trusses, rich mauve, double, frilly-edged, funnel-shaped flowers, ray of brown crimson markings within. Mid. AGM 1924 and 1959 H4

– 'Fire Bird' LS (E) ✗ ◑
Tall, vigorous. Long crimson bracts. Large trusses of salmon-red flowers. Mid. H3-4

– 'Fire Glow' MS (E) ✗ ◑
Fluted leaves. Racemes of slightly fragrant, trumpet-shaped, turkey-red flowers with ray of dark brown markings. Mid. AM 1935 H3

– Fittra SS (E) ✗ ◑
Compact habit. Abundant, dense trusses. Vivid deep rose flowers. Early-Mid. AM 1949 H4

– 'Fragrantissimum' MS (E) † ✗ ◑
Dark green, corrugated leaves. Flowers widely funnel-shaped, extremely fragrant, white flushed rose, green tinged inside. FCC 1868 H1

– 'Furnivall's Daughter' MS-LS (E) ✗ ◑
Widely funnel-shaped, light rose-pink flowers with splash of dark markings. Mid-Late. AMT 1958 FCCT 1961 H4

– 'Fusilier' LS (E) ✗ ◑
Long narrow leaves. Large trusses of brilliant red bell-shaped flowers. Mid. AM 1938 FCC 1942 H3

– Gladys MS (E) ✗ ◑
Widely funnel-shaped, slightly fragrant, pale cream flowers, marked with purple inside. Mid. AM 1926 H4. We recommend:

– – 'Rose' MS (E) ✗ ◑
Funnel-shaped, pale cream flowers with inner crimson basal blotch, light rosy pink in bud. Early-Mid. AM 1950

– 'Goldsworth Orange' SS (E) ✗ ◑
Spreading habit. Large trusses, pale orange flowers, tinged apricot. Late. AMT 1959 H4

– 'Goldsworth Yellow' SS (E) ✗ ◑
Dome-shaped. Rounded trusses, primrose yellow, funnel-shaped flowers with warm brown ray, apricot pink in bud. Mid. AM 1925 H4

– 'Gomer Waterer' (HH) LS (E) ✗ ◑
Large, rounded trusses, funnel-shaped flowers, white tinged mauve, with ochre basal blotch. Mid-Late. AM 1906 AGM 1969 H3

– 'Grenadier' LS (E) ✗ ◑
Compact growth. Huge trusses, deep blood red flowers. Mid-Late. FCC 1943 H3

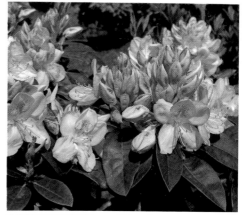

RHODODENDRON 'Gomer Waterer'

– 'Harvest Moon' MS (E) ✗ ◑
Creamy-white, bell-shaped flowers, inner ray of carmine spots. Mid. AMT 1948 H4

– 'Hawk' MS (E) ✗ ◑
Loose, flat-topped trusses, large, funnel-shaped, sulphur-yellow flowers, apricot in bud. Mid. AM 1949 H3

– 'Hugh Koster' (HH) MS (E) ✗ ◑
Stiff erect branches. Funnel-shaped, crimson-scarlet flowers, with black markings inside. Mid. AMT 1933 H4

– 'Humming Bird' SS (E) ✗ ◑
Compact dome-shaped habit. Widely bell-shaped carmine flowers, scarlet within the tube. Early. H3

– 'Intrifast' DS (E) ✗ ◑
Dense habit. Abundant, small violet-blue flowers in clusters. Mid. H4

– 'Isabella' LS-ST (E) ✗ ◑
Large trusses. Huge, trumpet-shaped, frilly-edged, fragrant, white flowers. Late. H3

– 'Jalisco' MS (E) ✗ ◑
Straw-coloured flowers, tinged orange-rose at tips. Late. H3-4. We recommend:

– – 'Elect' MS (E) ✗ ◑
Primrose-yellow flowers with paler lobes, brownish-red markings within. AM 1948

– – 'Janet' MS (E) ✗ ◑
Apricot-yellow flowers.

– 'Jenny' (*'Creeping Jenny'*) PS (E) ✗ ◑
Large, deep red, bell-shaped flowers. Mid. H4

– 'Jervis Bay' MS (E) ✗ ◑
Firm rounded trusses. Funnel-shaped primrose-yellow flowers, crimson basal flash. Mid. AM 1951 H3

– **'July Fragrance'** LS (E) ✕ ◑
Strong growth. Bronze flushed young leaves.
Large loose trusses, fragrant, trumpet-
shaped, white flowers, with inner crimson
basal stain. Late. H3
– **'Kluis Sensation'** MS (E) ✕ ◑
Bright scarlet flowers, darker spots on upper
lobes. Mid. AGM 1973 H4
– **'Kluis Triumph'** MS (E) ✕ ◑
Magnificent deep red flowers. Mid. AMT 1969
FCCT 1971 H4
– **Lady Bessborough** LS (E) ✕ ◑
Erect habit. Funnel-shaped, wavy-edged,
creamy flowers with maroon flash on deeper
cream interior, apricot in bud. Mid. FCC 1933
H4
– – **'Roberte'** LS (E) ✕ ◑
Loose trusses. Bright salmon, fringed flowers,
tinged apricot and spotted crimson in throat.
Mid. FCC 1933

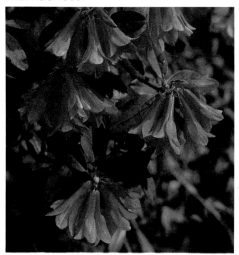

RHODODENDRON 'Lady Chamberlain'

– **Lady Chamberlain** LS (E) ✕ ◑
Stiffly branched. Clusters of long, waxy,
drooping, narrowly bell-shaped flowers,
typically mandarin-red, shading to
orange-buff. Mid. FCC 1933 H3
– – **'Chelsea'** LS (E) ✕ ◑
Orange-pink flowers.
– – **'Exbury'** LS (E) ✕ ◑
Yellow flowers, overlaid salmon-orange.
FCC 1931
– – **'Salmon Trout'** LS (E) ✕ ◑
Salmon-pink flowers.

– – **'Seville'** LS (E) ✕ ◑
Bright orange flowers.
– **'Lady Clementine Mitford'** (HH) LS (E) ✕ ◑
Large glossy leaves. Widely funnel-shaped
peach-pink flowers, shaded white; with pink,
green and brown inner markings. Mid-Late.
AMT 1971 H4
– **'Lady Eleanor Cathcart'** (HH) LS (E) ✕ ◑
Dome-shaped. Distinctive large glossy green
leaves. Widely funnel-shaped clear rose
flowers with darker veins, and maroon basal
blotch inside. Mid-Late. H4
– **Lady Roseberry** LS (E) ✕ ◑
Drooping, waxy, bell-shaped flowers typically
deep pink, lighter at margins. Mid. AM 1930
FCC 1932 H3
– – **'Pink Delight'** LS (E) ✕ ◑
Glistening pink flowers, paler inside.
– **'Laura Aberconway'** MS (E) ✕ ◑
Loose trusses. Frilly-edged, funnel-shaped
geranium-lake flowers. Mid. AM 1941
FCC 1944 H3
– **'Lavender Girl'** MS (E) ✕ ◑
Vigorous, compact habit. Dome-shaped
trusses, fragrant funnel-shaped lavender
flowers, lilac-mauve in bud. Mid. AMT 1950
FCCT 1967 AGM 1969 H4
– **'Letty Edwards'** MS (E) ✕ ◑
Compact habit. Sulphur-yellow,
funnel-shaped flowers, pale pink in bud.
Mid. AMT 1946 FCCT 1948 AGM 1969 H4
– **'Lionel's Triumph'** LS (E) ✕ ◑
Long leaves. Large trusses, bell-shaped,
Dresden-yellow flowers with inner crimson
spots at the base. Early-Mid. AM 1954 H3
– **'Little Ben'** DS (E) ✕ ◑
Spreading habit. Abundant, bell-shaped,
waxy, scarlet flowers; March-April. FCC 1937
H4
– **Lodauric** LS-ST (E) ✕ ◑
Nodding trusses, fragrant, trumpet-shaped
pure white flowers, streaked brownish-
crimson at the base inside. Late. H3
– **Loderi** LS-ST (E) ✕ ◑
Enormous trusses, fragrant, lily-like trumpet-
shaped flowers, 13-15cm across, varying
white to cream and soft pink. Early-Mid. H3
We recommend the clones:
– – **'Helen'** LS-ST (E) ✕ ◑
Pale pink, fading white.
– – **'Julie'** LS-ST (E) ✕ ◑
Cream, suffused sulphur-yellow. AM 1944

– – **'King George'** LS-ST (E) ✗ ◑
Pure white with pale green inner basal
markings, soft pink in bud. AM 1968
AGM 1969 FCC 1970
– – **'Pink Diamond'** LS-ST (E) ✗ ◑
Pale pink, with crimson basal markings,
turning to green, flushed brown. FCC 1914
AGM 1969

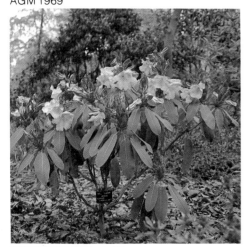

RHODODENDRON Loderi 'Venus'

– – **'Venus'** LS-ST (E) ✗ ◑
Rhodamine pink paling with age, deep pink in
bud. AGM 1969
– – **'White Diamond'** LS-ST (E) ✗ ◑
Pure white, flushed pink in bud. FCC 1914
– **'Loder's White'** (HH) LS (E) ✗ ◑
Conical trusses. Widely funnel-shaped, pure
white flowers, edged pink and marked with
crimson spots; mauve pink in bud. Mid.
AM 1911 AGM 1931 H4
– **'Lord Roberts'** (HH) MS (E) ✗ ◑
Erect habit. Dense rounded trusses. Dark
crimson, funnel-shaped flowers with black
markings. Mid-Late. H4
– **'Marcia'** MS (E) ✗ ◑
Abundant, compact trusses. Bell-shaped,
primrose-yellow flowers. Early-Mid. FCC 1944
H3
– **'Margaret Findlay'** MS (E) ✗ ◑
Flowers almost white, stained deep red at
base of throat. Mid. H3
– **'Marinus Koster'** MS (E) ✗ ◑
Large trusses, white flowers, shaded pink with
inner purple blotch, deep pink in bud. Mid.
AMT 1937 FCCT 1948 H4

– **'Matador'** MS (E) ✗ ◑
Spreading habit. Large, loose trusses, brilliant
dark orange-red, funnel-shaped flowers.
Early-Mid. AM 1945 FCC 1946 H3
– **'May Day'** MS (E) ✗ ◑
Wide spreading. Loose trusses, slightly
pendulous, funnel-shaped, signal-red or
orange-red flowers, with large calyces. Mid.
AGM 1969 H3
– **'Michael Waterer'** (HH) MS (E) ✗ ◑
Compact habit. Slow growth. Funnel-shaped,
crimson-scarlet flowers, fading rose-crimson.
Mid-Late. H4

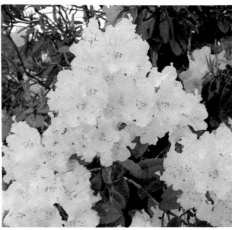

RHODODENDRON 'Loder's White'

– **'Midsummer Snow'** LS (E) ✗ ◑
Bright yellowish-green young shoots and
buds. Loose trusses, fragrant, trumpet-
shaped, pure white flowers. Late. H3
– **'Moonstone'** SS (E) ✗ ◑
Bell-shaped cream or pale primrose flowers,
rose-crimson in bud. Early-Mid. H3
– **'Moser's Maroon'** LS (E) ✗ ◑
Vigorous. Coppery-red young growths.
Maroon-red flowers, darker inner markings.
Mid. AM 1932 H4
– **'Mount Everest'** LS (E) ✗ ◑
Vigorous. Abundant, conical trusses.
Narrowly bell-shaped, white flowers,
speckled reddish-brown. Early. AMT 1953
FCCT 1958 AGM 1969 H4
– **'Mrs. A. M. Williams'** (HH) LS (E) ✗ ◑
Dense habit. Rounded trusses, frilly-edged,
funnel-shaped, crimson-scarlet flowers with
blackish spots. Mid. AM 1926 AMT 1933
FCCT 1954 H4

– **'Mrs. A. T. de la Mare'** (HH) MS (E) ⚘ ◑
Vigorous, upright habit. Dome-shaped
trusses, frilly-edged, funnel-shaped, white
flowers with greenish spots, pink tinted in bud.
Mid. AMT 1958 AGM 1969 H4

– **'Mrs. Charles E. Pearson'** (HH) MS (E) ⚘ ◑
Stout, erect branches. Conical trusses, widely
funnel-shaped, pale mauve-pink flowers
fading to white, with brown markings, mauve-
pink in bud. Mid. AMT 1933 FCCT 1955
AGM 1969 H4

– **'Mrs. C. Whitner'** LS (E) ⚘ ◑
Conical trusses, large trumpet-shaped, white
flowers suffused magenta, darker inner basal
stain. Mid. AM 1963 H3-4

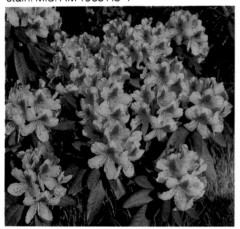

RHODODENDRON 'Mrs G W Leak'

– **'Mrs. G. W. Leak'** (HH) MS (E) ⚘ ◑
Lax, conical trusses, widely funnel-shaped
mottled rosy pink with crimson and brownish
black markings. Mid. FCCT 1934 AGM 1969
H4

– **'Mrs. Lionel de Rothschild'** MS (E) ⚘ ◑
Erect habit. Large trusses, widely funnel-
shaped, fleshy white flowers, edged pink, with
dark crimson markings. Mid. AM 1931 H4

– **'Mrs. P. D. Williams'** MS (E) ⚘ ◑
Flattened trusses; ivory flowers with brown
blotch on upper lobes, freely produced.
Mid-Late. AMT 1936 H4

– **Naomi** LS (E) ⚘ ◑
Large trusses. Fragrant, open flowers of soft
lilac shading to greenish-yellow, with faint
brown markings. Early-Mid. AM 1933 H3-4

– – **'Exbury'** LS (E) ⚘ ◑
Lilac flowers, tinged yellow.

– – **'Nautilus'** LS (E) ⚘ ◑
Deep rose, frilled flowers, flushed pale
orange-yellow, paling with age. AM 1938

– – **'Stella Maris'** LS (E) ⚘ ◑
Larger trusses. Buff flowers shaded lilac-pink.
FCC 1939

– **'New Comet'** MS (E) ⚘ ◑
Large globular trusses. Shallowly funnel-
shaped, mimosa-yellow flowers, flushed pale
pink. Early-Mid. AM 1957 H3

– **Nobleanum** (HH) LS-ST (E) ⚘ ◑
Slow growth. Compact trusses, widely funnel-
shaped, rich rose flowers, flushed white
inside, with crimson spots, rose-scarlet in
bud; January-March or earlier. AGM 1926 H4

– – **'Album'** (HH) MS (E) ⚘ ◑
White or blush flowers faintly marked
yellowish-green, pink in bud; January-March.
AGM 1969

– – **'Venustum'** (HH) MS (E) ⚘ ◑
Dome-shaped habit. Pink flowers shading to
white with inner dark crimson basal markings;
late winter. AGM 1969 AM 1973

– **Oreocinn** LS (E) ⚘ ◑
Slender, twiggy habit. Soft apricot-flowers.
Mid. H4

– **'Oudijk's Sensation'** SS (E) ⚘ ◑
Mound-forming habit. Loose trusses, bell-
shaped bright pink flowers. Mid. H4

– **Penjerrick (Cream)** LS (E) ⚘ ◑
Loose trusses. Fragrant, bell-shaped,
creamy-yellow flowers with crimson nectaries.
Early. AM 1923 H3

– **Penjerrick (Pink)** LS (E) ⚘ ◑
As above, but pale pink flowers with crimson
nectaries. Both forms are exquisite. AM 1923
H3

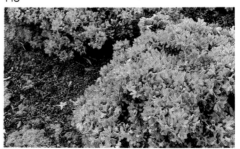

RHODODENDRON 'Pink Drift'

– **'Pink Drift'** DS (E) ⚘ ◑
Small aromatic leaves. Clusters of soft
lavender-rose flowers. Mid. H4

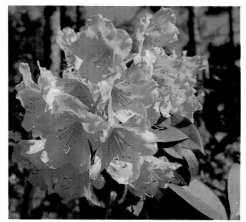

RHODODENDRON 'Pink Pearl'

– **'Pink Pearl'** (HH) LS (E) ✗ ◑
Strong-growing. Large trusses, widely funnel-shaped, lilac-pink flowers, fading white, with crimson-brown markings. Mid. AM 1897 FCC 1900 AGM 1952 H4

– **'Polar Bear'** LS-ST (E) ✗ ◑
Large leaves. Large trusses, fragrant, trumpet-shaped, white flowers, green flash inside. Late. FCC 1946 H3

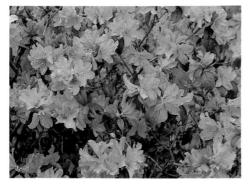

RHODODENDRON 'Praecox'

– **'Praecox'** SS Semi-(E) ✗ ◑
Leaves aromatic when crushed. Widely funnel-shaped, rosy-purple flowers; February-March. AGM 1926 FCC 1978 H4

– **'Princess Anne'** DS (E) ✗ ◑
Dense habit. Small, pale yellow, funnel-shaped flowers. Mid. AMT 1978 H4

– **'Ptarmigan'** DS (E) ✗ ◑
Spreading habit. Small neat heads of white flowers; March-April. FCC 1965 H4

– **'Purple Splendour'** (HH) LS (E) ✗ ◑
Erect branches. Widely funnel-shaped, rich purple flowers with black markings. Mid-Late. AM 1931 AGM 1969 H4

– **'Queen Elizabeth II'** MS (E) ✗ ◑
Fine clear yellow flowers. Mid. Strong-growing. AM 1967 FCC 1974

– **'Racil'** SS (E) ✗ ◑
Small leaves. Clusters of blush-pink flowers. Early. AM 1957 H4

– **'Remo'** SS (E) ✗ ◑
Compact habit. Loose trusses of bright yellow flowers. Early. H3

– **'Rocket'** MS (E) ✗ ◑
Flat-topped trusses. Bell-shaped, blood-red flowers, marked brown; late March-early April. AM 1954 H3-4

– **'Romany Chal'** LS (E) ✗ ◑ "Gypsy Girl"
Lax trusses. Bell-shaped, cardinal-red flowers with black markings. Mid-Late. AM 1932 FCC 1937 H3

– **'Rosy Bell'** MS (E) ✗ ◑
Loose terminal clusters of rose-pink, bell-shaped flowers. Early-Mid. AM 1894 H4

– **'Roza Stevenson'** (*Roza Harrison*) MS (E) ✗ ◑
Trusses of saucer-shaped, deep lemon-yellow flowers, darker in bud. Early-Mid. FCC 1968 H3

– **Russautinii** MS (E) ✗ ◑
Compact habit. Deep lavender-blue flowers. Mid. H4

– **'Saint Tudy'** SS (E) ✗ ◑
Dense bushy habit. Dense trusses, shallowly bell-shaped, lobelia-blue flowers. Early-Mid. AM 1960 FCCT 1973 H4

– **'Sapphire'** DS (E) ✗ ◑
Open habit. Small leaves. Pale lavender-blue flowers. Early. AMT 1967 H4

– **'Sappho'** (HH) MS ✗ ◑
Dome-shaped habit. Conical trusses. Widely funnel-shaped, white flowers, blotched purple-black, mauve in bud. Mid. AGM 1969 H4

– **Sarled** DS (E) ✗ ◑
Tiny leaves. Rounded trusses. Creamy-white flowers, pink in bud. Mid. H4

– **'Scarlet Wonder'** DS (E) ✗ ◑
Mound-forming. Loose terminal trusses, trumpet-shaped, frilly-edged, ruby-red flowers. Mid. AGM 1973 H4

– **'Seta'** MS (E) ✗ ◑
Erect habit. Narrowly bell-shaped flowers,

white shading to pink, in umbels; March-April.
AM 1933 FCC 1960 AGM 1969 H3-4
– **'Seven Stars'** LS (E) ✗ ◑
Vigorous. Bell-shaped, frilly-edged white
flowers flushed pink, reddish in bud. Mid.
AM 1967 H3-4
– **'Shilsonii'** LS (E) ✗ ◑
Rounded habit. Metallic coloured stems.
Loose trusses, bell-shaped, blood-red
flowers with darker veins and brown
markings. Large calyx. Early. AM 1900 H3-4
– **'Sir Frederick Moore'** LS (E) ✗ ◑
Long leaves. Large rounded trusses, widely
funnel-shaped wavy-edged, clear pink
flowers, spotted crimson. Mid. AM 1937 FCCT
1972 H3-4
– **'Snow Queen'** LS (E) ✗ ◑
Compact habit. Dome-shaped trusses, large
funnel-shaped, white flowers with inner red
basal blotch, dark pink in bud. Mid. AM 1934
AMT 1946 FCCT 1970 H3-4
– **'Solent Queen'** LS (E) ✗ ◑
Magnificent trusses. Large, widely funnel-
shaped, fragrant white flowers flushed pink
with green ray. Mid. AM 1939 H3
– **'Songster'** SS (E) ✗ ◑
Compact habit. Blue flowers freely borne.
Early. H4
– **'Souvenir de Dr. S. Endtz'** MS (E) ✗ ◑
Compact habit. Dome-shaped trusses.
Widely funnel-shaped, mottled pink flowers
marked crimson, rich rose in bud. Mid.
AM 1924 AGM 1969 FCCT 1970 H4
– **'Susan'** LS (E) ✗ ◑
Bushy habit. Large trusses of bluish-mauve
flowers, spotted purple. Early-Mid. AM 1930
AMT 1948 FCC 1954 AGM 1969 H4
– **'Tally Ho'** MS (E) ✗ ◑
Dome-shaped habit. Compact rounded
trusses, funnel-shaped, scarlet flowers. Mid-
Late. FCC 1933 H3
– **'Temple Belle'** SS (E) ✗ ◑
Neat rounded habit. Loose clusters of bell-
shaped, Persian-rose flowers. Early-Mid. H3
– **'Tessa'** SS (E) ✗ ◑
Up to 1 m. Loose flattened umbels of slightly
purplish-pink flowers with crimson spots;
March-early April. AM 1935 AGM 1969 H4
– **'Tortoiseshell Champagne'** MS (E) ✗ ◑
Funnel-shaped flowers, rich yellow, fading to
pale yellow tinged pink at the margins.
Mid-Late. AMT 1967 H3-4

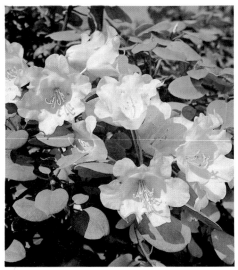

RHODODENDRON 'Temple Belle'

– **'Treasure'** DS (E) ✗ ◑
Mound-forming. Gnarled branches. Leaves
bronzed when young. Bell-shaped deep rose
flowers. Early-Mid. H3-4
– **'Trewithen Orange'** MS (E) ✗ ◑
Loose pendant trusses, deep orange-brown
flowers with rosy blush. Early-Mid. FCC 1950
H3-4
– **'Unique'** SS (E) ✗ ◑
Dense leafy habit. Dome-shaped trusses.
Funnel-shaped creamy flowers with crimson
spots. Early-Mid. AMT 1934 FCCT 1935 H4
– **'Unknown Warrior'** MS (E) ✗ ◑
Compact trusses. Widely bell-shaped, deep
rose flowers marked brown, crimson-scarlet
in bud. Early-Mid. H4
– **Vanessa** MS (E) ✗ ◑
Spreading habit. Loose trusses. Soft pink
flowers spotted carmine within. Mid-Late.
FCC 1929 H3-4
– – **'Pastel'** MS (E) ✗ ◑
Spreading habit. Cream flowers flushed
shell-pink, stained scarlet outside. Mid-Late.
AM 1946 FCCT 1971
– **'W.F.H.'** SS (E) ✗ ◑
Spreading habit. Clusters of funnel-shaped,
scarlet flowers. Mid. H3
– **'White Glory'** LS (E) ✗ ◑
Loose, globular trusses, large white, funnel-
shaped flowers, cream in bud. Early.
AM 1937 H3

RHODODENDRON – Cont.

– **'Winsome'** MS (E) ⚊ ◑
Deep coppery young growths. Loose
pendant trusses. Long wavy-edged, deep-
pink flowers. Mid. AM 1950 H3-4
– **'Yellow Hammer'** MS (E) ⚊ ◑
Slender habit. Tubular or narrowly bell-
shaped, bright yellow flowers in pairs from
terminal and axillary buds. Early. H3-4

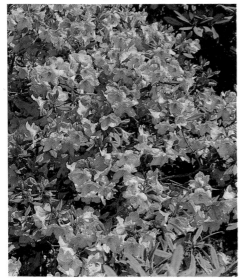

RHODODENDRON Vanessa 'Pastel'

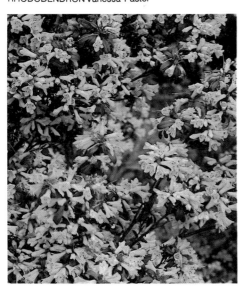

RHODODENDRON 'Yellow Hammer'

AZALEODENDRON

AZALEODENDRONS SS-MS Semi-(E) ⚊ ◑
*Hybrids between deciduous azaleas and
evergreen species of other series. Very hardy.
Flowering May-June. H4*
– **'Galloper Light'** MS Semi-(E) ⚊
Loose trusses of creamy-pink, funnel-shaped
flowers. May-early June. AM 1927
– **'Glory of Littleworth'** SS Semi-(E) ⚊
Stiff, erect habit. Fragrant funnel-shaped
flowers, cream turning milky white, with
conspicuous coppery blotch; May. AM 1911

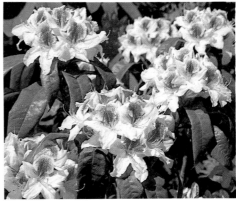

AZALEODENDRON 'Glory of Littleworth'

DECIDUOUS HYBRID AZALEAS SS-MS
*Generally trumpet-shaped, single flowers with
wide colour range. Many have rich autumn
leaf colour. Divided into groups of hybrids with
following characteristics:*
*Ghent Hybrids (Gh) – Usually fragrant, long-
tubed, honeysuckle-like flowers, produced
end of May onwards. Average height in an
open position 1.8 to 2.5m. H4*
*Knap Hill Hybrids (Kn) – Usually unscented,
colourful, trumpet-shaped flowers opening
May. Average height in an open position 1.8 to
2.5m. H4*
*Mollis Hybrids (M) – Scentless, vividly
coloured flowers in showy trusses before
leaves; generally May. Average height in
open position 1.2 to 1.8m. H4*
*Occidentale Hybrids (O) – Fragrant, pastel-
coloured flowers opening late May. Average
height in open position 1.8 to 2.5m. H4*
*Rustica Hybrids (R) – Sweetly-scented,
attractive double flowers, opening late May-
early June. Average height in open position.
1.2 to 1.5m. H4*
A (i) (k) all Azaleas

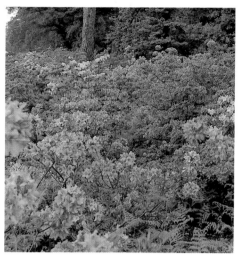

Massed DECIDUOUS AZALEAS

– **'Aida'** (R) SS
Deep peach-pink, deeper flush. Double.
– **'Ballerina'** (Kn) MS
White with orange flash, suffused flesh-pink in bud. Large, frilly-edged flowers.
– **'Beaulieu'** (Kn) MS
Salmon-pink with deep orange flash, deep salmon-pink in bud. Bronzy young foliage.
– **'Berryrose'** (Kn) MS
Rose-pink, yellow flash. Coppery young foliage. AM 1934
– **'Brazil'** (Kn) MS
Tangerine-red, darkening with age. Frilly-edged.

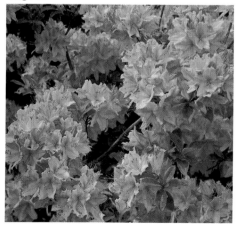

AZALEA 'Cecile'

– **'Cecile'** (Kn) MS
Salmon-pink, yellow flare; dark salmon pink in bud. Large. AGM 1969
– **'Christopher Wren'** (M) (*'Goldball'*) SS
Orange-yellow flushed flame, dark orange spotting.
– **'Coccinea Speciosa'** (Gh) MS
Brilliant orange-red. AGM 1960
– **'Corneille'** (Gh) MS
Cream, flushed pink; pink in bud. Excellent autumn leaf colour. AMT 1958 AGM 1969
– **'Daviesii'** (Gh) MS
White, yellow flare. Fragrant.
– **'Dr. M. Oosthoek'** (M) SS
Deep orange-red. AM 1920 AMT 1940 AGM 1969
– **'Embley Crimson'** (Kn) MS
Crimson, compact habit.
– **'Exquisitum'** (O) MS
Flesh pink, deep pink outside; orange flare. Frilly edged. Fragrant. AMT 1950 FCCT 1968
– **'George Reynolds'** (Kn) MS
Butter-yellow with chrome-yellow and green spotting. Flushed pink in bud. Large flowers. AM 1936

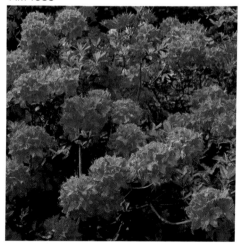

AZALEA 'Gibraltar'

– **'Gibraltar'** (Kn) MS
Flame orange, yellow flash, deep orange-crimson in bud. Large crinkly petals.
– **'Gloria Mundi'** (Gh) MS
Bright orange, yellow flare. Crinkly margins.
– **'Gog'** (Kn) MS
Orange-red, yellow flash, dark red flush outside.

– **'Goldball'** see *'Christopher Wren'*
– **'Golden Horn'** (Kn) MS
Straw yellow, deeper flash, rose flushed
outside, fading to ivory. Bronze tinted, hoary,
greyish leaves.

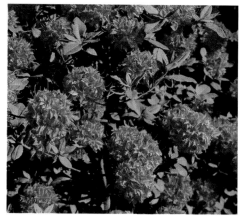

AZALEA 'Homebush'

– **'Homebush'** (Kn) MS
Rose-madder, paler shading. Semi-double.
AMT 1950 AGM 1969
– **'Hotspur'** (Kn) MS
Flame red, darker markings. AM 1934
– **'Irene Koster'** (O) MS
Rose-pink, yellow blotch. Late.
– **'Kathleen'** (Kn) MS
Salmon-pink, orange blotch; darker in bud.

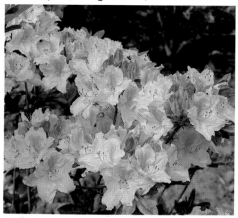

AZALEA 'Klondyke'

– **'Klondyke'** (Kn) MS
Glowing orange-gold, tinted red. Large
flowers. Coppery red young foliage.

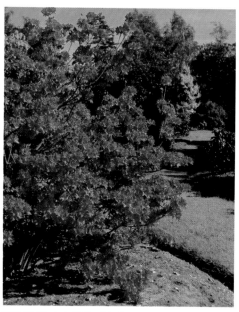

AZALEA 'Koster's Brilliant Red'

– **'Koster's Brilliant Red'** (M) SS
Glowing orange-red.
– **'Lemonara'** (M) SS
Apricot yellow, tinged red outside.
– **'Nancy Waterer'** (Gh) MS
Golden yellow. Large. AGM 1969
– **'Narcissiflorum'** (Gh) MS
Pale yellow, darker centre and outside.
Fragrant; double. Vigorous, compact habit.
AMT 1954 AGM 1969
– **'Persil'** (Kn) MS
White, orange flare.
– **'Satan'** (Kn) MS
Geranium red, darker buds.
– **'Silver Slipper'** (Kn) MS
White, flushed pink, orange flare. Copper
tinted young foliage. AMT 1962 FCCT 1963
– **'Spek's Orange'** (M) SS
Orange, deeper in bud. Late. AMT 1948 FCCT
1953 AGM 1969
– **'Strawberry Ice'** (Kn) MS
Flesh pink, deeper at margins, gold flare.
Deep pink in bud. AMT 1963 AGM 1969
– **'Tunis'** (Kn) MS
Deep crimson, orange flare, darker in bud.
– **'Whitethroat'** (Kn) MS
Pure white. Double, frilly edged. Compact
habit. AMT 1962

207

EVERGREEN HYBRID AZALEAS SS-MS (E)
⚘ ◑

*Low spreading shrubs. April, or more
generally May, flowering. Foliage is often
completely obscured by mass of flowers.
Some shelter from cold winds, and partial
shade is ideal. Average height 0.6-1.2m.
Main groups are:*

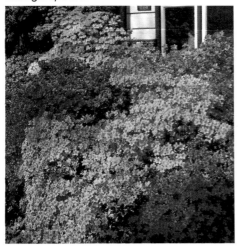

EVERGREEN HYBRID AZALEAS

*Glenn Dale Hybrids (GD) – flowers med. to
v.large 5-10cm across
Indian or Indica Hybrids (I) – flowers large 6 to
7.5cm across
Kaempferi Hybrids (Kf) – flowers medium 4 to
5cm across
Kurume Hybrids (K) – flowers small, 2.5 to
3.5cm across. Includes "Wilson's Fifty"
Oldhamii Hybrids (O) – flowers large 6 to
7.5cm across
Vuyk Hybrids (V) – flowers large 5 to 7.5cm
across
Wada Hybrids (W) – flowers medium to large*
– **'Addy Wery'** (K) SS (E) ⚘ ◑
Deep vermilion red. AMT 1950 H4
– **'Appleblossom'** see *'Hoo'*
– **'Atalanta'** (Kf) SS (E) ⚘ ◑
Soft lilac. H4
– **'Azuma-kagami'** (K) MS (E) ⚘ ◑
Phlox-pink, darker shading. Hose-in-hose.
AMT 1950 AGM 1969 H3
– **'Bengal Fire'** (O) MS (E) ⚘ ◑
Fiery orange. H4
– **'Benigiri'** (K) SS (E) ⚘ ◑
Bright crimson. H4

– **'Betty'** (Kf) SS (E) ⚘ ◑
Salmon pink, deeper centre. AMT 1940 FCCT
1972 H4
– **'Bijou de Ledeberg'** (I) SS (E) ⚘ ◑
Rose red. Leaves dark green with white
edges. H3
– **'Blaauw's Pink'** (K) SS (E) ⚘ ◑
Salmon pink, shaded paler; early. H4

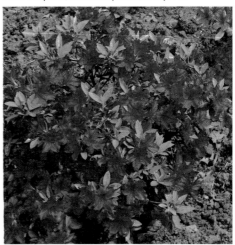

AZALEA 'Blue Danube'

– **'Blue Danube'** (V) SS (E) ⚘ ◑
Distinctive bluish violet. AMT 1970
– **'Bungo-nishiki'** (W) SS (E) ⚘ ◑
Orange-scarlet, semi-double; late. H4
– **'Chanticleer'** (GD) SS (E) ⚘ ◑
Amaranth purple, floriferous. Dense habit. H4

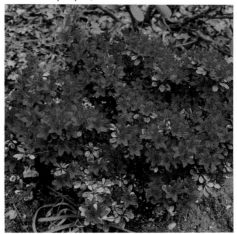

AZALEA 'Hinodegiri'

– **'Christmas Cheer'** see *'Ima-shojo'*
– **'Eddy'** (Kf) SS (E) ✗ ◑
Deep salmon-red. AM 1944 H3
– **'Favorite'** SS (E) ✗ ◑
Deep rose pink. H4
– **'Fedora'** (Kf) SS (E) ✗ ◑
Pale pink, darker flash. AM 1931 FCCT 1960
H4
– **'General Wavell'** (I) SS (E) ✗ ◑
Large, crimson flowers. Spreading. H3
– **'Hatsugiri'** (K) SS (E) ✗ ◑
Bright crimson-purple. AMT 1956 FCCT 1969
H4
– **'Hinodegiri'** (K) SS (E) ✗ ◑
Bright crimson. AMT 1965 AGM 1969 H4

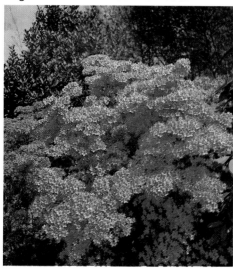

AZALEA 'Hinomayo'

– **'Hinomayo'** (K) SS (E) ✗ ◑
Clear pink. AM 1921 FCCT 1945 AGM 1954
H4
– **'Hoo'** (K) (*'Appleblossom'*) SS (E) ✗ ◑
Pale pink, white throat. AMT 1950 H4
– **'Ima-shojo'** (K) (*'Christmas Cheer'*) SS (E)
✗ ◑
Bright red, hose-in-hose. AMT 1959 H4
– **'Iro-hayama'** (K) SS (E) ✗ ◑
White, pale lavender margin, faint brown
centre. AMT 1952 H4
– **'John Cairns'** (Kf) SS (E) ✗ ◑
Dark orange-red. AMT 1940 AGM 1952 H4
– **'Kirin'** (K) SS (E) ✗ ◑
Deep rose, silvery rose shading; hose-in-
hose. AM 1927 AMT 1952 AGM 1969 H4

– **'Kure-no-yuki'** (K) (*'Snowflake'*) SS (E) ✗ ◑
White, hose-in-hose. AMT 1952 AGM 1969 H4
– **'Leo'** (O) SS (E) ✗ ◑
Bright orange. Late. H4
– **'Louise Dowdle'** (GD) SS (E) ✗ ◑
Brilliant Tyrian-pink with rose blotch, large.
AMT 1974 FCCT 1976 H4
– **'Miyagino'** (K) SS (E) ✗ ◑
Deep rose pink, hose-in-hose. H4
– **'Mother's Day'** SS (E) ✗ ◑
Rose red. AMT 1959 AGM 1969 FCCT 1970
H4
– **'Naomi'** (Kf) MS (E) ✗ ◑
Salmon-pink. Very late. H4
– **'Orange Beauty'** SS (E) ✗ ◑
Salmon-orange. AMT 1945 FCC 1958
AGM 1969 H4

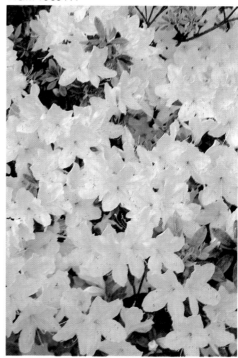

AZALEA 'Palestrina'

– **'Palestrina'** (V) SS (E) ✗ ◑
White, faint green ray. AM 1944 FCC 1967
AGM 1969 H4
– **'Polar Sea'** (GD) SS (E) ✗ ◑
White, pale green blotch, frilly edged. H4
– **'Purple Triumph'** (V) SS (E) ✗ ◑
Deep purple. AMT 1960 H4

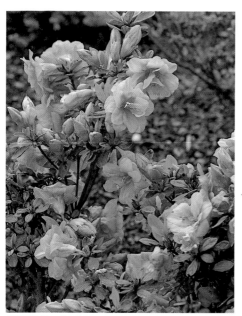

AZALEA 'Rosebud'

– **'Rosebud'** (K) SS (E) ⚬ ◑
Rose pink, hose-in-hose. Late. AMT 1972 H4
– **'Sakata Red'** SS (E) ⚬ ◑
Flame-red. H4
– **'Satsuki'** (I) SS (E) ⚬ ◑
Pink, dark blotch. H4
– **'Shin-seikai'** (K) SS (E) ⚬ ◑
White, hose-in-hose. AM 1921 AMT 1952 H4
– **'Silver Moon'** (GD) SS (E) ⚬ ◑
White, faint green blotch; frilly edged. H4

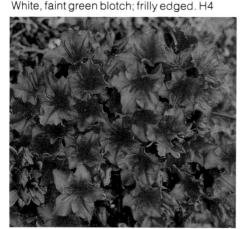

AZALEA 'Vuyk's Scarlet'

– **'Suga-no-ito'** (K) SS (E) ⚬ ◑
Lavender-pink, white throat. AMT 1952 H4
– **'Ukamuse'** (K) SS (E) ⚬ ◑
Light salmon-rose, darker flash; hose-in-hose.
AMT 1952 H4
– **'Vida Brown'** (K) SS (E) ⚬ ◑
Clear rose-pink, hose-in-hose. AMT 1960 H4
– **'Vuyk's Rosy Red'** (V) SS (E) ⚬ ◑
Deep rosy red. AMT 1962 H4
– **'Vuyk's Scarlet'** (V) SS (E) ⚬ ◑
Carmine red, fluted petals. AMT 1959
FCCT 1966 AGM 1969 H4
RHODORA canadensis see
RHODODENDRON canadense
RHODOTYPOS – Rosaceae SS ◑
*Montypic genus. Opposite leaves on erect
branches. Dog-rose-like white flowers. All
fertile soils.*
– **scandens** (*kerrioides*) SS ◑
Abundant paper-white flowers, May-July.
Shiny black conspicuous fruits.
RHUS – Anacardiaceae MS-ST "Sumachs"
*Grown primarily for pinnate, finely divided
foliage which colours richly in autumn. Male
and female flowers inconspicuous and
generally on separate plants. Easy cultivation,
any fertile soil – tolerant of atmospheric
pollution.*

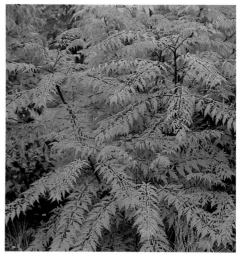

RHUS glabra 'Laciniata'

– **copallina** MS
Downy shrub with lustrous leaves. Greenish-
yellow flowers. Brilliant autumn foliage and
red fruit clusters. AM 1973

– **cotinoides** see *COTINUS obovatus*
– **cotinus** see *COTINUS coggygria*
– **glabra** MS "Smooth Sumach"
Wide-spreading habit. Smooth stems and
leaves. Fiery-red or orange-yellow autumn
foliage. Scarlet, erect, female fruit clusters.
– – **'Laciniata'** MS
Finely divided fern-like foliage. FCC 1867
– **trichocarpa** LS-ST ♥
Downy leaves, coppery-pink when young,
deep orange in autumn. Bristly, yellow fruits in
drooping clusters. AM 1979

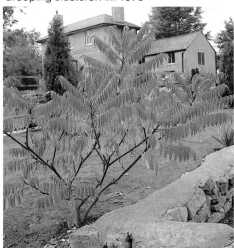

RHUS typhina

– **typhina** LS-ST ♥ "Stag's-horn Sumach"
Densely brown-felted stems. Leaves scarlet,
red, orange and yellow in autumn. Dense
cones of dark-crimson bristly fruits, retained
on female plants into winter. AGM 1969
– – **'Laciniata'** LS-ST ♥
Female form with deeply cut fern-like foliage.
AM 1910 AGM 1969
RIBES – Grossulariaceae DS-MS
*Flowering currants and ornamental
gooseberries. Generally spring flowering,
some evergreen. Easy cultivation – all soils.
Most are extremely hardy.*
(g) 5
– **alpinum** SS-MS
Densely twiggy habit. Small greenish-yellow
flowers. Red berries. Ideal for hedging.
– – **'Aureum'** SS
Young leaves yellow. FCC 1881
– **aureum** see *R. odoratum*

– **gayanum** SS (E)
Velvety, soft green leaves. Pale yellow, bell-
shaped, honey-scented flowers in erect
racemes; early June.
– **henryi** DS (E)
Bristly young shoots. Pale green leaves.
Drooping racemes of dioecious, greenish-
yellow flowers, February-March.
– **laurifolium** (*vicarii*) DS (E)
Large leathery leaves. Dioecious, greenish-
white flowers in drooping racemes; February-
March. Berries red, turning blackish. AM 1912
– **odoratum** (*aureum* HORT) MS "Buffalo
Currant"
Loose, erect habit. Shiny leaves, colouring
richly in autumn. Golden-yellow, clove-
scented flowers in lax racemes; April. Black
berries.
– **sanguineum** MS "Flowering Currant"
Flowers in drooping racemes, later
ascending; April. Black bloomy fruits.
Characteristic pungent smell. We
recommend the clones:

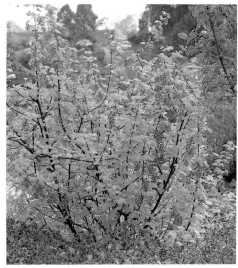

RIBES sanguineum 'Brocklebankii'

– – **'Brocklebankii'** SS ◑
Golden yellow leaves. Pink flowers. AM 1914
AGM 1973
– – **'Carneùm'** (*'Grandiflorum'*) MS
Deep flesh-pink flowers.
– – **'King Edward VII'** MS
Intense crimson flowers. Lower growing.
AM 1904 AGM 1969

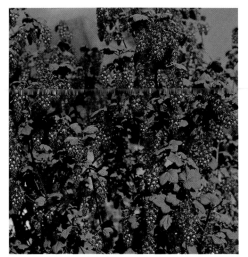

RIBES sanguineum 'Pulborough Scarlet'

– –**'Pulborough Scarlet'** MS
Deep red flowers. AM 1959 AGM 1969
– –**'Splendens'** MS
Longer racemes of rosy crimson flowers.
AGM 1928
– –**'Tydemans White'** MS
The best white-flowered, form and a distinct
improvement on *'Album'*.
– **speciosum** MS Semi-(E) "Fuchsia-
Flowered Gooseberry"
Glossy leaves. Spiny, bristly, red stems and
fruits. Pendulous clusters of rich red flowers;
April-May. Best against walls in cold areas.
AGM 1925
RICHEA – Epacridaceae SS (E) ✗
*Flowers in terminal panicles. Require moist,
preferably acid, soil.*
– **scoparia** SS (E) ✗
Spreading habit. Stiff, sharply pointed leaves,
covering stems. Pink flowers in erect, spike-
like panicles, May. AM 1942
ROBINIA – Leguminosae LS-MT ♥
*Attractive pinnate leaves, often spiny stems,
pea-flowers in hanging racemes. Hardy, fast-
growing and suitable for all soils, especially
useful for dry or sandy soils. Tolerate
atmospheric pollution.*
– × **ambigua** ST ♥
Slightly sticky young shoots. Racemes of pale
pink flowers, June. We recommend:
– –**'Bella-rosea'** ST ♥
Stickier shoots. Rather larger pink flowers.

– –**'Decaisneana'** MT ♥
Large racemes of pale pink flowers. Vigorous.
FCC 1865 AGM 1969
– **fertilis** MS
Suckering shrub. Bristly stems. Rose-pink
flowers, June. Bristly pods. We recommend
the form.
– –**'Monument'** LS
More compact form.

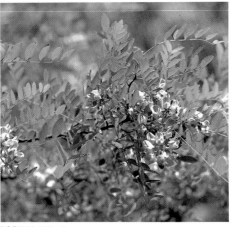

ROBINIA 'Hillieri'

– **'Hillieri'** ST ♥
Slightly fragrant lilac-pink flowers. June.
AM 1962 AGM 1973
– **hispida** LS "Rose Acacia"
Gladular-bristly branches. Large, deep rose
flowers in short racemes. Excellent against
sunny wall. AM 1934
– –**'Macrophylla'** LS
Larger leaflets and flowers. Less bristly.
– **kelseyi** LS-ST ♥
Slender branches, fairly brittle. Slightly
fragrant, lilac-pink flowers, June. Glandular-
bristly pods. AM 1910 FCC 1917
– **pseudoacacia** LT ♥ "Common Acacia"
"False Acacia" "Black Locust"
Suckering habit. Grooved and fissured bark.
Drooping racemes of white, slightly-scented
flowers along branches, June.
– –**'Bessoniana'** ST-MT ♥
Compact form, generally spineless.
– –**'Decaisneana'** see *R.* × *ambigua
'Decaisneana'*
– –**'Frisia'** ST-MT ♥
Rich golden-yellow foliage throughout spring
to autumn. AM 1964 AGM 1969

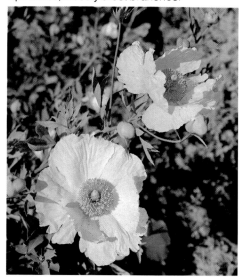

ROBINIA pseudoacacia 'Frisia'

– – **'Inermis'** ST ♥ "Mop-head Acacia"
Spineless branches. Compact rounded head.
Protect from strong winds. AGM 1969
– – **'Monophylla'** see *'Unifoliola'*
– – **'Pyramidalis'** (*'Fastigiata'*) MT ♦
Spineless, closely erect branches.

ROMNEYA coulteri

– – **'Rozynskyana'** ST ♥
Spreading branches, drooping at tips. large
drooping leaves, creating weeping effect.
– – **'Unifoliola'** (*'Monophylla'*)
Strange form with single large leaflets or
accompanied by one or two normal-sized
leaflets.
"ROCK ROSE" see *HELIANTHEMUM* and
CISTUS
ROMNEYA – Papaveraceae SS-MS ☼ "Tree
Poppy"
*Deeply-cut leaves. Large white poppy-like
flowers with central mass of golden stamens.
Spread quickly by rhizomes once
established.* A (c) 4
– **coulteri** SS-MS ☼
Large, solitary, fragrant flowers 10-15cm
across, July-October. FCC 1888 AGM 1929
– × **hybrida 'White Cloud'** SS-MS ☼
Large flowers. Strong growing.
ROSA – Rosaceae DS-LS The wild rose
species.
*Variable habit-low suckering shrubs to tall
climbers. Normally pinnate leaves, and
prickly stems. Flower colour varies from
delicate pastel shades to brilliant scarlet and
red. Generally colourful heps. Easy
cultivation, most soils, except very acid or wet.*
Shrub roses – A (g) 2
– **'Agnes'** MS
Erect habit. Arching branches and bright
green leaves. Deliciously-scented, double,
butter-yellow flowers, tinted amber. AM 1951
– × **alba** MS "White Rose of York" "Jacobite
Rose"
Strong prickly stems. Greyish-green leaves.
Richly-scented generally semi-double, white
flowers, 1.5cm across. Oblong red fruits.
– **'Albert Edwards'** MS
Arching branches. Abundant, fragrant,
lemon-yellow flowers, 5-6cm across; May.
– **alpina** see *R. pendulina*
– **altaica** see *R. pimpinellifolia altaica*
– **'Andersonii'** MS
Arching, prickly stems. Fragrant, clear, rose-
pink flowers, 5-7.5cm across, produced
abundantly over long period. Scarlet, urn-
shaped fruits.
– **anemoniflora** (*triphylla*)
Rambling or climbing habit. Anemone-like,
blush-white, double flowers, 2.5-4cm across.
Best against sunny wall.

– **'Apothecary's Rose'** see *R. gallica 'Officinalis'*

– **'Arthur Hillier'** LS
Vigorous, semi-erect habit. Large rose-crimson flowers, freely borne; June-July. Bright red, flask-shaped fruits. AM 1977

– **"Austrian Copper"** see *R. foetida 'Bicolor'*

– **"Austrian Yellow"** see *R. foetida*

– **banksiae** (*banksiae 'Alboplena'*) Semi-(E) ○ "Banksian Rose" "Lady Banks' Rose"
Vigorous climber 7.5m plus. Virtually thornless. Dense umbels of double, rosette-like, white flowers, 3cm across, violet scented, May-June.

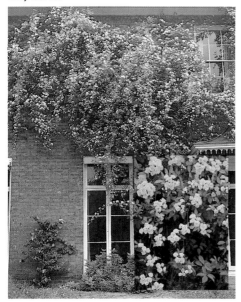

ROSA banksiae 'Lutea'

– – **'Lutea'** Semi-(E) ○ "Yellow Banksian"
Double yellow flowers. AM 1960

– – **lutescens** Semi-(E) ○
Single, yellow, fragrant flowers.

– – **normalis** Semi-(E) ○
Sweetly fragrant, single, creamy white flowers.

– **bracteata** MS-LS (E) † ○ "Macartney Rose"
Thick, stout, rambling stems. Deep green, glossy leaves. Lemon-scented, white flowers with gold anthers, 7.5 to 10cm across. Orange-red round fruits. Requires sunny, sheltered wall.

– **brunonii** (*moschata* HORT) ○ "Himalayan Musk Rose"
Vigorous climber, 9 to 12m. Richly fragrant, white flowers; June-July. We recommend the form:

– – **'La Mortola'** (*moschata 'La Mortola'*) ○
Larger leaves, greyish downy. Larger, pure white flowers in ample clusters. Hardier – but requires shelter.

– **"Burnet Rose"** see *R. pimpinellifolia*

– **"Burr Rose"** see *R. roxburghii*

– **"Cabbage Rose"** see *R. centifolia*

– **californica** MS
Stout prickly stems. Pink flowers in corymbs. Red, globose fruits. We recommend the clone:

– – **'Plena'** MS
Semi-double, dark pink flowers, fading pink and purple. AM 1958

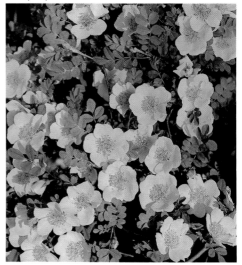

ROSA 'Canary Bird'

– **'Canary Bird'** MS
Arching stems. Small, fern-like, fresh green leaves. Abundant bright yellow flowers; late May-early June.

– **canina** MS-LS "Dog Rose"
Strong prickly stems. White or pink, scented flowers. Bright red, egg-shaped fruits.

– × **cantabrigiensis** MS
Bristly arching stems. Fragrant, fern-like leaves. Soft yellow flowers, 5cm across, changing to cream. AM 1931 AGM 1969

– **centifolia** SS "Cabbage Rose" "Provence Rose" "Rose des Peintres"
Erect prickly stems. Scented leaves. Large, fragrant, double, rose-pink flowers.
– – **'Cristata'** SS "Crested Cabbage Rose" "Crested Moss"
Crested sepals completely enveloping flower buds.
– – **'Muscosa'** (*R. muscosa*) SS "Moss Rose"
Stems, branches, leaf and flower stalks, and calyx tubes coated with moss-like glandular bristly covering. Richly scented, double, clear pink flowers.
– **"Cherokee Rose"** see *R. laevigata*
– **chinensis** SS -MS "China Rose"
Stout branches. Crimson, pink or occasionally white flowers June-September. Red obovoid fruits. We recommend:

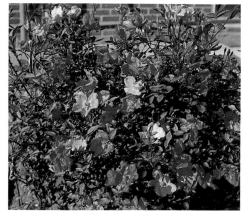

ROSA chinensis 'Mutabilis'

– – **'Mutabilis'** (*'Tipo Ideale'*) SS-MS
Vigorous, slender habit. Purplish young shoots and coppery young leaves. Richly tea scented, orange buds opening buff, shaded carmine, turning rose then crimson. AM 1957
– – **'Old Blush'** (*R. semperflorens* in part) (*chinensis 'Semperflorens'* in part) SS-MS "Monthly Rose"
Compact habit. Sweet-pea scented, pink flowers, darkening with age, produced over long period.
– – **'Viridiflora'** SS "Green Rose"
Double flowers of greenish, petal-like scales.
– **'Complicata'** MS
Scrambling habit. Very large, fragrant, deep peach pink flowers with white eye. AM 1951 FCC 1958 AGM 1965

– **damascena** SS "Damask Rose"
Very thorny stems. Greyish-green leaves. Fragrant, large flowers, varying white to red. Red, bristly, obovoid fruits. Petals are used in perfume manufacture. We recommend:
– – **'Trigintipetala'** SS
Richly scented, soft pink, loosely double flowers.

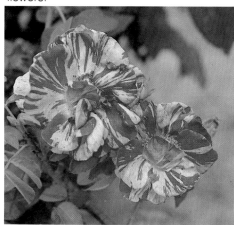

ROSA damascena 'Versicolor'

– – **'Versicolor'** SS "York and Lancaster Rose"
Loosely double, white flowers, blotched rose.
– **davidii** MS
Erect, open habit. Bright rose-pink flowers 4-5cm across in corymbs. Scarlet, long-necked, ovoid fruits. AM 1929
– **"Dog Rose"** see *R. canina*
– × **dupontii** (*moschata nivea*) MS
Strong gowing, loose habit. Large, fragrant, blush turning creamy-white flowers, 7.5cm across in corymbose clusters; July. AM 1954
– **ecae** SS
Dainty habit. Slender, arching, prickly, brown stems. Small buttercup-yellow flowers, late May-June. Small, rounded red fruits. AM 1933
– – **'Helen Knight'** SS
Flowers larger than the type and stronger growth.
– **eglanteria** see *R. rubiginosa*
– **"Eglantine"** see *R. rubiginosa*
– **fargesii** see *R. moyesii fargesii*
– **farreri** MS
Spreading habit. Fern-like leaves. Pale pink or white flowers, June. Coral-red fruits. We recommend:

– –**persetosa** MS "Threepenny-bit Rose"
Smaller leaves. Small, soft pink flowers, coral
red in bud.

–**fedtschenkoana** MS
Erect habit. White flowers, 5cm across;
throughout summer. Bristly, pear-shaped,
orange-red fruits.

–**ferruginea** see *R. rubrifolia*

–**filipes**
Strong rambling or climbing habit. Fragrant
white flowers in panicles; late June-July. Red,
globose fruits. We recommend the clone:

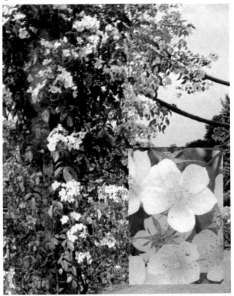

ROSA filipes 'Kiftsgate'

– –**'Kiftsgate'**
Very vigorous. Foliage copper-tinted when
young. Massive panicles of scented flowers.

–**foetida** (*lutea*) SS ○ "Austrian Yellow"
Erect, slender, prickly, brown stems. Rich
yellow flowers 5-6cm across. Requires well
drained site.

– –**'Bicolor'** SS ○ "Austrian Copper"
Brilliant coppery-red flowers with bright yellow
reverse.

– –**'Persiana'** SS "Persian Yellow Rose"
Double, golden yellow flowers.

–**foliolosa** SS
Suckering habit. Glossy green leaves.
Fragrant, bright pink flowers, 4-5cm across,
late July-September. Round red fruits. Good
autumn foliage colour.

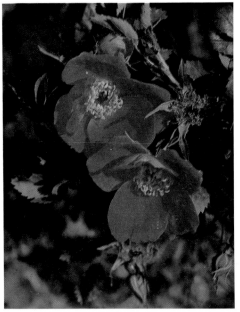

ROSA foetida 'Bicolor'

–**forrestiana** MS
Arching stems. Fragrant, rose-crimson
flowers in clusters. Enclosed by leafy bracts.
Bottle-shaped red fruits.

–**"Fortune's Yellow"** see *R. × odorata
'Pseudindica'*

–**gallica** (*rubra*) SS "French Rose"
Erect, slender, prickly stems. Deep pink
flowers, 5-7cm across. Rounded or top-
shaped, terracotta fruits. We recommend:

– –**'Officinalis'** (*R. officinalis*) SS
"Apothecary's Rose" "Red Rose of
Lancaster"
Fragrant, semi-double, rose-crimson flowers
with prominent yellow anthers.

– –**'Versicolor'** SS "Rosa Mundi"
Semi-double, rose-red striped white flowers,
with some entirely red. AM 1961

–**glauca** see *R. rubrifolia*

–**'Golden Chersonese'** MS
Slender arching stems. Frond-like small
leaves. Fragrant, buttercup-yellow flowers,
late May. AM 1966

–**"Green Rose"** see *R. chinensis 'Viridiflora'*

– × **hardii** SS-MS ○
Slender stems. Yellow flowers, 5cm across,
with red basal blotch to each petal. Requires
good drainage.

– **'Harrisonii'** MS "Harrison's Yellow"
Abundant, semi-double, brilliant yellow
flowers. Small blackish fruits. AM 1949
  'Headleyensis' M3
Vigorous habit. Fern-like leaves. Fragrant,
primrose-yellow flowers, May.
– **helenae**
Vigorous rambling or climbing habit, 6m or
more. Fragrant, creamy-white flowers in
dense corymbs, June. Orange red fruits in
hanging clusters.
– **'Highdownensis'** MS
Stout, semi-erect branches. Dainty leaves.
Light velvety crimson flowers with buff
anthers, 6cm across. Flagon-shaped orange-
scarlet fruits.
– × **hillieri** see *R.* × *pruhoniciana 'Hillieri'*
– **horrida** DS
Rigid, prickly stems, dense habit. White
flowers. Round red fruits.
– **hugonis** MS
Graceful arching habit. Fern-like leaves, often
bronzed in autumn. Abundant soft yellow
flowers, 5cm across, May. Small dark red
round fruits. AM 1917 AGM 1925
– **"Jacobite Rose"** see *R.* × *alba*
– **"Lady Banks' Rose"** see *R. banksiae*
– **laevigata** Semi-(E) "Cherokee Rose"
Strong growing rambler or climber. Glossy,
dark green leaves. Fragrant, white flowers,
7.5-10cm across, late May-June. Large bristly
fruits. AM 1954
– – **'Anemonoides'** LS
Silvery pink, rose shaded flowers, 10cm
across, produced for several weeks. AM 1900
– **longicuspis** (*lucens*) Semi-(E)
Vigorous rambler or climber. Glossy dark
green leaves. Large terminal panicles of
white, banana-scented flowers, 5cm across.
Scarlet-orange ovoid fruits. AM 1964
AGM 1969
– **lucida** see *R. virginiana*
– **lutea** see *R. foetida*
– **'Lutea Maxima'** see *R. pimpinellifolia 'Lutea'*
– **"Macartney Rose"** see *R. bracteata*
– **'Macrantha'** SS
Wide-spreading, prickly, arching branches.
Fragrant, large almond pink flowers fading
white, 7-10cm across. Conspicuous stamens.
Round red fruits.
– **macrophylla** MS-LS
Vigorous. Bright cerise-pink flowers, 7 to

10cm across. Bristly, pear-shaped, bright red
fruits. AM 1897. We recommend:
– – **'Master Hugh'** MS-LS
Deep pink flowers. Very large fruits, orange-
red turning bright red, AM 1966
– **'Max Graf'** PS GC
Long trailing stems. Fragrant, rose-pink,
golden centred flowers, 5cm across, over
extended period. AM 1964

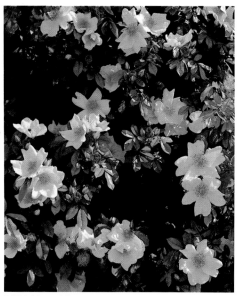

ROSA 'Mermaid'

– **'Mermaid'** (E) ◇
Rambling habit. Glossy green foliage. Sulphur
yellow flowers with golden stamens, 13 to
15cm across. Best against warm sunny wall.
– **microphylla** see *R. roxburghii*
– **"Monthly Rose"** see *R. chinensis 'Old
Blush'*
– **moschata** LS "Musk Rose"
Strong growing, lax habit. Musk-scented,
creamy-white flowers; late summer-autumn.
– **moschata** HORT see *R. brunonii*
– – **'La Mortola'** see *R. brunonii 'La Mortola'*
– **"Moss Rose"** see *R. centifolia 'Muscosa'*
– **moyesii** MS-LS
Loose open habit, erect branches. Rich
blood-crimson flowers, 6-7.5cm across; June-
July. Large, flagon-shaped, crimson fruits.
AM 1908 FCC 1916 AGM 1925
– – **fargesii** MS-LS
Glowing vivid carmine flowers. AM 1922

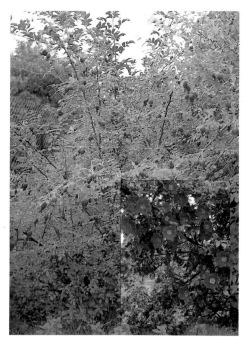

ROSA moyesii 'Geranium'

– – **'Geranium'** MS
More compact habit. Brilliant geranium-red flowers. Larger smoother fruits. AM 1950 AGM 1969

– **multibracteata** MS
Stout stems. Fragrant, fern-like leaves. Rose-lilac flowers, intermittently over long period. Bristly, round, red fruits. AM 1936

– **multiflora** (*polyantha*) LS
Vigorous shrub or rambler. Fragrant white flowers profusely borne. Small round fruits persisting into winter.

– **"Musk Rose"** see *R. moschata*

– **"Musk Rose, Himalayan"** see *R. brunonii*

– **mutabilis** see *R. chinensis 'Mutabilis'*

– **nitida** DS GC
Suckering habit. Slender, reddish stems with fine prickles. Rich autumn leaf colour. Rose-red flowers, 5cm across. Scarlet fruit.

– × **odorata** LS ○ "Tea Rose"
Group of old hybrids. We recommend the clone:

– – **'Pseudindica'** LS "Fortune's Double Yellow"
Flowers richly scented, semi-double, salmon- or coppery-yellow, flushed coppery scarlet.

– **omeiensis** (*sericea omeiensis*) MS "Mount Omei Rose"
Dense habit. Thorny stems. Generally white, four petalled flowers; May-early June. Pear-shaped fruits, red and yellow. We recommend:

– – **pteracantha** MS
Conspicuous flat, translucent, crimson thorns.

– × **paulii** SS GC
Vigorous, mound-forming habit. Thorny stems. White, clove scented flowers.

– **pendulina** SS
Semi-erect habit. Magenta-pink flowers, 4-5cm across. Flask shaped, red fruits.

– × **penzanceana** (*'Lady Penzance'*) MS
Arching branches. Fragrant leaves. Single, copper tinted flowers with yellow centre. AM 1891

– **pimpinellifolia** (*spinosissima*) SS "Scotch Rose" "Burnet Rose"
Suckering, thicket-forming habit. Abundant small white or pale pink flowers; May-June. Shiny, small, maroon-black or black fruits.

– – **altaica** (*R. altaica*) MS
More vigorous variety. Abundant large creamy-white flowers, 5-6cm across. Maroon-black fruits. Good for hedging. AGM 1925

– – **Double White** MS
Form with double white flowers.

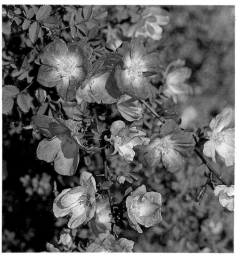

ROSA pimpinellifolia 'Glory of Edzell'

– – **'Glory of Edzell'** MS
Slender branches. Abundant, clear pink flowers, with lemon-yellow centre; May.

– – **'Lutea'** (*'Lutea Maxima'*) SS
Buttercup-yellow single flowers, 5cm across.
– – **'William III'** DS
Dense bushy habit. Greyish-green leaves.
Semi-double magenta-crimson flowers
turning to rich plum, paler reverse. Black
fruits.
– **polyantha** see *R. multiflora*
– **'Polyantha Grandiflora'** (*gentiliana*)
Climbing or rambling habit, to 6m. Strongly
scented creamy flowers, orange-yellow
stamens. Orange-red oval fruits, persisting
into winter. FCC 1888 AGM 1969
– **pomifera** see *R. villosa*
– **"Prairie Rose"** see *R. setigera*
– **primula** MS
Arching stems. Dark glossy leaves, aromatic
when crushed. Fragrant primrose-yellow
flowers, turning to white; mid May. Round red
fruits. AM 1962
– **"Provence Rose"** see *R. centifolia*
– × **pruhoniciana** LS
Strong growth. We recommend the clone:
– – **'Hillieri'** (*R. × hillieri*) LS
Elegant habit. Large, dark crimson, single
flowers.
– **"Ramanas Rose"** see *R. rugosa*
– **"Red Rose of Lancaster"** see *R. gallica*
'Officinalis'
– **'Rosa Mundi'** see *R. gallica 'Versicolor'*
– **'Rose d'Amour'** (*virginiana 'Plena'*) MS
"St Mark's Rose"
Almost thornless. Abundant, fragrant, double,
deep pink flowers; over long period mid-late
summer. FCC 1980
– **"Rose des Peintres"** see under *R. centifolia*
– **roxburghii** (*microphylla*) MS "Burr Rose"
"Chestnut Rose"
Viciously-armed shrub. Twisted cinnamon to
grey stems. Fragrant shell pink flowers with
prickly receptacles, calyces and pedicels.
Prickly orange-yellow fruits.
– **rubiginosa** (*eglanteria* L not MILL) Hdg
(0.6m) "Sweet Briar" Eglantine"
Stout, erect, prickly stems. Arching branches.
Aromatic leaves. Fragrant, clear pink flowers.
Oval, bright red, persistent fruits. Good for
hedging.
– **rubra** see *R. gallica*
– **rubrifolia** (*glauca*) (*ferruginea*) MS
Reddish-violet, almost thornless, stems.
Silvery-purple foliage. Clear pink flowers.
Red, ovoid fruits. AM 1949 AGM 1969

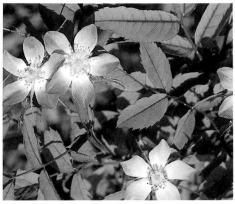

ROSA rubrifolia

– **rugosa** MS Hdg (0.6m) "Ramanas Rose"
Strong growing. Stout, prickly, bristly stems.
Fragrant, purplish rose flowers, 8-9cm across.
Recurrent. Bright red tomato-shaped fruits.
Excellent for hedging. AM 1896
– – **'Alba'** MS
Very vigorous. White flowers, tinted blush in
bud.
– – **'Blanc Double de Coubert'** MS
Semi-double white flowers, tinted blush in
bud. AM 1895 AGM 1969
– – **'Frau Dagmar Hastrup'** MS Hdg (0.6m)
Dense, compact habit. Pale rose-pink flowers,
with cream stamens, vivid pink in bud.
Abundant, large, crimson, round fruits.
AM1958 AGM 1969

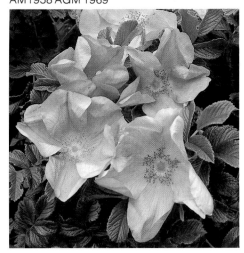

ROSA rugosa 'Frau Dagmar Hastrup'

––'**Roseraie de l'Hay**' MS Hdg (0.6m)
Vigorous growth. Double, crimson-purple
flowers with cream stamens 10-12cm across.
AGM 1969

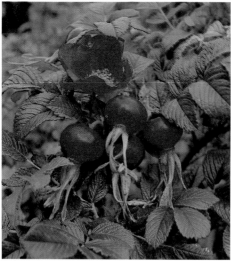

ROSA rugosa 'Rubra'

––'**Rubra**' MS
Fragrant, wine-crimson flowers. Conspicuous
large fruits.

––'**Scabrosa**' MS
Vigorous. Huge, violet-crimson flowers, to
14cm across. Large tomato-shaped fruits;
persistent sepals.

– "**Scotch Rose**" see *R. pimpinellifolia*

– **semperflorens** see *R. chinensis 'Old Blush'*

– **setigera** SS GS "Prairie Rose"
Wide spreading, trailing stems. Fragrant, rose
pink flowers, fading blush; July-August. Small,
round, red fruits.

– **setipoda** MS
Stout, erect stems. Leaves fragrant when
crushed. Abundant, clear pink flowers on
purplish stalks. Large, crimson, flagon-
shaped, bristly fruits.

– '**Silver Moon**' LS
Vigorous rambling habit, to 9m. Fragrant,
large, creamy flowers, yellow in bud.

– **soulieana** LS
Mound-forming, climbing stems. Grey-green
leaves. White flowers, creamy yellow in bud, in
large corymbs on mature plants. Small,
orange-red fruits.

– **spinosissima** see *R. pimpinellifolia*

– "**Sweet Briar**" see *R. rubiginosa*

– **sweginzowii** LS
Strong-growing. Bright rose-pink flowers,
usually in clusters. Bright red, bristly, flagon-
shaped fruits. AM 1922

– "**Tea Rose**" see *R.* × *odorata*

– "**Threepenny Bit Rose**" see *R. farreri
persetosa*

– **triphylla** see *R. anemoniflora*

– **villosa** (*pomifera*) MS "Apple Rose"
Vigorous. Leaves fragrant when crushed.
Clear pink flowers, carmine in bud. Large,
bristly, apple-shaped crimson fruits. AM 1955

– **virginiana** (*lucida*) SS
Suckering habit. Leaves colour well in
autumn. Bright pink flowers, 5-6cm across;
June-August. Small round red fruits. AM 1953
AGM 1969

– **webbiana** MS
Slender arching habit. Clear almond-pink
flowers, 4-5cm across; June. Shiny, sealing-
wax red, bottle-shaped fruits. AM 1955
AGM 1969

– '**Wedding Day**' LS
Vigorous climbing or rambling habit, to 10m.
Deeply-scented, large trusses of flowers,
cream with orange-yellow stamens, fading to
pink; deep yellow in bud. AM 1950

– "**White Rose of York**" see *R.* × *alba*

– **wichuraiana** PS Semi-(E) GC
Vigorous trailing stems, to 6m long. Fragrant
white flowers in clusters, late summer. Tiny,
round, red fruits. Excellent for covering tree-
stumps or eyesores. AGM 1973

– **willmottiae** MS
Graceful arching habit. Fern-like leaves,
fragrant when bruised. Lilac-pink flowers with
cream anthers. Pear-shaped orange-red
fruits. AM 1958

– × **wintonensis** MS
Fragrant foliage. Clusters of rich rose-pink
flowers.

– **woodsii** MS
Lilac-pink flowers. Red round fruits.
We recommend the form:

––**fendleri** MS
Dense leafy habit. Bright lilac-pink flowers.
Sealing-wax red persistent fruits.

– **xanthina** (*xanthina 'Flore Pleno'*) MS
Graceful arching habit. Fern-like leaves.
Semi-double golden-yellow flowers. AM 1945

– "**York and Lancaster Rose**" see *R.
damascena 'Versicolor'*

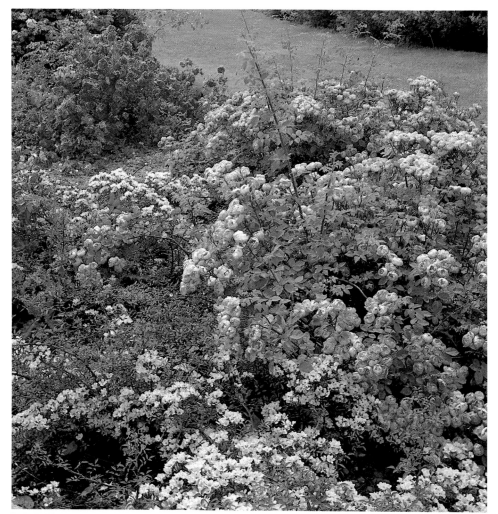

SHRUB ROSES as ground cover

SHRUB ROSES
Here are included other roses most suitable for growing in shrub borders or as hedges.

BOURBON
Flowering from early June. A very hardy class of strong-growing roses. The vigorous sorts are admirably suited for pergolas, arches etc., the others for pillars, massing in beds, pegging down etc.

ROSE 'Boule de Neige'
Creamy-white edged crimson in bud, opening to a round, camellia-like effect, very fragrant. Foliage smooth, leathery. Vigorous, erect.

– 'Coupe d'Hebe'
Rose-pink, large, full and quartered, very fragrant. Foliage fresh green. Vigorous.

– 'Gipsy Boy'
Dark crimson-purple, reflexed petals, flattish, robust, arching. A handsome bush.

– 'Honorine de Brabant'
Pale rosy lilac with crimson stripes and flecks, loosely double cupped, well quartered, fragrant; foliage light green. Strong.

– 'Kathleen Harrop'
Glowing shell pink, fragrant, thornless. A sport of *'Zephirine Drouhin'* but less vigorous.

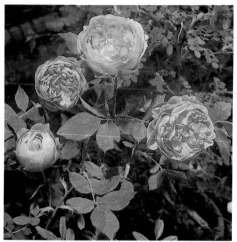

ROSA 'La Reine Victoria'

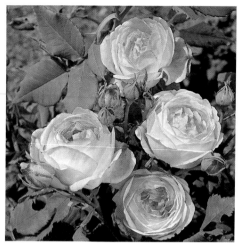

ROSA 'Madame Pierre Oger'

– 'La Reine Victoria'
Rich pink, exquisite cupped shape, fragrant. Foliage light green. Vigorous and erect.

– 'Louise Odier'
Deep rose-pink, sweetly scented, continuous. Foliage, rich. Vigorous, splendid constitution and shape.

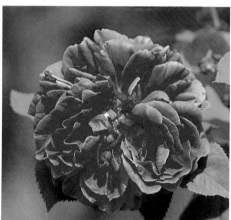

ROSA 'Madame Isaac Pereire'

– 'Madame Isaac Pereire'
Rose-carmine, very large, fully double, richly fragrant. Foliage handsome. Very vigorous – a large, free bush.

– 'Madame Pierre Oger'
Cream shades of pink shaded rosy-violet, globular, very fragrant, free intermittent flowering. Growth slender, erect. AM 1951

– 'Prince Charles'
Crimson-purple, flushed maroon-lilac, white centre, velvety sheen, double, fairly fragrant. Foliage dark grey-green, smooth. Vigorous.

– 'Queen of Bourbons' ('Souvenir de la Princesse de Lambelle')
Soft magenta-pink veined carmine, fairly double, flat, sweetly scented; scarlet heps. A vigorous pillar, wall or large bush rose, very free flowering.

– 'Souvenir de la Malmaison' (climbing form)
Soft creamy-blush large, flat and well quartered, delicate fragrance. Superb in a hot season. Strong growing to 3m.

– 'Variegata di Bologna'
White flecked deep carmine, globular, double, well filled, fragrant. Very vigorous, good for pegging down. The most distinct of the striped roses. Best in blackspot-free areas.

– 'Zephirine Drouhin'
Bright carmine pink, loosely double, sweetly scented, continuous. Very vigorous, tall, stems thornless. Can be pruned to form a large bush or hedge but best as a climber. AGM 1969

CHINA or MONTHLY
(Garden cultivars and hybrids of *Rosa chinensis*)
Flowering continuously from early June to late autumn. The most abundant of all roses, some being of unique colours, thriving best in a sunny position.

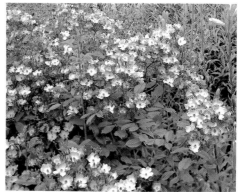
ROSE 'Ballerina'

ROSE 'Ballerina'
Apple-blossom pink, with white eye, small, single, very free flowering in large clusters, fragrant, recurrent flowers. Makes a neat bush.

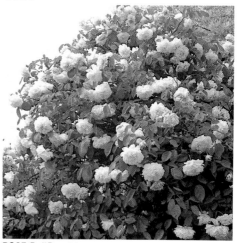
ROSE 'Buff Beauty'

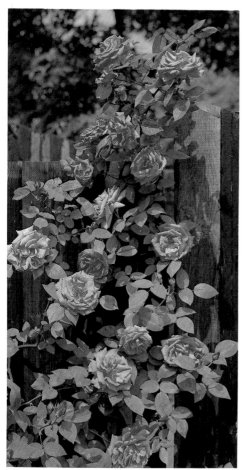
ROSA 'Zephirine Drouhin'

ROSE Blush or Common China see
R. chinensis 'Old Blush' under species
– 'Cecile Brunner'
Rose-pink shaded rose, small, in lax sprays; nearly thornless.
– 'Mevrouw Nathalie Nypels'
Clear rose-pink in clusters, semi-double, fragrant. Foliage glossy, dark green. Low growing, bushy.
– 'Perle d'Or'
Buff to pale yellow, beautifully formed, small, in large sprays.
HYBRID MUSK Hdg (0.6m)
Flowering June to late autumn. Perpetual flowering, cluster roses of bushy habit usually 1.2 to 2m high, all more or less musk scented.

– 'Buff Beauty'
Apricot yellow, lighter at the edges, double, prettily shaped, tea-scented, recurrent. Vigorous, spreading. AGM 1969
– 'Cornelia'
Coppery-pink with yellow base, double. Very fragrant; foliage dark green, ample; vigorous. A reliable, perpetual cluster rose.
– 'Felicia'
Salmon-pink shaded yellow, double, very fragrant in large clusters. Foliage abundant. An ideal, compact, bushy plant. AGM 1965

– 'Moonlight'

White flushed lemon, prominent golden stamens, semi-double sweetly scented, perpetual, foliage very dark green, stem dark mahogany. AM 1913

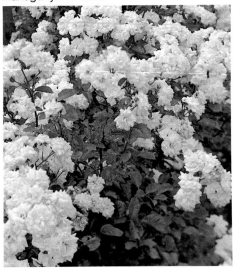

ROSE 'Penelope'

– 'Penelope'

Shell-pink shaded saffron with yellow stamens. Semi-double, strong musk fragrance, perpetual. Leaves broad, glossy. Sturdy and stout branching. AGM 1956

– 'Will Scarlet'

Glowing crimson-scarlet with a white eye, semi-double. Erect habit. AM 1954

MODERN SHRUB Hdg (0.6m)

(Including Scotch cultivars and hybrids. See also R. pimpinellifolia under species). Flowering June to late autumn. Strong bushes averaging 1.2 to 2.2m in height. Worthy inhabitants of the rose world.

ROSE 'Constance Spry'

Clear rose-pink, large cupped blooms of the old centifolia type, pronounced myrrh fragrance; attractive leaves, pointed, dark green, coppery when young. AM 1965 AGM 1969

– **Double White** see *R. pimpinellifolia Double White* under species

– 'Erfurt'

Clear pink, large white zone around yellow stamens; single, scented, perpetual, young foliage richly tinted.

– 'Fritz Nobis'

Pink, about 10cm across when fully open. H.T. shaped, clove-scented, free flowering. Very vigorous, bushy with arching branches. AM 1959 AGM 1969

– **'Fruhlingsgold'** (Pimpinellifolia Group) Butter-yellow, large, partially semi-double, fragrant, May-June. Very tall, arching branches. AM 1950 FCC 1955 AGM 1965

– **'Fruhlingsmorgen'** (Pimpinellifolia Group) Rose-pink with cream base, stamens dark purple, very large, single. May-June, repeating September; heps large, red. Foliage leaden green; vigorous. AM 1951

– **'Glory of Edzell'** see *R. pimpinellifolia 'Glory of Edzell'* under species.

– 'Golden Wings'

Yellow, mahogany-amber stamens, very large, single, deliciously scented, continuous flowering. Compact habit. AM 1965

– 'Heidelberg'

Dark, vivid scarlet-lake, large, double, in clusters, scented. Height 2m.

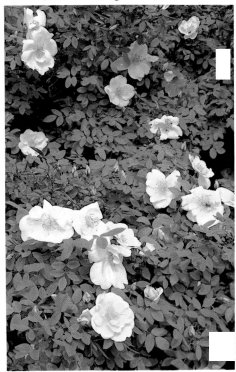

ROSE 'Fruhlingsgold'

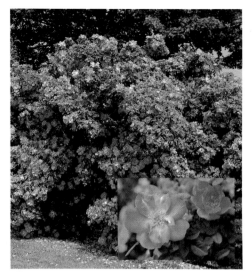

ROSE 'Marguerite Hilling'

– 'Marguerite Hilling'
Deep pink, single. Graceful bush. A sport of '*Nevada*' and similar in growth. AM 1960

– 'Nevada'
Creamy-white, pale in bud, single, up to 10cm across, recurrent. Very attractive bush, 2 to 2.5m high. AM 1949 FCC 1954 AGM 1969

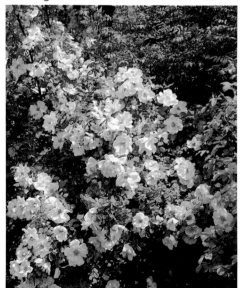

ROSE 'Nevada'

– 'Nymphenburg'
Salmon-pink with orange shadings and yellow base, fully double, very sweet fresh-apple scent. Foliage glossy, dark green. Large arching shrub. AM 1960

– 'Raubritter'
Pale silvery blush-pink outside, rose inside, cup-shaped, semi-double, 5cm across. Spreading habit forming a wide, low mound, suitable for a bank or covering drains or stumps. AM 1954

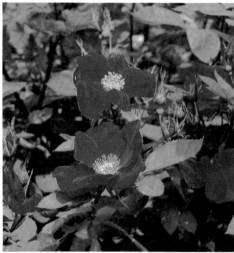

ROSE 'Scarlet Fire'

– 'Scarlet Fire' ('*Scharlachglut*')
Scarlet-flame, semi-double, limited flowering season. AM 1960 AGM 1969

– 'Stanwell Perpetual' (Pimpinellifolia Group)
Hdg (0.6m)
Blush, fading white, petals quilled and folded, large, double. Long flowering, slightly fragrant. Stems arching, thorny. Foliage greyish. Possibly a Damask hybrid.

– 'William III' see *R. pimpinellifolia 'William III'* under species

OLD FASHIONED
(Including Cabbage, Damask, Gallica, Moss and other roses which were favourites before the advent of the Hybrid Perpetuals.)
Flowering June and July. These old roses, mostly double flowered, have many charms, not the least of which is their unrivalled perfume. All grow best with liberal cultivation but after the first season only light pruning is necessary.

ROSE 'Belle de Crecy' (Gallica Group)
Mauve-pink passing to purple, very double, very fragrant; thornless. Elegant habit. Height 1.3m.
– **'Blanche Moreau'** (Moss Group)
Pure white with incurved petals, dark brownish moss. Height 2m.
– **'Camaieux'** (Gallica Group)
Crimson-purple splashed and striped white turning soft lilac-grey with white stripes with age. Height 1m.

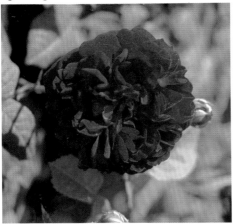

ROSE 'Cardinal de Richelieu'

– **'Cardinal de Richelieu'** (Gallica Group)
Deep purple-crimson, turning purplish, opening to a reflexed ball. Height 1.5m.
– **'Celestial'** (Alba Group)
Delicate soft pink, semi-double. Foliage grey-green off-setting the exquisite colour of the flowers. Healthy. Height 1.2 to 1.5m. AM 1948
– **'Charles de Mills'** (Gallica Group)
Very deep crimson shaded purple, flat, free, vigorous. Compact growth. Height 1.5m. A unique rose in this group.
– **'Comte de Chambord'** (Portland Group)
Rich pink fading to lilac, very full, flat, very fragrant, flowering intermittently through the season. Vigorous, upright. Height 1.2m
– **'Empress Josephine'** (Gallica Hybrid Group)
Beautiful rich pink, deeper veins, loosely shaped; few thorns; leaves folded. Height 1m. Well-branched rose.
– **'Fantin-Latour'** (Centifolia Group)
Blush, double, freely produced, foliage good, bushy. Height 2m. AM 1959 AGM 1969

– **'Gloire de Guilan'** (Damask Group)
Clear pink, cupped, petals quartered and folded, not fully double, very fragrant. Height 1.2m. Grown in Iran for perfume and rose water.
– **'Gloire des Mousseux'** (Moss Group)
Flesh pink, deeper at centre, quartered, with button eyes, long lasting. The largest flowers in Moss Group. Foliage light green. Height 1.2m
– **'Henri Martin'** (Moss Group)
Pure crimson, well shaped, in gracefully borne clusters. Height 1.5m. An elegant plant.
– **'Koenigin von Danemark'** (Alba Group)
Intense pink, deepest in the centre, well shaped, quartered and button eyed. Height 1.5m. Resembles *R.* × *alba* in foliage and habit but shows "Damask" influence.
– **'Madame Hardy'** (Damask Group)
Creamy white passing to pure white, incurved petals, flat, fully double, quartered, with button eye. Green, pointed, foliage. Height 2m. Sturdy growth.
– **'Maiden's Blush'** (Alba Group)
Blush pink, very double, in clusters, sweetly scented, the latest of the Alba Group to open. Foliage healthy, grey-green. Height 1.5m.
– **'Maxima'** (Alba Group)
White, tinged buff when first open, flat, very double. Vigorous. Height 2m or more. The "Jacobite Rose".

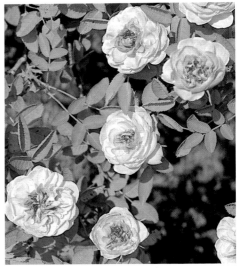

ROSE 'Rose de Meaux'

–**'Nuits de Young'** (Moss Group)
Deep maroon-purple, golden stamens, small, free flowering, foliage dark green; compact. Height 1.5m.
–**'Omar Khayyam'** (Damask Group)
Clear pink with rosette formation in centre, flat, fragrant. Prickly stems, foliage light greyish-green. Height 1m.
–**'Petite de Hollande'** (Centifolia Group)
Bright rose, small, full, fragrant, free flowering. Compact, height 1.2m. Of great beauty.
–**'Quatre Saisons Blanc Mousseux'**
(Damask Moss Group)
Blush white, perpetual, in clusters. Height 1.2m. Unusual cultivar with bristly green "moss" on stems and leaves.
–**'Rose de Meaux'** (Centifolia Group)
Clear pink, flat pompon double. Leaves small. Erect growing. Height 1.2m
–**'Tour de Malakoff'** (Centifolia Group)
Mauve-pink shaded purple, veined, loosely double paeony shaped, very fragrant. Height 2m.
–**'Tuscany Superb'** (Gallica Group)
Deep velvety purple on crimson ground, nearly double, golden stamens, fragrant. Height 1.2m

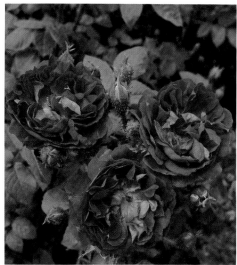

ROSE 'William Lobb'

–**'William Lobb'** (Moss Group)
Crimson, passing to slate-blue, flat, in clusters. Strong growing.
Height 2m. Suitable for the back of a border.

RUGOSA CULTIVARS AND HYBRIDS
(See also R. rugosa under species)
Flowering June to late autumn. Extremely ornamental and the hardiest of all roses, mostly making compact bushes with large flowers. Dark green, glossy foliage and very prickly stems. Height about 1.5m. Most make good hedges.
ROSE 'Agnes' see *R. 'Agnes'* under species
–**'Alba'** see *R. rugosa 'Alba'* under species.

–**'Blanc Double de Coubert'** see *R. rugosa 'Blanc Double de Coubert'* under species

–**'Conrad Ferdinand Meyer'**
Silvery-rose, double, fragrant, flowers early and late. A fine pillar or wall rose or for back of a border. AM 1901

–**'Frau Dagmar Hastrup'** see *R. rugosa 'Frau Dagmar Hastrup'* under species
–**'Max Graf'** see *R. 'Max Graf'* under species

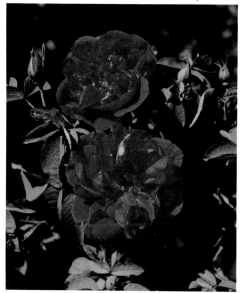

ROSE 'Mrs Anthony Waterer'

–**'Mrs Anthony Waterer'** Hdg (0.6m)
Magenta-crimson, large, loosely double, very fragrant. A large, arching shrub. AGM 1969
–**'Pink Grootendorst'** Hdg (0.6m)
Bright pink with fimbriated petals, small, double, in clusters. A very dainty rose, liking a good soil. AM 1953
–**'Roseraie de l'Hay'** see *R. rugosa 'Roseraie de l'Hay'* under species

– **'Rubra'** see *R. rugosa 'Rubra'* under species
– **'Sarah van Fleet'** Hdg (0.6m)
Pale rose-pink, very large, semi-double very
sweetly scented. Good foliage. Growth erect.
AM 1962
– **'Scabrosa'** see *R. rugosa 'Scabrosa'* under
species
– **'Schneezwerg'** Hdg (0.6m)
Pure white, golden stamens, semi-double
continuous, small, delicious scent. Orange
heps. Foliage neat. AM 1948

"ROSE OF SHARON" see *HYPERICUM
calycinum*

"ROSEMARY" see *ROSMARINUS*

ROSMARINUS – Labiatae PS-MS (E) ○
"Rosemary"
*Aromatic narrow leaves, used in cooking.
Blue flowers. Suits all well-drained soils.*
– **lavandulaceus** (*officinalis prostratus*
HORT) PS (E) † ○
Dense mat-forming habit. Clusters of flowers,
May-June. Excellent for tops of sunny wall.

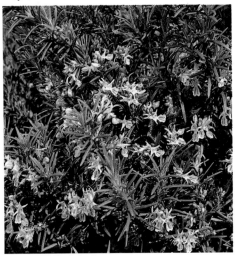

ROSMARINUS officinalis

– **officinalis** MS (E) ○ "Common Rosemary"
Dense habit. Green or grey-green leaves,
white beneath. Flowers in axillary clusters.
Good informal hedge.
– – **'Fastigiatus'** MS (E) ○ "Miss Jessop's
Variety"
Strong erect habit.
– – **'Severn Sea'** DS (E) ○
Arching branches. Brilliant flowers.

"ROWAN" see *SORBUS aucuparia*

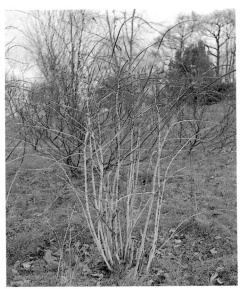

RUBUS cockburnianus

RUBUS – Rosaceae PS-MS "Ornamental
Brambles"
*Variable genus exhibiting variously attractive
foliage, flowers, or ornamental stems.
Generally prickly. Easy cultivation – some
excellent for poor soils.*
D 1, 2, 3
– **calycinoides** (*fockeanus* HORT) PS (E) GC
Dense mat-forming habit. Glossy green
leaves, white-felted beneath. White flowers,
summer.
– **cockburnianus** (*giraldianus*) MS
Strong arching habit. Purple stems clothed in
white bloom. Fern-like leaves, white or grey
beneath. Small purple flowers June. Bloomy
black fruits.
– **deliciosus** MS
Arching habit. Thornless stems. White, dog
rose-like flowers, May-June. Purplish fruits.
FCC 1881 AGM 1946
– **fockeanus** see *R. calycinoides*
– **giraldianus** see *R. cockburnianus*
– **microphyllus 'Variegatus'** SS
Mound-forming habit. Three-lobed leaves,
green mottled pink and cream.
– **nepalensis** PS (E) GC
Charming carpeting shrublet. Reddish,
bristly, procumbent shoots, small trifoliolate
leaves. White flowers. Raspberry-like orange-
red edible fruits.

– odoratus MS
Vigorous erect habit. Thornless, peeling stems. Large velvety leaves. Clusters of fragrant purplish-rose flowers, June-September. Edible red fruits.
– phoenicolasius MS "Wineberry"
Reddish glandular-bristly stems. Large trifoliolate leaves, white-felted beneath. Small, pale pink flowers in clusters, July. Sweet, edible, orange-red fruits. FCC 1894
– thibetanus (*veitchii*) MS
Semi-erect, purple-brown stems covered in blue-white bloom. Grey, silky, fern-like leaves, white or grey-felted beneath. Small purple flowers. Black or red fruits. AM 1915
– tricolor (*polytrichus*) PS (E) GC
Long, trailing, red bristly stems. Glossy green leaves, white-felted beneath. White flowers, July. Sometimes bears large red edible fruits.
– Tridel LS
Vigorous shrubs with tall, arching, spineless stems and 3 to 5-lobed leaves. We recommend the clone:

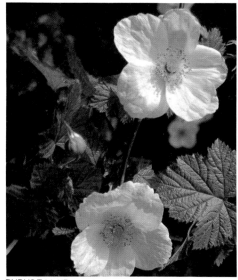

RUBUS Tridel 'Benenden'

– – 'Benenden' LS
Scented white flowers up to 5cm across, May. AM 1958 AGM 1962 FCC 1963
– ulmifolius LS
Vigorous, scrambling stems. Leaves, white-felted beneath. The cultivated form of this common bramble is:

– – 'Bellidiflorus' LS
Double pink flowers in large panicles, July-August. Exceedingly vigorous, suitable for a wild garden.

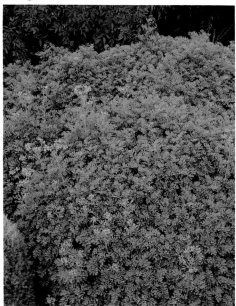

RUTA graveolens 'Jackman's Blue'

RUSCUS – Liliaceae DS-SS (E)
Dense clumps of stiff green stems. Leaves reduced to tiny scales. Apparent leaves are flattened stems. Tiny, dioecious flowers. Attractive fruits on female plants. For all soils.
– aculeatus SS (E) "Butcher's Broom"
Small, spine tipped "apparent" leaves, bright red cherry-like fruits where plants of both sexes are present.
– hypoglossum DS (E) GC
Large "apparent" leaves, with single tiny green flower on upper surface. Similarly large red fruits on female plants.
– racemosus see *DANAE racemosa*
RUTA – Rutaceae SS ○
Aromatic plants for well-drained situation in any soil.
– graveolens SS (E) ○ "Rue"
Fern-like, glaucous leaves. Small mustard-yellow flowers, June-August. We recommend the form:
– – 'Jackman's Blue' SS (E) ○
Compact, bushy habit. Vivid glaucous-blue foliage.

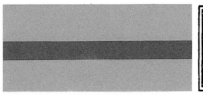

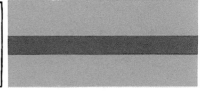

"ST JOHN'S WORT" see *HYPERICUM*
SALIX – Salicaceae PS-LT The "Willows"
Large diverse genus. Generally vigorous,
hardy and of easy cultivation – some excellent
for damp situations. They are dioecious, many
with attractive catkins, the male forms usually
more showy. Some have colourful stems in
winter; prune hard alternate years in March to
encourage these. B3
– acutifolia (*daphnoides acutifolia*)
(*pruinosa*) LS
Graceful habit. Long pointed leaves and
slender shoots. Catkins before the leaves. We
recommend:
– – 'Blue Streak' LS
Polished black-purple stems clothed in blue-
white bloom.
– aegyptiaca (*medemii*) LS-ST
Stout grey-felted twigs. Large conspicuous
bright yellow male catkins, February-March.
AM 1925 AM 1957 AGM 1969

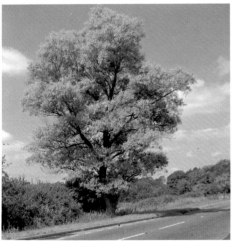

SALIX alba

– alba LT ♥ "White Willow"
Slender branches drooping at tips. Narrow
silver-backed leaves. Excellent for wet sites,
maritime exposure and as a wind break.
– – 'Caerulea' see *S. 'Caerulea'*

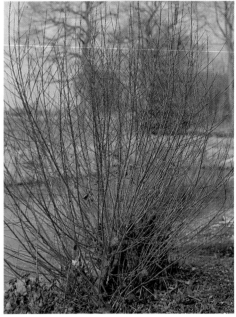

SALIX alba 'Chermesina'

– – 'Chermesina' (*'Britzensis'*) LT ♥ "Scarlet
Willow"
Conspicuous brilliant orange-scarlet young
stems in winter.
– – 'Sericea' (*'Argentea'*) (*'Regalis'*) MT ♥
Slower growing. Leaves intensely silvery.
– – 'Tristis' see *S. × chrysocoma*
– – 'Vitellina' (*S. vitellina*) MT ♥ "Golden
Willow"
Young shoots of brilliant egg-yolk yellow.
Male. AMT 1967 AGM 1969
– – 'Vitellina Pendula' see *S. × chrysocoma*
– amygdalina see *S. triandra*
– apoda PS
Shiny green leaves. Erect, furry, silver, male
catkins; early spring, before leaves, ripening
to reveal bright yellow anthers. AM 1948
AGM 1969 (male form)
– babylonica 'Ramulis Aureis' see
S. × chrysocoma

– **bockii** SS-MS
Neat spreading habit. Slender reddish twigs, greyish downy when young. Small greyish catkins, late summer-autumn.
– × **boydii** DS
Erect, gnarled habit. Slow growth. Grey downy leaves, turning green above. Small dark grey catkins, produced rarely. Female.
– **'Caerulea'** (*alba 'Caerulea'*) LT ♀ "Cricket Bat Willow"
Ascending branches. Sea-green lanceolate leaves, glaucous beneath. Best willow for cricket bats. Female.
– **caprea** LS-ST ♀ "Goat Willow" "Great Sallow"
Male form has large yellow spring catkins known as "Palm". Female, silvery catkins known as "Pussy Willow".

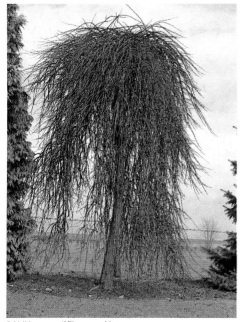

SALIX caprea 'Kilmarnock'

– – **'Kilmarnock'** ST ♠ "Kilmarnock Willow"
Stiffly pendulous branches. Male.
– × **chrysocoma** (*alba 'Vitellina Pendula'*) (*alba 'Tristis'*) (*babylonica 'Ramulis Aureis'*) MT ♠ "Golden Weeping Willow"
Wide-spreading. Strongly arching branches ending in golden yellow branchlets eventually to the ground. Slender bright green leaves.
AGM 1931

– **cinerea** LS-ST ♀ "Grey Sallow"
Grey downy stout twigs. Silky catkins, early spring before leaves.
– × **cottetii** PS GC
Vigorous carpet-forming habit. Trailing stems. Glossy dark green leaves, paler beneath. Catkins, early spring before leaves.

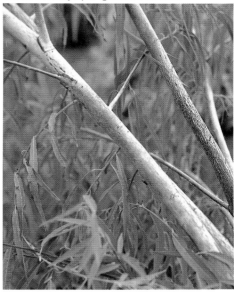

SALIX daphnoides

– **daphnoides** ST ♀ "Violet Willow"
Vigorous deep purple shoots, clothed in white bloom. Catkins in spring, before leaves.
AM 1957 AGM 1969
– **elaeagnos** (*incana*) (*rosmarinifolia* HORT) LS "Hoary Willow"
Dense, bushy habit. Slender reddish-brown stems. Linear leaves, greyish hoary, becoming green, white beneath. Catkins, with leaves, spring.
– × **erythroflexuosa** ST
Vigorous, contorted, orange-yellow, pendulous shoots. Twisted leaves.
– **exigua** LS-ST "Coyote Willow"
Slender greyish-brown branches. Linear, silky, silver leaves, minutely toothed. Slender catkins, with the leaves.
– **fargesii** MS-LS
Open habit. Stout shoots becoming polished reddish-brown. Conspicuous reddish winter buds. Slender, ascending catkins with or after leaves.

– **fragilis** LT ♥ "Crack Willow"
Rugged grooved bark. Brittle-jointed twigs.
Shiny, lanceolate leaves, green or bluish-
green below. Slender catkins, with leaves,
spring.

– **gracilistyla** MS
Vigorous. Grey downy young shoots and
leaves. Silky, grey, male catkins, with reddish
anthers, ripening to bright yellow; spring
before leaves. AM 1925 AGM 1969

– – **melanostachys** see *S. melanostachys*

– **hastata** SS
Leaves sea-green beneath. Catkins, before or
with leaves in spring. We recommend:

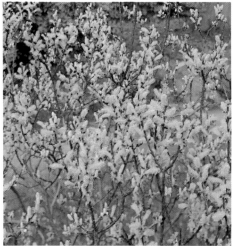

SALIX hastata 'Wehrhahnii'

– – **'Wehrhahnii'** (*S. wehrhahnii*) SS-MS
Spreading habit. Silver grey, male catkins,
turning yellow, spring. AM 1964 AGM 1969

– **helvetica** SS
Bushy habit. Soft greyish pubescence on
young stems, leaves and catkins. Grey green
leaves, white beneath. Catkins, with leaves in
spring.

– **humilis** MS "Prairie Willow"
Vigorous. Catkins before leaves, males have
brick-red anthers ripening yellow, females
have brick-red stigmas.

– **incana** see *S. elaeagnos*

– **integra** (*purpurea multinervis*) (*'Axukime'*)
LS-ST ♥
Graceful habit. Slightly drooping branches
and polished stems. Bright green leaves in
pairs. Slender catkins, before leaves. April.

– **irrorata** MS
Vigorous. Young green shoots turn purple
with white bloom. Catkins before leaves,
males have brick-red anthers ripening yellow.
AMT 1967

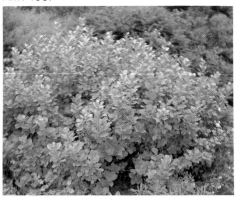

SALIX lanata

– **lanata** SS "Woolly Willow"
Slow spreading habit. Silvery grey downy
leaves. Erect, yellowish-grey, woolly catkins,
spring. AGM 1969

– **magnifica** LS-ST
Sparse habit. Large magnolia-like leaves.
Catkins with leaves, spring, females often
15-25cm long. AM 1913

– **matsudana** MT ♥ "Pekin Willow"
Slender stems. Narrow green leaves, grey
beneath. Catkins, with leaves in spring.
Excellent for dry soils and cold barren areas.

– – **'Pendula'** MT ♠
Graceful weeping habit.

– – **'Tortuosa'** MT ♥
Twisted and contorted branches and twigs,
especially noticeable in winter.

– **medemii** see *S. aegyptiaca*

– **melanostachys** (*gracilistyla
melanostachys*) SS-MS
Stout twigs. Catkins before the leaves, very
dark, with blackish scales and brick-red
anthers ripening yellow.

– **moupinensis** MS
Similar to *S. fargesii*, but smaller, generally
glabrous, leaves.

– **nitida** see *S. repens argentea*

– **pentandra** MT ♥ "Bay Willow"
Glossy twigs. Lustrous green, bay-like leaves,
aromatic when crushed. Catkins, late spring
with leaves, males yellow.

– **purpurea** MS-LS "Purple Osier"
Graceful arching shoots, often purplish. Narrow blue-green leaves. Slender catkins, before leaves in spring. Wood of young shoots is bright yellow beneath bark.
– – **'Eugenei'** ST
Slender habit. Abundant, grey-pink, male catkins.
– – **'Gracilis'** (*'Nana'*) SS
Compact habit. Good low hedge for damp sites.
– – **'Pendula'** ST
Long hanging branches. Excellent for a small garden.
– **repens** SS "Creeping Willow"
Creeping habit. Greyish green leaves, silvery beneath. Small catkins, before leaves in spring. We recommend:
– – **argentea** (*S. nitida*) SS
Silvery silky leaves. Revels in moist, sandy areas by the sea.
– – **subopposita** see *S. subopposita*
– **rosmarinifolia** see *S. elaeagnos*
– **sachalinensis** LS-ST
Spreading habit. Polished brown young shoots. Catkins before leaves, males large and conspicuous. We recommend the clone:
– – **'Sekka'** (*'Setsuka'*) LS
Occasional flattened and recurved stems, encouraged by hard pruning. Useful for 'Japanese' floral arrangements.
– **'Setsuka'** see *S. sachalinensis 'Sekka'*
– **subopposita** (*repens subopposita*) DS
Slender, erect, spreading stems. Small leaves, generally opposite. Catkins, early spring before leaves.

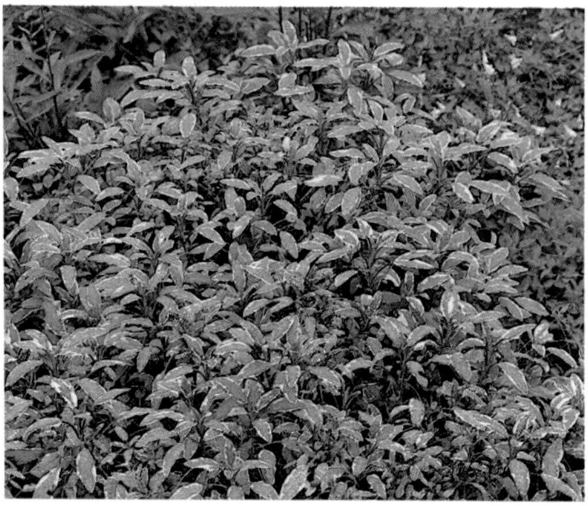
SALVIA officinalis 'Tricolor'

– **triandra** (*amygdalina*) LS-ST "Almond-leaved Willow"
Flaky bark. Glossy green almond-like leaves. Catkins, in spring with leaves. Males almost mimosa-like, fragrant.
– **uva-ursi** PS "Bearberry Willow"
Carpet forming habit. Small glossy green leaves. Catkins in spring with leaves.
– **viminalis** LS-ST "Common Osier"
Vigorous. Long straight shoots, grey tomentose when young. Long, narrow, dull green leaves, silvery silky beneath. Catkins before leaves. Cultivated for basket making.
– **wehrhahnii** see *S. hastata 'Wehrhahnii'*

"SALLOW" see *SALIX caprea* and *S. cinerea*

SALVIA – Labiatae DS-MS ☼
Aromatic sub-shrubs. Flowers normally in whorls along stems late summer-early autumn. Require a warm, dry, well-drained site. Tender species are ideal for cool conservatory.

– **gesneriiflora** SS † ☼
Heart shaped leaves. Long racemes of showy, intense scarlet flowers. AM 1950
– **guaranitica** (*ambigens*) (*caerulea*) SS † ☼
Erect habit. Downy, heart-shaped leaves. Deep azure-blue flowers in long racemes, late summer-autumn. AM 1926 AGM 1949
– **involucrata** SS † ☼
Racemes of rose-magenta flowers, sticky to the touch. We recommend the form:
– – **'Bethellii'** (*S. bethellii*) MS ☼
Large, heart-shaped leaves. Magenta-crimson flowers in stout racemes, mid-summer onwards. FCC 1880
– **microphylla** (*grahamii*) SS † ☼
Bright red flowers fading bluish-red, June-late autumn. We recommend the following:
– – **neurepia** (*S. neurepia*) SS † ☼
Larger leaves. Showier, rosy-red flowers, late summer-autumn.
– **officinalis** DS Semi-(E) ☼ "Common Sage"
Strongly aromatic, grey-green, leaves; used in cooking. Bluish-purple flowers, summer.
– – **'Icterina'** DS Semi-(E) ☼
Variegated leaves, green and gold.
– – **'Purpurascens'** DS Semi-(E) ☼ "Purple-Leaf Sage"
Stems and young foliage soft purple.
– – **'Tricolor'** DS Semi-(E) ☼
Grey-green leaves, splashed creamy white, suffused pink and purple.

– **rutilans** SS † ☼ "Pineapple Sage"
Downy, heart-shaped, pineapple-scented leaves. Magenta-crimson flowers, summer. Needs a sheltered south wall.

SAMBUCUS – Caprifoliaceae SS-ST "Elder"
Grown for ornamental foliage and fruit.
Pinnate leaves with serrated leaflets. Tolerate most situations and soils.

– **canadensis** MS "American Elderberry"
Strong, stout habit. White flowers in convex heads, July. Purplish black fruits. AM 1905 AM 1948. We recommend the forms:

– – **'Aurea'** MS
Yellow foliage. Red fruits.

– – **'Maxima'** MS-LS
Leaves 30-45cm long. Huge flower heads with attractive rose-purple stalks, which stay after flowers have fallen. AM 1951

– **nigra** LS-ST "Common Elder"
Fissured bark. Fragrant, cream flowers in flattened heads, June. Clusters of shiny black fruits. Good on chalk.

– – **'Albovariegata'** (*'Marginata'*) (*'Argenteomarginata'*) MS
Irregular creamy leaf margins. AM 1892

– – **'Aurea'** MS "Golden Elder"
Golden yellow leaves.

– – **'Aureomarginata'** MS
Irregular bright yellow leaf margins.

– – **'Laciniata'** MS "Fern-leaved Elder"
Finely cut, fern-like leaves.

– – **'Pulverulenta'** MS
Leaves mottled and striped white.

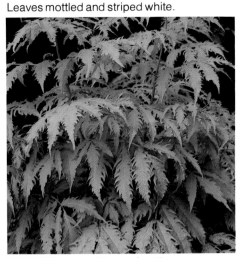

SAMBUCUS racemosa 'Plumosa Aurea'

– – **'Purpurea'** LS
Purple flushed leaves, particularly when young.

– **racemosa** MS-LS "Red-berried Elder"
Coarsely-serrated leaflets. Conical heads of yellowish white flowers, April. Bright scarlet fruit clusters. AM 1936

– – **'Plumosa Aurea'** (*'Serratifolia Aurea'*) SS
Deeply divided golden leaves. Rich yellow flowers. Slower growing. AM 1895 AM 1956

– – **'Tenuifolia'** SS
Mound-like habit. Arching branches. Fern-like, finely divided leaves. Slow growth. AM 1917

SANTOLINA – Compositae DS (E) ☼
"Cotton Lavender"
Mound-forming. Grey, green or silvery finely divided foliage. Dainty button-like flower heads on tall stalks, July. Needs well drained soil.

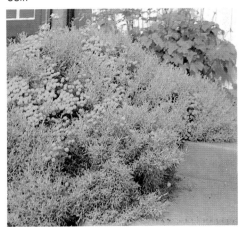

SANTOLINA chamaecyparissus

– **chamaecyparissus** (*incana*) DS (E) ☼
Woolly, silvery filigree foliage. Lemon-yellow flower heads. AGM 1969

– – **corsica** (*'Nana'*) DS (E) ☼
More compact, dwarf habit. AGM 1969

– **neapolitana** DS (E) ☼
Feathery silver leaves. Lemon-yellow flowers. We recommend:

– – **'Edward Bowles'** DS (E) ☼
Grey green foliage. Creamy white to pale primrose flower heads.

– **virens** (*viridis*) DS (E) ☼
Vivid green, filigree leaves. Lemon-yellow flower heads.

SAPIUM – Euphorbiaceae LS-ST
*Large, mostly tropical genus. One species
hardy in this country is recommended:*
– japonicum LS-ST
Smooth greyish branches. Dark green leaves,
crimson in autumn. Catkin-like racemes of
small, greenish yellow flowers, June.
Pendulous, caper-like green capsules,
turning brown.

SARCOCOCCA – Buxaceae DS-SS (E) ◑
"Christmas Box"
*Glossy foliage. Clusters of small, white,
fragrant flowers, late winter. For any fertile soil;
good on chalk.*
– confusa SS (E) ◑
Dense, spreading habit. Long, slender
pointed leaves. Very fragrant flowers, with
cream anthers. Shiny black fruits. AGM 1969
– hookerana SS (E) ◑
Erect habit. Hairy green stems. Lanceolate
leaves. Black berries. AM 1936
– – digyna SS (E) ◑
More slender habit. Narrower leaves.
AGM 1963 AM 1970
– – – 'Purple Stem' SS (E) ◑
Purple flushed young stems, petioles and
midribs.

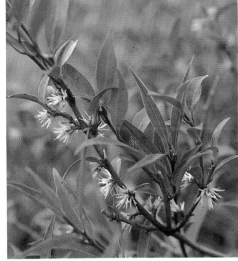

SARCOCOCCA humilis

– humilis DS (E) ◑ GC
Suckering, densely branched habit. Shiny
deep green leaves. Male flowers have pink
anthers. Black berries.

– ruscifolia SS (E)
Shiny dark green, thick leaves. Dark red
berries. Slow growth. AM 1908
– – chinensis SS (E)
More vigorous. Long, slender pointed leaves.
Dark red berries.

SASA – Gramineae DS-MS (E)
*Genus of thicket forming Bamboos, of low
habit. Usually solitary branches forming each
node. Broader leaves than most* Arundinarias.
– tessellata (*Arundinaria ragamowskii*) MS
(E)
Dense thickets of slender, arching, bright
green canes. Shining green leaves up to
60cm, largest of all hardy bamboos.

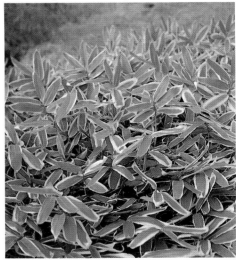

SASA veitchii

– veitchii (*albomarginata*) (*Arundinaria
veitchii*) DS-SS (E)
Thicket-forming. Deep purplish-green canes,
later dull purple. Leaves 10-25cm long, pale
straw or whitish along margins in autumn,
giving variegated effect through winter.
AM 1898

SASSAFRAS – Lauraceae MT ⟋ ⚑
*Require loamy, lime-free soil and the shelter of
woodland.*
– albidum (*officinale*) MT ⟋ ⚑
Distinctive aromatic tree. Flexuous branches,
particularly conspicuous in winter. Variously
shaped leaves, colouring well in autumn.
Inconspicuous racemes of greenish-yellow
flowers, May.

SCHIMA – Theaceae MS-LS (E) † ⟋ ◑
Require lime-free soil and woodland shelter.
– argentea MS-LS (E) † ⟋ ◑
Erect bushy habit. Dark green, glossy leaves, generally glaucous beneath. Creamy white flowers on young wood, late summer. AM 1955

"SEA BUCKTHORN" see *HIPPOPHAE rhamnoides*

SEDUM – Crassulaceae DS
Large genus, mainly herbaceous, with few hardy shrubby species.
– populifolium DS
Erect habit. Rufous, peeling bark. Pale green fleshy leaves, Flattened heads of hawthorn-scented, white or pink-tinged flowers with purple anthers; July-August.

SEMIARUNDINARIA fastuosa see *ARUNDINARIA fastuosa*

SENECIO – Compositae SS-MS (E) ○
Attractive, often grey, foliage. Daisy-like, white or yellow flowers, summer. Excellent wind resisters and maritime shrubs.
– compactus SS (E) † ○
Dense compact habit. Wavy-edged oval leaves, white felted beneath, as are flower stalks and young shoots. Bright yellow flower heads.
– elaeagnifolius MS (E) ○
Rigid dense habit. Glossy, oval, leathery leaves, buff-felted beneath, as are flower-stalks and young shoots.

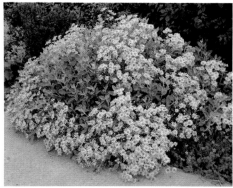

SENECIO 'Sunshine'

– greyi HORT see *S. 'Sunshine'*
– laxifolius SS (E) ○
Resembling *S. 'Sunshine'*, but smaller more slender pointed leaves. Yellow flower heads. Less hardy.

– leucostachys SS (E) † ○
Lax habit. Finely divided, pinnate silvery white leaves. Whitish flowers, summer. Requires sunny wall. AM 1973
– monroi SS (E) ○
Dense, dome-like habit. Oval wavy edged leaves, white felted beneath, as are flower stalks and young shoots. Yellow flower-heads.
– reinoldii (*rotundifolius*) MS (E) ○
Dense rounded habit. Thick, glossy green, rounded leaves, felted beneath. Yellowish flower-heads. Excellent for withstanding sea gales.
– 'Sunshine' (*greyi* HORT) SS (E) ○
Dense mound-like habit. Silvery grey leaves becoming green, white felted beneath. Yellow flower heads. AGM 1935

SHIBATAEA – Gramineae DS (E)
Low growing bamboo with creeping rootstock. Branches short. Leafy; clusters of three to five at each node.
– kumasasa (*Phyllostachys ruscifolia*) DS (E)
Compact. Dense leafy clumps. Zig-zag canes, pale green maturing dull brown. Leaves 5 to 10cm long. FCC 1896

SINOARUNDINARIA aurea see *PHYLLOSTACHYS aurea*
– murielae see *ARUNDINARIA murielae*
– nitida see *ARUNDINARIA nitida*

SKIMMIA – Rutaceae DS-SS (E)
Slow growing, aromatic shrubs. Compact habit. Dioecious, apart from S.reevesiana; both sexes necessary for production of bright, persistent, fruits. Excellent for maritime and industrial sites.
– fortunei see *S.reevesiana*
– japonica DS-SS (E)
Dense, dome-shaped habit. Leathery leaves. White, often fragrant flowers, April-May. Bright red, globular fruits on female plants. FCC 1863. AGM 1969. We recommend:
– – 'Foremanii' (*'Fisheri'*) (*'Veitchii'*) SS (E)
Vigorous. Broad leaves. Large bunches of brilliant fruits. Female. FCC 1888 AGM 1969
– – 'Fragrans' SS (E)
Dense panicles of "Lily-of-the-Valley" scented, white flowers. Male. AGM 1969
– – 'Nymans' SS (E)
Comparatively large fruits, freely borne. Female.
– – 'Rogersii' DS (E)
Slow, compact growth. Large red fruits.

Female. AGM 1969
– – **'Rogersii Nana'** DS (E)
Smaller leaves. Free flowering. Male.

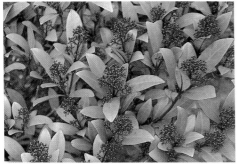

SKIMMIA japonica 'Rubella'

– – **'Rubella'** SS (E)
Large panicles of red buds, winter; opening to
white, yellow anthered flowers, early spring.
Male. AM 1962 AGM1969
– **laureola** SS (E)
Dense habit. Dark green leaves in terminal
clusters, pungent smelling when crushed.
Fragrant greenish yellow flower clusters,
spring. Bright red fruits on female plants.
– **reevesiana** (*fortunei*) DS (E) ↗
Low, mound-like habit. Hermaphrodite white
flowers in terminal panicles, May. Crimson
fruits persisting throughout winter.

"SLOE" see *PRUNUS spinosa*

"SMOKE TREE" see *COTINUS coggygria*

"SNOWBALL" see *VIBURNUM opulus
'Sterile'*

"SNOWBALL, JAPANESE" see *VIBURNUM
plicatum*

"SNOWBERRY" see *SYMPHORICARPOS
rivularis*

"SNOWDROP TREE" see *HALESIA carolina*

"SNOWY MESIPILUS" see *AMELANCHIER*

SOLANUM see under CLIMBERS

SOPHORA – Leguminosae SS-LT
*Elegant, pinnate leaves. Attractive pea-
flowers. Require well drained, fertile soil. Sun-
loving.*

– **japonica** MT-LT ♥ "Japanese Pagoda
Tree"
Leaves up to 30cm long. Creamy white
flowers in large terminal panicles, late
summer-autumn on mature trees.

– – **'Pendula'** ST ↑
Stiffly weeping branches, eventually touching
the ground.
– **microphylla** (*tetraptera microphylla*)
LS-ST (E). ♥ † ☼
Dense, wiry habit when juvenile. Leaves with
small, numerous leaflets. Drooping clusters of
yellow flowers May. AM 1951
– **tetraptera** LS-ST (E) ♥ † ☼ New Zealand
"Kowhai"
Spreading or drooping branches. Yellow,
slightly tubular flowers in hanging clusters,
May. Beaded, 4-winged seed pods. AM 1943.
We recommend the form:
– – **'Grandiflora'** LS-ST (E) ♥ † ☼
Large leaflets. Slightly larger flowers. AM1977

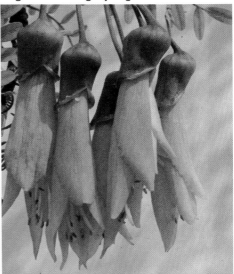

SOPHORA tetraptera 'Grandiflora'

– **viciifolia** (*davidii*) SS-MS ☼
Grey downy branches becoming spiny.
Leaves, silky hairy beneath. Terminal
racemes of small bluish-white flowers, June.
AM1933

SORBARIA – Rosaceae MS-LS
*Vigorous, elegant, pinnate leaves. Large
conical panicles of creamy white or white
flowers. Suitable for most soils. Best in full sun.
Associate well with water.*

– **aitchisonii** MS
Long, spreading branches, reddish when
young. Sharply serrated, tapering leaflets.
Flowers, July-August. AM 1905 AGM 1969

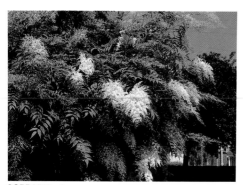

SORBARIA arborea

– arborea LS
Robust habit. Large leaves, downy beneath.
Flowers at ends of current year's growth, July-
August. AM 1963

SORBUS – Rosaceae DS-LT
*Ornamental foliage, often colouring richly in
autumn. Usually white flowers, May-June.
Colourful berry-like fruits; generally the yellow
or white forms remaining longer in winter, than
orange or red.*
*Mostly hardy and of easy cultivation on any
well drained fertile soil.*
*Majority fall into the first two of three groups:
Aria Section – Simple, toothed or lobed
leaves. Good on chalk "The Whitebeams"
Aucuparia Section – Pinnate leaves "The
Mountain Ashes"*
*Micromeles Section – Similar to Aria Section
but fruits with deciduous calyces.*
– alnifolia (Micromeles Section) ST-MT ♥
Dense purplish-brown branches. Heavily
veined, double toothed leaves, colouring
orange and scarlet, autumn. Small red fruits.
AM1924
– americana (Aucuparia Section) ST ♥
Vigorous, ascending branches. Red, sticky
buds. Leaves colouring well, autumn. Large
dense bunches of small red fruits. AM1950
– –'Nana' see *S.aucuparia 'Fastigiata'*
–'Apricot Lady' (Aucuparia Section) ST ♥
Bright green foliage, colouring richly, autumn.
Apricot yellow fruits. AM 1973
– aria ST-MT ♥ "Whitebeam"
Compact, rounded head. Greyish white, oval
leaves, becoming green, white beneath, then
russet and gold in autumn. Bunches of deep
crimson fruit. Tolerates industrial pollution and
sea winds. AGM 1969

– –'Chrysophylla' ST ♥
Yellowish leaves, turning rich butter-yellow,
autumn.
– –'Decaisneana' (*'Majestica'*) ST-MT ♥
Large leaves, 10-15cm long. Larger berries.
AGM 1969

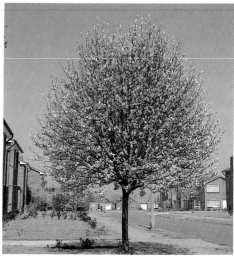

SORBUS aria 'Lutescens'

– –'Lutescens' ST ♥
Emerging leaves covered in dense, creamy-
white tomentum on upper surfaces, becoming
grey-green in summer. AM 1952 AGM 1969
– aucuparia ST-MT ♥ "Mountain Ash"
"Rowan"
Pinnate leaves. Large, dense bunches of
bright red fruits, autumn. Tolerant of extreme
acidity. Not for shallow chalk. AM 1962 AGM
1969
– –'Asplenifolia' (*'Laciniata'*) ST ♥
Fern-like leaves, deeply divided. AGM 1969
– –'Beissneri' ST ♦
Dark coral red young shoots and leaf petioles.
Trunk and stems, coppery russet. Yellowish-
green leaves, the leaflets varying deeply
incised to pinnately lobed. AGM 1969
– –'Edulis' (*'Moravica'*) (*dulcis*) MT ♥
Larger leaves. Heavy bunches of large,
sweet, edible fruits.
– –'Fastigiata' (*S. scopulina* HORT)
(*S. americana 'Nana'*)
(*S. decora 'Nana'*) ST ♦
Stiff, erect branches. Large, dark green
leaves. Dense bunches of large sealing wax
red berries. AM 1924 AGM 1969

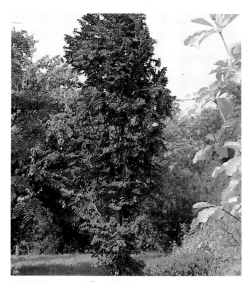

SORBUS aucuparia 'Fastigiata'

– – **'Sheerwater Seedling'** ST ❦
Vigorous, ascending branches. Orange red
berries in large clusters. Good street tree.
– – **'Xanthocarpa'** (*'Fructuluteo'*) ST ❦
Amber yellow fruits. AM 1895 AGM 1969
– **cashmiriana** (Aucuparia Section) ST ❦
Open branched habit. Pale pink flowers, May.
Gleaming white, marble-like fruits in hanging
clusters, persisting after leaf fall. AM 1952
FCC 1971
– **'Chinese Lace'** (Aucuparia Section) ST ❦
Upright habit. Lace-like, deeply divided
leaflets, reddish purple in autumn. Dark red
fruits.
– **commixta** (Aucuparia Section) ST ❦
Glossy green leaves, coppery when young,
colouring brightly in autumn. Erect bunches of
small, round, orange-red fruits. AM 1979
– **conradinae** see *S.esserteauana*
– **cuspidata** (Aria Section) (*vestita*) MT ❦
"Himalayan Whitebeam"
Bold, often rounded leaves, up to 25cm long;
greyish green, silvery or buff tomentose
beneath. Green fruits flushed russet
resembling miniature pears or "crabs".
– **decora 'Nana'** see *S.aucuparia 'Fastigiata'*
– **discolor** HORT see *S. 'Embley'*
– **domestica** MT ❦ "Service Tree"
Open habit. Scaly bark. Pinnate leaves.
Apple- or pear-shaped, edible, green fruits
flushed red, 2.5-3cm long.

– **'Eastern Promise'** (Aucuparia Section) ST
❦
Upright habit. Leaves turning purple then
flame in autumn. Heavy bunches of rose-pink
fruits.
– **'Embley'** (Aucuparia Section) (*discolor*
HORT) ST-MT ❦
Erect habit. Sticky winter buds. Leaves
colouring red in autumn. Heavy bunches of
orange red fruits. AGM 1930 AM1971
– **esserteauana** (Aucuparia Section)
(*conradinae* KOEHNE not HORT) ST ❦
Open habit. Large leafy stipules. Leaves
colour richly in autumn. Broad clusters of
small scarlet fruits. AM 1954
– – **'Flava'** ST ❦
Flattened corymbs of rich lemon yellow
berries. AM 1934
– **'Ethel's Gold'** (Aucuparia Section) ST ❦
Bright green leaves. Golden amber fruits,
persisting into the New Year.
– **folgneri** (Micromeles Section) ST ❦
Usually spreading or arching habit. Variable
leaves often colouring well in autumn.
Hanging clusters of dark red or purplish red
fruits. AM 1915
– × **hostii** ST ❦
Compact habit. Oval, sharply toothed leaves,
grey pubescent beneath. Soft pink flowers.
Red fruits. AM 1974

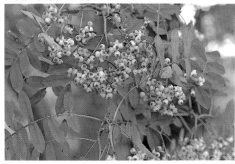

SORBUS hupehensis

– **hupehensis** (Aucuparia Section) ST ❦
Strong ascending purplish-brown branches.
Distinctive, bluish-green leaves. Loose,
drooping clusters of white or pink tinged fruits,
persisting late into winter. AM 1955 AGM 1969
– – **obtusa** (*S. oligodonta*) ST ❦
Attractive pink fruits.
– **hybrida 'Fastigiata'** see *S.* × *thuringiaca
'Fastigiata'*

– **insignis** (KW 7746) (Aucuparia Section) ST ♥
Stiffly ascending purplish-brown branches.
Large buds, conspicuous in winter. Large
heads of small pink fruits, persisting almost to
spring.

– **intermedia** (Aria Section) ST-MT ♥
"Swedish Whitebeam"
Dense, rounded head. Leaves, grey felted
beneath. Orange red fruits in bunches. Good
for town or city gardens.

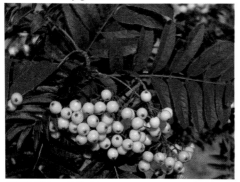

SORBUS 'Joseph Rock'

– **'Joseph Rock'** (Aucuparia Section) ST ♦
Erect, compact head. Leaves colouring fiery
red, orange, copper and purple in autumn.
Clusters of round, creamy yellow fruits,
maturing to amber. AM 1950 FCC 1962 AGM
1969

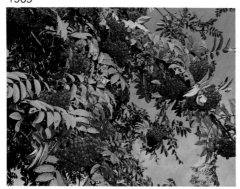

SORBUS × kewensis

– × **kewensis** (Aucuparia Section)
(*pohuashanensis* HORT) ST ♥
Heavy cropper. Dense bunches of orange-
red berries weigh down the branches in
September. AM 1947 AGM 1969 FCC 1973

– **megalocarpa** LS-ST ♥
Loose habit. Brown-purple twigs.
Conspicuous red sticky bud scales in spring.
Corymbs of pungent cream flowers, spring,
before leaves. Egg-like brown fruits.

– **meliosmifolia** (Micromeles Section) LS-ST
♥
Stiffly ascending purplish-brown branches.
Early flowering. Brownish red fruits.

– **'Mitchellii'** (Aria Section) MT-LT ♥
Large, rounded, green leaves, white
tomentose beneath, up to 15cm long and
across.

– **oligodonta** see *S. hupehensis obtusa*

– **'Pearly King'** (Aucuparia Section) ST ♥
Slender branched habit. Rose pink fruits,
turning white, flushed pink, in large hanging
clusters.

– **poteriifolia** HORT (Aucuparia Section) ST
♥
Slow growth. Erect purplish-brown branches.
Loose bunches of rosy pink round fruits.
AM 1951

– **'Red Marbles'** (Aucuparia Section) ST ♥
Stout twigs. Purple stalked leaves. Loose,
heavy bunches of pale spotted, red fruits.

– **reducta** (Aucuparia Section) DS
Thicket forming, suckering shrub. Red
stalked, shiny green leaves, bronze and
purplish in autumn. Small round fruits, white
flushed rose.

– **sargentiana** (Aucuparia Section) ST ♥
Rigidly branched habit. Large, sticky,
crimson, winter buds. Red-stalked leaves,
colouring red in autumn. Large rounded
heads of small scarlet fruits. AM 1954 FCC
1956 AGM 1969

– **scalaris** (Aucuparia Section) ST ♥
Wide-spreading habit. Dark glossy frond-like
leaves, grey downy beneath. Colouring
purple and red in autumn. Flattened heads of
small, red fruits. AM 1934 AGM 1969

– **scopulina** HORT see *S. aucuparia*
'*Fastigiata*'

– **'Signalman'** ST ♦
Densely arranged pinnate leaves. Dense
clusters of large bright orange fruits. Good for
street planting.

– **sp. Ghose** (Aucuparia Section) ST ♦
Large leaves, dull green leaflets, rusty
pubescent beneath. Large bunches of
persistent, small, rose-red fruits.

–'**Sunshine**' (Aucuparia Section) ST ♥
Erect habit when young. Large, lax, dense
bunches of golden yellow fruits.
–**thibetica** (KW21127) (Aria Section) ST ♦
Stiff, erect branches. Ribbed leaves, sparsely
hairy beneath, grey and downy when young.
Corymbs of amber fruits, speckled greyish
brown.
– × **thuringiaca** (*decurrens*) (*pinnatifida*)
(× *hybrida* HORT) ST ♥
Leaves divided to the midrib at the base,
shallowly lobed elsewhere. Bunches of
scarlet berries, lightly freckled. AM 1924. We
recommend the form:

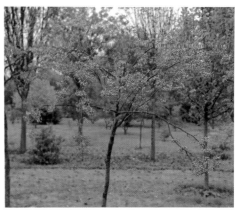
SORBUS vilmorinii

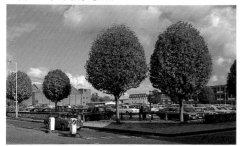
SORBUS × thuringiaca 'Fastigiata'

––'**Fastigiata**' (*hybrida 'Fastigiata'* HORT) ST
♦
Closely packed, stiffly ascending branches. A
good street tree.
–**torminalis** (Aria Section) MT ♥ "Wild
Service Tree"
Scaly bark. Twigs, woolly pubescent when
young. Dark, glossy, maple-like leaves,
bronzy yellow in autumn. Russety brown fruits.
–'**Tundra**' (Aucuparia Section) ST ♥
Erect habit. Drooping bunches of small, pale
green fruits, becoming pearly white, faintly
tinged green.
–**ursina** (*sp. Lowndes*) (Aucuparia Section)
ST ♦
Stout, ascending, greyish branches. Dense
bunches of white or pink-tinged fruits.
AM 1973
–**vilmorinii** (Aucuparia Section) ST ♥
Spreading habit. Leaves, red and purple in
autumn. Drooping clusters of rose-red fruits,
turning pink to white flushed rose. AM 1916
AGM 1953
–'**White Wax**' ST ♥
Fern-like leaves. Drooping clusters of white
berries.

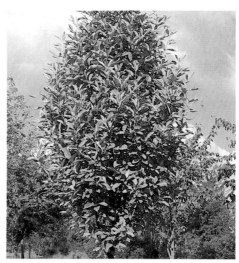
SORBUS 'Wilfred Fox'

–'**Wilfred Fox**' (Aria Section) MT ♦
Dense, ascending branches. Dark, glossy
green leaves, greyish white beneath. Marble-
like, green fruits turning deep amber flecked
grey.
–'**Winter Cheer**' (Aucuparia Section) ST ♥
Open branched habit. Large, flat bunches of
chrome yellow fruits, ripening orange-red,
persistent. AM 1971
"**SOUTHERNWOOD**" see *ARTEMISIA
abrotanum*
SPARTIUM – Leguminosae MS ○
*Monotypic genus. Revels in sunny, well
drained position. Good maritime shrub.*
(b) 3

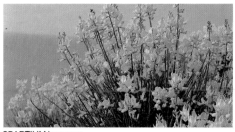
SPARTIUM junceum

– **junceum** MS ☼ "Spanish Broom"
Loose habit. Erect, green, rush-like stems.
Loose, terminal racemes of fragrant, yellow
pea-flowers, summer-early autumn.
AGM 1923 AM 1968
SPARTOCYTISUS – Leguminosae MS ☼
Monotypic genus. Requires well-drained site.
– **nubigenus** (*Cytisus supranubius*) MS ☼
"Teneriffe Broom"
Loose habit. Small trifoliolate leaves. Axillary
clusters of fragrant, white, tinted rose flowers;
May. AM 1924
"SPICE BUSH" see *LINDERA benzoin*
"SPINDLE" see *EUONYMUS*
SPIRAEA – Rosaceae DS-LS
*Variable flowering shrubs, some with
attractive foliage, of easy cultivation in
ordinary soil and a sunny site – a few dislike
shallow chalk.*
– **aitchisonii** see *SORBARIA aitchisonii*
– **albiflora** (*japonica alba*) DS
Compact habit. Angular shoots and serrated,
lanceolate leaves. White flowers in terminal
corymbs, late summer, on current season's
growth.
– **arborea** see *SORBARIA arborea*
– × **arguta** MS "Bridal Wreath" "Foam of May"
Dense habit. Graceful slender branches.
Small clusters of pure white flowers along
branches, April-May. AGM 1927 C or D 2 or 7

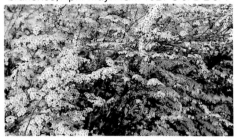
SPIRAEA × arguta

– × **billiardii** MS
Suckering habit. Erect hairy stems. Bright
rose flowers, summer. Not for shallow chalk.
We recommend the form:
– – **'Triumphans'** (*menziesii 'Triumphans'*)
MS
Purplish rose flowers in dense, conical
panicles, summer. Not for shallow chalk.
– **bracteata** see *S. nipponica*
– **bullata** see *S. japonica 'Bullata'*
– × **bumalda** DS
Sharply toothed leaves. Flattened terminal
panicles of deep pink flowers. Leaves often
variegated cream and pink. We recommend:

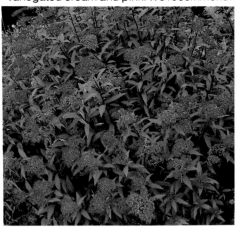
SPIRAEA × bumalda 'Anthony Waterer'

– – **'Anthony Waterer'** DS
Bright crimson flowers. Leaves occasionally
variegated cream and pink. FCC 1893 AGM
1969

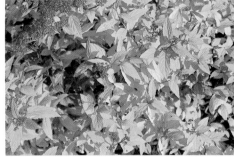
SPIRAEA × bumalda 'Goldflame'

– – **'Goldflame'** DS
Young growths gold and flame coloured in
spring, turning green. Best in moist soil.

– × cinerea SS
Arching stems. Narrow leaves, grey downy when young. Dense clusters of small white flowers along branches, late April-early May. We particularly recommend:

– –'Grefsheim' MS
Excellent free-flowering clone.

– crispifolia see *S. japonica 'Bullata'*

– discolor see *HOLODISCUS discolor*

– japonica (*callosa*) SS
Erect habit. Coarsely serrated, lanceolate to ovate leaves. Large, flattened heads of pink flowers, midsummer. Variable species, we recommend the forms:

– –alba see *S. albiflora*

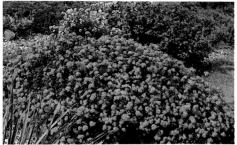

SPIRAEA japonica 'Alpina'

– –'Alpina' (*'Nana'*) DS
Mound-forming habit. Smaller leaves and flower-heads. Rose-pink flowers in tiny heads. AGM 1969

– –'Bullata' (*S. crispifolia*) (*S. bullata*) DS
Compact habit. Small, puckered leaves. Rose-crimson flowers in flat topped clusters. Slow growth. FCC 1884

– –'Little Princess' SS
Mound-forming habit. Rose-crimson flowers.

– –'Ruberrima' SS
Dense, rounded habit. Rose-red flowers.

– menziesii 'Triumphans' see *S. × billiardii 'Triumphans'*

– nipponica (*bracteata*) MS
Dense bushy habit. Long, arching stems. Clusters of white flowers, along upperside of branches, June. We recommend the form:

– –tosaensis (*'Snowmound'*) SS
Dense, mound-like habit. Abundant flowers, smothering branches, June. C or D 2 or 7

– salicifolia LS "Bridewort"
Vigorous, suckering habit. Erect stems. Pink flowers in dense, round downy panicles, June-July. Not for shallow chalk.

–'Snowmound' see *S. nipponica tosaensis*

– thunbergii SS-MS
Dense, twiggy, spreading habit. Wiry stems. Abundant, pure white flowers in clusters along branches, March-April. C or D 2 or 7

– × vanhouttei MS
Vigorous, arching habit. Dense umbels of white flowers along branches, June.

– veitchii LS
Arching, reddish branches. Dense corymbs of white flowers along branches, June-July. AM 1909. C or D 2 or 7

STACHYURUS – Stachyuraceae MS-LS
Stiffly pendulous racemes of flowers form in autumn and open early following spring. Suitable for all fertile soils.

– chinensis MS-LS
Spreading habit. Purplish branchlets. Tapering, dull green leaves, shiny pale green below. Soft yellow, cup-shaped flowers, February-March. AM 1925

– –'Magpie' MS
Variegated form, grey green leaves margined cream and tinged rose.

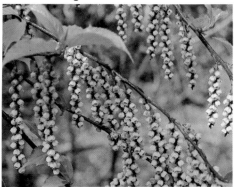

STACHYURUS praecox

– praecox (*japonicus*) MS-LS
Reddish brown branchlets. Broad, taper-pointed leaves. Short racemes of pale yellow, cup-shaped flowers, March or earlier. AM 1925 AGM 1964

STAPHYLEA – Staphyleaceae LS "Bladder Nut"
Hardy flowering shrubs. Curious inflated bladder-like fruits. For all fertile soils.

– colchica LS
Strong growing, erect habit. Conspicuous erect panicles of white flowers, May. Capsules up to 10cm long. FCC 1897

– **holocarpa** LS-ST ♀
Trifoliolate leaves. White flowers in drooping panicles, April-May. AM 1924. We recommend the form:
– – **'Rosea'** LS-ST ♀
Spreading branches. Young leaves bronze. Drooping clusters of soft pink flowers. AM 1953

STEPHANANDRA – Rosaceae DS-MS
Graceful habit. Leaves often colouring richly in autumn. Small greenish-white flowers. Suit most soils.
– **incisa** (*flexuosa*) MS
Dense habit. Slender, zig-zag stems. Ovate leaves, deeply toothed and lobed. Crowded flower panicles, June.

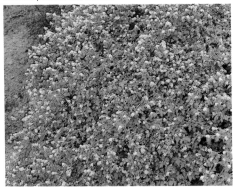
STEPHANANDRA incisa 'Crispa'

– – **'Crispa'** DS GC
Mound-forming habit. Small, crinkly leaves. Tiny creamy flowers, June.
– **tanakae** MS
Arching, brown stems. Broadly ovate or triangular leaves. Flowers slightly larger than *S. incisa.*

STEWARTIA (*STUARTIA*) – **Theaceae** LS-MT ⚲ ◑
Notable for flowers, autumn leaf colour and ornamental bark. White or cream, generally solitary, flowers produced in leaf axils. Short-lived but produced continuously, July-August. Need moist, loamy, lime-free soil, ideally in woodland conditions. Resent disturbance.
– **koreana** ST-MT ♀ ⚲ ◑
Attractive, flaking bark. Slender pointed leaves, colouring brightly, autumn. White flowers with spreading petals and central yellow stamens.

– **malacodendron** LS-ST ⚲ ◑
White flowers with purple stamens and bluish anthers. FCC 1934
– **ovata** (*pentagyna*) LS ⚲ ◑
Bushy habit. White, cup-shaped flowers with orange anthers.

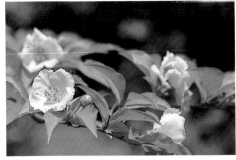
STEWARTIA pseudocamellia

– **pseudocamellia** (*grandiflora*) ST-MT ♀ ⚲ ◑
Open habit. Attractive, flaking bark. Leaves colouring red and yellow in autumn. White flowers with yellow anthers. FCC 1888
– **serrata** ST ♀ ⚲ ◑
Warm brown stems. Leathery leaves, colouring richly, autumn. White flowers with red basal stain outside, yellow anthers; June. AM 1932
– **sinensis** LS-ST ♀ ⚲ ◑
Attractive, flaking bark. Leaves, rich crimson in autumn. Cup-shaped, fragrant flowers.

STRANVAESIA – Rosaceae PS-ST (E)
Cotoneaster-like plants. White flower clusters, June. Red fruits, unattractive to birds. Easy cultivation – for any well drained soil in sun or shade. Tolerate atmospheric pollution. Ideal for informal hedging and screening.

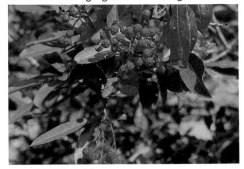
STRANVAESIA davidiana

– davidiana LS-ST (E) ♥
Vigorous, erect habit. Dark green leathery
leaves; old ones turn bright red, autumn.
Crimson fruits in hanging clusters. AM 1928
AGM 1964
– –'Fructuluteo' MS (E)
Bright yellow fruits.
– – salicifolia (*S. salicifolia*) LS-ST (E) ♥
Numerously veined, oblong or narrow
lanceolate leaves. AGM 1969
– – undulata 'Prostrata' PS (E) GC
Prostrate habit. Wavy-margined leaves.
× **STRANVINIA – Rosaceae** (*PHOTINIA* ×
STRANVAESIA)
*A remarkable hybrid raised in our nurseries of
which the following is the only form in general
cultivation.*

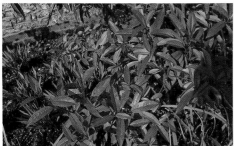

× STRANVINIA 'Redstart'

–'Redstart' LS-ST (E)
NEW A vigorous plant with narrow, glossy
green leaves tinted coppery-red when young,
a few turning to brilliant scarlet in autumn.
Dense, clusters of white flowers. June. Yellow-
tipped, red berries.
"STRAWBERRY TREE" see *ARBUTUS
unedo*
STUARTIA see *STEWARTIA*
STYRAX – Styraceae MS-ST ♥ "Snowbell"
*Pure white, pendulous flowers, late spring-
summer. Require moist, loamy, lime-free soil,
sun or semi-shade.*
– hemsleyana ST ♥
Open branched habit. Leaves almost round,
oblique at base. Lax, downy racemes of
flowers with central cone of yellow anthers,
June. AM 1930 FCC 1942 A (e) 3
– japonica ST ♥
Wide-spreading, fan-like branches. Bell-
shaped flowers with central cluster of yellow
stamens, hang along branches, June.
FCC 1885 AGM 1969. A (e) 3

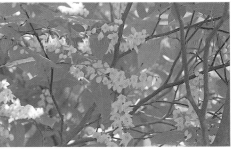

STYRAX japonica

– obassia LS-ST ♥
Large, almost round leaves, velvety beneath.
Long, lax, terminal racemes of fragrant, bell-
shaped flowers, June. FCC 1888
– wilsonii MS
Dense, twiggy habit. Tiny leaves. Pendulous
flowers, solitary or in clusters, June. Requires
a sheltered site. AM 1913
"SUMACH" see *COTINUS coggygria* and
RHUS typhina
"SUN ROSE" see *HELIANTHEMUM* and
CISTUS
"SWEET BRIAR" see *ROSA rubiginosa*
"SWEET CHESTNUT" see *CASTANEA sativa*
"SWEET GALE" see *MYRICA gale*
"SWEET GUM" see *LIQUIDAMBAR
styraciflua*
"SWEET PEPPER BUSH" see *CLETHRA
alnifolia*
"SYCAMORE" see *ACER pseudoplatanus*
SYCOPSIS – Hamamelidaceae LS-ST (E) ♥
*One species in general cultivation with
leathery, pointed, lanceolate leaves and early
spring flowers.*

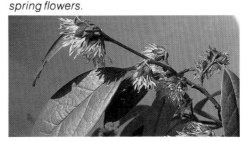

SYCOPSIS sinensis

– sinensis LS-ST (E) ♥
Monoecious flowers without petals, small
clusters of red-anthered, yellow stamens
surrounded by dark brown tomentose scales,
opening February-March.

SYMPHORICARPOS – Caprifoliaceae
DS-MS

Small flowers. Ornamental pink or white berries, abundantly produced autumn and persisting well into winter. Grow in all soils. Some are excellent for hedging.

– albus laevigatus see *S. rivularis*

– × chenaultii SS

Dense habit. Clusters or spikes of purplish red berries, pinkish white where unexposed. We recommend the form:

– –'Hancock' DS GC

Dwarf form, excellent as ground cover beneath trees.

– × doorenbosii MS

Strong growth. White fruits flushed rose. We recommend the following clones:

– –'Erect' MS Hdg (0.5m)

Vigorous. Compact, upright habit. Rose-lilac berries. Good hedger.

– –'Magic Berry' SS

Compact spreading habit. Abundant rose-pink berries.

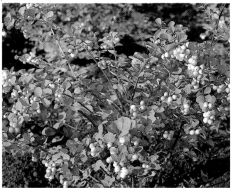

SYMPHORICARPOS × doorenbosii 'Mother of Pearl'

– –'Mother of Pearl' SS

Dense habit. Heavy crops of marble-like white berries flushed rose. AGM 1969 AM 1971

– –'White Hedge' SS Hdg (0.5m)

Strong, erect, compact growth. Erect clusters of abundant small white berries. Excellent hedger.

– orbiculatus (*vulgaris*) MS "Indian Currant" "Coral Berry"

Dense, bushy habit. Densely leafy stems. Very small purplish-rose berries in dense clusters along stems.

– –'Variegatus' MS

Leaves irregularly margined yellow.

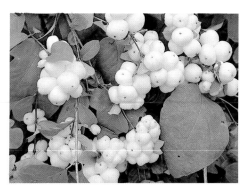

SYMPHORICARPOS rivularis

– rivularis (*albus laevigatus*) MS "Snowberry"

Dense, thicket-forming habit. Profuse, marble-like, glistening white berries. Excellent for poor soils and dense shade. FCC 1913 AGM 1931

SYMPLOCOS – Symplocaceae LS-ST ♥

Large genus, only one species is in general cultivation here.

– paniculata (*crataegoides*) LS-ST ⤢ ♥

Dense, twiggy habit. Fragrant, small, white flowers, May-June. Brilliant ultramarine fruits persisting into winter, most abundant after hot summer. Plant two or more for fertilisation. AM 1938 (flower) AM1947 (fruit) FCC 1954

SYRINGA-Oleaceae SS-LS ○ "Lilac"

Generally strong growing tree-like shrubs, flowering May-June. Many delightfully fragrant. Grow in most soils, especially good on chalk. A (j) (k) 2

– × chinensis MS "Rouen Lilac"

Dense bushy habit. Fragrant, lavender flowers in drooping panicles, May. AGM 1969 We recommend:

– –'Saugeana' (*'Rubra'*) MS

Lilac-red flowers. AGM 1969

– × hyacinthiflora LS

Early flowering, variable hybrid. We recommend the clone:

– –'Esther Staley' LS

Abundant, single, pink flowers, carmine in bud, late April-May. AM 1961 AGM 1969

– × josiflexa MS-LS

Deep green leaves. Loose plume like panicles of fragrant, rose-pink flowers. We particularly recommend:

– –'Bellicent' LS

Enormous flower panicles. FCC 1946 AGM 1969

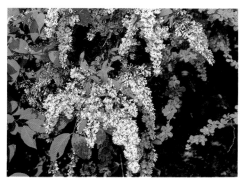

SYRINGA × josiflexa 'Bellicent'

– julianae MS
Graceful habit. Fragrant, pale lilac flowers in slender, erect panicles, May-early June. AM 1924
– laciniata (*afghanica* HORT) SS
Slender stems and dainty pinnately-divided leaves. Slender panicles of lilac flowers, May.
– microphylla MS
Small ovate leaves. Small panicles of fragrant, rosy-lilac flowers, June and September. We recommend the form:
– – 'Superba' MS
Abundant rosy-pink flowers, May and intermittently until October. AM 1957 AGM 1969
– palibiniana see *S. velutina*
– × persica MS "Persian Lilac"
Rounded, bushy habit. Slender branches. Small panicles of fragrant, lilac flowers, May.
– – 'Alba' MS
White flowers.
– × prestoniae "Canadian Hybrids"
Vigorous, late flowering hybrids. We recommend the forms:
– – 'Elinor' LS
Pale lavender flowers, purplish red in bud, in erect panicles. AM 1951
– – 'Isabella' LS
Mallow purple flowers in erect panicles. AM 1941
– reflexa LS
Large, rough, oval leaves, up to 20cm. Long narrow drooping panicles of purplish pink flowers, whitish within. AM 1914
– × swegiflexa MS
Strong growing, open habit. Large cylindrical panicles of generally pink flowers. We recommend:

– – 'Fountain' MS
Compact habit. Long drooping panicles of fragrant, soft pink flowers.
– sweginzowii MS
Vigorous. Elegant habit. Long loose panicles of fragrant, flesh-pink flowers. AM 1915. We recommend:

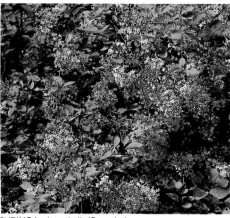

SYRINGA microphylla 'Superba'

– – 'Superba' MS
Larger flower panicles. AM 1918
– velutina (*palibiniana*) SS-MS "Korean Lilac"
Dense, compact habit. Velvety, dark green leaves. Abundant panicles of pale lilac or lilac pink flowers.
– vulgaris LS "Common Lilac"
Vigorous suckering habit. Richly scented flowers, May-June. Numerous cultivars have arisen from this. The following are recommended:
– – 'Charles Joly' LS
Double, dark purplish red, late.
– – 'Charles X' LS
Single, purplish red. Long panicles.
– – 'Condorcet' LS
Double, lavender. Massive, long panicles.
– – 'Congo' LS
Single, rich lilac-red, paling with age. Large, compact panicles.
– – 'Firmament' LS
Single, lilac-blue, early.
– – 'General Pershing' LS
Double, purplish-violet. Long panicles.
– – 'Katherine Havemeyer' LS
Double, lavender-purple, fading soft lilac-pink. Broad, compact panicles. AM 1933 AGM 1969

SYRINGA vulgaris – Continued

--**'Madame Antoine Buchner'** LS
Double, pink to rosy-mauve, late. Loose narrow panicles. AGM 1969

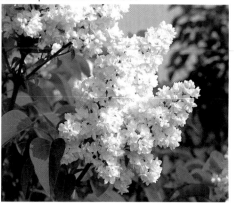

SYRINGA vulgaris 'Madame Lemoine'

--**'Madame Lemoine'** LS
Double, pure white, creamy yellow in bud. AM 1891 FCC 1894 AGM 1937
--**'Marechal Foch'** LS
Single, large carmine rose flowers. Broad, open panicles. AM 1935
--**'Maud Notcutt'** LS
Single, pure white. Large panicles, up to 30 cm. AM 1957
--**'Michel Buchner'** LS
Double. Soft rosy lilac. Large, dense panicles. AM 1891
--**'Mrs. Edward Harding'** LS
Double, claret red, shaded pink, late. Free-flowering. AGM 1969
--**'Paul Thirion'** LS
Double, claret rose, fading lilac-pink, carmine in bud. Late. AGM 1969

--**'Primrose'** LS
Single, pale primrose yellow. Small, dense panicles. AM 1950
--**'Sensation'** LS
Single, purplish red florets, margined white. Large panicles.

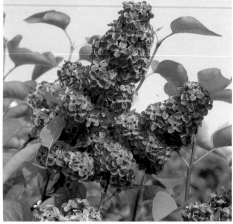

SYRINGA vulgaris 'Souvenir de Louis Spaeth'

--**'Souvenir d'Alice Harding'** LS
Double white. Tall panicles.
--**'Souvenir de Louis Spaeth'** LS
Single. Wine red. FCC 1894 AGM 1930
--**'Vestale'** LS
Single. Pure white. Densely packed, broad panicles. AGM 1931
--**yunnanensis** MS-LS "Yunnan Lilac"
Loose, open habit. Slender panicles of lilac-pink flowers, pink in bud; June. AM 1928 We recommend the form:
--**'Rosea'** MS-LS
Long slender panicles of rose-pink flowers.

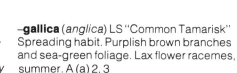

TAMARIX – Tamaricaceae LS "Tamarisks"
Graceful, slender branches. Feathery plume-like foliage and inflorescences. Tiny pink flowers in slender racemes. Excellent in windy or coastal sites. Any soils except shallow chalk.

--**gallica** (*anglica*) LS "Common Tamarisk"
Spreading habit. Purplish brown branches and sea-green foliage. Lax flower racemes, summer. A (a) 2, 3
--**germanica** see *MYRICARIA germanica*

– **parviflora** (*tetrandra purpurea*) LS
Brown or purple branches. Bright green
foliage. Deep pink flowers, May. AGM 1962
A (f) 7
– **pentandra** LS
Reddish-brown branches. Glaucous foliage.
Rose pink flowers, late summer – early
autumn. AM 1933 AGM 1962 A (a) 2, 3
– – **'Rubra'** LS
Darker coloured flowers. AGM 1969
A (a) 2, 3

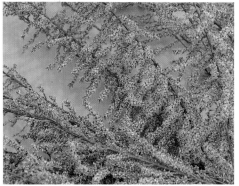

TAMARIX tetranda

– **tetrandra** (*caspica* HORT) LS
Loose, open habit. Dark branches. Light pink
flowers, May-early June. A (f) 7
TELOPEA – Proteaceae LS (E) ↙ ◑
*Require moist, well-drained, fertile, lime-free
soil.*

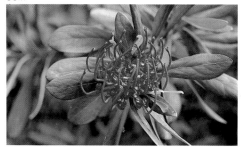

TELOPEA truncata

– **truncata** LS (E) ↙ ◑ "Tasmanian Waratah"
Stout, downy shoots. Thick leathery leaves.
Rich crimson flowers in dense terminal heads,
June. AM 1934 FCC 1938
TETRACENTRON – Tetracentraceae LS-MT
*Monotypic genus. Catkin-like inflorescences.
Prefers acid or neutral soil, but tolerates lime.
Revels in woodland situation.*

– **sinense** LS-MT ♥
Wide-spreading habit. Heart shaped or ovate
leaves, tinted red when young. Yellowish
catkins of minute flowers, summer.
TEUCRIUM – Labiatae DS-SS (E) ○
*Square stems. Double-lipped flowers. Need
well drained site in full sun.*

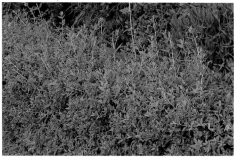

TEUCRIUM fructicans

– **fructicans** (*latifolium*) SS (E) † ○ "Shrubby
Germander" Dense, white tomentum on
stems and leaf undersides. Terminal racemes
of pale blue flowers. Needs wall shelter.
– **polium** DS (E) ○
Hummock-forming procumbent stems.
Narrow grey felted leaves. White or yellow
flowers.
– **subspinosum** DS (E) ○
Grey spiny shrublet. Mauve-pink flowers, late
summer.
THAMNOCALAMUS spathiflorus see
ARUNDINARIA spathiflora
THEA sinensis see *CAMELLIA sinensis*
"THORN" *see CRATAEGUS*
"THORN, CHRIST'S" see *PALIURUS spina-
christi*
"THORN, GLASTONBURY" see
CRATAEGUS monogyna 'Biflora'
TIBOUCHINA – Melastomataceae LS-ST †
*Not hardy. Suitable for sheltered warm wall in
very mild area, or conservatory.*
– **urvilliana** (*semidecandra* HORT) LS (E) †
Four-sided stems. Prominently veined,
velvety leaves. Large, rich purple flowers,
continuous summer-autumn. FCC 1868
TILIA – Tiliaceae ST-LT The "Limes" or
"Lindens"
*Basically heart-shaped leaves. Clusters of
small fragrant, greenish yellow flowers, July.
Suitable for all soils. Tolerant of atmospheric
pollution. May be hard pruned.*

– **americana** MT ♥ "American Lime"
Huge, coarsely toothed, broad leaves, up to
30cm long. We recommend the form:
– – **'Redmond'** MT ♦
Dense conical habit.
– **cordata** (*parvifolia*) MT-LT ♥ "Small-leaved
Lime"
Leathery, dark green leaves, pale green
beneath. Sweetly scented, tiny, ivory flowers.

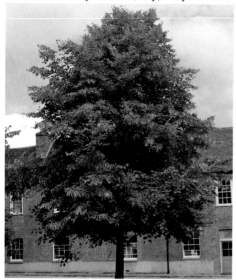

TILIA × euchlora

– × **euchlora** MT ♥
Elegant, arching, juvenile habit, densely
twiggy in maturity. Rounded, glossy green
leaves, paler beneath. Free from aphids and
associated stickiness. FCC 1890 AGM 1969
– × **europaea** LT ♥ "Common Lime"
Vigorous. Dense suckering habit. Greenish,
smooth, zig-zag shoots. Common avenue
tree. We recommend the forms:
– – **'Pallida'** MT ♥
Ascending branches forming broadly conical
crown. Wind resistant.
– – **'Wratislaviensis'** MT ♥
Golden yellow young leaves, becoming green
with maturity.
– **henryana** MT ♥
Softly downy, bristle-edged leaves, axillary
tufts beneath.
– × **moltkei** MT-LT ♥
Arching, slightly drooping branches. Leaves,
greyish downy beneath.

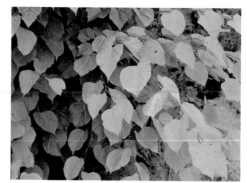

TILIA × europaea 'Wratislaviensis'

– **mongolica** ST ♥ "Mongolian Lime"
Compact, rounded head of branches.
Distinctive ivy-like, lobed leaves, glossy green
turning bright yellow in autumn.
– **oliveri** MT-LT ♥
Slightly pendulous shoots. Dark green finely
serrated leaves, silvery-white tomentose
beneath. AGM 1973
– **parvifolia** see *T. cordata*

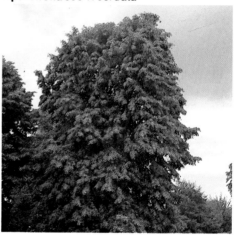

TILIA petiolaris

– **petiolaris** (*americana* 'Pendula' HORT) LT
♥ "Weeping Silver Lime"
Elegant, downward sweeping branches. Dark
green leaves, white felted beneath. Sweetly
scented flowers, narcotic to bees.
– **platyphyllos** (*grandifolia*) LT ♥ "Broad-
leaved Lime"
Vigorous, rounded habit. Downy shoots and
leaves. Relatively few suckers produced. FCC
1892

––**'Aurea'** (*'Aurantiaca'*) (*grandifolia 'Aurantia'*) LT ♥
Conspicuous yellow young shoots, maturing olive green.

––**'Fastigiata'** (*'Pyramidalis'*) LT ♦
Erect branches forming broadly conical head.

––**'Rubra'** (*'Corallina'*) LT ♥ "Red Twigged Lime"
Semi-erect branched habit. Conspicuous reddish young twigs. Good for industrial areas.

–**tomentosa** (*argentea*) (*alba*) LT ♥ "Silver Lime"
Strong ascending branches, often pendulous at tips. White-felted shoots. Dark green leaves, white-felted beneath.

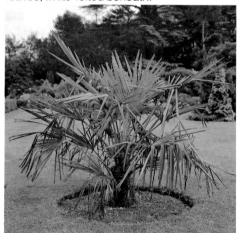

TRACHYCARPUS fortunei

TRACHYCARPUS – Palmaceae ST (E)
Palms with very large, fan-shaped leaves. Monoecious flowers.

–**fortunei** (*excelsus*) (*Chamaerops excelsa*) ST (E) ♥ "Chusan Palm"
Tall fibrous-coated trunk. Leaves, 1-1.5m across, borne in a cluster at trunk apex. Terminal panicles of numerous small yellow flowers. Bluish-black fruits. AM 1970

"TREE DAISY" see *OLEARIA*
"TREE OF HEAVEN" see *AILANTHUS altissima*
"TREE POPPY" see *ROMNEYA*
TRICUSPIDARIA see *CRINODENDRON*
TROCHODENDRON – Trochodendraceae LS (E) ✗
Monotypic genus. Suits most fertile soils except shallow chalk.

–**aralioides** LS (E) ✗
Slow, spreading growth. Aromatic bark. Bright apple-green, leathery, scallop-edged leaves. Erect terminal racemes of green flowers, spring-early summer.

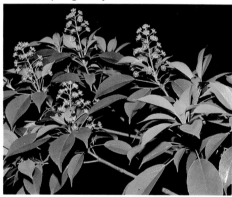

TROCHODENDRON aralioides

"TULIP TREE" see *LIRIODENDRON tulipifera*
"TUPELO" see *NYSSA sylvatica*

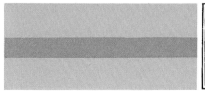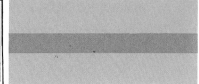

ULEX – Leguminosae SS-MS (E) "Furze" "Gorse" "Whin"
Revels in poor, dry, acid soils. Unsuitable for shallow chalk. Useful for clothing dry banks, and for gale swept, coastal sites.

–**europaeus** MS (E) "Common Gorse"
Green, viciously-spiny, densely branched shrub. Chrome-yellow pea flowers, March-May and intermittently at other times.

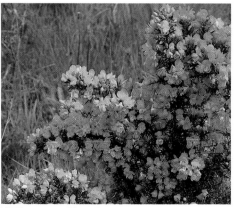

ULEX europaeus 'Plenus'

–– 'Plenus' SS (E)
Abundant, semi-double, persistent flowers,
April-May. AGM 1929 AM 1967
– gallii SS (E)
Low growing, often prostrate, spiny. Deep
golden flowers, August-October.
– minor (*nanus*) SS (E)
Often prostrate, softly spiny. Golden yellow
flowers, autumn.
ULMUS – Ulmaceae MS-LT "Elms"
*Hardy and fast growing. Grow in most soils,
and tolerate sea gales and atmospheric
pollution. As a result of "Dutch Elm Disease",
the planting of Elms has virtually ceased.*
– × elegantissima
Natural hybrid of which we recommend the
clone:

–– 'Jacqueline Hillier' MS
Dense suckering habit. Slender downy twigs.
Small double-toothed leaves, rough to the
touch. Good low hedge.
UMBELLULARIA – Lauraceae LS-ST (E) ☼
*Monotypic genus resembling 'Bay'. Requires
well drained soil.*
– californica LS-ST (E) ☼ "Californian Bay"
"Californian Laurel"
Dense, leafy habit. Bright green leaves,
pungent-smelling when crushed. Small
yellowish green flowers, April. Occasional
green fruits, purple when ripe.
"UMBRELLA TREE" see *MAGNOLIA
tripetala*

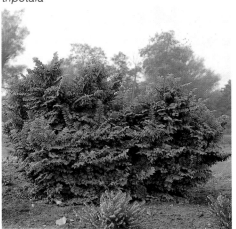

ULMUS × elegantissima 'Jacqueline Hillier'

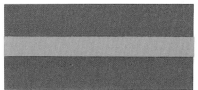

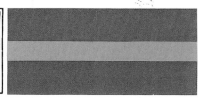

VACCINIUM – Ericaceae PS-LS ⚘
*Attractive, usually edible berries. Deciduous
species notable for autumn leaf colour. Thrive
in extremely acid soils. Generally prefer
moisture and some shade.*
– angustifolium (*pensylvanicum
angustifolium*) DS ⚘ "Low-bush Blueberry"
Compact habit. Thin wiry twigs. Lanceolate,
bristle-toothed leaves, colouring richly,
autumn. Clusters of white or red tinged

flowers, April-May. Sweet, edible; blue-black,
bloomy-berries.
– arctostaphylos MS ⚘ "Caucasian
Whortleberry"
Slow. Wide spreading habit. Large leaves,
purplish red in autumn. Racemes of waxy,
white or red tinted bell-shaped flowers,
summer and autumn. Shiny black berries.
AM 1970

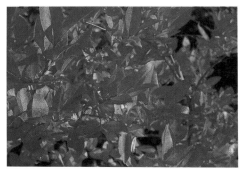

VACCINIUM corymbosum

– **corymbosum** MS ✗ "Swamp Blueberry"
Thicket forming shrub with erect stems. Bright green leaves turn scarlet and bronze in autumn. Pale pink or white flowers, May. Sweet, edible, usually black berries. Named, fruiting clones are usually cultivated.
– **cylindraceum** (*longiflorum*) LS ✗ Semi-(E)
Erect habit. Bright green leaves. Short racemes of cylindrical flowers, pale yellowish green, tinged red, red in bud. Blue-black, bloomy berries.
– **delavayi** MS (E) ✗
Compact habit. Leathery, box-like leaves. Hairy racemes of small white, pink tinged flowers, late spring-early summer. Purplish-blue berries. AM 1950
– **deliciosum** DS ✗
Solitary, globular, pinkish flowers, May. Sweet, edible, bloomy-black, berries.
– **floribundum** (*mortinia*) SS (E) ✗
Red young growths. Dark green leaves, purplish red when young. Dense racemes of cylindrical rose-pink flowers, June. Edible red berries. AM 1935
– **glaucoalbum** SS (E) ✗
Suckering habit. Grey green leaves, vivid blue-white beneath. Racemes of pink flowers amid conspicuous rosy, silvery bracts; May-June. Blue-black, bloomy berries. AM 1931
– **macrocarpum** (*Oxycoccus macrocarpus*) PS (E) ✗ "American Cranberry"
Creeping stems. Small leaves. Drooping pink flowers with recurved petals and yellow staminal beak. Edible, acid, red berries. Requires moist, boggy or peaty soil.
– **myrsinites** DS (E) ✗ "Evergreen Blueberry"
Spreading, compact habit. Small leaves. Clusters of white or pink tinged flowers, April-May. Blue-black berries.

– **myrtillus** DS ✗ "Bilberry" "Whortleberry" "Whinberry"
Dense suckering habit. Greenish pink, globular flowers, April-June. Edible, bloomy, black berries.
– **nummularia** DS (E) † ✗ ◑
Bristly-hairy, arching shoots. Small leathery leaves. Dense clusters of small, cylindrical, rose-red flowers, May-June. Edible black berries. AM 1932
– **ovatum** MS (E) ✗
Dense, compact habit. Dark green, glossy leaves, coppery-red when young. Racemes of white or pink, bell-shaped flowers, May-June. Red berries ripening to black.
– **oxycoccos** (*Oxycoccus palustris*) PS (E) ✗ "Cranberry"
Wiry stems. Tiny, silver-backed leaves. Tiny flowers with recurved, pink petals and yellow staminal beak; May-June. Edible, acid, red fruits. Needs moist, peaty soil.
– **praestans** PS ✗ ◑
Creeping habit. Leaves colour richly in autumn. Bell-shaped, white to red flowers, June. Fragrant, edible, sweet, red berries. Requires moist cool site.
– **vitis-idaea** DS (E) ✗ ◑ GC "Cowberry"
Creeping habit. Glossy, box-like leaves. Terminal racemes of bell-shaped, white tinged pink flowers; June-August. Edible, acid, red berries.

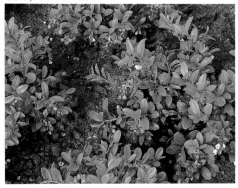

VACCINIUM vitis-idaea

VIBURNUM – Caprifoliaceae SS-LS
Easily cultivated shrubs. Some evergreen, often ornamental leaves. Deciduous species usually have rich autumn colour. Flowers usually white, often heavily fragrant. Some have brightly coloured fruits.

- **alnifolium** MS ⚋ ◑ "Hobble Bush"
Large, strongly veined leaves, claret red in autumn. Large, hydrangea-like inflorescences, marginal white sterile florets, May-June. Red fruits ripening blackish purple. Ideal for woodland. AM 1952
- **'Anne Russell'** MS (E)
Clusters of fragrant white flowers, pink in bud. AM 1957

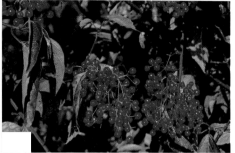
VIBURNUM betulifolium

- **betulifolium** LS
Coarsely-toothed leaves. White flowers in corymbs, June. Abundant clusters of persistent, redcurrant-like fruits. Several plants required to ensure pollination. AM 1936 FCC 1957 AGM 1960
- **bitchiuense** MS
Slender, open habit. Dark metallic green leaves. Clusters of sweetly fragrant, pink flowers, April-May. AGM 1948
- × **bodnantense** MS-LS
Strong, upright habit. Fragrant, rose-tinted flowers in dense clusters, October onwards. We recommend the clones:

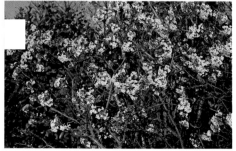
VIBURNUM × bodnantense 'Dawn'

- - **'Dawn'** MS-LS
Vigorous. Richly scented flowers, late autumn-winter. AM 1947 AGM 1960

- - **'Deben'** MS-LS
Sweetly fragrant white flowers, pink in bud, in mild weather October-April. AM 1962 FCC 1965 AGM 1969
- × **burkwoodii** MS (E)
Dark shiny leaves, brown-grey felted beneath. Fragrant white flower clusters, pink in bud; January-May. AM 1929 AGM 1956
- × **carlcephalum** MS
Compact habit. Often rich autumn leaf colour. Large, rounded flower corymbs, pink in bud; May. AM 1946 AGM 1969
- **carlesii** MS
Rounded habit. Downy leaves, greyish beneath, often colouring autumn. Heavily scented, rounded, white flower clusters, pink in bud; April-May. AM 1908 FCC 1909 AGM 1923
- - **'Aurora'** MS
Sweetly fragrant pink flowers, red in bud. AGM 1969

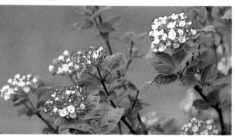
VIBURNUM carlesii 'Diana'

- - **'Diana'** MS
Compact habit. Strongly fragrant flowers, opening red turning pink. AGM 1969
- **cinnamomifolium** LS (E) ◑
Large, leathery, dark glossy leaves. Small, dull white flowers. Small, shiny, blue-black, egg-shaped fruits.
- **davidii** SS (E)
Wide-spreading, mound-like habit. Dark, glossy, leathery leaves, conspicuously three-veined. Bright turquoise berries when group-planted to ensure pollination. AM 1912 AGM 1969 AM 1971 (to female plant)
- **erubescens** MS †
Loose, pendulous clusters of fragrant, white, pink tinted flowers, July. Red fruits ripening black. We recommend the form:
- - **gracilipes** MS
Perfectly hardy. Longer flower panicles. Free-fruiting.

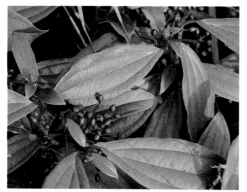

VIBURNUM davidii

– **farreri** (*fragrans*) MS-LS
Broad, rounded habit. Bronze young foliage.
Sweetly scented white flower clusters, pink in
bud; November onwards. Occasional red
fruits. AM 1921 AGM 1923
– **foetens** MS ◑
Loose, spreading habit. Fragrant white
flowers, sometimes blush in bud; January-
March. Red fruits turning black. Difficult plant.
– **fragrans** see *V. farreri*
– **furcatum** LS ✓
Upright habit. Leaves colouring richly in
autumn. Hydrangea like flowers with marginal
ray florets, May. Red fruits ripening black.
Good woodland shrub.
– × **globosum 'Jermyns Globe'** MS (E)
Dense, rounded habit. Dark green leathery
leaves on reddish petioles. Small, white
flowers May, and intermittently at other times;
blue fruits occasionally produced.
– **grandiflorum** (*nervosum*) MS
Upright habit. Dense clusters of fragrant
flowers, carmine in bud, opening pink fading
to blush; February-March. AM 1937
– **henryi** MS (E)
Open erect habit. Glossy, leathery leaves.
White flowers in pyramidal panicles, June.
Bright red fruits ripening black. FCC 1910
AGM 1936
– **hessei** see *V. wrightii 'Hessei'*
– × **hillieri** MS Semi-(E)
Spreading habit. Copper-tinted young
foliage, bronze-red in autumn. Abundant
creamy flowers in panicles, June. Bright red
fruits ripening black. We recommend:
– – **'Winton'** MS Semi-(E)
The only form in general cultivation. AM 1956

– **japonicum** (*macrophyllum*) MS (E)
Leathery, dark green leaves. Stout petioles.
Dense, rounded trusses of fragrant flowers,
on mature shrubs; June. Red fruits.
– **'Jermyns Globe'** see *V. × globosum
'Jermyns Globe'*
– × **juddii** MS
Bushy habit. Clusters of sweetly fragrant, pink
tinged flowers; April-May. AGM 1960
– **lantana** LS "Wayfaring Tree"
Native shrub common on chalk. Leaves
sometimes dark crimson in autumn. Creamy
flowers, May-June. Red fruits maturing black.
– **macrocephalum** (*macrocephalum 'Sterile'*)
MS Semi-(E)
Rounded habit. Large, rounded heads of
sterile, white flowers; May. Best against sunny
wall in cold areas. AM 1927
– **macrophyllum** see *V. japonicum*
– **odoratissimum** LS (E) †
Leathery, glossy leaves, often colouring,
winter. Large conical panicles of fragrant
white flowers, late summer on mature plants.
Red fruits ripening black.
– **opulus** LS "Guelder Rose" "Water Elder"
Maple-like leaves, colouring autumn.
Hydrangea-like flowers with marginal ray
florets; June-July. Persistent, red, translucent
fruit clusters. AGM 1969
– – **'Aureum'** LS ◑
Compact habit. Bright yellow leaves.
– – **'Compactum'** SS
Dense compact habit. AM 1962 AGM 1964
– – **'Notcutt's Variety'** LS
Larger flowers and fruits. AM 1930

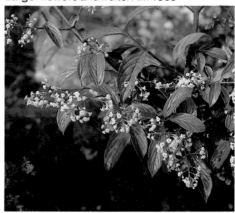

VIBURNUM × hillieri 'Winton'

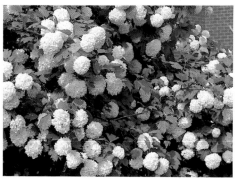

VIBURNUM opulus 'Sterile'

– – **'Sterile'** (*Roseum'*) LS "Snowball"
Conspicuous, creamy white, round heads of
sterile flowers. AGM 1964

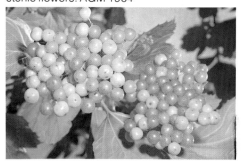

VIBURNUM opulus 'Xanthocarpum'

– – **'Xanthocarpum'** LS
Clear golden fruits, almost translucent when
ripe. AM 1932 FCC 1966 AGM 1969

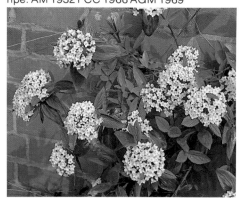

VIBURNUM 'Park Farm Hybrid'

– **'Park Farm Hybrid'** MS (E)
Strong, spreading habit. Fragrant white
flowers, pink in bud; April-May. AM 1949

– **plicatum** (*tomentosum 'Plicatum'*)
(*tomentosum 'Sterile'*) MS "Japanese
Snowball"
Dense, spreading habit. Globular heads of
white, sterile florets in double rows; May-June.
FCC 1893 AGM 1969
　'Grandiflorum' MS
Larger heads of flowers, tinged pink at
margins. AM 1961 AGM 1969
– – **'Lanarth'** MS
Strong growing. Characteristic, tiered
branching. (Form of *tomentosum*) AM 1930
AGM 1969

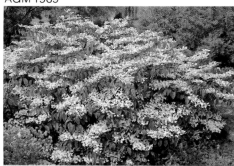

VIBURNUM plicatum 'Mariesii'

– – **'Mariesii'** MS
Distinctive horizontally tiered branches.
Abundant flowers. (Form of *tomentosum*)
AGM 1929

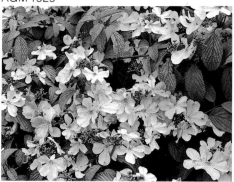

VIBURNUM plicatum 'Pink Beauty'

– – **'Pink Beauty'** MS
Ray florets turn pink with maturity. (Form of
tomentosum)
– – **'Rowallane'** MS
Similar to *'Lanarth'*. Conspicuous show of
fruits. (Form of *tomentosum*) AM 1942
FCC 1956 AGM 1969

––**tomentosum** (*V. tomentosum*) MS-LS
Tiered branches. Pleated leaves, often
colouring autumn. Flattened heads of creamy
flowers with marginal sterile ray florets, in
double rows on branch uppers; May-June.
Red fruits ripening black. AGM 1969
––**'Watanabe'** (*'Nanum Semperflorens'*) MS
Compact habit. Horizontal branching.
Flattened heads of flowers, intermittently
summer-late autumn. (Form of *tomentosum*)

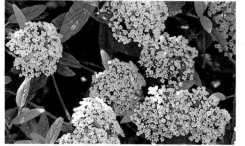

VIBURNUM 'Pragense'

– **'Pragense'** MS-LS (E)
Spreading habit. Elliptic, corrugated leaves to
10cm, glossy, dark green, white felted below.
Creamy white flowers, in terminal cymes, May.
– **propinquum** MS (E)
Dense, compact habit. Dark green, three-
nerved leaves. Greenish-white flowers,
summer. Blue-black, egg-shaped fruits.

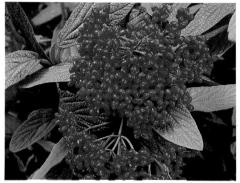

VIBURNUM rhytidophyllum

– **rhytidophyllum** LS (E)
Fast-growing. Glossy, corrugated leaves,
grey tomentose beneath. Heads of creamy
white flowers, May. Red fruits, turning black.
Plant two, to ensure fruiting. FCC 1907
––**'Roseum'** LS (E)
Flowers tinted rose-pink.

– **setigerum** (*theiferum*) MS
Open, lax habit. Distinctive leaves, altering
colour constantly, from metallic-blue-red
through greens to orange-yellow. Flowers
early summer. Orange yellow fruit clusters,
ripening bright red. AM 1925
– **tinus** LS (E) "Laurustinus" Hdg (0.5m)
Dense bushy habit. Dark glossy leaves.
Flattened heads of flowers, late autumn-early
spring. Metallic blue fruits ripening black.
Good for coastal sites. AGM 1969

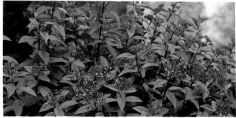

VIBURNUM tinus 'Eve Price'

––**'Eve Price'** MS (E)
Dense, compact habit. Carmine buds, flowers
pink-tinged. AM 1961
––**lucidum** LS (E)
Vigorous. Larger leaves. Larger flower heads;
March-April. AM 1972
––**'Purpureum'** LS (E)
Very dark leaves tinged purple when young.
––**'Variegatum'** MS (E) †
Leaves variegated creamy-yellow.
– **tomentosum** see *V. plicatum tomentosum*
––**'Plicatum'** see *V. plicatum*
– **wrightii** MS
Metallic green leaves, often colouring
autumn. Flowers, May. Glistening red fruits.
We recommend:
––**'Hessei'** SS
Broad, attractively-veined leaves.
Conspicuous sealing wax-red fruits.
VINCA – Apocynaceae PS (E) GC
"Periwinkle"
*Vigorous, trailing shrubs. Suitable for all fertile
soils.* A (f) 3
– **difformis** (*acutiflora*) (*media*) PS (E) GC
Glabrous plants, herbaceous in cold districts.
Solitary pale lilac blue flowers in leaf axils,
autumn-early winter.
– **major** PS (E) GC "Greater Periwinkle"
Rampant trailing habit, rooting at tips. Glossy,
hairy leaves. Bright blue flowers in leaf axils,
April-June.

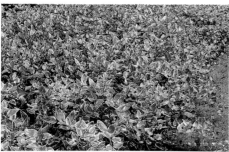

VINCA major 'Variegata'

––**'Variegata'** (*'Elegantissima'*) PS (E) GC
Leaves margined and mottled creamy white.

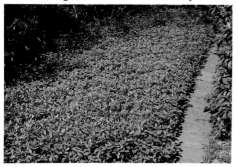

VINCA minor

– **minor** PS (E) GC "Lesser Periwinkle"
Trailing habit, rooting at intervals. Bright blue
flowers single in leaf axils; April-June, and
intermittently to autumn.
––**'Atropurpurea'** PS (E) GC
Plum-purple flowers.

––**'Aureovariegata'** PS (E) GC
Blue flowers. Leaves blotched yellow.
––**'Azurea Flore Pleno'** PS (E) GC
Sky blue, double flowers.
––**'Bowles' Variety'** PS (E) GC
Large blue flowers.
––**'Gertrude Jekyll'** PS (E) GC
White flowers. AGM 1962
––**'Multiplex'** PS (E) GC
Double, plum-purple flowers.
––**'Variegata'** PS (E) GC
Blue flowers. Leaves variegated creamy-
white.
VITEX – Verbenaceae MS ○
Requires good drainage and sun to ripen
growth and produce flowers. Excellent for
sunny wall.

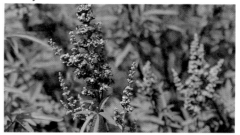

VITEX agnus-castus

– **agnus-castus** MS ○ "Chaste Tree"
Spreading habit. Aromatic. Grey downy
shoots. Slender racemes of fragrant, violet
flowers. September-October. AM 1934
––**'Silver Spire'** MS ○
Form with white flowers.

"WALNUT" see *JUGLANS*
"WATTLE" see *ACACIA*
"WAX MYRTLE" see *MYRICA cerifera*
"WAYFARING TREE" see *VIBURNUM*
lantana
WEIGELA – Caprifoliaceae SS-MS
Fresh green leaves. Funnel-shaped flowers
varying in colour, red-pink-white, produced

May-June. Easy cultivation, withstand
atmospheric pollution. C7
– **'Abel Carriere'** MS
Large, rosy carmine, yellow-throated flowers.
AGM 1939
– **'Avalanche'** MS
Vigorous. White flowers.

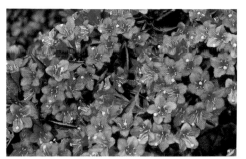

WEIGELA 'Bristol Ruby'

–**'Bristol Ruby'** MS
Vigorous, erect habit. Ruby red flowers.
AM 1954 AGM 1969
–**'Conquete'** MS
Very large, deep rose-pink flowers.
–**'Eva Rathke'** MS
Slow, compact growth. Red crimson flowers
with pale yellow anthers, over prolonged
period. FCC 1893
–**florida** (*amabilis* HORT) (*rosea*) MS
Reddish or rose-pink flowers, paler within. We
recommend the forms:
––**'Foliis Purpureis'** SS
Slower growing, compact habit. Purple-
flushed leaves. Pink flowers.

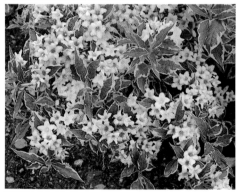

WEIGELA florida 'Variegata'

––**'Variegata'** MS
Compact. Leaves margined creamy white.
Pink flowers. AM 1968 AGM 1969

––**venusta** MS
Slightly larger, bright pink flowers, freely
borne.

––**'Versicolor'** MS
Flowers creamy-white changing to red.

–**hortensis** SS-MS
Leaves, white felted beneath. Reddish
flowers. We recommend the form:
––**'Nivea'** (*'Albiflora'*) MS
Comparatively large, white flowers. FCC 1891
–**'Looymansii Aurea'** MS ◑
Light golden foliage. Pink flowers.
–**'Majestueux'** MS

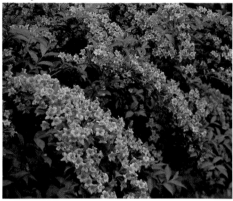

WEIGELA 'Majestueux'

Erect habit. Large madder pink, carmine-
throated flowers.
–**middendorffiana** SS ◑
Peeling bark. Bell-shaped sulphur yellow
flowers with dark orange markings. April-May.
Best given shelter. AM 1931
–**'Mont Blanc'** MS
Vigorous. Large, fragrant white flowers.
–**'Newport Red'** (*'Vanicek'*) MS
Large, bright red flowers.
–**praecox** MS
Vigorous. Honey scented, rose-pink flowers
with yellow markings, May onwards.
––**'Variegata'** MS
Leaves variegated creamy white.
–**rosea** see *W. florida*
"WHINBERRY" see *VACCINIUM myrtillus*
"WHITEBEAM" see *SORBUS aria*
"WHITEBEAM, SWEDISH" see *SORBUS
intermedia*
"WHORTLEBERRY" see *VACCINIUM
myrtillus*
"WINEBERRY" see *RUBUS phoenicolasius*
"WILLOW" see *SALIX*
"WING NUT" see *PTEROCARYA*
"WINTER JASMINE" see *JASMINUM
nudiflorum*
"WITCH HAZEL" see *HAMAMELIS*

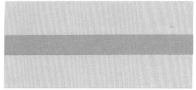

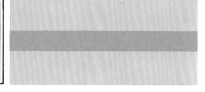

XANTHOCERAS – Sapindaceae LS
*Monotypic genus. Pinnate leaves and erect,
horse chestnut-like flower panicles. For all
fertile soils, good on chalk.*
– sorbifolium LS
Upright habit. White flowers with carmine eye,
May. Top shaped fruits. FCC 1876
XANTHORRHIZA (*ZANTHORRHIZA*) –
Ranunculaceae SS

*Monotypic genus. Suckering, thicket-forming
shrub. Requires a moist or clay soil – not for
shallow chalk.*
– simplicissima (*apiifolia*) SS "Yellow-root"
Pinnate leaves, burnished bronze-purple in
autumn. Drooping panicles of tiny purple
flowers, March-April. Bright yellow roots and
inner bark, bitter to the taste.
XANTHOXYLUM see *ZANTHOXYLUM*

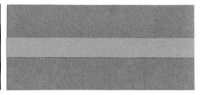

"YELLOW ROOT" see *XANTHORRHIZA
simplicissima*
"YELLOW WOOD" see *CLADRASTIS lutea*
YUCCA – Liliaceae DS-MS (E) ○
*Distinctive architectural plants. Long, sword-
like leaves in clumps or rosettes. Spectacular
panicles of drooping, lily-like, bell-shaped
flowers; July-August. Require hot, dry, well
drained site.*

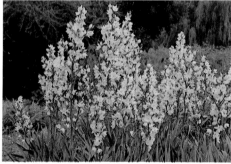

YUCCA filamentosa

– filamentosa DS (E) ○
Stemless. Dense clumps of leaves, margined
with curly white threads. Creamy-white
flowers in conical panicles 1–2m tall.
AGM 1969

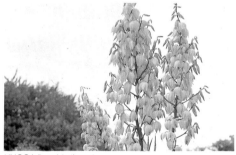

YUCCA flaccida 'Ivory'

– – 'Bright Edge' DS (E) ○
Leaves margined golden-yellow.
– – 'Variegata' DS (E) ○
Leaves striped and margined yellow.
– flaccida DS (E) ○
Stemless. Tufts of leaves with bent tips and
curly white threads along margins. Creamy
flowers in downy panicles 0.6–1.2m tall. We
recommend the clone:
– – 'Golden Sword' DS (E) ○
Leaves, with broad, central, yellow stripe.
– – 'Ivory' DS (E) ○
Large panicles of creamy white, green
stained flowers. AM 1966 FCC 1968
AGM 1969

– **glauca** (*angustifolia*) SS (E) ☼
Short stem. Rounded head of white margined, greyish leaves. Erect racemes of greenish white flowers, 1–1.5m tall.
– **gloriosa** MS (E) ☼ "Adam's Needle"
Trunk-like stem. Dense terminal head of vicious spine-tipped leaves. Creamy white flowers in erect conical panicles, 1–2m high.
– **recurvifolia** SS (E) ☼
Short stem. Long tapered leaves, recurved,

except for central leaves. Dense panicles of creamy white flowers, 0.6–1m high; late summer.
– **whipplei** (*Hesperoyucca whipplei*) SS (E) † ☼
Stemless. Dense globular clump of leaves. Dense panicles of large, fragrant greenish white flowers, edged purple – 1.8–3.6m tall; July-August. AM 1945
"YULAN" see *MAGNOLIA denudata*

ZANTHOXYLUM (*XANTHOXYLUM*) –
Rutaceae MS
Generally spiny branches. Leaves aromatic when crushed. Small insignificant flowers. Black or red fruits. For all soils, sun or shade.
– **piperitum** MS "Japan Pepper"
Neat compact habit. Pairs of flattened spines. Pinnate leaves, rich yellow in autumn. Greenish-yellow flowers, May-June. Reddish fruits, the black seeds ground for pepper in Japan.
– **schinifolium** MS
Single-thorned branches. Fern-like, pinnate leaves. Green-petalled flowers, late summer. Red fruits.
ZAUSCHNERIA – Onagraceae DS †
Excellent rock garden plants requiring warm, sunny, well drained sites.
– **californica** DS † "Californian Fuchsia"
Bushy habit. Downy, grey-green stems and leaves. Loose spikes of fuchsia-like red flowers with scarlet tubes, late summer-autumn.
– **cana** (*microphylla*) DS †
Grey stems and leaves. Loose spikes of red, scarlet tubed flowers, late summer-autumn. AM 1928
ZELKOVA – Ulmaceae MT-LT ♥
Smooth-barked trees. Simple toothed leaves. Small, monoecious, greenish flowers. Thrive in deep moist loamy soils, tolerate shade.

– **carpinifolia** (*crenata*) (*Planera richardii*) LT ♥
Slow growth. Smooth grey bark, flaking with age. Hairy shoots. Coarsely toothed leaves.
– **serrata** (*acuminata*) (*Planera acuminata*) MT ♥
Smooth, grey bark flaking with age. Coarsely-toothed leaves turn bronze or red, autumn.
ZENOBIA (*ANDROMEDA* in part) –
Ericaceae MS Semi-(E) ⚊ ☾
Monotypic genus. Requires lime-free soil, and preferably semi-shade.

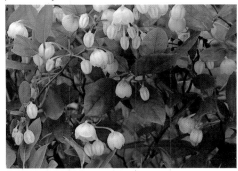

ZENOBIA pulverulenta

– **pulverulenta** (*speciosa*) MS Semi-(E) ⚊ ☾
Loose habit. Bloomy young shoots and leaves. Pendulous clusters of aniseed-scented, white, bell-shaped flowers; June-July. AM 1932 FCC 1934

Climbers
(including Wall Shrubs)

Contains some of the most beautiful of all woody plants. Reference is also made here to plants described in the Tree and Shrub section often treated as wall shrubs, including tender plants best grown against sheltered walls.

All climbers, even the self-clingers, require initial support until established. Many are useful ground cover plants.

ABELIA floribunda see Tree and Shrub section

ABUTILON see Tree and Shrub section

ACACIA see Tree and Shrub section

ACTINIDIA – Actinidiaceae
Vigorous climbers, often with edible fruit, suitable for walls, pergolas or tall stumps.

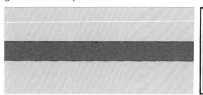

ACTINIDIA kolomikta

– **chinensis** "Chinese Gooseberry"
Large, heart-shaped leaves. Conspicuous creamy-white flowers in late summer. To secure edible fruits, both male and female plants are required. AM 1907

– **kolomikta**
Strikingly variegated leaves, white flushed pink in the terminal half, developing best in sun. Slightly fragrant white flowers, June. AM 1931

ADENOCARPUS see Tree and Shrub section

AKEBIA – Lardizabalaceae Semi-(E)
Vigorous, semi-evergreen twiners with attractive foliage. Good for training over hedges, small trees or old stumps. Unusual fruits, only produced after a mild spring and hot summer.

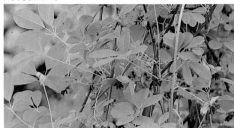

AKEBIA quinata

– **quinata** Semi-(E)
Leaves with five leaflets. Red-purple, fragrant flowers, April. Sausage-shaped, dark purple fruits. AM 1956

– **trifoliata** (*lobata*) Semi-(E)
Leaves with three leaflets. Dark purple flowers, April. Pale violet, sausage-shaped fruits.

AMPELOPSIS – Vitaceae
Ornamental vines climbing by tendrils. Good for covering walls, hedges etc. or training into trees. Attractive fruits formed after a long, hot summer and mild autumn. See also PARTHENOCISSUS *and* VITIS.
A (f) 12

– **brevipedunculata**
Vigorous climber, with "Hop"-like leaves. We recommend the following forms:

– –'Citrulloides'
Deeply five-lobed leaves. Attractive, small blue fruits.

– –'Elegans'
Leaves densely mottled white and tinged pink. Less vigorous habit.

– **megalophylla** (*Vitis megalophylla*) Large, bi-pinnate leaves up to 60cm long. Fruits purple, becoming black. A good specimen plant for a tall post or tree. AM 1903

– **sempervirens** HORT see *CISSUS striata*

– **veltchii** see *PARTHENOCISSUS tricuspidata 'Veitchii'*

ARISTOLOCHIA – Aristolochiaceae
Twining plants with mostly heart-shaped leaves and unusual flowers. Good for covering walls, fences or stumps or for training into trees.

– **heterophylla**
Rambling or climbing shrub with yellow flowers, blackish purple at the tip, June.

– **macrophylla** (*sipho*) "Dutchman's Pipe" Vigorous climber. Syphon-like, yellowish-green flowers, brownish purple flared mouth, June.

ASTERANTHERA – Gesneriaceae Cl (E) † ◑
A monotypic genus climbing by aerial roots. Best in leafy, acid or neutral soil.

– **ovata** Cl (E) † ◑
Trailing creeper, climbing walls or tree trunks in suitable conditions. Tubular, red flowers, white in throat, June. AM 1939

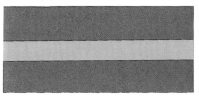

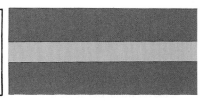

BERBERIDOPSIS – Flacourtiaceae (E) † ●
A monotypic genus. Best suited to a sheltered position in a moist, peaty soil.

– **corallina** (E) † ● "Coral Plant"
Leathery, dark green, spiny leaves, deep crimson flowers in pendant, terminal racemes, late summer. AM 1901

BIGNONIA – Bignoniaceae (E) ○
A monotypic genus related to Campsis *but climbing by tendrils.*

– **capreolata** (E) ○
Leaves with two leaflets 5-13cm long. Flowers tubular, orange-red in clusters, June. AM 1958

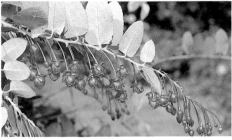
BERBERIDOPSIS corallina

"BLUEBELL CREEPER" see *SOLLYA heterophylla*

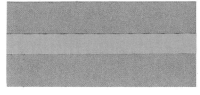

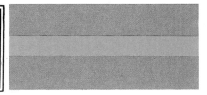

CALLISTEMON see Tree and Shrub section
CAMELLIA see Tree and Shrub section
CAMPSIS – Bignoniaceae ○

Two species of scandent shrubs with pinnate leaves and conspicuous, trumpet-shaped flowers August-September.

– grandiflora ○
Leaves with seven or nine glabrous leaflets.
Flowers deep orange and red in drooping
terminal panicles. Best on sheltered wall.
AM 1949
– radicans Cl ○ "Trumpet Vine"
Climbing by aerial roots but best given initial
support. Leaves with nine or eleven leaflets.
Flowers brilliant orange and scarlet in terminal
clusters.
– – 'Flava' (*'Yellow Trumpet'*) Cl ○
Flowers rich yellow. AM 1969
– × tagliabuana ○
A hybrid intermediate between the preceding
two species. We recommend the following
form:

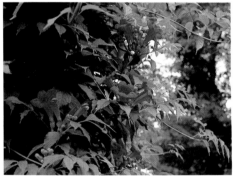

CAMPSIS × tagliabuana 'Madame Galen'

– – 'Madame Galen' ○
Panicles of salmon-red flowers. Vigorous.
Requires some support. AM 1959
CANTUA buxifolia see Tree and Shrub
section
CARPENTERIA californica see Tree and
Shrub section
CEANOTHUS see Tree and Shrub section
CELASTRUS – Celastraceae
*Vigorous, rampant climbers suitable for
growing over hedges, walls, tall shrubs or
trees.*
– orbiculatus
Twining, spiny shoots bear rounded leaves
which turn clear yellow in autumn. Scarlet and
gold-spangled split seed capsules in autumn.
Normally, male and female required for fruits if
hermaphrodite plants are also in cultivation.
CESTRUM see Tree and Shrub section
CHAENOMELES see Tree and Shrub section
CHIMONANTHUS see Tree and Shrub
section

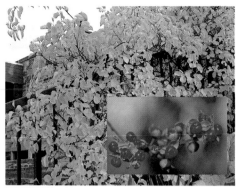

CELASTRUS orbiculatus

CISSUS – Vitaceae (E) †
*We recommend the following species for the
mildest areas only.*
– striata (*Vitis striata*) (*Ampelopsis
sempervirens* HORT) (E) † ○
Luxuriant climber for a sunny wall. Leaves with
five coarsely-toothed glossy, dark green
leaflets. Fruits like reddish-purple currants.
CLEMATIS – Ranunculaceae
The species of CLEMATIS *are in general of
easier cultivation than the large-flowered
hybrids. They are excellent climbers for
wooden supports, fences, or walls while the
more vigorous species are suitable for
training into large shrubs or trees. The flowers
are often followed by attractive, silken seed
heads. See also "Large Flowered Garden
Clematis".*

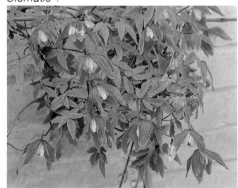

CLEMATIS alpina 'Frances Rivis'

– alpina
Blue or violet-blue flowers on long, slender
stalks, April-May. Good on a low wall or small
bush. AM 1894

– – 'Frances Rivis'
A vigorous, free flowering form with larger flowers. AM 1965

– armandii (E)
A vigorous and beautiful species. Flowers 5-6.5cm across in clusters, April-May. Best on a sunny wall. We recommend the following forms:

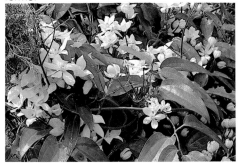

CLEMATIS armandii

– – 'Apple Blossom' (E)
Flowers white tinged pink. Young leaves bronze. AM 1926 FCC 1936 AGM 1938

– – 'Snowdrift' (E)
Flowers pure white. AGM 1969

– balearica see C. cirrhosa balearica

– campaniflora
A vigorous climber. Small, bowl-shaped, blue-tinted flowers, borne profusely, July-September.

– chrysocoma
Soft pink flowers 5 to 6.5cm across, borne profusely; early May-June, and again in late summer. AM 1936

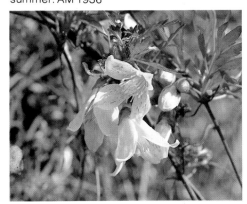

CLEMATIS cirrhosa balearica

– cirrhosa (E)
We recommend the following form:

– – balearica (C. balearica) (E) "Fern-leaved Clematis"
Prettily divided leaves, bronze in winter. Flowers 4 to 5cm across, pale yellow, spotted reddish purple within, throughout winter.

– colensoi see C. hookerana

– × durandii
Entire leaves up to 15cm long. Flowers dark blue, with central cluster of white stamens, often more than 10cm across. AGM 1942

– × eriostemon
Semi-herbaceous, reaching 2 to 2.5m, each year. We recommend the following form:

– – 'Hendersonii'
Flowers deep bluish-purple, widely bell-shaped and slightly fragrant. 5 to 6.5cm across, July-September.

– flammula
Vigorous, slender stems and bright green leaves making a dense tangle. Loose panicles of small, white, fragrant flowers. August to October. Good on tall hedges and walls.

– florida
We recommend the following form:

– – 'Sieboldii' (bicolor)
Flowers recalling a "Passion Flower", 8cm across, white with conspicuous central boss of violet-purple petaloid stamens, June-July. AM 1914

– hookerana (colensoi) (E) ☼
Fern-like, glossy green leaves. Yellowish-green, star-shaped fragrant flowers, 4cm across, May-June. AM 1961

– × jackmanii
A spectacular climber with violet-purple flowers 10 to 13cm across, July-October. FCC 1863 AGM 1930

– × jouiniana
Sub-shrubby climber, reaching 3.5m. We recommend the following form:

– – 'Cote d'Azur'
Small, azure-blue flowers, autumn. Excellent for covering low walls, mounds or tree stumps.

– macropetala
Relatively low growing climber to 2.5m with prettily divided leaves. Flowers 5.5 to 7.5cm across, violet-purple with conspicuous petaloid staminodes. Good on a low wall or fence. AM 1923 AGM 1934

– – 'Markham's Pink'
Flowers the shade of crushed strawberries.
AM 1935

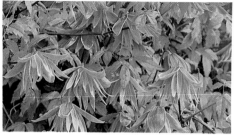

CLEMATIS macropetala 'Markham's Pink'

– – 'White Moth'
Flowers pure white.

– montana
Very vigorous. Trifoliolate leaves. Flowers 5-6.5cm across in profusion, May-June. Good for growing into trees, large shrubs or over hedges and walls. We recommend the following forms:

– – 'Alexander'
Creamy-white, sweetly-scented flowers.

– – 'Elizabeth'
Large, slightly fragrant, soft pink flowers.
AGM 1969

– – grandiflora
Vigorous form reaching 12m. Flowers white.
AGM 1969

– – rubens
Bronze-purple foliage, rose-pink flowers.
AM 1905 AGM 1969

– – 'Tetrarose'
Bronze foliage, lilac-rose flowers up to 7.5cm across.

– nutans see *C. rehderana*

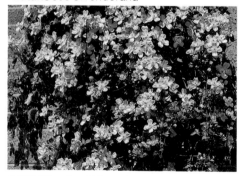

CLEMATIS montana 'Tetrarose'

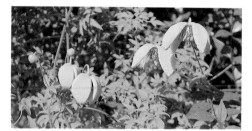

CLEMATIS orientalis

– orientalis "Orange-Peel Clematis"
Vigorous climber to 6m. Prettily divided, bluish leaves. Bell-shaped, nodding yellow flowers up to 5cm across with fleshy sepals, on slender stalks, August-September.
AM 1950

– rehderana (*nutans*)
Nodding, bell-shaped, soft primrose-yellow flowers up to 2cm long and cowslip-scented, in erect panicles, late summer and autumn.
AM 1936 AGM 1969

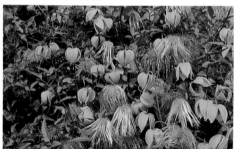

CLEMATIS tangutica

– tangutica
Prettily divided, sea-green leaves and nodding, rich-yellow, lantern-like flowers on long stalks – autumn. Silky seed heads. Good on low walls, fences, trellis and banks. AGM 1934

– viticella
Slender climber to 3.5m. Flowers violet, reddish-purple or blue, 4cm across, on slender stalks, summer-early autumn. We recommend the following forms:

– – 'Abundance'
Delicately veined flowers of soft purple.
AGM 1973

– – 'Alba Luxurians'
Flowers white, tinted mauve. AGM 1930

– – 'Kermesina'
Flowers crimson. AGM 1969

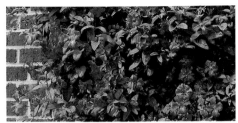
CLEMATIS viticella 'Abundance'

– – 'Royal Velours'
Flowers deep, velvety purple. AM 1948
AGM 1969

LARGE-FLOWERED GARDEN CLEMATIS
*Spectacular and colourful flowering climbers.
Best planted with the "heads" in sun and the
roots in shade in well-drained, good loamy
soil, to which has been added some well-
rotted manure and lime in some form. Can be
trained to wires on a wall or grown over
pergolas, trellises, tripods or into shrubs or
small trees but should be planted well away
from the roots of intended hosts. Respond well
to an annual mulch of well-rotted manure or
compost plus an ample supply of water.
Sometimes subject to "Clematis Wilt" for
which there is no known cure. This mainly
affects young plants with the sudden collapse
of a single shoot or the whole plant. Usually if
wilted shoots are pruned out, new young
growth will occur from the root or lower stem.*

Pruning
*a. LANUGINOSA (L) and PATENS (P)
groups. These normally flower in May and
June on the previous year's wood. Trim back
old flowering shoots immediately after
flowering. Old, dense habited plants may be ·
hard pruned in February, but the first crop of
flowers will be lost.
b. JACKMANII (J) and VITICELLA (V) groups.
These normally flower in late summer and
autumn on the current year's shoots. May be
hard pruned to within 30cm of the ground in
February or March. Old plants tend to become
bare at the base.*

– 'Barbara Dibley' (P)
Pansy-violet, striped deep carmine, May-
June, and again in September.

– 'Barbara Jackman' (P)
Deep violet, striped magenta, up to 15cm
across with 5 to 6 overlapping sepals. May-
June.

– 'Beauty of Worcester' (L)
Blue-violet, creamy-white stamens,
occasionally double, May-August.

– 'Bee's Jubilee' (L)
Blush-pink, banded carmine-rose.
Overlapping sepals.

– 'Blue Gem' (L)
Sky-blue, large. June-October.

– 'Comtesse de Bouchard' (J)
Soft rose-pink with yellow stamens, vigorous
and free flowering, June-August. AM 1936
AGM 1969

– 'Daniel Deronda' (P)
Large, violet-blue, paler at centre with creamy
stamens, often double. June-September.

– 'Ernest Markham' (V)
Glowing petunia-red, with a velvety sheen,
sepals rounded, June-September. AGM 1973

– 'Hagley Hybrid' (J)
Shell pink with chocolate-brown anthers, free
flowering. June-September.

– 'Henryi' (L)
Large, creamy-white with pointed sepals and
dark stamens, vigorous and free flowering;
May-June, and again in August-September.
AGM 1977

– 'H. F. Young' (L)
Large Wedgwood-blue, with broad,
overlapping, accuminate sepals and yellow
stamens.

– 'Huldine' (V) ☼
Pearly white, pointed sepals banded mauve
on the reverse; vigorous and free flowering,
July-October. AM 1934

– 'Jackmanii Superba' (J)
Large, rich, violet-purple with broad sepals;
vigorous and free flowering. July-September.

– 'Lady Betty Balfour' (V)
Deep velvety purple with golden stamens;
very vigorous, best in full sun, August-
October. AM 1912

– 'Lasurstern' (P)
Deep lavender blue, conspicuous white
stamens, broad, tapering, wavy-edged
sepals; May-June and again in early autumn.
AGM 1969

– 'Madam Edouard Andre' (J)
Rich crimson with yellow stamens and pointed
sepals, very free flowering. June-August.

– 'Marcel Moser' (P)
Mauve, tapered sepals with a deep carmine
bar. May-June. AM 1897

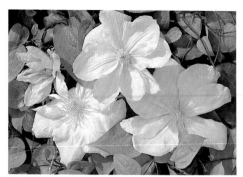

CLEMATIS 'Marie Boisselot'

– **'Marie Boisselot'** (P)
Large, pure white with cream stamens and broad, rounded, overlapping sepals; vigorous and free flowering. May-October.
– **'Mrs. Cholmondely'** (J)
Large, pale blue with long-pointed sepals vigorous and free flowering May-August. FCC 1873
– **'Mrs. N. Thompson'** (P)
Deep violet with a scarlet bar, pointed sepals. May-June, and September.

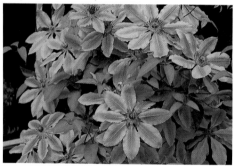

CLEMATIS 'Nelly Moser'

– **'Nelly Moser'** (L)
Large pale mauve-pink with carmine bar. Very free flowering. Best on a north wall, or in some shade. May-June, and again August-September. AGM 1969
– **'Perle d'Azur'** (J)
Light blue with broad sepals. Vigorous and free flowering, June-August. AGM 1973
– **'The President'** (P)
Deep purple-blue, silvery reverse, free flowering. June-September. FCC 1876
– **'Ville de Lyon'** (V)
Bright carmine-red, deeper at margins, with golden stamens. July-October. AM 1901

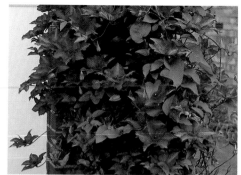

CLEMATIS 'The President'

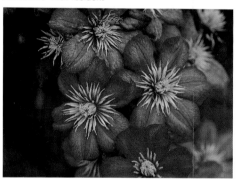

CLEMATIS 'Ville de Lyon'

– **'Vyvyan Pennell'** (P)
Deep violet blue suffused purple and carmine in the centre, fully double. May-July. Single flowers in autumn.
– **'W. E. Gladstone'** (L)
Very large, silky lavender with purple anthers. Vigorous and free flowering. June-September. FCC 1881
– **'William Kennet'** (L)
Lavender-blue with dark stamens, sepals with crimped margins. June-August.
CLIANTHUS puniceus see Tree and Shrub section
"CLIMBING HYDRANGEA" see HYDRANGEA petiolaris
CORONILLA glauca see Tree and Shrub section
COTONEASTER see Tree and Shrub section
CRINODENDRON see Tree and Shrub section
CYTISUS battandieri see Tree and Shrub section
– **'Porlock'** see Tree and Shrub section

DAPHNE odora see Tree and Shrub section
DECUMARIA – Hydrangeaceae Cl
Two species, climbing by aerial roots.
Succeed in sun or shade, on a wall or tree
trunk.
– **barbara** Cl Semi-(E)
Climber to 9m. Leaves ovate, to 13cm long.
Small, white flowers in small clusters, June-
July.

– **sinensis** Cl (E)
Climber to 5m, narrow leaves to 9cm long.
Small, green and white, honey-scented
flowers in clusters, May.
DENDROMECON see Tree and Shrub
section
DREGEA see *WATTAKAKA*
DRIMYS see Tree and Shrub section

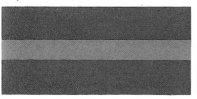

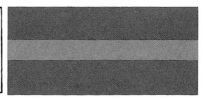

ECCREMOCARPUS – Bignoniaceae
The following species is hardy in a sheltered
corner in mild areas.
– **scaber**
Vigorous climber with bipinnate leaves

ending in slender tendrils. Scarlet to orange-
yellow, tubular flowers produced throughout
summer and autumn.
ERIOBOTRYA see Tree and Shrub section
ESCALLONIA see Tree and Shrub section

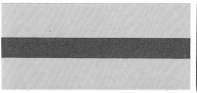

FEIJOA see Tree and Shrub section
FORSYTHIA suspensa and **cvs.** see Tree
and Shrub section

FREMONTODENDRON see Tree and Shrub
section

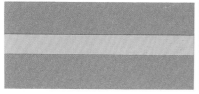

GARRYA elliptica see Tree and Shrub
section

"GRANADILLA" see *PASSIFLORA edulis*

HEDERA – Araliaceae "Ivy" CI (E)
*Evergreen climbers, clinging by aerial roots.
They thrive in almost any soil or situation, sun
or shade and are tolerant of atmospheric
pollution.* A (f) 2 and 5
– **canariensis** CI (E) GC "Canary Island Ivy"
Leaves bright, glossy green, up to 15 or 20cm
long, entire or obscurely three-lobed, often
bronze in winter.
– – **'Gloire de Marengo'** CI (E) GC
Leaves deep green in centre merging to
silvery-grey and margined creamy-white.
FCC 1880 AGM 1973 AMT 1980
– **chrysocarpa** see *H. helix poetica*
– **colchica** CI (E) GC "Persian Ivy"
Vigorous species. Dark green, thick, leathery
leaves up to 20cm or more long, usually entire.
We recommend the following forms:
– – **'Dentata'** CI (E) GC
Leaves very large, softer green more irregular
and occasionally toothed. AMT 1980

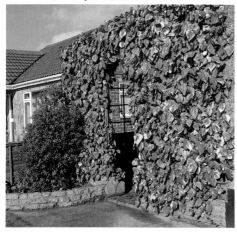

HEDERA colchica 'Dentata Variegata'

– – **'Dentata Variegata'** CI (E) GC
Leaves conspicuously margined creamy-
yellow, maturing creamy-white. AM 1907
AGM 1969 FCCT 1980
– – **'Sulphur Heart'** (*'Paddy's Pride'*) CI (E) GC
Large leaves, boldly marked with an irregular

central splash of yellow. AMT 1980
– **helix** CI (E) GC "Common Ivy"
A very variable climber useful for growing on
walls or trees or as ground cover, where little
else will grow. We recommend the following
forms:
– – **'Adam'** CI (E) GC
Leaves small, conspicuously margined with
white.
– – **'Arborescens'** SS (E)
A shrubby form, making a broad, densely
leafy mound.
– – **'Bird's Foot'** CI (E) GC
Leaves small, very deeply divided into linear
lobes.
– – **'Buttercup'** CI (E) GC
Leaves rich yellow, becoming yellowish-
green or pale green with age. AGM 1973
– – **'Caenwoodiana'** CI (E) GC
Small leaves regularly divided into narrow
lobes.
– – **'Cavendishii'** CI (E) GC
Small, angular leaves, mottled grey and
broadly margined creamy white.
– – **'Chicago'** CI (E) GC
Small, dark green leaves frequently blotched
bronze-purple.
– – **'Chicago Variegata'** CI (E) GC
Similar to *'Chicago'* with leaves broadly
margined creamy white.
– – **'Deltoidea'** CI (E) GC
Leaves with two rounded and overlapping
basal lobes, bronze tinged in winter. Neat,
close habit.
– – **'Digitata'** CI (E) GC
Leaves broad, divided into five finger-like
lobes.
– – **'Emerald Gem'** see under *poetica*
– – **'Feastii'** see *'Sagittifolia'*
– – **'Glacier'** CI (E) GC
Leaves silver-grey with a narrow white margin.
AMT 1980
– – **'Gold Child'** CI (E) GC
Leaves conspicuously margined with bright
yellow.

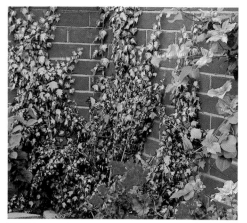

HEDERA helix 'Goldheart'

– – **'Goldheart'** Cl (E)
A striking form. Leaves with conspicuous
yellow central splash. AM 1970 AGM 1973
– – **'Green Ripple'** Cl (E) GC
Small jaggedly-lobed leaves, the central lobe
long and tapering. AMT 1980
– – **'Hibernica'** Cl (E) GC
Large, dark green, usually five-lobed leaves
up to 15cm across. Vigorous and particularly
useful as ground cover. AMT 1980
– – **'Ivalace'** Cl (E) GC
Glossy, green leaves, crimped at the margin.
FCCT 1980

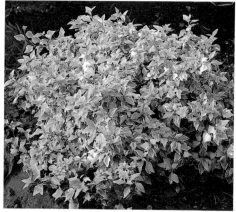

HEDERA helix 'Little Diamond'

– – **'Little Diamond'** (E) GC
Leaves green, mottled grey, with creamy-
white margin, entire or three-lobed. Dwarf,
bushy habit. AMT 1980

– – **'Manda's Crested'** Cl (E) GC
Bright green sharply pointed five-lobed
leaves, colouring reddish in winter. Neat,
mound forming habit. FCCT 1980
– – **'Marginata Elegantissima'** (*'Tricolor'*) Cl
(E) GC
Small, grey-green leaves margined white,
edged rose-pink in winter. *'Silver Queen'* is
similar.
– – **'Marmorata Minor'** Cl (E) GC
Leaves small, mottled with cream and grey,
occasionally pink tinged in winter.

– – **poetica** (*H. chrysocarpa*) Cl (E) GC
Bright green, shallowly lobed leaves, fruits
yellow. Older leaves bright copper, veined
green, in winter. *'Emerald Gem'* is a named
clone.
– – **'Sagittifolia'** (*'Feastii'*) Cl (E) GC
Five-lobed leaves, the central lobe long and
triangular.
– – **'Shamrock'** Cl (E) GC
Small, green, 3-lobed leaves, side lobes bent
forward, dense habit. Leaves copper tinged in
winter.
– – **'Silver Queen'** see under *'Marginata
Elegantissima'*
– – **'Sulphur Heart'** see *H. colchica 'Sulphur
Heart'*
– – **'Tres Coupe'** Cl (E) GC
Very small, five-lobed leaves, long pointed
centre lobe, small pointed basal lobes. Bushy.
Slow.
– – **'Tricolor'** see *'Marginata Elegantissima'*

– **hibernica** see *H. helix 'Hibernica'*
HOLBOELLIA – Lardizabalaceae (E) ☼
Twiners with compound leaves.

– **coriacea** (E) ☼ .
Vigorous climber to 6m or more. Leaves with
three glossy green leaflets. Small flowers
April-May; purplish, fleshy pods.
"HONEYSUCKLE" see *LONICERA*

"HONEYSUCKLE, CAPE" see *TECOMARIA
capensis*
"HOP" see *HUMULUS*
HUMULUS – Cannabidaceae
*The following species is herbaceous but
useful for covering hedges, shrubs etc.*
– **lupulus** "Hop"
Scrambling climber, three to five lobed,
coarsely toothed leaves. Small flowers in late
summer followed by "Hops".

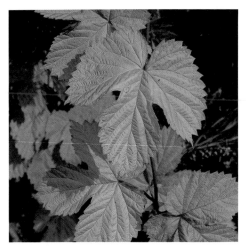

HUMULUS lupulus 'Aureus'

– –'Aureus'
Leaves soft yellow. Best in full sun.
HYDRANGEA – Hydrangeaceae Cl
*Climbing shrubs with aerial roots. Happy in
sun or shade in all soils. Tolerant of
atmospheric pollution.*
– petiolaris Cl "Climbing Hydrangea"
Vigorous climber, excellent on walls or trees.

Mound forming when grown as a shrub.
Greenish-white flowers, with several white
sterile florets; large clusters, June. AGM 1924
– serratifolia Cl (E)
Dark green, entire, leathery leaves. Small,
creamy-white flowers in dense panicles, late
summer. AM 1952

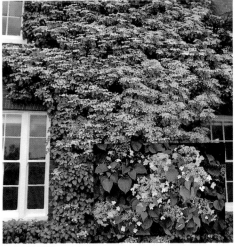

HYDRANGEA petiolaris

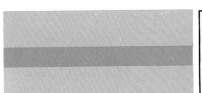

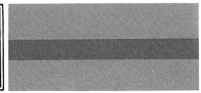

ITEA ilicifolia see Tree and Shrub section
"IVY" see *HEDERA*

"IVY, BOSTON" see *PARTHENOCISSUS
. tricuspidata*

"JASMINE" see *JASMINUM*

"JASMINE, CHILEAN" see *MANDEVILLA
suaveolens*

JASMINUM – Oleaceae "Jasmine"
"Jessamine"
*Twining, scandent shrubs. Small, trumpet-
shaped, usually fragrant flowers. Best in full
sun. Tender species are excellent for
conservatory.*

– azoricum (E) †
Trifoliolate leaves. Clusters of white, sweetly
scented flowers, purple flushed in bud,
summer and winter. AM 1934
– humile see Tree and Shrub section
– mesnyi (*primulinum*) Semi-(E) †
Four-angled shoots. Trifoliolate leaves. Bright
yellow, semi-double flowers 4cm long, March-
May. FCC 1903
– nudiflorum see Tree and Shrub section
– officinale "Common White Jasmine"
Vigorous twiner with pinnate leaves. Flowers
white, deliciously fragrant, in clusters, June-
September. AGM 1973 A (g) 10
– – 'Affine' (*'Grandiflorum'*)
Flowers slightly larger, pink tinged on the
outside.
– – 'Argenteovariegatum'
Leaves grey-green, margined creamy white.
– – 'Aureum'
Leaves blotched and suffused with yellow.

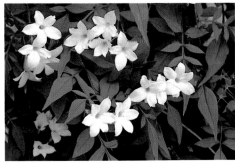
JASMINUM officinale

– polyanthum (E) †
Pinnate leaves with up to seven leaflets.
Flowers white, flushed pink, intensely
fragrant, throughout summer. AM 1941
FCC 1949
– × stephanense
Leaves simple or with up to five leaflets, often
variegated on vigorous shoots. Pale pink,
fragrant flowers, June-July. AM 1937
– suavissimum †
Slender, twining stems. Linear leaves up to
6cm long. Sweetly fragrant, white flowers in
loose panicles, late summer.

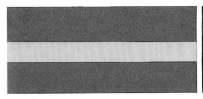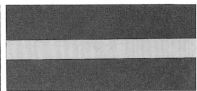

KERRIA japonica 'Pleniflora' see Tree and
Shrub section

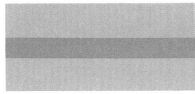

LAGERSTROEMIA see Tree and Shrub
section

LAPAGERIA – Philesiaceae (E) † ⟋ ◑
A monotypic genus; for a cool, moist soil, on a

sheltered wall. An excellent conservatory plant.

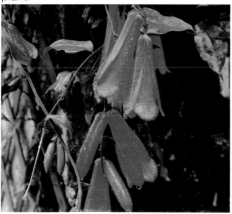

LAPAGERIA rosea

– rosea (E) † ⚹ ◑
Strong, wiry stems reaching 4 to 5m. Leathery leaves. Flowers rose-crimson, fleshy, bell-shaped, 7.5cm long by 5cm across, borne singly or in pendulous clusters, summer and autumn. FCC 1974

LONICERA – Caprifoliaceae "Honeysuckle"
Includes some of the loveliest and most popular of all climbers. Seen at their best when scrambling over bushes or tree stumps, trellises or pergolas.

– × americana (*grata*)
Vigorous, free-flowering. Flowers, 4 to 5cm long, fragrant, white, pale then deep yellow, tinged purple, June-July. AM 1937 AGM 1955

– × brownii "Scarlet Trumpet Honeysuckle"
Deciduous or Semi-(E). With long leaves, glaucous beneath. We recommend the following form:

– – 'Fuchsioides'
Flowers 2.5 to 4cm long, orange-scarlet in late spring and again in late summer. See also *L. 'Dropmore Scarlet'*.

– caprifolium (*'Early Cream'*) "Perfoliate Honeysuckle"
Vigorous. Glaucous leaves. Flowers fragrant, 4 to 5cm long creamy white, often tinged pink, June-July. Berries orange-red.

– – 'Pauciflora'
Flowers rose-tinted on the outside.

– 'Dropmore Scarlet'
Vigorous climber with clusters of bright scarlet, tubular flowers, July-October.

– etrusca
Vigorous, deciduous or semi-(E). Flowers fragrant, cream, becoming yellow, June-July. Best in full sun.

– flexuosa see *L. japonica repens*

– grata see *L. × americana*

– × heckrottii (*'Gold Flame'*)
Spreading shrub with scandent branches. Flowers fragrant, 4 to 5cm long, yellow, heavily flushed purple.

– henryi (E) or Semi-(E)
A vigorous climber. We recommend the following form:

– – subcoriacea (E) or Semi-(E)
Long, dark green, leathery leaves. Flowers yellow stained red, June-July. Black berries.

– japonica (E) or Semi-(E) GC
Vigorous. Useful for concealing unsightly objects. Flowers produced continuously from June onwards. We recommend the following forms:
A (g) or (b) 4

– – 'Aureoreticulata' (E) or Semi-(E)
Bright green leaves conspicuously veined with golden yellow. AGM 1969

– – 'Halliana' (E) or Semi-(E)
Flowers white, changing to yellow, very fragrant. AGM 1969

– – repens (*L. flexuosa*) (E) or Semi-(E)
Leaves and shoots flushed purple. Flowers very fragrant, flushed purple on the outside.

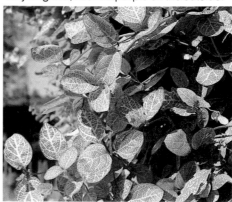

LONICERA japonica 'Aureoreticulata'

– periclymenum "Woodbine"
Our common, native honeysuckle. Vigorous. Richly fragrant flowers; red berries. We recommend the following forms:
C or E 8 or 9

– – **'Belgica'** "Early Dutch Honeysuckle"
Flowers reddish purple outside fading
yellowish, May-June, and again late summer.

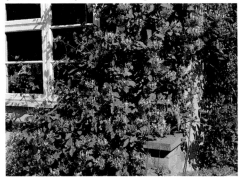

LONICERA periclymenum 'Serotina'

– – **'Serotina'** "Late Dutch Honeysuckle"
Flowers rich reddish purple outside, July-
October. AGM 1973

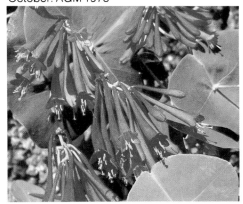

LONICERA sempervirens

– **sempervirens** (E) or Semi-(E) "Trumpet
Honeysuckle"
Rich green leaves. Flowers 4 to 5cm long rich
orange-scarlet outside, yellow within, late
summer-early autumn. AM 1964 A (g) or (b) 4
– **splendida** (E) or Semi-(E) †
A beautiful climber. Glaucous leaves.
Fragrant flowers, reddish purple outside,
yellowish-white within, summer.
– × **tellmanniana**
Flowers 5cm long, rich, coppery-yellow
flushed red in bud in large clusters, June-July.
Best with the roots in shade. AM 1931
AGM 1969

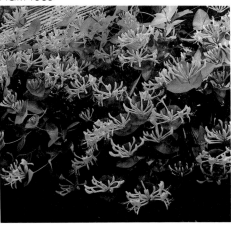

LONICERA tragophylla

– **tragophylla**
The largest flowered and most showy
climbing honeysuckle. Flowers 6 to 9cm long,
bright yellow in large clusters, June-July. At its
best with the roots in shade.

MAGNOLIA, in particular *M. delavayi* and *M. grandiflora* see Tree and Shrub section
MANDEVILLA – Apocynaceae
Mainly tropical climbers. The following succeeds on a sheltered wall in mild areas.

Makes an excellent conservatory plant.
– **suaveolens** † ○ "Chilean Jasmine"
Slender-stemmed climber with pointed, heart-
shaped leaves. Fragrant, white, periwinkle-
like flowers in clusters, summer. AM 1957

MICHELIA see Tree and Shrub section
MUEHLENBECKIA – Polygonaceae GC
Slender stemmed creepers or climbers with tiny flowers. Useful ground cover, or over tree stumps, etc.
– axillaris GC
Prostrate, forming dense carpets of intertwining, thread-like stems. Small, rounded leaves.
– complexa † GC
Slender, dark, interlacing stems reach 6m, on suitable support. Leaves variable, rounded to fiddle-shaped.

MUTISIA – Compositae (E) ☼ "Climbing Gazania"
Climbing or trailing shrubs. Colourful, gazania-like flowerheads produced singly on long stalks. Best in a well drained soil with the roots in shade.
– oligodon (E) ☼
Suckering, trailing shrub to 1.5m. Oblong, coarsely toothed leaves forming a low thicket. Flower heads 5 to 7.5cm across, salmon-pink petals, summer and intermittently into autumn. AM 1928
MYRTUS see Tree and Shrub section

PARTHENOCISSUS – Vitaceae
High climbing, mainly self-clinging vines, useful for covering large walls or tree trunks. Leaves often richly coloured in autumn. See also AMPELOPSIS *and* VITIS. A (f) 12

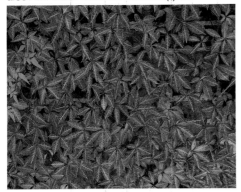

PARTHENOCISSUS henryana

– henryana (*Vitis henryana*) Cl
Leaves with three to five leaflets, dark green or bronze with silvery white veins, red in autumn. AM 1906 AGM 1936
– himalayana (*Vitis himalayana*) Cl
Vigorous climber, leaves with three dark green leaflets, rich crimson in autumn.
– – rubrifolia Cl
Leaflets smaller, purple when young.

– quinquefolia (*Vitis quinquefolia*) Cl "Virginia "Virginia Creeper"
Tall growing. Excellent for high walls, trees etc. Leaves with five leaflets, brilliant orange and scarlet in autumn. AGM 1969
– thomsonii (*Vitis thomsonii*)
Slender habit. Leaves of five, glossy green leaflets. Young growth purple, rich crimson and scarlet in autumn. Fruits black. FCC 1903

– triscuspidata (*Vitis inconstans*) Cl "Boston Ivy"
Vigorous climber commonly planted on old walls. Leaves very variable, ovate or trifoliolate on young plants, three lobed on mature plants, rich crimson and scarlet in autumn. Often incorrectly called "Virginia Creeper".

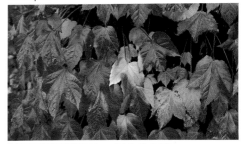

PARTHENOCISSUS tricuspidata 'Veitchii'

– – **'Veitchii'** (*Ampelopsis veitchii*) Cl
Smaller leaves, purple tinged when young.
PASSIFLORA (including *TACSONIA*) –
Passifloraceae † ○ "Passion Flower"
Climbing by tendrils, best on sunny, sheltered
wall. The unusual flowers are borne singly on
long stalks. Petals and sepals often similar
and known as tepals. Inside these is a
conspicuous ring of filaments (corona).
– **'Allardii'** † ○
Large, three-lobed leaves. Flowers 9 to
11.5cm across, tepals white shaded pink,
corona white and deep cobalt blue, summer-
autumn.
– **antioquiensis** (*Tacsonia vanvolxemii*) † ○
Leaves entire or deeply three-lobed. Flowers
pendulous 10 to 13cm across, tube rich rose
red, small, violet corona, late summer-
autumn.

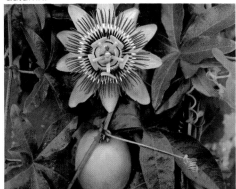

PASSIFLORA caerulea

– **caerulea** † ○ "Blue Passion Flower"
Vigorous, fairly hardy species. Dense habit.
Evergreen in mild areas. Leaves five to seven
lobed. Flowers slightly fragrant, 7.5 to 10cm
across, tepals white or pink tinged, corona
blue at tips, white in centre, purple at base;
summer-autumn.
– – **'Constance Elliott'** † ○
Flowers ivory white. FCC 1884
– **edulis** † ○ "Granadilla"
Vigorous. Deeply three-lobed leaves. Flowers
6cm across, tepals white, green without, curly
white filaments banded with purple,
throughout summer.
– **'Exoniensis'** (*Tacsonia 'Exoniensis'*) † ○
Beautiful hybrid. Deeply three-lobed leaves.
Flowers pendulous, 10 to 13cm across, tepals
rose-pink. Conservatory only.

– **racemosa** † ○ "Red Passion Flower"
Leaves usually three-lobed. Flowers vivid
scarlet with purple, white-tipped, outer
filaments, in drooping racemes – summer.
Conservatory only.
– **umbilicata** (*Tacsonia umbilicata*) † ○
Vigorous, fairly hardy species. Small violet
flowers.
"PASSION FLOWER" see *PASSIFLORA*
PILEOSTEGIA – Hydrangeaceae Cl (E)
*Evergreen climbers with aerial roots. The
following is suitable for wall or tree trunk.*

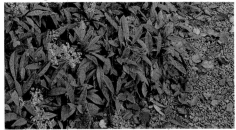

PILEOSTEGIA viburnoides

– **viburnoides** Cl (E)
Dark green, leathery leaves, up to 15cm long.
Flowers creamy-white in crowded, terminal
panicles – late summer-autumn. AM 1914
POLYGONUM – Polygonaceae
*Of the climbing species of this large genus we
recommend the following. Good for covering
unsightly objects, hedges, fences or for
growing into trees.*

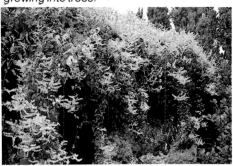

POLYGONUM baldschuanicum

– **baldschuanicum** "Russian Vine"
Very vigorous climber up to 12m.
Conspicuous panicles of tiny, pink-tinged
flowers, summer and autumn. AM 1899 AGM
1928
PUNICA see Tree and Shrub section
PYRACANTHA see Tree and Shrub section

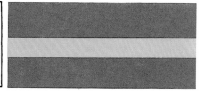

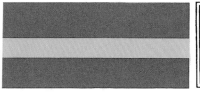

RAPHIOLEPIS see Tree and Shrub section
RUBUS – Rosaceae
Of the climbing species of this genus, we recommend the following:
– henryi bambusarum (E)
Long, scandent stems reaching 6m, on suitable support. Leaves with three narrow leaflets, glossy dark green above, white-felted beneath. Pink flowers, summer. Black fruits.
"RUSSIAN VINE" see *POLYGONUM baldschuanicum*

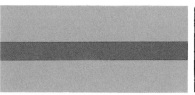

SCHISANDRA – Schisandraceae
Attractive, flowering climbers for walls, fences or for growing into shrubs or trees. Male and female flowers on separate plants. Females bear attractive berries.
– grandiflora
Leathery, conspicuously veined leaves, flowers up to 3cm across, May-June. Berries scarlet. We recommend the following:
– – cathayensis
Flowers clear rose-pink.
– – rubriflora (*S. rubriflora*)
Flowers deep crimson in late spring. AM 1925
– propinqua sinensis
Short-stalked, yellowish terracotta flowers – late summer-autumn. Berries scarlet.
SCHIZOPHRAGMA – Hydrangeaceae Cl
Ornamental climbers with aerial roots. Small creamy-white flowers in large heads, each head margined with several cream-coloured sterile florets. Suitable for walls, trees or stumps. Flower best in full sun.
– hydrangeoides Cl
Rounded, coarsely toothed leaves. Flower-heads up to 25cm across, July. FCC 1885
– – 'Roseum' Cl
Sterile florets rose-flushed. AM 1939

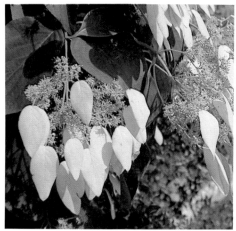
SCHIZOPHRAGMA integrifolium

– integrifolium Cl
Slender-pointed, entire or slightly toothed leaves. Flower-heads to 30cm across with large sterile florets up to 9cm long, July. AM 1936 FCC 1963 AGM 1969
SENECIO – Compositae
This large genus contains only a few climbers of which we recommend:

278

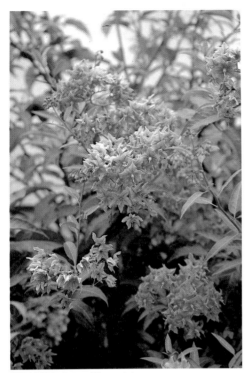

SOLANUM crispum 'Glasnevin'

SOLANUM – Solanaceae ○
The climbing members of this genus make spectacular wall plants given a sunny, sheltered position.
– crispum Semi-(E) ○
We recommend the following form:
– –'Glasnevin' (*'Autumnale'*) Semi-(E) ○
A vigorous scrambling shrub bearing loose corymbs of rich purple-blue, yellow centred flowers, summer and autumn. AM 1955 AGM 1969
– jasminoides Semi-(E) † ○
Fast-growing, twining shrub. Glossy green leaves. Flowers pale slate-blue, yellow in the centre, in loose clusters, summer-autumn.
– –'Album' Semi-(E) † ○
Flowers white with a yellow centre. AM 1977

SOLLYA – Pittosporaceae (E) † ○
Beautiful twining plants for very mild area or conservatory. We recommend the following:
– heterophylla (E) † ○ "Bluebell Creeper"
Slender stems to 2m or more. Nodding clusters of delicate, bell-shaped, sky-blue flowers, summer-autumn.

SOPHORA see Tree and Shrub section

STAUNTONIA – Lardizabalaceae (E)
Evergreen, twining shrubs. The following species requires a sheltered wall in sun or semi-shade.
– hexaphylla (E)
Vigorous climber to 10m or more. Leaves with three to seven, leathery leaflets. Flowers 2cm across, fragrant, white tinged violet, borne in racemes in spring. Edible, purple-tinged fruits produced after a warm, dry summer. AM 1960

– scandens Semi-(E) ○
Long scandent stems up to 6m. Coarsely toothed, often lobed leaves. Small, bright yellow flower-heads in large panicles, autumn. Best in a sheltered position and allowed to scramble over a bush or hedge.

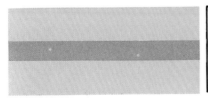

TACSONIA see *PASSIFLORA*
TECOMA see *CAMPSIS*
TECOMARIA – Bignoniaceae
The following species requires a warm, sunny wall in a sheltered position or a conservatory.
– capensis (E) † ○
Vigorous twining shrub with pinnate leaves. Brilliant scarlet, trumpet-shaped flowers, late

summer.
TIBOUCHINA see Tree and Shrub section
TRACHELOSPERMUM – Apocynaceae Cl (E) † ○
Beautiful, self clinging climbers with attractive sweetly-scented, jasmine-like flowers, suitable for a sheltered wall in all but the coldest localities.

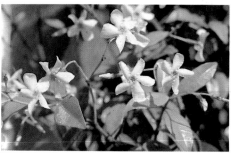

TRACHELOSPERMUM asiaticum

– asiaticum Cl (E) † ○
Dark, glossy green leaves, flowers 2cm
across creamy-white, buff yellow in centre,
becoming yellow, fragrant.
– jasminoides Cl (E) † ○
Dark, polished green leaves. Flowers 2.5cm
across, white becoming cream. Requires a
warm wall or conservatory. AM 1934
– – 'Variegatum' Cl (E) † ○
Leaves margined and splashed creamy-
white.

"VINE, TRUMPET" see *CAMPSIS radicans*
"VIRGINIA CREEPER" see
PARTHENOCISSUS quinquefolia and *P.
tricuspidata*
VITEX see Tree and Shrub section
VITIS – Vitaceae
*Ornamental vines, climbing by tendrils, often
giving rich autumn colour. Most effective
when growing into a large tree or covering an
old hedge or stump but can be trained to
cover walls, bridges or fences. Small greenish
flowers are followed by small grapes after a
hot, dry season.* (f) 12 or 1

– amurensis
Vigorous species with reddish young shoots.
Leaves up to 25cm across, three to five lobed,
rich crimson and purple in autumn. Fruits
black.
– betulifolia
Toothed or shallowly lobed leaves richly
coloured in autumn. Fruits blue-black. AM
1917
– 'Brant' (*vinifera 'Brant'*)
Popular, hardy, fruiting vine reaching 9m, or
more on suitable support. Dark purple-black,
bloomy, sweet grapes. AM 1970
– coignetiae
Possibly the most spectacular vine. Large
leaves up to 30cm across, brilliant crimson
and scarlet in autumn. Fruits 12mm across,
black, bloomed purple. AGM 1969

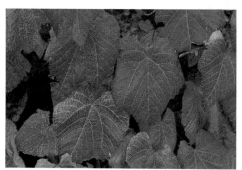

VITIS coignetiae

– davidii
Vigorous climber with spiny shoots. Leaves
heart-shaped, dark glossy green above,
glaucous and bristly beneath, rich crimson in
autumn. AM 1903
– henryana see *PARTHENOCISSUS
henryana*
– himalayana see *PARTHENOCISSUS
himalayana*
– inconstans see *PARTHENOCISSUS
tricuspidata*
– megalophylla see *AMPELOPSIS
megalophylla*
– pulchra
Reddish shoots and coarsely toothed leaves
reddish when young, brilliant scarlet in
autumn.

– **striata** see *CISSUS striata*
– **thomsonii** see *PARTHENOCISSUS
thomsonii*
– **vinifera** "Grape Vine"
We recommend the following forms which are
useful for ornamental foliage as well as fruits.
– – **'Brant'** see *V. 'Brant'*

– – **'Incana'** "Dusty Miller Grape"
Leaves grey-green, with a white, cobwebby
down. Fruits black.
– – **'Purpurea'** " Ieinturier Grape"
Leaves claret red when young becoming
deep vinous purple. AM 1958 AGM 1969

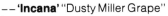

WATTAKAKA (*DREGEA*) – **Asclepiadaceae**
*We recommend the following species for a
warm, sheltered wall or conservatory.*
– **sinensis** (*Dregea sinensis*) †
Slender stemmed climber to 3m with ovate
leaves, grey felted beneath. Deliciously
scented white flowers with central zone of red
spots, in long-stalked umbels, summer. AM
1954
WISTERIA – Leguminosae
*Beautiful climbers with pinnate leaves and
long racemes of white, pink, blue or mauve
pea-flowers, May and June, and often later.
Best in full sun on a wall, pergola or into a tree.*
– **floribunda** "Japanese Wisteria"
Up to 4m or more. Leaves with thirteen to
nineteen leaflets. Flowers fragrant, with the
leaves. We recommend the following forms:

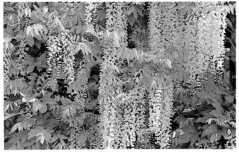

WISTERIA floribunda 'Alba'

– – **'Alba'**
Flowers white, tinted lilac in racemes 45 to
60cm long. AM 1931 AGM 1969
– – **'Issai'**
Flowers lilac blue in short trusses 18 to 25cm
long.

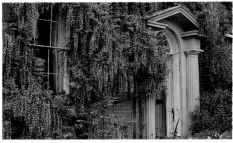

WISTERIA floribunda 'Macrobotrys'

– – **'Macrobotrys'**
Racemes up to 1m long or more. Flowers
fragrant, lilac tinged blue-purple. AGM 1969
– – **'Rosea'**
Flowers pale rose, tipped purple, in long
racemes.
– – **'Violacea Plena'**
Flowers violet blue, double.
– **sinensis** "Chinese Wisteria"
Perhaps the most popular wisteria, reaching
18 to 30m in a suitable tree. Leaves with nine
to thirteen leaflets. Flowers fragrant, mauve or
deep lilac in racemes up to 30cm long before
the leaves. AGM 1928
– – **'Alba'**
Flowers white. FCC 1892
– – **'Black Dragon'**
Flowers double, dark purple.
– – **'Plena'**
Flowers double, rosette shaped, lilac.
– **venusta**
Vigorous climber to 9m or more. Leaves with
nine to thirteen, downy leaflets. Flowers white,
slightly fragrant, racemes 10 to 15cm long.
AM 1945 FCC 1948

Conifers

The wide range of shape and colour shown by conifers make them valuable garden plants. Mainly evergreen, they range from prostrate and dwarf shrubs to large trees. Some are suitable for maritime exposures, hedging or ground cover. The deciduous conifers are no less attractive and contain several beautiful and unusual trees.

Apart from the naturally low growing species, several conifers have given rise to numerous dwarf forms which enables the beauty of these plants to be enjoyed in even the smallest of gardens.

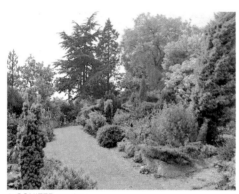

A CONIFER garden

ABIES – Pinaceae ST-LT (E) ♦ "Silver Firs"
Mainly conical trees with narrow flattened leaves often white beneath. Erect cylindrical cones, in some species attractively blue-purple or violet, when young. Require a deep, moist soil for best development. Apart from A. cephalonica and A. pinsapo they are largely intolerant of industrial atmosphere and shallow chalk soils.

– **amabilis** LT (E) ♦ ⚮ "Red Silver Fir"
A beautiful large tree of which we recommend the following form:

– – **'Spreading Star'** SS (E) ⚮
Wide-spreading, horizontally branched. Densely clothed with glossy, dark green leaves, white beneath.

– **arizonica** see *A. lasiocarpa arizonica*
– **balsamea** MT (E) ♦ ⚮ "Balsam Fir" "Balm of Gilead" We recommend the following form:

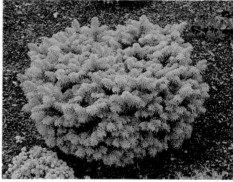

ABIES balsamea 'Hudsonia'

– – **'Hudsonia'** DS (E)
Dense, compact habit with densely arranged, short balsam-scented leaves. Fairly lime tolerant.

– **brachyphylla** see *A. homolepis*
– **bracteata** (*venusta*) LT (E) ♦
A very outstanding and distinct tree with long, rigid, spine tipped dark green leaves. Succeeds on deep soil over chalk. FCC 1915

– **cephalonica** LT (E) ♦ "Grecian Fir"
A handsome tree with rigid, pointed, glossy, green leaves, white beneath. One of the best for chalk soils.

--'**Nana**' DS (E)
A dwarf form with horizontally spreading branches, leaves shorter than type.
-**concolor** MT-LT (E) ♦ "Colorado White Fir"
Young trees with smooth, grey bark. Leaves 2-3cm, blue-green or grey-green. Cones cylindrical 16-25cm long.

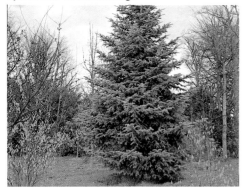

ABIES concolor 'Candicans'

--'**Candicans**' LT (E) ♦
Leaves vivid grey or silvery white.
--'**Glauca Compacta**' SS (E)
The most outstanding dwarf Silver Fir. Dense, irregular habit with greyish-blue foliage.
--'**Violacea**' LT (E) ♦
Leaves glaucous-blue.
--'**Wattezii**' ST-MT (E) ♦
Leaves creamy yellow when young becoming silvery-white.
-**delavayi** MT (E) ♦
Densely, set, glossy green leaves, gleaming silvery-white beneath. Barrel-shaped dark bluish-violet cones. AM 1980 We recommend:
--'**forrestii**' (A. forrestii) ST-MT (E) ♦
Dark green leaves, white beneath. Cones 8-9cm, sloe-black. Rich rusty red, young shoots. AM 1930
-**fargesii** MT (E) ♦
Vigorous tree with stout shoots and dark green notched leaves 3-5cm with two glaucous bands beneath. Cones 6 to 10cm purplish-brown when young.
-**firma** LT (E) ♦ ⊁ "Japanese Fir"
Comparatively broad leaves, glossy green or yellowish-green above, with two grey-green stripes beneath. Young cones yellowish green. FCC 1863
-**forrestii** see A. delavayi forrestii
-**gamblei** see A. pindrow brevifolia

-**grandis** LT (E) ♦ "Giant Fir"
Fast growing tree with dark, glossy green, horizontally arranged leaves with two glaucous-grey bands beneath. Cones bright green 7.5-10cm. Moderately lime tolerant.
-**holophylla** LT (E) ♦ "Manchurian Fir"
Leaves bright green above, densely arranged above the shoot, marked with grey-green bands beneath. Rare.
-**homolepis** (brachyphylla) LT (E) ♦ "Nikko Fir"
Leaves 1.5-3cm green above with two chalk-white bands beneath, crowded above the shoots. Cones cylindrical 7.5-9cm, purple when young.
-**intermedia** see A. pindrow intermedia

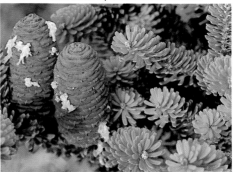

ABIES koreana

-**koreana** ST (E) ♦
Slow growing, neat habit. Dark green leaves, 1-2cm gleaming white beneath. Even young plants usually produce abundant small, violet-purple cylindrical cones, 5-7cm.
-**lasiocarpa** MT (E) ♦ "Alpine Fir"
We recommend the following forms:
--**arizonica** (A. arizonica) MT (E) ♦ "Cork Fir"
Thick, soft, corky bark, and conspicuously white resinous winter buds. Leaves 2.5-3.5cm silvery-grey. Cones purple when young.
--'**Compacta**' (arizonica 'Compacta') MS (E)
Slow growing. Dense, conical habit. Leaves blue-grey.
-**magnifica** LT (E) ♦ ⊁ "Californian Red Fir"
Slender tree with whitish bark when young. Leaves long and curved 2-4cm, grey-green or blue-green. Cones cylindrical 15-22cm, purple when young.
--'**Glauca**' LT (E) ♦ ⊁
Leaves deep glaucous green.

– nebrodensis ST-MT (E) ♦
Dark green, very stiff leaves densely arranged above the shoot. Cones cylindrical 2.5-3.5cm. Very rare.

– nobilis see *A. procera*

– nordmanniana LT (E) ♦ "Caucasian Fir"
Ornamental tree with tiered, down-sweeping branches. Leaves 2-3cm glossy green above white banded beneath, densely arranged. Cones cylindrical, greenish when young 15-20cm.

– –'Golden Spreader' (*'Aurea Nana'*) DS (E)
Slow growing, wide spreading form with light yellow leaves.

– numidica LT (E) ♦ "Algerian Fir"
Radially arranged leaves, 1-2cm, curving upwards, dark green above, white banded beneath. Cones cylindrical 12-18cm, brown. We recommend the form:

– –'Pendula' ST (E) ♠
Slow growing form with pendulous branchlets.

– pindrow LT (E) ♦ "West Himalayan Fir"
Rare, slender tree, stout young shoots and conspicuous orange-brown winter buds. Leaves bright glossy green above, banded grey-white beneath, up to 6cm long.

– –brevifolia (*A. gamblei*) LT (E) ♦
A distinct form with shorter leaves, 2-3.5cm.

– –intermedia LT (E) ♦
Long leaves, 4.5-6cm, dark green above, gleaming silvery-white beneath. AM 1944

– pinsapo MT-LT (E) ♦ "Spanish Fir"
Short, rigid, radially arranged, dark green leaves to 1.5cm. Cones cylindrical 10-15cm, purplish when young. One of the best for chalk.

– –'Glauca' LT (E) ♦
Leaves a striking blue-grey.

– procera (*nobilis*) LT (E) ♦ ⚲ "Noble Fir"
Bluish-green leaves, glaucous banded beneath, crowded above the shoots. Huge cylindrical cones up to 25cm long, green when young. AM 1973

– –'Glauca' LT (E) ♦ ⚲
Leaves blue-grey.

– –'Glauca Prostrata' DS (E)
Wide spreading or prostrate branches, glaucous leaves.

– sachalinensis MT (E) ♦ "Sachalin Fir"
Densely arranged leaves, 1.5-3.5cm, light

green above, grey-banded beneath. Conspicuous blue-white resinous winter buds. Cones cylindrical 7-8cm, olive green when young.

– spectabilis (*webbiana*) LT (E) ♦
"Himalayan Fir"
Densely two-ranked leaves up to 6cm long, glossy dark green above, silvery-white beneath. Cones cylindrical to 18cm, violet-purple when young. AM 1974

– squamata ST-MT (E) ♦ "Flaky Fir"
Distinct in its conspicuous shaggy, peeling, purplish-brown bark. Leaves 1-2.8cm, grey-green above, grey banded beneath. Very rare.

– sutchuenensis MT (E) ♦ "Szechwan Fir"
Pungently scented leaves 1-2.5cm, green above, glaucous banded beneath, crowded above the shoots. Deep violet or purplish-black cones, 7.5cm. Very rare.

– veitchii LT (E) ♦ ⚲
Fast growing. Densely arranged, upcurved leaves, 1-2.5cm, dark, glossy green above, silver-white beneath. Cones cylindrical 5-7cm, purplish when young. AM 1974

– venusta see *A. bracteata*

– webbiana see *A. spectabilis*

AGATHIS – Araucariaceae LT (E)
Genus related to Araucaria. *Only the following species is suitable for cultivation outside in this country:*

– australis ST (E) ♥ † "Kauri Pine"
Thick, spreading branches. Narrow, leathery leaves, often bronze or purple flushed. A small tree only in this country.

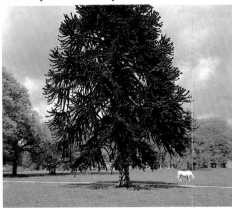

ARAUCARIA araucana

ARAUCARIA – Araucariaceae MT-LT (E) ♣
Remarkable trees of symmetrical appearance bearing whorled branches. The following is the only hardy species:
– **araucana** (*imbricata*) MT-LT (E) ♣ "Chile Pine" "Monkey Puzzle"
Long, spidery branches densely covered with overlapping, rigid, spine-tipped, dark green leaves. AM 1980.

ATHROTAXIS – Taxodiaceae ST-MT (E) ♦
"Tasmanian Cedars"
Slow growing trees with short, thick, overlapping leaves and small cones. Require a sheltered position.

– **cupressoides** ST (E) ♦
Very small, closely overlapping dark green, scale-like leaves.
– **laxifolia** ST-MT (E) ♦
Slightly spreading, pointed leaves. Laxer in habit than above.

AUSTROCEDRUS – Cupressaceae ST (E) ♣
A monotypic genus – allied to Libocedrus.
– **chilensis** (*Libocedrus chilensis*) ST (E) ♣
Remarkably hardy tree with flattened branchlets, bearing scale-like leaves marked with glaucous stomatic bands.

CALOCEDRUS – Cupressaceae ST-LT (E) ♣
A small genus of trees related to Thuja. *We recommend the following species and forms:*
– **decurrens** (*Libocedrus decurrens*) LT (E) ♣ "Incense Cedar"
Characteristic, columnar habit, with dark green leaves, arranged in dense, fan-like sprays. A good formal tree.
– –**'Aureovariegata'** MT (E) ♣
A form in which some leaf sprays are golden-yellow.
– –**'Nana'** (*'Intricata'*) MS (E)
Slow growing bush of dense, columnar habit.

CEDRUS – Pinaceae MT-LT (E) ♦ "Cedar"
A small genus of large trees ideally suited for specimen planting. Conical when young, spreading with age. Leaves in rosettes on short side shoots, single on young growths. Cones erect, barrel-shaped.
– **atlantica** LT (E) ♦ "Atlas Cedar"
Vigorous tree with green or grey-green leaves, 2–3.5cm, thickly covering the branches. Cones 5–7cm.
– –**'Fastigiata'** LT (E) ♦
Densely branched tree with ascending branches and short, erect branchlets. Leaves bluish green.

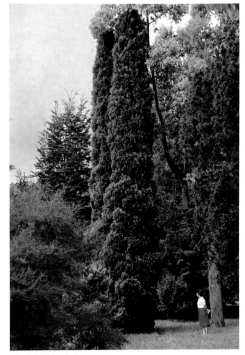

CALOCEDRUS decurrens

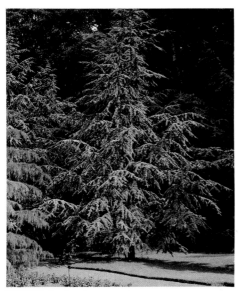

CEDRUS atlantica glauca

−−**glauca** LT (E) ♦ "Blue Cedar"
Spectacular form with silvery-blue leaves. A very effective specimen tree. FCC 1972 AGM 1973

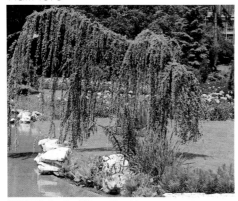

CEDRUS atlantica 'Glauca Pendula'

−−**'Glauca Pendula'** ST (E) ♠
Most effective when the long, weeping branches are supported. Leaves glaucous-blue.
−−**'Pendula'** ST (E) ♠
Weeping form with green or grey-green leaves.
−**brevifolia** MT (E) ♦ "Cyprian Cedar"
Slow growing tree similar to *C. libani* but with shorter leaves. Rare.

−**deodara** LT (E) ♦ "Deodar"
Very distinct tree of somewhat pendant habit with a drooping leader and shoot tips and leaves up to 5cm long, glaucous when young, becoming bright green. Cones 7–10cm.
−−**'Aurea'** MT (E) ♦ "Golden Deodar"
Young leaves golden yellow in spring.
−−**'Pendula'** ST (E) ♠
Weeping branches spread over the ground. Eventually produces a leader but can be kept as a spreading bush by pruning.
−−**'Pygmy'** (*'Pygmaea'*) DS (E)
Very slow growing, dwarf form, making a tiny hummock of blue-grey foliage. A rare gem for the rock garden.

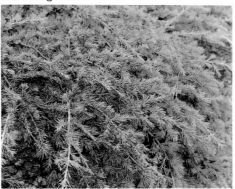

CEDRUS libani 'Sargentii'

−**libani** LT (E) ♦
Conical when young gradually developing flat-topped tiers of branches. Leaves green or grey-green.
−−**'Comte de Dijon'** MS (E)
Slow growing bush of dense, conical habit.
−−**'Nana'** MS (E)
A slow growing, dwarf form similar to *'Comte de Dijon'* but with broader, shorter leaves.
−−**'Sargentii'** (*'Pendula Sargentii'*) MS (E)
A prostrate form most effective when trained upwards to make a dense, weeping bush.
CEPHALOTAXUS – Cephalotaxaceae SS-ST (E)
Rather like large-leaved yews. Suitable for dense shade even under other conifers, as well as open sites. Excellent on chalk. Olive-like fruits on female plants.
−**fortuni** LS-ST (E) "Chinese Plum Yew"
Bushy spreading habit – usually wider than high. Dark green, narrow leaves 6–9cm, in two opposite rows. AM 1975

CEPHALOTAXUS fortuni – Cont.

--**'Prostrata'** (*'Prostrate Spreader'*) DS (E) GC
Low growing form of wide-spreading habit with deep green leaves. Superb ground-cover plant.

-**harringtonia** LS-ST (E)
Leaves 3.5–6.5cm. Paler green than *C. fortuni*. We recommend the following forms:

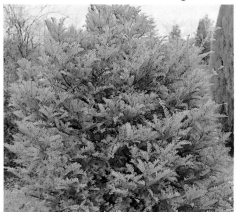

CEPHALOTAXUS harringtonia drupacea

--**drupacea** MS (E) "Cow's Tail Pine" "Japanese Plum Yew"
Makes a large mound of dense habit with elegant, drooping branchlets. Leaves 2 to 5cm.

--**'Fastigiata'** MS-LS (E)
Erect-branched habit, resembling the "Irish Yew". Almost black-green, radially arranged leaves.

CHAMAECYPARIS – Cupressaceae ST-LT
(E) "False Cypress"
Although containing only a few species this genus has contributed to gardens a vast number of forms ranging from dwarfs to large trees. Differing from Cupressus *in their flattened frond-like branchlets and smaller, globose cones.*

-**lawsoniana** LT (E) ♦ Hdg (0.6m) "Lawson Cypress"
Drooping branches. Broad, fan-like sprays of foliage, arranged in flattened planes. An excellent hedge even in exposed or shady positions.

--**'Allumigold'** ST (E) ♦
Similar to *'Allumii'* but slower growing with sprays of foliage edged golden yellow.

CHAMAECYPARIS lawsoniana – Cont.

--**'Allumii'** MT (E) ♦
Compact habit with ascending branches bearing soft, blue-grey foliage in flattened sprays.

--**'Aurea Densa'** MS (E)
Slow growing form of compact habit with golden-yellow foliage in short, flattened densely packed sprays. One of the best golden conifers for the rock garden.

--**'Backhouse Silver'** see *'Pygmaea Argentea'*

--**'Chilworth Silver'** LS (E)
Broadly columnar habit with densely packed, silvery-blue, juvenile foliage.

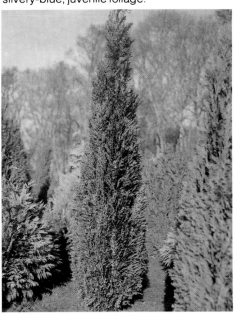

CHAMAECYPARIS lawsoniana 'Columnaris'

--**'Columnaris'** ST (E) ♦
Dense, narrow habit with ascending branches and flattened sprays of foliage, glaucous beneath and at the tips. AGM 1961

--**'Elegantissima'** ST (E) ♦
Broad, drooping sprays of silvery grey or grey-cream, foliage. AGM 1969

--**'Ellwoodii'** LS (E)
Closely columnar habit with short, feathery sprays of grey-green foliage, steel blue in winter. Slow growing. AM 1934 AGM 1969

--**'Ellwood's Gold'** MS-LS (E)
Similar to *'Ellwoodii'* but slower growing and with the tips of the sprays yellow tinged.

– –**'Erecta'** MT-LT (E) ❢

Dense compact habit. Columnar when young, wider when fully grown. Rich, bright green foliage in large, flattened, vertical sprays. FCC 1870

– –**'Erecta Witzeliana'** see *'Witzeliana'*

– –**'Fletcheri'** LS (E)

Broad, columnar habit with grey-green semi-juvenile foliage, bronze in winter.

– –**'Forsteckensis'** SS (E)

Very slow growing bush of dense, globular habit with grey-green foliage in congested, fern-like sprays.

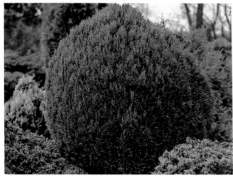

CHAMAECYPARIS lawsoniana 'Gimbornii'

– –**'Gimbornii'** SS (E)

Dense, slow growing bush with blue-green foliage, tipped mauve.

– –**'Golden King'** MT (E) ♦

Spreading branches. Large, flattened sprays of golden-yellow foliage, bronze in winter.

– –**'Green Globe'** SS (E)

Bun-shaped bush of tightly congested, deep green foliage.

– –**'Green Hedger'** MT-LT (E) ♦ Hdg (0.6m)

Dense habit with branches ascending from the base, rich green foliage. AGM 1973

– –**'Hillieri'** MT (E) ♦ ◑

Dense habit, foliage bright, golden yellow in large, drooping feathery sprays. Foliage, when young, prone to burn in full exposure.

– –**'Intertexta'** LT (E) ♦

Open, ascending habit. Branches loosely borne with widely spaced, drooping branchlets and dark, glaucous-green foliage. AGM 1969

– –**'Kilmacurragh'** MT-LT (E) ❢

Very narrow, columnar habit with irregular sprays of dark green foliage on short branches. AGM 1969

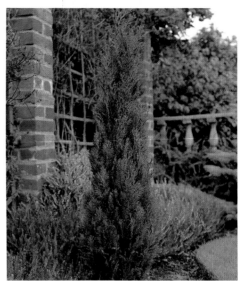

CHAMAECYPARIS lawsoniana 'Kilmacurragh'

– –**'Lane'** (*'Lanei'*) MT (E) ❢

Feathery sprays of golden-yellow foliage. One of the best golden Cypresses.

– –**'Lutea'** MT (E) ❢

Broad habit with a drooping, spire-like top. Foliage golden-yellow in feathery sprays. FCC 1872 AGM 1955

– –**'Lutea Nana'** SS (E)

Slow growing bush of conical habit with golden-yellow foliage in dense, short flattened sprays.

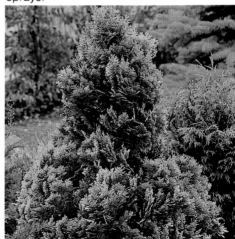

CHAMAECYPARIS lawsoniana 'Minima Aurea'

--**'Minima Aurea'** SS (E)
Conical bush of dense habit. Vertically held sprays of soft, golden-yellow foliage. One of the best golden conifers for the rock garden. AGM 1969

--**'Minima Glauca'** SS (E)
Slow growing bush of rounded habit with densely packed sprays of sea-green foliage.

--**'Moerheimii'** MT (E) ✦
Spreading branches and yellowish green foliage, golden at the tips.

--**'Naberi'** MT (E) ✦
Green foliage, sulphur-yellow at tips; creamy blue in winter.

--**'Parsons'** MS (E)
Slow growing bush of dense, dome-shaped habit with green foliage in large, flattened, arching and drooping sprays.

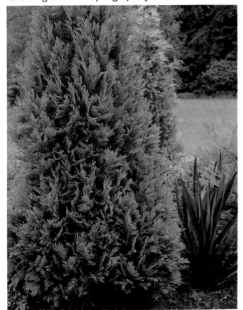

CHAMAECYPARIS lawsoniana 'Pembury Blue'

--**'Pembury Blue'** MT (E) ✦
Striking tree. Silvery-blue foliage. Perhaps the best blue "Lawson Cypress". AGM 1969

--**'Pendula'** MT (E) ✦
Open habit. Pendulous branches. Dark green foliage. FCC 1890

--**'Pottenii'** MT (E) ▮
Dense, slow growth. Sea-green, semi-juvenile foliage in soft, crowded, feathery sprays. AM 1916

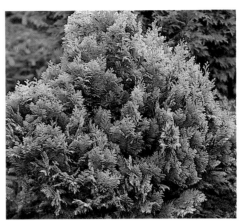

CHAMAECYPARIS lawsoniana 'Pygmaea Argentea'

--**'Pygmaea Argentea'** (*'Backhouse Silver'*) SS (E)
Slow growing rounded bush. Dark bluish-green foliage, creamy-white at the tips. Perhaps the best dwarf, white variegated conifer. AM 1900 AGM 1969

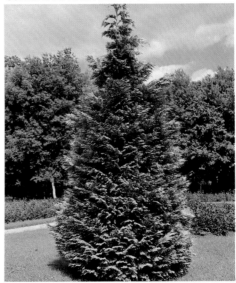

CHAMAECYPARIS lawsoniana 'Stewartii'

--**'Stardust'** MT (E) ✦
Narrow habit. Yellow foliage, bronze at the tips.

--**'Stewartii'** MT-LT (E) ✦
Elegant habit with semi-erect branches. Golden-yellow foliage.

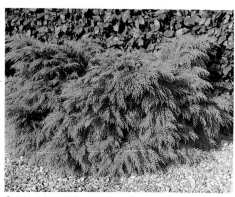

CHAMAECYPARIS lawsoniana 'Tamariscifolia'

– –**'Tamariscifolia'** MS-LS (E)
Slow growing, spreading bush with several
ascending stems, eventually umbrella
shaped. Foliage sea-green in fan-like sprays.
– – **'Triomf van Boskoop'** (*'Triomphe de
Boskoop'*) LT (E) ♦
Glaucous-blue foliage in large, lax sprays.
Needs trimming to retain density.
– –**'Westermannii'** MT (E) ♦
Dense, broad habit. Spreading branches
bearing large sprays of light yellow foliage
when young, becoming yellowish-green.
– –**'White Spot'** MT (E) ♦
Grey-green sprays of foliage, flecked creamy
white at the tips.
– –**'Winston Churchill'** ST-MT (E) ♥
Broadly columnar. Foliage rich, golden yellow
throughout the year. One of the best golden
Lawson Cypresses.
– –**'Wisellii'** MT-LT (E) ♦
Distinct tree of slender habit. Ascending
branches. Blue-green foliage borne in short,
crowded, fern-like sprays. AM 1899
AGM 1969
– –**'Witzeliana'** (*'Erecta Witzeliana'*) ST (E) ♥
Narrow habit with long, ascending branches.
Foliage vivid green, crowded sprays.
– –**'Yellow Transparent'** LS (E)
Similar to *'Fletcheri'* but slower growing, with
yellow young foliage, transparent in sunshine
– bronze in winter.
– **nootkatensis** LT (E) ♦ "Nootka Cypress"
Drooping branchlets. Long, flattened sprays
of green foliage, rough to the touch. AM 1978
– –**'Aureovariegata'** MT (E) ♦
Foliage conspicuously marked with deep
yellow. FCC 1872

– –**'Glauca'** MT-LT (E) ♦
Foliage dark sea-green.
– –**'Lutea'** (*'Aurea'*) MT (E) ♦
Foliage yellow when young becoming
yellowish green.

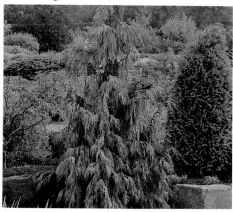

CHAMAECYPARIS nootkatensis 'Pendula'

– –**'Pendula'** MT-LT (E) ♦
Spreading and upcurved branches bearing
long, pendulous branchlets.
– **obtusa** (*Retinospora obtusa*) LT (E) ♦
"Hinoki Cypress"
Spreading branches with glossy green foliage
in thick, flattened sprays. We recommend the
following forms:
– –**'Caespitosa'** (*'Nana Caespitosa'*) DS (E)
A slow-growing, bun-shaped bush with light
green foliage in short, crowded, shell-like
sprays.

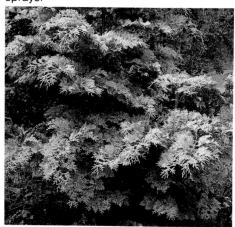

CHAMAECYPARIS obtusa 'Crippsii'

––**'Crippsii'** ST (E) ✦
Frond-like sprays of rich golden-yellow foliage. One of the best small golden conifers. FCC 1899

––**'Densa'** (*'Nana Densa'*) DS (E)
Slow growing miniature bush of dome shaped habit with foliage in densely crowded cockscombs.

––**'Juniperoides Compacta'** DS (E)
Very slow growing miniature bush. Dense, globular habit small, cup-shaped sprays of foliage.

––**'Mariesii'** (*'Nana Variegata'*) SS (E)
Small, slow growing bush of conical habit, foliage creamy white in summer, yellowish green in winter.

––**'Minima'** (*'Nana Minima'*) DS (E)
Very dwarf habit forming a moss-like flat pin-cushion with green foliage in upright sprays. Perhaps the smallest of its type.

––**'Nana'** SS (E)
Flat-topped dome with densely packed tiers of black-green foliage.

––**'Nana Aurea'** MS (E)
A slow growing bush, ideal for the rock garden, golden-yellow foliage. Perhaps the best dwarf golden conifer. AGM 1973

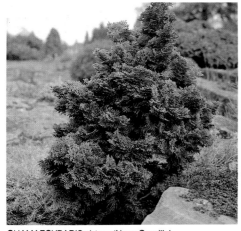

CHAMAECYPARIS obtusa 'Nana Gracilis'

––**'Nana Gracilis'** MS (E)
Slow growing bush of compact habit. Dark green foliage in short, neat, shell-like sprays. AGM 1969

––**'Pygmaea'** SS (E)
Spreading bush. Loose sprays of bronze-green foliage, reddish-bronze in winter.

––**'Spiralis'** DS (E)
Stiff, upright habit. Attractively twisted branchlets.

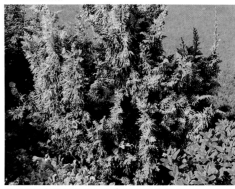

CHAMAECYPARIS obtusa 'Tetragona Aurea'

––**'Tetragona Aurea'** LS-ST (E) ✦
Congested, angular habit with wide-spreading branches, bearing moss-like sprays of golden-yellow foliage. FCC 1876

–**pisifera** (*Retinospora pisifera*) LT (E) ✦
"Sawara Cypress"
Horizontally flattened sprays of dark green foliage with sharply pointed, scale-like leaves. FCC 1861. We recommend the following forms:

––**'Aurea Nana'** DS (E)
Slow growing. Flattened, globular habit. Rich golden yellow foliage. FCC 1861

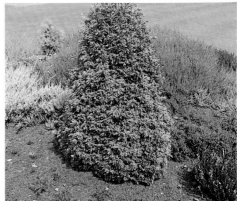

CHAMAECYPARIS pisifera 'Boulevard'

––**'Boulevard'** (*'Cyanoviridis'*) LS (E)
Dense, narrowly columnar habit. Steel-blue foliage, soft to the touch. One of the most popular of conifers. AGM 1973

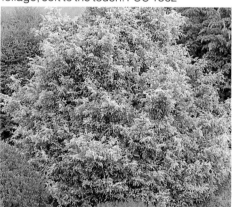

CHAMAECYPARIS pisifera 'Filifera Aurea'

‒‒**'Filifera Aurea'** MS-LS (E)
Spreading branches. Long, drooping whip-like branchlets. Golden-yellow foliage. AGM 1973
‒‒**'Filifera Nana'** SS (E)
A dense, rounded bush with long, string-like branchlets.
‒‒**'Nana'** DS (E)
Slow growing bush making a flat-topped dome. Flattened sprays of dark green foliage.
‒‒**'Nana Aureovariegata'** DS (E)
Similar to *'Nana'* but with golden tinged foliage. Excellent for the rock garden.
‒‒**'Plumosa'** ST-MT (E) ♦
Densely packed branchlets. Plumose sprays of bright green, juvenile foliage, soft to the touch. FCC 1866

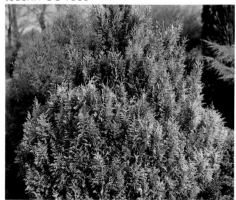

CHAMAECYPARIS pisifera 'Plumosa Aurea'

‒‒**'Plumosa Aurea'** ST (E) ♦
Similar to *'Plumosa'* with young foliage bright yellow.

‒‒**'Plumosa Aurea Compacta'** MS (E)
Dense, conical bush of slow growth. Soft yellow foliage.
‒‒**'Plumosa Aurescens'** ST (E) ♦
Plumose branchlets, light yellow at the tips in summer, becoming bluish-green.
‒‒**'Plumosa Compressa'** DS (E)
Slow growing, flat-topped bush making a tight, rounded bun. Moss-like foliage. AM 1925
‒‒**'Snow'** DS (E)
Bun-shaped bush. Mossy foliage, blue-grey tipped creamy-white.
‒‒**'Squarrosa'** ST-MT (E) ♦
Dense, billowy sprays of glaucous, juvenile foliage, soft to the touch. FCC 1862

CHAMAECYPARIS pisifera 'Squarrosa Sulphurea'

‒‒**'Squarrosa Sulphurea'** ST (E) ♦
Similar to *'Squarrosa'* with sulphur yellow foliage. AM 1894
‒**thyoides** ST-MT (E) ♦ ✗ "White Cypress"
Erect, fan-shaped sprays of aromatic, glaucous-green foliage. We recommend the following forms:
‒‒**'Andeleyensis Nana'** (*'Leptoclada Nana'*) SS (E)
Dense, flat topped bush. Mostly juvenile foliage. Slow.
‒‒**'Ericoides'** SS (E) ✗
Compact, conical bush with sea-green juvenile foliage, soft to the touch, becoming bronze-purple in winter.
‒‒**'Glauca'** ST-MT (E) ♦ ✗
Foliage glaucous-blue.
‒‒**'Purple Heather'** (*'Heatherbun'*) DS (E) ✗
Dense, round-topped bush with juvenile foliage rich plum-purple in winter.

CRYPTOMERIA – Taxodiaceae
A monotypic genus. Cones solitary, globular.
– **japonica** LT (E) ✿ "Japanese Cedar"
Vigorous tree with reddish, shredding bark and densely crowded, awl-shaped leaves on long, slender branchlets.
– – **'Bandai-sugi'** SS-MS (E)
A dense, slow growing bush with foliage in congested clusters, bronze-purple in winter.

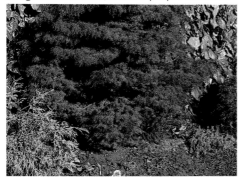

CRYPTOMERIA japonica 'Elegans'

– – **'Elegans'** ST (E) ✿
Bushy tree with soft, feathery, juvenile foliage red-bronze in winter. FCC 1862
– – **'Elegans Compacta'** MS (E)
Dense billowy bush with very soft, plumose foliage rich purple in winter.
– – **'Elegans Nana'** SS (E)
Very dense, rounded habit with, juvenile foliage, bronze in winter. Differs from *'Elegans Compacta'* in its straight fairly stiff leaves.
– – **'Lobbii'** MT-LT (E) ♦
Leaves deep, rich green on long branchlets clustered at the ends of the shoots.
– – **'Nana'** MS (E)
Dense bush with slender shoots arching at the tips bearing short leaves.
– – **'Spiralis'** SS (E) "Grannies Ringlets"
Slow growing bush of dense, spreading habit. Bright green leaves, spirally twisted round the stems.
– – **'Vilmoriniana'** DS (E)
Very slow growing bush with short, crowded branchlets, making a dense, rigid globe, reddish-purple in winter. AGM 1973
CUNNINGHAMIA – Taxodiaceae ST-MT (E) ✿

Two species of trees recalling Araucaria. The following is hardy but best planted in a sheltered position.

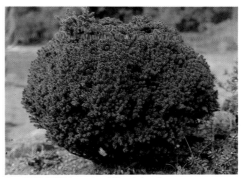

CRYPTOMERIA japonica 'Vilmoriniana'

– **lanceolata** ST-MT (E) ✿ "Chinese Fir"
Lanceolate leaves, 3-7cm, emerald green above, marked with two white bands beneath, becoming bronzy by autumn.
× **CUPRESSOCYPARIS** (*CUPRESSUS* × *CHAMAECYPARIS*) – **Cupressaceae** MT-LT (E) ✿
Fast growing, popular trees with many uses.

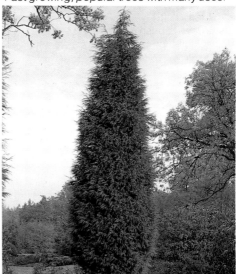

× CUPRESSOCYPARIS leylandii

– **leylandii** LT (E) ✿ Hdg (0.6m) "Leyland Cypress"
Vigorous tree of dense habit. Foliage in irregular, slightly drooping sprays. Excellent for tall hedges and screens and tolerant of coastal conditions and chalk soils. The fastest growing conifer in this country. AM 1941 AGM 1969

--**'Castlewellan'** MT (E) ❦

A form with yellow foliage.

--**'Robinsons Gold'** MT (E) ❦

Close, compact habit. Yellow foliage, golden-bronze in spring.

-**notabilis** MT (E) ❦

Sinuous, unswept branches with flattened sprays of dark grey-green foliage.

CUPRESSUS – Cupressaceae ST-LT (E)

Impressive trees differing from Chamaecyparis *in their usually rounded branchlets and larger cones.*

-**bakeri matthewsii** MT (E) ✦

Bark flaking, reddish-grey. Branches spreading with drooping branchlets divided into grey-green, thread-like sections.

-**cashmeriana** ST-MT (E) ✦ † "Kashmir Cypress"

Ascending branches draped with long pendulous branchlets with conspicuously blue-grey foliage in flattened sprays. FCC 1971

-**glabra** (*arizonica* HORT) MT (E) ✦

We recommend the following form:

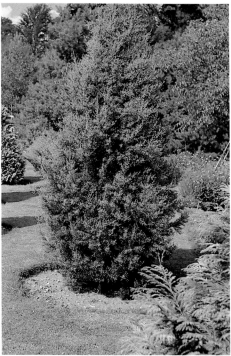

CUPRESSUS glabra 'Pyramidalis'

--**'Pyramidalis'** MT (E) ✦

Dense, conical habit with conspicuous, blue-grey foliage. An excellent formal tree. AGM 1969

-**lusitanica** MT-LT (E) ❦ † "Mexican Cypress" "Cedar of Goa"

Graceful tree with rich brown peeling bark. We recommend the following form:

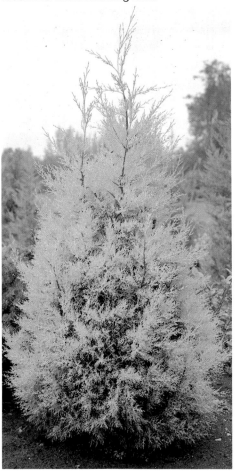

CUPRESSUS macrocarpa 'Goldcrest'

--**'Glauca Pendula'** ST (E) ❦ †

Spreading. Drooping, glaucous-blue branchlets. AM 1944

-**macnabiana** LS-ST (E) ✦ "McNab's Cypress"

Branches spreading with age, conspicuous red-tinged branchlets, pale, glaucous-green foliage.

– **macrocarpa** MT-LT (E) ⬆ "Monterey Cypress"
Vigorous tree becoming broad-crowned with age. Bright green foliage, densely packed sprays. Excellent for shelter in coastal areas. The yellow forms are best in full sun.
– – **'Donard Gold'** MT (E) ⬆
Foliage rich, deep golden-yellow.
– – **'Goldcrest'** MT (E) ⬆
Dense, narrow habit with rich yellow, feathery, juvenile foliage.
– – **'Golden Cone'** MT (E) ♦
A form of conical habit with golden foliage.
– – **'Golden Pillar'** MT (E) ⬆
A very narrow tree with golden-yellow foliage.
– – **'Lutea'** MT (E) ⬆
Foliage soft yellow, becoming green.
– **sempervirens** MT (E) ❘ "Italian Cypress" "Mediterranean Cypress"
The familiar narrow cypress of the Mediterranean region. Branches strictly ascending with dark green foliage.
– – **'Green Spire'** MT (E) ❘
Selected clone of closely erect habit.
– – **'Swane's Golden'** ST (E) ❘
Slow growing form of compact habit. Golden tinged foliage.
"CYPRESS" see *CUPRESSUS* and *CHAMAECYPARIS*

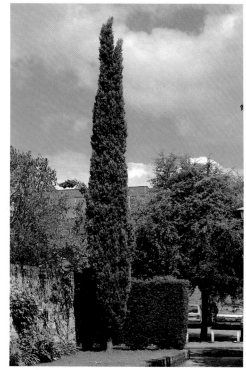

CUPRESSUS sempervirens

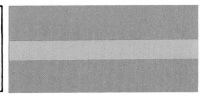

DACRYDIUM – Podocarpaceae PS-ST (E)
A small genus of mainly Australasian conifers. We recommend the following:
– **franklinii** LS-ST (E) ♦ † "Huon Pine"
Slender, drooping branches; bright green, scale-like leaves.
– **laxifolium** PS (E)
The smallest known conifer, making a mat of slender stems with tiny, scale-like leaves, turning plum purple in winter.
DISELMA – Cupressceae MS-LS (E)
A monotypic genus.
– **archeri** MS-LS (E)
Erect branched shrub of lax habit with closely appressed, scale like leaves. Rare.

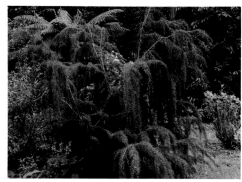

DACRYDIUM franklinii

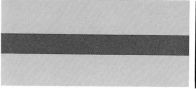

"FIR" see *ABIES*
FITZROYA – Cupressaceae LS-ST (E) ⚘
A monotypic genus.
– cupressoides LS-ST (E) ⚘
Dense habit. Scale-like leaves, banded white,
drooping branchlets.
FOKIENIA – Cupressaceae MS (E)
Genus related to Cupressus *and* Calocedrus.

*The following species is best planted in a
sheltered position in woodland.*
– hodginsii MS (E)
Slow growing. Spine-tipped, scale-like
leaves, bright glossy green above, silvery-
white bands beneath, in flattened sprays.
Rare. AM 1911

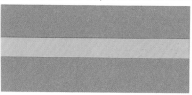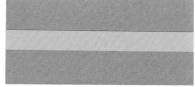

GINKGO – Ginkgoaceae MT-LT ♠
*The only member of this genus is the sole
living representative of a large group of plants
which occurred throughout the world in
prehistoric times.*

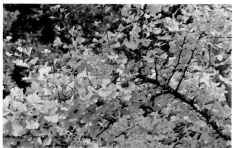

GINKGO biloba

– biloba (*Salisburia adiantifolia*) MT-LT ♠
"Maidenhair Tree"
A remarkable, deciduous tree with bi-lobed
fan-like leaves, clear yellow in autumn.
Tolerant of industrial areas. AGM 1969
– –'Fastigiata' MT ⚘
A columnar form with semi-erect branches.
– –'Tremonia' MT ♠
A form of narrowly conical habit.
– –'Variegata' ST ♠
Leaves banded with creamy white.

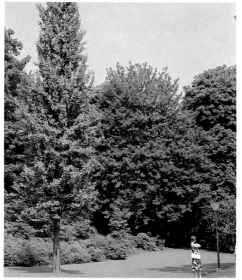

GINKGO biloba 'Tremonia'

GLYPTOSTROBUS - Taxodiaceae
A monotypic genus related to Taxodium. *Best
given a sheltered position in a moist soil.*
– lineatus (*pencilis*) ST ♠ †
A very rare, deciduous conifer with narrow,
sea-green leaves rich brown in autumn.

"HEMLOCK" see *TSUGA*

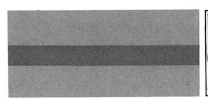

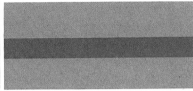

JUNIPERUS – Cupressaceae PS-LT (E)
"Juniper"
A large group of plants of varying habit.
Leaves narrow and pointed on juvenile plants,
usually scale-like on adult plants. Excellent on
chalk.
– **chinensis** MT-LT (E) ⚑
Variable tree, normally of columnar habit.
Generally both adult and juvenile foliage. We
recommend the following forms:
– – **'Aurea'** ST (E) ⚑ "Young's Golden
Juniper"
Foliage golden-yellow. Inclined to burn in full
sun. FCC 1871
– – **'Expansa'** see *J. × davurica 'Expansa'*
– – **'Kaizuka'** LS-ST (E) ♦
A very distinct form of architectural quality.
Long, spreading branches; dense bright
green foliage.
– – **'Kaizuka Variegata'** LS (E)
Similar to *'Kaizuka'* but slower growing with
foliage splashed creamy white.
– – **'Keteleeri'** (*virginiana 'Keteleeri'*) ST (E) ♦
Dense, narrow habit with crowded masses of
vivid green, scale-like leaves.
– – **'Obelisk'** MS (E)
Erect, columnar habit with densely packed,
bluish-green, juvenile foliage.
– – **'Oblonga'** SS (E)
Irregular, rounded habit with densely
crowded branches. Foliage juvenile,
becoming adult towards the top of the plant.
– – **'Parsonsii'** see *J. × davurica 'Expansa'*
– – **'Pfitzerana'** see *J. × media 'Pfitzerana'*
– – **'Plumosa'** see *J. × media 'Plumosa'*

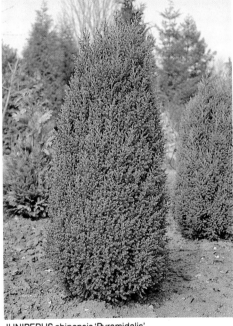
JUNIPERUS chinensis 'Pyramidalis'

– – **procumbens** see *J. procumbens*
– – **'Pyramidalis'** MS (E)
Slow growing, conical bush of dense habit,
almost all juvenile foliage. FCC 1868
– – **sargentii** see *J. sargentii*
– **communis** MS-LS (E) "Common Juniper"
Narrow, prickly silver-backed leaves. The
prostrate forms make excellent ground cover
in full sun. AM 1890

297

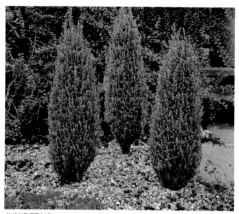
JUNIPERUS communis 'Compressa'

– – **'Compressa'** DS (E)
Slow growing narrow column. A gem for the
rock garden.
– – **depressa** DS (E) GC "Canadian Juniper"
Wide spreading. Tightly packed, slightly
ascending stems. Leaves yellowish or
brownish-green, bronze above in winter.

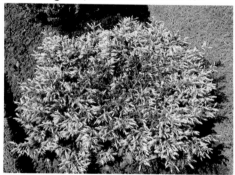
JUNIPERUS communis 'Depressa Aurea'

– – **'Depressa Aurea'** DS (E) GC
Similar to *depressa* with young foliage golden
yellow.
– – **'Hibernica'** (*'Stricta'*) (*J. hibernica*) LS (E)
"Irish Juniper"
Dense form of slender, columnar habit. An
excellent formal specimen.
– – **'Hornibrookii'** PS (E) GC
Prostrate form. Rather small, sharply pointed
leaves, silvery beneath. AGM 1973
– – **'Repanda'** PS (E) GC
Densely packed, semi-prostrate stems.
Loosely arranged leaves, soft to the touch.
– – **'Stricta'** see *'Hibernica'*

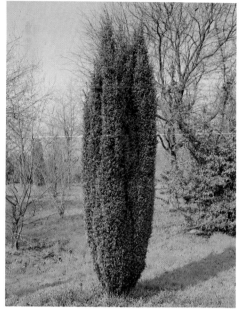
JUNIPERUS communis 'Hibernica'

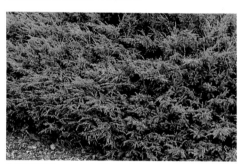
JUNIPERUS communis 'Repanda'

– **conferta** PS (E) GC "Shore Juniper"
Apple-green, prickly leaves banded white
above. Excellent cover in full sun where it will
form large patches.
– – **'Blue Pacific'** PS (E) GC
Shorter and broader, less prickly leaves,
deeper green.
– × **davurica** DS (E)
A variable hybrid of which the following forms
are cultivated:
– – **'Expansa'** (*chinensis 'Parsonsii'*)
(*chinensis 'Expansa'*) DS (E)
Wide spreading almost horizontal rigid
branches, with scale-like, sage-green leaves
in dense, spray-like clusters.

--**'Expansa Aureospicata'** DS (E)
Similar to *'Expansa'* in habit. Foliage grey-green with scattered yellow splashes, mainly juvenile.

--**'Expansa Variegata'** DS (E)
Similar to *'Expansa'* in habit and foliage but with scattered, creamy-white sprays.

-**drupacea** ST (E) ⚑ "Syrian Juniper"
Distinctive narrow columnar habit. Short, densely crowded branches. Leaves awl shaped, sharply pointed, broadly banded white above.

-**'Grey Owl'** (*virginiana 'Grey Owl'*) MS (E)
Vigorous shrub with wide-spreading branches and soft, silvery grey foliage. AM 1968

-**hibernica** see *J. communis 'Hibernica'*

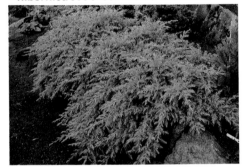

JUNIPERUS conferta

-**horizontalis** PS-DS (E) GC "Creeping Juniper"
Long, usually creeping branches, forming large carpets. Excellent, dense ground cover. AGM 1969. We recommend the following forms:

--**'Bar Harbor'** PS (E) GC
Branches closely ground hugging. Short, ascending branchlets, bearing glaucous, grey-green scale-like leaves.

--**'Blue Chip'** PS (E) GC
Foliage bright blue throughout the year.

--**'Blue Rug'** see *'Wiltonii'*

--**'Coast of Maine'** PS (E) GC
Low growing, forming flattened mounds. Leaves awl-shaped, grey-green, purple tinted in winter.

--**'Douglasii'** PS (E) GC
Long, spreading branches. Sprays of both adult and juvenile leaves, bright glaucous-green in summer, purple tinged in autumn and winter.

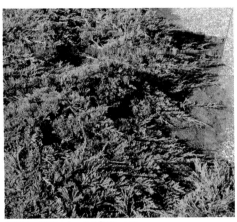

JUNIPERUS horizontalis 'Glauca'

--**'Glauca'** PS (E) GC
Long branches with slender "whipcord" tips hugging the ground. Leaves steel-blue in slender sprays.

--**'Hughes'** DS (E) GC
Wide-spreading, slightly ascending branches with grey-green foliage.

--**'Montana'** PS (E) GC
Long, slender branches with densely packed scale-like leaves of an intense, glaucous-blue.

--**'Wiltonii'** (*'Blue Rug'*) PS (E) GC
Long, prostrate branches with glaucous-blue foliage.

-**japonica** HORT see *J. × media 'Plumosa'*

-× **media** SS-LS (E)
A variable hybrid, usually of wide-spreading habit. Several forms make excellent ground cover and are plants of architectural quality. The following are recommended:

--**'Blaauw'** SS (E)
Strongly ascending branches densely clothed with feathery sprays of mainly scale-like, greyish-blue leaves.

--**'Hetzii'** MS-LS (E)
Wide-spreading habit similar to *'Pfitzerana'* but branches more ascending with glaucous, mainly adult foliage.

--**'Mint Julep'** MS (E)
Wide spreading habit with arching shoots. Foliage rich green.

--**'Old Gold'** MS (E) GC
Similar to *'Pfitzerana'* but of more compact habit with bronze-gold foliage throughout the year.

– – **'Pfitzerana'** MS (E) GC

One of the most popular of all conifers. A wide-spreading shrub with stout, ascending, arm-like branches drooping at the tips. An excellent specimen plant with many landscape possibilities. Often used to cover low, unsightly objects. AGM 1969

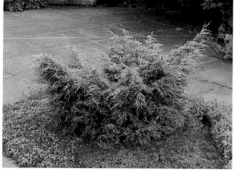

JUNIPERUS × media 'Pfitzerana Aurea'

– – **'Pfitzerana Aurea'** SS (E) GC "Golden Pfitzer"

A low growing, flat-topped form of *'Pfitzerana'* with the young foliage golden yellow.

– – **'Pfitzerana Compacta'** DS (E) GC

A low growing but wide-spreading form of *'Pfitzerana'* with mainly juvenile, prickly leaves.

– – **'Plumosa'** (*chinensis 'Plumosa'*) (*J. japonica* HORT) SS (E)

Wide spreading branches bear crowded plume-like sprays of densely set, green, scale-like leaves.

– – **'Plumosa Aurea'** MS (E)

Ascending branches arching at the tips with dense, plume-like sprays of yellow foliage, bronze-gold in winter.

– – **'Sulphur Spray'** SS (E)

Foliage pale sulphur yellow, brighter in summer. Spreading. Sport of *'Hetzii'*.

– **procumbens** (*chinensis procumbens*) PS (E) GC "Creeping Juniper"

Wide-spreading, mound-forming shrub with long, stiff branches bearing glaucous-green, sharply pointed leaves.

– – **'Nana'** (*'Bonin Isles'*) PS (E) GC

A more compact form with shorter branches.

– **recurva** LS-ST (E) ♦ "Drooping Juniper"

Drooping branchlets with awl-shaped green or grey-green leaves, usually white above. We recommend the following forms:

– – **'Castlewellan'** ST (E) ♦

Loose, open habit. Lax branches with long, drooping branchlets. Foliage in soft, thread-like sprays.

– – **coxii** ST (E) ♦

Gracefully drooping branchlets with loosely arranged, sage-green leaves.

– – **'Embley Park'** (*viridis* HORT) SS (E)

A distinct form with ascending branches and rich, grass green, awl-shaped leaves.

– **rigida** LS-ST (E) ♥

Elegant, spreading branches and drooping branchlets bearing rigid, sharply pointed leaves, bronze-green in winter.

– **sabina** SS (E) GC "Savin"

Variable shrubs of usually wide-spreading habit with green or grey-green, mainly scale-like leaves. We recommend the following forms:

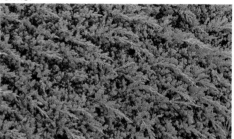

JUNIPERUS procumbens 'Nana'

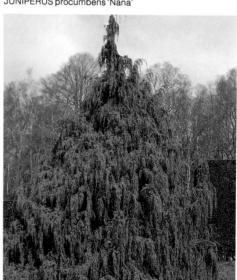

JUNIPERUS recurva coxii

--**'Hicksii'** SS (E) GC
Wide-spreading, semi-prostrate shrub with semi-erect plume-like branchlets crowded with grey-blue, awl-shaped leaves.

--**'Skandia'** (*'Scandens'*) DS (E) GC
Low growing but wide-spreading bush with dark green, mainly awl-shaped leaves.

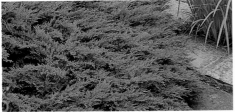

JUNIPERUS sabina tamariscifolia

--**tamariscifolia** DS (E) GC
Compact habit, making a wide-spreading, flat-topped bush with horizontally packed branches. A plant of architectural quality. AGM 1969

-**sargentii** (*chinensis sargentii*) PS (E) GC
Spreading shrub making dense carpets. Leaves mostly scale-like green and bloomy.

--**'Glauca'** PS (E) GC
A more compact form with ascending branches and glaucous-green foliage.

-**scopulorum** ST (E) ♦ "Rocky Mountain Juniper"
Cypress-like tree with reddish-brown, shredding bark and slender branchlets. Tightly appressed, scale-like leaves. We recommend the following:

--**'Springbank'** ST (E) ♦
Ascending and spreading branches bear silvery grey-green foliage.

-**squamata** PS-ST (E)
A variable species. Shoots with characteristic, nodding tips. Leaves short, awl-shaped, white or pale green above. We recommend:

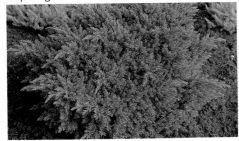

JUNIPERUS squamata 'Blue Star'

--**'Blue Star'** DS (E)
Dense bush with silvery-blue, awl-shaped leaves.

--**'Chinooo Silver'** MS-LS (E)
Many-stemmed shrub of dense habit with awl-shaped leaves, intense silvery blue-green.

--**'Meyeri'** LS (E)
Vigorous, semi-erect shrub with ascending, angular branches and densely-packed, glaucous-blue leaves. AM 1931

-**virginiana** MT-LT (E) ♦ "Pencil Cedar"
Slender branchlets with small, sharp-pointed scale-like leaves, and scattered, glaucous, awl-shaped leaves. We recommend:

--**'Burkii'** MT-LT (E) ♦
Compact habit with ascending branches and steel-blue leaves, bronze-purple in autumn.

--**'Canaertii'** ST (E) ♦
Dense, slender habit with bright green foliage. Bears numerous small, blue-purple, bloomed cones.

--**'Glauca'** ST-MT (E) ♥
Dense, narrow habit with silvery-grey, mainly scale-like leaves.

--**'Grey Owl'** see *J. 'Grey Owl'*
--**'Keteleeri'** see *J. chinensis 'Keteleeri'*
--**'Skyrocket'** ST (E) ♦
Very narrow habit with erect branches and blue-grey foliage. One of the narrowest of conifers. AGM 1973

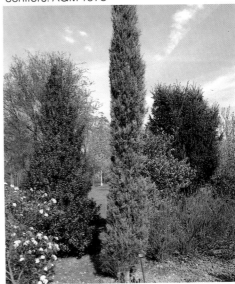

JUNIPERUS virginiana 'Skyrocket'

LARIX – Pinaceae MT-LT ♦ "Larch"
Vigorous, deciduous trees with linear leaves borne in dense rosettes on short shoots and singly on young shoots, turning yellow in autumn. Suitable for most soils except very wet or dry, shallow chalk.
– **dahurica** see *L. gmelinii*
– **decidua** (*europaea*) LT ♦ "European Larch" "Common Larch"
Crown slender conical when young. Branches and branchlets drooping on older specimens. Shoots yellowish or grey. Leaves light green.
– × **eurolepis** LT ♦ "Hybrid Larch" "Dunkeld Larch"
Vigorous hybrid between the European and Japanese larches. Shoots and leaves slightly glaucous. An important forestry tree.

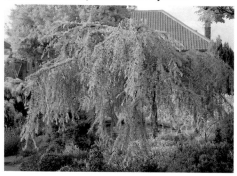

LARIX kaempferi 'Pendula'

– **europaea** see *L. decidua*
– **gmelinii** (*dahurica*) MT ♦ "Dahurian Larch"
A variable species of which we recommend the following form:
– – **principis-ruprechtii** MT ♦
Vigorous tree with reddish-brown shoots and bright green leaves, up to 10cm long on young shoots.
– **griffithii** (*griffithiana*) MT ♦ † "Himalayan Larch"
Long, drooping branchlets and downy shoots, reddish-brown the second year. Leaves bright green. AM 1974
– **kaempferi** (*leptolepis*) LT ♦ "Japanese Larch"
Vigorous tree with reddish shoots and sea-green leaves. Commonly used in forestry plantations withstanding exposure well.
– – **'Blue Haze'** LT ♦
Leaves an attractive glaucous-blue.
– – **'Pendula'** LT ♠
A form with long, weeping branches.
– **leptolepis** see *L. kaempferi*
"LEYLAND CYPRESS" see × *CUPRESSOCYPARIS leylandii*
LIBOCEDRUS chilensis see *AUSTROCEDRUS chilensis*
– **decurrens** see *CALOCEDRUS decurrens*
– **tetragona** see *PILGERODENDRON uviferum*

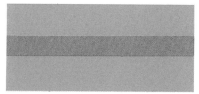

"MAIDENHAIR TREEE" see *GINKGO biloba*
METASEQUOIA – Taxodiaceae MT-LT ♦
A monotypic genus. The first living representative was found in China in 1941, the same year in which the genus was named from fossil specimens. It has quickly become a very popular conifer.

– **glyptostroboides** MT-LT ♦ "Dawn
Redwood"
Vigorous, deciduous tree conical when
young, developing a rounded head with age.
Bright green, linear leaves borne on short,
deciduous branchlets resembling a pinnate
leaf, pink and old gold in autumn. Best in a
moist, well-drained soil. AM 1969 AGM 1973
We recommend the following form:

– – **'Emerald Feathers'** MT-LT ♦
A form, selected for vegetative propagation,
of regular habit with dense, lush-green
foliage.

MICROBIOTA – Cupressaceae DS (E)
A monotypic genus related to Juniperus.
– **decussata** DS (E)
Densely branched, spreading habit. Leaves
mostly scale-like, brownish in winter. Very rare.

MICROCACHRYS – Podocarpaceae PS (E)
A monotypic genus related to Podocarpus.

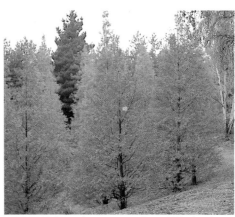

METASEQUOIA glyptostroboides 'Emerald Feathers'

– **tetragona** PS (E)
Spreading bush with 4-angled arching shoots
bearing minute, scale-like leaves. Rare.

PHYLLOCLADUS – Podocarpaceae
SS-ST (E)
*Unusual shrubs or small trees with whorled
branches and leaf-like, flattened shoots
(cladodes). We recommend the following;*
– **alpinus** SS-MS (E) "Alpine celery-topped
Pine"
Erect, narrowly conical habit. Numerous,
small, green, diamond-shaped cladodes. A
splendid miniature tree for the rock garden.

PICEA – Pinaceae MT-LT (E) ♦ "Spruce"
*Ornamental trees usually of conical habit with
whorled branches and needle-like, usually
sharp pointed leaves. Cones pendulous. Not
recommended (apart from the dwarf forms)
for poor, shallow, chalky or dry soils or very
exposed situations.*
– **abies** (*excelsa*) LT (E) ♦ "Common Spruce"
"Norway Spruce" "Christmas Tree"
Orange or reddish-brown shoots and bright
green leaves. It has given rise to numerous
forms.

– – **'Acrocona'** LS-ST (E)
Branches semi-pendulous usually
terminating in a large cone even when young.

– – **'Clanbrassiliana'** SS (E)
Slow growing, dense, flat-topped bush, wider
than high. Many brown buds, conspicuous in
winter.

– – **'Gregoryana'** DS (E)
Very dense, dome-shaped bush with radially
arranged, sea-green leaves. One of the most
popular dwarf forms.

– – **'Humilis'** DS (E)
Slow growing bush of compact, conical habit
with crowded and congested branchlets.

– – **'Inversa'** (*'Pendula'*) ST (E) ♦
Branches pendulous. Needs to be trained
when young to reach tree form.

– – **'Little Gem'** DS (E)
A dwarf, bun-shaped plant of very slow
growth with tiny, densely crowded leaves.

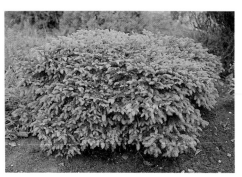

PICEA abies 'Nidiformis'

--**'Nidiformis'** DS (E)
A flat-topped bush of dense spreading habit with branches in horizontal layers.
--**'Pseudoprostrata'** (*'Prostrata'*) DS (E)
Spreading, flat-topped bush of dense habit with short, ascending branches.
--**'Pumila'** SS (E)
Slow growing, flat-topped bush of dense, irregular habit.
--**'Pyramidata'** LT (E) ♦
Vigorous tree of narrow habit with strongly ascending branches.

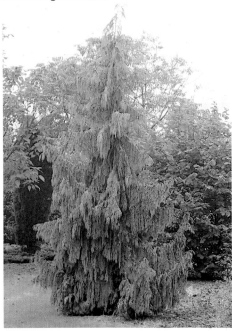

PICEA brewerana

--**'Reflexa'** PS (E)
A wide-spreading, creeping bush making a low dome with long, prostrate branches. Can be trained to make a weeping tree.
--**'Rubra Spicata'** MT-LT (E) ♦
Red tipped young growth in spring.
--**'Tabuliformis'** SS (E)
A slow-growing, wide spreading, flat-topped bush with layered branches.
-**alba** see *P. glauca*
-**asperata** MT (E) ♦
Pale, yellowish-brown shoots and more or less radially arranged grey-green or blue-green, sharply pointed leaves. Lime tolerant.
-**brachytyla** MT-LT (E) ♦
Long, spreading and gracefully ascending branches. Shining, pale brown or nearly white shoots and green or yellowish-green leaves, vivid white beneath.
-**brewerana** ST-MT (E) ♦ "Brewer's Weeping Spruce"
Spreading branches bear long, slender, hanging, tail-like branchlets. Leaves flattened, shining dark blue-green above, white beneath, Perhaps the most beautiful of all spruces. FCC 1974
-**engelmannii** ST-MT (E) ♦ ∠ "Engelmann Spruce"
Finely downy, pale yellow-brown young shoots. Leaves four-angled sharply pointed, grey-green. Not for dry or shallow chalk soils. We recommend the following form:
--**glauca** ST-MT (E) ♦
Leaves glaucous.
-**excelsa** see *P. abies*
-**glauca** (*alba*) LT (E) ♦ "White Spruce"
Dense habit with decurved branches ascending at the tips. Leaves four-angled, glaucous-green and densely arranged. Very hardy and suitable for exposed positions. We recommend the following forms:
--**albertiana 'Conica'** MS (E)
Slow growing, perfectly cone-shaped bush of dense habit. A deservedly popular form. AM 1933 AGM 1969
--**'Caerulea'** LT (E) ♦
Densely arranged, silvery, grey-blue leaves.
--**'Echiniformis'** DS (E)
Slow growing, globular bush of dense habit with glaucous, grey-green leaves. A first class rock garden miniature.
-**jezoensis** MT-LT (E) ♦ "Yezo Spruce"
We recommend the following form:

– – **hondoensis** LT (E) ♦ "Hondo Spruce"
Yellowish-brown to pale brown shoots and
flattened, dull green leaves, white beneath.
Cones crimson when young. AM 1974

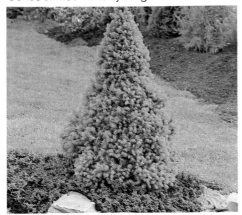

PICEA glauca albertiana 'Conica'

– **koyamae** ST-MT (E) ♦
Densely branched, narrow habit with reddish-
orange young shoots and densely packed,
four angled, green or slightly glaucous leaves.
Rare.

– **likiangensis** MT (E) ♦
Vigorous, ornamental tree with pale brown or
reddish young shoots. Leaves flattened,
green or bluish green above, glaucous
beneath. Young cones and male flowers
brilliant red in April-May.

– – **purpurea** (*P. purpurea*) MT (E) ♦
A form with a narrower crown and small,
darker green leaves. Cones violet-purple.

– **mariana** (*nigra*) MT (E) ♦ "Black Spruce"
Narrow habit with densely hairy, brown
shoots. Leaves dark bluish-green. Cones
dark purple when young.

– – **'Nana'** DS (E)
Globular bush of dense habit with grey-green
leaves. Suitable for the rock garden.
AGM 1973

– **morinda** see *P. smithiana*

– **omorika** MT-LT (E) ♦ "Serbian Spruce"
A graceful tree of slender habit with relatively
short, drooping branches curving upwards at
the tips. Leaves flattened, dark green above,
glaucous beneath. AGM 1969

– – **'Pendula'** MT (E) ♦
Tree of very slender habit with pendulous
branches. AGM 1969

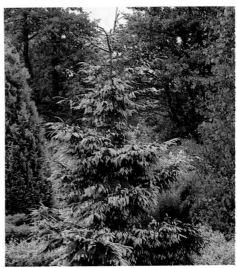

PICEA omorika

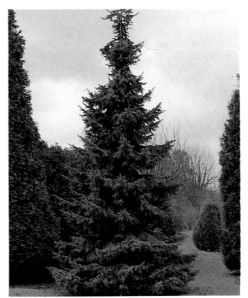

PICEA orientalis 'Aurea'

– **orientalis** LT (E) ♦ "Oriental Spruce"
Densely branched tree of broad habit,
branched to the ground. Leaves glossy dark
green, short and blunt, very densely
arranged.

– – **'Aurea'** MT (E) ♦
Young shoots creamy yellow, becoming
golden yellow and finally green. FCC 1893

--**'Pendula'** MT (E) ♦
A compact, slow growing form with weeping branches.
-**pungens** MT-LT (E) "Colorado Spruce"
Stout, orange-brown young shoots and rigid, sharply pointed green to grey leaves.
FCC 1887
More common in cultivation are forms belonging to var. *glauca* ("Blue Spruce") of which a selection is given below.

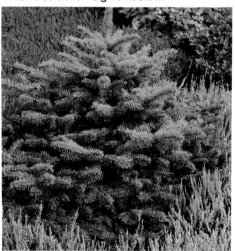

PICEA pungens 'Globosa'

--**'Globosa'** (*'Glauca Globosa'*) SS (E)
Flat-topped, globular bush of dense habit with glaucous-blue leaves.
--**'Hoopsii'** ST-MT (E) ♦
Dense habit with vividly glaucous-blue leaves.
--**'Koster'** ST-MT (E) ♦
Leaves an intense silvery-blue.
--**'Moerheimii'** ST-MT (E) ♦
Dense habit with intensely glaucous-blue leaves.
--**'Pendula'** ST (E) ♦
Branches pendulous, the lower ones eventually spreading over the ground. Leaves glaucous-blue.
--**'Procumbens'** (*'Glauca Procumbens'*)
PS (E) GC
Low growing, wide spreading shrub with glaucous-blue foliage.
--**'Spekii'** ST-MT (E) ♦
Leaves glaucous-blue.
-**purpurea** see *P. likiangensis purpurea*

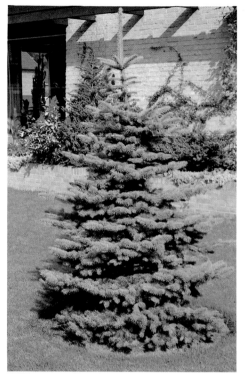

PICEA pungens 'Koster'

-**sitchensis** LT (E) ♦ "Sitka Spruce"
Vigorous tree with pale brown shoots and rigid, sharply pointed leaves glaucous beneath. The most commonly planted forestry tree in the British Isles, particularly in wetter areas.
-**smithiana** (*morinda*) LT (E) ♦ "West Himalayan Spruce"
Branches upcurved at tips bearing long, pendulous branchlets. Leaves relatively long, needle-like and dark green.
-**spinulosa** MT-LT (E) ♦
Rare tree with spreading branches and pendulous branchlets. Leaves flattened, green below, glaucous above.
PILGERODENDRON – Cupressaceae ST (E) ♥
A monotypic genus related to Libocedrus.
-**uviferum** (*Libocedrus tetragona*) ST (E) ♥
"Alerce"
Slow growing tree of stiff, upright habit when young. Leaves scale-like in four ranks, giving the shoots a quadrangular appearance. Rare.

PINUS – Pinaceae ST-LT (E) "Pine"
A large genus of evergreen trees. Normally conical when young, broadening in maturity. Leaves long and needle-like, borne in bundles of 2-5. Some survive in the poorest soils, acid or alkaline but generally the 5-needled species are not satisfactory on shallow chalk soils. Some make excellent windbreaks especially in coastal districts. All dislike shade and few will tolerate a smoke-polluted air. Numerous dwarf forms are cultivated.

– **albicaulis** ST (E) ♠
Young shoots, reddish-brown, eventually white. Leaves 4-6cm long in fives, green or grey-green. We recommend the following form:

– – **'Nana'** (*'Nobles Dwarf'*) DS (E)
A shrubby form of compact habit. Rare.

– **aristata** LS-ST (E) "Bristlecone Pine"
Dense habit. Stout, reddish-brown, young shoots. Leaves in fives, tightly bunched, dark green, flecked with white resin spots. Specimens up to 2000 years old have been recorded in the wild.

– **armandii** MT (E) ♣ "Armand's Pine"
An ornamental tree with drooping, slender, glaucous leaves borne in fives. Long, decorative, eventually pendulous cones.

– **ayacahuite** LT (E) ♣
Young shoots pale brown or greyish. Leaves in fives, long and slender, glaucous-green. Cones long and pendulous, resin-smeared. AM 1960 FCC 1961

– **banksiana** MT (E) ♠ ⸙ "Jack Pine"
Smooth, yellowish-green young shoots. Leaves in pairs, short, curved or twisted. Cones small and curved in pairs.

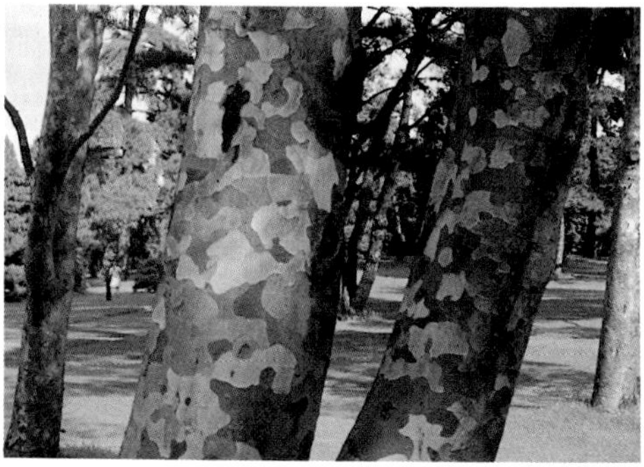

PINUS bungeana

– **bungeana** ST-MT (E) ♠ "Lace-bark Pine"
Often branched from near the base with characteristic, patchwork bark like a "London Plane". Shoots grey-green, leaves in threes, rigid.

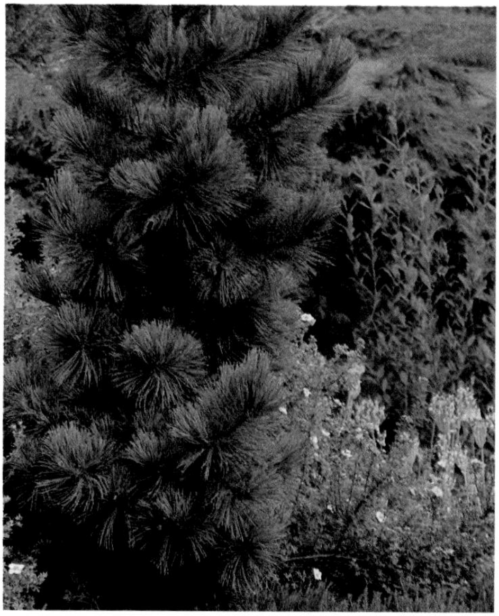

PINUS cembra

– **cembra** ST-MT (E) ♠ "Arolla Pine"
Characteristic, dense conical or columnar habit. Young shoots densely rusty - hairy. Leaves in fives, densely crowded, dark blue-green, glaucous on the inner surface. Cones deep blue, never opening. A good formal tree.

– – **pumila** see *P. pumila*

– – **'Stricta'** (*'Columnaris'*) ST (E) ♦
A form of narrow habit with closely ascending branches.

– **cembroides** ST (E) ♣ "Mexican Nut Pine"
Young shoots glaucous. Leaves, normally in threes, sharply pointed. Cones with large, edible seeds. We recommend the following form:

– – **edulis** (*P. edulis*) MT (E) ♣ "Two-leaved Nut Pine"
Leaves normally in pairs, sometimes in threes.

– **contorta** MT-LT (E) ♠ ⸙ "Beach Pine"
Young shoots green. Leaves in pairs, yellowish-green and characteristically twisted. We recommend the following form:

– – **latifolia** MT (E) ♠ ⸙ "Lodgepole Pine"
Leaves longer and slightly broader.

– **coulteri** MT-LT (E) ♠ "Big-Cone Pine"
Striking tree with stout, glaucous shoots. Leaves in threes, very long, grey-green, stiff and curved. Cones huge but rarely produced in this country. AM 1961

– **densiflora** MT (E) ♣ ⁄ "Japanese Red Pine"
Reddish, flaking bark. Leaves in pairs, slender and dark green.

– – **'Oculus Draconis'** ST (E) ♣ ⁄ "Dragon-eye Pine"
A slow growing form with the terminal leaves banded yellow.

– – **'Pendula'** PS (E) ⁄
A form with prostrate branches. Can be trained to make a dwarf, weeping tree.

– – **'Umbraculifera'** ST (E) ⁄
A slow growing, miniature tree eventually reaching about 3m with a dense, umbrella-like head of branches. Tiny cones often freely produced.

– **excelsa** see *P. wallichiana*

– **flexilis** MT (E) ♠ "Limber Pine"
Very flexible, glossy green young shoots. Leaves in fives, crowded at the ends of the branches.

– **griffithii** see *P. wallichiana*

– **halepensis** MT (E) ♣ "Aleppo Pine"
Young shoots glaucous. Leaves usually in pairs bright green, very slender. Ideally suited to southern, coastal areas and dry, shallow, chalk soils.

– × **holfordiana** LT (E) ♣
A vigorous hybrid with wide-spreading branches, long, silvery-green leaves in fives and long, banana-shaped, resin-flecked cones. AM 1977

– × **hunnewellii** MT (E) ♠
A vigorous tree of loose open habit with grey-green leaves, 7.5-8.5cm long, borne in fives.

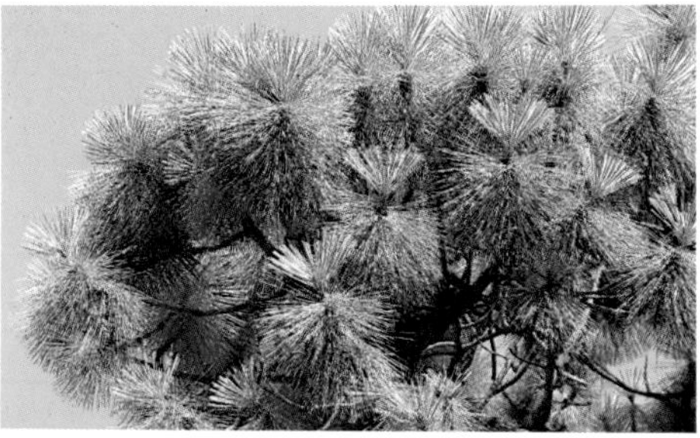

PINUS montezumae

– **insignis** see *P. radiata*

– **jeffreyi** (*ponderosa jeffreyi*) LT (E) ♠ "Jeffrey Pine"
Narrow, spire-like crown. Young shoots stout and glaucous. Leaves to 20cm long, bluish-green, in threes, crowded at the ends of the branchlets.

– **koraiensis** MT (E) ♠ "Korean Pine"
Open-branched tree with densely rusty hairy young shoots. Leaves usually in fives, blue-green, stiff and rough to the touch.

– – **'Compacta Glauca'** (*cembra 'Compacta Glauca'* HORT) ST (E) ♠
Compact form with short, stout branches and densely packed, conspicuously glaucous foliage.

– – **'Winton'** MS (E)
Slow growing, bushy form eventually wider than tall with glaucous leaves.

– **lambertiana** MT (E) ♠ "Sugar Pine"
Leaves in fives, sharp pointed and conspicuously twisted, blue-green. Cones pendulous, up to 50cm long on the upper branches but rarely produced in this country.

– **laricio** see *P. nigra maritima*

– **leucodermis** MT (E) ♠ "Bosnian Pine"
Dense, ovoid habit. Young shoots glaucous. Leaves in pairs, very dark green, rigid and erect. Young cones bright blue. Suitable for dry and shallow chalk soils.

– – **'Pygmy'** (*'Schmidtii'*) DS (E)
Very slow growing, dense bush with bright green leaves.

– **longifolia** see *P. palustris*

– **maritima** see *P. pinaster*

– **montana** see *P. mugo*

– **montezumae** MT-LT (E) ♣ † "Montezuma Pine"
Magnificent tree. Large, domed crown. Young shoots stout, orange-brown. Leaves to 25cm long, usually in fives, blue-grey, spreading or drooping.

– **monticola** MT-LT (E) ♠ ⁄ "Western White Pine"
Narrowly conical habit. Leaves in fives, dark blue-green, white on the inner surface. Cones long, eventually pendulous.

– **mugo** (*mughus*) (*montana*) LS-ST (E) ♣ "Mountain Pine"
Dense, bushy habit. Leaves in pairs, dark green, short, rigid and curved. Succeeds in almost all soils including chalk.

– – **'Gnom'** MS (E)
A compact form making a dark green, globular mound.
– – **'Mops'** M3 (E)
Slow growing, dense bush of rounded habit.

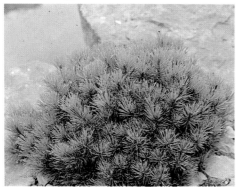

PINUS mugo pumilio

– – **pumilio** PS-MS (E)
Branches prostrate or ascending to 2m.
– – **rostrata** see *P. uncinata*
– **muricata** MT-LT (E) ♥ ⚉ "Bishop Pine"
Crown dense and often flat-topped. Young shoots green. Leaves 10-15cm in pairs, dark green and rigid. Cones with stout spines, often remaining unopened for many years. Suitable for exposed positions and coastal areas.
– **nigra** (*nigra austriaca*) LT (E) ♦ "Austrian Pine"
Commonly planted tree with dark bark and yellowish-brown young shoots. Leaves in pairs, dark green and rigid, densely crowded. Good in exposed positions as a windbreak, on chalky soils and coastal areas.
– – **calabrica** see *maritima*
– – **'Hornibrookiana'** SS (E)
A slow growing form of spreading habit with many stout, ascending branches.
– – **maritima** (*calabrica*) (*P. laricio*) LT (E) ♦ "Corsican Pine"
Differs from the "Austrian Pine" in its straighter, more openly branched trunk and more flexible, grey-green leaves. A common forestry tree happy in almost any soil and situation.
– – **'Pygmaea'** MS (E)
Slow-growing, dense globular bush or miniature tree with the foliage turning yellow-green in winter.

– **palustris** (*longifolia*) ST-MT (E) ♦ ⚉
"Southern Pitch Pine"
Slow growing tree with stout orange-brown young shoots. Leaves in threes, 20-25cm long and flexible. Requires a moist soil in a mild area.

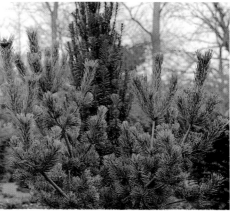

PINUS parviflora

– **parviflora** ST-MT (E) ♦ "Japanese White Pine"
A slow growing, bushy tree becoming flat-topped with age. Leaves in fives, slightly curved, deep blue-green, blue-white on the inner surface.
– – **'Adcock's Dwarf'** MS (E)
A compact, slow growing bush with very short leaves produced in congested bunches at the shoot tips.
– – **'Brevifolia'** ST (E) ♦
Sparsely branched tree of narrow habit with tight bunches of short, stiff, blue-green leaves.
– – **'Glauca'** ST-MT (E) ♦
Leaves rigid and conspicuously glaucous.
– **patula** ST-MT (E) ♥ ⚉ †
A very beautiful tree with reddish bark and spreading branches. Leaves normally in threes, 15-30cm long, slender and pendulous. Requires a sheltered position or mild area.
– **pinaster** (*maritima*) MT-LT (E) ♦ "Maritime Pine" "Bournemouth Pine"
Fast-growing, sparsely branched tree. Leaves in pairs to 25cm long, rigid and curved, dull grey. Excellent for sandy soils and coastal areas particularly in the south and west.

–**pinea** ST-MT (E) ♥ "Umbrella Pine" "Stone Pine"
Distinct tree with a characteristic dense flat-topped head. Leaves in pairs, to 15cm long, stiff and sharply pointed. Particularly suitable for sandy soils and coastal areas.

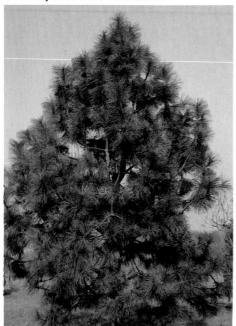

PINUS ponderosa

–**ponderosa** LT (E) ♦ "Western Yellow Pine"
Stately tree with a tall, straight trunk, and relatively short spreading or drooping branches. Leaves in threes to 25cm long and stiff. AM 1980.
––**jeffreyi** see *P. jeffreyi*
–**pumila** (*cembra pumila*) DS-MS (E) ⚲ "Dwarf Siberian Pine"
Usually a wide -spreading dwarf shrub occasionally medium sized and bushy. Leaves in fives, green outside, glaucous on the inner surfaces, densely crowded.
––**'Compacta'** SS (E) ⚲
Dense, erect, bushy habit with crowded bunches of glaucous leaves.
–**radiata** LT (E) ♥ "Monterey Pine"
Thick, rugged, dark brown bark. Leaves in threes, bright green and densely crowded. Cones often remaining intact for many years. Grows rapidly in coastal areas of the south and west where it is suitable for a windbreak.

–**rigida** MT (E) ♦ ⚲ "Northern Pitch Pine"
Strongly ridged, green young shoots. Leaves in threes, dark green and rigid. Shoots are occasionally produced on the trunk and older branches.
–**strobus** LT (E) ♦ "Weymouth Pine" "White Pine"
Older trees develop a rounded head. Leaves in fives, slender and glaucous-green. A fast growing, ornamental tree.

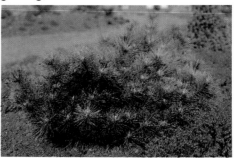

PINUS strobus 'Nana'

––**'Nana'** SS (E)
A dwarf form of dense habit.
––**'Nivea'** ST (E) ♦
Slow growing tree with glaucous leaves tipped milky-white.
––**'Prostrata'** PS (E) GC
Wide-spreading, prostrate shrub making a low mound.
–**sylvestris** LT (E) ♦ "Scots Pine"
Common tree with characteristic, reddish young bark. Leaves in pairs, twisted, grey-green or blue-green. Suitable for all soils AGM 1969
––**'Argentea'** LT (E) ♦
Leaves silvery blue-green. AGM 1969
––**'Aurea'** ST (E) ♦
Slow growing tree with leaves golden yellow in winter. AM 1964
––**'Beuvronensis'** SS (E)
A compact, dome-shaped bush, ideal for the rock garden. AM 1968 AGM 1969
––**'Doone Valley'** SS (E)
A dwarf form of dense, somewhat conical habit. Leaves glaucous.
––**'Fastigiata'** ST (E) ❶
A remarkable form of very narrow habit with erect branches. A superb tree where space is limited.
––**'Nana'** DS (E)
A dwarf, bushy form of slow growth.

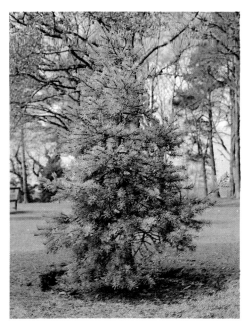

PINUS sylvestris 'Aurea'

– –**'Pumila'** see *'Watereri'*
– –**'Virdis Compacta'** MS (E)
A compact bush of conical habit with long, vivid grass-green leaves.
– –**'Watereri'** (*'Pumila'*) LS-ST (E) ♥
A slow growing bush or small tree of dense, rounded habit. AGM 1969.
–**tabuliformis** ST-MT (E) ♥ "Chinese Pine"
A rare species of which we recommend the following form:
– –**yunnanensis** (*P. yunnanensis*) ST-MT (E) ♥
Usually relatively low growing and flat headed. Leaves usually in threes, long, slender and drooping.
–**thunbergii** LT (E) ♦ "Black Pine"
Distinct tree with stout, twisted branches. Leaves in pairs, rigid and twisted. Useful as a windbreak in coastal areas and suitable for poor, sandy soils.
– –**'Oculus-draconis'** ST (E) ♦
Leaves with two yellow bands.
–**uncinata** (*mugo rostrata*) MT (E) ♦
"Mountain Pine"
Bushy tree related to *P. mugo*. Habit broadly conical, leaves in pairs. Suitable for all soils including shallow chalk and excellent for a windbreak in exposed positions.

–**wallichiana** (*griffithii*) (*excelsa*) LT (E) ♥
"Bhutan Pine"
Vigorous broad-headed tree. Young shoots glaucous. Leaves in fives to 20cm long, slender, blue-green, drooping with age. Long, banana-shaped resin-smeared cones. AM 1979.
– –**Nana'** MS (E)
A dome-shaped bush of dense habit with drooping, glaucous leaves.
–**yunnanensis** see *P. tabuliformis yunnanensis*

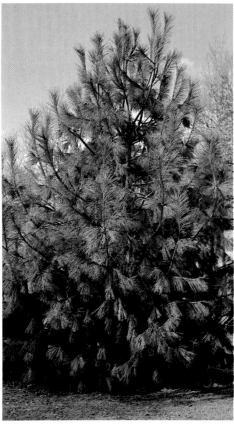

PINUS wallichiana

PODOCARPUS – Podocarpaceae PS-LT (E)
A large genus of trees and shrubs from the southern hemisphere containing several hardy species. Mainly suitable for most soils, acid or alkaline.
–**alpinus** SS (E) GC
Mound-forming, spreading shrub with yew-like, blue or grey-green leaves crowding the stems.

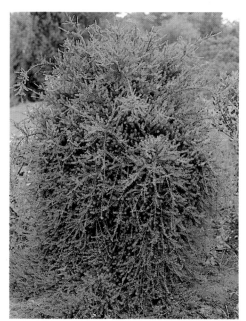

PODOCARPUS andinus

– **andinus** (*Prumnopitys elegans*) LS-MT (E)
🌂 "Plum-fruited Yew" "Chilean Yew"
Yew-like plant with linear leaves, bright green
above, glaucous-green beneath. Fruits
glaucous black, like small damsons. Excellent
on good soils over chalk. FCC 1864
– **chilinus** see *P. salignus*
– **macrophyllus** LS-ST (E) 🌂 ⚹ "Kusamaki"
One of the hardiest species with leaves to
13cm long, bright green, glaucous beneath.
– **nivalis** DS-MS (E) GC "Alpine Totara"
A variable shrub, usually low and spreading
but sometimes up to 2m. Leaves narrow and
leathery, olive green, crowded. Very hardy
and excellent on chalk.
– **nubigenus** LS-ST (E) 🌂
Usually a slow growing shrub with narrow
leaves, deep green above and glaucous
beneath. At its best in mild, wet areas.
– **salignus** (*chilinus*) LS-ST ✦ †
Usually a large shrub with drooping branches
and bright green willow-like leaves. Hardy
given evergreen protection but at its best in
the south-west.
PRUMNOPITYS elegans see
PODOCARPUS andinus
PSEUDOLARIX – Pinaceae MT ✦ ⚹
A monotypic genus related to Larix.

– **amabilis** (*fortunei*) (*kaempferi*) MT ✦ ⚹
"Golden Larch"
A beautiful and very hardy slow growing
deciduous tree. Leaves in clusters on short
shoots as the Larch, golden yellow in autumn.
Cones like pale green artichokes, reddish
brown when ripe.
PSEUDOTSUGA – Pinaceae ST-LT (E) ✦ ⚹
Evergreen trees with whorled branches and
spindle-shaped buds. Leaves linear, soft to
the touch, with glaucous bands beneath.
– **macrocarpa** MT (E) ✦ ⚹ "Large-coned
Douglas Fir"
Leaves arranged in two ranks, cones very
long. Rare.
– **menziesii** (*taxifolia*) (*douglasii*) LT (E) ✦ ⚹
"Douglas Fir"
A vigorous tree with downswept lower
branches and pendulous branchlets. A
commonly planted and very important forestry
tree. Many trees have exceeded 45m in this
country.

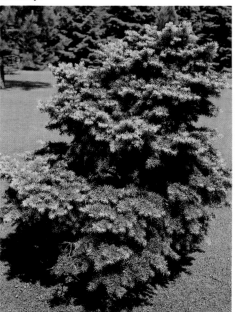

PSEUDOTSUGA menziesii 'Fletcheri'

– – **'Fletcheri'** MS (E)
A slow growing, rounded or flat-topped bush
with blue-green leaves. AM 1912
– – **'Glauca Pendula'** ST (E) ✦ ⚹
A weeping tree of graceful habit with blue-
green leaves.

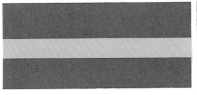

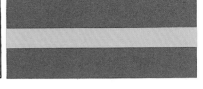

"REDWOOD" see *SEQUOIA sempervirens*
RETINISPORA *(RETINOSPORA)*
An obsolete generic name at one time

including several conifers with permanently
juvenile foliage, now mainly assigned to
CHAMAECYPARIS.

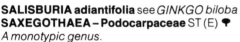

SALISBURIA adiantifolia see *GINKGO biloba*
SAXEGOTHAEA – Podocarpaceae ST (E) ♥
A monotypic genus.
– conspicua ST (E) ♥ "Prince Albert's Yew"
A perfectly hardy, unusual tree with spreading
branches and drooping branchlets. Leaves
narrow, dark green above, glaucous-banded
beneath.
SCIADOPITYS – Pinaceae MT (E) ♦ ✗
A monotypic genus.
– verticillata MT (E) ♦ ✗ "Umbrella Pine"
A very distinct, slow growing tree of dense
habit. Leaves long and linear, in dense whorls
like the spokes of an umbrella. AM 1979.
SEQUOIA – Taxodiaceae LT (E) ♦
*A monotypic genus. The world's tallest tree
reaching more than 100m in the wild.*
– sempervirens (*Taxodium sempervirens*)
LT (E) ♦ "Californian Redwood"
A very large tree which has reached more
than 40m in this country. Bark soft, reddish-
brown. Leaves dark green above with two
white bands beneath.
– –'Adpressa' (*'Albospica'*) ST (E) ♦
A slow growing form with the young shoots
tipped creamy white. FCC 1890
– –'Prostrata' PS-DS (E)
Prostrate or, if trained, a dwarf bush with
spreading branches. Leaves comparatively
broad, glaucous-green. AM 1951

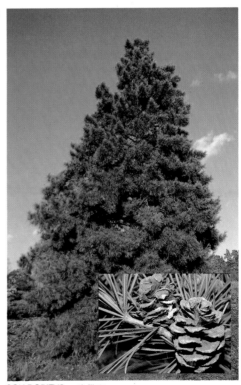

SCIADOPITYS verticillata

– **wellingtonia** see *SEQUOIADENDRON giganteum*
SEQUOIADENDRON – Taxodiaceae LT (E) ♦

A monotypic genus. Not as tall in the wild as the "Californian Redwood" but more massive and acknowledged to be the world's largest living thing.

– **giganteum** (*Sequoia gigantea*) (*Sequoia wellingtonia*) LT (E) ♦
"Wellingtonia" "Mammoth Tree" "Big Tree" Vigorous tree of dense habit with downswept branches. Bark deeply furrowed, reddish-brown. Leaves awl-shaped, bright green, prickly pointed.

– – **'Pendulum'** ST (E) ♥
An unusual tree of unique appearance. Usually forming a narrow column with long branches hanging down along the trunk. FCC 1882

"SPRUCE" see *PICEA*

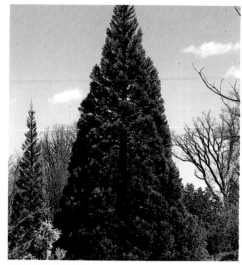

SEQUOIADENDRON giganteum

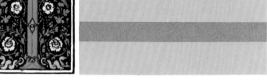

TAIWANIA – Taxodiaceae ST (E) ♦
Related to and generally resembling Cryptomeria. *Male and female strobili on same tree.*

– **cryptomerioides** ST (E) † ♦
Sparsely branched. Drooping whip-like branchlets clothed in green, sickle-shaped, pointed leaves, more scale-like on mature specimens. Round cones. Needs well-drained, moist soil and shelter. AM 1931

TAXODIUM – Taxodiaceae ST-LT ✗
Deciduous. Attractive, frond-like, feathery foliage. Male and female strobili on same tree. Grow on all soils except chalk. Tolerant of waterlogged conditions.

– **ascendens** ST-MT ✗ ♦
Bright green awl-shaped leaves, rich brown in autumn. Round cones, purple and resinous when young. We recommend:

– – **'Nutans'** ST-MT ✗ ♥
Shortly spreading or ascending branches. Branchlets erect at first, later nodding.

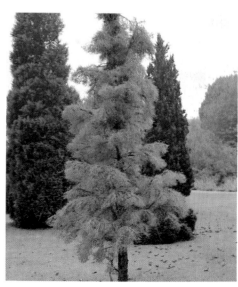

TAXODIUM ascendens 'Nutans'

TAXODIUM ascendens – Continued

– – **distichum** LT ✗ ♦ "Deciduous Cypress" "Swamp Cypress"
Fibrous, reddish-brown bark, buttressed trunk. Bright green feathery foliage, bronze in autumn. Small round cones, purple when young. Best conifer for wet or swampy soils. AM 1973

– – **'Pendens'** LT ✗ ♦
Drooping branch tips and branchlets.

– **sempervirens** see *SEQUOIA sempervirens*

TAXUS – Taxaceae MS-ST (E) "Yew"
Dark green leaves with two grey-green or yellow-green bands beneath. Male and female strobili usually on separate plants. Fruits with fleshy cup containing single poisonous seed. Tolerate most soils and situations. Good for hedging.

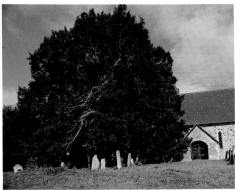

TAXUS baccata

– **baccata** ST-MT (E) ♀ Hdg (0.6m) "Common Yew" "English Yew"
Dark green leaves, yellowish-green beneath. Fruits with red cup. Needs good drainage. Will grow on shallow chalk or very acid soil. Good for hedging.

– – **'Adpressa'** LS-ST (E) ♀
Dense, spreading habit. Small, dark green leaves. Female.

– – **'Adpressa Variegata'** LS (E)
Young leaves old gold turning yellow, restricted to margins as they age. Male. FCC 1889

– – **'Argentea Minor'** (*'Dwarf White'*) SS (E)
Slow growth. Drooping branchlets. Leaves margined white. Female.

– – **'Aurea'** LS (E) "Golden Yew"
Compact habit. Golden yellow leaves, green by second year.

TAXUS baccata – Continued

– – **'Cavendishii'** SS (E) GC
Wide spreading branches, drooping at tips. Excellent ground cover. Female.

– – **'Dovastoniana'** ST (E) ♀ "Westfelton Yew"
Long, horizontal branches and weeping branchlets. Blackish green leaves. Generally female. AGM 1969

– – **'Dovastonii Aurea'** LS (E)
Leaves margined yellow. Male. AGM 1969

– – **'Elegantissima'** LS (E)
Dense habit. Ascending branches. Yellow young leaves turning paler, confined to margins with age. Female. AGM 1969

– – **'Erecta'** LS (E) "Fulham Yew"
Broadly columnar habit. Female

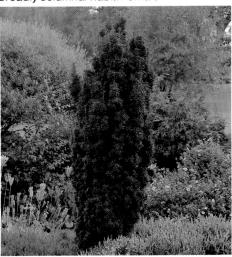

TAXUS baccata 'Fastigiata'

– – **'Fastigiata'** LS (E) "Irish Yew"
Erect, broadly columnar habit. Black green leaves. Female FCC 1863 AGM 1969

– – **'Fastigiata Aureomarginata'** LS (E) "Golden Irish Yew"
Similar in habit to the "Irish Yew". Leaves margined yellow. Male.

– – **'Lutea'** (*'Fructoluteo'*) (*'Xanthocarpa'*) ST-MT (E) ♀ "Yellow-berried Yew"
Fruits with yellow cups. AM 1929 AGM 1969

– – **'Pygmaea'** DS (E)
Slow. Dense, conical habit. Glossy, black green leaves.

– – **'Repandans'** DS (E) GC
Long spreading branches, often drooping at tips. Female. AGM 1969

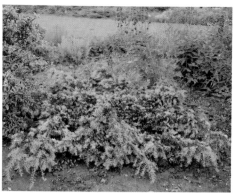

TAXUS baccata 'Repens Aurea'

– –**'Repens Aurea'** DS (E)
Low spreading habit. Leaves yellow margined when young, cream later.
– –**'Semperaurea'** MS (E)
Slow. Ascending branches. Young leaves old gold, turning rusty yellow. Male. AGM 1969
– –**'Standishii'** (*'Fastigiata Standishii'*) MS (E)
Slow. Dense columnar habit. Golden leaves. Female. AGM 1969
– –**'Xanthocarpa'** see *'Lutea'*
– × **media** MS-LS (E)
Vigorous, spreading habit. We recommend:
– –**'Hicksii'** LS (E) Hdg (0.6m)
Broadly columnar habit. Female. Good for hedging.

THUJA (*THUYA*) – **Cupressaceae** DS-LT (E)
"Arbor-vitae"
Aromatic foliage. Small scale-like leaves often borne in flattened, fan-like sprays. Male and female strobili on same tree. Small cones.
Thrive in almost any well-drained soil.
– **japonica** see *T. standishii*
– **koraiensis** LS-ST (E) ❦ "Korean Arborvitae"
Dark brown, peeling bark. Frond-like sprays of green foliage, white beneath, pungently aromatic when crushed.
– **lobbii** see *T. plicata*
– **occidentalis** MT (E) ❦ "American Arborvitae"
Reddish brown peeling bark. Branches up-curved at tips. Flattened sprays of dark green foliage, paler beneath, usually bronze in winter.
– –**'Danica'** DS (E)
Dense, round habit. Erect, flattened sprays of foliage.

– –**'Fastigiata'** (*'Columnaris'*) ('Pyramidalis') (*'Stricta'*) ST (E) ❦ Compact form of narrow habit. A good formal tree.
– –**'Holmstrupii'** (*'Holmstrupensis'*) MS-LS (E)
Slow. Dense conical habit. Erect sprays of rich green foliage.
– –**'Indomitable'** LS-ST (E) ❦
Dark green foliage, reddish bronze in winter.
– –**'Little Gem'** DS (E)
Slightly flat-topped, rounded habit. Crowded, crimpled sprays of deep green foliage.
– –**'Malonyana'** ST-MT (E) ❦
Short, dense, crowded sprays of rich green foliage.

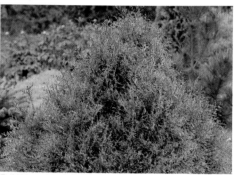

THUJA occidentalis 'Rheingold'

– –**'Rheingold'** LS (E)
Slow. Ovoid or conical habit. Rich old gold-amber foliage. AM 1902 AGM 1969
– –**'Sunkist'** SS (E)
Slow growing, bushy shrub with golden-yellow foliage.
– –**'Wareana Lutescens'** (*'Lutescens'*) SS (E)
Compact conical habit. Thickened sprays of pale yellow foliage.
– –**'Woodwardii'** SS (E)
Dense ovoid habit. Green foliage throughout year.
– **orientalis** LS (E) "Chinese Arbor-vitae"
Dense, conical or columnar habit. Erect branches and branchlets. Frond-like vertical sprays of small green leaves. Less aromatic than other species.
– –**'Aurea Nana'** DS (E)
Dense, round habit. Light yellow-green foliage. AGM 1969
– –**'Conspicua'** MS-LS (E)
Compact, conical habit. Golden yellow foliage.

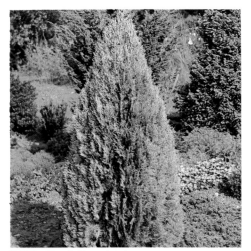

THUJA orientalis 'Conspicua'

– – **'Elegantissima'** MS-LS (E)
Dense, columnar habit. Golden yellow foliage,
tinged old gold turning green in winter.
AGM 1973.
– – **'Juniperoides'** (*'Decussata'*) DS (E)
Rounded habit. Juvenile foliage greyish green
in summer, turning deep purplish-grey in
winter. Protect from cold winds. AM 1973
– – **'Meldensis'** DS (E)
Dense, globular habit. Sea green, semi-
juvenile foliage, plum-purple in winter.
– – **'Minima Glauca'** DS (E)
Dense globular habit. Semi-juvenile sea-
green foliage, warm yellow-brown in winter.
– – **'Rosedalis'** (*'Rosedalis Compacta'*) SS (E)
Dense ovoid habit. Soft juvenile foliage
changes from canary yellow in spring, to sea-
green then plum-purple in winter.
– – **'Semperaurea'** MS (E)
Dense rounded habit. Yellow foliage
throughout summer, bronzed later. FCC 1870
– **plicata** (*lobbii*) (*gigantea*) LT ❢ (E) Hdg
(0.6m) "Western Red Cedar"
Reddish brown shredding bark. Bright, glossy
green leaves in flattened, drooping sprays,
fruity when crushed. Tolerates shallow chalk.
Excellent for hedging.
– – **'Aureovariegata'** see '*Zebrina*'
– – **'Aurea'** LT (E) ❢
Rich old gold foliage. FCC 1897
– – **'Cuprea'** SS (E)
Slow, dense conical habit. Growth tips old
gold-cream.

– – **'Fastigiata'** (*'Stricta'*) LT (E) ❢
Slender ascending branches, densely
arranged.

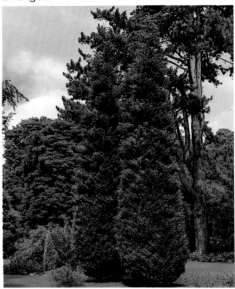

THUJA plicata 'Fastigiata'

– – **'Hillieri'** (*'Nana'*) MS (E)
Slow. Dense rounded habit. Moss-like
clusters of green foliage.
– – **'Rogersii'** (*'Aurea Rogersii'*) SS (E)
Slow. Compact conical habit. Golden and
bronze densely packed foliage.
– – **'Semperaurescens'** LT (E) ❢
Vigorous. Young growths and leaves tinged
golden yellow, bronze-yellow in winter.

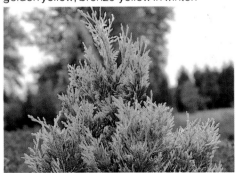

THUJA plicata 'Stoneham Gold'

– – **'Stoneham Gold'** SS (E)
Slow. Dense conical habit. Bright golden
foliage, tipped coppery bronze.

– –**'Zebrina'** (*'Aureovariegata'*) LT (E) ❢
Sprays of green foliage, banded creamy
yellow. Strong growth. FCC 1869
– **standishii** (*japonica*) ST-MT (E) ♦
"Japanese Arbor-vitae"
Loosely spreading or upcurved branches,
drooping branchlets. Drooping sprays of
yellowish green foliage, smelling of lemon
verbena when crushed.
THUJOPSIS – Cupressaceae ST-MT (E) ♦
Monotypic genus. Related to Thuja *but longer
leaves and broader, flatter branchlets. For all
well-drained soils.*
– **dolabrata** (*Thuja dolabrata*) ST-MT (E) ♦
Dense habit. Large flattened sprays of dark
green, silver-backed leaves. FCC 1864

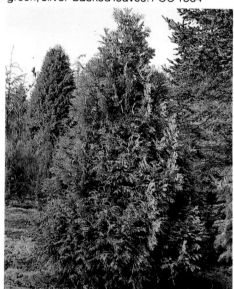

THUJOPSIS dolabrata 'Aurea'

– –**'Aurea'** ST (E) ♦
Leaves suffused golden yellow.
THUYA see *THUJA*
TORREYA – Taxaceae LS-MT (E) ♦
*Rigid, linear, spine-tipped leaves with two
bands beneath. In cultivation, male and
female strobili sometimes on same tree.
Fleshy, plum-like, one-seeded fruits. Good for
chalk soils.*
– **californica** (*myristica*) ST-MT (E) ♦
"Californian Nutmeg"
Branches to ground level. Shiny dark green
leaves. Green fruits, streaked purple when
ripe.

– **nucifera** LS-ST (E) ♦
Slender habit. Sickle shaped leaves, pungent
when crushed. Green fruits clouded purple
when ripe.
TSUGA – Pinaceae LS-LT (E) "Hemlock"
*Spreading branches and drooping or arching
branchlets. Short, linear leaves. Male and
female strobili on same tree. Small, pendulous
cones. Thrive in well-drained, moist loamy
soil. Not for shallow chalk. Shade tolerant.*
– **albertiana** see *T. heterophylla*
– **canadensis** LT (E) ♦ "Eastern Hemlock"
Trunk often forked near base. Densely hairy,
greyish-brown young shoots. Leaves with two
whitish bands beneath.
– –**'Bennett'** (*'Bennett's Minima'*) DS (E)
Slow, spreading habit. Dense growth.
– –**'Dwarf Whitetip'** SS (E)
Broadly conical habit. Young shoots creamy
white, green in late summer.
– –**'Horsford'** (*'Horsford's Dwarf'*) DS (E)
Densely packed, rounded habit.
– –**'Lutea'** LT (E) ♦
Slow. Bright yellow foliage.
– –**'Minuta'** DS (E)
Extremely slow. Tightly congested growth.
– –**'Nana Gracilis'** SS (E)
Mound-like habit. Slender, arching stems.

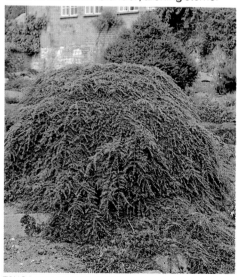

TSUGA canadensis 'Pendula'

– –**'Pendula'** MS (E)
Mound-like habit, overlapping, drooping
branches. AGM 1973

– –**'Prostrata'** PS (E)
Slow. Mat-like habit. Prostrate stems.
–**caroliniana** LS-ST (E) ✗ ✦ "Carolina Hemlock"
Young shoots grey, reddish brown or yellowish brown. Soft yellowish green leaves, with two white bands beneath. Oblong or ovoid cones.
–**chinensis** ST (E) ✦
Yellowish young shoots. Comparatively broad leaves with two greyish bands beneath. Ovoid cones.
–**heterophylla** (*albertiana*) LT (E) ✦
"Western Hemlock"
Fast growing. Spreading branches. Greyish

hairy young shoots. Leaves with two white bands beneath. Good specimen tree. AGM 1969
– –**'Greenmantle'** LT (E) 🌢
Graceful pendulous branches. Narrow habit.
– –**'Laursen's Column'** LT (E) ❢
Loosely columnar habit with erect branches.
–**mertensiana** LT (E) ✦
Spire-like habit. Densely hairy, greyish brown young shoots. Grey-green or blue-grey leaves. Comparatively large cones. We recommend:
– –**'Glauca'** LT (E) ✦
Delightful form with glaucous leaves.

"WELLINGTONIA" see *SEQUOIADENDRON giganteum*

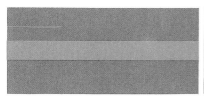

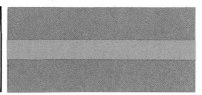

"YEW" see *TAXUS*

lossary of Botanical Terms

Throughout this book, certain accepted botanical terms have been used as an aid to precise description, and/or for the sake of brevity.

The following glossary explains those terms and some others which you may find useful if your interest in trees and shrubs inspires you to further reading.

Acicular – Needle-shaped
Acuminate – Tapering at the end, long pointed
Acute – Sharp pointed
Anther – The pollen-bearing part of the stamen
Adpressed – Lying close and flat against
Aristate – Awned, bristle-tipped
Articulate – Jointed
Ascending – Rising somewhat obliquely and curving upwards
Auricle – An ear-shaped projection or appendage
Awl-shaped – Tapering from the base to a slender and stiff point
Axil – The angle formed by a leaf or lateral branch with the stem, or of a vein with the midrib
Axillary – Produced in the axil

Bearded – Furnished with long or stiff hairs
Berry – Strictly a pulpy, normally several seeded, indehiscent fruit
Bifid – Two-cleft
Bipinnate – Twice pinnate
Bisexual – Both male and female organs in the same flower
Blade – The expanded part of a leaf or petal
Bloomy – With a fine powder-like waxy deposit
Bole – Trunk, of a tree
Bract – A modified, usually reduced leaf at the base of a flower-stalk, flower-cluster, or shoot
Bullate – Blistered or puckered

Calcareous – Containing carbonate of lime or limestone, chalky or limey
Calcifuge – Avoiding calcareous soils
Calyx – The outer part of the flower, the sepals
Campanulate – Bell-shaped

Capitate – Head-like, collected into a dense cluster
Capsule – A dry, several-celled pod
Catkin – A normally dense spike or spike-like raceme of tiny, scaly-bracted flowers or fruits
Ciliate – Fringed with hairs
Cladode – Flattened leaf-like stems
Clone – A new individual plant formed by separation and independent growth of a vegetative part of the parent plant. Its genetic factors are thus exactly the same as those of the parent plant
Columnar – Tall, cylindrical or tapering, column-like
Compound – Composed of two or more similar parts
Compressed – Flattened
Conical – Cone-shaped
Cordate – Shaped like a heart, as base of leaf
Coriaceous – Leathery
Corolla – The inner normally conspicuous part of a flower, the petals
Corymb – A flat-topped or dome-shaped flower head with the outer flowers opening first
Corymbose – Having flowers in corymbs
Crenate – Toothed with shallow, rounded teeth, scalloped
Cultivar – Garden variety, or form found in the wild and maintained as a clone in cultivation
Cuneate – Wedge-shaped
Cuspidate – Abruptly sharp pointed
Cyme – A flat-topped or dome-shaped flower head with the inner flowers opening first
Cymose – Having flowers in cymes

Deciduous – Soon or seasonally falling, not persistent
Decumbent – Reclining, the tips ascending
Decurrent – Extending down the stem
Deltoid – Triangular
Dentate – Toothed with teeth directed outward
Denticulate – Minutely dentate
Depressed – Flattened from above
Diffuse – Loosely or widely spreading
Digitate – With the members arising from one point (as in a digitate leaf)
Dioecious – Male and female flowers on different plants
Dissected – Divided into many narrow segments
Distichous – Arranged in two vertical ranks: two-ranked
Divaricate – Spreading far apart

Divergent – Spreading

Divided – Separated to the base

Double – (flowers) with more than the usual number of petals, often with the style and stamens changed to petals

Doubly Serrate – Large teeth and small teeth alternating

Downy – Softly hairy

Elliptic – Widest at or about the middle, narrowing equally at both ends **'Elongate** – Lengthened

Emarginate – With a shallow notch at the apex

Entire – Undivided and without teeth

Evergreen – Remaining green during winter

Exfoliating – Peeling off in thin strips

Exserted – Projecting beyond (stamens from corolla)

Falcate – Sickle-shaped

Fascicle – A dense cluster

Fastigiate – With branches erect and close together

Fertile – Stamens producing good pollen or fruit containing good seeds, or of stems with flowering organs

Ferruginous – Rust-coloured

Filament – The stalk of a stamen

Filiform – Thread-like

Fimbriate – Fringed

Flexuous – Wavy or zig-zag

Floccose – Clothed with flocks of soft hair or wool

Florets – Small, individual flowers of a dense inflorescence

Floriferous – Flower-bearing

Form – Although 'forma' is a recognised .botanical category below 'variety', the term is used more loosely in this book and may refer to a species, subspecies or cultivar.

Genus – An assemblage of closely related species

Gibbous – Swollen, usually at the base (as in corolla)

Glabrous – Hairless

Glandular – With secreting organs

Glaucous – Covered with a 'bloom', bluish-white or bluish-grey

Glutinous – Sticky

Habit – General form of a plant

Hermaphrodite – Bisexual, both male and female organs in the same flower

Hirsute – With rather coarse or stiff hairs

Hispid – Beset with rigid hairs or bristles

Hoary – Covered with a close whitish or greyish-white pubescence

Hybrid – A plant resulting from a cross between different species

Imbricate – Overlapping, as tiles on a roof

Impressed – Sunken (as in veins)

Incised – Sharply and usually deeply and irregularly cut

Indehiscent – Fruits which do not (burst) open

Indumentum – Dense hairy covering

Inflorescence – The flowering part of the plant

Internode – The portion of stem between two nodes or joints

Involucre – A whorl of bracts surrounding a flower or flower cluster

Keel – A central ridge

Lacerate – Torn, irregularly cut or cleft

Laciniate – Cut into narrow pointed lobes

Lanceolate – Lance-shaped, widening above the base and long tapering to the apex

Lanuginose – Woolly or cottony

Lateral – On or at the side

Lax – Loose

Leaflet – Part of a compound leaf

Linear – Long and narrow with nearly parallel margins

Lip – One of the parts of an unequally divided flower

Lobe – Any protruding part of an organ (as in leaf, corolla or calyx)

Lustrous – Shining

Membranous – Thin and rather soft

Midrib – The central vein or rib of a leaf

Monoecious – Male and female flowers separate, but on the same plant

Monotypic – Of a single species (genus)

Mucronate – Terminated abruptly by a spiny tip

Nectary – A nectar-secreting gland, usually a small pit or protuberance

Node – The place upon the stem where the leaves are attached, the 'joint'

Nut – A non-splitting, one-seeded, hard and bony fruit

Oblanceolate – Inversely lanceolate
Oblique – Unequal-sided
Oblong – Longer than broad, with nearly parallel sides
Obovate – Inversely ovate
Obtuse – Blunt (as in apex of leaf or petal)
Orbicular – Almost circular in outline
Oval – Broadest at the middle
Ovary – The basal 'box' part of the pistil, containing the ovules
Ovate – Broadest below the middle (like a hen's egg)
Ovule – The body which, after fertilisation, becomes the seed

Palmate – Lobed or divided in hand-like fashion, usually five or seven-lobed
Panicle – A branching raceme
Paniculate – Having flowers in panicles
Parted – Cut or cleft almost to the base
Pea-Flower – Shaped like a sweet pea blossom
Pectinate – Comb-like (as in leaf margin)
Pedicel – The stalk of an individual flower in an inflorescence
Peduncle – The stalk of a flower cluster or of a solitary flower
Pellucid – Clear, transparent (as in gland)
Pendulous – Hanging, weeping
Perfoliate – A pair of opposite leaves fused at the base, the stem appearing to pass through them
Perianth – The calyx and corolla together ; also commonly used for a flower in which there is no distinction between corolla and calyx
Persistent – Remaining attached
Petal – One of the separate segments of a corolla
Petaloid – Petal-like (as in stamen)
Petiole – The leaf-stalk
Pilose – With long, soft straight hairs
Pinnate – With leaflets arranged on either side of a central stalk
Pinnatifid – Cleft or parted in a pinnate way
Pistil – The female organ of a flower comprising ovary, style and stigma
Plumose – Feathery, as the down of a thistle
Pollen – Spores or grains contained in the anther, containing the male element
Polygamous – Bearing bisexual and uni-sexual flowers on the same plant
Procumbent – Lying or creeping
Prostrate – Lying flat on the ground
Pruinose – Bloomy
Puberulent – Minutely pubescent
Pubescent – Covered with short, soft hairs, downy

Punctate – With translucent or coloured dots or depressions
Pungent – Ending in a stiff, sharp point, also acid (to the taste) or strong smelling
Pyramidal – Pyramid-shaped (broad at base tapering to a point)

Raceme – A simple elongated inflorescence with stalked flowers
Racemose – Having flowers in racemes
Rachis – An axis bearing flowers or leaflets
Recurved – Curved downward or backward
Reflexed – Abruptly turned downward
Reniform – Kidney-shaped
Reticulate – Like a network (as in veins)
Revolute – Rolled backwards, margin rolled under (as in leaf)
Rib – A prominent vein in a leaf
Rotund – Nearly circular
Rufous – Reddish-brown
Rugose – Wrinkled or rough
Runner – A trailing shoot taking root at the nodes

Sagittate – Shaped like an arrow-head
Scabrous – Rough to the touch
Scale – A minute leaf or bract, or a flat gland-like appendage on the surface of a leaf, flower or shoot
Scandent – With climbing stems
Scarious – Thin and dry, not green
Semi-evergreen – Normally evergreen but losing some or all of its leaves in a cold winter or cold area
Sepal – One of the segments of a calyx
Serrate – Saw-toothed (teeth pointing forward)
Serrulate – Minutely serrate
Sessile – Not stalked
Setose – Clothed with bristles
Sheath – A tubular envelope
Shrub – A woody plant which branches from the base with no obvious trunk
Simple – Said of a leaf that is not compound or an unbranched inflorescence
Sinuate – Strongly waved (as in leaf margin)
Sinus – The recess or space between two lobes or divisions of a leaf, calyx or corolla
Spatulate – Spoon-shaped
Species – A group of plants of similar genetical constitution
Spicate – Flowers in spikes
Spike – A simple, elongated inflorescence with sessile flowers
Spine – A sharp-pointed end of a branch or leaf
Spur – A tubular projection from a flower ; or a short stiff branchlet
Stamen – The male organ of a flower comprising filament and anther
Staminode – A sterile stamen, or a structure resembling a stamen, sometimes petal-like

Standard – The upper, normally broad and erect petal in a pea-flower ; also used in nurseries to describe a tall single stemmed young tree

Stellate – Star shaped

Stigma – The summit of the pistil which receives the pollen, often sticky or feathery

Stipule – Appendage (normally two) at base of some petioles

Stolon – A shoot at or below the surface of the ground which produces a new plant at its tip

Striate – With fine, longitudinal lines

Strigose – Clothed with flattened fine, bristle-like, hairs

Style – The middle part of the pistil, often elongated between the ovary and stigma

Subulate – Awl-shaped

Succulent – Juicy, fleshy, soft and thickened in texture

Suckering – Producing underground stems ; also the shoots from the stock of a grafted plant

Tendril – A twining thread-like appendage

Ternate – In threes

Tessellated – Mosaic-like (as in veins)

Tomentose – With dense, woolly pubescence

Tomentum – Dense covering of matted hairs

Tree – A woody plant that produces normally a single trunk and an elevated head of branches

Trifoliate – Three-leaved

Trifoliolate – A leaf with three separate leaflets

Turbinate – Top-shaped

Type – Strictly the original (type) specimen, but used in a general sense to indicate the typical form in cultivation

Umbel – A normally flat-topped inflorescence in which the pedicels or peduncles all arise from a common point

Umbellate – Flowers in umbels

Undulate – With wavy margins

Unisexual – Of one sex

Urceolate – Urn-shaped

Velutinous – Clothed with a velvety indumentum

Venation – The arrangement of the veins

Verrucose – Having a wart-like or nodular surface

Verticillate – Arranged in a whorl or ring

Villous – Bearing long and soft hairs

Viscid – Sticky

Whorl – Three or more flowers or leaves arranged in a ring